# Brief Contents

# Contents

**CHAPTER 7**

CHAPTER 8

# Modern Psychology: A History

## TENTH EDITION

**DUANE P. SCHULTZ**
*University of South Florida*

**SYDNEY ELLEN SCHULTZ**

WADSWORTH

A ...apore • Spain • United Kingdom • United States

**WADSWORTH**
CENGAGE Learning

**Modern Psychology: A History,
Tenth Edition, International Edition**
Duane P. Schultz and Sydney Ellen
Schultz

Senior Publisher: Linda Schreiber-Ganster

Executive Editor: Jon-David Hague

Editorial Assistant: Sheli DeNola

Senior Marketing Manager: Elizabeth
Rhoden

Marketing Communications Manager:
Laura Localio

Marketing Coordinator: Janay Pryor

Media Editor: Lauren Keyes

Senior Art Director: Pamela Galbreath

Print Buyer: Karen Hunt

Rights Acquisition Specialist, Text/Image:
Dean Dauphinais

Photo Researcher: PreMediaGlobal

Text Researcher: PreMediaGlobal

Compositor: PreMediaGlobal

Cover Image: © Kim D. French/Shutterstock

Cover Designer: William Stanton

*To Russ Nazzaro*

*who asked the department's
newest assistant professor,
one day long ago*

*"How would you like to teach
the history of psychology?"*

For permission to use material from this text or product,
submit all requests online at **www.cengage.com/permissions**
Further permissions questions can be emailed to
**permissionrequest@cengage.com**

Library of Congress Control Number: 2011921415

International Edition:

ISBN-13: 978-1-111-34498-6

ISBN-10: 1-111-34498-1

Cengage Learning International Offices

**Asia**
www.cengageasia.com
tel: (65) 6410 1200

**Australia/New Zealand**
www.cengage.com.au
tel: (61) 3 9685 4111

**Brazil**
www.cengage.com.br
tel: (55) 11 3665 9900

**India**
www.cengage.co.in
tel: (91) 11 4364 1111

**Latin America**
www.cengage.com.mx
tel: (52) 55 1500 6000

**UK/Europe/Middle East/Africa**
www.cengage.co.uk
tel: (44) 0 1264 332 424

**Represented in Canada by
Nelson Education, Ltd.**
www.nelson.com
tel: (416) 752 9100/(800) 668 0671

Cengage Learning is a leading provider of customized learning solutions with office locations around the globe, including Singapore, the United Kingdom, Australia, Mexico, Brazil, and Japan. Locate your local office at: **www.cengage.com/global**

For product information: **www.cengage.com/international**
Visit your local office: **www.cengage.com/global**
Visit our corporate website: **www.cengage.com**

Printed in Canada
2 3 4 5 6 7 15 14 13 12

## CHAPTER 10

## CHAPTER 11

**CHAPTER 15**

# In Their Own Words

# Preface

The focus of this book is the history of modern psychology, the period beginning in the late 19th century, when psychology became a separate and independent discipline. Although we briefly review earlier philosophical thought, we concentrate on issues directly related to the establishment of psychology as a new and distinct field of study. Our purpose is to present a history of *modern* psychology, not the centuries of philosophical work that preceded it.

We recount the history of psychology in terms of people, ideas, and schools of thought, as well as the times that influenced their development. Since the formal beginning of the field in 1879, psychology's methods and subject matter have changed as each new idea captured the loyalty of adherents and dominated the field. Our interest, then, is in the developing sequence of approaches that have defined psychology over the years.

Each school of thought is discussed as a movement arising within a historical and social context. Contextual forces include the intellectual spirit of the times (the *Zeitgeist*), plus social, political, and economic factors such as the effect of war, prejudice, and discrimination.

Although the chapters are organized in terms of the schools of thought, we also recognize that these systems resulted from the work of scholars, researchers, organizers, and promoters. It is people, not abstract forces, who write articles, conduct research, present papers, popularize ideas, and teach the next generation of psychologists. We discuss the contributions of the pivotal men and women, noting that their work was often affected not only by the times in which they flourished but also by their personal experiences.

We describe each school of thought in terms of its connection to the scientific ideas and discoveries that preceded and followed it. Each school evolved from or revolted against the existing order, and in its turn inspired viewpoints that challenged, opposed, and eventually replaced it. With the hindsight of history, then, we can trace the pattern and the continuity of the development of modern psychology.

## New to the Tenth Edition

- *Thorough update of all subject areas, especially more recent movements in psychology.*
- *New introduction to Chapter 1 to show the relevance of the past for the present by discussing similarities in the results of two experiments that explore the concept of multitasking. One is a classic study from 1861 and the other is dated 2009.*
- *An overview of metaphors for the human mind, from the clockwork universe and automata to modern-day computers.*
- *Early 19th-century neurasthenia and its relationship to multitasking.*
- *Evidence of mechanical computers as early as 100 B.C.*
- *The mechanization of phrenology – a highly successful business in its day – with the development of a machine to read the bumps and indentations on the human skull.*
- *The contemporary relevance of Wilhelm Wundt's research on the personal equation.*
- *The phenomenon of simultaneous discovery.*
- *The contributions of Charles Darwin.*
- *New biographical material on William James, Sigmund Freud, Herbert Spencer, James McKeen Cattell, Alfred Binet, Henry Goddard, Ivan Pavlov, John B. Watson, Abraham Maslow, Carl Jung, and other important figures.*

- *The dominance of psychological research by psychologists at universities and laboratories in the United States: Can the results of these findings, influenced by American culture and using Americans as subjects, be generalized to people in other parts of the world?*
- *The controversial use of IQ tests at Ellis Island, New York, to process new immigrants to the United States.*
- *Psychological testing in World War I.*
- *The stunning change in the role and importance of clinical psychology as a result of World War II.*
- *The dispute between Lightner Witmer and Wilhelm Wundt about the proper use of introspective data.*
- *John B. Watson's behaviorist child-rearing techniques and their effects on his family.*
- *The Brelands and the IQ Zoo – pigs, chickens, raccoons, rabbits, ducks, dolphins, and whales – and what they meant for psychology.*
- *Early research on sex and on dreams that pre-dated the work of Sigmund Freud.*
- *New information on the so-called cure of Freud's famous patient Anna O.*
- *Social self-efficacy and the modeling effects of viewing violence on television and in video games.*
- *The variability hypothesis, or the functional inequality of women (the notion that men were inherently intellectually superior to women).*
- *The influence of video games on dreams and on behavior.*
- *The psychodynamics of gum chewing.*
- *Topics in cognitive psychology including embedded cognition, cognitive neuroscience, neuroprosthetics, evolutionary psychology, animal personality and intelligence, artificial intelligence, and unconscious cognition.*
- *Current developments in positive psychology.*

As we prepared the tenth edition of this textbook many years after writing the first one, we were struck anew by the dynamic nature of the history of psychology. This history is not fixed or finished but in a continuing state of growth. An enormous amount of scholarly work is continually being produced, translated, and reevaluated. Information from nearly 180 new sources has been added, some published as recently as 2010, and revisions have been made to material from the previous edition.

We have included information on websites that provide additional material on the people, theories, movements, and research discussed in this book. We have explored hundreds of sites and chosen the most informative, reliable, and current, as of the time of publication. The **In Their Own Words** sections provide original writings by the key figures in the history of psychology, presenting in each theorist's distinctive personal style – and the style of the times – a unique perspective on psychology's methods, problems, and goals. These sections have been reevaluated and edited for clarity and comprehension.

At the beginning of each chapter we offer a teaser, a brief narrative built around a person or event designed to introduce the major theme of the chapter. These sections immediately define the subject matter and tell the student that history is about real people and real situations. These topics include, among others:

- *The mechanical duck that ate, digested, and defecated on a silver platter. All the rage in Paris in 1739, it was to become a metaphor for a new conception of the functioning of the human body as a machine.*
- *The campus clown and perception*
- *Charles Darwin's fascination with Jenny the Orangutan, who wore a frilly dress and drank tea from a cup*

- *Why Wilhelm Wundt couldn't multitask, and what that meant for the new psychology*
- *The 1909 Tennessee drug bust against the deadly substance caffeine, and the psychologist who proved the government wrong*
- *Why John B. Watson held the hammer while his pretty young graduate assistant held the baby*
- *The IQ Zoo, Priscilla the Fastidious Pig, and Bird Brain, who beat B. F. Skinner at a game of tic-tac-toe*
- *What Wolfgang Köhler was really doing on the most famous island in the history of psychology*
- *Sigmund Freud's boyhood dream about his mother and what it really meant*

New photographs, tables, and figures have been chosen for this new edition. Chapters contain outlines, discussion questions, and annotated reading lists. Important terms are boldfaced in the text and defined in the margin glossary and back of the book. The following supplements are available:

### For instructors (www.cengage.com/international):

- *Instructor's Manual with Test Bank by Wendi Everton of Eastern Connecticut State University.*
- *ExamView, computerized testing software that includes content from the test bank.*
- *Book companion website for instructors that includes electronic files of the print Instructor's Manual, PowerPoint lecture slides, and more.*

### For students (www.cengage.com/international):

- *Free book companion website that provides flashcards, crossword puzzles, tutorial quizzes, and web links.*

## Acknowledgments

We are grateful to the many instructors and students who have contacted us over the years with valuable suggestions. We are pleased to acknowledge the assistance of David Baker, director of the Archives of the History of American Psychology at the University of Akron, and his staff, for providing gracious and valuable assistance with the photographs.

D.P.S., S.E.S.

CHAPTER **1**

# The Study of the History of Psychology

## Did You See the Clown?

Suppose you were walking across the campus and you were approached by a person dressed like a clown. He is wearing bright purple and yellow clothing with oversize sleeves decorated with polka dots, red shoes, wild eye make-up, a white wig, a large red nose, and floppy blue shoes—and he is riding a unicycle. We don't know about your campus, but we rarely see clowns around ours. If we did, we probably would notice them, wouldn't you? How could you not notice something as obvious and odd as a clown? That was what Ira Hyman, a psychologist at Western Washington University, wanted to find out. He asked a student to dress up like a clown and ride around the main campus square where hundreds of people were walking to and from classes (Hyman, Boss, Wise, McKenzie & Caggiano, 2009; Parker-Pope, 2009).

When students reached the edge of the quadrangle, trained observers asked 151 of them if they had seen anything unusual, such as a clown. Only half of the students who were walking by themselves said they noticed the clown. More than 70 percent of those walking with another person saw the clown. Only 25 percent of those who were talking on their cell phones were aware of the clown. In other words, 3 of every 4 students talking on their phones were oblivious to the appearance of a clown on a unicycle right in front of them. They had been so distracted by their conversations or their texting that they could not recollect the bizarre sight. Now you might be thinking that this would be a disappointment to a clown who is trying to attract attention, but more importantly, what does it have to do with the history of psychology?

Consider what the results of this experiment tell us about ourselves. They suggest that we may find it difficult, if not impossible, to pay attention to more than one stimulus at a time. In other words, it is really hard to focus on more than one thing.

Does this make you question the value of multitasking, something you most likely do routinely? You probably consider it normal to listen to music while you write a paper, or send a text message while you eat, but are you truly concentrating on either of these activities? Scientists in many fields are investigating the usefulness and effectiveness of multitasking, just as the researchers did in the gorilla study, but their conclusions are not new. Similar results were demonstrated more than 150 years ago, in 1861, by a German psychologist.

That long-ago experiment (described in Chapter 4) also shows us that the study of the past is relevant for the present, but first we must become aware of what was done in the past. History has much to tell us about the world today, and early developments in the field of psychology help us understand the nature of psychology in the twenty-first century. That is one answer to the question you may be asking yourself: namely, "Why am I taking this course?"

## Why Study the History of Psychology?

We just noted one example of how understanding the past can be useful. Another example is the fact that this course is being offered at your school at all. It indicates that the faculty believes it is important to learn about the history of the field. Courses in the history of psychology have been taught since 1911, and many colleges require them for psychology majors.

A survey of 374 colleges, taken in 2005, found that 83 percent provided coursework in the history of psychology (Stoloff et al., 2010). Another survey of 311 psychology departments reported that 93 percent offered such courses (Chamberlin, 2010). Of all the sciences, psychology is unique in this regard. The majority of science departments do not offer studies in the history of their fields, nor do the faculty of those departments consider that history to be vital to their students' development.

The history of psychology is a significant area of study within the discipline of psychology with its own journals, its own division (Division 26) within the American Psychological Association, and its own research center (The Archives of the History of American Psychology) at the University of Akron, Ohio (www3.uakron.edu/ahap/).

The Archives contains the world's largest collection of material on the history of psychology, including more than 50,000 books, 15,000 photographs, 6,000 films, audio and video tapes, hundreds of thousands of letters, manuscripts, lecture notes, testing apparatus, and laboratory equipment. The American Psychological Association (APA), founded in 1892, also maintains historical archives about the organization and its membership. Its Web site, www.apa.org/archives/apa-history.aspx, will direct you to oral histories, photos, biographies, obituaries, and relevant material in the Library of Congress collections.

In determining how all of this academic interest in the history of the field helps you understand psychology today, consider what you already know from taking other psychology courses: namely, that there is no single form, approach, or definition of psychology on which all psychologists agree. You have learned that there is an enormous diversity, even divisiveness and fragmentation, in professional and scientific specialization and in subject matter.

Some psychologists focus on cognitive functions, others deal with unconscious forces, and still others work only with overt behavior or with physiological and biochemical processes. Modern psychology includes many subject areas that seem to have little in common beyond a broad interest in human nature and behavior and an approach that attempts in some general way to be scientific.

The only framework that binds these diverse areas and approaches and gives them a coherent context is their history, the evolution over time of psychology as an independent discipline. Only by exploring psychology's origins and development can we see clearly the nature of psychology today. Knowledge of history brings order to disorder and imposes meaning on what appears to be chaos, putting the past into perspective to explain the present.

Many psychologists practice a similar technique, agreeing that the influence of the past helps shape the present. For example, some clinical psychologists attempt to understand their adult clients by exploring their childhood and examining the forces and events that may cause their patients to behave or think in certain ways. By compiling case histories, clinicians reconstruct the evolution of their clients' lives, and often that process leads to explanations of present behaviors and patterns of thought.

Behavioral psychologists also accept the influence of the past in shaping the present. They believe that behavior is determined by prior conditioning and reinforcing experiences. In other words, the current state of a person can be explained by his or her history—the way we were can tell us something about the way we are now.

So it is with the field of psychology. This book will show you that studying the history of psychology is the most systematic way to integrate the areas and issues of modern psychology. This course will enable you to recognize relationships among ideas, theories, and research efforts and to understand how pieces of the psychology puzzle come together to form a coherent picture. You might consider this course to be a case study, an exploration of the people, events, and experiences that have made psychology what it is today.

We should add that the history of psychology is a fascinating story on its own, offering drama, tragedy, heroism, and revolution—and its share of sex, drugs, and really weird behavior. Despite false starts, mistakes, and misconceptions, overall there is a clear and continuing evolution that has shaped contemporary psychology and provides us with an explanation for its richness.

# The Development of Modern Psychology

Here is another question. For our study of the history of psychology, where do we start? The answer depends on how we define *psychology*. The origins of the field we call psychology can be traced to two different time periods, some 2,000 years apart. Thus, psychology is among the oldest of all scholarly disciplines as well as one of the newest.

First, we can trace ideas and speculations about human nature and behavior back to the fifth century BC, when Plato, Aristotle, and other Greek philosophers were grappling with many of the same issues that concern psychologists today. These ideas include some of the basic topics you covered in your introductory psychology classes: memory, learning, motivation, thought, perception, and abnormal behavior. There seems to be little disagreement among historians of psychology that the "views of our forebears over the past 2,500 years set the framework within which practically all subsequent work has been done" (Mandler, 2007, p. 17). Thus, one possible starting point for a study of the history of psychology would take us back to ancient philosophical writings about problems that later came to be included in the formal discipline we know as psychology.

Conversely, we could choose to view psychology as one of the newer fields of study and begin our coverage approximately 200 years ago, when modern psychology emerged from philosophy and other early scientific approaches to claim its own identity as a formal field of study.

How should we distinguish between modern psychology, which we cover in this book, and its roots—that is, the prior centuries of its intellectual forerunners? The distinction has less to do with the kinds of questions asked about human nature than with the methods used to seek the answers to those questions. It is the approach taken and the techniques employed that distinguish the older discipline of philosophy from modern psychology and mark the emergence of psychology as a separate, primarily scientific, field of study.

Until the last quarter of the nineteenth century, philosophers studied human nature by speculating, intuiting, and generalizing based on their own experience. However, a major transformation occurred when philosophers began to apply the tools and methods already successful in the biological and physical sciences to explore questions about human nature. Only when researchers came to rely on carefully controlled observation and experimentation to study the human mind did psychology begin to attain an identity separate from its philosophical roots.

The new discipline of psychology needed precise and objective ways of dealing with its subject matter. Much of the history of psychology, after its separation from its roots in philosophy, is the story of the continuing development of tools, techniques, and methods to achieve this increased precision and objectivity, refining not only the questions psychologists asked but also the answers they obtained.

If we seek to understand the complex issues that define and divide psychology today, then a more appropriate starting point for the history of the field is the nineteenth century, the time when psychology became an independent discipline with distinctive methods of inquiry and theoretical rationales. Although it is true, as we noted, that philosophers such as Plato and Aristotle concerned themselves with problems that are still of general interest, they approached these problems in ways vastly different from those of today's psychologists. Those scholars were not *psychologists* in the contemporary usage of the term.

A noted scholar of the history of psychology, Kurt Danziger, refers to the early philosophical approaches to questions of human nature as the "prehistory" of modern psychology. He believes that the "history of psychology is limited to the period when psychology recognizably emerges as a disciplinary subject matter and that it is extremely problematical to talk about psychology as having a history before that" (Danziger, quoted in Brock, 2006, p. 12).

The idea that the methods of the physical and biological sciences could be applied to the study of mental phenomena was inherited from both philosophical thought and physiological investigations of the seventeenth to nineteenth centuries. That exciting era forms the immediate background out of which modern psychology emerged. We shall see that while the nineteenth-century philosophers were clearing the way for an experimental attack on the functioning of the mind, physiologists were independently approaching some of the same problems from a different direction. The nineteenth-century physiologists were making great strides toward understanding the bodily mechanisms underlying mental processes. Their methods of study differed from those of the philosophers, but the eventual union of these disparate disciplines—philosophy and physiology—produced a new field of study that quickly earned its own identity and stature. This new field grew rapidly to become one of the most popular subjects for college students today.

# The Data of History: Reconstructing Psychology's Past

## Historiography: How We Study History

In this book, *A History of Modern Psychology,* we are dealing with two disciplines, history and psychology, using the methods of history to describe and understand the development of psychology. Because our coverage of the evolution of psychology depends on the methods of history, let us introduce briefly the notion of **historiography**, which refers to the techniques and principles employed in historical research.

**Historiography:** The principles, methods, and philosophical issues of historical research.

Historians face several problems that psychologists do not share. The data of history—that is, the materials historians use to reconstruct lives, events, and eras—differ markedly from the data of science. The most distinctive feature of scientific data is the way they are gathered. For example, if psychologists want to investigate the circumstances under which people act to help those in distress, or the impact of variable reinforcement schedules on the behavior of laboratory rats, or whether children imitate aggressive behavior they see on television or in videogames, then they will construct situations or establish conditions from which data can be generated.

The psychologists may conduct a laboratory experiment, observe behavior under controlled real-world conditions, take a survey, or calculate the statistical correlation between two variables. In using these methods, scientists have a measure of control over the situations or events they choose to study. In turn, those events can be reconstructed or replicated by other scientists at other times and places. Thus, the data can be verified later by establishing conditions similar to those of the original study and repeating the observations.

In contrast, the data of history cannot be reconstructed or replicated. Each situation occurred at some time in the past, perhaps centuries ago, and historians might not have bothered to record the particulars of the event at the time or even to record the details accurately.

Today's researchers cannot control or reconstruct past events to examine them in the light of present knowledge. If the historical incident itself has been lost to view, then how can historians deal with it? What data can they use to describe it, and how can we possibly know for sure what happened?

Although historians cannot repeat a situation to generate pertinent data, they still have significant information to consider. The data of past events are available to us as fragments, descriptions written by participants or witnesses, letters and diaries, photographs and pieces of laboratory equipment, interviews, and other official accounts. It is from these sources, these data fragments, that historians try to recreate the events and experiences of the past.

This approach is similar to that of archaeologists who work with fragments of past civilizations—such as arrowheads, shards of clay pots, or human bones—and try to describe the characteristics of those civilizations. Some archaeological excavations yield more detailed data fragments than others, allowing for more accurate reconstructions. Similarly, with excavations in history the data fragments may be so great as to leave little doubt about the accuracy of the account. In other instances, however, the data fragments may be lost, distorted, or otherwise compromised.

## HISTORY ONLINE

**www.cengagebrain.com/international**
Check the publisher's Web site, www.cengagebrain.com, and enter ISBN 1-111-34498-1 to find companion materials for this text.

**www3.uakron.edu/ahap/**
The Archives of the History of American Psychology holds an outstanding collection of documents and artifacts, including the professional papers of prominent psychologists, laboratory equipment, posters, slides, and films.

**www.apa.org/about/archives/index.aspx**
This link to the historical archives of the APA will help you locate APA-relevant historical material held by the Library of Congress in Washington, D.C. as well as oral histories, photos, biographies, and obituaries.

**psychclassics.yorku.ca/ [companion site: psychclassics.asu.edu/]**
This amazing site is maintained by psychologist Christopher Green at York University in Toronto, Canada. It includes the complete text of books, book chapters, and articles of importance in the history of psychology. Google *York University History and Theory of Psychology Question & Answer Forum* to post questions about the history of psychology, answer questions that other people have submitted, or browse the site to find out what people are saying. Green offers a blog and a weekly podcast, *This Week in the History of Psychology*, at **yorku.ca/christo/podcasts**.

**historyofpsychology.org/**
The Web site for the Society for the History of Psychology (Division 26 of the American Psychological Association) offers student resources, online books and journals, and an etail shop selling posters, T-shirts, coffee mugs, baseball caps, and more featuring great men and women from psychology's past.

## Lost or Suppressed Data

In some cases, the historical record is incomplete because data have been lost, sometimes deliberately. Consider the case of John B. Watson, the founder of the behaviorism school of thought. Before he died in 1958, at the age of 80, he systematically burned his letters, manuscripts, and research notes, destroying the entire unpublished record of his life and career. Thus, these data are forever lost to history.

Sometimes data have been misplaced. In 2006 more than 500 handwritten pages were discovered in a household cupboard in England. They were determined to be the official minutes of Royal Society meetings for the years 1661 to 1682, recorded by Robert Hooke, one of the most brilliant scientists of his time. The papers revealed early work done with a new scientific tool, the microscope, and detailed the discovery of bacteria and spermatozoa. Also included was Hooke's correspondence with Isaac Newton about the subject of gravity and the movement of the planets (see Gelder, 2006; Sample, 2006).

In 1984, the papers of Hermann Ebbinghaus, who was prominent in the study of learning and memory, were found some 75 years after his death. In 1983, 10 large boxes were uncovered that contained the handwritten diaries of Gustav Fechner, who developed psychophysics. These diaries covered the period from 1828 to 1879, a significant time in the early history of psychology, yet for more than 100 years psychologists were unaware of their existence. Many authors had written books about the work of Ebbinghaus and Fechner without having access to these important collections of personal papers.

Charles Darwin has been the subject of more than 200 biographies. Surely we can assume that the written record of Darwin's life and work would be accurate and complete by now. Yet as recently as 1990, well over 100 years after Darwin's death, large amounts of new material became available, including notebooks and personal letters that were not available for consideration by earlier biographers. Uncovering these new fragments of history means that more pieces of the puzzle can be set in place.

In rare and bizarre instances, the data of history may be stolen and not recovered, if at all, for many years. In 1641, an Italian mathematician stole more than 70 letters written by the French philosopher Rene Descartes. One of the letters was discovered in 2010 in a collection housed at a college in the United States. It was subsequently returned to France (Smith, 2010).

Other data may be hidden deliberately or altered to protect the reputation of the people involved. Sigmund Freud's first biographer, Ernest Jones, intentionally minimized Freud's use of cocaine, commenting in a letter, "I'm afraid that Freud took more cocaine than he should, though I'm not mentioning that [in my biography]" (Isbister, 1985, p. 35). We will see when we discuss Freud (Chapter 13) that recently uncovered data confirm Freud's cocaine use for a longer period than Jones was willing to admit in print.

When the correspondence of the psychoanalyst Carl Jung was published, the letters were selected and edited in such a way as to present a favorable impression of Jung and his work. In addition, it was revealed that Jung's so-called autobiography was written not by him but by a loyal assistant. Jung's words were "altered or deleted to conform to the image preferred by his family and disciples. ... Unflattering material was, of course, left out" (Noll, 1997, p. xiii).

In a similar instance, a scholar who catalogued the papers of Wolfgang Köhler, a founder of the school of thought known as Gestalt psychology, was perhaps too devoted an admirer. When he oversaw the selection of materials for publication, he restricted selected information to enhance Köhler's image. The papers had been "carefully selected to present a favorable profile of Köhler." A later historian reviewing the papers confirmed the basic problem with the data of history, "namely, the difficulty of determining the extent to which a set of papers is a true representation of a person or a slanted one, either favorable or unfavorable, biased by the person who selected the papers to be made public" (Ley, 1990, p. 197).

These instances illustrate the difficulties faced by scholars in assessing the worth of historical materials. Are the documents or other data fragments accurate representations of the person's life and work, or have they been chosen to foster a certain impression, whether positive, negative, or something in between? Another biographer stated the problem as follows: "The more I study human character, the more convinced I become that all records, all reminiscences, are to a greater or lesser degree based on illusions. Whether the distorting lens is that of bias, vanity, sentimentality, or simple inaccuracy, there is no Absolute Truth" (Morris, quoted in Adelman, 1996, p. 28).

Let us offer one more example of suppressed data fragments. The father of psychoanalysis, Sigmund Freud, died in 1939, and in the more than 70 years since his death many of his papers and letters have been published or released to scholars. A large collection of papers is held by the Library of Congress in Washington, D.C. Some of these documents will not be made available for many more years, at the request of the Freud estate. The formal reason for this restriction is to protect the privacy of Freud's patients and their families, and perhaps the reputation of Freud and his family as well.

A noted Freud scholar found considerable variation in the release dates of this material. For example, one letter to Freud from his eldest son is sealed until the year 2032. A letter from one of Freud's mentors will not be released until 2102, some 177 years after the man's death, leaving us to wonder what could be so remarkable about that letter as to require such secrecy for such a long period of time. Psychologists do not know how these archival documents and manuscripts will affect our understanding of Freud and his work. Until these data fragments are available for study, however, our knowledge of one of psychology's pivotal figures remains incomplete and perhaps inaccurate.

## Data Distorted in Translation

Another problem with the data of history relates to information that comes to the historian in distorted form. Here the data are available, but they have been altered in some way, perhaps through faulty translation from one language to another or through distortions introduced deliberately or carelessly by a participant or observer recording the relevant events.

We refer to Freud again for examples of the misleading impact of translations. Not many psychologists are sufficiently fluent in the German language to read Freud's original work. Most people rely on a translator's choice of the most appropriate words and phrases, but the translation does not always convey the original author's intent.

Three fundamental concepts in Freud's theory of personality are id, ego, and superego, terms with which you are already familiar. However, these words do not represent Freud's ideas precisely. These words are the Latin equivalents of Freud's German words: id for *Es* (which literally translates as "it"), ego for *Ich* ("I"), and superego for *Über-Ich* ("above-I").

Freud wanted to describe something intimate and personal with his use of *Ich* (I) and to distinguish it from *Es* (it), the latter being something distinct from or foreign to "I." The translator's use of the words *ego* and *id* instead of *I* and *it* turned these personal concepts into "cold technical terms, which arouse no personal associations" (Bettelheim, 1982, p. 53). Thus, the distinction between I and it (ego and id) is not as forceful for us as Freud intended.

Consider Freud's term *free association*. Here the word *association* implies a connection between one idea or thought and another, as though each one acts as a stimulus to elicit the next one in a chain. This is not what Freud proposed. His term in German was *Einfall,* which does not mean association. Literally, it means an intrusion or an invasion. Freud's idea was not to describe a simple linking of ideas but rather to denote something from the unconscious mind that is uncontrollably intruding into or invading conscious thought. Thus, our historical data—Freud's own words—were misinterpreted in the act of translation. An Italian proverb, *Traditore—Tradutore* (to translate is to betray), makes this point clearly.

## Self-Serving Data

The data of history also may be affected by the actions of the participants themselves in recounting pivotal events. People may, consciously or unconsciously, produce biased accounts to protect themselves or enhance their public image. For example, the behavioral psychologist B. F. Skinner described in his autobiography his rigorous self-discipline as a graduate student at Harvard University in the late 1920s:

> *I would rise at six, study until breakfast, go to classes, laboratories, and libraries with no more than fifteen minutes unscheduled during the day, study until exactly nine o'clock at night and go to bed. I saw no movies or plays, seldom went to concerts, had scarcely any dates and read nothing but psychology and physiology* (Skinner, 1967, p. 398).

This description seems a useful data fragment providing insight into Skinner's character. However, 12 years after this material was published and 51 years after the events described, Skinner denied that his graduate school days had been so difficult. He said, "I was recalling a pose rather than the life I actually led" (Skinner, 1979, p. 5).

Although Skinner's school days are of minor importance in the history of psychology, his differing versions illustrate the difficulty that historians face. Which set of data, or which version of the incident, is more accurate? Which characterization comes closer to reality? Which has been influenced by vague or self-serving memories? And how are we to know?

In some cases it is possible to seek corroborating evidence from colleagues or observers. If Skinner's graduate school regimen were significant for historians of psychology, they could try to locate Skinner's classmates or their diaries or letters and compare their recollections of Skinner's Harvard days with his own. One biographer attempting to do so was told by a former classmate that Skinner finished his laboratory work sooner than other graduate students and liked to spend his afternoons playing Ping-Pong (Bjork, 1993).

Thus, some distortions in history can be investigated and the controversies resolved by consulting other sources. This method was applied to Freud's account of certain life events. Freud liked to depict himself as a martyr to his psychoanalytic cause, a visionary scorned, rejected, and vilified by the medical and psychiatric establishment. Freud's first biographer, Ernest Jones, reinforced these claims in his books (Jones, 1953, 1955, 1957).

Data uncovered later revealed a different situation. Freud's work had not been ignored during his lifetime. By the time Freud was middle-aged his ideas were exerting an immense influence on the younger generation of intellectuals. His clinical practice was thriving, and he could be described as a celebrity. Freud himself had clouded the record. The false impression he fostered was perpetuated by several biographers, and for decades our understanding of Freud's influence during his lifetime was inaccurate.

What do these problems with the data of history tell us about our study of the history of psychology? They show primarily that our understanding of history is dynamic. The story constantly changes and grows, and is refined, enhanced, and corrected whenever new data are revealed or reinterpreted. Therefore, history cannot be considered finished or complete. It is always in progress, a story without an ending. The historian's narrative may only approximate or approach the truth, but it does so more fully with each new finding or new analysis of the data fragments of history.

# Contextual Forces in Psychology

A science such as psychology does not develop in a vacuum, subject only to internal influences. Because it is part of the larger culture, psychology also is affected by external forces that shape its nature and direction. An understanding of psychology's history must consider the context in which the discipline evolved, the prevailing ideas in the science and culture of the day—the **Zeitgeist** or intellectual climate of the times—as well as the existing social, economic, and political forces.

**Zeitgeist:** The intellectual and cultural climate or spirit of the times.

We will see instances throughout this book of how these contextual forces influenced psychology's past and continue to shape its present and future. Let us consider a few examples of contextual forces, including economic opportunity, the world wars, and prejudice and discrimination.

## Economic Opportunity

The early years of the twentieth century saw dramatic changes in the nature of psychology in the United States and in the type of work that psychologists were doing. Largely because of economic forces, increasing opportunities emerged for psychologists to apply their knowledge and techniques to solve real-world problems. The primary explanation for this situation was practical. As one psychologist said, "I became an applied psychologist in order to earn a living" (H. Hollingworth, quoted in O'Donnell, 1985, p. 225).

Toward the end of the nineteenth century, the number of psychology laboratories in the United States was rising steadily, but so was the number of psychologists competing for jobs. By 1900, there were three times as many psychologists with doctoral degrees as there were labs to employ them. Fortunately, the number of teaching jobs was increasing as states throughout the Midwest and the West established universities. At most of them, however, psychology, as the newest science, received the smallest amount of financial support. Compared to more established departments such as physics and chemistry, psychology consistently ranked low in annual appropriations. There was little money for research projects, laboratory equipment, and faculty salaries.

Psychologists quickly realized that if their academic departments, budgets, and incomes were ever to improve, they would have to prove to college administrators and state legislators that psychology could be useful in solving social, educational, and industrial problems. So, in time, psychology departments came to be judged on the basis of their practical worth.

At the same time, because of social changes in the American population, psychologists were presented with an exciting opportunity to apply their skills. The influx of immigrants to the United States, along with their high birth rate, made public education a growth industry. Public school enrollments increased 700 percent between 1890 and 1918, and high schools were being built at the rate of one a day. More money was being spent on education than on defense and welfare programs combined.

Many psychologists took advantage of this situation and actively pursued ways to apply their knowledge and research methods to education. This pursuit marked a fundamental shift of emphasis in American psychology, from experimentation in the academic laboratory to the application of psychology to the issues of teaching and learning.

## The World Wars

War is another contextual force that helped shape modern psychology by providing job opportunities for psychologists. We will see in Chapter 8 that the experiences of American psychologists in aiding the war effort in World Wars I and II accelerated the growth of applied psychology by extending its influence into such areas as personnel selection, psychological testing, and engineering psychology. This work demonstrated to the psychological community at large, and to the public, how useful psychology could be.

World War II also altered the face and fate of European psychology, particularly in Germany (where experimental psychology began) and in Austria (the birthplace of psychoanalysis). Many prominent researchers and theorists fled the Nazi menace in the 1930s, and most of them settled in the United States. Their forced exile marked the final phase of psychology's relocation from Europe to the United States.

War had a personal impact on the ideas of several major theorists. After witnessing the carnage of World War I, for example, Sigmund Freud proposed aggression as a significant motivating force for the human personality. Erich Fromm, a personality theorist and antiwar activist, attributed his interest in abnormal behavior to his exposure to the fanaticism that swept his native Germany during the war.

## Prejudice and Discrimination

Another contextual factor is discrimination by race, religion, and gender. For many years, such prejudice influenced basic issues such as who could become a psychologist and where he or she could find employment.

***Discrimination against women***   Widespread prejudice against women has existed throughout psychology's history. We will see numerous instances in which women were denied admission to graduate school or excluded from faculty positions. Even when women were able to obtain such appointments, they were paid lower salaries than men and encountered barriers to promotion and tenure. For many years, the only academic jobs typically open to women were at women's colleges, although these schools often practiced their own form of prejudice by refusing to hire married women. The reasoning was that a woman was incapable of managing both a husband and a teaching career.

Eleanor Gibson received awards from the APA as well as several honorary doctorates and the National Medal of Science for her work on perceptual development and learning. When Gibson applied to graduate school at Yale University in the 1930s, she was told that the director of the primate laboratory would not permit women in his facility. She also was barred from attending seminars on Freudian psychology. Further, women were not allowed to use the graduate students' library or cafeteria, which were reserved for men only.

Thirty years later, the situation had not changed very much. Sandra Scarr, a developmental psychologist, recalled her 1960 admission interview for graduate school at Harvard University. Gordon Allport, the eminent personality psychologist, told her that Harvard loathed accepting women. He said, "Seventy-five percent of you get married, have kids and never finish your degrees, and the rest of you never amount to anything anyway!" Scarr added:

*Then, I did get married, and I had a baby in my third year of graduate school, and I was immediately written off. No one would take me seriously as a scientist; no one would do anything for me—write letters, help me find a job. No one believed that a woman with young kids would do anything. So I went and beat on doors and said, "Okay, here I am" until I got hired. Finally, after about 10 years and after I published a lot of articles, my colleagues began to treat me seriously as a psychologist* (Scarr, 1987, p. 26).

Despite such examples of obvious discrimination, psychology's record for equitable treatment of men and women is far more enlightened than that of other scholarly disciplines and professions. By the beginning of the twentieth century, 20 women had earned doctoral degrees in psychology. In the 1906 edition of the reference work *American Men of Science* (note the title), 12 percent of the listed psychologists are women, a high figure considering the barriers to their graduate education. These women were actively encouraged to join the APA.

James McKeen Cattell, a pioneer in the mental testing movement (see Chapter 8), took the lead in urging the acceptance of women in psychology, reminding male colleagues that they ought not "draw a sex line" (unpublished letter quoted in Sokal, 1992, p. 115). At the APA's second annual meeting in 1893, Cattell nominated two women for membership. Largely because of his efforts, the APA was the first scientific society to admit women. Between 1893 and 1921, the APA elected 79 women to membership, 15 percent of the total of new members during that period. By 1938, 20 percent of all psychologists listed in *American Men of Science* were women, and women accounted for almost one-third of the membership of the APA. By 1941, more than 1,000 women had earned graduate degrees in psychology, and one-fourth of all psychologists who held Ph.D.s were women (Capshaw, 1999).

As early as 1905, Mary Whiton Calkins became APA's first woman president; in 2007, Sharon Brehem became APA's eleventh woman president. Other professional societies denied women full participation for many years. Female doctors were not permitted to join the American Medical Association until 1915 (Walsh, 1977). Female lawyers were excluded from the American Bar Association until 1918; the ABA did not elect its first female president until 1995 (Furumoto, 1987; Scarborough, 1992).

***Discrimination based on ethnic origin***    Well into the 1960s, Jewish men and women faced admissions quotas in colleges and graduate schools. A study of discrimination against Jews during that time at three elite universities—Harvard, Yale, and Princeton—found exclusionary practices to be widespread. Admissions officers and college presidents routinely spoke of keeping the "Jewish invasion" under control. In 1922 the director of admissions at Yale University wrote a report entitled "The Jewish Problem." He described Jews as an "alien and unwashed element" (Friend, 2009, p. 272). In the 1920s the policy at Harvard University was to accept no more than 10 to 15 percent of the Jews who applied for admission to each entering class. Jews who were admitted to these elite schools were often segregated, not allowed to join fraternities or prestigious dining and social clubs. Too high a percentage of Jewish students was seen as a threat; "If Jews get in," one researcher was told, "they would ruin Princeton" (Karabel, 2005, p. 75).

Those Jewish students who did gain admission and eventually earn a doctoral degree in psychology still experienced anti-Semitism. The late 1800s saw the founding of Johns Hopkins University in Baltimore, Maryland, and of Clark University in Worcester, Massachusetts, both important institutions in the early history of psychology. It was their policy to exclude Jewish professors from faculty positions. In other colleges, academic jobs for Jewish psychologists were rare. Julian Rotter, a leading personality theorist who received his doctoral degree in 1941, recalled that he "had been warned that Jews simply could not get academic jobs, regardless of their credentials" (Rotter, 1982, p. 346). He began his professional career working at a state mental hospital instead of a university.

When Isadore Krechevsky was unable to find a teaching appointment after he earned his Ph.D., he changed his name to David Krech. Toward the end of his distinguished career in social psychology, he recalled, "I had suffered too many indignities because of the name 'Krechevsky' " (Krech, 1974, p. 242).

David Bakanovsky, a graduate student at the University of Iowa in the 1940s, was told that he would never be able to obtain an academic position. "His progress was blocked by several faculty members who believed that Iowa had graduated too many Jewish students" (Weizmann & Weiss, 2005, p. 317). He changed his name to Bakan and went on to a distinguished career.

Harry Israel was Protestant, but his name made him an obvious target for discrimination. Two of his graduate professors at Stanford University suggested that he change it (Vicedo, 2009). When they later recommended Israel for a faculty position at a large university, the dean of that school replied, "It makes no difference about his qualification. I simply can't take a man with that name" (Leroy & Kimble, 2003, p. 280). Harry Israel adopted his father's middle name and had a highly successful psychology career as Harry Harlow.

Abraham Maslow was urged by his professors at the University of Wisconsin to change his first name to "something less obviously Jewish" so that he would have a better chance of obtaining an academic job (Hoffman, 1996, p. 5). Maslow refused to do so.

After receiving his doctorate from Columbia University in 1931, Daniel Harris was told by Robert Woodworth that he could not become Woodworth's assistant during the next academic year because he was Jewish. Woodworth said Harris "shouldn't be too hopeful in an academic career" (Harris, quoted in Winston, 1996, p. 33).

Writing about one of his graduate students, Harvard psychologist E. G. Boring noted, "He is a Jew, and on this account we have not found it so far easy to place him in a college teaching position in psychology, because of the personal prejudice that exists against Jews in many academic circles and possibly especially in psychology" (quoted in Winston, 1998, pp. 27–28). These and similar incidents drove many Jewish psychologists into clinical psychology, which offered greater job opportunities, rather than the more futile pursuit of an academic career.

In 1945 the editor of the *Journal of Clinical Psychology* proposed that a limit be placed on Jewish applicants to graduate training in that specialty area. He argued that it would be unwise to allow any one group to "take over" the field, and that if too many Jews were allowed to become clinical psychologists it could jeopardize public acceptance of clinical work. To their credit, a majority of the psychology community voiced strong opposition to the proposal (Harris, 2009).

African Americans have faced considerable prejudice from mainstream psychology. In 1940, only four black colleges in the United States offered undergraduate degree programs in psychology. In those instances when blacks were permitted to enroll at predominantly white universities, they confronted a variety of barriers to achievement. In the 1930s and 1940s, many colleges did not even allow black students to live on campus. Francis Sumner, the first black student to earn a doctoral degree in psychology, received what was considered in 1917 to be a highly positive letter of recommendation to graduate school. His advisor described him as "a colored man ... relatively free from those qualities of body and mind which many persons of different race find so objectionable" (Sawyer, 2000, p. 128). When Sumner enrolled at Clark University as a graduate student, the administration arranged a separate table in the dining hall for him—and those few students who were willing to eat with him.

The major university providing psychology instruction for black students was Howard University in Washington, D.C. In the 1930s, the school was known as the "Black Harvard" (Phillips, 2000, p. 150). Between 1930 and 1938, only 36 black students were enrolled in graduate psychology programs in universities outside the American South; the majority of these students were at Howard. Between 1920 and 1950, 32 blacks earned doctoral degrees in psychology. From 1920 to 1966, the 10 most prestigious psychology departments in the United States awarded 8 doctorates to blacks, out of a total of more than 3,700 doctoral degrees granted (Guthrie, 1976; Russo & Denmark, 1987). In 1933

Inez Beverly Prosser became the first black woman to earn a Ph.D. in psychology. However, her career was restricted to teaching at small southern, historically black colleges (Benjamin, 2008).

Kenneth Clark, later noted for his research on the effects of racial segregation on children, graduated from Howard University in 1935 with a bachelor of science degree in psychology. He was often refused service at restaurants in the Washington, D.C., area because of his race. He organized a student protest demonstration against segregation in 1934 and was arrested and charged with disorderly conduct. He noted that this was the beginning of his career as an activist on behalf of integration (Phillips, 2000). Clark's application for admission to graduate school at Cornell University was rejected on the basis of race because, he was told, Ph.D. candidates "developed a close interpersonal, social relationship. They worked very closely with the professors and they were sure that I would be uncomfortable, that I would feel awkward in the situation" (Clark, quoted in Nyman, 2010, p. 84). In 1940 Clark became the first African American to earn a doctoral degree from Columbia University and the first to receive a permanent professorship at the City College of New York (Philogene, 2004).

Mamie Phipps Clark also earned a doctoral degree at Columbia but faced both race and sex discrimination. She wrote that "following my graduation it soon became apparent to me that a black female with a Ph.D. in psychology was an unwanted anomaly in New York City in the early 1940s" (M. P. Clark, quoted in Cherry, 2004, p. 22). Although her husband Kenneth Clark was on the faculty at City College, Mamie Phipps Clark was effectively barred from academic jobs. She found work analyzing research data, a minor position she described as "humiliating" for a Ph.D. psychologist (M. P. Clark, quoted in Guthrie, 1990, p. 69).

Working with Kenneth Clark, Mamie Clark opened a storefront center to provide psychological services, including testing, to children. Their efforts prospered and became the noted Northside Center for Child Development. In 1939 and 1940, the Clarks conducted an important research program on racial identity and self-concept in black children. The results of their work were cited in the 1954 U.S. Supreme Court's landmark decision to end racial segregation in public schools. In 1971, Kenneth Clark served as president of the APA, the first African American to be elected to that post.

Despite his considerable accomplishments, Clark considered his life to be a series of "magnificent failures." At the age of 78 he said that he was "more pessimistic now than I was two decades ago" (K. Clark, quoted in Severo, 2005, p. 23).

Earning a Ph.D. was only the first hurdle for blacks; next was finding a suitable job. Few universities hired blacks as faculty members, and most business organizations that employed applied psychologists (a major source of jobs for female psychologists) were effectively closed to African Americans. The historically black colleges were the primary sources of employment, but working conditions rarely afforded opportunities for the kind of scholarly research that led to professional visibility and recognition. In 1936, a professor at a black college described the situation as follows: "Lack of money, overwork, and other unpleasant factors make it practically impossible for him to do anything outstanding in the field of pure scholarship. He cannot buy books on a large scale himself, and he cannot get them at his school libraries, because there are no really adequate libraries in the Negro schools. Probably the worst handicap of all is the lack of a scholarly atmosphere about him. There is no incentive, and, of course, no money for research in most schools" (A. P. Davis, quoted in Guthrie, 1976, p. 123).

Since the 1960s, the APA has made determined efforts to bring greater diversity to the field by expanding opportunities for ethnic minorities to attend graduate schools and to increase their presence among college faculty. Despite these initiatives, minority representation of Ph.D. faculty on campus has not kept pace with the proportion of African

Americans or Hispanic Americans in the general population. For example, according to data issued by the APA in 2007, 66 percent of the current Ph.D. graduate students in psychology were white; 7.4 percent were black, 7.6 percent Hispanic, and 6 percent Asian.

When we consider the effects of prejudice as a contextual factor restricting the access of women and minorities to education and employment opportunities in psychology, it is important to note the following. Yes, the history of psychology as described in this and other textbooks includes the contributions of few female and minority scholars because of the discrimination they faced. However, it is also true that few white men are singled out for attention, relative to their numbers in the field. This is not the result of deliberate discrimination. Rather, it is a function of the way history in any field is written.

> *The history of a discipline such as psychology involves describing major discoveries, illuminating questions of priority, and identifying "great individuals" in the context of a national or international Zeitgeist. Those who carry out the day-to-day work of a discipline are unlikely to find themselves in this spotlight. Psychologists who bring considerable talent to bear behind the scenes—teaching courses, seeing clients, performing experiments, sharing data with colleagues seldom are publicly recognized beyond a small group of peers.* (Pate & Wertheimer, 1993, p. xv)

Thus, history ignores the everyday work of the *majority* of psychologists, regardless of their race, gender, or ethnic origin.

## Conceptions of Scientific History

Two ways to view the historical development of scientific psychology are the personalistic approach and the naturalistic approach.

### The Personalistic Theory

**Personalistic theory:** The view that progress and change in scientific history are attributable to the ideas of unique individuals.

The **personalistic theory** of scientific history focuses on the achievements and contributions of specific individuals. According to this viewpoint, progress and change are attributable directly to the will and charisma of unique persons who alone redirected the course of history. A Napoleon or a Hitler or a Darwin was, so this theory goes, the prime mover and shaper of great events. The personalistic conception implies that the events never would have occurred without the appearance of these monumental figures. The theory says, in effect, that the person makes the times.

At first glance, it seems clear that science is the work of the intelligent, creative, and energetic men and women who alone determine its direction. We often define an era by the name of the person whose discoveries, theories, or other contributions mark the period. We talk of physics "after Einstein" or of sculpture "after Michelangelo." It is apparent in science, in the arts, and in popular culture that individuals have produced dramatic—sometimes traumatic—changes that have altered the course of history.

Therefore, the personalistic theory has obvious merit, but is it sufficient by itself to explain entirely the development of a science or a society? No. Often, the contributions of scientists, artists, and scholars were ignored or suppressed during their lifetimes, only to be recognized long afterward. These instances imply that the intellectual, cultural, or spiritual climate of the times can determine whether an idea will be accepted or rejected, praised or scorned. The history of science is also the story of discoveries and insights that were initially rejected. Even the greatest thinkers and inventors have been constrained by the Zeitgeist, by the spirit or climate of the times.

Thus, the acceptance and application of a great person's discovery or idea may be limited by prevailing thought, but an idea too unorthodox for one time and place may be readily received and supported a generation or a century later. Slow change is often the rule for scientific progress.

## The Naturalistic Theory

**Naturalistic theory:**
The view that progress and change in scientific history are attributable to the Zeitgeist, which makes a culture receptive to some ideas but not to others.

We can see, then, that the notion that the person makes the times is not entirely correct. Perhaps, as the **naturalistic theory** of history proposes, the times make the person, or at least make possible the recognition and acceptance of what that person has to say. Unless the Zeitgeist and other contextual forces are receptive to the new work, its proponent may not be heard, or they may be shunned or put to death. Society's response, too, depends on the Zeitgeist.

Consider the example of Charles Darwin. The naturalistic theory suggests that if Darwin had died young, someone else would have developed a theory of evolution in the mid-nineteenth century because the intellectual climate was ready to accept such a way of explaining the origin of the human species. (Indeed, someone else did develop the same theory at the same time, as we see in Chapter 6.)

The inhibiting or delaying effect of the Zeitgeist operates not only at the broad cultural level but also within science itself, where its effects may be more pronounced. The concept of the conditioned response was suggested by the Scottish scientist Robert Whytt in 1763, but no one was interested then. Well over a century later, when researchers were adopting more objective research methods, the Russian physiologist Ivan Pavlov elaborated on Whytt's observations and expanded them into the basis of a new system of psychology. Thus, a discovery often must await its time. One psychologist wisely noted, "There is not much new in this world. What passes for discovery these days tends to be an individual scientist's rediscovery of some well-established phenomenon" (Gazzaniga, 1988, p. 231).

Instances of simultaneous discovery also support the naturalistic conception of scientific history. Similar discoveries have been made by individuals working far apart geographically, often in ignorance of one another's work. In 1900, three investigators unknown to one another coincidentally rediscovered the work of Austrian botanist Gregor Mendel, whose writings on genetics had been largely ignored for 35 years.

Other examples of simultaneous discovery in science and technology include calculus, oxygen, logarithms, sun spots, and the conversion of energy, as well as the invention of color photography and the typewriter, all discovered or promoted at approximately the same time by at least two researchers (Gladwell, 2008; Ogburn & Thomas, 1922).

Nevertheless, the dominant theoretical position in a scientific field may obstruct or prohibit consideration of new viewpoints. A theory may be believed so strongly by the majority of scientists that any investigation of new issues or methods is stifled.

An established theory can determine the ways in which data are organized and analyzed as well as the research results permitted to be published in mainstream scientific journals. Findings that contradict or oppose current thinking may be rejected by a journal's editors, who function as gatekeepers or censors, enforcing conformity of thought by dismissing or trivializing revolutionary ideas or unusual interpretations.

An analysis of articles that appeared in two psychology journals (one published in the United States and the other in Germany) over a 30-year period from the 1890s to 1920 examined the question of how important each article was considered to be at the time of publication and at a later date. Level of importance was measured by the number of citations to the articles in subsequent publications. The results showed clearly that by this measure, the level of scientific importance of the articles depended on whether the "research topics [were] in the focus of scientific attention at the time" (Lange, 2005, p. 209). Issues not in keeping with currently accepted ideas were judged to be less important.

In the 1970s, psychologist John Garcia attempted to publish the results of research that challenged the prevailing stimulus-response (S-R) learning theory. Major journals refused to accept his articles, even though the work was judged to be well done and had received professional recognition. Garcia, a Hispanic American, was elected to the Society of Experimental Psychologists and received the APA's Distinguished Scientific Contribution Award for his research. Eventually his work was published in lesser-known, smaller-circulation journals, but this situation delayed the dissemination of his ideas.

The Zeitgeist within science can have an inhibiting effect on methods of investigation, theoretical formulations, and the definition of the discipline's subject matter. For example, we will describe the tendency in early scientific psychology to focus on consciousness and subjective aspects of human nature. Not until the 1920s could it be said, as some joked, that psychology finally "lost its mind" and then lost consciousness altogether. But a half century later under the impact of a different Zeitgeist, psychology regained consciousness as an acceptable subject for investigation, responding to the changing intellectual climate of the times.

Perhaps we can more readily comprehend this situation if we make an analogy with the evolution of a living species. Both science and species change or adapt in response to the demands of their environment. What happens to a species over time? Very little, as long as its environment remains largely constant. When conditions change, however, the species must respond appropriately or face extinction.

Similarly, a science exists in the context of an environment, its Zeitgeist, to which it must be responsive. The Zeitgeist is not so much physical as it is intellectual, but like the physical environment, it is subject to change. We see evidence of this evolutionary process throughout the history of psychology. When the Zeitgeist favored speculation, meditation, and intuition as paths to truth, psychology also favored those methods. Later, when the intellectual spirit of the times dictated an observational and experimental approach to truth, the methods of psychology moved in that direction. At the beginning of the twentieth century, when one form of psychology was transplanted to a different intellectual soil, it became two distinct species of psychology. (This move occurred when psychologists brought the original German psychology to the United States, where it was modified to become a uniquely American psychology.)

Our emphasis on the Zeitgeist does not negate the importance of the personalistic conception of scientific history—that is, the significant contributions of great men and women—but it does require us to consider their ideas in context. A Charles Darwin or a Sigmund Freud does not single-handedly alter the course of history through sheer force of genius. He or she does so only because the path has already been cleared.

Therefore, in this book we approach the historical development of psychology in terms of both personalistic and naturalistic viewpoints, although the Zeitgeist plays the major role. When scientists propose ideas that are too far out of phase with accepted intellectual and cultural thought, their insights are likely to die in obscurity. Individual creative work is more like a prism that diffuses, elaborates, and magnifies current though, rather than a beacon. Remember, however, that both viewpoints will shed light on the path ahead.

# Schools of Thought in the Evolution of Modern Psychology

During the last quarter of the nineteenth century—the initial years of psychology's evolution as a distinct scientific discipline—the direction of the new psychology was influenced by Wilhelm Wundt. A German physiologist, Wundt had definite ideas about the form this new science (*his* new science) should take. He determined its goals, subject matter, research methods, and topics to be investigated. In this pursuit he was influenced by the spirit of his times, by the current thinking in philosophy and physiology. Nevertheless, it was Wundt in his role as the agent of the Zeitgeist who drew together threads of philosophical and scientific thought. Because he was such a compelling promoter of the inevitable, psychology for some time was shaped by his vision.

Before long, however, controversy arose among the growing numbers of psychologists. New social and scientific ideas were being advanced. Some psychologists, reflecting more modern currents of thought, disagreed with Wundt's version of psychology and proposed their own. By around 1900, several systematic positions and schools of thought coexisted uneasily. We may think of them as differing definitions of the nature of psychology.

The term *school of thought* refers to a group of psychologists who become associated ideologically, and sometimes geographically, with the leader of a movement. Typically the members of a school of thought share a theoretical or systematic orientation and investigate similar problems. The emergence of the various schools of thought and their subsequent decline and replacement by others is a striking characteristic of the history of psychology.

This stage in the development of a science, when it is still divided into schools of thought, has been referred to as "preparadigmatic." (A paradigm—a model or pattern—is an accepted way of thinking within a scientific discipline that provides essential questions and answers.) The notion of paradigms in scientific evolution was advanced by Thomas Kuhn, a historian of science, whose 1970 book, *The Structure of Scientific Revolutions,* has sold more than a million copies.

The more mature or advanced stage in the development of a science is reached when it is no longer characterized by competing schools of thought—that is, when the majority of the scientists agree on theoretical and methodological issues. At that stage, a common paradigm or model defines the entire field.

We can see paradigms at work in the history of physics. The Galilean-Newtonian concept of mechanism was accepted by physicists for 300 years, during which time virtually all physics research was conducted within that framework. Then, when a majority of physicists came to accept Einstein's model—a new way of viewing the subject matter—the approach of Galileo and Newton was replaced. This replacement of one paradigm by another is what Kuhn meant by a scientific revolution.

Psychology has not yet reached the paradigmatic stage. Throughout psychology's history, scientists and practitioners have been seeking, embracing, and rejecting various definitions of the field. No single school or viewpoint has succeeded in unifying these assorted positions. Cognitive psychologist George Miller said that "no standard method or technique integrates the field. Nor does there seem to be any fundamental scientific principle comparable to Newton's laws of motion or Darwin's theory of evolution" (Miller, 1985, p. 42).

More than 15 years later, the state of psychology had changed little. Scholars referred to the history of the field as a "sequence of failed paradigms" (Sternberg & Grigorenko, 2001, p. 1075). Noted historian Ludy Benjamin wrote, "A common lament among psychologists today … is that the field of psychology is far along a path of fragmentation or disintegration [with] a multitude of independent psychologies that soon will be or already are incapable of communicating with one another" (Benjamin, 2001, p. 735).

Another contemporary psychologist described the field "not as a unified discipline but as a collection of psychological sciences" (Dewsbury, 2009, p. 284). Yet another acknowledged "fragmentation, hyperspecialization, and ostensible incommensurability among our theories, areas of research, and methodologies" (Hunt, 2005, p. 358).

Thus, psychology may be more fragmented today than at any time in its history, with each faction clinging to its theoretical and methodological orientation, approaching the study of human nature with different techniques and promoting itself with specialized jargon, journals, and the trappings of a school of thought.

Each of the early schools of thought within psychology was a protest movement, a revolt against the prevailing systematic position. Each school loudly criticized what it saw as the weaknesses of the older system and offered new definitions, concepts, and research strategies to correct the perceived failures. When a new school of thought captured the attention of a segment of the scientific community, those scholars rejected the previous viewpoint. Typically these intellectual conflicts between old and new positions were fought with righteous fervor.

Sometimes leaders of the older school of thought never became convinced of the worth of the new system. Usually more advanced in age, these psychologists remained too deeply committed to their position, intellectually and emotionally, ever to change. Younger, less committed adherents of the old school were more easily attracted to fresh ideas and became supporters of the new position, leaving the others to cling to their traditions and their work in increasing isolation. The German physicist Max Planck wrote, "A new scientific truth does not triumph by convincing its opponents and making them see the light, but rather because its opponents eventually die, and a new generation grows up that is familiar with it" (Planck, 1949, p. 33). Charles Darwin wrote, at a young age, "What a good thing it would be if every scientific man was to die when 60 years old, as afterwards he would be sure to oppose all new doctrines" (Darwin, quoted in Boorstin, 1983, p. 468).

Different schools of thought have developed during the course of the history of psychology, each an effective protest against what had gone before. Each new school used its older opponent as a base against which to push and gain momentum. Each position proclaimed what it was not and how it differed from the established theoretical system. As the new system developed and attracted supporters and influence, it inspired opposition, and the whole combative process began anew. What was once a pioneering, aggressive revolution became, with its own success, the established tradition, and inevitably it then succumbed to the vigorous force of the next youthful protest movement. Success destroys vigor. A movement feeds on opposition. When the opposition has been defeated, the passion and ardor of the once-new movement die.

It is in terms of the historical development of the schools of thought that we describe the advance of psychology. Great men and women have made inspiring contributions, but the significance of their work is most easily understood when examined within the context of the ideas that preceded theirs, the ideas on which they built, and the work their contributions eventually inspired.

## Plan of the Book

We describe the philosophical and physiological precursors of experimental psychology in Chapters 2 and 3. The psychology of Wilhelm Wundt (Chapter 4) and the school of thought called **structuralism** (Chapter 5) developed from these philosophical and physiological traditions.

Structuralism was followed by **functionalism** (Chapters 6, 7, and 8), **behaviorism** (Chapters 9, 10, and 11), and **Gestalt psychology** (Chapter 12), all of which evolved from or revolted against structuralism. On a roughly parallel course in time, though not in subject matter or methodology, **psychoanalysis** (Chapters 13 and 14) grew out of ideas about the nature of the unconscious and the medical interventions to treat the mentally ill.

Psychoanalysis and behaviorism instigated a number of sub-schools. In the 1950s, **humanistic psychology**, incorporating principles of Gestalt psychology, developed in

---

**Structuralism:** E. B. Titchener's system of psychology, which dealt with conscious experience as dependent on experiencing persons.

**Functionalism:** A system of psychology concerned with the mind as it is used in an organism's adaptation to its environment.

**Behaviorism:** Watson's science of behavior, which dealt solely with observable behavioral acts that could be described in objective terms.

**Gestalt psychology:** A system of psychology that focuses largely on learning and perception, suggesting that combining sensory elements produces new patterns with properties that did not exist in the individual elements.

**Psychoanalysis:** Sigmund Freud's theory of personality and system of psychotherapy.

**Humanistic psychology:** A system of psychology that emphasizes the study of conscious experience and the wholeness of human nature.

**Cognitive psychology:**
A system of psychology that focuses on the process of knowing, on how the mind actively organizes experiences.

reaction to behaviorism and psychoanalysis (Chapter 14). Around 1960, **cognitive psychology** challenged behaviorism to revise psychology's definition once again. The major focus of the cognitive system is a return to the study of conscious processes. That idea, along with contemporary developments such as evolutionary psychology, cognitive neuroscience, and positive psychology, is the subject of Chapter 15.

# Discussion Questions

1. Describe the cyclical process by which schools of thought begin, prosper, and then fail.

2. Describe the differences between personalistic and naturalistic conceptions of scientific history. Explain which approach is supported by cases of simultaneous discovery.

3. Describe the obstacles faced by women, Jews, and African Americans in pursuing careers in psychology, especially during the first half of the twentieth century.

4. How does the process of writing history in any field necessarily restrict the number of people whose work can be singled out for attention?

5. In what ways do the data of history differ from the data of science? Give examples of how historical data can be distorted.

6. In what ways have contextual forces influenced the development of modern psychology?

7. What can we learn from studying the history of psychology?

8. What is meant by the term "school of thought"? Has the science of psychology reached the paradigmatic stage of development? Why or why not?

9. What is the Zeitgeist? How does the Zeitgeist affect the evolution of a science? Compare the growth of a science with the evolution of a living species.

10. Why can psychologists claim that psychology is one of the oldest scholarly disciplines as well as one of the newest? Explain why modern psychology is a product of both nineteenth-century and twentieth-century thought.

## CHAPTER 2

# Philosophical Influences

## The Defecating Duck and the Glory of France

It looked like a duck. It quacked like a duck. It rose up on its legs when the keeper held out his hand to offer it kernels of grain. It stretched its neck forward, grabbed the grain in its beak, and swallowed it, just like a duck. And then it defecated onto a silver platter—just like a duck? Only it was not a duck, at least not a real one. It was a mechanical duck, a machine full of levers and cogs and springs that caused it to move and to imitate a duck's behavior. One wing alone contained more than 400 parts. It was considered one of the great wonders of its time.

The duck's inventor, Jacques de Vaucanson, charged an admission fee equivalent to the average of one week's wages to view this marvel of the age. He quickly became rich as a result, and his mechanical model became "the talk of all the salons, as the nation's leaders debated how it worked and just what it signified for politics, philosophy, and life itself" (Singer, 2009, p. 43). That is a lot to ask of a defecating duck!

The year was 1739; the place was Paris, France. The defecating duck drew enormous crowds from many European countries. People marveled that inventors could fashion such a lifelike creation. They watched it move and eat and swallow and defecate, in awe that such a glorious, miraculous machine had been made possible. Even the great philosopher Voltaire beheld the duck and wrote, "Without the shitting duck, there would be nothing to remind us of the glory of France" (Voltaire, quoted in Wood, 2002, p. 27). More than 100 years later, the great scientist Hermann von Helmholtz (see Chapter 3) wrote that the duck was "the marvel of the last century" (quoted in Riskin, 2004, p. 633).

Well, you might ask, what is the big deal? Why was this mechanical toy considered such a wonder? Today we can see far more complicated and realistic figures at any theme park. But remember, this was the eighteenth century, and such a contraption had rarely been seen. The great public interest in the amazing French duck was part of a newfound fascination with all sorts of machines that were being invented and perfected for use in science, industry, and entertainment.

## The Spirit of Mechanism

Throughout England and Western Europe, a vast number of machines were put to daily use to extend human muscle power. Pumps, levers, pulleys, cranes, wheels, and gears powered water mills and windmills to grind grain, saw wood, weave textiles, and accomplish other forms of labor-intensive work, thus freeing European society from its dependence on human brawn. Machines became familiar to people at all levels of society, from peasant to aristocrat, and soon they were accepted as a natural part of everyday life.

In the royal gardens of the day, mechanical devices were being built to provide whimsical forms of amusement. Water running through underground pipes operated mechanical figures that performed an astonishing variety of movements, played musical instruments, and produced sounds approximating human speech. As people strolled through the gardens they would unwittingly step on hidden pressure plates, activating the mechanisms and sending water coursing through the pipes to set the figures in motion. Of all the new devices, however, it was the mechanical clock that would have the greatest impact on scientific thought.

You may wonder what this massive growth of technology has to do with the history of modern psychology. We are referring to a time 200 years before the formal founding of psychology as a science, and to physics and mechanics, disciplines far removed from the study of human nature. Nevertheless, the relationship is compelling and direct because the principles embodied by those machines, mechanical figures, and clocks that first appeared in the seventeenth century influenced the direction of the new psychology.

The Zeitgeist of the seventeenth to nineteenth centuries was the intellectual soil that nourished the new psychology. The underlying philosophy—the basic contextual force—of the seventeenth century was the spirit of **mechanism**, the image of the universe as a great machine. This doctrine held that all natural processes are mechanically determined and are capable of being explained by the laws of physics and chemistry.

**Mechanism:** The doctrine that natural processes are mechanically determined and capable of explanation by the laws of physics and chemistry.

The idea of mechanism originated in physics, then called natural philosophy, as a result of the work of the Italian physicist Galileo Galilei (1564–1642) and the English physicist and mathematician Isaac Newton (1642–1727), who had been trained as a clockmaker. Everything that existed in the universe was assumed to be composed of particles of matter in motion. According to Galileo, matter was made up of discrete corpuscles or atoms that affected one another by direct contact. Newton revised Galileo's version of mechanism by suggesting that movement was communicated not by actual physical contact but by forces that acted to attract and repel the atoms. Newton's idea, although important in physics, did not radically change the basic concept of mechanism and the way it was applied to problems of a psychological nature.

If the universe consists of atoms in motion, then every physical effect (the movement of each atom) follows from a direct cause (the movement of the atom that strikes it). Because the effect is subject to the laws of measurement, it should be predictable. The operation of the physical universe was thus considered to be orderly, like a smoothly running clock or any other good machine. It was thought that once scientists grasped the laws by which the world functioned, they could determine how it would run in the future.

The methods and findings of science were growing apace with technology during this period, and the two meshed effectively. Observation and experimentation became the distinguishing features of science, followed closely by measurement. Scholars attempted to define and describe every phenomenon by assigning it a numerical value, a process that was vital to the study of the machinelike universe. Thermometers, barometers, slide rules, micrometers, pendulum clocks, and other measuring devices were perfected, and they reinforced the notion that it was possible to measure every aspect of the natural universe. Even time, previously deemed incapable of being reduced to smaller units, could now be measured with precision.

The precise measurement of time had both scientific and practical consequences. "Without accurate time-keeping instruments, there could be no measurement of small increments of time elapsed between observations and thus no consolidation of the advances in scientific understanding begun with the help of the telescope and microscope" (Jardine, 1999, pp. 133–134). In addition, astronomers and navigators needed exact time-measuring devices to accurately record the movements of celestial bodies. These data were vital to determining the location of ships on the open seas.

# The Clockwork Universe

The mechanical clock was the ideal metaphor for the seventeenth-century spirit of mechanism. Historian Daniel Boorstin referred to the clock as the "mother of machines" (Boorstin, 1983, p. 71). Clocks in the seventeenth century were a technological sensation, as astonishing and influential as computers would become in the twentieth century. No other mechanical device had such an impact on human thought at all levels of society. In Europe, clocks were being produced in great quantity and variety.

Note that the Chinese had devised huge mechanical clocks as early as the tenth century. It is possible that news of their invention stimulated the development of clocks in Western Europe. However, the Europeans' refinement of clockwork mechanisms and their enthusiasm for elaborate, even fanciful, clocks was unmatched (Crosby, 1997).

Some were small enough to fit on a tabletop or even to be carried on one's person. With advancing technology, portable clocks were developed that were small enough to be carried around. At first they were worn on a chain around the neck as a symbol of the person's wealth. They became such a status symbol that members of the Calvinist and Puritan religious sects, "objecting to such ostentatious display, began carrying them in their pockets. Thus was born the pocket watch, popular until well into the twentieth century" (Newton, 2004, p. 62).

Larger clocks, housed in church towers and government buildings, could be seen and heard by residents for miles around. In this way, clocks became available to everyone, regardless of social class or economic circumstances. Also, however, people came to depend on clocks and to be governed by them. For the first time, punctuality became part of daily life. Activities came to be measured in units of time. Life was "regularized and became more orderly" and, as a result, more predictable (Shorto, 2008, p. 208).

Because of the regularity, predictability, and precision of clocks, scientists and philosophers began to think of them as models for the physical universe. Perhaps the world itself was a vast clock made and set in motion by the Creator. Scientists such as the British physicist Robert Boyle, the German astronomer Johannes Kepler, and the French philosopher René Descartes agreed with this idea, expressing the belief that the harmony and order of the universe could be explained in terms of the clock's regularity—which is built into the machine by the clockmaker just as the regularity of the universe was thought to be built into it by God.

This idea also became a model in the founding of the United States and the development of American politics. A commentator observed 200 years later that the Founding Fathers "who were influenced by Newtonian physics and the deist idea of God as cosmic clockmaker, devised a constitutional system of separated powers, checking and balancing one another, mimicking what they considered our solar system's clockwork mechanics" (Will, 2009, np). Thus, the idea of a clockwork universe transformed nearly every aspect of human experience.

## Determinism and Reductionism

**Determinism:** The doctrine that acts are determined by past events.

When seen as a clocklike machine, the universe—once it was created by God and set in motion—would continue to function efficiently without any outside interference. Thus, the clock metaphor for the universe encompasses the idea of **determinism**, the belief that every act is determined or caused by past events. In other words, we can predict the changes that will occur in the operation of the clock—as well as in the universe—because we understand the order and regularity with which its parts function.

**Reductionism:** The doctrine that explains phenomena on one level (such as complex ideas) in terms of phenomena on another level (such as simple ideas).

It was not difficult to gain insight into the structure and workings of a clock. Anyone could easily disassemble a clock and see exactly how its springs and gears operated. This led scientists to popularize the notion of **reductionism.** The workings of machines such as clocks could be understood by reducing them to their basic components.

Similarly, we could understand the physical universe (which, after all, was just another machine) by analyzing or reducing it to its simplest parts—its molecules and atoms. Eventually, reductionism would come to characterize every science, including the new psychology.

Some obvious questions followed: If the clock metaphor and the methods of science could be used to explain the workings of the physical universe, would they also be appropriate for the study of human nature? If the universe was a machine—orderly, predictable, observable, and measurable—could human beings be considered in the same way? Were people, and even animals, also some type of machine?

## Automata

The intellectual and social aristocrats of the seventeenth century already had the models for this idea in their water-powered garden figures, and the proliferation of clocks provided similar models for everyone else. As the technology was refined, more sophisticated mechanical contraptions, built to imitate human movement and action, were offered for popular entertainment. These devices were called *automata,* and they were capable of performing marvelous and amusing feats with precision and regularity.

Automata had been developed much earlier than the seventeenth century. Ancient Greek and Arabic manuscripts contain descriptions of mechanized figures. China also excelled in constructing automata; Chinese literature tells of mechanical animals and fish and of human figures devised to pour wine, carry cups of tea, sing, dance, and play musical instruments. In the sixth century, a large clock had been built in what was then called Palestine. When it struck the hours, an elaborate set of mechanical figures was set in motion. As a result, the art of creating automata spread through much of the Islamic world (Rossum, 1996). But more than a thousand years later, when seventeenth-century Western European scientists, intellectuals, and artisans devised automata, they were thought to be new. The fundamental work of those earlier civilizations had been lost.

Two of the most complex and spectacular European automata were the defecating duck and an animated flute player, which contained "an infinity of wires and steel chains [that] form the movement of the fingers, in the same way as in living man, by the dilation and contraction of the muscles. It is doubtless the knowledge of the anatomy of man that guided the author in his mechanics" (Riskin, 2003, pp. 601–602). The flute player not only produced sounds, which popular musical toys could do, but it played the instrument. Standing five-and-a-half feet tall, the height of the average man of the day, this automaton contained a mechanical part that duplicated every muscle or other body part needed to play the flute.

Nine bellows pumped differing amounts of air into the figure's chest, depending on which of the 12 tunes it was programmed to perform. The air was forced through a single pipe (corresponding to a human trachea) and into the mouth, where it was controlled by the metal tongue and lips before entering the flute, thus giving the impression that the figure was actually breathing. Fingers opened and closed over the instrument's holes to produce precise sounds. Both of these automata "blurred the line between man and machine, between the animate and the inanimate" (Wood, 2002, p. xvii).

Another musical automaton, the so-called "Lady Musician," played five different melodies on a harpsichord. Her mechanical eyes followed mechanical fingers as they moved over the keys, and she appeared to be breathing in time with the music. Another marvel was the figure of a small boy seated at a desk, programmed to move its hand as if writing letters.

Automata can be seen today in the central squares of many European cities, where mechanical figures in the town hall's clock tower march in circles, bang drums, and strike bells with hammers on the quarter hour. In France's Strasbourg Cathedral, representations of Biblical figures bow hourly to a statue of the Virgin Mary, while a rooster opens its beak, sticks out its tongue, flaps its wings, and crows. At England's Wells Cathedral, pairs of knights in armor circle each other in mock combat. As the clock strikes the hour, one knight knocks the other off his horse. The Bavarian National Museum in Munich, Germany, houses a parrot 16 inches tall. As the clock strikes the hour, the parrot whistles, flaps its mechanical wings, rolls its eyes, and drops a small steel ball from its tail.

The accompanying photo shows the inner workings of a 16-inch figure of a monk, now in the collection of the National Museum of American History in Washington, D.C. The monk is programmed to move within the space of a two-foot square. Its feet appear to kick out from beneath its robe, but actually the statue is moving on wheels. It beats its chest with one arm and waves with the other, nods its head, and opens and shuts its mouth.

The philosophers and scientists of the time believed that this kind of clockwork technology might fulfill their dream of creating an artificial being. Clearly, many of the early automata give that appearance. We could think of them as the Disney figures of their era, and it is easy to understand why people reached the conclusion that living beings were simply another kind of machine.

## People as Machines

Look again at the inner workings of the monk in the photo. A person examining it could clearly understand the functioning of the gears, levers, and ratchets that accounted for the figure's movements. The English philosopher Thomas Hobbes (1588–1679) wrote, "for what is the heart but a spring, and the nerves but so many strings; and the joints but so many wheels, giving motion to the whole body" (Hobbes, quoted in Zimmer, 2004, p. 97).

Descartes and other philosophers also adopted automata as models for human beings. Not only was the universe a clockwork machine, so too were its people. Descartes wrote that this idea would not "appear at all strange to those who are acquainted with the different automata, or moving machines, fabricated by human industry … such persons will look upon this body as a machine made by the hands of God, which is incomparably better arranged and adequate to movements more admirable than in any machine of human invention" (Descartes, 1637/1912, p. 44). People might be better and more efficient machines than the ones the clockmakers built, but they were machines nonetheless.

Thus, clocks and automata paved the way for the ideas that human functioning and behavior were governed by mechanical laws and that the experimental and quantitative methods so successful in uncovering the secrets of the physical universe could be applied to human nature. In 1748, the French physician Julien de La Mettrie (who died of an overdose of pheasant and truffles) reported a hallucination he had experienced during a high fever. The dream persuaded him that people were machines, albeit enlightened ones, like a watch that wound its own springs (Mazlish, 1993).

This notion became a driving force of the Zeitgeist in science and philosophy and, for a considerable time, altered the prevailing image of human nature, even among the general population. For example, during the U.S. Civil War (1861–1865), a Northern military officer, commenting on the death of a friend, wrote that nothing was left of him "but the broken machine that the soul once put in motion" (Lyman, quoted in Agassiz, 1922, p. 332).

The mechanical image of human beings permeated the literature of the nineteenth and early twentieth centuries in novels and children's tales. People were fascinated by the idea that lifelike figures could be recreated by machines. Hans Christian Andersen,

Automaton figure of a monk.

the Danish storyteller, wrote *The Nightingale* about a mechanical bird. The English novelist Mary Wollstonecraft Shelley's perennially popular book, *Frankenstein,* features a machine-monster that destroys its creator. The famous Oz books for children by the American writer L. Frank Baum—the basis for the classic movie *The Wizard of Oz*—are full of mechanical men.

And so the legacy of the seventeenth to nineteenth centuries includes the conception of humans operating as machines, along with the scientific method by which human functioning could be investigated. Bodies were likened to machines, the scientific outlook was dominant, and life was subject to mechanical laws. In a rudimentary way, mechanism also was applied to human mental functioning. The result was a machine that supposedly could think.

## The Calculating Engine

Charles Babbage (1791–1871) developed a fascination with clocks and automata as a boy. He was attracted particularly to the mechanical figure of a dancing lady, an object he managed to purchase later in life. Babbage was unusually intelligent and gifted in mathematics, which he studied on his own as an adolescent. When he enrolled at Cambridge University, he was disappointed to discover that he understood more about math than the faculty did. He later became a mathematics professor at Cambridge as well as a

Fellow of the Royal Society and one of the best-known intellectuals of the age. His life-long quest was to develop a calculating machine that could perform mathematical operations faster than humans and then print the results. In pursuing this goal, Babbage formulated the basic principles that drive modern computers.

We note that Babbage may not have been the first to develop a mechanical computing machine. The so-called Antikythera computer was discovered in 1900 in the wreckage of a ship sunk around the year 100 BC off the Greek island of Antikythera. The gadget was about the size of a modern laptop and contained a series of 37 gears which, when a date was entered, could crank out information about the position of the sun, moon, and other planets (Seabrook, 2007).

Whereas the automata we discussed above imitated human physical actions, Babbage's calculator imitated human mental actions. In addition to tabulating the values of mathematical functions, the machine could play chess, checkers, and other games. It even had a memory that held intermediate results until they were needed to complete a given calculation. Babbage called his calculator "the difference engine" (see accompanying photo), and he referred to himself as "the programmer." The difference engine consisted of some 2,000 precisely engineered brass and steel parts—shafts, gears, and disks—all of which were powered, or set into motion, by a hand crank. This machine, which still works, marks the beginning of the development of today's sophisticated computers. It is considered to represent a major breakthrough in the attempt to simulate human thought, to fabricate a mechanism that would display "artificial" intelligence (see Chapter 15).

One of Babbage's biographers noted, "The significance of the machine being automatic cannot be overstated. By cranking the handle, that is, by exerting a *physical* force, you could for the first time achieve results that up to that point in history could only have been arrived at by *mental* effort—thinking. It was the first successful attempt to externalize a faculty of thought in an inanimate machine" (Swade, 2000, p. 83).

Babbage planned to promote his new machine to the most influential people of the day and to garner their support so that he could construct an even more advanced device. He held grand parties at his London house, inviting up to 300 of the social, intellectual, and political elite. Charles Darwin was a guest; the writer Charles Dickens attended. Important people were eager to be seen at the home of the brilliant raconteur, inventor, and celebrity, to be in the presence of Babbage and his marvelous machine. The complete engine was too big to exhibit at home, however, so Babbage had a working model of a portion of it built to entertain his visitors. The model was two-and-a-half feet tall, two feet wide, and two feet deep.

After 10 years, Babbage was forced to abandon his work on the difference engine because of high cost overruns, to the point where the government withdrew its support. A British government official said that if the machine ever were completed, it should "first be set to calculating how much money went into its construction!" (quoted in Green, 2001, p. 136).

Babbage turned his attention to designing a larger device, which he called "the analytical engine." This machine could be programmed, through the use of punch cards, and had a separate memory and information processing capability. It also had an output capability for printing the results of its tabulations. The analytical engine has been likened to a "general purpose digital computing machine" (Swade, 2000, p. 115). Unfortunately, the machine was never built due to lack of funds. The government declined to get involved with Babbage's projects again.

One of Babbage's loyal supporters—and one of the few people who understood the machine's operation—was the 18-year-old math prodigy, Ada, Countess of Lovelace (1815–1852). Babbage called her his "Enchantress of Numbers." She referred to herself as the

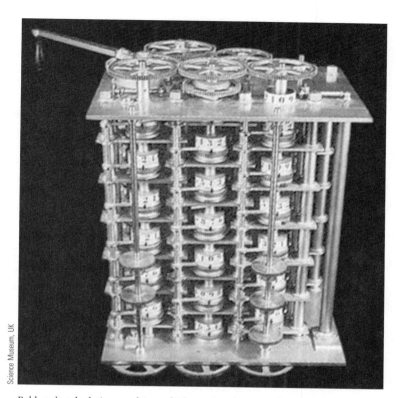

Science Museum, UK

Babbage's calculating machine, which survives intact at the Science Museum in London, England.

"Bride of Science" (Babbage, quoted in Johnson, 2008, p. 76). Ada had been a willful child, and her mother had tried to discipline her wild tendencies by prescribing the study of mathematics. Her independent tendencies were not dampened, but she turned out to be a mathematical genius. Later in life she developed extreme mood swings, became addicted to opium and morphine, and lost considerable money through gambling (Lewis, 2009).

Ada was fascinated by Babbage's machine and published a clear explanation of how the calculating machine functioned and its potential uses and philosophical implications. She was the first to recognize the fundamental limitation of a "thinking" machine, which is that it cannot, on its own, originate or create anything new. The machine can do only what it is instructed—or programmed—to do.

It is also interesting to note that she was the daughter of the poet Lord Byron (George Noel Gordon), whose memorable lines include, " 'Tis strange, but true; for truth is always strange,—Stranger than fiction." In 1980, the U.S. Department of Defense named the programming language for its military computer control system "Ada."

Babbage never explicitly stated that his machines could think, but he did not dissuade others from making such a claim. One historian observed that Babbage invariably referred to his machines' actions as capable of "replacing" or "substituting" for certain types of mental activities, such as performing mathematical calculations more rapidly than humans (Green, 2005).

Babbage became despondent when he could no longer obtain funding for his work, and after Ada's death from cancer at age 37 he turned bitter and resentful. He reportedly said that he had never known one happy day in his entire life. He "hated mankind in general, Englishmen in particular, and the English government and organ-grinders most of all" (Morrison & Morrison, 1961, p. xiii). His battle against organ-grinders and other street musicians brought him considerable notoriety among Londoners, many of whom derided him as a "crackpot." He frequently wrote letters of protest to the newspapers, complaining that the grating noise from the street dampened his mental powers and interfered with his work.

Overall, he came to believe that his efforts to develop a calculating machine had been wasted and that the importance of his contributions would never be recognized. Nevertheless, Babbage did eventually receive ample credit for his work. In 1946, when the first fully automatic computing machine was developed at Harvard University, one computer pioneer referred to that accomplishment as the realization of Babbage's dream. In 1991, to commemorate the bicentennial of Babbage's birth, a team of British scientists constructed a duplicate of one of Babbage's dream machines, based on his original drawings. The device consists of 4,000 parts and weighs three tons. It performs calculations flawlessly (Dyson, 1997).

Charles Babbage, who typified the nineteenth-century notion of humans operating as machines, clearly was far ahead of his times. His calculating machine, a forerunner of the modern computer, marked the first successful attempt to duplicate human cognitive processes and develop a form of artificial intelligence. Scientists and inventors of Babbage's day predicted that there would be no limit to what machines might be designed to do or to the humanlike functions they might perform.

# The Beginnings of Modern Science

We noted that the seventeenth century saw far-ranging developments in science. Until that time, philosophers had looked to the past for answers, to the works of Aristotle and other ancient scholars, and to the Bible. The ruling forces of inquiry were dogma (the doctrine proclaimed by the established church) and authority figures. In the seventeenth century, a new force became important: **empiricism**, the pursuit of knowledge through observation and experimentation. Knowledge handed down from the past became suspect. In its place, the golden age of the seventeenth century became illuminated by discoveries and insights that reflected the changing nature of scientific inquiry.

Among the many scholars whose creativity marked that period, the French mathematician and philosopher René Descartes contributed directly to the history of modern psychology. His work helped to free scientific inquiry from the control of rigid, centuries-old theological and intellectual beliefs. Descartes symbolized the transition to the modern era of science, and he applied the idea of the clockwork mechanism to the human body. For these reasons, we can say that he inaugurated the era of modern psychology.

**Empiricism:** The pursuit of knowledge through the observation of nature and the attribution of all knowledge to experience.

## René Descartes (1596–1650)

Descartes was born in France on March 31, 1596. He inherited enough money from his father to finance a life of intellectual pursuits and travel. From 1604 to 1612, he was a pupil at a Jesuit school, where he studied mathematics and the humanities. He also displayed considerable talent in philosophy, physics, and physiology. Because Descartes's health was poor, the school's director excused the young man from morning religious services and permitted him to lie in bed until noon, a habit Descartes retained all his life. During these quiet mornings he did his most creative thinking.

After completing his formal education, Descartes chose to sample the pleasures of life in Paris. Eventually he found this tiresome and chose a quieter life devoted to the study of mathematics. At the age of 21, he served as a gentleman-volunteer in the armies of Holland, Bavaria, and Hungary, and was known as a fine swordsman and adventurer. He loved to dance and to gamble; he proved a successful gambler because of his mathematical skills.

RENÉ DESCARTES

Descartes was attracted to women who squinted, and on that basis he offered the following explanation to people who fall in love. He wrote, "When I was a boy I fell in love with a girl who had a bit of a squint, and for a long time afterwards, whenever I saw someone with a squint I felt the passion of love. … So if we love someone without knowing why, we can assume that that person is somehow similar to someone else whom we loved before, even if we don't know precisely how" (Descartes, quoted in Buckley, 2004, pp. 107–108).

His only lasting romantic attachment was a three-year affair with a Dutch woman, Helene Jans, who gave birth to their daughter Francine. Descartes adored the child and was heartbroken when she died in his arms at the age of five. A biographer wrote that Descartes was inconsolable, experiencing "the deepest regret he had ever felt in his life" (quoted in Rodis-Lewis, 1998, p. 141). Descartes remained celibate for the rest of his life.

Descartes was keenly interested in applying scientific knowledge to practical concerns. He investigated ways to keep his hair from turning gray and conducted experiments on the maneuverability of wheelchairs. He also anticipated the notion of conditioning in dogs, some 200 years before Pavlov refined the concept (see Chapter 9). According to one biographer, Descartes, in 1630, told a friend that "after you whip a dog six or eight times to the sound of a violin, the sound of the violin alone will make the dog whimper and tremble with fear" (quoted in Watson, 2002, p. 168).

While on duty with the army, Descartes had several dreams that changed his life. As he recalled, he spent the day of November 10 alone in a stove-heated room, deep in thought about his mathematical and scientific ideas. He fell asleep, and in his dreams—as he later interpreted it—he was rebuked for his idleness. The "Spirit of Truth" took possession of his mind and persuaded him to devote his life's work to the proposition that mathematical principles can be applied to all the sciences and thus produce certainty of knowledge. He resolved to doubt everything, particularly dogma and lore from the past, and accept as true only that of which he could be absolutely certain.

Returning to Paris, he again found life too distracting. By selling the estates he had inherited from his father, Descartes was able to afford to move to a country house in Holland. His need for solitude was so great that he lived in 13 towns and two dozen houses over 20 years, keeping his address secret from all but close friends, with whom he corresponded frequently. His only apparent requirements were proximity to a Roman Catholic church and to a university. According to one biographer, Descartes' motto was, "He lives well who is well hidden" (Gaukroger, 1995, p. 16).

A more recent biographer described Descartes at this stage of his life as follows:

> … *a man of immense self-regard and of immeasurable ambition … a proud, excitable, egotistical little man. Dogmatic about his own views, he accused everyone who disagreed with him of misunderstanding or of being stupid. He was suspicious, quick to take offense and to anger, slow to cool. He insisted that he was unaffected by personal attacks but he never forgot an insult, slight, or an injury.* (Watson, 2002, pp. 165, 187–188)

Descartes wrote extensively on mathematics and philosophy, and his growing fame from these writings caught the attention of 20-year-old Queen Christina of Sweden, who requested that he instruct her in philosophy. Although exceedingly reluctant to abandon his freedom and privacy, and fearing that he would die in Sweden, he nevertheless had great respect for royal demands.

On September 7, 1649, Descartes boarded a ship, "dressed up in his new green silk suit, white collar, lace-spangled gloves, curly wig, and boots with turned up toes," prepared for the month-long voyage to Stockholm (Watson, 2002, p. 290). His appearance at the royal court was not a success, however. The queen insisted on having her lessons at 5 o'clock in the morning in a poorly heated library during an unusually bitter winter. "I am not in my element here," Descartes wrote to a friend, "and I want only peace and quiet" (quoted in Rodis-Lewis, 1998, p. 196). To another friend he wrote, "I think that in winter men's thoughts here freeze like the water" (quoted in Watson, 2002, p. 304). The increasingly frail Descartes withstood the early hour and extreme cold for nearly four months before contracting pneumonia. He died on February 11, 1650.

An interesting postscript to the death of a man who, as we will see, devoted considerable thought to the interaction between the mind and the body is the disposition of his own body. Sixteen years after Descartes's death, his friends decided that the body should be returned to France. They sent a coffin to Sweden, but it was too short to contain the remains, so the solution reached by Swedish authorities was to cut off the head and bury it until other arrangements could be made.

While the rest of the corpse was being prepared for the journey home, France's ambassador to Sweden decided he wanted a souvenir, and he severed the right forefinger. The body, now minus its head and one finger, was buried in Paris amid much pomp and ceremony. Some time later, an army officer in Sweden dug up Descartes's skull as a memento. For 150 years, it passed from one Swedish collector to another until it was finally interred in Paris.

Descartes's notebooks and manuscripts were shipped to Paris after his death, but the boat sank just before docking. The papers lay submerged for three days. It took 17 years of restoration work before they could be published. Almost 200 years after Descartes's death, an Italian mathematician stole 72 of his letters and took them to England, providing another example of data lost to history. Only 45 of these letters have been recovered, the latest in 2010 (Cohen, 2010). Fortunately, Descartes's ideas have fared better than the remains of his corpse and his writings.

## The Contributions of Descartes: Mechanism and the Mind-Body Problem

**Mind-body problem:**
The question of the distinction between mental and physical qualities.

Descartes's most important work for the development of modern psychology was his attempt to resolve the **mind-body problem**, an issue that had been controversial for centuries. Throughout the ages scholars had argued about how the mind, or mental qualities, could be distinguished from the body and all other physical qualities. The basic, deceptively simple question was this: Are mind and body—the mental world and the material world—distinct from each other? For thousands of years, scholars had taken a dualistic position, arguing that the mind (the soul or spirit) and the body had different natures. However, accepting the dualistic position raises other questions. If the mind and body are of different natures, what is their relationship? How do they interact? Are they independent, or does one influence the other?

Before Descartes, the accepted theory was that the interaction between mind and body flowed essentially in one direction. The mind could exert an enormous influence on the body, but the body had little effect on the mind. One view is that the body and mind are related in the same way that a puppet and its puppeteer are joined. The mind is like the puppeteer, pulling the strings of the body.

Descartes accepted this position; in his view, mind and body were indeed of different essences. But he deviated from tradition by redefining the relationship. In Descartes's theory of mind-body interaction, the mind influences the body but the body exerts a greater influence on the mind than previously supposed. The relationship is not in one direction only, but rather is a mutual interaction. This idea, considered radical in the seventeenth century, has important implications for psychology.

After Descartes published his doctrine, many of his contemporaries decided they could no longer support the conventional idea that the mind was the master of the two entities—the puppeteer pulling the strings—functioning almost independently of the body. As a result, scientists and philosophers came to assign a greater importance to the physical or material body. Functions previously attributed to the mind were now considered functions of the body.

For example, the mind was believed to be responsible not only for thought and reason, but also for reproduction, perception, and movement. Descartes disputed this belief, arguing that the mind had only a single function, that of thought. To Descartes, all other processes were functions of the body.

Thus, he introduced an approach to the long-standing mind-body problem that focused attention on a physical-psychological duality. In so doing, he redirected the attention of scholars from the abstract theological concept of soul to the scientific study of the mind and mental processes. The outcome was that methods of inquiry shifted from subjective metaphysical analysis to objective observation and experimentation. Whereas people could only speculate about the nature and existence of the soul, they could actually observe the operations and processes of the mind.

So, scientists accepted mind and body as two separate entities. Matter, the body's material substance, can be said to have extension (in that it takes up space) and to operate according to mechanical principles. The mind, however, is free; it is unextended and lacks physical substance. Descartes's revolutionary idea is that mind and body, although distinct, are capable of interacting within the human organism. The mind can influence the body, and the body can influence the mind.

## The Nature of the Body

Descartes argued that because the body is composed of physical matter, it must possess those characteristics common to all matter; that is, extension in space and the capacity for movement. If the body is matter, then the laws of physics and mechanics that account for movement and action in the physical world must apply to the body as well. Therefore, the body is like a machine whose operation can be explained by the mechanical laws that govern the movement of all objects in space. Following this line of reasoning, Descartes proceeded to explain the physiological functioning of the body in terms of physics.

He was clearly influenced by the mechanistic spirit of the age, as reflected by the development of automata and mechanical clocks. When he lived in Paris, he had been fascinated by the mechanical marvels installed in the royal gardens. He spent many hours treading on the pressure plates that caused water jets to activate the figures, making them move and utter sounds.

When Descartes described the operation of the human body, he referred directly to the mechanical figures he had seen. He compared the body's nerves to the pipes through which the water passed, and the body's muscles and tendons to engines and springs. The movements of the automata were not caused by voluntary action on their part but by external forces such as the water pressure. The involuntary nature of this movement was reflected in Descartes's observation that bodily movements frequently occur without a person's conscious intention.

**Reflex action theory:** The idea that an external object (a stimulus) can bring about an involuntary response.

From this line of reasoning he arrived at the idea of the *undulatio reflexa,* a movement not supervised or determined by a conscious will to move. For this conception, Descartes is often called the author of the **reflex action theory**. This theory is a precursor of modern behavioral stimulus-response (S-R) psychology, in which an external object (a stimulus) brings about an involuntary response, such as the jerk of your leg when the doctor taps your knee with a hammer. Reflexive behavior involves no thought or cognitive process; it appears to be completely mechanical or automatic.

Descartes's work also supported the growing trend in science toward the notion that human behavior is predictable. The mechanical body operates in ways that can be expected or anticipated, as long as the inputs are known. In one example, Descartes compared the control of muscular movement to the mechanical functioning of the choir organs he had seen in church:

> *If you have ever had the curiosity to examine the organs in our churches, you know how the bellows push air into receptacles called (presumably for this reason) wind-chests. And you know how the air passes from these into one or other of the pipes, depending on how the organist moves his fingers on the keyboard. You can think of our machine's heart and arteries, which push the animal spirits into the cavities of its brain, as being like the bellows, which push air into the wind-chests; and of external objects, which stimulate certain nerves and cause spirits contained in the cavities to pass into particular pores, as being like the fingers of the organist, which press certain keys and cause the air to pass from the wind-chests to particular pipes.* (quoted in Gaukroger, 1995, p. 279)

Descartes found confirmation in contemporary physiology for his mechanical interpretation of the workings of the human body. In 1628, the English physician William Harvey uncovered the basic facts about blood circulation within the body. Other physiologists were studying the digestive processes. Scientists had determined that the muscles of the body worked in opposing pairs, and that sensation and movement depended somehow on the nerves.

Although researchers were making great strides in describing the functions and processes of the human body, their findings often were inaccurate and incomplete. For example, the nerves were believed to be hollow tubes through which liquid animal spirits flowed, not unlike water flowing in the pipes that powered mechanical figures. However, our concern here is not with the accuracy or completeness of seventeenth-century physiology, but rather with its support for a mechanical interpretation of the body.

Established church dogma held that animals did not possess souls. Therefore, they were assumed to be automata. This idea preserved the difference between humans and animals so essential to Christian thought. If animals were automata and did not have souls, then they did not have feelings either. So the researchers of Descartes' time could conduct their research on live animals, before anesthesia was available. One writer described their amusement "at [the animals'] cries and yelps since these were nothing but the hydraulic hisses and vibrations of machines" (Jaynes, 1970, p. 224). Thus, animals belonged entirely to the category of physical phenomena. They had no immortality, no thought processes, and no free will. Their behavior could be explained wholly in mechanistic terms.

## The Mind-Body Interaction

According to Descartes, the mind is nonmaterial—it lacks physical substance—but it is capable of thought and other cognitive processes. Consequently, the mind provides human beings with information about the external world. In other words, while the mind has none of the properties of matter, it does have the capacity to think, and it is this characteristic that sets the mind apart from the material or physical world.

Because the mind thinks, perceives, and wills, it must somehow influence and be influenced by the body. For example, when the mind decides to move from one place to another, this decision is carried out by the body's muscles, tendons, and nerves. Similarly, when the body is stimulated—for example, by light or heat—it is the mind that recognizes and interprets these sensory data and determines the appropriate response.

Before Descartes could complete his theory about the interaction of mind and body, he needed to locate the actual physical part of the body where the mind and the body mutually interacted. He conceived of the mind as unitary, which meant that it must interact with the body only at a single point. He also believed that the interaction occurred somewhere within the brain because research had shown that sensations travel to the brain and movement originates within the brain. It was obvious to Descartes that the brain had to be the focal point for the mind's functions. The only structure of the brain that is single and unitary (that is, not divided and duplicated in each hemisphere) is the pineal body or *conarium,* and Descartes chose this as the logical site of the interaction.

Descartes used mechanistic terms to describe how the mind-body interaction occurs. He suggested that the movement of animal spirits in the nerve tubes makes an impression on the conarium and from this impression the mind produces a sensation. In other words, a quantity of physical motion (the flow of animal spirits) produces a mental quality (a sensation). The reverse can also occur: The mind can make an impression on the conarium (in some way Descartes never made clear), and by inclining to one direction or another, the impression can influence the flow of animal spirits to the muscles, resulting in a physical or bodily movement.

### The Doctrine of Ideas

Descartes's doctrine of ideas also had a profound influence on the development of modern psychology. He suggested that the mind produces two kinds of ideas: derived and innate. **Derived ideas** arise from the direct application of an external stimulus, such as the sound of a bell or the sight of a tree. Thus, derived ideas (the idea of the bell or the tree) are products of the experiences of the senses. **Innate ideas** are not produced by objects in the external world impinging on the senses but develop instead out of the mind or consciousness. Although the potential existence of innate ideas is independent of sensory experiences, they may be realized in the presence of appropriate experiences. Among the innate ideas Descartes identified are God, the self, perfection, and infinity.

In later chapters we note how the concept of innate ideas led to the nativistic theory of perception (the idea that our ability to perceive is innate rather than learned) and also influenced the Gestalt school of psychology, which, in turn, influenced the more contemporary cognitive movement in psychology. The doctrine of innate ideas is also important because it inspired opposition among early empiricists and associationists, such as John Locke, and among later empiricists, such as Hermann von Helmholtz and Wilhelm Wundt.

Descartes's work served as a catalyst for many trends that would converge in the new psychology. His noteworthy systematic contributions include the following:

- *The mechanistic conception of the body*
- *The theory of reflex action*
- *The mind-body interaction*
- *The localization of mental functions in the brain*
- *The doctrine of innate ideas*

With Descartes we see the idea of mechanism applied to the human body. So widespread was the mechanistic philosophy in defining the Zeitgeist of that era that it was inevitable that someone would decide to apply it to the human mind. Let us now turn to that significant event: the reduction of the human mind to a machine.

# Philosophical Foundations of the New Psychology: Positivism, Materialism, and Empiricism
## Auguste Comte (1798–1857)

By the middle of the nineteenth century, 200 years after Descartes' death, the long period of prescientific psychology had come to an end. During this time, European philosophical thought had become infused with a new spirit: **positivism**. The term and the concept are

**Derived and innate ideas:** Derived ideas are produced by the direct application of an external stimulus; innate ideas arise from the mind or consciousness, independent of sensory experiences or external stimuli.

**Positivism:** The doctrine that recognizes only natural phenomena or facts that are objectively observable.

the work of the French philosopher Auguste Comte, who, when he learned he was dying, said that his death would be an irreparable loss to the world.

Comte undertook a systematic survey of all human knowledge. To make this ambitious task more manageable, he decided to limit his work to facts that were beyond question; that is, those facts that had been determined solely through the methods of science. Thus, his positivistic approach referred to a system based exclusively on facts that are objectively observable and not debatable. Everything of a speculative, inferential, or metaphysical nature he declared illusory, and thus rejected.

Comte believed that the physical sciences had already reached a positivist stage, no longer dependent on unobservable forces or religious beliefs to explain natural phenomena. However, for the social sciences to reach a more advanced stage of development, they, too, would have to abandon metaphysical questions and explanations and build solely on observable facts. So influential were Comte's ideas that positivism became a popular and dominant force in the European Zeitgeist of the late 1800s. "*Everyone* was a positivist, or at least professed to be" (Reed, 1997, p. 156).

It is amazing that Comte was able to exert such a major and lasting influence over European thought, considering his financial and emotional problems. He never held a formal academic position. His writings provided little more than subsistence income, supplemented by fees for public lectures and occasional gifts from admirers. He was brilliant but troubled, and he struggled with frequent periods of dementia.

> *[He] would often crouch behind doors and act more like an animal than a human.... Every lunch and dinner, he would announce he was a Scottish Highlander from one of Walter Scott's novels, stick his knife into the table, demand a juicy piece of pork, and recite verses of Homer. ... One day, when his mother joined [Comte and his wife] for a meal, an argument broke out at the table, and Comte took a knife and slit his throat. The scars were visible for the rest of his life.* (Pickering, 1993, p. 392)

Early in his career Comte had supported the notion of equality for women, as well as other feminist causes, but he changed his mind when he married a strong-willed, highly intelligent woman. He described his marriage as the biggest mistake of his life. (His ideas on positivism fared better than his personal life.)

The widespread acceptance of positivism meant that scholars would consider two types of propositions. A historian described them as follows: "One refers to the objects of sense, and it is a scientific statement. The other is nonsense!" (Robinson, 1981, p. 333). Knowledge derived from metaphysics and from theology was the "nonsense." Only knowledge derived from science was held to be valid.

**Materialism:** The doctrine that considers the facts of the universe to be sufficiently explained in physical terms by the existence and nature of matter.

Other ideas in philosophy also supported anti-metaphysical positivism. The doctrine of **materialism** stated that the facts of the universe could be described in physical terms and explained by the properties of matter and energy. The materialists proposed that even human consciousness could be understood in terms of the principles of physics and chemistry. The materialists' work on mental processes focused on physical properties— the anatomical and physiological structures of the brain.

A third group of philosophers, those who advocated empiricism, were concerned with how the mind acquires knowledge. They argued that all knowledge is derived from sensory experience. Positivism, materialism, and empiricism became the philosophical foundations of the new science of psychology. Of these three philosophical orientations, empiricism played the major role. Empiricism could be related to the growth of the mind; that is, to how the mind acquires knowledge. According to the empiricist view, the mind grows through the progressive accumulation of sensory experiences. This idea contrasts with the nativistic view exemplified by Descartes, which holds that some ideas are innate.

We consider some of the major British empiricists: John Locke, George Berkeley, David Hartley, James Mill, and John Stuart Mill.

JOHN LOCKE

## John Locke (1632–1704)

John Locke, the son of a lawyer, studied at universities in London and Oxford and received his bachelor's degree in 1656 and his master's degree shortly thereafter. At first he was an indifferent student, amusing himself by "reading, romance, and writing flirtatious letters to women he never actually pursued. He developed an amateur's curiosity about medicine, filling notebooks with recipes that called for hedgehog grease and carved-up puppies. He once took the heart out of a frog and watched the animal leap about until it died. Locke did these things more to pass the time than with any pretense of practicing the new science" (Zimmer, 2004, p. 241).

After several years as a student, he finally showed a serious interest in one subject: natural philosophy. He remained at Oxford a few more years, tutoring in Greek, writing, and philosophy, and then took up the practice of medicine. He developed an interest in politics and in 1667 went to London to become secretary to the Earl of Shaftesbury and, in time, the confidant and friend of this controversial statesman.

Shaftesbury's influence in the government declined, and in 1681 he fled to Holland after participating in a plot against King Charles II. Although Locke was not involved in the plot, his relationship with the earl brought him under suspicion, and so he, too, left for Holland. Several years later, Locke was able to return to England, where he became commissioner of appeals and wrote books on education, religion, and economics. He was concerned about religious freedom and the right of people to govern themselves. His writings brought him much fame and influence, and he was known throughout Europe as a champion of liberalism in government. Some of his work had an impact on the writers of the American Declaration of Independence.

Locke's major work of importance to psychology is *An Essay Concerning Human Understanding* (1690), which was the culmination of 20 years of study. This book, which appeared in four editions by 1700 and was translated into French and Latin, marks the formal beginning of British empiricism.

***How the mind acquires knowledge.***    Locke was concerned primarily with cognitive functioning; that is, the ways in which the mind acquires its knowledge. In tackling this issue, he rejected the existence of innate ideas, as proposed by Descartes, and argued that humans are born without any knowledge whatsoever. Aristotle had held a similar notion centuries before, that the mind at birth was a *tabula rasa,* a blank or clean slate on which experience would write. Locke admitted that certain concepts—such as the idea of God— may seem to us as adults to be innate, but that is only because we were taught those ideas in childhood and cannot remember a time when we were unaware of them. Thus, Locke explained the apparent inherent nature of some ideas in terms of learning and habit. How, then, does the mind acquire knowledge? To Locke, as for Aristotle earlier, the answer was that the mind acquired knowledge through experience.

***Sensation and reflection.***    Locke recognized two kinds of experiences, one deriving from sensation and the other from reflection. The ideas that derive from sensation—from direct sensory input from physical objects in the environment—are simple sense impressions. These sense impressions operate on the mind, and the mind itself also operates on the sensations, reflecting on them to form ideas. This mental or cognitive function of reflection as a source of ideas depends on sensory experience because the ideas produced by the mind's reflection are based on impressions already experienced through the senses. In the course of human development, sensations appear first. They are a necessary forerunner of reflections because there must first be a reservoir of sense impressions for the mind to be able to reflect on. In reflecting, we recall past sensory impressions and combine them to form abstractions and other higher-level ideas. Thus, all ideas arise from sensation and reflection, but the ultimate source remains our sensory experiences.

You may wonder why we are asking you to read something that Locke wrote more than 300 years ago. After all, you are reading about Locke in this section of the textbook, and your instructor is discussing him in class. Remember, however, that textbook authors and teachers provide you with their own versions, visions, and perceptions. Authors and teachers must reduce, abstract, and synthesize the original data of history to distill them to manageable proportions. In that process, something of the unique form, style, and even content of the original may be lost.

To understand fully any system of thought, one should, ideally, read the original data of history on which writers base their books and professors create their lectures. In practice, of course, this is rarely possible. That is why we are providing you with samples of the original data—the theorists' own words—for many of the contributors to the development of psychological thought. These excerpts show you how the theorists presented their ideas and acquaint you with the explanatory style previous generations of students were required to study.

## IN THEIR OWN WORDS

### Original Source Material on Empiricism from *An Essay Concerning Human Understanding* (1690)

**John Locke**

Let us then suppose the Mind to be, as we say, white Paper, void of all Characters, without any *Ideas;* How comes it to be furnished? Whence comes it by that vast store, which the busy and boundless Fancy of Man has painted on it, with an almost endless variety? Whence has it all the materials of Reason and Knowledge? To this I answer, in one word, From *Experience.* In that, all our Knowledge is founded; and from that it ultimately derives it self. Our observation employ'd either about external, sensible Objects; or about the internal Operations of our Minds, perceived and reflected on by our selves, is that which supplies our Understandings with all the materials of thinking. These two are the Fountains of Knowledge from whence all the Ideas we have, or can naturally have, do spring.

First, Our Senses, conversant about particular sensible Objects, do convey in to the Mind several distinct perceptions of things, according to those various ways wherein those Objects do affect them: And thus we come by those ideas we have of Yellow, White, Heat, Cold, Soft, Hard, Bitter, Sweet, and all those which we call sensible qualities, which when I say the senses convey into the mind, I mean they from external Objects convey into the mind what produces there those *Perceptions.* This great Source of most of the ideas we have, depending wholly upon our Senses, and derived by them to the Understanding, I call *Sensation.*

Secondly, The other Fountain from which Experience furnisheth the Understanding with Ideas, is the Perception of the Operations of our own Minds within us, as it is employ'd about the Ideas it has got: which Operations, when the Soul comes to reflect on and consider do furnish the Understanding with another set of Ideas, which could not be had from things without: and such are Perception, Thinking, Doubting, Believing, Reasoning, Knowing, Willing, and all the different actings of our own Minds; which we being conscious of and observing in our selves do from these receive into our Understandings as distinct Ideas, as we do from Bodies affecting our Senses. This Source of Ideas every Man has wholly in himself: And though it be not Sense, as having nothing to do with external Objects; yet it is very like it and might properly enough be call'd internal Sense. But as I call the other *Sensation,* so I call this *Reflection,* the Ideas it affords being such only as the Mind gets by reflecting on its own Operations within it self. By *Reflection,* then, I would be understood to mean that notice which the Mind takes of its own Operations and the manner of them, by reason whereof there come to be Ideas of these Operations in the Understanding. These two, I say—External, Material things as the objects of *Sensation;* and the Operations of our own Minds within as the Objects of *Reflection*—are, to me, the only Originals from whence all our Ideas take their beginnings.

*Simple ideas and complex ideas.*    Locke distinguished between simple ideas and complex ideas. **Simple ideas** can arise from both sensation and reflection and are received passively by the mind. Simple ideas are elemental; they cannot be analyzed or reduced to even simpler ideas. Through the process of reflection, however, the mind actively creates new ideas by combining simple ideas. These new, derived ideas are what Locke called **complex ideas**. They are compounded of simple ideas, and hence they are capable of being analyzed or resolved into their simpler component ideas.

*The theory of association.*    The notion of combining or compounding ideas and the reverse notion of analyzing them marks the beginning of the mental-chemistry approach to the problem of association. In this view, simple ideas may be linked or associated to form complex ideas. **Association** is an early name for the process psychologists call "learning." The reduction or analysis of mental life into simple ideas or elements, and the association of these elements to form complex ideas, became central to the new scientific psychology. Just as clocks and other mechanisms could be disassembled—reduced to their component parts—and reassembled to form a complex machine, so could human ideas.

Locke treated the mind as though it behaved in accordance with the laws of the natural universe. The basic particles or atoms of the mental world are the simple ideas, conceptually analogous to the atoms of matter in the mechanistic universe of Galileo and Newton. These elements of the mind cannot be broken down into simpler elements, but, like their counterparts in the material world, they can combine, or be associated, to form more complex structures. Thus, association theory was a significant step in the direction of considering the mind, like the body, to be a machine.

*Primary and secondary qualities.*    Another proposition important to early psychology is Locke's distinction between primary and secondary qualities as they apply to simple sensory ideas. **Primary qualities** exist in an object whether or not we perceive them. The size and shape of a building are primary qualities, whereas the building's color is a secondary quality. Color is not inherent in the object itself but rather depends on the experiencing person, and not all people perceive a particular color in the same way. **Secondary qualities** such as color, odor, sound, and taste exist not in the object but in a person's perception of the object. The tickle of a feather is not in the feather but in our reaction to the feather's touch. The pain inflicted by a knife is not in the knife but in our experience in response to the wound.

A popular experiment described by Locke illustrates these ideas. Prepare three containers of water: one cold, one lukewarm, and one hot. Place your left hand in the cold water and your right hand in the hot water, then put both hands in the lukewarm water. One hand will perceive this water as warm and the other will perceive it as cool. The lukewarm water itself is the same temperature for both hands; it cannot be both warm and cool at the same time. The secondary qualities or experiences of warmth and coolness exist in our perception and not in the object (in this case, the water).

Consider another example. If we did not bite into an apple, its taste would not exist. Primary qualities, such as the size and shape of the apple, exist whether or not we perceive them. Secondary qualities, such as the taste, exist only in our act of perception.

Locke was not the first scholar to distinguish between primary and secondary qualities. Galileo had proposed essentially the same notion:

> *I think that if ears, tongues, and noses were removed, shapes and numbers and motions [primary qualities] would remain, but not odors nor tastes nor sounds [secondary*

*qualities]. The latter, I believe, are nothing more than names when separated from living beings* (quoted in Boas, 1961, p. 262).

The distinction between primary and secondary qualities is consonant with the mechanistic position, which holds that matter in motion constitutes the only objective reality. If matter were all that existed objectively, then our perception of anything else—such as colors, odors, and tastes—must be subjective. Only primary qualities can exist independently of the perceiver.

In making this distinction between objective and subjective qualities, Locke was recognizing the subjectivity of much human perception, an idea that intrigued him and stimulated his desire to investigate the mind and conscious experience. He proposed secondary qualities in an attempt to explain the lack of precise correspondence between the physical world and our perception of it.

Once scholars accepted the theoretical distinction between primary and secondary qualities—that some existed in reality and others existed only in our perception—it was inevitable that someone would ask whether there was any real difference between them. Perhaps all perception exists only in terms of secondary qualities, those qualities that are subjective and dependent on the observer. The philosopher who did ask, and answer, this question was George Berkeley.

## George Berkeley (1685–1753)

George Berkeley was born and educated in Ireland. A deeply religious man, he was ordained a deacon in the Anglican Church at the age of 24. Shortly thereafter, he published two philosophical works that were to exert an influence on psychology, *An Essay Towards a New Theory of Vision* (1709) and *A Treatise Concerning the Principles of Human Knowledge* (1710). With these books, his contribution to psychology ended.

Berkeley traveled extensively throughout Europe and held a number of jobs in Ireland, including a teaching position at Trinity College in Dublin. He became financially independent when he received a sizable gift of money from a woman he met once at a dinner party. After spending three years in Newport, Rhode Island, Berkeley donated his house and library to Yale University. For the last years of his life, he served as Bishop of Cloyne. When he died, his body was left untended in bed until it began to decompose, in accordance with his instructions. Berkeley believed that putrefaction was the only sure sign of death, and he did not wish to be buried prematurely.

Berkeley's fame—or at least his name—remains known in the United States today. In 1855, a Yale University clergyman, the Reverend Henry Durant, established a school in California. He named it "Berkeley" in honor of the good bishop, or perhaps in recognition of Berkeley's poem, "On the Prospect of Planting Arts and Learning in America," which includes the oft-quoted line, "Westward the course of empire takes its way."

**Mentalism:** The doctrine that all knowledge is a function of mental phenomena and dependent on the perceiving or experiencing person.

***Perception is the only reality.*** Berkeley agreed with Locke that all knowledge of the external world comes from experience, but he disagreed with Locke's distinction between primary and secondary qualities. Berkeley argued that there were no primary qualities. There were only what Locke called secondary qualities. To Berkeley, all knowledge was a function of—or depended on—the experiencing or perceiving person. Some years later, his position was given the name **mentalism**, to denote its emphasis on purely mental phenomena.

Berkeley suggested that perception is the only reality of which we can be sure. We cannot know with certainty the nature of physical objects in the experiential world—the world that is derived from or based on our own experiences. All we can know is how we perceive or experience those objects. Thus, because perception is subjective—that is, within ourselves—it does not mirror the external world. A physical object is nothing more than an accumulation of sensations we experience concurrently, so that they become associated in our mind by habit. According to Berkeley, then, the world of our experiences becomes the summation of our sensations.

There is no material substance of which we can be certain because if we take away the perception, the quality disappears. Thus, there can be no color without our perception of color, no shape or motion without the perception of shape or motion.

Berkeley was not saying that real objects exist in the physical world only when they are perceived. His theory was that because all experience is within ourselves, relative to our own perception, we can never know precisely the physical nature of objects. We can rely only on our own unique perception of them.

He recognized, however, that there was stability and consistency in the objects of the material world and that objects existed independent of our perception of them, and so he had to find some way to account for this. He did so by invoking God; Berkeley was, after all, a bishop. God functioned as a kind of permanent perceiver of all the objects in the universe. If a tree fell in the forest (as the old riddle goes), it would make a sound even if no one were there to hear it, because God would always be perceiving it.

### The association of sensations.
Berkeley applied the principle of association to explain how we come to know objects in the real world. This knowledge is essentially a construction or composition of simple ideas (mental elements) bound by the mortar of association. Complex ideas are formed by joining the simple ideas that are received through the senses, as he explained in *An Essay Towards a New Theory of Vision*:

> *Sitting in my study I hear a coach drive along the street; I look through the [window] and see it; I walk out and enter it. Thus, common speech would incline one to think I heard, saw, and touched the same thing … the coach. It is nevertheless certain the ideas [admitted] by each sense are widely different, and distinct from each other; but, having been observed constantly to go together, they are spoken of as one and the same thing.* (Berkeley, 1709/1957a)

The complex idea of the coach is fashioned from the sound of its wheels on the cobblestone street, the sturdy feel of its frame, the fresh smell of its leather seats, and the visual image of its boxy shape. The mind constructs complex ideas by fitting together these basic mental building blocks—the simple ideas. The mechanical analogy in the use of the words "constructs" and "building blocks" is not coincidental.

Berkeley also used association to explain visual depth perception. He examined the problem of how we perceive the third dimension of depth given that the human eye has a retina of only two dimensions. His answer was that we perceive depth as a result of our experience. We associate visual impressions with the sensations that occur as our eyes adjust to seeing objects at different distances and with the movements we make in approaching or retreating from the objects we see. In other words, the continuous sensory experiences of walking toward or reaching for objects, plus the sensations from the eye muscles, become linked to produce the perception of depth. When an object is brought closer to the eyes, the pupils converge; when the object is moved away, this convergence diminishes. Thus, depth perception is not a simple sensory experience but an association of ideas that must be learned.

Berkeley was continuing the growing associationist trend within empirical philosophy by attempting to explain a purely psychological, or cognitive, process in terms of the association of sensations. His explanation accurately anticipated the modern view of depth perception in its consideration of the physiological cues of accommodation and convergence.

### David Hartley (1705–1757)

David Hartley was prepared to follow his father's career path and become a minister, but because he quarreled frequently with established church doctrine, he wisely turned to medicine instead. He led a quiet and uneventful life working as a doctor, even though he never completed his medical degree, and on his own pursued the study of philosophy. In 1749, he published *Observations on Man, His Frame, His Duty, and His Expectations,* considered by many scholars to be the first systematic treatise on association.

*Association by contiguity and repetition.*   Hartley's fundamental law of association is contiguity, by which he attempted to explain the processes of memory, reasoning, emotion, and voluntary and involuntary action. Ideas or sensations that occur together, simultaneously or successively, become associated so that the occurrence of one is connected with the occurrence of the other. Further, Hartley proposed that **repetition** of sensations and ideas is necessary for associations to be formed.

**Repetition:** The notion that the more frequently two ideas occur together, the more readily they will be associated.

Hartley agreed with Locke that all ideas and knowledge are derived from experiences conveyed to us through the senses; there are no innate associations, no knowledge present at birth. As children grow and accumulate a variety of sensory experiences, mental connections of increasing complexity are established. In this way, higher systems of thought have been developed by the time we reach adulthood. This higher-order mental life—skills such as thinking, judging, and reasoning—may be analyzed or reduced to the mental elements or simple sensations from which it was compounded. Hartley was the first to apply the theory of association to explain all types of mental activity.

*The influence of mechanism.*   Like other philosophers before him, Hartley viewed the mental world in mechanistic terms. In one respect, he exceeded the aims of other empiricists and associationists: Not only did Hartley attempt to explain psychological processes in light of mechanical principles, but he also tried to similarly explain their underlying physiological processes.

Isaac Newton had asserted that one characteristic of impulses in the physical world is that they vibrate. Hartley applied this idea to the functioning of the human brain and nervous system. He suggested that the nerves were solid structures (not hollow tubes, as Descartes believed), and that vibrations of the nerves transmitted impulses from one part of the body to another. These vibrations initiated smaller vibrations in the brain, which were the physiological counterparts of ideas. The importance of Hartley's doctrine for psychology is that it is yet another attempt to use scientific ideas about the mechanical universe as a model for understanding human nature.

### James Mill (1773–1836)

James Mill was born in Scotland, the son of a shoemaker, which ordinarily would have limited his job prospects considerably. His mother, however, refused to permit that. She had "great ambitions for him, and from the very first, James was made to feel that he was superior and the center of attention" (Capaldi, 2004, p. 1). She insisted that he stay away from other children and devote his time to study. This proved to be a Spartan regimen, and one to which he would later subject his son.

Mill was educated at the University of Edinburgh in Scotland and served for a short time as a clergyman. When he discovered that no one in his congregation understood his sermons, he left the Church of Scotland to earn his living as a writer. His most famous literary work is the *History of British India,* which took 11 years to complete. His most important contribution to psychology is *Analysis of the Phenomena of the Human Mind* (1829).

### The mind as a machine.

James Mill applied the doctrine of mechanism to the human mind with a rare directness and comprehensiveness. His stated goal was to destroy the illusion of all subjective or psychic activities and to demonstrate that the mind was nothing more than a machine. Mill believed that empiricists who argued that the mind was merely similar to a machine in its operations had not gone far enough. The mind *was* a machine—it functioned in the same predictable, mechanical way as a clock. It was set in operation by external physical forces and run by internal physical forces.

According to this view, the mind is a totally passive entity that is acted on by external stimuli. We respond to these stimuli automatically; we are incapable of acting spontaneously. Mill therefore had no place in his theory for the concept of free will.

As the title of Mill's major work suggests, he proposed that the mind be studied by the method of analysis; that is, by reducing the mind to its elementary components. You will recognize that this is the mechanistic doctrine. To understand complex phenomena, whether in the mental or the physical worlds—whether ideas or clocks, for example—it is necessary to break them down into their smallest component parts. Mill wrote that a "distinct knowledge of the elements is indispensable to an accurate conception of that which is compounded of them" (Mill, 1829, Vol. 1, p. 1).

To Mill, sensations and ideas are the only kinds of mental elements that exist. In the familiar empiricist-associationist tradition, all knowledge begins with sensations from which are derived, through the process of association, higher-level complex ideas. Association was a matter of contiguity or concurrence alone, and it could be simultaneous or successive.

Mill believed that the mind had no creative function because association is a totally automatic, passive process. The sensations that occur together in a certain order will be reproduced mechanically as ideas, and these ideas occur in the same order as their corresponding sensations. In other words, association is mechanical, and the resulting ideas are merely the accumulation or sum of the individual mental elements.

## John Stuart Mill (1806–1873)

James Mill agreed with Locke's suggestion that the human mind at birth was like a blank slate on which experience would write. When his son John was born, Mill vowed that he would determine the experiences that would fill the boy's mind, and he embarked on a rigorous program of private tutoring. Every day, for up to five hours, he drilled the child in Greek, Latin, algebra, geometry, logic, history, and political economy, questioning young John repeatedly until he answered correctly (Reeves, 2009).

He was kept away from the distraction of other children, frequently admonished and corrected for making mistakes, and never praised for his achievements. He once described his father as "excessively severe. No fault, however trivial, escaped his notice; none goes without reprehension or punishment of some sort" (quoted in Capaldi, 2004, p. 10).

In his autobiography, John Stuart Mill wrote that his father "demanded of me not only the utmost that I could do, but much that I could by no possibility have done … no holidays were allowed, lest the habit of work should be broken and a taste for idleness acquired" (J. S. Mill, 1873/1909, pp. 10, 27). Although his was a harsh upbringing, he succeeded in learning all his father thought he should know.

At the age of three, John Stuart Mill could read Plato in the original Greek. At 11, he wrote his first scholarly paper, and by 12 he had mastered the standard university

National Portrait Gallery, London

JOHN STUART MILL

curriculum. At 18, he described himself as a "logical machine," and by 21 he suffered from major depression. He wrote of his mental breakdown: "I was in a dull state of nerves … the whole foundation on which my life was constructed fell down. … I seemed to have nothing left to live for" (Mill, 1873/1909, p. 83). It was several years before he recovered a sense of self-worth. Later in life he blamed his parents for his mental difficulties, his father for his strictness and his mother who, as he said, never showed any regard for him. "I thus grew up in the absence of love and in the presence of fear" (J. S. Mill, quoted in Kamm, 1977, p. 15).

Mill worked for the East India Company, handling routine correspondence about England's governance of India. "He was such a demon for work that growing overheated through feverish memo-writing he would gradually strip off his clothes and work gravely at his stool without waistcoat or pants, as his colleagues watched in prim Victorian wonder" (Gopnik, 2009, p. 86).

At the age of 25, Mill fell in love with Harriet Taylor, a beautiful and intelligent married woman. Mrs. Taylor would have a major influence on Mill's work and life. The two developed a close friendship and mutual affection that became widely known. Even by today's standards, it was an unusual relationship. After repeated demands from her husband that she stop spending so much time with Mill, Harriet negotiated a compromise. She and Mill would continue to see one another but she would live with her husband, vowing to be loyal and faithful to both men by abstaining from sexual activities with either. This situation continued for 20 years, until Harriet's husband died. After the socially acceptable two-year mourning period, Harriet and John Stuart Mill were able to marry.

She assisted in his work, so much that he referred to her as the "chief blessing of my existence" (Mill, 1873/1909, p. 111). He was heartbroken when she died only seven years later. He built a cottage for himself from which he could gaze upon her grave. "It is doubtful," he wrote, "if I shall ever be fit for anything public or private again … the spring of my life is broken" (quoted in Capaldi, 2004, p. 246). This quotation is important because of the mechanical image Mill used; a spring was the engine, the motivating force of machines such as clocks and automata, and by extension, of humans as well. At the age of 52 he found a new "spring" in Harriet's 27-year-old daughter, Helen, who remained his companion for the rest of his life. In letters he referred to her as his daughter, but in reality she acted more like a governess. "He had adored being dominated by Harriet; he enjoyed being dominated by Helen" (Kamm, 1977, p. 133).

Mill later published an essay entitled "The Subjection of Women," written at Helen's suggestion and inspired by Harriet's marital experiences with her first husband. He was appalled that women had no financial or property rights, and he compared the plight of women to that of other disadvantaged groups. He condemned the ideas that a wife was expected to submit to sex with her husband on demand, even against her will, and that divorce on the grounds of incompatibility was not then permitted. He proposed that marriage be more a partnership between equals than a master/slave relationship (Rose, 1983). Sigmund Freud later translated Mill's essay on women into the German language, and in letters to his fiancée sneered at Mill's notion of equality of the sexes. Freud wrote, "The position of woman cannot be other than what it is: to be an adored sweetheart in youth, and a beloved wife in maturity" (Freud, 1883/1964, p. 76). We can see that Mill was more advanced in his thinking on this issue than was Freud.

***Mental chemistry.***   Through his writings on various topics, John Stuart Mill became an influential contributor to what was soon to become formally the new science of psychology. He argued against the mechanistic position of his father, James Mill, who viewed the mind as passive, something acted upon by external stimuli. To John Stuart Mill, the mind played an active role in the association of ideas.

He proposed that complex ideas are not merely the summation of simple ideas through the process of association. Complex ideas are more than the sum of the individual parts (the simple ideas). Why? Because they take on new qualities that are not found in the simple elements. For example, if you mix blue, red, and green light in the proper proportion, you end up with white, which is an entirely new quality. According to this view—which came to be known as **creative synthesis**—the proper combining of mental elements always produces some distinct quality that was not present in the elements themselves.

Thus, John Stuart Mill was influenced in his thinking by the research then being undertaken in chemistry, which provided him with a different model for his ideas than the physics and mechanics that formed the context for the ideas of his father and the earlier empiricists and associationists. Chemists were demonstrating the concept of synthesis, in which chemical compounds were found to exhibit attributes and qualities not present in their component parts or elements. For example, the proper mixture of the elements hydrogen and oxygen produces water, which has properties not found in either of the elements. Similarly, complex ideas formed by combining simple ideas take on characteristics not found in their elements. Mill called this approach to the association of ideas "mental chemistry."

John Stuart Mill also made a significant contribution to psychology by arguing that it was possible to make a scientific study of the mind. He made this assertion at a time when other philosophers, notably Auguste Comte, were denying that the mind could be examined by the methods of science. In addition, Mill recommended a new field of study, which he called "ethology," devoted to factors that influence the development of the human personality.

> **Creative synthesis:** The notion that complex ideas formed from simple ideas take on new qualities; the combination of the mental elements creates something greater than or different from the sum of the original elements.

# Contributions of Empiricism to Psychology

With the rise of empiricism, many philosophers turned away from earlier approaches to knowledge. Although concerned with some of the same problems, their methods for considering these problems became atomistic, mechanistic, and positivistic.

Reconsider the principles of empiricism:

- *The primary role of the process of sensation*
- *The analysis of conscious experience into elements*
- *The synthesis of elements into complex mental experiences through the process of association*
- *The focus on conscious processes*

The major role that empiricism was playing in shaping the new scientific psychology was about to become evident, and we will see that the concerns of the empiricists formed psychology's basic subject matter.

By the middle of the nineteenth century, philosophers had established the theoretical rationale for a natural science of human nature. What was needed next, to translate theory into reality, was an experimental attack on the same subject matter. And that was soon to occur, thanks to the physiologists, who supplied the kind of experimentation that would complete the foundation for the new psychology.

## Discussion Questions

1. Compare the explanations of association offered by Hartley, James Mill, and John Stuart Mill.
2. Contrast and compare the positions of James Mill and John Stuart Mill on the nature of the mind. Which view had the more lasting impact on psychology?
3. Define positivism, materialism, and empiricism. What contributions did each viewpoint make to the new psychology?
4. Describe Locke's definition of empiricism. Discuss his concepts of sensation and reflection, and of simple and complex ideas.
5. Explain the concept of mechanism. How did it come to be applied to human beings?
6. How did Berkeley's ideas challenge Locke's distinction between primary and secondary qualities? What did Berkeley mean by the phrase "perception is the only reality"?
7. How did Descartes explain the functioning and interaction of the human body and the human mind? What is the role of the *conarium*?
8. How did Descartes distinguish between innate ideas and derived ideas?
9. How did Descartes's views on the mind-body issue differ from earlier views?
10. How did Hartley's work exceed the aims of the other empiricists and associationists? How did Hartley explain association?
11. How did the development of clocks and automata relate to the ideas of determinism and reductionism?
12. What is the mental-chemistry approach to association? How does it relate to the idea that the mind is like a machine?
13. What were the implications of Babbage's calculating engine for the new psychology? Describe the contribution of Ada Lovelace to Babbage's work.
14. Why was the defecating duck such a sensation in Paris in 1739? What did it have to do with the development of the new psychology?
15. Why were clocks considered to be models for the physical universe?

## CHAPTER 3

# Physiological Influences

## David K. Makes a Mistake: The Importance of the Human Observer

David Kinnebrook got his shoes shined every night, but that was the only perk he received from his job. Otherwise his work was lonely, tedious, and highly demanding. He had to live in the same building where he worked and to be available from 7 in the morning until 10 at night, seven days a week. In addition, many nights an alarm bell rang in his tiny bedroom, summoning him to work again. For this he was paid a tiny salary, given three meals a day, and, oh yes, he had his shoes shined.

What were the qualifications for this dream job? One of the scientists who operated the facility wrote, "I want indefatigable, hard-working, and above all obedient drudges, men who will be contented to pass their day in using their hands and eyes in the mechanical act of observing and the remainder of it in the dull process of calculations" (quoted in Croarken, 2003, p. 286).

After Kinnebrook finally left, his replacement described the job as follows:

*Nothing can exceed the tediousness and ennui of the life the assistant leads in this place, excluded from all society, except perhaps that of a poor mouse which may occasionally sally forth from a hole in the wall. … Here forlorn, he spends his days, weeks, and months, in the same long wearisome computations, without a friend to shorten the tedious hours, or a soul with whom he can converse"* (quoted in Croarken, 2003, p. 285).

The place was the Royal Observatory in Greenwich, England; the year was 1795. Kinnebrook worked as assistant to the Reverend Nevil Maskelyne (1732–1811), the Royal Astronomer. He held the job one year, eight months, and 22 days before he was fired—and he never knew how losing his job would play such an important role in the founding of the new science of psychology.

It all began with a difference of five-tenths of a second. That is not much, you may be thinking, but it was too much for the Royal Astronomer. Maskelyne, when he noticed that Kinnebrook's observations of the time required for a star to pass from one point to another were slower than his own, rebuked the man for his mistakes and warned him to be more careful. Kinnebrook tried, but the differences increased. Maskelyne wrote:

*I think it necessary to mention that my assistant, Mr. David Kinnebrook, who had observed the transits of the stars and planets very well, in agreement with me, all the year 1794, and for the great part of the present year, began, from the beginning of August last, to set them down half a second of time later than he should do, according to my observations; and in January of the succeeding year, 1796, he increased his error to eight-tenths of a second.*

Angelo Hornak/CORBIS

Old Royal Observatory, Greenwich, England.

> *As he had unfortunately continued a considerable time in this error before I noticed it, and did not seem to me likely ever to get over it, and return to a right method of observing, therefore, though with reluctance, as he was a diligent and useful assistant to me in other respects, I parted with him (quoted in Howse, 1989, p. 169).*

And so Kinnebrook was fired. He took a job as a schoolmaster until his death 14 years later, and thus he passed into that crowded place known as obscurity, never to know that he had not really made errors after all (Rowe, 1983).

For 20 years the Kinnebrook incident was ignored, until the phenomenon was investigated by Friedrich Wilhelm Bessel (1784–1846), a German astronomer interested in errors of measurement. He suspected that the so-called mistakes made by Maskelyne's assistant were attributable to individual differences—personal differences among people over which they have no control. If so, Bessel reasoned, then differences in observation times would be found among all astronomers, a phenomenon that came to be called the "personal equation." Bessel proceeded to test his hypothesis and found it to be correct. Even among the most experienced astronomers, disagreements were common.

Bessel's finding led to two conclusions. First, astronomers would have to take into account the nature of the human observer because personal characteristics and perceptions would necessarily influence the reported observations. Second, if the role of the human observer had to be considered in astronomy, then surely it was also important in every other science that relied on observational methods.

Empirical philosophers such as Locke and Berkeley had discussed the subjective nature of human perception, arguing that there is not always—or even often—an exact correspondence between the nature of an object and our perception of it. Bessel's work provided data from a hard science—astronomy—to illustrate and support that point. As a result, scientists were forced to focus on the role of the human observer to account fully for the results of their experiments. They began to study the human sense organs—those physiological mechanisms through which we receive information about our world—as a way of investigating the psychological processes of sensing and perceiving. Once the physiologists began to study sensation in this manner, a science of psychology was but a short and inevitable step away.

# Developments in Early Physiology

The physiological research that stimulated and guided the new psychology was a product of the scientific work of the late nineteenth century. As with all such endeavors, it had its antecedents—earlier work on which it built. Physiology became an experimentally oriented discipline during the 1830s, primarily under the influence of the German physiologist Johannes Müller (1801–1858), who advocated the use of the experimental method. Müller held the prestigious position of professor of anatomy and physiology at the University of Berlin. He was phenomenally productive, publishing on the average one scholarly paper every seven weeks. He maintained this pace for 38 years before committing suicide during a bout of depression.

One of his most influential publications was the *Handbook of the Physiology of Mankind,* published between 1833 and 1840. These volumes summarized the physiological research of the period and systematized a large body of knowledge. They cited many new studies, indicating the rapid growth in experimental work. The first volume was translated into English in 1838 and the second in 1842, which attests to the interest in physiological research shown by scientists in many countries outside Germany.

Müller is also noteworthy in physiology and psychology for his theory of the specific energies of nerves. He proposed that the stimulation of a particular nerve always leads to a characteristic sensation, because each sensory nerve has its own specific energy. This idea stimulated a great deal of research aimed at localizing functions within the nervous system and pinpointing sensory receptor mechanisms on the periphery of the organism.

## Research on Brain Functions: Mapping from the Inside

Several early physiologists made substantial contributions to the study of brain functions by conducting research directly on brain tissue. Their efforts constituted the first attempts to map the brain's functions; that is, to determine the specific parts of the brain that controlled different cognitive functions. This work is significant for psychology not only because it delimited the brain's specialized areas, but also because it refined the research methods that later became widespread in physiological psychology.

A pioneer in the investigation of reflex behavior was Marshall Hall (1790–1857), a Scottish physician working in London. Hall observed that decapitated animals would continue to move for some time when he stimulated various nerve endings. He concluded that different levels of behavior arise from different parts of the brain and nervous system. Specifically, Hall postulated that voluntary movement depends on the cerebrum, reflex movement on the spinal cord, involuntary movement on direct stimulation of the muscles, and respiratory movement on the medulla.

The research of Pierre Flourens (1794–1867), a professor of natural history at the Collège de France in Paris, involved systematically destroying parts of the brain and spinal cord in pigeons and observing the consequences. Flourens concluded that the cerebrum controls higher mental processes, parts of the midbrain control visual and auditory reflexes, the cerebellum controls coordination, and the medulla governs heartbeat, respiration, and other vital functions.

**Extirpation:** A technique for determining the function of a given part of an animal's brain by removing or destroying it and observing the resulting behavior changes.

The findings of Hall and Flourens, although generally considered valid, are for our purposes second in importance to their use of the **extirpation** method. In extirpation, the researcher attempts to determine the function of a given part of the brain by removing or destroying it and observing the resulting changes in the animal's behavior.

**Clinical method:** Posthumous examination of brain structures to detect damaged areas assumed to be responsible for behavioral conditions that existed before the person died.

The mid-nineteenth century saw the introduction of two additional experimental approaches to brain research: the clinical method and the electrical stimulation technique. The **clinical method** was developed in 1861 by Paul Broca (1824–1880), a surgeon at a hospital for the insane near Paris. Broca performed an autopsy on a man who for many years had been unable to speak intelligibly. The clinical examination revealed a lesion in the third frontal convolution of the left hemisphere of the cerebral cortex. Broca labeled this section of the brain the speech center; later it came to be known, appropriately, as *Broca's area.*

The clinical method is a useful supplement to extirpation because it is difficult to secure human subjects who agree to the removal of parts of their brain, even for extra credit in their psych lab. As a sort of posthumous extirpation, the clinical method provides the opportunity to examine the damaged area of the brain, the area assumed to be responsible for a behavioral condition that existed while the patient was still alive. (Broca's own brain has been preserved in the Musee de l'Homme in Paris.)

**Electrical stimulation:** A technique for exploring the cerebral cortex with weak electric current to observe motor responses.

The **electrical stimulation** technique for studying the brain was first promoted in 1870 by Gustav Fritsch and Eduard Hitzig. This technique involves the use of weak electrical currents to explore the cerebral cortex. Fritsch and Hitzig found that stimulating certain cortical areas in rabbits and dogs resulted in motor responses, such as movements of the front and back legs. With the development of increasingly sophisticated electronic equipment, electrical stimulation has become a productive technique for studying brain functions.

## Research on Brain Functions: Mapping from the Outside

Among the scientists attempting to map the brain from the inside was the German physician Franz Josef Gall (1758–1828), who dissected the brains of deceased animals and humans. His work confirmed the existence of both white and gray matter in the brain, the nerve fibers connecting each side of the brain to the opposite side of the spinal cord, and the fibers connecting both halves of the brain.

After completing this painstaking research program, Gall turned his attention to the outside of the brain. He wanted to find out if the size and shape of the brain would reveal information about brain faculties. With regard to brain size, his studies on animals showed the tendency for species with larger brains to display more intelligent behavior than species with smaller brains. When he began to investigate the shape of the brain, however, Gall ventured into controversial territory. He founded a movement called cranioscopy, later known as phrenology, which proposed that the shape of a person's skull revealed his or her intellectual and emotional characteristics. In promoting this idea, Gall's reputation plummeted; he was no longer viewed by his colleagues as a respected scientist but rather as a quack and a fraud.

Gall believed that when a mental characteristic—such as conscientiousness, benevolence, or self-esteem—was particularly well developed, there would be a corresponding protrusion or bulge on the surface of the skull in the area controlling that characteristic. If that ability was weak, there would be an indentation in the skull. After examining the bumps and dents of a great many people, Gall mapped the location of 35 human attributes (see Figure 3.1).

Johann Spurzheim, a student of Gall, and George Combe, a Scottish phrenologist, did much to popularize the movement. They traveled throughout Europe and the United States, giving lectures and demonstrations on phrenology. Their success was rapidly overshadowed by two brothers, Orson and Lorenzo Fowler, well-educated sons of a farmer in upstate New York. The Fowler brothers became interested in phrenology from reading the works of Spurzheim and Combe, and they went on to develop an amazingly

**FIGURE 3.1** The power and organs of the mind.

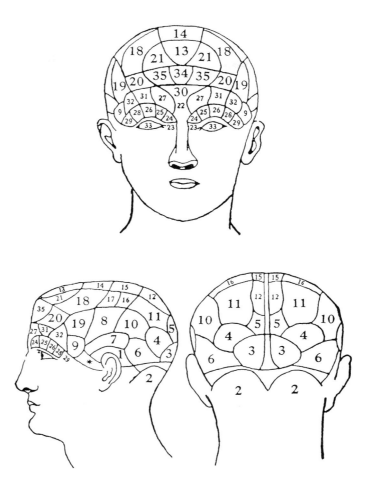

| AFFECTIVE FACULTIES | | INTELLECTUAL FACULTIES | |
|---|---|---|---|
| PROPENSITIES | SENTIMENTS | PERCEPTIVE | REFLECTIVE |
| ? Desire to live | 10 Cautiousness | 22 Individuality | 34 Comparison |
| * Alimentiveness | 11 Approbativeness | 23 Configuration | 35 Causality |
| 1 Destructiveness | 12 Self-Esteem | 24 Size | |
| 2 Amativeness | 13 Benevolence | 25 Weight and | |
| 3 Philoprogenitiveness | 14 Reverence | Resistance | |
| 4 Adhesiveness | 15 Firmness | 26 Coloring | |
| 5 Inhabitiveness | 16 Conscientiousness | 27 Locality | |
| 6 Combativeness | 17 Hope | 28 Order | |
| 7 Secretiveness | 18 Marvelousness | 29 Calculation | |
| 8 Acquisitiveness | 19 Ideality | 30 Eventuality | |
| 9 Constructiveness | 20 Mirthfulness | 31 Time | |
| | 21 Imitation | 32 Tune | |
| | | 33 Language | |

Source: Suggested by J. Spurzheim. *Phrenology, or the Doctrine of Mental Phenomena,* 1834.

successful business enterprise. Millions of Americans had their heads examined and the bumps on their skulls read by the Fowlers and their associates. The brothers:

*opened clinics in New York, Boston, and Philadelphia in the late 1830s. They franchised their business to other cities, principally through the training of phrenological examiners, and provided phrenological supplies … such as busts for display and teaching, calipers of varying sizes for measurements, display charts for the wall, manuals to sell, and, for the itinerant phrenologists, carrying cases for tools and supplies (Benjamin & Baker, 2004, pp. 4–5).*

Theirs was an incredibly profitable business that remained successful well into the twentieth century. In 1838 they started a magazine, the *American Phrenological Journal,* which was published for more than 70 years. Clients arrived in such huge numbers that the practice often resembled a carnival sideshow. Phrenologists went from town to town, "visiting during market days, setting themselves up for a short time, and offering their services for a fee … they sold books and charts, much as today's rock groups sell T-shirts and posters at their concerts" (Sokal, 2001, p. 25).

Phrenological societies were formed, and the reading of heads became so widespread that many American businesses used the technique to select their employees. Phrenology practitioners claimed they could use it to assess a child's level of intelligence and to counsel couples experiencing marriage difficulties. Thus, the belief that phrenology could be applied to practical problems was a major reason for its success in the United States. In 1929 Charles Lavery and Frank White established the Psycograph Company of Minneapolis and developed a machine to read the bumps on people's heads. The device, consisting of nearly 2,000 parts, was lowered over the client's skull and measured 32 separate points. The machine printed out a report that gave scores on 32 mental attributes ranging from self-esteem to combativeness. This mechanical phrenologist became so popular that 33 machines were built and used with great financial success for several years (Joyce & Baker, 2008).

The most effective criticism of Gall's original cranioscopy theory grew out of the brain research conducted by Pierre Flourens. By systematically destroying parts of the brain (using the method of extirpation), Flourens found that the shape of the skull did not match the contours of the underlying brain tissue. In addition, brain tissue was too soft to produce changes such as bulges and dents in the bony surface of the skull. Flourens and other physiologists also demonstrated that the areas Gall designated for specific mental functions were in error. So while you may now be feeling your own skull for bumps, you can be assured that they do not reveal anything about your intellectual or emotional functioning.

Gall failed in his attempt to map the brain from the outside, but his ideas reinforced the growing belief among scientists that through the application of extirpation, clinical, and electrical stimulation methods, it was possible to localize specific brain functions.

There is a lesson to be learned from the success and later failure of phrenology that is applicable to all movements in all time periods. There is not necessarily a relationship between the popularity of an idea, trend, or school of thought and its validity. Daniel Robinson, a noted historian of psychology, observed that "Gall's phrenology flourished as long as has psychoanalytic theory [and] its findings and sayings filled a score of journals…. Educated citizens in all the right and interesting centers of culture were serious about palpating each other's heads. Thus does another moral lesson intrude itself: Impact *per se* establishes nothing regarding the validity or adequacy of works" (Robinson, 2003, p. 200). In other words, just because something is popular does not mean it is true.

## Research on the Nervous System

Considerable research on the structure of the nervous system and the nature of neural activity also was being conducted during this period. Recall the two early descriptions of neural activity: Descartes's nerve tube theory and Hartley's theory of vibrations.

Toward the end of the eighteenth century, the Italian researcher Luigi Galvani (1737–1798) had suggested that nerve impulses were electrical. Galvani's work was continued by his nephew, Giovanni Aldini. One historian wrote that Aldini "mixed serious research with showmanship. One of the more gruesome of Aldini's displays, designed to emphasize the effectiveness of electrical stimulation for obtaining spasmodic movements from muscles, involved using the recently severed heads of two criminals" (Boakes, 1984, p. 96).

Experimental work proceeded so rapidly that by the middle of the nineteenth century, scientists accepted as fact the electrical nature of nerve impulses. They came to believe that the nervous system was essentially a conductor of electrical impulses and that the central nervous system functioned like a switching station, shunting the impulses onto either sensory or motor nerve fibers.

Although this position was a great advance over Descartes's nerve tube theory and Hartley's theory of vibrations, it was conceptually similar. Both the newer and the older viewpoints were reflexive: Something from the external world (a stimulus) made an impact on a sense organ and thereby excited a nerve impulse. The nerve impulse traveled to the appropriate place in the brain or central nervous system. There, in response to the impulse, a new impulse was generated and transmitted along the motor nerves to trigger the organism's response.

The direction of travel for nerve impulses in the brain and spinal cord was revealed by the Spanish physician Santiago Ramón y Cajal (1852–1934), a professor of anatomy at the medical school of the University of Zaragoza and director of the Zaragoza Museum. For his discoveries, he received the Helmholtz Medal from the Royal Academy of Sciences in Berlin in 1905 and the Nobel Prize in 1906. Because the Spanish language was not used in the scientific journals of the day, however, Ramón y Cajal had difficulty communicating his findings to the scholarly community. Frustrated, he "was often saddened to read of 'new' discoveries in English, German, or French journals that were really rediscoveries of his own work published much earlier in Spanish" (Padilla, 1980, p. 116). His situation presents another instructive example of the barriers faced by scientists who work outside the mainstream culture.

Researchers also were investigating the anatomical structure of the nervous system. They found that nerve fibers were composed of separate structures (neurons) that somehow were connected at specific points (synapses). These findings were consistent with a mechanistic image of human functioning. Scientists believed that the nervous system, like the mind, was made up of atomistic structures, bits of matter that combined to produce a more complex product.

## The Mechanistic Spirit

The spirit of mechanism was dominant in nineteenth-century physiology, as it was in the philosophy of that time. Nowhere was this spirit more pronounced than in Germany. In the 1840s, a group of scientists, many of them former students of Johannes Müller, founded the Berlin Physical Society. These scientists, all in their twenties, were committed to a single proposition: that all phenomena could be accounted for by the principles of physics.

What they hoped to do was connect physiology with physics; that is, to develop a physiology in the framework of mechanism. In a dramatic gesture, four of the scientists swore a solemn oath, signing it, according to legend, with their own blood. Their declaration stated that the only forces active within an organism are the common physicochemical ones. And so the threads came together in nineteenth-century physiology: materialism, mechanism, empiricism, experimentation, and measurement.

The developments in early physiology indicate the kinds of research techniques and the discoveries that supported a scientific approach to the psychological investigation of the mind. While philosophers were paving the way for an experimental attack on the mind, physiologists were experimentally investigating the mechanisms that underlie mental phenomena. The next step was to apply the experimental method to the mind itself.

The British empiricists had argued that sensation was the only source of knowledge. The astronomer Bessel had demonstrated the impact on observation of individual differences in sensation and perception. Physiologists were defining the structure and function of the senses. It was time to experiment with and to quantify this doorway to the mind: the subjective, mentalistic experience of sensation. Techniques had been available to investigate the body, and now they were being developed to explore the mind. Experimental psychology was ready to begin.

# The Beginnings of Experimental Psychology

Four scientists can be credited with the initial applications of the experimental method to the mind, the subject matter of the new psychology: Hermann von Helmholtz, Ernst Weber, Gustav Theodor Fechner, and Wilhelm Wundt. All were German scientists who had been trained in physiology, and all were aware of the impressive developments in modern science.

## Why Germany?

The sciences were developing in most of Western Europe in the nineteenth century, particularly in England, France, and Germany. No one nation had a monopoly on the enthusiasm, conscientiousness, or optimism with which the tools of science were being applied to a variety of research problems. Why, then, did experimental psychology begin in Germany and not in England, France, or elsewhere? The answer seems to lie in certain unique characteristics that made German science a more fertile breeding ground for the new psychology.

***The German Approach to Science***   For a century, German intellectual history had paved the way for an experimental science of psychology. Experimental physiology was firmly established and recognized to a degree not yet achieved in France and England. The so-called German temperament was well suited to the precise description and classification work needed in biology, zoology, and physiology. Whereas scientists in France and England favored the deductive, mathematical approach, German scientists—with their emphasis on the careful, thorough collection of observable facts—adopted an inductive approach.

Because biological and physiological sciences do not lend themselves to grand generalizations from which facts can be deduced, biology was accepted only slowly by the scientific communities of England and France. In contrast, Germany, with its faith in taxonomic description and classification, welcomed biology to its family of sciences.

Further, the Germans defined science broadly. Science in France and England was limited to physics and chemistry, which could be approached quantitatively. Science in Germany included such areas as phonetics, linguistics, history, archaeology, esthetics, logic, even literary criticism. French and English scholars were skeptical about applying science to the complex human mind. Not so the Germans, and they plunged ahead, unconstrained, using the tools of science to explore and measure all facets of mental life.

***The Reform Movement in German Universities***   In the early nineteenth century, a wave of educational reform swept over German universities devoted to the principles of academic freedom. Professors were encouraged to teach whatever they wished, without outside interference, and to conduct research on topics of their choice. Students were free to take whatever courses they preferred, unrestricted by a fixed curriculum. This freedom—unknown in English and French universities—also extended to the consideration of new areas of scientific inquiry, such as psychology.

The German style of university provided the ideal environment for the flourishing of scientific inquiry. Professors could not only lecture on whatever interested them, but they could also direct students in experimental research in well-equipped laboratories. No other country actively promoted such an approach to science (Watson, 2010).

Germany also provided greater opportunities to learn and practice new scientific techniques; here we see the impact of prevailing economic conditions (a contextual factor). Germany had many universities. Prior to 1870, the year it became a unified nation with a central government, Germany had consisted of a loose confederation of autonomous kingdoms, duchies, and city-states. Each of these districts had a well-financed university with a highly paid faculty and state-of-the-art laboratory equipment.

England at that time had only two universities—Oxford and Cambridge—and neither facilitated, encouraged, or supported scientific research in any discipline. Further, they opposed adding new fields of study to the curriculum. In 1877, Cambridge vetoed a request to teach experimental psychology because it would "insult religion by putting the human soul on a pair of scales" (Hearnshaw, 1987, p. 125). Experimental psychology would not be taught at Cambridge for another 20 years and was not offered at Oxford until 1936. The only way to practice science in England was in the manner of the gentleman-scientist, living on an independent income, the way of Charles Darwin or Francis Galton (see Chapter 6). The situation was similar in France.

The United States had no universities devoted to research until 1876, when Johns Hopkins University was founded in Baltimore, Maryland. This new university was based on the German model; its primary goal was to make scientific research the core and focus of graduate student training. Indeed, Baltimore itself was considered "a little fragment of Germany that had resettled on the Eastern seaboard." According to the psychologist and philosopher John Dewey (see Chapter 7), "students and teachers [in the club room at Hopkins] met to drink German beer and sing German songs" (quoted in Martin, 2002, p. 56).

The founding of Hopkins has been called the "beginning of the great transformation in American higher learning," and it served as the model for other U.S. universities that were emerging by the beginning of the twentieth century (Cole, 2009, p. 20).

Before that time, however, there were more opportunities for scientific research in Germany than in other countries. In pragmatic terms, we may say that a person could make a living as a research scientist in Germany but not in France, England, or the United States. Thus, the chances of becoming a well-paid, respected professor were higher in Germany than elsewhere, although it remained difficult to attain the very top positions. The promising university scientist was required to produce research judged by peers to be a major contribution, research more significant than the typical doctoral dissertation. Consequently, most of the people selected for university careers were of extremely high caliber. Once these scientists joined the faculty, the pressure on them to publish was fierce.

Although the competition was intense and the demands high, the rewards were more than worth the effort. Only the best succeeded in nineteenth-century German science, and the result was a series of breakthroughs in all sciences, including the new psychology. Thus, it is no coincidence that the people directly responsible for the growth of scientific psychology were German university professors.

# Hermann von Helmholtz (1821–1894)

One of the greatest scientists of the nineteenth century, Hermann von Helmholtz was a prolific researcher in physics and physiology. Psychology ranked third among his areas of scientific contribution, yet his work, together with that of Fechner and Wundt, was instrumental in beginning the new psychology. He emphasized a mechanistic and deterministic approach, assuming that the human sense organs functioned like machines. He also liked technical analogies, such as comparing the transmission of nerve impulses to the operation of the telegraph (see Ash, 1995).

HERMANN VON
HELMHOLTZ

## Helmholtz's Life

Born in Potsdam, Germany, where his father taught at the *Gymnasium* (in Europe, a high school/junior college preparatory for the university), Helmholtz was tutored at home because of his delicate health. At 17, he enrolled in a Berlin medical institute where no tuition was charged to students who agreed to become army surgeons after graduation. Helmholtz served for seven years, during which time he continued his studies in mathematics and physics and published several articles. In a paper on the indestructibility of energy, he mathematically formulated the law of the conservation of energy. After leaving the army, Helmholtz accepted a position as associate professor of physiology at the University of Königsberg. Over the next 30 years, he held academic appointments in physiology at universities in Bonn and Heidelberg, and in physics at Berlin.

The tremendously energetic Helmholtz delved into several scholarly areas. In doing research on physiological optics, he invented the ophthalmoscope, a device still used to examine the retina of the eye. This revolutionary instrument made possible the diagnosis and treatment of retinal disorders. As a result, Helmholtz's name "spread quickly throughout the academic and public worlds. At a stroke he achieved career advancement and worldly recognition," all by the age of 30 (Cahan, 1993, p. 574).

Helmholtz's three-volume work on physiological optics (*Handbook of Physiological Optics,* 1856–1866) proved to be so influential and enduring that it was translated into English 60 years later. He published research on acoustical problems in *On the Sensations of Tone* (1863), which summarized his own findings plus the rest of the available literature. He also wrote on such diverse subjects as afterimages, color blindness, the Arabian-Persian musical scale, human eye movements, the formation of glaciers, geometrical axioms, and hay fever. In later years, Helmholtz contributed indirectly to the invention of wireless telegraphy and radio.

In the fall of 1893, returning from a trip to the United States that included a visit to the Chicago World's Fair, Helmholtz suffered a fall aboard ship. Less than a year later he had a stroke that left him semiconscious and delirious. His wife wrote, "His thoughts ramble on confusedly, real life and dream life, time and scene, all float mistily by in his brain… It is as if his soul were far, far away, in a beautiful ideal world, swayed only by science and the eternal laws" (quoted in Koenigsberger, 1965, p. 429).

Archives of the History of American Psychology/University of Akron

The Helmholtz motor, powered by an electromagnetic device, generated energy for many laboratory instruments.

### Helmholtz's Contributions to the New Psychology

Of major importance to psychology are Helmholtz's investigations of the speed of the neural impulse and his research on vision and hearing. Scientists had assumed that the nerve impulse was instantaneous, or at least that it traveled too fast to be measured. Helmholtz provided the first empirical measurement of the rate of conduction by stimulating a motor nerve and the attached muscle in the leg of a frog. He arranged the demonstration so that the precise moment of stimulation and of the resulting movement could be recorded. Working with nerves of different length, he recorded the delay between stimulation of the nerve near the muscle and the muscle's response, and did the same for stimulation farther from the muscle. These measurements yielded the conduction speed of the neural impulse: 90 feet per second.

Helmholtz also experimented on the reaction times for sensory nerves in human subjects, studying the complete circuit from stimulation of a sense organ to the resulting motor response. The findings showed such enormous individual differences—as well as differences for the same person from one trial to the next—that he abandoned the research.

Helmholtz's demonstration that the speed of conduction was not instantaneous suggested that thought and movement follow each other at a measurable interval and do not occur simultaneously, as had been thought. However, Helmholtz was interested in the measurement itself and not its psychological significance. Later, the implications of his research for the new psychology were recognized by others, who made reaction-time experiments a fruitful line of research. Helmholtz's work was one of the earliest instances of experimentation and measurement for a psychophysiological process.

His studies on vision also had an impact on the new psychology. Helmholtz investigated the external eye muscles and the mechanism by which internal eye muscles focus the lens. He revised and extended a theory of color vision published in 1802 by Thomas Young, and this work is now known as the Young-Helmholtz theory of color vision. No less important is Helmholtz's research on audition, specifically the perception of tones, the nature of harmony and discord, and the problem of resonance. The enduring influence of his ideas and experiments is evident from the fact that they are still cited in modern psychology textbooks.

He focused on the applied or practical benefits of scientific research. Helmholtz did not believe in conducting experiments just to accumulate data. In his view, the mission of a scientist was to gather information and then to extend or apply that growing body of knowledge to practical problems. We will see the further development of this approach in the functionalist school of psychology that took root in the United States (see Chapters 7 and 8).

Helmholtz was not a psychologist, nor was psychology his major interest, but he contributed a large and important body of knowledge to the study of the human senses. Thus, his work helped strengthen the experimental approach to the study of topics that would become central to the new psychology.

# Ernst Weber (1795–1878)

Ernst Weber, the son of a theology professor, was born in Wittenberg, Germany. He earned his doctorate at the University of Leipzig in 1815 and taught anatomy and physiology there from 1817 until his retirement in 1871. His primary research interest was the physiology of the sense organs, an area in which he made outstanding contributions. Thus, he applied physiology's experimental methods to problems of a psychological nature. Previous research on the sense organs had been conducted almost exclusively on the higher senses of vision and hearing. Weber explored new fields, notably cutaneous (skin) senses and muscular sensations.

ERNST WEBER

## Two-Point Thresholds

A significant contribution to the new psychology involved Weber's experimental determination of the accuracy of the two-point discrimination of the skin—that is, the distance between two points that must be spanned before subjects report feeling two distinct sensations. Without looking at the apparatus, which resembles a drawing compass, subjects are asked to report whether they feel one or two points touching the skin. When the two points of stimulation are close together, subjects report a sensation of being touched at only one point. As the distance between the two sources of stimulation is increased, subjects report uncertainty about whether they feel one or two sensations. Finally, a distance is reached where subjects report two distinct points of touch.

**Two-point threshold:** The threshold at which two points of stimulation can be distinguished as such.

This procedure demonstrates the **two-point threshold**, the point at which the two separate sources of stimulation can be distinguished. Weber's research marks the first systematic, experimental demonstration of the concept of threshold (the point at which a psychological effect begins to be produced), an idea widely used in psychology from its beginnings to the present day. (In chapter 13 we discuss the concept of threshold as it applies to consciousness—to that point at which unconscious ideas in the mind become conscious).

## Just Noticeable Differences

Weber's research led to the formulation of psychology's first quantitative law. He wanted to determine the **just noticeable difference** (jnd)—that is, the smallest difference between weights that could be detected. He asked his subjects to lift two weights—a standard weight and a comparison weight—and to report whether one felt heavier than the other. Small differences between the weights resulted in judgments of sameness; large differences resulted in judgments of disparity between the weights.

**Just noticeable difference:** The smallest difference that can be detected between two physical stimuli.

As his research program progressed, Weber found that the just noticeable difference between two weights was a constant ratio, 1:40, of the standard weight. In other words, a weight of 41 grams was reported to be "just noticeably different" from a standard weight of 40 grams, and an 82-gram weight was just noticeably different from a standard weight of 80 grams.

Weber then asked how muscle sensations might contribute to a person's ability to distinguish between the weights. He found that subjects could make such discriminations much more accurately when they lifted the weights themselves (by receiving muscular sensations in hands and arms) than when the experimenter placed the weights in their hands. Actually hefting the weights involved tactile (touch) and muscular sensations, whereas when the weights were placed in the palms, only tactile sensations were experienced.

Because subjects could detect smaller differences between the weights when the weights were lifted (a ratio of 1:40) than when the weights were placed in the hand (a ratio of 1:30), Weber concluded that the internal muscular sensations in the first instance must have an influence on the subjects' ability to discriminate.

From these experiments, Weber suggested that discrimination among sensations depended not on the absolute difference between two weights but on their relative difference or ratio. His experiments on visual discrimination found that the ratio was smaller than for the muscle sense experiments. He then proposed a constant ratio for the just noticeable difference between two stimuli that would be consistent for each of the human senses.

Weber's research showed that there is not a direct correspondence between a physical stimulus and our perception of it. Like Helmholtz, however, Weber was interested only in the physiological processes and did not appreciate the significance of his work for psychology. His research provided a method for investigating the relationship between body and mind—between the stimulus and the resulting sensation. This was a vital breakthrough; what was required now was for someone to act on its importance.

Weber's experiments stimulated additional research and focused the attention of later physiologists on the usefulness of the experimental method for studying psychological phenomena. Weber's research on thresholds and the measurement of sensations was of paramount importance to the new psychology and has influenced virtually every aspect of psychology to the present day.

# Gustav Theodor Fechner (1801–1887)

GUSTAV THEODOR
FECHNER

Archives of the History of American Psychology/
University of Akron

Gustav Theodor Fechner was a scholar who followed diverse intellectual pursuits during a remarkably active life. He was a physiologist for seven years, a physicist for 15, a psychophysicist for 14, an experimental estheticist for 11, a philosopher for 40—and an invalid for 12. Of these endeavors, the work on psychophysics brought his greatest fame, although he did not wish to be so remembered by posterity.

## Fechner's Life

Fechner was born in a village in southeastern Germany where his father was the minister. He began medical studies at the University of Leipzig in 1817, and while there he attended Weber's lectures on physiology. Fechner remained at Leipzig for the rest of his life.

Even before he graduated from medical school, Fechner's humanistic viewpoint rebelled against the prevailing mechanism of his scientific training. Under the pen name "Dr. Mises" he wrote satirical essays ridiculing medicine and science. This conflict between the two sides of his personality persisted throughout his life—his interest in science and his interest in the metaphysical. Obviously troubled by the current atomistic approach to science, he subscribed to what he called his "day view"—that the universe can be regarded from the standpoint of consciousness. This stood in opposition to the prevailing "night view"—that the universe, including consciousness, consisted of nothing but inert matter.

After completing his medical studies, Fechner began a career in physics and mathematics at Leipzig and also translated handbooks of physics and chemistry from French into German. By 1830, he had translated more than a dozen volumes, and this activity brought him recognition as a physicist. In 1824, he began lecturing in physics at the university and conducting his own research. By the late 1830s he had become interested in the problem of sensation, and while investigating visual afterimages he seriously injured his eyes by looking directly at the sun through colored glasses.

In 1833, Fechner obtained the prestigious appointment of professor at Leipzig, whereupon he fell into a depression that endured for several years. He complained of exhaustion and had difficulty sleeping. He could not digest food, and even though his body approached starvation, he felt no hunger. He was unusually sensitive to light and spent most of his time in a darkened room whose walls were painted black, listening while his mother read to him through a narrowly opened door.

He tried to take long walks—at first only at night, when it was dark, and then in daylight with his eyes bandaged—hoping to ease the boredom and gloom. As a form of catharsis, he composed riddles and poems. He dabbled in alternative medical therapies, including laxatives, electric shock, steam treatments, and the application of burning substances to the skin; none of them provided a cure.

Fechner's illness may have been neurotic in nature. This idea is supported by the bizarre way in which he recovered. A friend reported a dream in which she prepared him a meal of raw spiced ham marinated in Rhine wine and lemon juice. The next day she fixed the dish and brought it to Fechner. He tasted it, reluctantly, but ate more and more of the ham every day, declaring that he felt somewhat better. The improvement in his condition was short lived, and after six months the symptoms worsened to the point where he feared for his sanity. Fechner wrote, "I had the distinct feeling that my mind was hopelessly lost unless I could stem the flood of disturbing thoughts. Often the least important matters bothered me in this manner and it took me often hours, even days, to rid myself of these worries" (Kuntze, 1892, quoted in Balance & Bringmann, 1987, p. 42).

Fechner forced himself to undertake routine chores—a sort of occupational therapy—but was limited to tasks that did not make demands on his mind or his eyes. "I made strings and bandages, dipped candles ... rolled yarn and helped in the kitchen sorting [and] cleaning lentils, making bread crumbs, and grinding a sugarloaf into powdered sugar. I also peeled and chopped carrots and turnips ... a thousand times I wished to be dead" (Fechner in Kuntze, 1892, quoted in Balance & Bringmann, 1987, p. 43).

In time, Fechner's interest in the world around him revived, and he maintained the diet of wine-soaked ham. He had a dream in which the number 77 appeared, persuading him that he would be well in 77 days—and of course he was. His depression turned to euphoria and delusions of grandeur, and he claimed God had chosen him to solve all the world's mysteries. Out of this experience he developed the notion of the pleasure principle, which many years later influenced the work of Sigmund Freud (see Chapter 13).

Fechner lived to the age of 86, in excellent health, and made major contributions to science, despite the fact that more than 40 years earlier the University of Leipzig had declared him an invalid and paid him an annual pension for the rest of his life.

## Mind and Body: A Quantitative Relationship

October 22, 1850, is a significant date in the history of psychology. While lying in bed that morning, Fechner had a flash of insight about the connection between mind and body: It could be found, he said, in a quantitative relationship between a mental sensation and a material stimulus.

An increase in the intensity of a stimulus, Fechner argued, does not produce a one-to-one increase in the intensity of the sensation. Rather, a geometric series characterizes the stimulus and an arithmetic series characterizes the sensation. For example, adding the sound of one bell to that of an already ringing bell produces a greater increase in sensation than adding one bell to 10 others already ringing. Therefore, the effects of stimulus intensities are not absolute but are relative to the amount of sensation that already exists.

What this simple yet brilliant revelation means is that the amount of sensation (the mental quality) depends on the amount of stimulation (the physical quality). To measure the change in sensation, we must measure the change in stimulation. Thus, it is possible to formulate a quantitative or numerical relationship between the mental and material worlds. Fechner crossed the barrier between body and mind by relating one to the other empirically, making it possible to conduct experiments on the mind.

Although the concept was now clear to Fechner, how was he to proceed? A researcher would have to measure precisely both the subjective and the objective, the mental sensation and the physical stimulus. To measure the physical intensity of the stimulus—such as the level of brightness of a light or the weight of a standard object—was not difficult, but how could one measure sensation, the conscious experiences the subjects reported when they responded to the stimulus?

Fechner proposed two ways to measure sensations. First, we can determine whether a stimulus is present or absent, sensed or not sensed. Second, we can measure the stimulus intensity at which subjects report that the sensation first occurs; this is the **absolute threshold** of sensitivity—a point of intensity below which no sensation is reported and above which subjects do experience a sensation.

Although the idea of an absolute threshold is useful, its usefulness is limited because only one value of a sensation—its lowest level—can be determined. To relate both intensities, we must be able to specify the full range of stimulus values and their resulting

**Absolute threshold:** The point of sensitivity below which no sensations can be detected and above which sensations can be experienced.

**Differential threshold:**
The point of sensitivity at which the least amount of change in a stimulus gives rise to a change in sensation.

sensation values. To accomplish this, Fechner proposed the **differential threshold** of sensitivity: the least amount of change in a stimulus that gives rise to a change in sensation. For example, by how much must a weight be increased or decreased before subjects will sense the change—before they will report a just noticeable difference in sensation?

To measure how heavy a particular weight feels to a person (how heavy a subject senses it to be), we cannot use the physical measurement of the object's weight. However, we can use that physical measurement as a basis for measuring the sensation's psychological intensity. First, we measure by how much the weight must be decreased in intensity before a subject is barely able to discriminate the difference. Second, we change the weight of the object to this lower value and measure the size of the differential threshold again. Because both weight changes are just barely noticeable to the subject, Fechner assumed they were subjectively equal.

This process can be repeated until the object is barely felt by the subject. If every decrease in weight is subjectively equal to every other decrease, then the number of times the weight must be decreased—the number of just noticeable differences—can be taken as an objective measure of the subjective magnitude of the sensation. In this way we are measuring the stimulus values necessary to create a difference between two sensations.

Fechner suggested that for each of the human senses there is a certain relative increase in stimulus intensity that always produces an observable change in the intensity of the sensation. Thus, the sensation (the mind or mental quality) as well as the stimulus (the body or material quality) can be measured. The relationship between the two can be stated in the form of an equation: $S = K \log R$, in which $S$ is the magnitude of the sensation, $K$ is a constant, and $R$ is the magnitude of the stimulus. The relationship is logarithmic; one series increases arithmetically and the other geometrically.

In his later writings, Fechner noted that this idea for describing the mind-body relationship had not been suggested to him by Weber's work, even though he had attended Weber's lectures at the University of Leipzig and Weber had published on the topic a few years earlier. Fechner maintained that he did not discover Weber's work until after he had begun the experiments designed to test his hypothesis. It was only some time later that Fechner realized that the principle to which he gave mathematical form was essentially what Weber's work had shown.

## Methods of Psychophysics

**Psychophysics:** The scientific study of the relations between mental and physical processes.

The immediate result of Fechner's insight was his research on **psychophysics**. (The word defines itself: the relationship between the mental [*psycho-*] and material [*physics*] worlds.) In the course of this work, which included experiments on lifted weights, visual brightness, visual distance, and tactile distance, Fechner developed one and systematized two of the three fundamental methods used in psychophysics research today.

The method of average error, or method of adjustment, consists in having subjects adjust a variable stimulus until they perceive it to be equal to a constant standard stimulus. Over a number of trials, the mean, or average, value of the differences between the standard stimulus and the subjects' setting of the variable stimulus represents the error of observation. This technique is useful for measuring reaction times as well as visual and auditory discriminations. In a larger sense, it is basic to much psychological research; every time we calculate a mean we are essentially using the method of average error.

The method of constant stimuli involves two constant stimuli, and the aim is to measure the stimulus difference required to produce a given proportion of correct judgments. For example, subjects first lift a standard weight of 100 grams and then lift a comparison weight of, say, 88, 92, 96, 104, or 108 grams. The subjects must judge whether the second weight is heavier, lighter, or equal to the first.

In the method of limits, two stimuli (for example, two weights) are presented to the subjects. One stimulus is increased or decreased until subjects report that they detect a difference. Data are obtained from a number of trials, and the just noticeable differences are averaged to determine the differential threshold.

Fechner's psychophysics research program lasted seven years. He published two brief papers in 1858 and 1859, and in 1860 he offered the complete exposition in the *Elements of Psychophysics,* a textbook of the exact science of the "functionally dependent relations … of the material and the mental, of the physical and psychological worlds" (Fechner, 1860/1966, p. 7). This book is an outstanding original contribution to the development of scientific psychology. Fechner's statement of the quantitative relationship between stimulus intensity and sensation was considered, at the time, to be of comparable importance to the discovery of the laws of gravity.

The following material is a portion of *Elements of Psychophysics,* in which Fechner discussed the difference between matter and mind, between the stimulus and the resulting sensation. In the section reprinted here, Fechner also distinguishes between what he called "inner" and "outer" psychophysics. Inner psychophysics refers to the relationship between the sensation and the accompanying brain and nerve excitation. It was not possible, in Fechner's day, to measure precisely such physiological processes. Therefore, he chose to deal with outer psychophysics, the relationship between the stimulus and the subjective intensity of the sensation, as measured by his psychophysical methods.

## IN THEIR OWN WORDS

### Original Source Material on Psychophysics from *Elements of Psychophysics* (1860)

**Gustav Fechner**

Psychophysics should be understood here as an exact theory of the functionally dependent relations of body and soul or, more generally, of the material and the mental, of the physical and the psychological worlds.

We count as mental, psychological, or belonging to the soul, all that can be grasped by introspective observation or that can be abstracted from it; as bodily, corporeal, physical, or material, all that can be grasped by observation from the outside or abstracted from it. These designations refer only to those aspects of the world of appearance, with whose relationships psychophysics will have to occupy itself, provided that one understands inner and outer observation in the sense of everyday language to refer to the activities through which alone existence becomes apparent.

In any case, all discussions and investigations of psychophysics relate only to the apparent phenomena of the material and mental worlds, to a world that either appears directly through introspection or through outside observation, or that can be deduced from its appearance or grasped as a phenomenological relationship, category, association, deduction, or law. Briefly, psychophysics refers to the *physical* in the sense of physics and chemistry, and to the *psychical* in the sense of experiential psychology, without referring back in any way to the nature of the body or of the soul beyond the phenomenal in the metaphysical sense.

In general, we call the psychic a dependent function of the physical, and vice versa, insofar as there exists between them such a constant or lawful relationship that, from the presence and changes of one, we can deduce those of the other.

The existence of a functional relationship between body and mind is, in general, not denied; nevertheless, there exists a still unresolved dispute over the reasons for this fact, and the interpretation and extent of it.

With no regard to the metaphysical points of this argument (points which concern rather more the so-called essence than the appearance), psychophysics undertakes to determine the actual functional relationship between the modes of appearance of body and mind as exactly as possible.

What things belong together quantitatively and qualitatively, distant and close, in the material and in the mental world? What are the laws governing their changes in the same or in opposite directions? These are the questions in general that psychophysics asks and tries to answer with exactitude.

In other words, but still with the same meaning: what belong together in the inner and outer modes of appearance of things, and what laws exist regarding their respective changes?

Insofar as a functional relationship linking body and mind exists, there is actually nothing to prevent us from looking at it and pursuing it from the one direction rather than from the other. One can illustrate this relationship suitably by means of a mathematical function, an equation between the variables x and y, where each variable can be looked upon at will as a function of the other, and where each is dependent upon the changes of the other. There is a reason, however, why psychophysics prefers to make the approach from the side of the dependence of the mind on the body rather than the contrary, for it is only the physical that is immediately open to measurement, whereas the measurement of the psychical can be obtained only as dependent on the physical …

By its nature, psychophysics may be divided into an outer and an inner part, depending on whether consideration is focused on the relationship of the psychical to the body's external aspects, or on those internal functions with which the psychic are closely related …

The truly basic empirical evidence for the whole of psychophysics can be sought only in the realm of outer psychophysics, inasmuch as it is only this part that is available to immediate experience. Our point of departure therefore has to be taken from outer psychophysics. However, there can be no development of outer psychophysics without constant regard to inner psychophysics, in view of the fact that the body's external world is functionally related to the mind only by the mediation of the body's internal world …

Psychophysics, already related to psychology and physics by name, must on the one hand be based on psychology, and on the other hand promises to give psychology a mathematical foundation. From physics outer psychophysics borrows aids and methodology; inner psychophysics leans more to physiology and anatomy, particularly of the nervous system, with which a certain acquaintance is presupposed …

Sensation depends on stimulation; a stronger sensation depends on a stronger stimulus; the stimulus, however, causes sensation only via the intermediate action of some internal process of the body. To the extent that lawful relationships between sensation and stimulus can be found, they must include lawful relationships between the stimulus and this inner physical activity, which obey the same general laws of interaction of bodily processes and thereby give us a basis for drawing general conclusions about the nature of this inner activity …

Quite apart from their import for inner psychophysics, these lawful relationships, which may be ascertained in the area of outer psychophysics, have their own importance. Based on them, as we shall see, physical measurement yields a psychic measurement, on which we can base arguments that in their turn are of importance and interest.

---

At the beginning of the nineteenth century, the German philosopher Immanuel Kant insisted that psychology could never be a science because it was impossible to experiment on or measure psychological processes (Sturm, 2006). Because of Fechner's work—which, indeed, made it possible to measure mental phenomena—Kant's assertion could no longer be taken seriously. It was largely because of Fechner's psychophysical research that Wilhelm Wundt conceived his plan for an experimental psychology. Fechner's methods have proved applicable to a wider range of psychological problems than he ever imagined. Most important, he gave psychology what every discipline must possess if it is to be called a science: precise and elegant techniques of measurement.

# The Formal Founding of Psychology

By the middle of the nineteenth century, the methods of the natural sciences were being used to investigate purely mental phenomena. Techniques had been developed, apparatus devised, important books written, and widespread interest aroused. British empirical philosophers and astronomers emphasized the importance of the senses, and German scientists were describing how the senses functioned. The positivist intellectual spirit of the times, the Zeitgeist, encouraged the convergence of these two lines of thought. Still lacking, however, was someone to bring them together, someone to "found" the new science. This final touch was provided by Wilhelm Wundt.

# Discussion Questions

1. Describe Gall's cranioscopy method and the popular movement that derived from it. How were they discredited?

2. Describe Weber's research on two-point thresholds and on just noticeable differences. What was the importance of these ideas for psychology?

3. Discuss the methods that scientists developed to map brain functions.

4. Do you think experimental psychology would have developed when it did without Fechner's work? Without Weber's work? Why?

5. Explain how developments in physiology combined with British empiricism to produce the new psychology.

6. For what reasons did experimental psychology emerge in Germany and not elsewhere?

7. How did developments in early physiology support the mechanistic image of human nature?

8. What is the difference between inner psychophysics and outer psychophysics? Which was Fechner forced to focus on? Why?

9. What is the significance of Helmholtz's research on the speed of the neural impulse?

10. What is the relationship between the intensity of the stimulus and the intensity of the sensation, as represented by the equation $S = K \log R$?

11. What psychophysical methods did Fechner use? How did psychophysics influence the development of psychology?

12. What was David Kinnebrook's role in the development of the new psychology?

13. What was Fechner's insight on October 22, 1850? How did Fechner measure sensations?

14. What was the ultimate goal of the Berlin Physical Society?

15. What was the significance of Bessel's work for the new psychology? How did it relate to the work of Locke, Berkeley, and other empirical philosophers?

# CHAPTER 4
# The New Psychology

## No Multitasking Allowed

Wilhelm Wundt had never heard of multitasking. Even if he had, he would not have believed it was possible to pay attention to more than one stimulus or to engage in more than one mental activity at precisely the same moment in time, such as sending a text message and noticing a clown on the campus. Of course, no one had heard of multitasking in the middle of the nineteenth century before there were phones of any kind, much less instant messages, e-mail, videogames, and other electronic gadgets simultaneously claiming our time and attention.

The year was 1861, and in the United States the Civil War was beginning. In Germany, an ambitious Wilhelm Wundt was a 29-year-old researcher in physiology and a part-time lecturer at the University of Heidelberg. Described by colleagues as absentminded and given to daydreaming, he was trying to make his way in the world by teaching basic laboratory techniques to undergraduate students. In his makeshift lab at home, he was attempting to conduct research to spark the development of the new science of psychology.

Lately Wundt had been thinking about what Friedrich Bessel, the German astronomer, had called the "personal equation," the errors of measurement among astronomers that had led to the firing of David Kinnebrook back in 1796. As explained by one historian of psychology, Wundt was intrigued by the

> systematic differences between astronomers in their measures of the passage of stars across grid lines in telescopes. These slight differences [a mere half-second with Kinnebrook and Maskelyne] depended on whether the astronomer first focused his attention on the star or on his timing device. (Blumenthal, 1980, p. 121)

If the observer looked first at the star, he obtained one reading; if he looked at the grid line first, he made a slightly different reading. It was impossible for the observer to focus his attention on both objects at the same instant. Wundt's interest in this problem led him to modify a pendulum clock so that it presented both an auditory and a visual stimulus, in this case a bell and a pendulum swinging past a fixed point. He called the instrument a *Gedankenmesser,* meaning "thought meter" or "mind gauge," and he used it to measure the mental process of perceiving the two stimuli.

Choosing himself as the only subject in this experiment, he concluded that it was impossible to perceive these two things at the same moment. He could either attend to the sound of the bell or to the sight of the pendulum passing a specific point. The results of his measurements showed that it took one-eighth of a second to register both stimuli sequentially. To the casual observer, the stimuli appeared to occur simultaneously, but not to the trained researcher.

Wundt's finding that we cannot attend to or focus clearly on more than one thing at a time has, as we noted, a strikingly contemporary application. A rapidly growing body of

Research Topics of the
Würzburg Laboratory

**Comment**

**Discussion Questions**

literature demonstrates consistently the distracting effects of text messaging while driving, for example, and that multitasking, in the words of one writer, can "make you stupid" because we cannot effectively manage more than one cognitive task at a time (see Gorlick, 2009; Hosking, Young, & Regan, 2009; Lin, 2009; Richtel, 2010; and Shellenbarger, 2004).

Thus, Wundt was far ahead of his time when he wrote that "consciousness holds only a single thought, a single perception. When it appears as if we have several percepts simultaneously, we are deceived by their quick succession" (quoted in Diamond, 1980b, p. 39). With that discovery, Wilhelm Wundt had measured the mind. Yes, Fechner had done it before him, but it was Wundt who used the experiment as the basis for a new science. (And David Kinnebrook never knew the part he played.)

# The Founding Father of Modern Psychology

Wundt was the founder of psychology as a formal academic discipline. He established the first laboratory, edited the first journal, and began experimental psychology as a science. The areas he investigated—sensation and perception, attention, feeling, reaction, and association—became basic chapters in textbooks yet to be written. That so much of the history of psychology after Wundt is characterized by opposition to his view of psychology does not detract from his stature or achievements as its founder.

Why have the honors for founding the new psychology fallen to Wundt and not Fechner? Fechner's *Elements of Psychophysics* was published in 1860, approximately 15 years before Wundt began psychology. Wundt himself wrote that Fechner's work represented the "first conquest" in experimental psychology (Wundt, 1888, p. 471). When Fechner died, his papers were left to Wundt, who offered a eulogy at Fechner's funeral. In addition, Wundt's disciple, E. B. Titchener, referred to Fechner as the father of experimental psychology (Benjamin, Bryant, Campbell, Luttrell, & Holtz, 1997). Historians agree on Fechner's importance; some even question whether psychology could have begun when it did, if not for Fechner's work. So why don't historians credit Fechner with founding psychology?

The answer lies in the nature of the process of founding a school of thought. Founding is a deliberate and intentional act. It involves personal abilities and characteristics that differ from those necessary for brilliant scientific contributions. Founding requires the integration of prior knowledge and the publication and promotion of the newly organized material. One historian of psychology wrote:

> When the central ideas are all born, some promoter takes them in hand, organizes them, adding whatever else seems . . . essential, publishes and advertises them, insists upon them, and in short "founds" a school. (Boring, 1950, p. 194)

A more recent commentary on the nature of founding speaks of the necessity of selling an idea to the scientific community: "To make a great contribution to knowledge, successfully completing the task of assuring the impact of an idea is as important as the idea's originality. Successfully selling the idea is perhaps even more important" (Berscheid, 2003, p. 110).

Wundt's contribution to the founding of modern psychology stems not so much from any unique scientific discovery as from his vigorous promotion, or selling, of the idea of systematic experimentation. Thus, founding is quite different from originating, although the distinction is not intended to be a disparaging one. Founders and originators are both essential to the formation of a science, as indispensable as the architect and the builder in the construction of a house.

With this distinction in mind, we can understand why Fechner is not identified as the founder of psychology. Stated simply, he was not trying to found a new science. His goal was to understand the relationship between the mental and material worlds. He sought to describe a unified conception of mind and body that had a scientific basis.

Wundt, however, set out deliberately to found a new science. In the preface to the first edition of his *Principles of Physiological Psychology* (1873–1874), he wrote, "The work I here present to the public is an attempt to mark out a new domain of science." Wundt's goal was to promote psychology as an independent science. Nevertheless, it bears repeating that although Wundt is considered to have founded psychology, he did not originate it. We have seen that psychology emerged from a long line of creative efforts.

During the last half of the nineteenth century, the Zeitgeist was ready for the application of experimental methodology to problems of the mind. Wundt was a vigorous agent of what was already developing, a gifted promoter of the inevitable.

# Wilhelm Wundt (1832–1920)
## Wundt's Life

WILHELM WUNDT

Wilhelm Wundt spent his early years in small towns near Mannheim, Germany. His childhood was lonely (his older brother was at boarding school), and his sole diversion seemed to be the fantasy of becoming a famous writer. His grades in school were poor. Wundt's father was a pastor, and although both parents were described as sociable, Wundt's memories of his father were unpleasant. Wundt recalled that one day his father visited the school and smacked him across the face for not paying attention to the teacher. Beginning in the second grade, his education was turned over to his father's assistant, a young vicar for whom the boy developed a strong emotional attachment. When the vicar was transferred to a neighboring town, Wundt became so upset that he was allowed to live with the vicar until the age of 13.

A strong tradition of scholarship was prevalent in the Wundt family, with ancestors of intellectual renown in virtually every field. Nevertheless, it seemed that this impressive line would not be continued by young Wundt. He spent more time daydreaming than studying, and he failed his first year at *Gymnasium*. He did not get along with his classmates and was ridiculed by his teachers. Gradually, however, Wundt learned to control his reveries and even became relatively popular. Although he always disliked school, he worked to develop his intellectual interests and abilities. By the time he graduated at the age of 19, he was prepared for university studies.

Wundt decided to become a physician, to pursue the twin goals of working in science and earning a living. He undertook medical training at the University of Tübingen and the University of Heidelberg; at the latter he studied anatomy, physiology, physics, medicine, and chemistry. He came to realize that the practice of medicine would not be to his liking, and he changed his major to physiology.

After a semester of study at the University of Berlin with the great physiologist Johannes Müller, Wundt returned to the University of Heidelberg to complete his doctorate in 1855. He held an appointment as lecturer in physiology at Heidelberg from 1857 to 1864 and was appointed laboratory assistant to Helmholtz. Wundt found it dreary to spend his time drilling undergraduates in their laboratory fundamentals, so he resigned from that duty. In 1864, he was promoted to associate professor, and he remained at Heidelberg for another 10 years.

While engrossed in his research in physiology, Wundt began to conceive of the study of psychology as an independent experimental scientific discipline. He first outlined his ideas in a book entitled *Contributions to the Theory of Sensory Perception*, published in sections between 1858 and 1862. He described his own original experiments, conducted in a makeshift laboratory built in his house, and he described the methods he considered appropriate for the new psychology, using the term "experimental psychology" for the first time. Along with Fechner's *Elements of Psychophysics* (1860), Wundt's *Contributions* book is considered to mark the literary birth of the new science.

The following year, Wundt published *Lectures on the Minds of Men and Animals* (1863). An indication of this book's importance was its revision almost 30 years later, with an English translation and repeated reprintings even after Wundt's death. In it Wundt discussed many issues—such as reaction time and psychophysics—that were to occupy the attention of experimental psychologists for years to come.

Beginning in 1867, Wundt taught a course at Heidelberg on physiological psychology, the first formal offering of such a course in the world. Out of his lectures came another significant book, *Principles of Physiological Psychology,* published in two parts in 1873 and 1874. Wundt revised the book in six editions over 37 years, the last published in 1911. Indisputably his masterpiece, the *Principles* firmly established psychology as an independent laboratory science with its own problems and methods of experimentation.

For many years, successive editions of the *Principles of Physiological Psychology* served as a storehouse of information and a record of psychology's progress for experimental psychologists. The term "physiological psychology" in the title may be misleading. At the time, the word "physiological" was used synonymously with the German word meaning "experimental." Wundt was actually teaching and writing about experimental psychology, not physiological psychology as we know it today (Blumenthal, 1998).

## The Leipzig Years

Wundt began the longest and most important phase of his career in 1875 when he became professor of philosophy at the University of Leipzig, where he worked prodigiously for 45 years. He established a laboratory at Leipzig shortly after he arrived, and in 1881 he founded the journal *Philosophical Studies,* the official publication of the new laboratory and the new science. He had intended to call the journal *Psychological Studies,* but he changed his mind apparently because there already was such a journal (although it dealt with occult and spiritualistic issues). In 1906, Wundt was able to rename his journal *Psychological Studies.* Now equipped with a handbook, a laboratory, and a scholarly journal, psychology was well under way.

Wundt's lab and his growing reputation drew a large number of students to Leipzig to work with him. Among these were many students who became pioneers, spreading their versions of psychology to subsequent generations. They included several Americans, most of whom returned to the United States to begin laboratories of their own. Thus, the Leipzig laboratory exerted an immense influence on the development of modern psychology, serving as the model for new laboratories and continuing research. "Wundt and the psychological laboratory at Leipzig were known worldwide as a modern and outstanding scientific institution that provided an excellent introduction to the new experimental psychology" (Muhlberger, 2008, p. 169).

In addition to facilities established in the United States, laboratories were founded by Wundt's students in Italy, Russia, and Japan. More of Wundt's books were translated into Russian than any other language, and Russian adulation of Wundt led Moscow psychologists to construct a virtual duplicate of Wundt's lab in 1912. Another replica was built by Japanese students at Tokyo University in 1920, the year Wundt died, but it was destroyed during a student riot in the 1960s.

Wundt was a popular lecturer. At one time the enrollment in his Leipzig courses exceeded 600 students. His classroom manner was described in 1890 by his student E. B. Titchener:

*The [attendant] swung the door open, and Wundt came in. All in black, of course, from boots to necktie; a spare, narrow-shouldered figure, stooping a little from the hips; he gave the impression of height, though I doubt if in fact he stands more than 5 ft. 9.*

*He clattered—there is no other word for it—up the side-aisle and up the steps of the platform; slam bang, slam bang, as if his soles were made of wood. There was something positively undignified to me about this stamping clatter, but nobody seemed to notice it.*

*He came to the platform, and I could get a good view of him. Hair iron-grey, and a fair amount of it, except on the top of his head—which was carefully covered by long wisps drawn up from the side. …*

*The lecture was given without reference to notes: Wundt, so far as I could tell, never looked down once at the bookrest, though he had some little shuffle of papers there between his elbows. …*

*Wundt did not keep his arms lying on the rest: the elbows were fixed, but the arms and hands were perpetually coming up, pointing and waving. … the movements were subdued, and seemed in some mysterious way to be illustrative. …*

*He stopped punctually at the stroke of the clock, and clattered out, stooping a little, as he had clattered in. If it wasn't for this absurd clatter I should have nothing but admiration for the whole proceeding. (Baldwin, 1980, pp. 287–289)[1]*

In his personal life, Wundt was quiet and unassuming, and his days were carefully regimented. In the morning, Wundt worked on a book or article, read student papers, and edited his journal. In the afternoon, he attended exams or went to the laboratory. An American student recalled that Wundt's laboratory visits were limited to five or 10 minutes. Apparently, despite his faith in laboratory research, "he was not himself a laboratory worker" (Cattell, 1928, p. 545).

Later in the day, Wundt would take a walk and mentally prepare his afternoon lecture, which he habitually delivered at four o'clock. Evenings were devoted to music, politics, and—in his younger years—activities concerned with student and worker rights. He earned a comfortable living, and the family employed household servants and frequently entertained.

## Cultural Psychology

With the laboratory and the journal established and an immense amount of research under direction, Wundt turned his energy to philosophy. During the years from 1880 to 1891, he wrote on ethics, logic, and systematic philosophy. He published the second edition of *Principles of Physiological Psychology* in 1880 and the third edition in 1887, and he continued to contribute articles to his journal.

Another field on which Wundt focused his considerable talent had been sketched in his first book: the creation of a social psychology. When he returned to this project, he produced a 10-volume work, *Cultural Psychology,* published between 1900 and 1920. (The title is often translated inaccurately as *Folk Psychology.*)

Cultural psychology dealt with the various stages of human mental development as manifested in language, art, myths, social customs, law, and morals. The implications of this publication for psychology are of greater significance than the actual content; it served to divide the new science of psychology into two major parts: the experimental and the social.

Wundt believed that the simpler mental functions, such as sensation and perception, must be studied through laboratory methods. For investigating the higher mental processes, such as learning and memory, however, scientific experimentation is impossible because these processes are conditioned by language and other aspects of our cultural

---

[1]From "In Memory of William Wundt," in W. G. Bringmann and R. D. Tweney (eds.) *Wundt Studies: A Centennial Collection,* pp. 280–308. Reprinted by permission of the American Psychological Association.

Archives of the History of American Psychology/University of Akron

Wundt and his graduate students conduct an experiment on reaction time.

training. To Wundt, the higher thought processes could be approached only by the non-experimental means used in sociology, anthropology, and social psychology. The suggestion that social forces are significant in the development of cognitive processes is still considered important, but Wundt's conclusion that these processes cannot be studied experimentally was soon challenged and disproved.

Wundt devoted 10 years to the development of his cultural psychology, which provided him "the most satisfying experience in his working life" (Wong, 2009, p. 232). However, the field as he envisioned it had little impact on American psychology. A survey covering 90 years of articles published in the *American Journal of Psychology* showed that, of all the citations to Wundt's publications, fewer than 4 percent were to *Cultural Psychology*. In contrast, Wundt's *Principles of Physiological Psychology* accounted for more than 61 percent of the references to his works (Brozek, 1980).

One probable reason for the lack of interest in Wundt's cultural psychology among American psychologists was the timing of its publication: the period between 1900 and 1920. As we shall see, a new psychology was flourishing in the United States, an approach quite different from Wundt's. American psychologists had developed confidence in their own ideas and educational institutions by then and saw little need to pay attention to developments from Europe. One prominent researcher of that era noted that cultural psychology was of no interest because it "came at a stage of the maturity of American psychology in which American workers were far less open to foreign impressions than they had been" in the 1880s and 1890s (Judd, 1961, p. 219).

Wundt continued with his systematic research and theoretical work until his death in 1920. Consistent with his well-regulated lifestyle, he managed to complete his psychological reminiscences shortly before he died. Analyses of his productivity showed that he wrote 54,000 pages between 1853 and 1920, an output of 2.2 pages per day (Boring, 1950; Bringmann & Balk, 1992). His childhood fantasies of becoming a famous writer had been realized.

## The Study of Conscious Experience

Wundt's psychology relied on the experimental methods of the natural sciences, particularly the techniques used by the physiologists. Wundt adapted these scientific methods of investigation for the new psychology and proceeded to study its subject matter in the same way physical scientists were studying their own subject matter. Thus, the Zeitgeist in physiology and philosophy helped shape both the methods of investigation of the new psychology and its subject matter.

The subject matter of Wundt's psychology was, in a word, consciousness. In a broad sense, the impact of nineteenth-century empiricism and associationism was at least partly reflected in Wundt's system. In Wundt's view, consciousness included many different parts and could be studied by the method of analysis or reduction. Wundt wrote, "The first step in the investigation of a fact must therefore be a description of the individual elements … of which it consists" (quoted in Diamond, 1980a, p. 85).

Beyond that point, however, there is little similarity between Wundt's approach and the viewpoint of the majority of the empiricists and associationists. Wundt did not agree with the idea that the elements of consciousness were static (so-called atoms of the mind), which were passively connected by some mechanical process of association. Instead, Wundt believed that consciousness was active in organizing its own content. Hence, the study of the elements, content, or structure of consciousness alone would provide only a beginning to understanding psychological processes.

**Voluntarism:** The idea that the mind has the capacity to organize mental contents into higher-level thought processes.

*Voluntarism*  Because Wundt focused on the mind's self-organizing capacity, he labeled his system **voluntarism**, a term he derived from the word *volition,* defined as the act or power of willing. Voluntarism refers to the power of the will to organize the mind's contents into higher-level thought processes. Wundt emphasized not the elements themselves, as had the British empiricists and associationists (and as Wundt's student Titchener would later do), but rather the process of actively organizing or synthesizing those elements. It is important to remember, however, that although Wundt claimed that the conscious mind had the power to synthesize elements into higher-level cognitive processes, he nevertheless recognized that the elements of consciousness were basic. Without the elements, there would be nothing for the mind to organize.

**Mediate and immediate experience:** Mediate experience provides information about something other than the elements of that experience; immediate experience is unbiased by interpretation.

*Mediate and immediate experience*  According to Wundt, psychologists should be concerned with the study of immediate experience rather than mediate experience. **Mediate experience** provides us with information or knowledge about something other than the elements of an experience. This is the usual form in which we use experience to acquire knowledge about our world. When we look at a rose and say, "The rose is red," for example, this statement implies that our primary interest is in the flower and not in the fact that we are perceiving something called "redness."

However, the **immediate experience** of looking at the flower is not in the object itself but is instead in the experience of something that is red. For Wundt, immediate experience is unbiased or untainted by any personal interpretations, such as describing the experience of the rose's red color in terms of the object—the flower—itself. Similarly, when we describe our own feelings of discomfort from a toothache, we are reporting our immediate experience. If we were simply to say, "I have a toothache," then we would be concerned with mediate experience.

In Wundt's view, basic human experiences—such as the experiences of redness or of discomfort—form the states of consciousness (the mental elements) that the mind actively organizes. Wundt's goal was to analyze the mind into its elements, its component parts, just as the natural scientists were working to break down their subject matter—the physical universe. The ideas of the Russian chemist Dimitri Mendeleev in developing the periodic table of chemical elements supported Wundt's aim. Historians have suggested that Wundt may have been striving to develop a "periodic table" of the mind (Marx & Cronan-Hillix, 1987).

## The Method of Introspection

Wundt described his psychology as the science of conscious experience, and therefore the method of a scientific psychology must involve observations of conscious experience. However, only the person having such an experience can observe it. Wundt decided that the method of observation must necessarily involve **introspection**—the examination of one's own mental state. Wundt referred to this method as internal perception. The method of introspection did not originate with Wundt; its use can be traced to Socrates. Wundt's innovation was the application of precise experimental control over the conditions under which introspection was performed.

In physics, introspection had been used to study light and sound; in physiology, it had been applied to research on the sense organs. To obtain information about the senses, for example, an investigator applied a stimulus and asked the subject to report on the sensation produced. You will recognize this as similar to Fechner's psychophysics research methods. When subjects compared two weights and reported whether one was heavier, lighter, or equal in weight to the other, they were introspecting; that is, they were reporting on their conscious experiences.

Introspection, or internal perception, as practiced in Wundt's laboratory at the University of Leipzig, was conducted under Wundt's explicit rules and conditions:

- *Observers must be able to determine when the process is to be introduced.*
- *Observers must be in a state of readiness or strained attention.*
- *It must be possible to repeat the observation several times.*
- *It must be possible to vary the experimental conditions in terms of the controlled manipulation of the stimuli.*

The last condition invokes the essence of the experimental method: varying the conditions of the stimulus situation and observing the resulting changes in the subjects' reported experiences. Wundt believed that his form of introspection—internal perception—would provide all the raw data necessary for the problems of interest to psychology, just as external perception provided data for sciences such as astronomy and chemistry. In external perception, the focus of observation is outside of the observer, such as a star or the reaction produced by mixing chemicals in a test tube. With internal perception, the focus is within the observer: his or her conscious experiences.

The purpose of practicing internal perception under stringent experimental conditions is to produce accurate observations that are capable of being replicated, the way external perception yields observations for the natural sciences that can be repeated independently by other researchers. To achieve that goal, Wundt insisted that his observers be carefully and rigorously trained to perform internal perceptions properly. Observers were required to complete a staggering 10,000 individual introspective observations before they were judged sufficiently prepared to supply meaningful data for Wundt's laboratory research.

Through such persistent, repetitive training, subjects would be able to make observations mechanically and would quickly attend to the conscious experience being observed. In theory, Wundt's trained observers would not need to pause—to think about or reflect on the process (and possibly introduce some personal interpretation)—but could report on their conscious experience almost immediately and automatically. Thus, the interval between the acts of observing and reporting the immediate experience would be minimal.

**Introspection:** Examination of one's own mind to inspect and report on personal thoughts or feelings.

Wundt rarely accepted the kind of qualitative introspection in which subjects simply described their inner experiences. The type of introspective report he sought dealt primarily with the subjects' conscious judgments about the size, intensity, and duration of various physical stimuli; these are the kinds of quantitative judgments made in psychophysical research. Only a small number of Wundt's laboratory studies used reports of a subjective or qualitative nature, such as the pleasantness of a stimulus, the intensity of an image, or the quality of a sensation. Most of Wundt's research involved objective measurements provided by sophisticated laboratory equipment, and many of these measurements were of reaction times recorded quantitatively.

One historian investigated Wundt's use of qualitative versus quantitative data, and he found that "in the nearly 180 experimental studies published between 1883 and 1903 in the 20 volumes of the *Philosophische Studien* [Wundt's first journal, *Philosophical Studies*], there are just four which use qualitative introspective data" (Danziger, 1980, p. 248). When sufficient objective data had been accumulated, Wundt drew inferences from them about the elements and processes of conscious experience.

## Elements of Conscious Experience

Having defined the subject matter and methodology for his new science of psychology, Wundt outlined his goals as follows:

- *Analyze conscious processes into their basic elements.*
- *Discover how these elements are synthesized or organized.*
- *Determine the laws of connection governing the organization of the elements.*

*Sensations*   Wundt suggested that sensations were one of two elementary forms of experience. Sensations are aroused whenever a sense organ is stimulated and the resulting impulses reach the brain. Sensations can be classified by intensity, duration, and sense modality.

Wundt recognized no fundamental difference between sensations and images because images are also associated with excitation of the cerebral cortex.

*Feelings*   Feelings are the other elementary form of experience. Sensations and feelings are simultaneous aspects of immediate experience. Feelings are the subjective complements of sensations but do not arise directly from a sense organ. Sensations are accompanied by certain feeling qualities; when sensations combine to form a more complex state, a feeling quality will result.

**Tridimensional theory of feelings:** Wundt's explanation for feeling states based on three dimensions: pleasure/ displeasure, tension/ relaxation, and excitement/depression.

Wundt proposed a **tridimensional theory of feelings**, based on his personal introspective observations. Working with a metronome (a device that can be programmed to produce audible clicks at regular intervals), he reported that after experiencing a series of clicks, he felt that some rhythmic patterns were more pleasant or agreeable than others. He concluded that part of the experience of any pattern of sound is a subjective feeling of pleasure or displeasure. (Note that the subjective feeling occurred at the same time as the physical sensations associated with the clicks.) Wundt then suggested that this feeling state could be located on a continuum ranging from highly agreeable to highly disagreeable.

Continuing the experiments, Wundt noticed a second kind of feeling while listening to the metronome's clicks: a slight tension in anticipation of each successive sound, followed by relief after the awaited click had occurred. From this he concluded that in addition to a pleasure/displeasure continuum, feelings had a tension/relaxation dimension. Further, he felt mildly excited when he increased the rate of clicks, and calmer, even somewhat depressed, when he reduced the rate of clicks.

Thus, by varying the speed of the metronome and introspecting and reporting on his immediate conscious experiences (his sensations and feelings), Wundt arrived at three independent dimensions of feeling: pleasure/displeasure, tension/relaxation, and excitement/depression. Every elementary feeling could be effectively described by determining its location within this three-dimensional space—that is, its position on each of the dimensions.

Because Wundt considered emotions to be complex compounds of elementary feelings, if one could pinpoint the elementary feelings within the three-dimensional grid, then emotions could be reduced to these mental elements. Although the tridimensional theory of feelings stimulated a great deal of research at Leipzig and other European laboratories of the day, it has not withstood the test of time.

## Organizing the Elements of Conscious Experience

Despite his emphasis on the elements of conscious experience, Wundt did recognize that when we look at objects in the real world, our perceptions have a unity or wholeness. When we look out the window we see a tree, for example, not individual sensations or conscious experiences of brightness, color, or shape that trained observers in a laboratory report as a result of their introspections. Our visual experience in the real world comprehends the tree as a whole, not as the elementary sensations and feelings that constitute the tree.

**Apperception:** The process by which mental elements are organized.

How is the unified conscious experience compounded from the elementary parts? Wundt explained the phenomenon through his doctrine of **apperception**. The process of organizing mental elements into a whole is a creative synthesis (also known as the law of psychic resultants), which creates new properties from the building up or combining of the elements. Wundt wrote, "Every psychic compound has characteristics which are by no means the mere sum of the characteristics of the elements" (Wundt, 1896, p. 375). You have probably heard the saying that the whole is different from the sum of its parts. This is the idea promoted by the Gestalt psychologists (see Chapter 12). The notion of creative synthesis has its counterpart in chemistry. Combining chemical elements produces compounds or resultants that contain properties not found in the original elements.

To Wundt, apperception is an active process. Our consciousness is not merely acted on by the elemental sensations and feelings we experience. Instead, the mind acts on these elements in a creative way to make up the whole. Thus, Wundt did not conceive of the process of association in the passive, mechanical way favored by most of the British empiricists and associationists.

## IN THEIR OWN WORDS

### Original Source Material on the Law of Psychic Resultants and the Principle of Creative Synthesis from *Outline of Psychology* (1896)

**Wilhelm Wundt**

*The law of psychical resultants* finds its expression in the fact that every psychical compound shows attributes which may indeed be understood from the attributes of its elements after these elements have once been presented, but which are by no means to be looked upon as the mere sum of the attributes of these elements. A compound clang is more in its ideational and affective attributes than merely a sum of single tones. In spacial and temporal ideas the spacial and temporal arrangement is conditioned, to be sure, in a perfectly regular way by the cooperation of the elements that make up the idea, but still the arrangement itself can by no means be regarded as a property belonging to the sensational elements themselves. The nativistic theories that assume this implicate themselves in contradictions that cannot be solved; and besides, insofar as they admit subsequent changes in the original space-perceptions and time-perceptions, they are ultimately driven to the assumption of the rise, to some extent at least, of new attributes.

Finally, in the apperceptive functions and in the activities of imagination and understanding, this law finds expression in a clearly recognized form. Not only do the elements united by apperceptive synthesis gain, in the aggregate idea that results from their combination, a new significance which they did not have in their isolated state, but what is of still greater importance, the aggregate idea itself is a new psychical content that was made possible, to be sure, by these elements, but was by no means contained in them. This appears most strikingly in the more complex productions of apperceptive synthesis, as, for example, in a work of art or a train of logical thought.

The law of psychical resultants thus expresses a principle which we may designate, in view of its results, as a *principle of creative synthesis*. This has long been recognized in the case of higher mental creations, but generally not applied to the other psychical processes. In fact, through an unjustifiable confusion with the laws of psychical causality, it has even been completely reversed.

A similar confusion is responsible for the notion that there is a contradiction between the principle of creative synthesis in the mental world and the general laws of the natural world, especially that of the conservation of energy. Such a contradiction is impossible from the outset because the points of view for judgment, and therefore for measurements wherever such are made, are different in the two cases, and must be different since natural science and psychology deal not with different contents of experience but with one and the same content viewed from different sides....

*Physical measurements* have to do with objective masses, forces, and energies. These are supplementary concepts which we are obliged to use in judging objective experience; and their general laws, derived as they are from experience, must not be contradicted by any single case of experience. *Psychical measurements,* which are concerned with the comparison of psychical components and their resultants, have to do with subjective values and ends. The subjective value of a whole may increase in comparison with that of its components; its purpose may be different and higher than theirs without any change in the masses, forces, and energies concerned. The muscular movements of an external volitional act, the physical processes that accompany sense-perception, association, and apperception, all follow invariably the principle of the conservation of energy. But the mental values and ends that these energies represent may be very different in quality even while the quantity of these energies remains the same.

## The Fate of Wundt's Psychology in Germany

Although Wundtian psychology spread rapidly, it did not immediately or completely transform the nature of academic psychology in Germany. In Wundt's lifetime—indeed, as late as 1941, two decades after Wundt's death—psychology in German universities remained primarily a subspecialty of philosophy, in part because some psychologists and philosophers argued against separating psychology and philosophy. However, it also was attributable to a significant contextual factor; namely, the government officials in charge of funding German universities did not see sufficient practical value in psychology to warrant supplying the money to establish independent academic departments and laboratories.

When the Society for Experimental Psychology held a meeting in Berlin in 1912, psychologists formally urged government officials to provide increased financial support. In response, Berlin's mayor implied that first he would need to see some useful results from all this psychological research. The message was clear: "If psychology were to get more support, its representatives would have to prove its usefulness to society" (Ash, 1995, p. 45).

The difficulty was that Wundt's psychology, with its focus on describing and organizing the elements of consciousness, was not appropriate for solving real-world problems. Perhaps that was one reason why Wundt's psychology did not take root in the pragmatic climate of the United States. Wundt approached psychology as a pure academic science; he had no interest in applying his psychology to practical concerns. Therefore, despite its widespread acceptance at universities in many other countries, Wundtian psychology at home in Germany was relatively slow to develop as a distinct science.

By 1910, 10 years before Wundt died, German psychology had three journals and several textbooks and research laboratories, but only four scholars listed themselves in official directories as psychologists rather than philosophers. By 1925, only 25 people in Germany called themselves psychologists, and only 14 of 23 universities had established separate psychology departments (Turner, 1982).

At the same time in the United States, there were many more psychologists and psychology departments. Psychological knowledge and techniques were being applied to practical problems in business and education, yet we shall see that these departures from Wundt's agenda still owe their origins to his viewpoint.

## Criticisms of Wundtian Psychology

Wundt's position, like that of any innovator, was open to criticism. Especially vulnerable was his method of internal perception or introspection. Critics asked: When introspection by different observers provides differing results, how do we decide who is correct? Experiments using the introspection technique cannot always yield agreement because introspective observation is self-observation—decidedly a private experience. As such, disagreements cannot be settled by repeating the observations. Wundt recognized this fault but believed that the method could be improved by providing greater training and experience for the observers.

Wundt's personal opinions on political matters also offered a target for criticism and may explain what one historian described as "the precipitous decline of Wundtian psychology between the World Wars [1918–1939]. ... The massive body of Wundtian research and writings all but disappeared in the English-speaking world" (Blumenthal, 1985, p. 44). Scholars have speculated that the decline is related to Wundt's outspoken remarks about World War I. He blamed England for starting the war, and he defended Germany's invasion of Belgium as an act of self-defense. These statements were self-serving and incorrect, and they turned many American psychologists against Wundt and his psychology (see Benjamin, Durkin, Link, Vestal, & Acord, 1992; Muhlberger, 2009; Sanua, 1993).

His political stance may also have cost him a Nobel Prize. Wundt had been nominated twice before, in 1907 and 1909, and in 1915 was one of six finalists. Although he was "the best known psychologist in the world at the time and a person of considerable accomplishments" he did not win (Benjamin, 2003, p. 735). World War I was in its second bloody year, and anti-German sentiment was strong. Wundt's sometimes vitriolic defense of his homeland may well have contributed to his rejection for the prize.

Wundt's system also faced increasing competition in the German-speaking world following World War I. During Wundt's later years, two other schools of thought arose in Europe to overshadow his views: Gestalt psychology in Germany and psychoanalysis in Austria. In the United States, functionalism and behaviorism eclipsed the Wundtian approach.

In addition, the prevailing economic and political contextual forces contributed to the disappearance of the Wundtian system in Germany. The economy's collapse after Germany's defeat in World War I left its universities in financial ruin. The University of Leipzig could not even afford to purchase copies of Wundt's latest books for its library. Wundt's laboratory, at which he trained the first generation of psychologists, was destroyed during World

War II in a British and American bombing raid on December 4, 1943. Thus, the nature, content, form, and even the home of Wundtian psychology have been lost.

### Wundt's Legacy

Wundt began a new domain of science, as he had announced he would, and conducted research in a laboratory he designed exclusively for that purpose. He published the results in his own journal and tried to develop a systematic theory of the nature of the human mind. Some of his students went on to found laboratories to continue experimenting on the problems by using the techniques that Wundt set forth. Thus, Wundt provided psychology with all the trappings of a modern science.

Of course, the times were ready for the Wundtian movement. It was the natural outgrowth of the development of the physiological sciences, particularly in German universities. However, that Wundt's work was the culmination of this movement and not its origin does not diminish its stature. The founding of psychology did require a great deal of dedication and courage to bring such a movement to fulfillment, and thus the results of Wundt's efforts represent an achievement of such overwhelming importance that we must accord Wundt a stature unique among psychologists of the modern period. A survey of 49 American historians of psychology that was conducted 70 years after Wundt's death revealed that he was still considered the most important psychologist of all time, quite an honor for a scholar whose system had long ago faded from view (Korn, Davis, & Davis, 1991).

Wundt's monumental contributions are not diminished by the fact that much of the history of psychology after Wundt consists of rebellion against the limitations he placed on the field. Instead, we may consider that these developments enhanced his greatness. Revolutions must have some target, something to push against, and as that target Wundt's work provided a compelling and magnificent beginning to modern experimental psychology.

## Other Developments in German Psychology

Wundt had a monopoly on the new psychology for only a short time; the science was also beginning to flourish at other German laboratories. Although Wundt was obviously the most important organizer and systematizer in the early days of psychology, others were also influential in the field's early development. Researchers who did not subscribe to Wundt's viewpoint proposed different ideas, but all were engaged in the common enterprise of expanding psychology as a science. Their work, along with Wundt's work, made Germany the undisputed center of the movement.

Developments in England would give psychology a radically different theme and direction (see Chapter 6). Charles Darwin proposed a theory of evolution, and Francis Galton began work on a psychology of individual differences. These ideas influenced the direction of psychology when it came to the United States, even more than the pioneering work of Wilhelm Wundt.

In addition, early American psychologists, most of whom had studied under Wundt at Leipzig, returned to the United States and made of Wundtian psychology something uniquely American. Thus, shortly after Wundt founded psychology, it divided into factions, and soon his approach was only one of several.

## Hermann Ebbinghaus (1850–1909)

Only a few years after Wundt claimed it was impossible to conduct experiments on the higher mental processes, a German psychologist working alone, isolated from any academic center of psychology, began to experiment successfully on the higher mental

HERMANN
EBBINGHAUS

processes. Hermann Ebbinghaus became the first psychologist to investigate learning and memory experimentally. In doing so, he not only showed that Wundt was wrong on that point but also changed the way in which association, or learning, could be studied.

## Ebbinghaus's Life

Ebbinghaus was born near Bonn, Germany, in 1850 and undertook his college studies first at the University of Bonn and then at universities in Halle and Berlin. During his academic training his interests shifted from history and literature to philosophy, in which he received his degree in 1873, following military service in the Franco-Prussian War. He devoted seven years to independent study in England and France, where his interests changed again, this time leading him toward science.

Three years before Wundt established his laboratory at Leipzig, Ebbinghaus bought at a London bookstore a secondhand copy of Fechner's great work, *Elements of Psychophysics.* This chance encounter profoundly affected his thinking and, ultimately, the direction of the new psychology.

Fechner's mathematical approach to psychological phenomena was an exciting revelation to Ebbinghaus, and he resolved to do for psychology what Fechner had done for psychophysics, using rigid and systematic measurement. His goal was nothing less than to apply the experimental method to the higher mental processes. Most likely influenced by the popularity of the work of the British associationists, Ebbinghaus chose to undertake his breakthrough research in the area of human learning.

## Research on Learning

Before Ebbinghaus began his work, the customary way to study learning was to examine associations that were already formed. This was the approach of the British associationists. In a sense, investigators were working backward, attempting to determine how the connections had been established.

Ebbinghaus's focus was different; he began his study with the initial formation of the associations. In this way he could control the conditions under which the chains of ideas were formed and thus make the study of learning more objective.

Ebbinghaus's work on learning and forgetting has been judged one of the great instances of original genius in experimental psychology. It was the first venture into a truly psychological problem area, one that was not part of physiology, as was true with so many of Wundt's research topics. Thus, Ebbinghaus's revolutionary research broadened considerably the scope of experimental psychology. Recall that learning and memory had never been studied experimentally. Indeed, the eminent Wilhelm Wundt had said they could not be. Ebbinghaus set out to do so, even though he had no academic appointment, no university setting in which to conduct his work, no teacher, no students, and no laboratory. Nevertheless, over a period of five years, he carried out alone a series of carefully controlled and comprehensive studies using himself as the only subject.

For the basic measure of learning Ebbinghaus adapted a technique from the associationists who had proposed frequency of associations as a condition of recall. Ebbinghaus reasoned that the difficulty of learning material could be measured by this frequency; that is, by counting the number of repetitions needed for one perfect reproduction of the material. Here we see the influence of Fechner, who measured sensations indirectly by measuring the stimulus intensity necessary to produce a just noticeable difference in sensation. Ebbinghaus approached the problem of measuring memory similarly, by counting the number of trials or repetitions required to learn the material.

For the material to be learned, Ebbinghaus devised similar, but not identical, lists of syllables. He repeated the task often enough to be confident of the accuracy of his results.

Thus, he could cancel out variable errors from trial to trial and obtain an average measure. So systematic was Ebbinghaus in his experimentation that he regulated his personal habits as well, keeping them as constant as possible and following an unvarying routine, always learning the material at the same time each day.

## Research with Nonsense Syllables

**Nonsense syllables:**
Syllables presented in a meaningless series to study memory processes.

For the subject matter of his research—the material to be learned—Ebbinghaus invented **nonsense syllables**, which revolutionized the study of learning. Wundt's student, E. B. Titchener (see Chapter 5), noted that the use of nonsense syllables marked the first significant advance in the field since the time of Aristotle.

Ebbinghaus was looking for some alternatives to everyday words for his subject matter because he recognized an inherent difficulty in using stories or poetry as stimulus materials. Meanings or associations have already been attached to words by people familiar with the language. These existing associations can facilitate the learning of material. These connections are already present at the time of the experiment, so they cannot be controlled by the experimenter. Ebbinghaus wanted to use material that would be uniformly unassociated, completely homogeneous, and equally unfamiliar—material with which there could be few, if any, past associations. The nonsense syllables he created, typically formed of two consonants with a vowel in between (as in *lef, bok,* or *yat*), satisfied these criteria. He wrote all possible combinations of consonants and vowels on cards, yielding a supply of 2,300 syllables from which he drew at random the stimulus materials to be learned.

Later data of history—supplied a century later, in the 1980s, by a German psychologist who read all the footnotes in Ebbinghaus's publications and in the workbook for a set of his experiments, and who then compared the English translations with the original German—provide us with a new interpretation to our understanding of nonsense syllables (Gundlach, 1986). They were not always limited to three letters, and they were not necessarily nonsense.

This meticulous investigation of the data of history—in this case using Ebbinghaus's own writings—revealed that some of the syllables were four, five, or six letters long. More important, what Ebbinghaus called a "meaningless series of syllables" as the subject matter of his research was incorrectly translated into English as a "series of nonsense syllables." To Ebbinghaus, it was not the individual syllables that were designed to be meaningless (although many were), but rather that the entire list of stimulus words would be meaningless—deliberately constructed to be free of prior connections or associations.

This reinterpretation of Ebbinghaus's writings also revealed that he was fluent in English and French as well as German and had studied Latin and Greek. Therefore, he would have had a difficult time deriving syllables that would have had no meaning for him. The researcher concluded: "The vain struggle for the definitively nonsensical, association-free syllable is the endeavor of some of [Ebbinghaus's] followers" (Gundlach, 1986, pp. 469–470).

Ebbinghaus designed several studies using his meaningless series of syllables to determine the influence of various experimental conditions on human learning and retention. One study investigated the difference between the speed of memorizing lists of syllables versus the speed of memorizing material that had more apparent meaning. To determine the difference, Ebbinghaus memorized stanzas of Byron's poem, "Don Juan." Each stanza has 80 syllables, and Ebbinghaus found that it required approximately nine readings to memorize one stanza. He then memorized a meaningless series of 80 syllables and discovered that the task required nearly 80 repetitions. He concluded that meaningless or unassociated material is approximately nine times harder to learn than meaningful material.

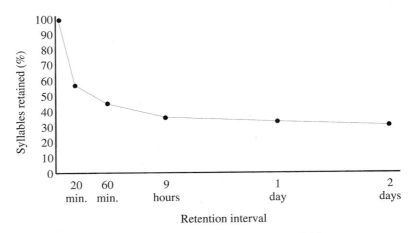

**FIGURE 4.1** Ebbinghaus's forgetting curve for nonsense syllables.

He also studied the effect of the length of the material to be learned on the number of repetitions necessary for a perfect reproduction. He found that longer material requires more repetitions and, consequently, more time to learn. When Ebbinghaus increased the number of syllables to be learned, the average time to memorize a syllable increased. Of course these results are predictable in a general way: The more we have to learn, the longer it will take us. The significance of Ebbinghaus's work is in his careful control of the experimental conditions, his quantitative analysis of the data, and his conclusion that learning time per syllable as well as total learning time both increase with longer lists of syllables.

Ebbinghaus studied other variables he expected would also influence learning and memory: the effects of overlearning (repeating the lists more times than necessary for one perfect reproduction), associations within lists, reviewing material, and the time elapsed between learning and recall. His research on the effect of time yielded the famous Ebbinghaus's forgetting curve, which shows that material is forgotten rapidly in the first few hours after learning and more slowly thereafter (see Figure 4.1).

Ebbinghaus published his research results in a book titled *On Memory: A Contribution to Experimental Psychology* (1885), which may be the most brilliant single investigation in the history of experimental psychology. In addition to beginning a new field of study that remains important today, his research program is an example of technical skill, perseverance, and ingenuity. We cannot find in the history of psychology any other investigator working alone who subjected himself to such a painstaking regimen of experimentation. The research was so exacting, thorough, and systematic that it continues to be cited in psychology textbooks well over a century later.

## Other Contributions to Psychology

Ebbinghaus, with the physicist Arthur König, founded in 1890 a journal called the *Journal of Psychology and Physiology of the Sense Organs*. A new journal was welcome in Germany at the time because Wundt's journal, the primary outlet for research reports from the Leipzig laboratory, could not handle all of the work being produced. The need for a new publication, a mere nine years after Wundt had begun his, is significant testimony to the phenomenal growth of psychology in both size and diversity.

In their first issue, Ebbinghaus and König made a bold claim for the two disciplines named in the journal's title: psychology and physiology. These fields have "consequently grown together ... to form one whole; they promote and presuppose one another, and so constitute two coequal members of one great double science" (quoted in Turner, 1982, p. 151). This declaration, only 11 years after Wundt established his experimental laboratory, also shows how far Wundt's idea of psychology as a science had come.

In 1902 Ebbinghaus wrote a successful textbook, *The Principles of Psychology,* which he dedicated to Fechner's memory, and in 1908 he published *A Summary of Psychology,* intended for a broader audience. Both books appeared in several editions. After Ebbinghaus's death from pneumonia in 1909, the books were revised by other writers.

Ebbinghaus did not make theoretical contributions to psychology. He created no formal system and had no disciples. He did not found a school of thought, nor did he seem to want to do so. Yet he is of importance not only to the study of learning and memory, which he began, but also to experimental psychology as a whole.

One measure of a scientist's overall historical worth is how well his or her position stands the test of time. By that standard, Ebbinghaus can be seen as more influential than Wundt. Ebbinghaus's research brought objectivity, quantification, and experimentation to the study of learning, a topic that remained central to much of twentieth-century psychology. It is because of Ebbinghaus's vision and dedication that work on association shifted from speculation about its attributes to formal scientific investigation. Many of his conclusions about the nature of learning and memory remain valid more than a century after he offered them.

National Library of Medicine

FRANZ BRENTANO

# Franz Brentano (1838–1917)

At about the age of 16, Franz Brentano began training for the priesthood. He studied at universities in Berlin, Munich, and Tübingen in Germany, receiving a degree in philosophy from Tübingen in 1864. He was ordained the same year, and two years later he began teaching philosophy at the University of Würzburg, where he also wrote and lectured on the work of Aristotle. In 1870, the Vatican Council in Rome accepted the doctrine of papal infallibility, an idea Brentano opposed. He resigned his professorship, to which he had been appointed as a priest, and formally left the church.

Brentano's most famous book, *Psychology from an Empirical Standpoint,* was published in 1874, the year in which the second part of Wundt's *Principles of Physiological Psychology* appeared. Brentano's book directly contradicted Wundt's views, attesting to the dissent already apparent in the new psychology. Also in that year, Brentano was appointed professor of philosophy at the University of Vienna. He remained in Austria for 20 years, and his influence grew considerably. He was a popular lecturer, and a number of his students later achieved prominence in psychology, notably Christian von Ehrenfels and Sigmund Freud. Freud took five courses with Brentano and later referred to him as a "genius" and "a damned clever fellow" (Gay, 1988, p. 29). In 1894, Brentano retired from teaching but continued to study and write, dividing his time between Switzerland and Italy.

Brentano is considered one of the more important early psychologists because of his diverse interests. We will see that he is an intellectual precursor of the Gestalt psychology and humanistic psychology schools, and he also shared with Wundt the goal of making psychology a science. Whereas Wundt's psychology was experimental, Brentano's was empirical. According to Brentano, the primary method for psychology should be observation, not experimentation, although he did not totally reject the experimental method. He considered an empirical approach to be generally broader in scope because it accepts data from observation and individual experience as well as from experimentation.

## The Study of Mental Acts

Brentano opposed Wundt's fundamental idea that psychology should study the content of conscious experience. He argued that the proper subject matter for psychology is

**Act psychology:**
Brentano's system of psychology, which focused on mental activities (e.g., seeing) rather than on mental contents (e.g., that which is seen).

mental activity, such as the mental action of seeing rather than the mental content of what a person sees. Thus, Brentano's **act psychology** questioned the Wundtian view that mental processes involve contents or elements.

He argued that a distinction should be drawn between experience as a structure or content, and experience as an activity. In looking at a red flower, for example, the sensory content of redness is different from the act of experiencing or sensing redness. To Brentano, that act of experiencing redness is an example of the true subject matter of psychology. He stated that color is a physical quality, but the act of seeing the color is a mental quality or activity. Of course, an act necessarily involves an object; some sensory content must be present because the act of seeing is meaningless without something to be seen.

Brentano's redefinition of psychology's subject matter required a different method of study because acts, unlike sensory contents, are not accessible through introspection, the internal perception method Wundt and his students were practicing at the Leipzig laboratory. The study of mental acts required observation on a larger scale. Thus, we see Brentano's preference for more empirical rather than experimental methods for his act psychology. He was not proposing a return to speculative philosophy. Remember that although Brentano's methodology was not experimental, he did rely on systematic observation.

Brentano advanced two ways to study mental acts:

1. Through memory (recalling the mental processes involved in a particular mental state).
2. Through imagination (imagining a mental state and observing the accompanying mental processes).

Although Brentano's position attracted its share of followers, Wundtian psychology maintained prominence. Because Wundt published so much more than Brentano, his position was the better known. Also, psychologists admitted that it was easier to study sensations or conscious contents with the methods of psychophysics than it was to use observation to study the more elusive acts.

CARL STUMPF

# Carl Stumpf (1848–1936)

Born into a medical family in Bavaria, Carl Stumpf became acquainted with science at an early age but developed a greater interest in music. At the age of seven, he began studying the violin and eventually mastered five other instruments. By age 10, he was composing music. As a student at the University of Würzburg, he became interested in Brentano's work and focused his attention on philosophy and science. At Brentano's suggestion, Stumpf attended the University of Göttingen, where he received his doctoral degree in 1868.

In 1894, Stumpf was awarded the most prized professorship in German psychology, an appointment at the University of Berlin. His years there were extremely productive. He developed his original laboratory of three small rooms into a large and important institute. Although his research programs never equaled Wundt's in scope, Stumpf has been considered Wundt's major rival. Stumpf trained two of the psychologists who later founded Gestalt psychology (see Chapter 12), a school of thought that opposed Wundt's views.

Stumpf's early writings in psychology were concerned with the perception of space, but his most influential work, in keeping with his lifelong interest in music, is *Psychology of Tone,* published in two volumes (1883 and 1890). This work and later studies of music earned him a place second only to Helmholtz in the field of acoustics, and they were considered a pioneering effort in the psychological study of music.

## Phenomenology

The influence of Brentano may explain why Stumpf accepted a less-rigorous approach to psychology than what Wundt considered appropriate. Stumpf argued that the primary

**Phenomenology:**
Stumpf's introspective method that examined experience as it occurred and did not try to reduce experience to elementary components. Also, an approach to knowledge based on an unbiased description of immediate experience as it occurs, not analyzed or reduced to elements.

data for psychology are phenomena. **Phenomenology**, the kind of introspection Stumpf favored, refers to the examination of unbiased experience; that is, experience just as it occurs. He disagreed with Wundt about breaking experience down into elements. Stumpf believed that to analyze experience by reducing it to mental contents or elements is to make that experience artificial and abstract and thus no longer natural. Later, Edmund Husserl, a student of Stumpf's, proposed a philosophy of phenomenology, considered a precursor of Gestalt psychology (see Chapter 12).

In a series of publications, Stumpf and Wundt waged a bitter fight about the introspection of tones. Stumpf initiated the debate on a theoretical level, but Wundt made it personal, spicing the controversy with "scathing invectives" (Stumpf, 1930/1961, p. 441). Essentially, the question was: Whose introspection reports are more credible? When reporting on the experience of hearing musical tones, should we accept the results of Wundt's highly trained laboratory observers or the results of Stumpf's expert musicians? Stumpf simply refused to accept the results obtained at Wundt's Leipzig laboratory.

While continuing to write about music and acoustics, Stumpf established a center for the collection of recordings of primitive music from many countries throughout the world. He founded the Berlin Association for Child Psychology, and he published a theory of emotion that attempted to reduce feelings to sensations, an idea relevant to contemporary cognitive theories of emotion. Thus, Stumpf was one of several German psychologists working independently of Wundt to expand psychology's boundaries.

# Oswald Külpe (1862–1915)

Archives of the History of American Psychology/University of Akron

OSWALD KÜLPE

Initially a follower of Wundt, Oswald Külpe led a group of students in a protest movement against what he saw as the limitations of Wundtian psychology. Throughout his career in psychology, Külpe worked on problems that Wundt's psychology ignored.

In 1881, Külpe began his studies at the University of Leipzig. He planned to study history, but under Wundt's influence he switched to philosophy and experimental psychology, the latter then in its infancy. After receiving his degree, he became assistant professor and assistant to Wundt, carrying on research in the psychology laboratory. A student called him the "kind mother" of Wundt's lab because he was always ready to help students with their problems (Kiesow, 1930/1961, p. 167).

Külpe wrote an introductory textbook, *Outline of Psychology* (1893), and dedicated it to Wundt. In the book, Külpe defined psychology as the science of the facts of experience that are dependent on the experiencing person.

In 1894 Külpe accepted a professorship at the University of Würzburg, and two years later he established a psychology laboratory that soon would rival Wundt's in importance. Among the students attracted to Würzburg were several Americans, including James Rowland Angell who became a pivotal figure in the development of the functionalist school of thought (see Chapter 7). Külpe remained devoted to his students and to his research throughout his life. Never married, he was fond of explaining that "science is my bride" (quoted in Ogden, 1951, p. 4).

## Külpe's Differences with Wundt

In the *Outline of Psychology,* Külpe did not discuss the process of thought; at that time, his position was still compatible with Wundt's view that it was impossible to experiment on the higher mental processes. Only a few years later, however, Külpe had become convinced that thought processes could indeed be studied experimentally. After all, Ebbinghaus was studying memory, another of the higher mental processes. If memory could be assessed in the laboratory, why not thought? Asking this question obviously meant that Külpe was challenging Wundt's definition of the scope of psychology.

## Systematic Experimental Introspection

**Systematic experimental introspection:** Külpe's introspective method that used retrospective reports of subjects' cognitive processes after they had completed an experimental task.

Another difference between psychology as practiced at Würzburg and at Leipzig related to introspection. Külpe developed a method he called **systematic experimental introspection**, which involved, first, performing a complex task (such as establishing logical connections between concepts), then having the subjects provide a retrospective report about their cognitive processes during the task. In other words, subjects undertook some mental process, such as thinking or judging, after which they examined *how* they had thought or judged. Wundt prohibited the use of such retrospective, or after-the-fact, reporting in his laboratory. Wundt studied conscious experience as it occurred, not the memory of it after it had occurred. He was so displeased with Külpe's methodology that he referred to it as "mock" introspection.

Külpe's approach was systematic because the total experience could be described precisely by dividing it into time periods. Similar tasks were repeated many times so that the introspective reports could be corrected, corroborated, and amplified. These reports were usually supplemented by additional questions, directing the subjects' attention to specific points.

Other differences existed between the introspective approaches of Külpe and Wundt. Wundt was opposed to having his subjects describe their subjective conscious experiences in detail. Most of his research focused on objective, quantitative measurements, such as reaction times or the judgments of weights in psychophysical research. In contrast, Külpe's systematic experimental introspection emphasized detailed subjective, qualitative reports from subjects about the nature of their thought processes. Külpe's subjects were expected to do more than make simple judgments about stimulus intensity. They were asked to describe the complex mental operations they performed during their exposure to the experimental task.

In Külpe's systematic experimental introspection, the experimenter assumes a more active role in the research process. In Wundt's laboratory, the experimenter's involvement was limited to presenting the stimulus material and recording the results of the subject's observations. Therefore, Wundt's experimenters did not intrude on the actual observations. In Külpe's approach, however, the experimenters asked direct questions of the observers to elicit the details of their reactions to the experimental stimuli.

Such questioning demanded that the observers work harder to describe carefully and accurately the complex mental events they had experienced. Külpe required more information from them than reaction times, judgments of heavier versus lighter weights, or other quantitative measurements. One historian suggested that Külpe was truly pushing the narrow limits of Wundt's form of introspection (Danziger, 1980).

In summary, then, Külpe's approach was aimed directly at investigating what was going on in a subject's mind during a conscious experience. His stated goals were to expand Wundt's conception of psychology's subject matter to encompass the higher mental processes and to refine the introspective method.

## Imageless Thought

**Imageless thought:** Külpe's idea that meaning in thought can occur without any sensory or imaginal component.

What was the outcome of Külpe's campaign to expand and refine psychology's subject matter and method? Wundt attempted to reduce conscious experience to its component parts; that is, to its sensations and images. All experience, Wundt stated, is composed of sensations and images. Yet the results of Külpe's direct introspection of the thought processes supported the opposite viewpoint—that thought can occur without any sensory or imaginal content. This finding came to be identified as **imageless thought**, to represent the idea that meanings in thought do not necessarily involve specific images. Külpe's research had identified a non-sensory aspect of consciousness.

It is interesting to note another instance of simultaneous discovery. Imageless thought was proposed independently at about the same time by the American psychologist Robert Woodworth (see Chapter 7) and by the French psychologist Alfred Binet (see Chapter 8).

### Research Topics of the Würzburg Laboratory

Külpe and his students conducted research on a variety of topics. One significant contribution was a study by Karl Marbe on the comparative judgment of weights. Although sensations and images were present during the task, Marbe found that they seemed to play no part in the process of judgment. Subjects were unable to report on how their judgments of lighter or heavier weights came into their minds. This contradicted the accepted notion that in making such judgments, subjects retained a mental image of the first weight and compared it with a sensory impression of the second weight.

A study by Henry Watt demonstrated that in a word-association task (i.e., asking subjects to respond to a stimulus word), subjects had little relevant information to report about their conscious process of judgment. This finding reinforced Külpe's contention that conscious experience could not be reduced solely to sensations and images. Watt's subjects were able to respond correctly without being consciously aware of any intention to do so at the time they made their response. Watt concluded that their conscious work was done before the task was performed, at the time when the instructions were given and understood.

Watt's subjects apparently established an unconscious set or determining tendency to respond in the desired way, once they comprehended the instructions. When the rules for the task had been understood and the determining tendency adopted, the actual task was performed with little conscious effort. This research suggested that predispositions outside of consciousness were somehow able to control conscious activities. Thus, experience depended not only on conscious elements but also on unconscious determining tendencies, suggesting that the unconscious mind can have an influence on human behavior. This idea was later adopted by Sigmund Freud for his psychoanalytic school of thought.

## Comment

We can see that divisions and controversies engulfed psychology shortly after its formal founding. For all their differences, however, the early psychologists were united in the goal of developing an independent science of psychology. Even with their varying views of psychology's subject matter and methods, Wundt, Ebbinghaus, Brentano, Stumpf, and others together irrevocably changed the study of human nature. One writer noted that because of the efforts of these scholars, psychology was no longer

> *a study of the soul [but] a study, by observation and experiment, of certain reactions of the human organism not included in the subject matter of any other science. The German psychologists, in spite of their many differences, were to this extent engaged in a common enterprise; and their ability, their industry, and the common direction of their labors all made the developments in the German universities the center of the new movement in psychology. (Heidbreder, 1933, p. 105)*

Germany did not remain the center of the new movement for long. Soon, Wundt's student E. B. Titchener brought a different version of the founder's psychology to the United States.

## Discussion Questions

1. Describe Ebbinghaus's research on learning and memory. How was it influenced by the work of Fechner?

2. Describe the differences between "founding" and "originating" in science.

3. Describe Wundt's cultural psychology. How did it lead to division within psychology?

4. Describe Wundt's methodology and his rules for introspection. Did he favor quantitative or qualitative introspection? Why?

5. Despite their many differences, what did the works of Wundt, Ebbinghaus, Brentano, and Stumpf have in common?

6. Distinguish between internal and external perception. What is the purpose of apperception?

7. Distinguish between mediate and immediate experience.

8. How did apperception relate to the work of James Mill and John Stuart Mill?

9. How did Stumpf differ with Wundt on introspection and on the reduction of experience to elements?

10. How did the idea of imageless thought challenge Wundt's conception of conscious experience?

11. How does Brentano's act psychology differ from Wundtian psychology?

12. How was Wundt's psychology influenced by the work of the German physiologists and the British empiricists? Describe the concept of voluntarism.

13. On what basis did Wundt conclude that a person cannot engage in more than one mental activity at precisely the same moment in time?

14. Trace the fate of Wundtian psychology in Germany. On what grounds was Wundt's system criticized?

15. What are elements of consciousness? What is their role in mental life?

16. What did Külpe mean by systematic experimental introspection? How did Külpe's approach differ from Wundt's?

17. Why did cultural psychology have little impact on American psychology?

18. Why is Wundt, and not Fechner, considered the founder of the new psychology?

## CHAPTER 5

# Structuralism

## Swallow the Rubber Tube—A College Prank?

Would you volunteer to swallow a rubber tube that goes down to your stomach? And then have hot water poured down the tube? And then ice-cold water? All for the glory of psychological research? Do you need more time to decide on your answer?

If you had been a graduate student in psychology at Cornell University in upstate New York around the beginning of the twentieth century, you would have been asked, or urged, to do just that. Professor Edward Bradford Titchener, the psychologist conducting the experiment, was such a formidable being that nearly all of his students agreed to the often outrageous things he asked them to do in the name of science. The students were providing data for the psychological system he was developing. How? They were undertaking a form of introspection.

Introspection was a serious endeavor at Cornell in those days, and Titchener's graduate students were dedicated to their work. Consider the stomach tube, for example; they were asked to swallow the tube to study the sensitivity of their internal organs. Students swallowed the tubes in the morning, and they remained in place throughout the day. You can imagine that it was not easy to carry out ordinary activities with a tube down your throat, and many students vomited before they were able to keep the tubes down. At specified times, throughout the day the students went to the laboratory to have hot water poured through the tubes, and then they reported on the sensations they were experiencing. Later they repeated the process with cold water. In another experiment students carried notebooks with them to the bathroom so they could record their feelings and sensations whenever they urinated or defecated.

Then there was the sex study, another example of data lost to history for many years before being recovered. Married students were asked to make notes of their elementary sensations and feelings during sexual intercourse and to attach measuring devices to their bodies to record physiological responses. This research was little publicized at the time. It was revealed in 1960 by Cora Friedline, one of Titchener's students, in a lecture she gave at Randolph-Macon College in Lynchburg, Virginia.[1] The study did become common knowledge around the Cornell campus at the time, however, giving the psychology laboratory a reputation as an immoral place. The housemother in the women's dormitory would not allow her students to visit the lab after dark. When word spread that condoms had been attached to the stomach tubes that the graduate students were swallowing, the talk in the dorm, Friedline said, was that the lab "wasn't a safe place for anyone to go."

---

[1]We are grateful to F. B. Rowe for providing a copy of Friedline's remarks, delivered in April 1960.

EDWARD BRADFORD
TITCHENER

# Edward Bradford Titchener (1867–1927)

Although E. B. Titchener professed to be a loyal follower of Wilhelm Wundt, Titchener dramatically altered Wundt's system of psychology when he brought it from Germany to the United States. Titchener offered his own approach, which he called structuralism, yet claimed it represented psychology as set forth by Wundt. In reality, the two systems were radically different, and the label "structuralism" can properly be applied only to Titchener's psychology. Structuralism attained a prominence in the United States and lasted some two decades before it was overthrown by newer movements.

Wundt had recognized the elements or contents of consciousness, but his overriding concern was their organization; that is, their synthesis into higher-level cognitive processes through apperception. In Wundt's view, the mind had the power to organize mental elements voluntarily, a position that contrasted with the passive, mechanistic explanation favored by most of the British empiricists and associationists.

Titchener focused on mental elements or contents, and their mechanical linking through the process of association, but he discarded Wundt's doctrine of apperception. Titchener's work concentrated on the elements themselves. In Titchener's view, psychology's fundamental task was to discover the nature of the elementary conscious experiences—to analyze consciousness into its component parts and thus determine its structure.

Titchener spent his most productive years at Cornell University. He wore his Oxford University academic gown to class and made every lecture a dramatic production. The stage was carefully prepared by assistants under his watchful eye. The junior faculty, required to attend all the lectures, filed through one door to take front row seats. Professor Titchener entered through another door leading directly to the lecture platform. Although he had studied with Wundt for only two years, he resembled his mentor in many ways, copying the authoritative style, the formal lecture manners, even the beard. Although Titchener was English by birth, he was "often mistaken by those who knew him slightly, or who knew only about him, for a German" (Boring, 1927, p. 493). A former student, E. G. Boring, who later became a noted historian of psychology, observed that Wundt and Titchener had similar personalities in that both were autocratic and domineering. Titchener seemed to become more arrogant as he grew older, and "he became progressively more intolerant of others' dissent" (Jeshmaridian, 2007, p. 20).

## Titchener's Life

Born in Chichester, England, into a family with impressive lineage but little money, Titchener relied on his considerable intellectual abilities to win scholarships to college. He attended Malvern College and later Oxford University, where he studied philosophy and the classics and worked as a research assistant in physiology. He won many academic prizes along the way and was seen as a brilliant student with a flair for languages, including Latin, Greek, German, French, and Italian. An Oxford professor once gave Titchener a research article written in the Dutch language and asked him to report on it in a week's time. Titchener protested that he did not know Dutch. The professor told him to learn it—and he did.

Titchener became interested in Wundtian psychology while at Oxford, an enthusiasm not shared or encouraged by anyone else at the university. Obviously, then, he would have to journey to Leipzig—the mecca for scientific pilgrims—to study under Wundt himself. Titchener earned his doctoral degree at Leipzig in 1892. During his student years, Titchener developed a close relationship with Wundt and his family. Titchener was often invited to their home, and he spent at least one Christmas holiday with them at their mountain retreat (Leys & Evans, 1990).

Once Titchener received his doctorate, he hoped to become the English pioneer of Wundt's new experimental psychology. When Titchener returned to Oxford, however, his colleagues remained skeptical of any so-called scientific approach to their favorite philosophical topics. After staying only a few months, Titchener realized that better opportunities lay elsewhere. He left England for Cornell University in the United States to teach psychology and direct the laboratory. He was then 25 years old, and he remained at Cornell for the rest of his life. He died of a brain tumor at age 60; his brain has been preserved in a glass jar on display at Cornell, part of a collection begun in 1889 to study differences in brain characteristics (Young, 2010).

Titchener spent the years 1893 to 1900 establishing his laboratory, conducting research, and writing scholarly articles; he eventually published more than 60. As his brand of psychology attracted more students to Cornell, he relinquished the task of participating personally in the research studies, leaving his students to conduct the experiments. Thus, his systematic position reached its fullest development through the direction of his students' research. In 35 years at Cornell, he supervised more than 50 doctoral candidates in psychology, and most of their dissertations bear the imprint of his ideas. Titchener exercised clear authority in selecting research problems for his students, assigning topics related to issues about which he was curious. In this way he built his system of structuralism, which he later referred to as the "only scientific psychology worthy of the name" (quoted in Roback, 1952, p. 184).

Titchener translated Wundt's books from German into English. By the time he had completed work on the third edition of Wundt's *Principles of Physiological Psychology,* Wundt had already finished the fourth edition. Titchener translated the fourth edition, only to learn that the tireless Wundt had published a fifth edition.

Titchener's own books include *An Outline of Psychology* (1896), *Primer of Psychology* (1898b), and the four-volume *Experimental Psychology: A Manual of Laboratory Practice* (1901–1905). These *Manuals,* as the individual volumes of that work came to be called, stimulated the growth of laboratory work in psychology in the United States and influenced a generation of experimental psychologists. Titchener's textbooks were widely used and were translated into Russian, Italian, German, Spanish, and French.

Like Wundt, Titchener was praised as an outstanding teacher whose lectures were always well attended; often the halls were filled to overflowing. When Boring went to attend his first class by Titchener, he found students "spilling over into all the adjacent rooms. I cannot exaggerate the magnetism of the lecturer. … I remember the lecture on tonal beats as especially exciting; imagine making tonal beats exciting! I was then an engineering student, and yet it was the memory of these lectures that caused me to change to psychology five years later" (Boring, 1927, p. 494).

As Titchener aged, his hobbies diverted time and energy from his work in psychology. He conducted a small musical ensemble at his home on Sunday evenings, and for many years he was Professor in Charge of Music at Cornell before a music department was formally established. His interest in coin collecting led him to learn Chinese and Arabic so that he could decipher the characters on the coins. He corresponded frequently with colleagues; most of the letters were typewritten, with additional notes written by hand. Almost by accident he added the word "empathy" to the English language. In another example of translation altering a word's original intent (see Chapter 1), Titchener translated the German word for sympathy, from a paper written by a German psychologist, into English as empathy, giving it quite a different meaning (Jahoda, 2005).

Eventually Titchener withdrew from social and university life and achieved the status of a living legend at Cornell, though many faculty members had never met him or even seen him. He preferred to work in his study at home. After 1909, he lectured only on Monday evenings during each spring semester. His wife screened all callers and protected him from intrusions; it was understood that no student would phone him except in an emergency.

Although he was autocratic in the manner of the stereotypical German professor, Titchener was also helpful to students and colleagues, as long as they accorded him the deference and respect he believed were his due. Stories are told of how junior faculty members and graduate students washed his car and installed window screens at his house in the summer, not on command but out of admiration.

Karl Dallenbach, a former student, quoted Titchener as saying that "a man could not hope to become a psychologist until after he had learned to smoke" (Dallenbach, 1967, p. 85). Accordingly, many students took to smoking cigars, at least in Titchener's presence. (Dallenbach also reported that he became quite ill from his first cigar.)

Cora Friedline reported the following experience with Titchener:

> *[She] was discussing her research in Titchener's office when his ever-present cigar caught his beard on fire. He was talking at the time and his imposing manner made her reluctant to interrupt. Finally she said, "I beg your pardon, Dr. Titchener, but your whiskers are on fire." By the time he extinguished the flames, the fire had burned through his shirt and his underwear.[2]*

Titchener's concern for his students did not end when they left Cornell, nor did his impact on their lives. Dallenbach, on receiving his Ph.D., intended to go to medical school, but Titchener obtained a teaching position for him at the University of Oregon. Dallenbach had thought Titchener would approve of medical school, but he was wrong. "I had to go to Oregon, as [Titchener] did not intend to have his training and work with me wasted" (Dallenbach, 1967, p. 91).

E. G. Boring recalled that not all students reacted positively to Titchener's attempts to direct their lives. "Many of his more able graduate students came to resent his interference and control and eventually rebelled, to find themselves suddenly on the outside, excommunicated, bitter, with return impossible" (Boring, 1952, pp. 32–33).

Also, Titchener's relations with psychologists outside his own group were sometimes strained. Elected to the APA by the charter members in 1892, he resigned shortly thereafter because the association declined to expel a member whom Titchener accused of plagiarism. The story is told that a friend paid Titchener's dues for many years so he would continue to be listed as a member.

## Titchener's Experimentalists: No Women Allowed!

In 1904, a group of psychologists from Cornell, Yale, Clark, Michigan, and Princeton, among others, who called themselves the Titchener Experimentalists, began meeting regularly to compare research notes. Titchener selected the topics and the guests and generally dominated the meetings. One of his rules was that no women were allowed. E. G. Boring reported that Titchener wanted "oral reports that could be interrupted, dissented from, and criticized in a smoke-filled room with no women present. Women were considered too pure to smoke" (Boring, 1967, p. 315).

Some women students from Bryn Mawr College in Pennsylvania attempted to attend the group's meetings, but they were quickly ordered to leave. Once they hid under a table during a session while Boring's fiancée, Lucy May, and another woman waited in the next room "with the door ajar to hear what unexpurgated male psychology was like." Boring recalled that they came through "unscathed" (Boring, 1967, p. 322).

---

[2]From L. T. Benjamin, Jr., based on material in the Cora Friedline papers, Archives of the History of American Psychology, University of Akron, Ohio.

Titchener Experimentalists pose during a meeting in 1916; at least five members can be seen with cigars.
SOURCE: Archives of the History of American Psychology/University of Akron

Lucy May Boring, who lived for 110 years (1886 to 1996), earned her Ph.D. from Cornell in 1912 and taught briefly at Vassar College and Wells College before choosing marriage over a career in psychology. Like many middle-class married women with high-level academic training and credentials at that time, she worked quietly on her husband's projects. She read and advised on his publications, though her contributions were generally unacknowledged.

For the 1912 meeting of the Experimentalists, Christine Ladd-Franklin (1847–1930) wrote to Titchener to request the opportunity to read a paper on her experimental psychology research. She had worked on problems of color vision in G. E. Müller's laboratory at the University of Göttingen in Germany and at Helmholtz's laboratory in Berlin. Previously she had completed the requirements for a Ph.D. in mathematics at Johns Hopkins University, but she had been denied the degree because she was a woman; the Hopkins administration finally relented, awarding her the doctorate 44 years later.

When Titchener refused her request to participate in the 1912 meeting, she wrote, "I am shocked to know that you are still—at this year—excluding women from your meeting of experimental psychologists. It is such a very old-fashioned standpoint!" (quoted in Furumoto, 1988, p. 107). Not to be deterred in her campaign to participate, she continued her protests for years, calling Titchener's policy immoral and unscientific.

Titchener wrote to a friend, "I have been pestered by abuse by Mrs. Ladd-Franklin for not having women at the meetings, and she threatens to make various scenes in person and in print. Possibly she will succeed in breaking us up, and forcing us to meet—like rabbits—in some dark place underground" (quoted in Scarborough & Furumoto, 1987, p. 126).

Although Titchener continued to exclude women from the Experimentalists' meetings, he encouraged and supported their advancement in psychology. He accepted women in his graduate studies program at Cornell, while Harvard and Columbia universities refused them admission.

More than one-third of the 56 doctorates Titchener awarded were to women. More women completed doctoral degrees with Titchener than with any other male psychologist of the day. Titchener also favored the hiring of women faculty, an idea many of his

MARGARET FLOY
WASHBURN

colleagues considered radical. In one instance, he insisted on hiring a female professor despite the objection of the dean.

The first woman to earn a doctoral degree in psychology was Margaret Floy Washburn; she was also Titchener's first doctoral student. She recalled, "He did not quite know what to do with me" (Washburn, 1932, p. 340). After Washburn received her degree, she wrote an important book on comparative psychology (*The Animal Mind*, 1908) and became the first female psychologist elected to the National Academy of Sciences. She also served as president of the APA.

We mention Washburn's success briefly to highlight Titchener's continuing support for women in psychology. Although he did not relent about permitting women to attend meetings of the Titchener Experimentalists, he did work to open doors to women that were kept firmly closed by most other male psychologists.

In 1929, two years after Titchener's death, the Experimentalists were reborn as the Society of Experimental Psychologists, which is still active today (www.sepsych.org). The new organization admitted women members (Washburn was one of two female charter members), and today it holds annual meetings to discuss the research of those invited to attend (see Goodwin, 2005). In 2004, "the Society of Experimental Psychologists held its centennial meeting on the campus at Cornell University. One of the faculty members at Cornell brought a guest to the meeting: Titchener's brain" (Benjamin, 2006a, p. 137).

## The Content of Conscious Experience

According to Titchener, the subject matter of psychology is conscious experience as that experience is dependent on the person who is actually experiencing it. This kind of experience differs from that studied by scientists in other fields. For example, light and sound can be studied by physicists and by psychologists. Physicists examine the phenomena from the standpoint of the physical processes involved, whereas psychologists consider the light and sound in terms of how humans observe and experience these phenomena.

Other sciences are independent of experiencing persons. Titchener offered, from physics, the example of temperature. The temperature in a room may be measured at 85 degrees Fahrenheit, for example, whether or not anyone is in the room to experience it. When observers are present in that room and report that they feel uncomfortably warm, however, that feeling—that experience of warmth—is dependent on the experiencing individuals, the people in the room. To Titchener, this type of conscious experience was the only proper focus for psychological research. Titchener described the difference between dependent and independent experience in his 1909 book, *A Textbook of Psychology*.

## IN THEIR OWN WORDS

### Original Source Material on Structuralism from *A Textbook of Psychology* (1909)

E. B. Titchener[3]

All human knowledge is derived from human experience; there is no other source of knowledge. But human experience, as we have seen, may be considered from different points of view. Suppose that we take two points of view, as far as possible apart, and discover for ourselves what experience looks like in the two cases. First, we will regard experience as altogether independent of any particular person; we will assume that it goes on whether or not anyone is there to have it. Secondly, we will regard experience

---

[3]Reprinted with permission of Macmillan Publishing Co. Inc., from *A Textbook of Psychology* by E. B. Titchener (pp. 6–9). Copyright 1909 by Macmillan Publishing Co. Inc. Revised 1937 by Sophia K. Titchener.

as altogether dependent upon the particular person; we will assume that it goes on only when someone is there to have it. We shall hardly find standpoints more diverse. What are the differences in experience, as viewed from them?

Take, to begin with, the three things that you first learn about in physics: space, time, and mass. Physical space, which is the space of geometry and astronomy and geology, is constant, always and everywhere the same. Its unit is the centimeter, and the centimeter has precisely the same value wherever and whenever it is applied. Physical time is similarly constant, and its constant unit is the second. Physical mass is constant; its unit, the gram, is always and everywhere the same. Here we have experience of space, time, and mass considered as independent of the person who experiences them.

Change, then, to the point of view which brings the experiencing person into account. The two vertical lines in [Figure 5.1] are physically equal; they measure alike in units of one centimeter. To you, who see them, they are not equal. The hour that you spend in the waiting room of a village station and the hour that you spend in watching an amusing play are physically equal; they measure alike in units of one second. To you, the one hour goes slowly, the other quickly; they are not equal. Take two circular cardboard boxes of different diameter (say, two centimeters and eight centimeters) and pour sand into them until they both weigh, say, fifty grams.

The two masses are physically equal; placed on the pans of a balance [a scale], they will hold the beam level. To you, as you lift them in your two hands, or raise them in turn by the same hand, the box of smaller diameter is considerably the heavier. Here we have experience of space, time, and mass considered as dependent upon the experiencing person. It is the same experience that we were discussing just now. But our first point of view gives us facts and laws of physics; our second gives us facts and laws of psychology.

Now take three other topics that are discussed in the physical textbooks: heat, sound, and light. Heat proper, the physicists tell us, is the energy of molecular motion; that is to say, heat is a form of energy due to a movement of the particles of a body among themselves. Radiant heat belongs, with light, to what is called radiant energy— energy that is propagated by wave movements of the luminiferous ether with which space is filled. Sound is a form of energy due to the vibratory movements of bodies, and is propagated by wave movements of some elastic medium, solid, liquid, or

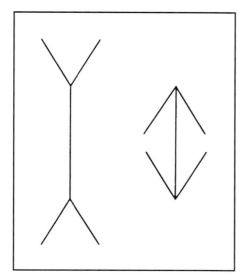

**FIGURE 5.1**

gaseous. In brief, heat is a dance of molecules; light is a wave motion of the ether; sound is a wave motion of the air.

The world of physics, in which these types of experience are considered as independent of the experiencing person, is neither warm nor cold, neither dark nor light, neither silent nor noisy. It is only when the experiences are considered as dependent upon some person that we have warmth and cold, blacks and whites and colors and grays, tones and hisses and thuds.

And these things are the subject matter of psychology.

**Stimulus error:**
Confusing the mental process under study with the stimulus or object being observed.

In studying conscious experience, Titchener warned against committing what he called the **stimulus error**, which confuses the mental process with the object we are observing. For example, observers who see an apple and then describe that object as an apple—instead of reporting the elements of color, brightness, and shape they are experiencing—are guilty of committing the stimulus error. The object of our observation is not to be described in everyday language but rather in terms of the elementary conscious content of the experience.

When observers focus on the stimulus object instead of on the conscious content, they fail to distinguish what they have learned in the past about the object (for example, that it is called an apple) from their own direct and immediate experience. All that observers can really know about the apple is that it is red, shiny, and round. When they describe anything other than color, brightness, and spatial characteristics, they are interpreting the object, not observing it. Thus, they would be dealing with mediate, not immediate, experience.

Titchener defined consciousness as the sum of our experiences as they exist at a given time. The mind is the sum of an individual's experiences accumulated over a lifetime. Consciousness and mind are similar, except that consciousness involves mental processes occurring at the moment whereas mind involves the total of these processes.

Structural psychology as Titchener envisioned it was a pure science. He was not concerned with applying psychological knowledge. Psychology, he said, was not in the business of curing sick minds or reforming society. Psychology's only legitimate purpose was to discover the facts of the structure of the mind. He believed scientists should remain free of speculation about the practical worth of their work. For this reason he opposed the development of child psychology, animal psychology, and all other areas that did not fit with his introspective experimental psychology of the content of conscious experience.

## Introspection

Titchener's form of introspection, or self-observation, relied on observers who were rigorously trained to describe the elements of their conscious state rather than reporting the observed or experienced stimulus by a familiar name. Titchener realized that everyone learns to describe experience in terms of the stimulus—such as calling a red, shiny, and round object an apple—and that in everyday life this is beneficial and necessary. In his psychology laboratory, however, this practice had to be unlearned.

Titchener adopted Külpe's label, systematic experimental introspection, to describe his method. Like Külpe, Titchener used detailed, qualitative, subjective reports of his subjects' mental activities during the act of introspecting. He opposed Wundt's approach, with its focus on objective, quantitative measurements, because he believed it was not useful for uncovering the elementary sensations and images of consciousness that were the core of his psychology.

In other words, Titchener differed from Wundt in that Titchener was interested in the analysis of complex conscious experience into its component parts, not in the synthesis

Archives of the History of American Psychology, University of Akron

Titchener often met with students in his home study.

of the elements through apperception. Titchener emphasized the parts, whereas Wundt emphasized the whole. In line with most of the British empiricists and associationists, Titchener's goal was to discover the so-called atoms of the mind.

His approach to introspection apparently had been formed before he went to Leipzig to study with Wundt. One historian suggested that while Titchener was still enrolled at Oxford, he had been influenced by the writings of James Mill (Danziger, 1980).

Titchener also was influenced by philosophy's mechanistic spirit, as is evident in his image of the observers who supplied the data in his laboratory. In Titchener's published research reports, subjects are called *reagents,* a term used by chemists to denote substances that, because of their capacity for certain reactions, are used to detect, examine, or measure other substances. A reagent is usually passive, an agent used to elicit or prompt responses from some other substance.

Applying this concept to the human observers in Titchener's laboratory, we see that he considered his subjects to be like mechanical recording instruments, objectively reacting and responding by noting the characteristics of the stimulus they are observing. The subjects were to be nothing more than impartial, detached machines. In keeping with Wundt's idea, the trained observations would become so mechanized and habitual that the subjects would no longer be aware that they were carrying out a conscious process. Titchener wrote:

> In his attention to the phenomena under observation, the observer in psychology, no less than the observer in physics, completely forgets to give subjective attention to the state of observing … observers, as we know them, are already trained; the "state of observing" has already been mechanized. (Titchener, 1912a, p. 443)

If observers in the laboratory are considered to be machines, then it is easy to suggest that all human beings are machines. This thinking shows the continuing influence of the Galilean-Newtonian mechanical view of the universe, an idea that did not disappear with the eventual death of structuralism. As the history of psychology unfolds, we will see that this image of human-as-machine continued to characterize experimental psychology through the first half of the twentieth century.

Titchener proposed taking an experimental approach to introspective observation in psychology. He diligently followed the rules of scientific experimentation, noting that

> *an experiment is an observation that can be repeated, isolated, and varied. The more frequently you can repeat an observation, the more likely are you to see clearly what is there and to describe accurately what you have seen. The more strictly you can isolate an observation, the easier does your task of observation become, and the less danger is there of your being led astray by irrelevant circumstances, or of placing emphasis on the wrong point. The more widely you can vary an observation, the more clearly will the uniformity of experience stand out, and the better is your chance of discovering laws. (Titchener, 1909, p. 20)*

The reagents or subjects in Titchener's laboratory introspected on a variety of stimuli and provided lengthy, detailed observations of the elements of their experiences. For example, a chord would be struck on a piano; the chord consisted of three individual notes sounded together. The subjects would report on how many separate tones they could distinguish, the mental characteristics of the sounds, and whatever other basic atoms or elements of consciousness they could detect.

Another experiment involved a given word spoken aloud. As Titchener described it, the reagent was asked to "observe the effect which this stimulus produces upon consciousness: how the word affects you, what ideas it calls up, and so forth" (Titchener, 1910, quoted in Benjamin, 1997, p. 174). You can see from these examples why the introspectors in Titchener's laboratory had to be thoroughly trained, and how subjective, or qualitative, their judgments necessarily were.

## The Elements of Consciousness

Titchener posed three essential problems for psychology:

1. Reduce conscious processes to their simplest components.
2. Determine laws by which these elements of consciousness were associated.
3. Connect the elements with their physiological conditions.

Thus, the aims of Titchener's structural psychology coincide with those of the natural sciences. After scientists decide which part of the natural world they wish to study, they proceed to discover its elements, to demonstrate how those elements are compounded into complex phenomena, and to formulate laws governing those phenomena. The bulk of Titchener's research was devoted to the first problem, to discovering the elements of consciousness.

Titchener defined three elementary states of consciousness: sensations, images, and affective states. Sensations are the basic elements of perception and occur in the sounds, sights, smells, and other experiences evoked by physical objects in our environment. Images are the elements of ideas, and they are found in the process that reflects experiences that are not actually present at the moment, such as a memory of a past experience. Affective states, or affections, are the elements of emotion and are found in experiences such as love, hate, and sadness.

In *An Outline of Psychology* (1896), Titchener presented a list of the elements of sensation uncovered through his research. The list includes nearly 44,500 individual sensation qualities; of these, 32,820 were identified as visual sensations and 11,600 were identified as auditory sensations. Each element was believed to be conscious and distinct from all others, and each could be combined with others to form perceptions and ideas.

Although basic and irreducible, mental elements could be categorized, just as chemical elements are grouped into classes. Despite their simplicity, mental elements have attributes that allow us to distinguish among them. Titchener added duration and clearness to the Wundtian attributes of quality and intensity. He considered these four to be fundamental to all sensations in that they are present, to some degree, in all experiences.

- *Quality is the characteristic—such as "cold" or "red"—that clearly distinguishes each element from every other element.*
- *Intensity refers to a sensation's strength, weakness, loudness, or brightness.*
- *Duration is the course of a sensation over time.*
- *Clearness refers to the role of attention in conscious experience; experience that is the focus of our attention is clearer than experience toward which our attention is not directed.*

Sensations and images possess all four of these attributes, but affective states have only three: quality, intensity, and duration. Affective states lack clearness. Why? Titchener believed it was impossible to focus attention directly on an element of feeling or emotion. When we try to do so, the affective quality—such as the sadness or the pleasantness—disappears. Some sensory processes, particularly those involving vision and touch, possess another attribute, extensity, in that they take up space.

All conscious processes can be reduced to one of these attributes. The findings on the problem of imageless thought from Külpe's laboratory at Würzburg did not cause Titchener to modify his position. He recognized that some poorly defined qualities may occur during thought, but he suggested that these were still sensations or images. It was obvious to Titchener that Külpe's subjects had succumbed to the stimulus error because they paid more attention to the stimulus object than to their conscious processes.

The graduate students at Cornell carried out a great deal of research on affective states, and their findings led Titchener to reject Wundt's tridimensional theory of feelings. Titchener suggested that affections had only one dimension, that of pleasure/displeasure. He denied Wundt's dimensions of tension/relaxation and excitement/depression.

In later years, Titchener began to modify his structural psychology in fundamental ways. He dropped the concept of mental elements from his lectures around 1918, suggesting that psychology should study not basic elements but the larger dimensions or processes of mental life, which he listed as quality, intensity, duration, clearness, and extensity. A few years later he wrote to a graduate student, "You must give up thinking in terms of sensations and affections. That was all right ten years ago; but now it is wholly out of date. You must learn to think in terms of dimensions rather than in terms of systematic constructs like sensation" (Evans, 1972, p. 174).

By the 1920s, Titchener even began to question the term "structural psychology," and he took to calling his approach an existential psychology. He was reconsidering his introspective method in favor of a phenomenological approach, examining experience just as it occurs without trying to break it down into elements.

Had Titchener lived long enough to implement them, these dramatic shifts in viewpoint might have altered radically the face and fate of structural psychology. These ideas suggest a flexibility and openness to change that scientists like to think they possess, but which not all can demonstrate. The evidence for these alterations was pieced together by historians from a meticulous examination of Titchener's letters and lectures (see Evans, 1972; Henle, 1974). Although these ideas were not incorporated formally into Titchener's system, they indicate the direction in which he was moving. Death prevented him from reaching his goal.

# Criticisms of Structuralism

People often gain prominence in history because they oppose an older viewpoint, but with Titchener the situation was reversed. He stood firm when everyone else had moved beyond him. By the second decade of the twentieth century, the intellectual climate of thought in American and European psychology had changed, but the formal published statement of Titchener's system had not. As a result, many psychologists came to regard his structural psychology as a futile attempt to cling to antiquated principles and methods. Psychologist James Gibson, who met Titchener toward the end of the great man's life, noted that although Titchener "inspired genuine awe … my generation had no need for his theory or his method. His influence was on the wane" (Gibson, 1967, p. 130).

Titchener believed he was establishing a foundation for psychology, but his efforts proved to be only one phase in its history. The era of structuralism collapsed when Titchener died, and that it was sustained for so long is an effective tribute to his commanding personality.

## Criticisms of Introspection

The criticisms directed at the method of introspection are more relevant to the kind of observation practiced at Titchener's and Külpe's laboratories, which dealt with subjective reports of the elements of consciousness, than to Wundt's internal perception method, which dealt with more objective and quantitative responses to external stimuli.

Introspection, broadly defined, had been in use for decades, and attacks on the method were not new. A century before Titchener's work, the German philosopher Immanuel Kant had written that any attempt at introspection necessarily altered the conscious experience being studied because it introduced an observing variable into the content of the conscious experience.

The positivist philosopher Auguste Comte attacked the introspective method, arguing that if the mind were capable of observing its own activities, it would have to divide itself into two parts—one doing the observing and the other being observed. Obviously, Comte claimed, this was impossible (Wilson, 1991):

> The mind may observe all phenomena but its own. … The observing and observed organ are here the same, and its action cannot be pure and natural. In order to observe, your intellect must pause from activity; yet it is this very activity that you want to observe. If you cannot effect it, you cannot observe; if you do effect it, there is nothing to observe. The results of such method are in proportion to its absurdity. (Comte, 1830/1896, Vol. 1, p. 9)

Additional criticism of introspection came from the English physician Henry Maudsley who wrote about psychopathology:

> There is little agreement among introspectionists. Where agreement does occur, it can be attributed to the fact that introspectionists must be meticulously trained, and thereby have a bias built into their observations. … Due to the extent of the pathology of mind, self-report is hardly to be trusted. (Maudsley, 1867, quoted in Turner, 1967, p. 11)

Thus, there were substantial doubts about introspection long before Titchener modified and refined the method to make it conform to the requirements of science. Even as his approach to introspection became more precise, the attacks continued.

One point relates to definition. Titchener apparently had difficulty defining exactly what he meant by the introspective method. He attempted to do so by relating it to specific experimental conditions:

> The course that an observer follows will vary in detail with the nature of the consciousness observed, with the purpose of the experiment, [and] with the instruction given by

*the experimenter. Introspection is thus a generic term, and covers an indefinitely large group of specific methodical procedures. (Titchener, 1912b, p. 485)*

A second point of attack on Titchener's methodology involves the question of precisely what the structuralist introspectors were trained to do. Titchener's graduate student observers were instructed to ignore certain classes of words (so-called meaning words) that had become a fixed part of their vocabulary. For example, the phrase "I see a table" has no scientific meaning to a structuralist; the word "table" is a meaning word, based on previously established and generally agreed-upon knowledge about the specific combination of sensations we learn to identify and call a table. Thus, the observation "I see a table" told the structural psychologist nothing about the elements of the observers' conscious experience. The structuralist was interested not in the collection of sensations summarized in a meaning word but in the specific elementary forms of the experience. Observers who said "table" were committing what Titchener called the stimulus error.

If ordinary words were stricken from the vocabulary, how should trained observers describe their experiences? An introspective language would have to be developed. Because Titchener (and Wundt) emphasized that external experimental conditions had to be carefully controlled so that conscious experience could be determined precisely, any two observers should have identical experiences; that is, their results should corroborate one another. Because these highly similar experiences occurred under controlled conditions, it was theoretically possible to develop a working vocabulary for the observers that was free of meaning words. After all, it is because of our shared experiences in everyday life that we are able to agree on common meanings for familiar words.

The idea of developing an introspective language was never realized. Observers frequently disagreed, even when experimental conditions were most rigidly controlled. Introspectors at different laboratories reported different results. Even subjects at the same lab introspecting on the same stimulus material often failed to make similar observations. Nevertheless, Titchener maintained that agreement would be reached eventually. Had there been sufficient uniformity in introspective findings, perhaps the school of structuralism might have lasted longer than it did.

Critics also charged that introspection was really a form of *retro*spection because some time elapsed between the experience and the reporting of it. Recall that Ebbinghaus had demonstrated that our rate of forgetting is most rapid immediately following an experience, so it seemed likely that some of the experience would be lost before introspection could be performed and reported. Structural psychologists answered this charge in two ways: first, by specifying that observers work with the briefest time intervals, and, second, by proposing the existence of a primary mental image that was alleged to maintain the experience for the observers until it could be reported.

We noted earlier that the very act of examining an experience in an introspective manner may in some way alter it. For example, consider the difficulty of introspecting the conscious state of anger. In the process of rationally paying attention to and trying to dissect the experience into its elementary components, our anger is likely to subside or disappear. Titchener maintained his belief, however, that his trained introspectors would with continued practice perform their observational task automatically without consciously altering the experience.

The notion of the unconscious mind, as proposed by Sigmund Freud in the early years of the twentieth century (see Chapter 13), prompted another criticism of the introspective method. If, as Freud claimed, part of our mental functioning is unconscious, then clearly introspection is of no use in exploring it. One historian wrote:

*The foundation of introspective analysis was the belief that all of the mind's functioning was accessible to conscious observation, for unless every aspect of human thought and emotion could be observed, introspection could provide at best only an incomplete and fragmented picture of mental functioning. If consciousness represented only the visible tip of the iceberg, with vast areas of the mind permanently curtained off behind powerful defensive barriers, then introspection was clearly doomed. (Lieberman, 1979, p. 320)*

### Additional Criticisms of Titchener's System

Introspection was not the only target. The structuralist movement was accused of artificiality and sterility for attempting to analyze conscious processes into elements. Critics charged that the whole of an experience cannot be recaptured by any later association or combination of elementary parts. They argued that experience does not come to us in individual sensations, images, or affective states but in unified wholes. Something of the conscious experience is inevitably lost in any artificial effort to analyze it. The Gestalt school of psychology (see Chapter 12) made effective use of this point in launching its revolt against structuralism.

The structuralist definition of psychology also came under attack. By Titchener's later years, the scope of psychology included several specialties that the structuralists chose to exclude because these areas did not fit their view of psychology. We noted that Titchener regarded animal psychology and child psychology as not psychology at all. His conception of the field was too limited to embrace the new work being done and the new directions being explored. Psychology was moving beyond Titchener, and moving quickly.

## Contributions of Structuralism

Despite these criticisms, historians give due credit to the contributions of Titchener and the structuralists. Their subject matter—conscious experience—was clearly defined. Their research methods, based on observation, experimentation, and measurement, were in the highest traditions of science. Because consciousness can only be perceived by the person having the conscious experience, the most appropriate method for studying that experience and that subject matter was some form of self-observation.

Although the subject matter and aims of the structuralists are no longer vital, the method of introspection—more broadly defined as the giving of a verbal report based on experience—continues to be used in many areas of psychology. Researchers in psychophysics still ask subjects to report whether a second tone sounds louder or softer than the first. Self-reports are requested from people exposed to unusual environments, such as weightlessness for space flight. Clinical reports from patients, and responses on personality tests and attitude scales, are introspective in nature.

Introspective reports involving cognitive processes such as reasoning are frequently used in psychology today. For example, industrial/organizational psychologists obtain introspective reports from employees about their interaction with computer terminals. This information can be used to develop user-friendly computer components and ergonomic chairs. Such verbal reports based on personal experience are legitimate forms of data collecting. Also, cognitive psychology, with its renewed interest in conscious processes, has conferred greater legitimacy on introspection (see Chapter 15). Thus, the introspective method, though not the same as Titchener envisioned it, remains alive and well.

A significant contribution of structuralism was its service as a target of criticism. Structuralism provided a strong, established orthodoxy against which newly developing movements in psychology could array their forces. These newer schools of thought owed their existence in no small measure to their progressive reformulation of the structuralist position. We noted that advances in science require something to oppose. With Titchener's structuralism as an idea to oppose, psychology moved far beyond the initial boundaries of his system.

# Discussion Questions

1. According to Titchener, what is the proper subject matter for psychology? How does it differ from the subject matter of other sciences?

2. Contrast and compare Titchener's and Wundt's approaches to psychology.

3. Describe the difference between experience as *independent* of the experiencing person and experience as *dependent* on the experiencing person. Give examples. According to Titchener, which type provides the data for psychology?

4. Describe the paradoxical views of Titchener regarding the place of women in psychology. Did he act to assist them in their careers or discriminate against them?

5. Describe Titchener's method of introspection. How did it differ from Wundt's?

6. Describe Titchener's three elementary states of consciousness and the four attributes of mental elements.

7. How did Titchener distinguish between inspection and introspection?

8. In what ways did Titchener begin to alter his system late in his career?

9. On what grounds was Titchener's approach to introspection criticized? How did he answer his critics?

10. What additional criticisms have been made of Titchener's structuralism? What contributions has Titchener's structuralism made to psychology?

11. What criticisms had been made of the method of introspection before the work of Titchener?

12. What did Titchener's use of the term *reagent* indicate about his views of human subjects and of people in general?

13. What distinction did Titchener draw between consciousness and mind?

14. What is the stimulus error? Give an example. How, in Titchener's view, could the stimulus error be avoided?

15. What was the role of *retrospection* in psychological research, according to Titchener?

16. Why did some of Titchener's graduate students swallow rubber tubes, take notebooks to the bathroom, and record their feelings during intercourse?

## CHAPTER 6

# Functionalism: Antecedent Influences

## Scientist Captivated by Childlike Jenny

Jenny was dressed much like any typical two-year-old and certainly behaved the way two-year-old kids behaved. People flocked by the thousands to see her. They stared in wonder, in awe, because Jenny—so childlike, so human—was actually an orangutan, an ape, as most people called her. Jenny was on display in the giraffe cage at the London Zoo. The year was 1838.

Few people in England, or anywhere in Europe, had ever seen such a creature, and those who came to watch Jenny were amazed, even disconcerted, at her all-too-human mannerisms. Outfitted in a frilly girl's dress, she sat at a table, used a spoon to eat from a plate, drank tea from a cup, and appeared to understand what her keeper told her. She also seemed to recognize what she was and was not permitted to do.

One visitor wrote:

*The keeper showed her an apple, but would not give it to her, whereupon she threw herself on her back, kicked and cried, precisely like a naughty child. The keeper said, "Jenny, if you will stop bawling and be a good girl, I will give you the apple." She certainly understood every word of this, and though like a child, she had great work to stop whining, she got the apple. (quoted in Aydon, 2002, p. 128)*

Apparently Jenny reminded that visitor of his two young children, and he returned to the zoo a few months later, bringing with him a mouth organ (a harmonica) and a mirror. He played the instrument in front of her cage and then handed it through the bars to her. She immediately put it to her lips, just as he had done. When he gave her the mirror, she kept looking at it again and again, as though astonished by her reflection, just as the man's children had done the first time they saw a mirror.

He watched her take bread from another visitor, glancing first at her keeper to see if it was all right for her to eat it. But Jenny also showed willful and disobedient behavior. Often she would

*… do a thing, which she has been told not to do. When she thinks [the] keeper will not see her, then knows she has done wrong, and will hide herself. … When she thinks she is going to be whipped, will cover herself with straw or a blanket. (quoted in Keynes, 2002, p. 50)*

Observing Jenny's actions had a profound effect on the visitor. He wrote the following comment in his notebook: "Let man visit Orang-outang in domestication, see its intelligence … and then let him boast of his proud pre-eminence. … Man in his arrogance thinks himself a great work, worthy the interposition of a deity. More humble, and I believe true, to consider him created from animals" (quoted in Ridley, 2003, p. 9).

Who was this distinguished visitor so impressed with Jenny? His name was Charles Darwin.

## The Functionalist Protest

Charles Darwin, and his notion of evolution, changed the focus of the new psychology from the *structure* of consciousness to its *functions*. It was then inevitable that a functionalist school of thought would develop.

Functionalism is concerned with how the mind functions or how it is used by an organism to adapt to its environment. The functional psychology movement focused on a practical question: What do mental processes accomplish? Functionalists studied the mind not from the standpoint of its composition—its mental elements or its structure—but rather as a conglomerate or accumulation of functions and processes that lead to practical consequences in the real world. The research undertaken by Wundt and by Titchener revealed nothing of the outcomes or accomplishments of human mental activity, but that was not their goal. Such utilitarian concerns were inconsistent with their purely scientific approach to psychology.

As the first uniquely American system of psychology, functionalism was a deliberate protest against Wundt's experimental psychology and Titchener's structural psychology, both of which were seen as too restrictive. These early schools of thought could not answer the questions the functionalists were asking: What does the mind do? And how does it do it?

As an outgrowth of this emphasis on mental functions, the functionalists became interested in the potential applications of psychology to everyday problems of how people function in and adapt to different environments. The rapid development of applied psychology in the United States may be considered the most important legacy of the functionalist movement.

We consider in this chapter the roots of the functional psychology movement, including the works of Darwin, Galton, and early students of animal behavior. It is important to note the time when these forerunners of functionalism were developing their ideas: the period prior to and during the years in which the new psychology was first developing.

Darwin's pioneering book about evolution, *On the Origin of Species* (1859), was published a year before Fechner's *Elements of Psychophysics* (1860) and 20 years before Wundt established his laboratory at the University of Leipzig. Galton began work on the problem of measuring individual differences in 1869, before Wundt wrote his *Principles of Physiological Psychology* (1873–1874). Animal psychology experiments were conducted in the 1880s, before Titchener journeyed from England to Germany to study under Wundt.

Thus, major work on the functions of consciousness, on individual differences, and on animal behavior was being performed at the same time Wundt and Titchener chose to exclude these areas from their definitions of psychology. Not until psychologists brought the new science to the United States would mental functions, individual differences, and laboratory rats attain prominence in psychology.

## The Evolution Revolution: Charles Darwin (1809–1882)

The idea of evolution did not begin with Darwin. By the time he published his theory in 1859, there was really nothing new about it (see Gribbin, 2002). The suggestion that living things change with time, which is the fundamental notion of evolution, can be traced to the fifth century BC, although it was not until the late eighteenth century that the theory was investigated systematically. The English physician Erasmus Darwin (grandfather of

Charles Darwin and Francis Galton) wrote that all warm-blooded animals had evolved from a single living filament and were given animation by God.

Erasmus Darwin believed there was a God who had originally set life on earth in motion but who did not intervene thereafter to alter animal or plant species or create new ones. Changes in animal forms, he suggested, developed in accordance with natural laws in which species were continually adapting to changes in their environment. We noted that Erasmus was a huge man who gave up weighing himself when he reached 336 pounds. His driver (also a sizable man) always preceded the doctor into a patient's house to make sure the floor would hold him. In his spare time Erasmus wrote erotic poetry and fathered 14 children by two wives and one governess (see www.ucmp.berkeley.edu/history/Edarwin.html).

In 1809, the French naturalist Jean-Baptiste Lamarck formulated a behavioral theory of evolution that emphasized the modification of an animal's bodily form through its efforts to adapt to its environment. Lamarck suggested that these modifications were inherited by succeeding generations. For example, the giraffe developed its long neck over generations of having to reach for higher and higher branches to find food.

In the mid-1800s, the British geologist Charles Lyell introduced the notion of evolution into geological theory, arguing that the earth had passed through various stages of development in evolving to its present structure. In 1844, a 400-page book appeared, *Vestiges of the Natural History of Creation*, describing the evolution of plant and animal life. It argued that people were descended from primates, and it quickly became a bestseller in Europe and the United States. Among its readers were U.S. President Abraham Lincoln and Britain's Queen Victoria, along with leading philosophers, scientists, and theologians. Naturally the subject matter aroused considerable controversy and helped spread the notion of evolution to all segments of society (Caton, 2007).

After so many centuries of accepting the biblical account of creation, why were scholars driven to seek an alternative explanation? One reason is that scientists were learning more about the other species that inhabited the earth. Explorers were discovering forms of animal life that were previously unknown. Therefore, it was inevitable that someone should ask how the biblical Noah could possibly have put a pair of each of these animals into the ark. Too many species had been identified to allow scholars to continue to believe in that story.

As early as 1501, Italian explorer Amerigo Vespucci wrote after his third voyage around the coast of South America: "What should I tell of the multitude of wild animals, the abundance of pumas, of panthers, of wild cats, not like those of Spain, but of the Antipodes; of so many wolves, red deer, monkeys, and felines, marmosets of many kinds, and many large snakes? … So many species could not have entered Noah's Ark" (quoted in Boorstin, 1983, p. 250).

In the 1830s, people in England and Europe began to see, for the first time, animal species that appeared to be disconcertingly similar to human beings. Prior to that time, only a few intrepid explorers had glimpsed such animals as orangutans or chimpanzees. In 1835, a year before Darwin returned from his five-year voyage of exploration, a chimpanzee named Tommy was exhibited at the London Zoo. In 1837, Jenny the orangutan was put on display, with a second one following two years later. In the 1850s, a male orangutan was taken on tour to cities throughout England and Scotland. It was advertised as displaying intelligent behaviors that were barely inferior to those of humans.

In 1853, the British Museum displayed a gorilla skeleton alongside a human skeleton. The resemblance was so striking that many viewers reported feeling uncomfortable. Could they still insist that humans were unique creatures, totally unlike other species? Perhaps not.

Explorers had also uncovered fossils and bones of creatures that did not match those of existing species—bones that apparently belonged to animals that once roamed the earth but had since disappeared. Such findings fascinated scientists and laypersons alike, and a great many people began to collect fossils.

*In eighteenth-century Britain it was a mark of refinement and impeccable good taste to own and display a collection of fossils. Not only were the objects themselves rare and beautiful … the simple possession of them hinted at a thirst for knowledge, an awareness of natural philosophy, a sympathetic understanding of the mysterious processes of the earth. (Winchester, 2001, p. 106)*

People wanted to know what those fossils and bones might reveal about the origins of man. To scientists, the growing accumulation of these artifacts meant that living forms could no longer be seen as constant, as unchanged since the beginning of time, but rather must be viewed as subject to modification and change. Old species had clearly become extinct and new species had appeared, some of them altered versions of current forms. It was possible that everything in nature resulted from change and was still in the process of evolving.

The impact of unceasing change was observed not only in intellectual and scientific circles but also in everyday life. The social Zeitgeist was being transformed by the Industrial Revolution. Values, relationships, and cultural norms, constant for generations, were suddenly disrupted as masses of people migrated from rural areas and small towns to the rapidly developing urban manufacturing centers.

The growing domination of science permeated popular attitudes. People were less content to base their ideas about human nature and about society on what the Bible or ancient authorities claimed was true. Instead, they were ready, even eager, to shift their allegiance—to put their faith in science.

Change was the order of the day. It affected the peasant farmer, whose life now pulsed to the ticking of the clock and the rhythm of the machine instead of to the seasons, as much as it affected the scientist, whose time was spent puzzling over a newly unearthed set of bones. The intellectual climate of the times rendered the idea of evolution not only scientifically respectable but also necessary. For a long time, however, scholars thought and speculated and hypothesized but offered little supporting evidence. Then Darwin's *On the Origin of Species* provided so much well-organized data that evolutionary theory could no longer be ignored. The Zeitgeist demanded such a theory, and Charles Darwin became its agent.

## Darwin's Life

*He was one of the luckiest men who ever lived. His grandfathers were two of the most famous men in England. Thanks to them, he was from his earliest years accustomed to the company of clever and artistic people. He grew up in a comfortable home, filled with affection, in which his imagination was free to roam. His father was a wealthy man, and in his late teens he realized he would never have to do anything he did not want to do. For the rest of his life he did exactly as he pleased. And to the end of his days, he was surrounded by the same atmosphere of love and protection he had known as a child. (Aydon, 2002, p. xxiii)*

As a boy, however, Charles Darwin gave little indication of becoming the keen, hardworking scientist the world would later know. He was boisterous and mischievous, playing pranks, lying, and stealing to get attention. One of his early memories was of trying to break the windows in a room in which he had been locked as punishment for misbehaving (see Desmond & Moore, 1991). He showed so little promise that his father, a physician, worried that young Charles would disgrace the family name.

Although he did poorly in school, Charles showed an interest in natural history and in collecting things—coins, shells, and minerals. Sent to the University of Edinburgh to study medicine, he soon pronounced it dull. His father's response was that Charles

CHARLES DARWIN

should become a clergyman. He spent three years at Cambridge University and thought the experience a waste of time, at least from an academic standpoint. Socially, however, it was wonderful—the happiest period of his life. He spent his days and nights drinking, singing, and playing cards, part of a group he described as dissipated and low-minded. He also collected beetles.

The botanist John Stevens Henslow, one of Darwin's teachers, secured Darwin's appointment as a naturalist aboard *HMS Beagle,* a vessel that the British government was preparing for a scientific voyage around the world. This famous excursion, which lasted from 1831 to 1836, explored South American waters, then proceeded to Tahiti and New Zealand, and returned to England by way of Ascension Island and the Azores. However, Darwin was almost rejected for the shipboard job because of the shape of his nose. The captain, Robert Fitzroy, prided himself on his ability to judge character by facial features, and he was certain Darwin's nose indicated laziness. Darwin managed to persuade him otherwise. Fitzroy, a deeply religious man, had wanted a naturalist on board during the journey to find evidence to support the biblical theory of creation. He chose the wrong man.

The journey afforded Darwin a unique opportunity to observe a variety of plant and animal life, and he was able to collect various specimens and an immense amount of data. The trip also seemed to alter Darwin's character. No longer the pleasure-loving dilettante, he returned to England a dedicated scientist with a single passion: to develop a theory of evolution.

Darwin married in 1839, and three years later he and his wife moved to the village of Down, 16 miles from London, where he could concentrate on his work without the distractions of city life. Never a person of robust health, Darwin now began to be plagued by physical ailments, complaining of vomiting, flatulence, boils, skin rashes, dizziness, trembling, and depression. His home became an "infirmary where no one got well; here illness was the norm and health a strange affliction" (Desmond, 1997, p. 291).

Darwin's symptoms were apparently neurotic in origin, triggered by stress and any disruption to his daily routine (see Sheehan, Meller, & Thurber, 2008). Whenever the outside world intruded and prevented him from working, he suffered another attack. Illness became a useful device, protecting Darwin from mundane affairs and allowing him the solitude and concentration he needed to create and develop his theory. Conversely, even though he was able to work no more than one day of every three, he viewed work as an escape from his gloomy feelings. "Work is the only thing which makes life enjoyable to me," he wrote (cited in Lehrer, 2010, p. 40). Another writer termed Darwin's condition a "creative malady" (Pickering, 1974).

> He cut himself off, ducked parties, and declined engagements; he even installed a mirror outside his study window to spy on visitors as they came up his drive. Day after day, week after week, his stomach plagued him. … This was a worried man. (Desmond & Moore, 1991, pp. xviii–xix)

Darwin had good reason to be worried. The idea of evolution was being condemned by conservative authorities in the church and even in some academic circles. The clergy, viewing it as morally degenerative and subversive, preached that if people were depicted as no different from animals, they would behave accordingly. The result of such savagery would surely cause civilization to collapse.

Darwin referred to himself as the devil's chaplain, telling a friend that working on a theory of evolution was like confessing to murder. Darwin knew that when he finally published his book, he would be damned as a heretic. He realized that the anxiety brought on by these concerns were a cause of his persistent physical complaints—"the main part of the ills to which my flesh is heir" (quoted in Desmond, 1997, p. 254). He waited 22 years before presenting his ideas to the public, wanting to be certain that when he did publish, the theory would be supported by irrefutable scientific evidence. So Darwin proceeded slowly, with painstaking caution.

In 1842, Darwin wrote a 35-page sketch of his evolutionary theory. Two years later he expanded this into a 200-page essay, but still he was not satisfied. He continued to keep much of his work secret, sharing his ideas privately only with close friends—the geologist Charles Lyell and the botanist Joseph Hooker. For an additional 15 years, Darwin fretted and labored over his data, rechecking, elaborating, revising, and insisting that all aspects of his position be unassailable.

No one knows how much longer Darwin might have delayed had he not received, in June of 1858, a shocking letter from one Alfred Russel Wallace, a poor, struggling naturalist 14 years younger than Darwin (see Rosen, 2007). While Wallace was in the East Indies recovering from malaria, he had outlined a theory of evolution remarkably similar to Darwin's, although it did not rest on the wealth of data Darwin had accumulated. Worse, Wallace said his theory had come to him fully developed in less than three days! Wallace's biographer wrote:

> In the space of two hours that had elapsed between the onset of chills and then subsidence in a pool of sweat [symptoms of malaria], Wallace said that he had devised the entire theory of natural selection, which, despite physical exhaustion, he sketched out that same evening. It was a spark of inspiration that brought together years of experience and contemplation. Over the next two evenings he wrote the theory out in full. (Slotten, 2004, p. 144)

In his letter to Darwin, Wallace asked for Darwin's opinion about his ideas and for help in getting the work published. Wallace wrote years later that the effect of his brief paper on Darwin was "almost paralyzing," as if Darwin was reading his own work. "Any idea of [Darwin's] priority vanished; his originality was smashed" (quoted in Raby, 2001, p. 137).

Like many scientists, Darwin was highly ambitious. He wrote in his diary: "I wish I could set less value on the bauble fame. ... I rather hate the idea of writing for priority, yet I certainly should be vexed if anyone were to publish my doctrines before me" (quoted in Merton, 1957, pp. 647–648). Darwin told his friend Lyell that if he helped Wallace get his paper published, then all his years of hard work—and, more important, the credit for originating evolutionary theory—would be forfeited (Benjamin, 1993).

While Darwin struggled with questions of how much to assist Wallace and whether to rush his own work into print, his 18-month-old son died of scarlet fever. In despair, Darwin brooded about the implications of Wallace's letter and the options open to him. Finally, with an enviable sense of fair play, he decided: "It seems hard on me that I should lose my priority of many years' standing, but I cannot feel at all sure that this alters the justice of the case ... It would be dishonorable in me now to publish" (quoted in Merton, 1957, p. 648).

Lyell and Hooker suggested that both Wallace's paper and portions of Darwin's forthcoming book be read at a meeting of the Linnaean Society (a scientific society named after the Swedish naturalist Linnaeus) on July 1, 1858, the same day Darwin's son was buried. The rest is history. Each one of the 1,250 copies of the first printing of Darwin's *On the Origin of Species* was sold on the day of publication. The book generated immediate excitement and controversy, and Darwin, although the object of considerable criticism, won his "bauble fame."

When the book was published, Darwin was beset by new infirmities. He described a "terrible long fit of vomiting," "a rash and fiery boils," and feeling "miserably unwell and shattered" (quoted in Desmond, 1997, p. 257). He fled to a spa in the north of England, where he hid from the world for two months.

Wallace never expressed bitterness about not receiving commensurate recognition for developing a theory so similar to Darwin's. In fact, quite the opposite was true. When he learned that his work and Darwin's were to be read to the Linnaean Society, Wallace said that he had received "more honour and credit than I deserved." He expressed satisfaction at knowing that by sending his paper to Darwin, he was "the unconscious means of leading [Darwin] to concentrate himself on the task" of completing one of the most influential books in history (Wallace, quoted in Raby, 2001, pp. 141–142). On April 15, 2000, the Linnaean Society assumed the care of Wallace's tombstone as a way of honoring his accomplishments. The grave, in Broadstone Cemetery in Dorset, England, features a seven-foot tall fossil tree trunk.

After he read Darwin's book, Wallace wrote to a friend, "I could never have approached the completeness of his book, its vast accumulation of evidence, its overwhelming argument, and its admirable tone and spirit. … Mr. Darwin has created a new science." In a personal note to Darwin he offered similar praise, and he preserved Darwin's reply among his papers. Darwin responded, "How nobly free you seem to be of this common failing of mankind. But you speak far too modestly of yourself; you would, if you had had my leisure, have done the work just as well, perhaps better, than I have done it" (Slotten, 2004, pp. 172–173).

## On the Origin of Species by Means of Natural Selection

The Darwinian theory of evolution is so well known that only an overview of the fundamental points is necessary here. Starting with the obvious fact of variation among individual members of a species, Darwin reasoned that this spontaneous variability was inheritable. In nature, a process of natural selection results in the survival of those organisms best suited for their environment and the elimination of those not fit. A continuing struggle for survival takes place, and those life forms that do survive are the ones that have made successful adaptations or adjustments to the environmental circumstances to which they are exposed. In brief, species that cannot adapt do not survive.

Darwin formulated the ideas of the struggle for survival, and the "survival of the fittest," after reading *Essay on the Principle of Population* (1789) by the economist Thomas Malthus who noted that the world's food supply increases arithmetically, whereas the human population tends to increase geometrically. The inevitable result—which Malthus described as having a "melancholy hue"—is that many human beings will live under near-starvation conditions. Only the most forceful, cunning, and adaptable will survive. (Alfred Russel Wallace had also been inspired by the Malthus book.)

Darwin extended the Malthusian principle to all living organisms to develop his concept of natural selection. Those life forms that survive the struggle and reach maturity tend to transmit to their offspring the skills or advantages that enabled them to thrive. Further, because variation is one of the general laws of heredity, offspring will show variation among themselves; that is, some will possess the useful qualities developed to a higher degree than their parents. The qualities tend to survive, and in the course of many generations changes may occur. These changes can be so extensive as to account for the differences among species found today.

Natural selection was not the only mechanism of evolution Darwin recognized. He also subscribed to Lamarck's doctrine that changes in form brought about by experience during an animal's lifetime can be passed to subsequent generations.

***Thomas Henry Huxley and the Evolution Controversy***    As scholars in many fields rose to support the theory of evolution, or to decry it as evil, Darwin himself remained in the background, uninterested in participating in the growing argument. One vigorous defender of the theory, eager to be involved in the controversy, was Thomas

Henry Huxley (1825–1895), an ambitious biologist who was the driving force of England's scientific establishment. (Huxley's grandsons include Julian, a prominent biologist, and Aldous, author of the futuristic novel *Brave New World*.)

Darwin called Huxley his "good and kind agent for the propagation of the gospel [of evolution]" (quoted in Desmond, 1997, p. xiii). Huxley was always delighted to do battle with the enemies of science—and now with the enemies of evolution—and was a powerful, charismatic speaker. His popular appeal was immense, especially among blue-collar workers. To them he promoted science as a new religion, a new path to salvation. Huxley's biographer wrote: "Bushy-bearded labourers with blistered hands flocked to his talks. … He drew the sort of crowds that are reserved for evangelists or rock stars today" (Desmond, 1997, p. xvii). People stopped him on the street to ask for his autograph, and taxi drivers refused to charge him for riding in their cab.

Within a year of the publication of *On the Origin of Species,* the British Association for the Advancement of Science hosted a debate on evolution at Oxford University. Darwin's supporters and friends urged him to attend, but he could not bear the thought of having to defend himself in a public setting. His friends persisted, and the conflict became almost unbearable. Finally, a biographer wrote, "His stomach saved him. Two days before the meeting his health broke down completely. Never had a bout of sickness been more welcome" (Browne, 2002, p. 118).

At the meeting, the speakers were Huxley, who defended Darwin and evolution, and Bishop Samuel Wilberforce (nicknamed Soapy Sam, because of his long-winded speeches) who defended the Bible.

> *Referring to the ideas of Darwin, [Wilberforce] congratulated himself … that he was not descended from a monkey. The reply came from Huxley: "If I had to choose, I would prefer to be a descendant of a humble monkey rather than of a man who employs his knowledge and eloquence in misrepresenting those who are wearing out their lives in the search for truth." (White, 1896/1965, p. 92)*

Robert Fitzroy, captain of the *Beagle* during Darwin's voyage, was among those in the audience for the debate. Fitzroy blamed himself for aiding Darwin's research by approving his selection as the ship's naturalist (despite the shape of his nose). Fitzroy waved a Bible as he spoke at the debate, urging the audience to believe the word of God and expressing his profound sorrow and regret at having provided Darwin with the opportunity to collect data to support his theory. No one was interested in hearing Fitzroy's regrets. "The room fell silent," wrote Darwin's biographer, and Fitzroy "slumped back in his chair almost unheard" (Browne, 2002, p. 123).

Life had become difficult for Fitzroy since the voyage of the *Beagle*. After service in Parliament and a brief, unsuccessful stint as Governor of New Zealand, he returned to England to devote himself to the study of meteorology. He "developed the fundamental techniques of weather forecasting [and] invented the system of storm warnings and signals which saved countless lives in the ensuing decades, and issued the first daily weather forecasts. Indeed, he invented the term 'weather forecast'" (Gribbin & Gribbin, 2004, p. 5). However, his obsession cost him the family fortune.

Fitzroy remained haunted by his role in enabling Darwin to produce the theory of evolution. He was firm in his belief that had he not chosen Darwin to accompany him on the *Beagle*, there would have been no such theory. When Darwin sent him a copy of *On the Origin of Species,* he replied, "I *cannot* find anything 'ennobling' in the thought of being a descendant of even the most ancient Ape" (quoted in Nichols, 2003, p. 311).

Five years after the Oxford debate, on a Sunday morning amid his preparations to go to church, the brooding captain committed suicide by cutting his throat with a razor. Mrs. Darwin wrote that Darwin was "very sorry about Fitzroy, but not much surprised.

He remembered [Fitzroy] almost insane once in the *Beagle*" (quoted in Browne, 2002, p. 264). Darwin later sent Fitzroy's destitute widow a considerable sum of money.

***Darwin's Other Work***    Darwin's second major book on evolution, *The Descent of Man* (1871), gathered the evidence for human evolution from lower life forms, emphasizing the similarity between animal and human mental processes. The book quickly became popular. A prominent magazine writer noted, "In the drawing room it is competing with the latest novel, and in the study it is troubling alike the man of science, the moralist, and the theologian. On every side it is raising a storm of mingled wrath, wonder, and admiration" (quoted in Richards, 1987, p. 219).

Darwin made an intensive study of emotional expressions in humans and animals. He suggested that the changes in gestures and postures typical of various emotional states could be interpreted in evolutionary terms. In *The Expression of the Emotions in Man and Animals* (1872), he explained emotional expressions as remnants of movements that once had served some practical function. Emotional expressions have thus evolved over time and only those that proved useful have survived (see Hess & Thibaut, 2009; Nesse & Ellsworth, 2009).

He also argued that facial expressions and so-called body language were "innate and uncontrollable manifestations" of internal emotional states. For example, pain was accompanied by a grimace; pleasure by a smile. Darwin proposed that these kinds of expressions in humans and in other animal species had come about through evolutionary means. His biographer wrote, "The expressions that pass over human faces were, to him, a daily, living proof of animal ancestry" (Browne, 2002, p. 369).

Darwin made an early contribution to the child psychology literature with his diary about his infant son. Darwin carefully recorded the child's development and published the material in the journal *Mind* as "A Biographical Sketch of an Infant" (1877). The diary is an important precursor to developmental psychology, illustrating Darwin's thesis that children pass through a series of developmental stages that parallel the stages of human evolution.

Darwin's books, papers, notebooks, and correspondence can be viewed at www.darwin-online.org.uk. This site provides access to publications, manuscripts, biographies, obituaries and recollections, illustrations of collections of specimens, and audio mp3 files available for downloading, including a reading of his diary of the *Beagle* voyage.

## The Finches' Beaks: Evolution at Work

Darwin had made many of his observations of variation among and within species while visiting the Galápagos Islands in the Pacific Ocean, off the South American coast. He had seen how animals of the same species had evolved in different ways in response to differing environmental conditions.

Following in Darwin's path, Princeton University biologists Peter and Rosemary Grant, along with a dedicated corps of graduate students, visited the islands to monitor the modifications found in succeeding generations of 13 species of finches as the birds adapted to dramatic changes in the environment. The research program, which began in 1973, lasted more than 30 years. The researchers were witnessing evolution in action, observing the differences in the small songbirds from one generation to the next. The Grants concluded that Darwin had underestimated the power of natural selection. In the case of the finches, evolution was occurring faster than expected.

The variations seen in one species of finch began during severe drought conditions that affected the birds' food supply, reducing it to tough spiky seeds. Only those finches with the thickest beaks—approximately 15 percent of the population—were able to break open the seeds. Many of the birds with more slender beaks, which were unable to crack the seeds, soon died. Thus, under these dry conditions, thicker beaks were a necessary adaptation tool.

When the thick-beaked birds reproduced, their offspring inherited that characteristic, possessing beaks 4 percent to 5 percent larger than those of their ancestors before the drought. In only a single generation, natural selection had produced a hardier, better-adapted species.

Then it began to rain. Heavy storms and floods struck the islands, sweeping away the larger seeds, leaving only tiny seeds as the birds' major source of nourishment. Now the thick-beaked birds were at a disadvantage, unable to gather adequate amounts of food. Obviously, slender beaks were necessary for survival. You can guess what happened. Peter Grant wrote, "Natural selection had swung around against the birds from the other side. Big birds with big beaks were dying. Small birds with small beaks were flourishing. Selection had flipped" (quoted in Weiner, 1994, p. 104).

By the following generation, the average beak size was measurably smaller. A decade later, in response to a drought in 2003 and 2004, another evolution in beak size was observed in response to that changed environment (Grant & Grant, 2006). Once again the species had evolved, adapting to changes in its environment. As Darwin predicted, only the most fit survived, and in 2006 researchers were able to identify the specific molecule that "turns on" the genes responsible for altering the length of the beaks of the finches (Cromie, 2006).

## Darwin's Influence on Psychology

"In the distant future," Darwin wrote in 1859, "I see open fields for more important researches. Psychology will be based on a new foundation" (quoted in Dewsbury, 2009a, p. 67). Today we can see that Darwin's work influenced contemporary psychology in the following ways:

- *A focus on animal psychology, which formed the basis of comparative psychology.*
- *An emphasis on the functions rather than the structure of consciousness.*
- *The acceptance of methodology and data from many fields.*
- *A focus on the description and measurement of individual differences.*

The theory of evolution raised the intriguing possibility of continuity in mental functioning between humans and the lower animals. If the human mind had evolved from more primitive minds, did it follow that there were similarities in mental functioning between animals and humans? Two centuries earlier, Descartes had insisted on a gap between animal and human functioning. Now the issue was about to be revisited.

Psychologists realized that the study of animal behavior was vital to their understanding of human behavior, and they focused their research on the mental functioning of animals, thus introducing a new topic into the psychology laboratory. The investigation of animal psychology would have far-reaching implications for the development of the field. "Early functionalists and behaviorist psychologists embraced the commitment to strong continuity derived from experimental studies of animals to accommodate virtually all forms of human psychology and behavior" (Greenwood, 2008, p. 103).

Evolutionary theory also brought about a change in psychology's subject matter and goal. The structuralist school of thought focused on analyzing the contents of consciousness. Darwin's work inspired some psychologists working in the United States to consider the functions that consciousness might serve. To many researchers this aspect seemed to be more important than uncovering any so-called structural elements of consciousness. Gradually, as psychology came to be more concerned with how humans and animals functioned in adapting to their environment, the detailed investigation of mental elements—begun by Wundt and Titchener—lost its appeal. "Functionalism was not merely 'influenced' by Darwinian theory, but constituted a radical attempt to start over by establishing a new scientific basis for psychology" (Green, 2009, p. 75).

Darwin's ideas influenced psychology by broadening the methods the new science could legitimately use. The methods employed in Wundt's laboratory at Leipzig were derived primarily from physiology, notably Fechner's psychophysical methods. Darwin's methods, which produced results that could be applied to both humans and animals, bore no resemblance to physiologically based techniques. Darwin's data came from a variety of sources, including geology, archeology, demography, observations of wild and domesticated animals, and research on breeding. Information from all these fields provided support for his theory.

Here was tangible and impressive evidence that scientists could study human nature by applying techniques other than experimental introspection. Following Darwin's example, psychologists who accepted evolutionary theory and its emphasis on the functions of consciousness became more eclectic in their research methods, thus expanding the kinds of data that psychologists could collect.

Another effect of evolution on psychology was the growing focus on individual differences. During the voyage of the *Beagle* Darwin had observed many species and forms, so the fact of variation among members of the same species was obvious to him. If each generation were identical to its forebears, then evolution could not occur. Therefore, these variations—these individual differences—were an important principle of evolutionary theory.

While the structural psychologists continued to search for general laws that encompassed all minds, the psychologists influenced by Darwin's ideas searched for ways in which individual minds differed, and soon they proposed techniques for measuring those differences.

Now, for a change of pace, we have selected material from Darwin's autobiography. This passage is not about his research or theory but about his self-image and his view of the personal qualities to which he attributed his success.

## IN THEIR OWN WORDS

### Original Source Material from *The Autobiography of Charles Darwin* (1876)

My books have sold largely in England, have been translated into many languages, and passed through several editions in foreign countries. I have heard it said that the success of a work abroad is the best test of its enduring value. I doubt whether this is at all trustworthy; but judged by this standard my name ought to last for a few years. Therefore it may be worth while to try to analyse the mental qualities and the conditions on which my success has depended; though I am aware that no man can do this correctly.

I have no great quickness of apprehension or wit which is so remarkable in some clever men, for instance, Huxley. I am therefore a poor critic: a paper or book, when first read, generally excites my admiration, and it is only after considerable reflection that I perceive the weak points. My power to follow a long and purely abstract train of thought is very limited; and therefore I could never have succeeded with metaphysics or mathematics. My memory is extensive, yet hazy: it suffices to make me cautious by vaguely telling me that I have observed or read something opposed to the conclusion which I am drawing, or on the other hand in favour of it; and after a time I can generally recollect where to search for my authority. So poor in one sense is my memory, that I have never been able to remember for more than a few days a single date or a line of poetry. …

On the favourable side of the balance, I think that I am superior to the common run of men in noticing things which easily escape attention, and in observing them carefully. My industry has been nearly as great as it could have been in the observation and collection of facts. What is far more important, my love of natural science has been steady and ardent.

This pure love has, however, been much aided by the ambition to be esteemed by my fellow naturalists. From my early youth I have had the strongest desire to understand or explain whatever I observed, that is, to group all facts under some general laws. These causes combined have given me the patience to reflect or ponder for any number of years over any unexplained problem. As far as I can judge, I am not apt to follow blindly the lead of other men. I have steadily endeavoured to keep my mind free so as to give up any hypothesis, however much beloved (and I cannot resist forming one on every subject), as soon as facts are shown to be opposed to it. Indeed, I have had no choice but to act in this manner, for with the exception of the Coral Reefs, I cannot remember a single first formed hypothesis which had not after a time to be given up or greatly modified. This has naturally led me to distrust greatly, deductive reasoning in the mixed sciences. On the other hand, I am not very sceptical, a frame of mind which I believe to be injurious to the progress of science. A good deal of scepticism in a scientific man is advisable to avoid much loss of time, [but] I have met with not a few men, who, I feel sure, have often thus been deterred from experiment or observations, which would have proved directly or indirectly serviceable....

My habits are methodical, and this has been of not a little use for my particular line of work. Lastly, I have had ample leisure from not having to earn my own bread. Even ill health, though it has annihilated several years of my life, has saved me from the distractions of society and amusement.

Therefore, my success as a man of science, whatever this may have amounted to, has been determined, as far as I can judge, by complex and diversified mental qualities and conditions. Of these, the most important have been the love of science, unbounded patience in long reflecting over any subject, industry in observing and collecting facts, and a fair share of invention as well as of common sense. With such moderate abilities as I possess, it is truly surprising that I should have influenced to a considerable extent the belief of scientific men on some important points.

# Individual Differences: Francis Galton (1822–1911)

Francis Galton's work on mental inheritance and the individual differences in human capacities effectively brought the spirit of evolution to bear on the new psychology. Before Galton, the phenomenon of individual differences had rarely been considered an appropriate subject for study.

One of the few early scientists to recognize individual differences in abilities and attitudes was the Spanish physician Juan Huarte (1530–1592). Three hundred years before Galton's efforts in this area, Huarte published a book titled *The Examination of Talented Individuals,* in which he proposed a wide range of individual differences in human capacities (cited in Diamond, 1974). Huarte suggested that children be studied early in life so that their education could be planned, individually, in accordance with their abilities. After proper assessment, for example, a student with a high musical aptitude could be provided with opportunities for study in music and allied fields.

Huarte's book achieved some popularity, but his ideas were not formally pursued until the time of Galton. Although Weber, Fechner, and Helmholtz did report individual differences in their experimental results, they did not investigate these findings systematically, and Wundt and Titchener did not even consider individual differences to be a legitimate part of psychology.

## Galton's Life

Francis Galton possessed an extraordinary intelligence (an estimated IQ of 200) and a wealth of novel ideas. A few of the topics he investigated are fingerprints (which the police adopted for identification purposes), fashions, the geographical distribution of beauty, weightlifting, and the effectiveness of prayer. He invented an early version of

FRANCIS GALTON

the teletype printer, a device for picking locks, and a periscope to enable him to see over the heads of the crowd while watching a parade.

The youngest of nine children, Galton was born in 1822 near Birmingham, England. His father was a prosperous banker whose wealthy and socially prominent family included people in major spheres of influence: the government, the church, and the military. Francis was a precocious child who learned quickly. A biographer wrote:

> ... *at 12 months Galton could recognize all the capital letters; at 18 months he was comfortable with both the English and Greek alphabets, and cried if they were removed from sight; at 2½ he read his first book. ... At the age of 5 he was already well acquainted with the works of Homer. (Brookes, 2004, p. 18)*

At the age of 16, at his father's insistence, Galton began medical training at Birmingham General Hospital as an apprentice to the physicians. He dispensed pills, studied medical books, set broken bones, amputated fingers, pulled teeth, vaccinated children, and amused himself by reading the literary classics. Overall, however, it was not a pleasant experience for him, and only the continued pressure from his father kept him there.

One incident during this medical apprenticeship illustrates Galton's curiosity. Wanting to learn the effects of the various medications in the pharmacy, Galton began taking small doses of each and noting his reaction, beginning in systematic fashion with those under the letter "A." This scientific venture ended at the letter "C" when he took a dose of croton oil, a powerful laxative.

After a year at the hospital, Galton continued his medical education at King's College, London. The next year he changed his plans and enrolled at Trinity College of Cambridge University. There, under the gaze of a bust of Sir Isaac Newton, he pursued his interest in mathematics. Although his work was interrupted by a severe mental breakdown, he did manage to earn his degree. He returned to the hated study of medicine, until his father's death finally released him from that profession.

A phrenologist had told Galton that his head was not the proper shape for a life of scholarly activity but was just right for an active outdoor life. To test this idea, travel and exploration next claimed Galton's attention. He journeyed throughout Africa, making difficult and dangerous journeys to areas few white men had gone or visited. He found it all very exciting and invigorating, except perhaps for one incident recounted by his biographer:

> *Alone and far from home it seems that Galton may have overcome his shyness and procured the services of a prostitute. His courage may have been rewarded with a bad dose of venereal disease that would plague him intermittently for years to come. Wherever the truth lies, Galton's attitude toward women cooled noticeably after 1846, the year in question. (Brookes, 2004, p. 60)*

When he returned to England he published accounts of his trips, which earned him a medal from the Royal Geographic Society. In the 1850s he stopped traveling—because of marriage and poor health, he said—but maintained his interest in exploration and wrote a popular guidebook called *The Art of Travel*. The book was so successful that it was published in eight editions in eight years and reprinted as recently as 2001. Galton also organized expeditions for explorers and lectured on camp life to soldiers training for overseas duty.

Mental restlessness led him next to meteorology and the design of instruments to plot weather data. His work in this field led to the development of the type of weather map still in use today. Galton summarized his findings in a book considered to be a significant attempt to chart large-scale weather patterns.

When his cousin Charles Darwin published *On the Origin of Species*, Galton was fascinated by the new theory. He wrote that it "made a marked epoch in my own mental development, as it did in human thought generally" (quoted in Gillham, 2001, p. 155).

The biological aspect of evolution captivated him first, and he undertook an investigation of the effects of blood transfusions between rabbits to determine whether acquired characteristics could be inherited. Although the genetic side of evolutionary theory did not hold his interest for long, the social implications guided Galton's subsequent work and determined his influence on modern psychology.

## Mental Inheritance

Galton's first important book for psychology was *Hereditary Genius* (1869). When Darwin read it, he wrote to Galton that "I do not think I ever in my life read anything more interesting and original. I congratulate you on producing what I am convinced will be a memorable work" (quoted in Fancher, 2009, p. 89). In *Hereditary Genius* Galton sought to demonstrate that individual greatness or genius occurred within families far too often to be explained solely by environmental influences. Briefly, his thesis was that eminent men have eminent sons. (At that time, daughters had few opportunities to achieve eminence except through marriage to a man of importance.)

Most of the biographical studies Galton reported in *Hereditary Genius* were investigations of the ancestries of his contemporaries—influential scientists and physicians. The data showed that each famous person inherited not only genius but a specific form of genius. For example, a great scientist was born into a family that had already attained eminence in science.

Galton's goal was to encourage the birth of the more eminent or fit individuals in a society and to discourage the birth of the unfit. Toward this end he founded the science of "eugenics," a word he coined. Eugenics, he wrote, dealt with "questions bearing on what is termed in Greek, *Eugenes,* namely, good in stock, hereditarily endowed with noble qualities" (quoted in Gillham, 2001, p. 207). Galton wanted to foster the improvement of the inherited qualities of the human race. He argued that humans, not unlike farm animals, could be improved by artificial selection. If people of considerable talent were selected and mated generation after generation, the result would be a highly gifted human race. He proposed the development of intelligence tests to choose exceptional men and women designated for selective breeding, and he recommended that those who scored high be offered financial incentives for marrying and producing children. Galton himself, however, fathered no children; the problem could have resulted from disease he contracted in Africa—or it could have been genetic!

In attempting to verify his eugenic theory, Galton studied issues in measurement and statistics. In the book *Hereditary Genius,* he applied statistical concepts to problems of heredity, sorting the prominent men in his sample into categories according to the frequency with which their level of ability occurred in the population. His data showed that eminent men have a higher probability of fathering eminent sons than do average men. The sample consisted of 977 famous men, each so outstanding as to be one in 4,000. On a chance basis, this group would be expected to have only one important relative; instead it had 332.

The probability of eminence in certain families was not high enough for Galton to consider seriously any possible influence of a superior environment, better educational opportunities, or social advantages. He argued that eminence—or the lack of it—was solely a function of heredity, not of opportunity.

Galton wrote *English Men of Science* (1874), *Natural Inheritance* (1889), and more than 30 papers on problems of inheritance. He published a journal, *Biometrika,* established the Eugenics Laboratory at University College, London, and founded an organization for promoting his ideas on improving the mental qualities of the human race. In this excerpt from *Hereditary Genius,* Galton discusses the limits to both physical and mental development that he believed were set in place for each of us by heredity. He notes that no amount of mental or physical exertion will enable a person to rise above his or her genetic endowment.

# IN THEIR OWN WORDS

## Original Source Material from *Hereditary Genius: An Inquiry into Its Laws and Consequences* (1869)

### Francis Galton

I have no patience with the hypothesis occasionally expressed, and often implied, especially in tales written to teach children to be good, that babies are born pretty much alike, and that the sole agencies in creating differences between boy and boy, and man and man, are steady application and moral effort. It is in the most unqualified manner that I object to pretensions of natural equality. The experiences of the nursery, the school, the University, and of professional careers, are a chain of proofs to the contrary. I acknowledge freely the great power of education and social influences in developing the active powers of the mind, just as I acknowledge the effect of use in developing the muscles of a blacksmith's arm, and no further. Let the blacksmith labour as he will, he will find there are certain feats beyond his power that are well within the strength of a man of herculean make, even although the latter may have led a sedentary life. ...

Everybody who has trained himself to physical exercises discovers the extent of his muscular powers to a nicety. When he begins to walk, to row, to use the dumb-bells, or to run, he finds to his great delight that his [muscles] strengthen and his endurance of fatigue increases day after day. So long as he is a novice, he perhaps flatters himself there is hardly an assignable limit to the education of his muscles; but the daily gain is soon discovered to diminish, and at last it vanishes altogether. His maximum performance becomes a rigidly determinate quantity. He learns to an inch how high or how far he can jump, when he has attained the highest state of training. He learns to half a pound the force he can exert on the dynamometer by compressing it. He can strike a blow against the machine used to measure impact and drive its index to a certain gradation, but no further. So it is in running, in rowing, in walking, and in every other form of physical exertion. There is a definite limit to the muscular powers of every man, which he cannot by any education or exertion overpass.

This is precisely analogous to the experience that every student has had of the working of his mental powers. The eager boy, when he first goes to school and confronts intellectual difficulties, is astonished at his progress. He glories in his newly developed mental grip and growing capacity for application, and, it may be, fondly believes it to be within his reach to become one of the heroes who have left their mark upon the history of the world. The years go by; he competes in the examinations of school and college, over and over again with his fellows, and soon finds his place among them. He knows he can beat such and such of his competitors; that there are some with whom he runs on equal terms, and others whose intellectual feats he cannot even approach. ...

Accordingly, with newly furbished hopes, and with all the ambition of twenty-two years of age, he leaves his University and enters a larger field of competition. The same kind of experience awaits him here that he has already gone through. Opportunities occur—they occur to every man—and he finds himself incapable of grasping them. He tries, and is tried in many things. In a few years more, unless he is incurably blinded by self-conceit, he learns precisely of what performances he is capable and what other enterprises lie beyond his compass. When he reaches mature life, he is confident only within certain limits and knows, or ought to know, himself just as he is probably judged of by the world, with all his unmistakeable weakness and all his undeniable strength. He is no longer tormented into hopeless efforts by the fallacious promptings of overweening vanity, but he limits his undertakings to matters below the level of his reach, and finds true moral repose in an honest conviction that he is engaged in as much good work as his nature has rendered him capable of performing.

## Statistical Methods

Galton was never fully satisfied with a problem until he had found some way to quantify the data and analyze them statistically. When necessary, he even developed his own methods.

A Belgian mathematician, Adolph Quetelet (1796–1874), who was also a skilled painter, poet, and writer, was a great believer in the utility of statistics, "convinced that statistics provided an insight into human behavior and the understanding of society" (Cohen, 2005, p. 126). Quetelet was the first to use statistical methods and the normal curve of distribution with biological and social data. The normal curve had been used in work on the distribution of measurements and errors in scientific observation, but it had not been applied to human variability until Quetelet showed that measures of height taken from 10,000 subjects approximated the normal curve. His phrase *l'homme moyen* (the average man) expressed the finding that most physical measurements cluster around the average or center of the distribution, and fewer are found toward either extreme.

Galton was impressed by Quetelet's data and assumed that similar results would hold for mental characteristics. For example, Galton found that the grades given in university examinations followed the normal curve. Because of the simplicity of the normal curve and its consistency over a variety of traits, Galton suggested that any large set of measurements or values for human characteristics could be meaningfully described by two numbers: the average value of the distribution (the arithmetic mean) and the dispersion or range of variation around this average value (the standard deviation).

Galton's work in statistics yielded one of science's most important measures: the correlation. The first report of what he called "co-relations" appeared in 1888. Modern statistical techniques for determining test validity and reliability, as well as factor-analytic methods, are direct outgrowths of Galton's research on correlation, which were based on his observation that inherited characteristics tend to regress toward the mean. For example, he noted that, on the average, tall men are not as tall as their fathers, whereas the sons of very short men are taller than their fathers. He represented the basic properties of the correlation coefficient graphically and developed a formula for its calculation, although the formula is no longer in use.

With Galton's encouragement, his student Karl Pearson (1857–1936) developed the current formula for calculating the correlation coefficient (the Pearson product-moment coefficient of correlation). The symbol for the correlation coefficient, *r,* is taken from the first letter of the word "regression," in recognition of Galton's discovery of the tendency of inherited human traits to regress toward the mean. For many years Pearson worried that his scientific reputation would always be that of a mere "footnote to a formula. ... That fear has largely come true" (E. Baumgartner, 2005, p. 84).

Correlation is a fundamental tool in the social and behavioral sciences as well as in engineering and the natural sciences. In addition, other statistical techniques have been developed from Galton's pioneering work.

## Mental Tests

**Mental tests:** Tests of motor skills and sensory capacities; intelligence tests use more complex measures of mental abilities.

The term **mental tests** was coined by James McKeen Cattell, an American disciple of Galton and student of Wundt (see Chapter 8). However, it was Galton who originated the concept of mental tests. Galton assumed that intelligence could be measured in terms of a person's sensory capacities, and that the higher the intelligence, the higher the level of sensory functioning. He derived this idea from John Locke's empiricist view that all knowledge comes through the senses. If Locke was correct, it followed that the smartest people would have the keenest senses.

To carry out his aim, Galton needed to invent the apparatus with which sensory measurements could be taken quickly and accurately from large numbers of people. To determine the highest frequency of sound that could be detected, for example, he invented a whistle, which he tested on animals as well as on humans. He strolled through London's zoo with the whistle affixed to a hollow walking stick; he would squeeze a rubber bulb to activate the whistle and observe the animals' reactions. Galton's whistle became a standard piece of psychology laboratory equipment until it was replaced in the 1930s by a more sophisticated electronic device.

Other instruments that Galton used included a photometer to measure the precision with which a subject could match two spots of color, a calibrated pendulum to measure the speed of reaction to lights and sounds, and a series of weights to be arranged in order of heaviness to measure kinesthetic or muscle sensitivity. He provided a bar with a variable distance scale to test the estimation of visual extension and sets of bottles containing various substances to test olfactory discrimination. Most of Galton's tests served as prototypes for what later became standard laboratory equipment.

Armed with his new tests, Galton proceeded to collect a mass of data. He established the Anthropometric Laboratory in 1884 at the International Health Exhibition and later moved it to London's South Kensington Museum. During the six years the laboratory remained active, Galton collected data from more than 9,000 people. He arranged the instruments for the anthropometric and psychometric measurements on a long table at one end of a narrow room, six-feet wide and 36-feet long. After paying a small admission fee, a person would pass down the length of the table to be assessed by an attendant who recorded the data on a card.

Archives of the History of American Psychology/University of Akron

Galton established his Anthropometric Laboratory to collect data on human psychometric capacities.

In addition to the measurements just mentioned, the laboratory workers recorded height, weight, breathing power, strength of pull and squeeze, quickness of blow, hearing, vision, and color sense. Each person took a total of 17 tests. Galton's purpose in this large-scale testing program was no less than the definition of the range of human capacities of the entire British population to determine its collective mental resources.

A century later, a group of psychologists in the United States analyzed Galton's data (Johnson et al., 1985). They found substantial test/retest correlations, indicating that the data were statistically reliable. In addition, Galton's data provided information on developmental trends for childhood, adolescence, and maturity within the population tested. Measures such as weight, arm span, breathing power, and strength of squeeze were shown to be similar to those reported in the recent psychology literature, except that the rate of development in Galton's time appears to have been slightly slower. The psychologists concluded that Galton's data continue to be instructive.

## The Association of Ideas

Galton worked on two problems in the area of association: the diversity of associations of ideas and reaction time (the time required to produce associations). One of his methods for studying the diversity of associations was to walk 450 yards along Pall Mall (the London street between Trafalgar Square and St. James's Palace), focusing his attention on an object until it suggested one or two associated ideas to him.

The first time he tried this, he was amazed at the number of associations that developed from the nearly 300 objects he had seen. Many of these associations were recollections of past experiences, including incidents he thought he had long forgotten. Repeating the walk a few days later, he found considerable repetition of the associations from his first walk, which quashed his interest in the problem. He turned to reaction-time experiments, which produced more useful results.

Galton prepared a list of 75 words and wrote each one on a separate slip of paper. After a week he viewed them one at a time and used a chronometer to record the time it took for him to produce two associations for each word. Many of his associations were single words, but some were images or mental pictures that required several words to describe. His next task was to determine the origin of these associations. He traced approximately 40 percent to events in childhood and adolescence, an early demonstration of the influence of childhood experiences on the adult personality.

Galton was also highly impressed by the influence of his unconscious thought processes, which brought to the level of conscious awareness incidents he had considered long forgotten. He came to believe, he said, "that my best brain work is wholly independent of [consciousness]" (quoted in Gillham, 2001, p. 221). He wrote about the importance of the unconscious in an article published in the journal *Brain* (1879). In Vienna, Sigmund Freud, who had his own ideas about the importance of the unconscious, subscribed to the journal and was obviously influenced by Galton's work.

Of greater importance than Galton's results is the experimental method he developed to study associations, which is now well known as the word-association test. Wilhelm Wundt at his Leipzig laboratory adopted the technique, as we noted in Chapter 4, limiting his subjects' responses to a single word. The analyst Carl Jung (Chapter 14) elaborated on the technique for his own word-association research on personality.

## Mental Imagery

Galton's investigation of mental images marks the first extensive use of the psychological questionnaire. Subjects were asked to recall a scene, such as their breakfast table that morning, and to try to elicit images of it. They were told to report whether the images were dim or clear, bright or dark, colored or not colored, and so on. To Galton's amazement, his first group of subjects, scientific acquaintances, reported no clear images at all. Some were not even sure what Galton was talking about.

Turning to a broader cross section of the population, Galton obtained reports of clear and distinct images, full of color and detail. The imagery described by women and by children was particularly concrete and detailed. Through statistical analysis, Galton determined that mental imagery, like so many other human characteristics, was distributed in the population in accordance with the normal curve.

More than 150 years later, two American psychologists repeated Galton's experiment, comparing the mental imagery of scientists and college undergraduates. They found no differences between the two groups. The scientists (physicists and chemists) displayed ample visual imagery in response to the same questions Galton had asked, such as images of their breakfast table that morning (see Brewer & Schommer-Aikins, 2006).

Galton's work on imagery was rooted in his continuing attempt to demonstrate hereditary similarities. He found that similar images were more likely to occur between siblings than between people who were unrelated.

## Arithmetic by Smell and Other Topics

The richness of Galton's talent is evident in the variety of his research studies. He tried to put himself in the state of mind of people suffering from paranoid disorders by imagining that everyone or everything he saw was spying on him. One historian noted that when Galton attempted this during his morning walk, "every horse seemed to be watching him either directly or, just as suspicious, disguising their espionage by elaborately paying no attention" (Watson, 1978, pp. 328–329).

With the controversy between Darwin's evolutionary theory and fundamentalist theology at its height, Galton studied the issue with typical objectivity and concluded that although large numbers of people held strong religious beliefs, this was not sufficient evidence that those beliefs were valid.

He investigated the power of prayer to produce results and decided it was of no use to physicians in curing patients or to meteorologists in invoking weather changes, or even to ministers in affecting their everyday lives. He believed that little difference existed between people who professed a religious belief and those who did not in terms of how long they lived, how they interacted with other people, or how they dealt with their own problems. Galton expressed the hope that a more effective set of beliefs could be structured in terms of science. He believed that the evolutionary development of an improved human race, through eugenics, should be society's goal rather than a place in heaven.

Galton's interest in quantification and statistical analysis often expressed itself in a fondness for counting. He occupied himself at lectures or the theater by counting the yawns and coughs of the audience, describing the results as a measure of boredom. While having his portrait painted, he counted the artist's brush strokes—some 20,000. He decided to count by odors instead of numbers and trained himself to forget what numbers meant; he assigned numerical values to odors, such as peppermint, and learned to add and subtract by thinking of them. Out of this intellectual exercise came a paper titled "Arithmetic by Smell," published in the first issue of the American journal *Psychological Review.*

## Comment

Galton spent 15 years investigating psychological issues, and his efforts had a significant impact on the direction of the new psychology even though he was not truly a psychologist. He was an extremely gifted person whose talent and temperament were not bound by any single discipline. Consider the scope of his interests and methods: adaptation, heredity versus environment, comparison of species, child development, the questionnaire method, statistical techniques, individual differences, and mental tests. We will see that Galton's work had a greater influence on developments in American psychology than the work of psychology's founder, Wilhelm Wundt.

# Animal Psychology and the Development of Functionalism

Darwin's theory of evolution proved to be a stimulus for the development of animal psychology. "In no other area of psychology did Darwin have a more immediate and profound effect than in the study of the behavior of animals" (Burghardt, 2009, p. 102). Before Darwin published *On the Origin of Species,* there was no reason for scientists to be concerned about the animal mind because animals were considered to be automata with no minds or souls. After all, Descartes had stated emphatically that animals had no similarity with humans.

Darwin's work altered this comforting view. His evidence pointed to the conclusion that no sharp distinction existed between human minds and animal minds. Therefore, scientists could propose a continuity between all mental and physical aspects of humans and animals because humans were believed to be derived from animals by the continuous evolutionary developmental process. Darwin wrote, "There is no fundamental difference between man and the higher mammals in their mental faculties" (1871, p. 66). He believed that the lower animals experience pleasure and pain, happiness and sadness. They have vivid dreams and even some degree of imagination. Even worms, Darwin wrote, show pleasure from eating and demonstrate sexual passion and social feeling, all evidence of some form of animal mind.

If mental abilities could be shown to exist in animals, and if continuity between animal minds and human minds could be demonstrated, such evidence would disprove the human/animal dichotomy espoused by Descartes. Thus, scientists were challenged to seek evidence of intelligence in animals.

Darwin defended his ideas on animal intelligence in his book, *The Expression of the Emotions in Man and Animals* (1872), in which he argued that human emotional behavior stems from inherited behavior that was once useful to animals but is no longer relevant for humans. One example is the way people curl their lips when they sneer. Darwin said this gesture was a remnant of the way enraged animals bare their canine teeth.

In the years following the publication of *On the Origin of Species,* the topic of animal intelligence grew in popularity, not only among scientists but also with the general public. In the 1860s and 1870s, many people wrote to scientific and popular magazines to claim instances of animal behavior believed to support previously unsuspected mental abilities. Stories circulated about remarkable feats of intelligence of pet cats and dogs, horses and pigs, snails and birds.

Even the great experimentalist Wilhelm Wundt was not immune to this trend. In 1863—before he became the world's first psychologist—Wundt wrote about the intellectual abilities of a wide range of beings, from beetles to beavers. He assumed that animals that displayed even minimal sensory capacities must also possess powers of judgment and conscious inference. Indeed, the lower animals should not be considered inferior or less intelligent. They differed from humans not so much in their abilities as in the fact that they had received less education and training! Thirty years later Wundt was less generous in attributing intelligence to animals, but for a time his voice was added to the many suggesting that animals might be as mentally well endowed as humans.

## George John Romanes (1848–1894)

The British physiologist George Romanes formalized and systematized the study of animal intelligence (see Thomas, 2000). As a child, Romanes had been considered by his parents to be "a shocking dunce" (Richards, 1987, p. 334). As a young man, Romanes had been impressed by Darwin's writings. He and Darwin became friends, and Darwin gave Romanes his notebooks on animal behavior. Thus, Darwin chose Romanes to carry on that aspect of his work, applying the theory of evolution to the mind as Darwin applied it to the body. Romanes was a worthy successor. Being wealthy, he did not have to be concerned about earning a living. The only job he held was part-time lecturer at the University of Edinburgh, which required his presence two weeks a year. He spent winters in London and Oxford and summers on the seacoast, where he built a private laboratory as well equipped as that of a university.

Romanes published *Animal Intelligence* (1883), generally considered to be the first book on comparative psychology. He collected data on the behavior of protozoa, ants, spiders, reptiles, fish, birds, elephants, monkeys, and domestic animals. His purpose was to demonstrate the high level of animal intelligence and its similarity to human intellectual functioning, thus illustrating the continuity in mental development. As Romanes put it, he wanted to show that there is "no difference in kind between the acts of reason performed by the crab and any act of reason performed by a man" (quoted in Richards, 1987, p. 347).

He developed what he called a "mental ladder," on which he arrayed the various animal species in the order of their degree of mental functioning (Table 6.1). Romanes credited even low life forms (such as jellyfish, sea urchins, and snails) with high levels of mental functioning. He formed these somewhat startling opinions by collecting data by the **anecdotal method** defined as the use of observational, often casual, reports or narratives about animal behavior. Many of the reports Romanes accepted came from uncritical, untrained observers, whose observations could be careless or biased.

Romanes derived his findings on animal intelligence from these anecdotal observations through a curious and eventually discarded technique called **introspection by analogy**. In this approach, investigators assume that the same mental processes that occur in their own minds must also occur in the minds of the animals being observed. Thus, the presence of specific mental functions is inferred by observing the animal's behavior and drawing an analogy—a correspondence or a relationship—between known human mental processes and the processes assumed to be taking place in the animal's mind:

**Anecdotal method:** The use of observational reports about animal behavior.

**Introspection by analogy:** A technique for studying animal behavior by assuming that the same mental processes that occur in the observer's mind also occur in the animal's mind.

### TABLE 6.1 ROMANES'S LADDER OF MENTAL FUNCTIONING

| SPECIES | LEVEL OF INTELLECTUAL DEVELOPMENT |
|---|---|
| Apes, dogs | Indefinite morality |
| Monkeys, elephants | Use of tools |
| Birds | Recognition of pictures, understanding of words |
| Bees, wasps | Communication of ideas |
| Reptiles | Recognition of persons |
| Lobsters, crabs | Reason |
| Fish | Association by similarity |
| Snails, squids | Association by contiguity |
| Starfish, sea urchins | Memory |
| Jellyfish, sea anemones | Consciousness, pleasure, pain |

*Note:* Adapted from *Feral Children and Clever Animals: Reflections on Human Nature* (p. 192), by D. K. Candland, 1993, New York: Oxford University Press.

*Starting from what I know subjectively of the operations of my own individual mind, and of the activities which in my own organism these operations seem to prompt, I proceed by analogy to infer from the observable activities displayed by other organisms the fact that certain mental operations underlie or accompany these activities. (Romanes, quoted in Mackenzie, 1977, pp. 56–57)*

Through the introspection-by-analogy technique, Romanes suggested that animals are capable of the same kinds of rationalization, ideation, complex reasoning, information processing, and problem-solving abilities as humans. Some of his followers even credited animals with a level of intelligence far superior to that of the average human.

Romanes believed that cats were more intelligent than all other animals except monkeys and elephants. He wrote extensively about the behavior of the cat that belonged to his driver. Through an intricate series of movements, this cat was able to open the latched door that led to the stables. Introspecting by analogy, Romanes concluded:

*Cats in such cases have a very definite idea as to the mechanical properties of a door; they know that to make it open, even when unlatched, it requires to be pushed. ... First the animal must have observed that the door is opened by the hand grasping the handle and moving the latch. Next she must reason, by "the logic of feelings," if a hand can do it, why not a paw? ... The pushing with the hind feet after depressing the latch must be due to adaptive reasoning. (Romanes, 1883, pp. 421–422)*

Romanes's work falls far short of modern scientific rigor. Often, the line between fact and subjective interpretation in his data is unclear. However, although scientists recognize the deficiencies in his data and method, Romanes is respected for his pioneering efforts in stimulating the development of comparative psychology and preparing the way for the experimental study of animal behavior. We have seen that in many areas of science, a reliance on observational data precedes the development of more refined experimental methodology. It was Romanes who launched the observational stage of comparative psychology.

## C. Lloyd Morgan (1852–1936)

**Law of parsimony:**
*(Lloyd Morgan's Canon):* The notion that animal behavior must not be attributed to a higher mental process when it can be explained in terms of a lower mental process.

The weaknesses inherent in the anecdotal and introspection-by-analogy methods were recognized formally by Conwy Lloyd Morgan (1852–1936), whom Romanes designated as his successor. Morgan, a student of Thomas Henry Huxley, became professor of psychology and education at the University of Bristol, England, and he was one of the first people to ride a bicycle within the city limits. He was also interested in geology and zoology. Morgan proposed a **law of parsimony** (also called Lloyd Morgan's Canon) to counteract the prevailing tendency to attribute excessive intelligence to animals.

The law of parsimony states that an animal's behavior must not be interpreted as the outcome of a higher mental process when it can be explained in terms of a lower mental process. Morgan advanced this idea in 1894 and may have derived it from a similar law of parsimony described by Wundt two years earlier. Wundt had noted that "complex explanatory principles can be used only when the simpler [principles] have proved insufficient" (Richards, 1980, p. 57).

It was not Morgan's intent to exclude anthropomorphism completely from reports of animal behavior but rather to reduce its use and to give the methods of comparative psychology a more scientific basis. Morgan agreed with Romanes that subjective reports could not be avoided, but he attempted in his work to keep anecdotal inferences to a minimum. Morgan wrote:

*With regard to Romanes' collection of anecdotes ... I felt, as no doubt he did, that not on such anecdotal foundations could a science of comparative psychology be built. Most of the stories were merely casual records, supplemented by amateurish opinions of*

C. LLOYD MORGAN

*passing observers whose psychological training was well-nigh negligible. I then entertained doubts whether one could extract from the minds of animals … the data requisite for a science. (1930/1961, pp. 247–248)*

In essence, Morgan followed Romanes's approach in observing an animal's behavior and explaining it through an introspective examination of his own mental processes. By applying his law of parsimony, however, Morgan refrained from ascribing higher-level mental processes to animals when their behavior could be explained in terms of lower-level processes.

He believed that most animal behavior resulted from learning or association based on sensory experience; this type of learning was a lower-level process than rational thought or ideation. With the acceptance of Morgan's canon, the method of introspection by analogy was refined and provided more useful data, but eventually it was superseded by more objective methods.

Morgan was the first scientist to conduct large-scale experimental studies in animal psychology. Although his experiments were not performed under the rigid scientific conditions required today, they did involve careful observations of animal behavior, mostly in natural environments but with some artificial modifications. Although these studies did not permit the same degree of control as laboratory experiments, they were an important advance over Romanes's anecdotal method.

### Comment

The initial work in comparative psychology was carried out in England, but leadership in the field quickly passed to the United States. Romanes died in his forties from a brain tumor, and Morgan abandoned his research for a career in university administration.

Comparative psychology emerged from the excitement and controversy engendered by Darwin's suggestion of a continuity between human and animal species. Basic to Darwinian theory are the notion of function and the assertion that as a species evolves, its physical structure is determined by the requirements for its survival. This premise led biologists to regard each anatomical structure as a functioning or utilitarian element in a total living, adapting system. When psychologists began to examine mental processes in the same way, they laid the groundwork for a new movement: functional psychology.

# Discussion Questions

1. Describe the anecdotal method and introspection by analogy. Explain Romanes's mental ladder.
2. Describe the role of Thomas Henry Huxley in promoting Darwin's theory.
3. Describe the work of Juan Huarte in anticipating the contributions of Galton.
4. Explain how the study of bird beaks supports evolutionary theory.
5. Explain the approaches to evolution taken by Erasmus Darwin and Jean-Baptiste Lamarck.
6. How did Darwin's evolutionary theory stimulate the development of animal psychology? What was Wundt's initial reaction to this development?
7. How did Galton study the association of ideas? How did he test for intelligence?
8. How did increasing travel and exploration, and the public fascination with fossils, influence attitudes toward the idea of evolution?
9. How did Morgan limit the use of introspection by analogy? Which of the following techniques did Morgan use to study the animal mind: (a) collecting anecdotes, (b) experimental studies, (c) the method of extirpation, (d) electrical stimulation?
10. How was Darwin's concept of natural selection influenced by Malthus's doctrine of population and food supply?
11. How was Galton's work on mental tests influenced by Locke's empiricist view?

12. In what ways did Darwin's data and ideas alter the subject matter and methods of psychology?
13. On what grounds did the functionalists protest against Wundt's psychology and Titchener's structuralism?
14. What aspects of consciousness did the functionalists deal with?
15. What did Darwin mean when he referred to himself as the "devil's chaplain" and said that his work was like confessing to murder?

16. What statistical tools did Galton develop to measure human characteristics? Describe Galton's research on hereditary genius.
17. Why did it seem inevitable that a theory of evolution would be proposed and accepted by the middle of the nineteenth century? How did the Zeitgeist influence the success of Darwin's ideas?
18. Why did some people find it such a disturbing experience to see Jenny the Orangutan in the London Zoo? How did her behavior affect Charles Darwin?

## CHAPTER 7

# Development and Founding of Functionalism

## Evolution's Neurotic Philosopher

He was one of the most famous men in the world, yet he frequently walked the streets of London wearing earmuffs to keep the sound of other people's voices from disturbing his thoughts. Whenever noise intruded, he considered the day to be ruined. Charles Darwin referred to him as "our philosopher," and he often wandering aimlessly, "unable to concentrate, unable to write, unable even to read" (Coser, 1977, pp. 104–105).

At home he kept his large collection of books hidden behind curtains drawn across the bookshelves so that he would not be distracted by the titles printed on the spines. When he traveled by train, he carried the manuscript of his current book project tied around his waist with string; the pages could be seen flapping beneath his coat. Whenever he felt the need to take his pulse, he would simply stop his carriage, even on a crowded London street, oblivious of the traffic jam he was creating (Francis, 2007).

In the summer of 1882 he arrived in the United States, to be greeted as an international celebrity. He was met in New York by Andrew Carnegie, multimillionaire patriarch of the American steel industry, who praised him as a messiah. In the estimation of many leaders of business, science, politics, and religion, this eccentric English philosopher was indeed a savior. He was wined and dined, and honors and appreciation were lavished upon him. Yet he remained a "semi-invalid and psychic cripple throughout the rest of his life. Suffering from acute insomnia, which he at times attempted to overcome with a fairly heavy dose of opium, [he] was henceforth never able to work more than a few hours a day. To work longer would lead to undue nervous excitement" (Coser, 1977, pp. 104–105). Although hailed as the outstanding thinker of his day, he was "nearing the pitch of despair," lonely, disappointed, and depressed (Werth, 2009, p. ix).

Before he became so incapacitated he had been one of the most prolific writers of the nineteenth century. He had written many books, dictated to a secretary as rapidly as she could record the words, sometimes while he was between sets of tennis or lounging in a rowboat. His writings were serialized in popular magazines, and his books sold hundreds of thousands of copies. The system of philosophy he proposed was soon part of the standard curriculum of nearly every university.

No doubt he would have published even more books had he not developed the intense neurotic symptoms that limited his work to a few hours a day. At age 35, in a situation that reminds us of Darwin's predicament, our philosopher developed not only insomnia but also heart palpitations and digestive disorders whenever the outside world intruded. Again like Darwin, the onset of his symptoms coincided with the development of the system of thought to which he would devote his life, the system that would profoundly influence the direction of the new American psychology. His name was Herbert Spencer.

HERBERT SPENCER

# Evolution Comes to America: Herbert Spencer (1820–1903)

The philosophy that brought Herbert Spencer recognition and acclaim was Darwinism, the notion of evolution and the survival of the fittest. Spencer extended it far beyond Darwin's own work.

Interest in Darwin's theory of evolution was intense in the United States, and Darwin's ideas had been accepted eagerly. Evolutionary theory was embraced not only in universities and scholarly societies but also in popular magazines and even some religious publications.

## Social Darwinism

Spencer argued that the development of *all* aspects of the universe is evolutionary, including human character and social institutions, in accordance with the principle of "survival of the fittest" (a phrase Spencer coined). It was this emphasis on what came to be called social Darwinism—applying the theory of evolution to human nature and society—that met with such enthusiasm in America.

In Spencer's utopian view, if the principle of survival of the fittest were allowed to operate freely, then only the best would survive. Therefore, human perfection was inevitable as long as no action was taken to interfere with the natural order of things. Individualism and a *laissez-faire* economic system were vital, whereas governmental attempts to regulate business and industry and welfare (even subsidies for education, housing, and the poor) were opposed.

People and organizations were to be left alone to develop themselves and society in their own ways, just as other living species were left to develop and adapt to their natural environments. Any assistance from the state would interfere with the natural evolutionary process.

People, programs, businesses, or institutions that could not adapt were unfit for survival and should be allowed to perish (to become "extinct") for the betterment of society as a whole. If government continued to support poorly functioning enterprises, then these enterprises would endure, ultimately weakening society and violating the basic law of nature that only the strongest and most fit shall survive. Again, Spencer's idea was that by ensuring that only the best survived, society could eventually achieve perfection.

This message was compatible with America's individualistic spirit, and the phrases "survival of the fittest" and "the struggle for existence" quickly became part of the national consciousness. Railroad tycoon James J. Hill reiterated Spencer's message: "The fortunes of railroad companies are determined by the law of the survival of the fittest." From John D. Rockefeller: "The growth of a large business is merely a survival of the fittest" (Hill and Rockefeller as quoted in Hofstadter, 1992, p. 45). Clearly the phrases reflected the American society of the late nineteenth century; the United States was a living embodiment of Spencer's ideas.

This pioneer nation was being settled by hardworking people who believed in free enterprise, self-sufficiency, and independence from government regulation. And they knew all about the survival of the fittest from their daily lives. Land was freely available to those with the courage, cunning, and ability to take it and to make a living from it. The principles of natural selection were vividly demonstrated in everyday experiences, particularly on the Western frontier, where survival and success depended on one's ability to adapt to the demands of a hostile environment. Those who could not adapt did not survive.

The American historian Frederick Jackson Turner described the survivors in these terms:

> *"That coarseness and strength combined with acuteness and inquisitiveness; that practical, inventive turn of mind, quick to find expedients; that masterful grasp of material things ... powerful to effect great ends; that restless, nervous energy; that dominant individualism" (Turner, 1947, p. 235).*

The people of the United States were oriented toward the practical, the useful, and the functional. In its pioneering stages, American psychology mirrored these qualities. For this reason the United States was more accepting than other nations of evolutionary theory. American psychology became a functional psychology because evolution and the functional spirit were in keeping with Americans' basic temperament. Spencer's views were compatible with the American ethos, and that is why his philosophical system influenced every field of learning. The famous American preacher Henry Ward Beecher wrote to Spencer: "The peculiar condition of American society has made your writings far more fruitful and quickening here than in Europe" (Beecher, quoted in Hofstadter, 1992, p. 31).

### Synthetic Philosophy

**Synthetic philosophy:** Herbert Spencer's idea that knowledge and experience can be explained in terms of evolutionary principles.

Spencer formulated a system he called **synthetic philosophy**. (He used the word "synthetic" in the sense of synthesizing or combining, not to mean something artificial or unnatural.) He based this all-encompassing system on the application of evolutionary principles to human knowledge and experience. His ideas were published in a series of 10 books between 1860 and 1897. The volumes were hailed by many leading scholars of the time as works of genius. Conwy Lloyd Morgan wrote to Spencer: "To none of my intellectual masters do I owe a larger debt of gratitude than to you." Alfred Russel Wallace named his first son after Spencer. After reading one of Spencer's books, Darwin said that Spencer was "a dozen times my superior" (quoted in Richards, 1987, p. 245). Although Darwin appreciated Spencer's work, he did not like him personally: "I think that he was extremely egotistical" (Darwin, quoted in Werth, 2009, p. 101).

Two of the volumes on synthetic philosophy constitute *The Principles of Psychology*, published first in 1855 and later used by William James as a textbook for the first psychology course he taught at Harvard. In this book Spencer discussed the notion that the mind exists in its present form because of past and continuing efforts to adapt to various environments. He emphasized the adaptive nature of nervous and mental processes and wrote that an increasing complexity of experiences, and hence of behavior, is part of the normal evolutionary process. The organism needs to adapt to its environment if it is to survive.

## The Continuing Evolution of Machines

We noted in Chapter 2 that machines had been created to duplicate human movement (recall the automata) as well as human thought (such as Babbage's calculating engine). Was it possible that machines could evolve to higher forms the way humans and animals were said to do? At the time Darwin's theory was published in 1859, the mechanical metaphor for human life had become so widely accepted in intellectual and social circles that the question seemed inevitable.

The person who asked the question, and who extended the theory of evolution to machines, was Samuel Butler (1835–1902), an eccentric English writer, painter, and musician who in 1859 immigrated to New Zealand to raise sheep. Butler and Darwin carried on an extensive correspondence.

In an essay titled "Darwin Among the Machines," Butler wrote that the evolution of machines had already occurred. We had only to compare primordial, rudimentary items such as levers, wedges, and pulleys with the complex machinery of industrial factories and the great steam-driven locomotives and ocean liners.

Butler proposed that mechanical evolution was occurring through the same processes that guided human evolution: natural selection and the struggle for existence. Inventors are constantly creating new machines to gain some competitive advantage. The new machines eliminate or render extinct the older, inferior machines that can no longer adapt or compete in the struggle for life—for a share of the marketplace. As a result, the obsolete machines disappear, just as the dinosaurs did.

The rapid development of technology made it clear to Butler that machines had made greater evolutionary strides than animals, and he predicted that machines would one day become capable of simulating human mental processes—a kind of intelligence. Within Butler's lifetime his prediction came true, at least for the mental process of making calculations.

By the end of the nineteenth century, Babbage's type of calculating engine was no longer adequate. The demands being made on both human and mechanical calculators required more appropriate, and more highly evolved, machines. One event that highlighted this need was the 1890 U.S. population census.

The census of 10 years earlier was so complex that it had taken a full seven years to complete. Fifteen hundred clerks tallied by hand data on age, sex, ethnic origin, residence, and other characteristics for (they hoped) every U.S. citizen. The results filled a report totaling more than 21,000 pages. In the interim, the population had grown so rapidly that a change in procedures was obviously required; otherwise, the 1890 census would not be finished before the 1900 census was due to start. A new and improved information-processing machine was necessary.

## Henry Hollerith and the Punched Cards

Henry Hollerith (1859–1929) was an engineer who developed a new and improved way of processing information. Hollerith's innovative approach was recorded as follows by two historians of the origin of computers:

> ... to record the census return for each individual as a pattern of holes on punched paper tape or a set of punched cards, similar to the way music was recorded on a string of punched cards on fairground organettes [like player pianos] of the period. It would then be possible to use a machine to automatically count the holes and produce the tabulations. (Campbell-Kelly & Aspray, 1996, p. 22)

Hollerith used 56 million cards to tally the results obtained from 62 million people. Each card could store the equivalent of up to 36 eight-bit bytes of information. Thus, the 1890 U.S. census yielded more information than ever previously amassed and was completed in only two years at a cost savings of $5 million over the hand-tallied method. Hollerith's punched card system radically altered the processing of this type of information and led to renewed hopes (and fears) that machines, in time, would duplicate human cognitive functioning. An article in the popular magazine *Scientific American* was subtitled "How Strips of Paper Can Endow Inanimate Machines with Brains of Their Own" (Dyson, 1997).

In 1896, Hollerith established his own business, the Tabulating Machine Company, which he sold in 1911. The new corporation, the Computing-Tabulating-Recording Company, was renamed in 1924. We know it today as IBM.

WILLIAM JAMES

# William James (1842–1910): Anticipator of Functional Psychology

Much is paradoxical about William James and his role in American psychology. His work was the major American precursor of functional psychology, and he was a pioneer of the new scientific psychology as it developed in the United States. A survey of historians of psychology 80 years after James's death revealed that James ranked second only to Wilhelm Wundt among psychology's important figures and was the leading American psychologist listed (Korn, et al., 1991). The eminent philosopher and psychologist John Dewey called James "far and away the greatest of American psychologists … in any country … perhaps of any time." John B. Watson, the founder of behaviorism, referred to James as "the most brilliant psychologist the world has ever known" (both quoted in Leary, 2003, pp. 19–20).

However, some of James's colleagues viewed him as a negative force in the development of a scientific psychology because he maintained a widely publicized interest in mental telepathy, clairvoyance, spiritualism, communication with the dead at séances, and other mystical events. Many American psychologists, including Titchener and Cattell, criticized James for his enthusiastic espousal of the very mentalistic and psychical phenomena that they, as experimental psychologists, were trying to banish from the field.

James founded no formal system of psychology and trained no disciples; there would be no Jamesian school of thought. Although the form of psychology with which he was associated attempted to be scientific and experimental, James himself was not an experimentalist in attitude or deed. Psychology—which he once called that "nasty little science"—was not his lifelong passion, as it was for Wundt and Titchener.

James worked in psychology for a while and moved on. Later in life, this fascinating and complex man who contributed so much to psychology turned his back on it. (Once when he was about to give a talk at Princeton University, he asked that he not be introduced as a psychologist.) He even insisted that psychology was merely "an elaboration of the obvious." Although he allowed the field to stumble on without his commanding presence, his place in the history of psychology is significant and assured.

James did not found functional psychology, but he presented his ideas clearly and effectively within the functionalist atmosphere that was pervading American psychology. In doing so, he influenced the functionalist movement by inspiring subsequent generations of psychologists.

## James's Life

William James was born in the Astor House, a New York City hotel, into a prominent and wealthy family. His father (at the time, the second richest man in the United States) devoted himself enthusiastically, though erratically, to the children's education, which alternated between Europe and the United States. Thus, James's early schooling took place in England, France, Germany, Italy, Switzerland, and the United States. These stimulating experiences exposed James to the intellectual and cultural advantages of England and the rest of Europe.

Throughout his life James made frequent journeys abroad. His father's favorite method for dealing with a family illness was to send the ailing member to Europe rather than to a hospital. And his mother provided her children with affection and attention only when they were sick. Perhaps it is no surprise that James's health was seldom good.

Although the elder James did not expect any of the children to be concerned with earning a living, he did try to encourage William's early interest in science. He gave the boy a chemistry set, a "Bunsen burner and vials of mysterious liquids which he mixed, heated, and transfused, staining his fingers and clothes, to his father's annoyance, and sometimes even causing alarming explosions" (Allen, 1967, p. 47).

At age 18, James decided to become an artist. Six months at the Newport, Rhode Island, studio of the painter William Hunt persuaded James that although his technique was good, he lacked sufficient talent to be a truly great artist. He decided instead to enroll at the Lawrence Scientific School at Harvard. Civil war between North and South had broken out in the United States, and James reported later that he had wanted to join the army. His father forbade it, saying that no government or cause was worth the sacrifice of William's life. We note that William's brother Henry, the novelist, also did not serve in the war, but the two younger James brothers did.

Shortly after William arrived at Harvard, his health and self-confidence began to decline, transforming him into the intensely troubled neurotic he remained for most of his life. He abandoned his interest in chemistry, apparently because of the exacting demands of laboratory work, and tried medical school. However, he had little enthusiasm for medicine, noting:

> There is much humbug therein … With the exception of surgery, in which something positive is sometimes accomplished, a doctor does more by the moral effect of his presence on the patient and family, than by anything else. He also extracts money from them. (James, quoted in Allen, 1967, p. 98)

James left his medical studies to assist the zoologist Louis Agassiz on an expedition to Brazil's Amazon River basin to collect specimens of marine animals. The trip gave James the opportunity to sample a career in biology, but he quickly found out that he could not tolerate the precise collecting and categorizing or the physical demands of field work. In a letter home he admitted, "My coming was a mistake. I am convinced now, for good, that I am cut out for a speculative rather than an active life" (quoted in Simon, 1998, p. 93). His reaction to work in the chemical and biological sciences was prophetic of his later distaste for experimentation in the field of psychology.

Although medicine proved no more attractive after the 1865 expedition to Brazil than it had been before, James reluctantly resumed his studies mainly because nothing else appealed to him. He was frequently ill, complaining of depression, digestive disorders, insomnia, visual disturbances, and a weak back. "It was obvious to everyone that he was suffering from America; Europe was the only cure" (Miller & Buckhout, 1973, p. 84).

James recuperated at a German spa, dabbled in literature, and wrote long letters to friends, but his depression persisted. He attended physiology lectures at the University of Berlin, which led him to speculate that perhaps it was time for "psychology to begin to be a science" (quoted in Allen, 1967, p. 140). He also said that—assuming he survived his illness and lived through the winter!—he might be interested in learning more about psychology from the great Helmholtz and, as he put it, some man named Wundt. James did live through the winter, but he did not meet Wundt at that time. However, the fact that he had heard of Wundt shows James's awareness of scientific and intellectual trends some 10 years before Wundt began his laboratory.

James earned his medical degree from Harvard in 1869, but his insecurities and depression had worsened. Plagued by nameless and horrible dreads, he even considered suicide. So intense was his fear that he was unable to go out at night alone. He had himself committed to an asylum in Somerville, Massachusetts, but whatever treatment he was offered there did nothing to lessen his misery. A biographer noted that during this time James was "an accomplished complainer. During 1870 and 1871 we hear endlessly about his eyes, his back, his low spirits, his aimless existence" (Richardson, 2006, p. 128). But then William James was not the only person suffering such problems at that time.

***An epidemic of neurasthenia***   An American neurologist, George Beard, had coined the term "neurasthenia" and referred to the condition as a peculiarly American nervousness. He listed a variety of symptoms: insomnia, hypochondria, headache, skin rash, nervous exhaustion, and something called brain collapse (Lutz, 1991). James called the syndrome "Americanitis" (Ross, 1991).

> *During the second half of the nineteenth century, what many observers called an "epidemic of neurasthenia" swept through the upper classes. Neurasthenia was, literally, a lack of nerve force—an immobilizing depression, a loss of will. The most educated and self-conscious were among the most likely to succumb. Postponement of career choice became a common experience among these disabled sons of the bourgeoisie. (Lears, 1987, p. 87)*

Beard also noted that neurasthenia occurred most frequently among "brain workers, that the condition was usually found in the northern and eastern states, and that it resulted in a depletion of a person's nervous energy." Beard related it to the rapid development of clocks and the resulting emphasis on keeping to a schedule and increasing time pressures, particularly in the workplace. "Punctuality," Beard wrote, "is a greater thief of nervous force than is procrastination. We are under constant strain, mostly unconscious, oftentimes in sleeping as well as in waking hours, to get somewhere or do something at a definite moment" (quoted in Freeman, 2009, p. 78).

This notion of working at too frantic a pace as a danger to mental health was reinforced by Spencer in an 1882 speech at New York's famous Delmonico's Restaurant. He told the audience, comprised of the titans of American business and industry, that "for Americans, work had become a pathological obsession. Americans were endangering their mental and physical health through overwork" (quoted in Shapin, 2007, p. 75). Note that Spencer made this point long before our current obsession with multitasking and taking our work with us 24/7.

At any rate, the symptoms of neurasthenia spread far and wide in the United States in the early nineteenth century. Many of James's friends, relatives, and colleagues suffered these debilitating symptoms. A friend wrote, "I wonder if anybody ever reached 35 in New England without wanting to kill himself." And James noted, "I take it that no man is educated who has never dallied with the thought of suicide" (quoted in Townsend, 1996, pp. 32–33). The condition was so widespread among the affluent and highly educated segment of American society that a popular publication was titled "Anybody Who Was Anybody Was Neurasthenic" (Miller, 1991). Obviously William James was in good company.

The Rexall drug company capitalized on the opportunity afforded by this illness. It introduced a patent medicine called Americanitis Elixir, recommended for nervous disorders, exhaustion, and all troubles arising from Americanitis (Marcus, 1998). Female sufferers, notably intellectuals and feminists, were advised to "spend six weeks or more in bed without any work, reading, or social life, and to gain large amounts of weight on a high-fat diet." Men were not expected to so restrict their lifestyle. Their recommended course of treatment included "travel, adventure, [and] vigorous physical exercise" (Showalter, 1997, pp. 50, 66).

***Discovering psychology***   During the dark months of 1869, James began to construct a philosophy of life, compelled not so much by intellectual curiosity as by despair. He read much philosophy, including essays by Charles Renouvier on freedom of the will, which persuaded James of its existence. He decided that his first act of free will would be to believe in free will. Next, he resolved to believe that he could cure himself of his depression by believing in the power of the will. Apparently he succeeded to some extent because in 1872 he accepted a teaching position at Harvard in physiology, commenting that "it is a noble thing for one's spirits to have some responsible work to do" (James, 1902, p. 167). However, after only a year on the job he took time off to visit Italy, but then he did return to teaching.

At about the same time, James became interested in the effects of certain mind-altering chemicals. He read about the revelations people experienced under the influence of nitrous oxide (so-called "laughing gas") and amyl nitrite, which affect oxygen delivery to the brain and so can cause a rush. He decided to try these substances himself. This was, a biographer wrote, "the first of [James's] many experiments with altered states of consciousness, which fascinated him because of the way bodily changes influenced consciousness" (Croce, 1999, p. 7).

During the 1875–1876 academic year, James taught his first psychology course, which he called "The Relations Between Physiology and Psychology." Thus, Harvard became the first university in the United States to offer instruction in the new experimental psychology. James had never taken formal courses in psychology; the first psychology lecture he attended was his own. He asked the college for money to purchase laboratory and demonstration equipment for his classes and was given $300.

In 1878, two important events occurred in James's life: he married Alice Howe Gibbens, the woman chosen for him by his father, and he signed a publishing contract with Henry Holt, which resulted in one of psychology's classic books. It took James 12 years to write the book, which he began on his honeymoon.

James was a compulsive traveler, which is one reason he spent so many years preparing the book. When not in Europe, he usually could be found in the mountains of New York or New Hampshire.

> *His letters give the impression that family relationships were fatiguing and that he often felt the need to be alone. Travel was a crucial means of coping with this restlessness. He arranged a journey in the aftermath of the birth of each of his children, and then, of course, felt guilty. He was often absent, if only as far away as Newport, on holidays such as Christmas, New Year's Day, and birthdays. … James's flights from his family were escapes from human entanglements to nature, solitude, and mystical relief. (Myers, 1986, pp. 36–37)*

The births of his children were particularly unsettling to James's sensitive temperament. He found it impossible to work, and he resented his wife's attention to the newborns. After the second child was born James went abroad for a year, roaming from one city to another. From Venice he wrote to his wife that he had fallen in love with an Italian woman. "You will get used to these enthusiasms of mine and like them," he promised (quoted in Lewis, 1991, p. 344). He also told Alice that she had no right to be upset or to resent his falling in love with other women because he had once felt the same way about her; no doubt this statement was of no great comfort to her.

There were many other women with whom James fell in love, including the poet and writer Emma Lazarus. (She wrote the immortal lines inscribed on the Statue of Liberty: "Give me your tired, your poor … .") And James dutifully told Alice about each and every one. At age 53, James met a 21-year old woman whom he described as "a perfect little serious rosebud," and he met and corresponded with her for the rest of his life (Fisher, 2008, p. 539). Alice was less than happy with his "tendency to flirt casually with acquaintances and even family servants." Yet James was of the opinion that his affectionate nature should please his wife (Simon, 1998, pp. 215–216).

James continued to teach at Harvard when he was in town, and in 1885 he was promoted to professor of philosophy. Four years later, that title was changed to professor of psychology. By that time James had met many European psychologists, including

Wundt, who "made a pleasant and personal impression on me, with his agreeable voice and ready, tooth-showing smile." A few years later, however, James noted that Wundt "isn't a genius, he is a professor—a being whose duty is to know everything, and have his own opinion about everything" (James, quoted in Allen, 1967, pp. 251, 304).

James's book, *The Principles of Psychology,* was finally published in 1890, in two volumes. It was a tremendous success and a significant contribution to the field. Almost 80 years after its publication, one psychologist wrote, "James's *Principles* is without question the most literate, the most provocative, and at the same time the most intelligible book on psychology that has ever appeared in English or in any other language" (MacLeod, 1969, p. iii). For several generations of students, *The Principles* was the most influential textbook ever written in psychology. It is still read today by people who are not required to do so.

Not everyone reacted favorably to the book. Wundt and Titchener, whose views James attacked in *The Principles,* did not like it. Wundt wrote, "It is literature, it is beautiful, but it is not psychology" (Wundt, quoted in Bjork, 1983, p. 12). Wundt remained highly critical of James's work in psychology. According to C. H. Judd, an American student at Wundt's Leipzig laboratory, there was

> very little respect for the leaders in American psychology who had received their train-
> ing elsewhere than Leipzig. Especially was there a very pronounced antipathy to James.
> James had done what was thought to be quite out of order; not only had he criticized
> Wundt ... he had allowed his criticism to take the form of witty sarcasm. This was too
> much. ... James was not regarded as a thinker of the first order. (1930/1961, p. 215)

James's own reaction to the book was not favorable either. In a letter to his publisher he described the manuscript as a "loathsome, distended, tumefied, bloated, dropsical mass, testifying to nothing but two facts: first, that there is no such thing as a science of psychology, and second, that [William James] is an incapable" (James, quoted in Allen, 1967, pp. 314–315).

With the publication of *The Principles,* James decided that he had nothing more to say about psychology. Further, he was no longer interested in supervising Harvard's psychology laboratory. He arranged for Hugo Münsterberg, then at the University of Freiburg, Germany, to become director of the laboratory and to teach the psychology courses, freeing James for work in philosophy. Münsterberg never fulfilled the role James intended for him, to provide leadership in experimental research for Harvard. Instead, Münsterberg pursued a variety of real-world problems and paid scant attention to the laboratory. He is important for helping to popularize psychology and to make it a more applied discipline (see Chapter 8).

Although James began and equipped Harvard's psychology laboratory, he was not an experimentalist. He was never convinced of the value of laboratory work and did not like it personally. He said that American universities had too many laboratories, and in *The Principles* he remarked that the results of laboratory work were not in proportion to the amount of painstaking effort required. Therefore, it is not surprising that he contributed little important experimental work to psychology.

James spent the last 20 years of his life refining his philosophical system, and by the 1890s he was recognized as America's leading philosopher. Among his several major published works in philosophy is *The Varieties of Religious Experience* (1902). His book *Talks to Teachers* (1899) marked the beginning of educational psychology and offered James's ideas about how psychology could be applied to the classroom learning situation.

### The Principles of Psychology

Why is James considered by so many scholars to be the greatest American psychologist? Three reasons have been suggested for his overwhelming stature and influence. First,

James wrote with a clarity that is rare in science. His writing style has magnetism, spontaneity, and charm. Second, he opposed Wundt's goal for psychology; namely, the analysis of consciousness into elements. Third, James offered an alternative way of looking at the mind, a view congruent with the functional approach to psychology. In brief, the times in American psychology were ready for what James had to say.

In *The Principles of Psychology,* James presents what eventually became the central tenet of American functionalism—that the goal of psychology is not the discovery of the elements of experience but rather the study of living people as they adapt to their environment. The function of consciousness is to guide us to those ends required for survival. Consciousness is vital to the needs of complex beings in a complex environment; without it, human evolution could not have occurred.

James also emphasized nonrational aspects of human nature. People are creatures of emotion and passion as well as of thought and reason. Even when discussing purely intellectual processes, James stressed the nonrational. He noted that intellect can be affected by the body's physical condition, that beliefs are determined by emotional factors, and that reason and concept formation are influenced by human wants and needs. Thus, James did not consider people to be wholly rational beings. The following sections describe several of the areas James wrote about in *The Principles.*

## The Subject Matter of Psychology: A New Look at Consciousness

James stated at the beginning of *The Principles* that "Psychology is the Science of Mental Life, both of its phenomena and their conditions" (James, 1890, Vol. 1, p. 1). In terms of subject matter, the key words are *phenomena* and *conditions*. The term *phenomena* is used to indicate that the subject matter of psychology is to be found in immediate experience; the term *conditions* refers to the importance of the body, particularly the brain, in mental life.

According to James, the physical substructures of consciousness form a basic part of psychology. Consciousness must be considered in its natural setting, which is the physical human being. This awareness of biology—of the action of the brain on consciousness—is a unique feature of James's approach to psychology.

James rebelled against the artificiality and narrowness of the Wundtian position. He believed that conscious experiences are simply what they are, and they are not groups or collections of elements. The discovery of discrete elements of consciousness through introspective analysis does not show that these elements exist independently of a trained observer. Psychologists may read into an experience whatever their systematic position or viewpoint tells them should be there.

A trained food taster learns to discriminate individual elements in a flavor that might not be perceived by an untrained person. An untrained person experiences a fusion of flavor elements, a total blend of ingredients not capable of analysis. Similarly, the fact that some trained observers can analyze their conscious experiences in a psychology laboratory does not mean that the elements they report are present in the consciousness of anyone else exposed to the same experience. James considered such an assumption to be the "psychologists' fallacy."

Striking at the heart of Wundt's approach to psychology, James declared that simple sensations do not exist in conscious experience but exist only as the result of some convoluted process of inference or abstraction. In a blunt and eloquent statement, James wrote:

> *No one ever had a simple sensation by itself. Consciousness, from our natal day, is of a teeming multiplicity of objects and relations, and what we call simple sensations are results of discriminative attention, pushed often to a very high degree. (James, 1890, Vol. 1, p. 224)*

**Stream of consciousness:** William James's idea that consciousness is a continuous flowing process and that any attempt to reduce it to elements will distort it.

In place of the artificial analysis and reduction of conscious experience to its alleged elements, James called for a new program for psychology. Mental life is a unity, a total experience that changes. Consciousness is a continuous flow, and any attempt to divide it into temporally distinct phases can only distort it. James coined the phrase **stream of consciousness** to express this idea.

Because consciousness is always changing, we can never experience the same thought or sensation more than once. We may think about an object or a stimulus on more than one occasion, but our thoughts each time will not be identical. They will differ because of the effect of intervening experiences. Thus, our consciousness can be described as cumulative and not recurrent.

The mind is also continuous. There are no sharp disruptions in the flow of consciousness. We may notice gaps in time, such as when we are asleep, but on our awakening we have no difficulty making connection with our ongoing stream of consciousness. In addition, the mind is selective. Because we can pay attention to only a small part of the world of our experiences, the mind chooses from among the many stimuli to which it is exposed. It filters out some experiences, combines or separates others, selects or rejects still others. The most important criterion for selection is relevance. The mind selects relevant stimuli to attend to so that our consciousness can operate logically and a series of ideas can lead to a rational conclusion.

Overall, James emphasized the function or purpose of consciousness. He believed that consciousness must have some biological utility or it would not have survived over time. The function of consciousness is to enable us to adapt to our environment by allowing us to choose. Pursuing this idea, James distinguished between conscious choice and habit; he believed habits to be involuntary and nonconscious. When we encounter a new problem and need to choose a new way of coping, consciousness comes into play. This emphasis on purposefulness reflects the impact of evolutionary theory.

## IN THEIR OWN WORDS

### Original Source Material on Consciousness from *Psychology (Briefer Course)* (1892)

**William James**

*Consciousness is in constant change.* I do not mean by this to say that no one state of mind has any duration—even if true, that would be hard to establish. What I wish to lay stress on is this, that no state once gone can recur and be identical with what it was before. Now we are seeing, now hearing; now reasoning, now willing; now recollecting, now expecting; now loving, now hating; and in a hundred other ways we know our minds to be alternately engaged. But all these are complex states, it may be said, produced by combination of simpler ones; do not the simple ones follow a different law? Are not the *sensations* which we get from the same object, for example, always the same? Does not the same piano key, struck with the same force, make us hear in the same way? Does not the same grass give us the same feeling of green, the same sky the same feeling of blue, and do we not get the same olfactory sensation no matter how many times we put our nose to the same flask of cologne? It seems a piece of metaphysical sophistry to suggest that we do not; and yet a close attention to the matter shows that there is no proof that an incoming current ever gives us just the same bodily sensation twice.

What is got twice is the same *object*. We hear the same *note* over and over again; we see the same *quality* of green, or smell the same objective perfume, or experience the same *species* of pain. The realities, concrete and abstract, physical and ideal, whose permanent existence we believe in, seem to be constantly coming up again before our thought, and lead us, in our carelessness, to suppose that our "ideas" of them are the same ideas. ... The grass out of the window now looks to me of the same green in the sun as in the shade, and yet a painter would have to paint one part of it dark brown, another part bright yellow, to give its real sensational effect. We take no heed, as a rule, of the different way in which the same things look and sound and smell at different distances and under different circumstances. The sameness of the *things* is what we are concerned to ascertain; and any sensations that assure us of that will probably be considered in a rough way to be the same with each other.

This is what makes offhand testimony about the subjective identity of different sensations well-nigh worthless as a proof of the fact. The entire history of what is called *sensation* is a commentary on our inability to tell whether two sensible qualities received apart are exactly alike. What appeals to our attention far more than the absolute quality of an impression is its *ratio* to whatever other impressions we may have at the same time. When everything is dark a somewhat less dark sensation makes us see an object white. Helmholtz calculates that the white marble painted in a picture representing an architectural view by moonlight is, when seen by daylight, from ten to twenty thousand times brighter than the real moonlit marble would be.

Such a difference as this could never have been *sensibly* learned; it had to be inferred from a series of indirect considerations. These make us believe that our sensibility is altering all the time, so that the same object cannot easily give us the same sensation over again. We feel things differently accordingly as we are sleepy or awake, hungry or full, fresh or tired; differently at night and in the morning, differently in summer and in winter; and above all, differently in childhood, manhood, and old age. And yet we never doubt that our feelings reveal the same world, with the same sensible qualities and the same sensible things occupying it. The difference of the sensibility is shown best by the difference of our emotion about the things from one age to another, or when we are in different organic moods. What was bright and exciting becomes weary, flat, and unprofitable. The bird's song is tedious, the breeze is mournful, the sky is sad ...

[I]t is obvious and palpable that our state of mind is never precisely the same. Every thought we have of a given fact is, strictly speaking, unique, and only bears a resemblance of kind with our other thoughts of the same fact. When the identical fact recurs, we *must* think of it in a fresh manner, see it under a somewhat different angle, apprehend it in different relations from those in which it last appeared. And the thought by which we cognize it is the thought of it-in-those-relations, a thought suffused with the consciousness of all that dim context. Often we are ourselves struck at the strange differences in our successive views of the same thing. We wonder how we ever could have opined as we did last month about a certain matter. We have outgrown the possibility of that state of mind, we know not how. From one year to another we see things in new lights. What was unreal has grown real, and what was exciting is insipid. The friends we used to care the world for are shrunken to shadows; the women once so divine, the stars, the woods, and the waters, how now so dull and common!

## The Methods of Psychology

Because psychology deals with a personal and immediate consciousness, introspection must be a basic method. James wrote, "Introspective observation is what we have to rely on first and foremost and always; the looking into our own minds and reporting what we there discover. Everyone agrees that we there discover states of consciousness" (James, 1890, Vol. 1, p. 185). James was aware of the difficulties of introspection, and he accepted it as a less-than-perfect form of observation. However, he believed that introspective results could be verified by appropriate checks and by comparing the findings obtained from several observers.

Although James did not make widespread use of the experimental method, he acknowledged it as an important path to psychological knowledge, primarily for psychophysics research, the analysis of space perception, and research on memory.

To supplement introspective and experimental methods, James recommended the comparative method. By inquiring into the psychological functioning of different populations—such as animals, infants, preliterate peoples, or emotionally disturbed individuals—psychology could uncover meaningful variations in mental life.

The methods James cited in *The Principles* point to a major difference between structural and functional psychologies: The functionalist movement would not be restricted to a single method, such as Wundt's or Titchener's forms of introspection. Functionalism would accept and apply other methods as well. This eclectic approach broadened considerably the scope of American psychology.

## Pragmatism

**Pragmatism:** The doctrine that the validity of ideas is measured by their practical consequences.

James emphasized the value for psychology of **pragmatism**, the basic tenet of which is that the validity of an idea or conception must be tested by its practical consequences. The popular expression of the pragmatic viewpoint is "anything is true if it works."

Pragmatism had been advanced in the 1870s by Charles Sanders Peirce, a mathematician and philosopher and a lifelong friend of James. Peirce's work remained largely unrecognized until James wrote a book titled *Pragmatism* (1907), which formalized the doctrine as a philosophical movement. (It was Peirce who first wrote about the new psychology of Fechner and Wundt in an article published for American scholars in 1869.)

## The Theory of Emotions

James's theory of emotions, published in an article in 1884 and later in *The Principles,* contradicted current thinking about the nature of emotional states. Psychologists assumed that the subjective mental experience of an emotion preceded the bodily expression or action. The traditional example—we see a wild animal, we feel fear, and we run away—illustrates the idea that the emotion (the fear) comes before the body's reaction (running away).

James reversed the order. He stated that the arousal of the physical response precedes the appearance of the emotion, especially for what he termed "coarser" emotions such as fear, rage, grief, and love. For example, we see the wild animal, we run, and *then* we experience the emotion of fear. "Our feeling of the [bodily] changes as they occur *is* the emotion" (James, 1890, Vol. 2, p. 449).

To support this idea, James noted the introspective observation that if bodily changes such as rapid heart rate, shallow breathing, and muscle tension did not occur, then there would be no emotion. James's views on emotions have stimulated considerable controversy and a great deal of research. In an instance of simultaneous discovery, the Danish physiologist Carl Lange published a similar theory in 1885. The correspondence between the two theories has led to the designation "James-Lange theory of emotions."

## The Three-Part Self

James suggested that a person's sense of self is made up of three aspects or components. The *material* self consists of everything we call uniquely our own, such as our body, family, home, or style of dress. He thought that our choice of clothing was particularly important. He wrote that "the old saying that the human person is composed of three parts—soul, body, and clothes—is more than a joke. We appropriate our clothes and identify ourselves with them" (James, 1890, Vol. 1, p. 292). The *social* self refers to the recognition we get from other people. James pointed out that we have many social selves; we present different sides of ourselves to different people. For example, you will probably behave differently with parents than with acquaintances or lovers. Each will see you in a different way. The third component, the *spiritual* self, refers to our inner or subjective being.

Psychologists have suggested that our choice of clothing and manner of dress influence and reflect not only our material self, as James believed, but also our social and spiritual selves. Further, how we are perceived, recognized, and judged by other people can all be influenced by how we dress.

Thus, clothing can be a form of self-expression, as it appears to have been for James. He tended to dress in a way that was noticeably different from the norm for his position and social class. He favored polka-dot bow ties and brightly-colored checkered pants, definitely a "deviation from the polite standard" (Watson, 2004, p. 218). He was considered "quite conspicuous in his dress," contrary to the fashion standards of the day. Obviously he wanted to stand out in a crowd.

### Habit

The chapter in *The Principles* dealing with habit reaffirms James's interest in physiological influences. He describes all living creatures as "bundles of habits" (James, 1890, Vol. 1, p. 104). Repetitive or habitual actions involve the nervous system and serve to increase the plasticity of neural matter. As a result, habits become easier to perform on subsequent repetitions and require less conscious attention.

Habits have enormous social implications. The following passage illustrates this point:

> *Habit ... alone is what keeps us all within the bounds of ordinance. ... It dooms us all to fight out the battle of life upon the lines of our nurture or our early choice, and to make the best of a pursuit that disagrees, because there is no other for which we are fitted, and it is too late to begin again.*
>
> *Already at the age of twenty-five you see the professional mannerism settling down on the young commercial traveler, on the young doctor, on the young minister, on the young counselor-at-law. You see the little lines of cleavage running through the character, the tricks of thought, the prejudices from which the man can by-and-by no more escape than his coat sleeve can suddenly fall into a new set of folds. On the whole, it is best he should not escape. It is well for the world that in most of us, by the age of thirty, the character has set like plaster, and will never soften again. (James, 1890, Vol. 1, p. 121)*

*The Principles* was a major influence on American psychology, and its publication inspired tributes even a century later (Donnelly, 1992; Johnson & Henley, 1990). It affected the views of thousands of students and inspired psychologists to shift the new science of psychology away from the structuralist view and toward the formal founding of the functionalist school of thought.

## The Functional Inequality of Women
### Mary Whiton Calkins (1863–1930)

James was instrumental in facilitating the graduate education of Mary Whiton Calkins and helping her overcome barriers of prejudice and discrimination. Calkins later developed the paired-associate technique used in the study of memory and made significant and lasting contributions to psychology (Madigan & O'Hara, 1992). She became the first woman president of the APA and in 1906 ranked twelfth among the 50 most important psychologists in the United States—high praise from colleagues for a person who was refused her Ph.D. (Furumoto, 1990).

Archives of the History of American Psychology/
University of Akron

MARY WHITON
CALKINS

Calkins had never been allowed to enroll formally at Harvard University, but William James welcomed her to his seminars and urged the university to grant her the degree. When the administration resisted, James wrote to Calkins that it was "enough to make dynamiters of you and all women. I hope and trust that your application will break the barrier. I will do what I can" (James, quoted in Benjamin, 1993, p. 72). Despite James's efforts, Harvard declined to grant a doctoral degree to a woman, even though Calkins's examination (administered informally by James and other faculty members) was described as the "most brilliant examination for the Ph.D. that we have had at Harvard" (James, quoted in Simon, 1998, p. 244).

Seven years later, when Calkins was a professor at Wellesley and undertaking her memory research, Harvard offered her a degree from Radcliffe College, which had been established by Harvard to provide undergraduate education for women. Calkins refused; she had completed the graduate degree requirements at Harvard, not Radcliffe. Harvard was discriminating against her only because she was a woman. Harvard ignored her repeated requests for the degree she had earned. She eventually was awarded an honorary degree by Columbia University (Denmark & Fernandez, 1992). Harvard, on the other hand, did not award doctoral degrees to women until 1963.

We mention Calkins's experience as an example of the discrimination women faced in higher education, a condition that persisted well into the twentieth century. Even so, Calkins was fortunate compared with previous generations of women, who were not admitted to universities at all. In most academic fields of study in Europe and the United States, women were traditionally excluded from colleges and universities. When Harvard was founded in 1636, it did not accept women as students. Not until the 1830s did some colleges in the United States relax their prohibition and admit women as undergraduates.

The primary reason for this restriction was a generally held belief in the so-called natural intellectual superiority of men. Even if women were granted educational opportunities similar to those available to men, so this argument ran, women's innate intellectual deficiencies would prevent them from reaping the benefits. Prominent nineteenth-century scientists such as Darwin, and most of the psychologists of the time, agreed with this view.

Today, the majority of graduates who receive Ph.D.s in psychology are women, as are the majority of psychology graduate and undergraduate students. However, we have seen that the history of psychology is dominated by men. Recall that Margaret Washburn was not allowed to enroll at Columbia University because she was a woman. Not until 1892 did Yale, the University of Chicago, and a few other institutions agree to accept female graduate students. For nearly 20 years after the formal founding of psychology as a scientific discipline, women faced barriers in becoming psychologists and thus having a chance to make a significant contribution to the development of the field.

**Variability hypothesis:** The notion that men show a wider range and variation of physical and mental development than women; the abilities of women are seen as more average.

Much of the myth of the intellectual superiority of men derived from the so-called **variability hypothesis**, based on Darwinian ideas of male variability (Shields, 1982; Shields & Bhatir, 2009). Darwin found that in many species, males showed a wider range of development of physical characteristics and abilities than females. The characteristics and abilities of females were found to be clustered around the average, or mean, value. This female tendency toward averageness was thought to make women less likely to benefit from education and less likely to achieve in intellectual or scholarly work. It was a small step from that proposition to the idea that female brains were less highly evolved than male brains. Because males showed a greater range of talents, it was believed they could adapt to and benefit from varied, stimulating environments. Thus, women were considered inferior to men in both the physical and the mental functioning needed to adapt successfully to the demands of the environment. The result was widespread acceptance of the idea of a functional inequality between the sexes.

It was widely believed that "at maturity, women's brain and nervous system were limited in their capacity to support the higher mental processes, specifically objective rationality and true creativity" (Shields, 2007, p. 96). Even the pseudoscience of phrenology supported the notion of male intellectual superiority. "Women's smaller brains, the shallowness of the grey matter, the numbers of convolutions, all proved that women were intellectually inferior and childlike in their nature" (Appignanesi, 2008, p. 110).

A popular related theory was that women who were exposed to education beyond basic schooling would suffer physical and emotional damage. Some psychologists argued that educating women endangered their biological imperative to motherhood by disrupting the menstrual cycle and weakening the maternal urge. If women were to be educated at all, one psychologist wrote, "they should be educated to motherhood" (G. S. Hall, quoted in Diehl, 1986, p. 872).

A Harvard Medical School professor wrote that education for women would produce "monstrous brains and puny bodies; abnormally active cerebration and abnormally weak digestion; flowing thought and constipated bowels" (E. Clarke, quoted in Scarborough & Furumoto, 1987, p. 4). The professor also warned, "Identical education of the sexes is a crime before God and humanity" (Clarke, 1873, p. 127).

In the early years of the twentieth century, two female psychologists successfully challenged the notion of the functional inequality of the sexes. Using the empirical techniques of functional psychology, Helen Bradford Thompson Woolley and Leta Stetter Hollingworth demonstrated that Darwin and others were wrong about women.

### Helen Bradford Thompson Woolley (1874–1947)

HELEN BRADFORD
THOMPSON
WOOLLEY

Helen Bradford Thompson was born in Chicago in 1874. Her parents supported the idea of education for women; all three Thompson daughters attended college. Helen Thompson received her undergraduate degree at the University of Chicago in 1897 and her Ph.D. in 1900. Her major professors were James Rowland Angell and John Dewey; Dewey called Thompson one of his most brilliant students (quoted in James, 1994). After a postgraduate fellowship in Paris and Berlin, Thompson became director of the psychological laboratory at Mount Holyoke College in Massachusetts.

She married Paul Woolley, a physician, and accompanied him to the Philippines where he was director of a laboratory. In 1908, the couple moved to Cincinnati, Ohio, where Helen accepted the directorship of the vocation bureau of the public school system, concerned with child welfare issues. Her research on the effects of child labor led to changes in the state's labor laws. (In many states, children as young as eight years old were working in factories 10 hours a day, six days a week. Few states had protective legislation regarding age, working hours, or minimum wages for children.)

In 1921, Helen served as president of the National Vocational Guidance Association. That year the Woolleys relocated to Detroit, Michigan, where she joined the staff of the Merrill-Palmer Institute and established a nursery school program to study child development and mental abilities. In 1924 she became director of the new Institute of Child Welfare Research at Columbia University, continuing her work on learning in early childhood, vocational education, and school guidance counseling.

Helen Woolley's doctoral dissertation at the University of Chicago was the first experimental test of the Darwinian notion that women were biologically inferior to men, an idea assumed at the time to be so obvious that it needed no scientific study (James, 1994). She administered a battery of tests to 25 male and 25 female subjects to measure motor abilities, sensory thresholds (taste, smell, hearing, pain, and vision), intellectual abilities, and personality traits.

The results showed no sex differences in emotional functioning and only small, insignificant differences in intellectual abilities. The data also revealed that women were slightly superior to men in abilities such as memory and sensory perception. Woolley took the then unprecedented step of attributing these differences to social and environmental factors—the differences in child-rearing practices and expectations for boys and for girls—rather than to biological determinants (Rossiter, 1982).

Woolley published her results in *The Mental Traits of Sex: An Experimental Investigation of the Normal Mind in Men and Women* (Thompson, 1903). Her conclusions were not well received by male academic psychologists. G. Stanley Hall accused her of giving a feminist interpretation to the data (Hall, 1904). The fact that it was a woman whose research showed that women were not biologically inferior to men was seen as a tainting factor that biased the results (James, 1994). She later wrote two reviews of the growing research literature on the psychology of sex differences for the prestigious journal *Psychological Bulletin* (Woolley, 1910, 1914). By then, perhaps goaded by all the arguments that male psychologists kept making against her findings, she wrote, "There is perhaps no field aspiring to be scientific where flagrant personal bias, logic martyred in the course of supporting a prejudice, unfounded assertions, and even sentimental rot and drivel, have run riot to such an extent as here" (quoted in Milar, 2010, p. 26).

For 30 more years Woolley worked as teacher, researcher, and mentor for female psychologists in the areas of child development and education. When poor health and a traumatic divorce forced her to retire prematurely, the focus on the psychology of women passed to others.

### Leta Stetter Hollingworth (1886–1939)

LETA STETTER
HOLLINGWORTH

Leta Stetter grew up in Nebraska in a family of limited financial means. Her home was a sod hut, and she attended a one-room school. Her mother died when she was three years old, and her father left her to be raised by her grandparents. When he reappeared 10 years later, he took her from that secure home to live with him and his wife, who treated Leta badly. She never forgave him. Despite this unpromising beginning, she enrolled at the University of Nebraska, graduating in 1906 with Phi Beta Kappa honors. She taught high school for two years while her fiancé, Harry Hollingworth, completed his Ph.D. in psychology with James McKeen Cattell at Columbia University. Leta and Harry married in 1908. He taught at Barnard College in New York City, but by law married women were not permitted to teach in public schools, to Leta's surprise and regret.

She turned to writing fiction but was unable to find a publisher for her short stories. With no outlet for her talent and energy, she grew sad and embittered. Harry later wrote that Leta would "unaccountably burst into tears. … Later on she said it was because she could not bear being strong and able, with a good mind and a sound education, and yet being so unable to contribute materially toward our welfare" (quoted in Klein, 2002, p. 65).

The couple lived frugally, and Harry accepted consulting jobs to save enough money for Leta to attend graduate school. In 1916, she earned her Ph.D. from Teacher's College, Columbia University, studying with Edward L. Thorndike, and worked as a psychologist for the civil service in New York City. Five years later she was cited in *American Men of Science* for her contributions to the psychology of women.

Leta Hollingworth conducted extensive empirical research on the variability hypothesis: the idea that for physical, psychological, and emotional functioning, women were a more homogeneous and average group than men and thus showed less variation. Hollingworth's research between 1913 and 1916 focused on physical and sensorimotor functioning and intellectual abilities in a variety of subjects: infants, male and female college students, and women during their menstrual period (when it was assumed their mental and emotional conditions were affected by their natural bodily processes). Her data refuted the variability hypothesis and other notions of female inferiority. For example, she found that the menstrual cycle was not related to performance deficits in perceptual and motor skills or in intellectual abilities, as had long been assumed (Hollingworth, 1914).

Further, she challenged the concept of an innate instinct for motherhood, questioning the idea that women could find satisfaction only through bearing children, and she dismissed the notion that a woman's desire to achieve in other fields, outside of marriage and family, was somehow abnormal or unhealthy. She suggested that social and cultural attitudes rather than biological factors were influential in keeping women from becoming fully contributing members of society (Benjamin & Shields, 1990; Shields, 1975). Hollingworth also cautioned vocational and guidance counselors against advising women that they should restrict their aspirations to the then socially acceptable fields of childrearing and housekeeping, where prominence and visibility are denied. "No one knows who is the best housekeeper in America," she wrote. "Eminent housekeepers do not and cannot exist" (quoted in Benjamin & Shields, 1990, p. 177).

Leta Hollingworth also made significant contributions to clinical, educational, and school psychology, especially the educational and emotional needs of so-called "gifted" children, a term she coined (Benjamin, 1975). Despite the breadth and quality of her research, she was never able to obtain research grant support (Hollingworth, 1943). She was active in the woman's suffrage movement, campaigning for women's right to vote (finally achieved in 1920) and taking part in parades and demonstrations in New York. She died at the relatively young age of 53 from stomach cancer, "which, for unexplained reasons she endured and concealed from everyone for 10 years" (Stanley & Brody, 2004, p. 4).

# Granville Stanley Hall (1844–1924)

Although William James was the first truly notable American psychologist, the tremendous growth of psychology in the United States between 1875 and 1900 was hardly the work of James alone. Another remarkable figure in the history of American psychology, and a worthy and influential contemporary of James, was G. Stanley Hall.

Hall compiled an outstanding record of firsts in American psychology. He received the first American doctoral degree in psychology, and he claimed to be the first American student in the first year of the first psychology laboratory. (Later data of history reveal that he was the second; see Benjamin, Durkin, Link, Vestal, & Acord, 1992.) Hall began what is often considered to be the first psychology laboratory in the United States as well as the first American journal of psychology. He was the first president of Clark University, the organizer and first president of the APA, and one of the first applied psychologists.

## Hall's Life

Hall was born on a farm in Massachusetts. His mother was a pious, kind, and gentle woman; his father was stern and demanding and sometimes beat the young Hall. At the age of 14, after his father slapped him hard, Hall "stepped back in anger, partly real and—I distinctly remember—partly feigned for effect, doubled my fists and glared at him as if I were strongly tempted to hit back. I shall never forget his amazed look. I was never hit again" (Hall, quoted in Hulbert, 2003, p. 53).

An intensely ambitious boy, Hall pledged to "do and be something in the world" (quoted in Ross, 1972, p. 12). At 17 he was deeply ashamed when, at the onset of the American Civil War, his father purchased a draft exemption for him. Hall said he felt the need to do penance, to atone for not doing his duty by serving in the army (Vande Kemp, 1992).

In 1863, Hall entered Williams College. By the time he graduated, he had won a number of honors and had been voted the smartest man in his class. He developed an

GRANVILLE STANLEY
HALL

enthusiasm for evolutionary theory, which would influence his career in psychology. Hall wrote, "As soon as I first heard it in my youth, I think I must have been hypnotized by the word 'evolution,' which was music to my ear" (Hall, 1923, p. 357). After graduation, still unclear about his vocation, he enrolled in the Union Theological Seminary in New York City. He had no strong commitment to the ministry, and his interest in evolution was surely no advantage. It quickly became clear that he would not be noted for his religious orthodoxy. The story is told that when Hall gave his trial sermon to the faculty and students, the seminary president knelt and prayed for Hall's soul. "I do not think I have got the requirements for a pastor," he wrote to his parents (quoted in Hulbert, 2003, p. 55).

On the advice of the famous preacher Henry Ward Beecher, Hall went to the University of Bonn, Germany, to study philosophy and theology. In Berlin, he added studies in physiology and physics. He supplemented this phase of his education with visits to theaters and beer gardens, daring experiences for a young man of pious upbringing. He wrote of his amazement at seeing a theology professor drinking beer on a Sunday. Hall also recorded romantic interludes, noting that two passionate affairs revealed capacities in himself "hitherto unusually dormant and repressed and [that] thus made life seem richer and more meaningful" (quoted in Lewis, 1991, p. 317). Apparently Hall's European sojourn was quite a time of liberation.

He returned home reluctantly in 1871 because, one biographer suggested, his parents would no longer support him (White, 1994). By then Hall was 27 years old, with no degree and heavily in debt. He completed his seminary studies (though he was not ordained) and preached in a country church in Cowdersport, Pennsylvania, leaving that position after only 10 weeks. After working as a private tutor for more than a year, Hall secured a teaching job at Antioch College in Ohio. He taught English literature, French and German languages and literature, and philosophy. He also served as librarian, led the choir, and preached in the chapel.

In 1874, Wundt's book *Physiological Psychology* aroused Hall's interest in the new science, causing him additional uncertainty about his career. He took a leave of absence from Antioch, settled in Cambridge, Massachusetts, and became a tutor in English at Harvard. He began graduate studies and conducted research at the medical school. He also worked with William James. The two became close friends, even taking vacations together. James described Hall as "a more learned man than I ever hope to become" (quoted in Leary, 2009, p. 11). In 1878, Hall presented his dissertation on space perception and was awarded the first doctoral degree in psychology in the United States.

Immediately after receiving his degree, Hall left for Europe again, first to study physiology at Berlin and then to become Wundt's student at Leipzig, where he found himself living next door to Fechner. The anticipation of working with Wundt was greater than the reality. Although Hall dutifully attended Wundt's lectures and served as a subject in the laboratory, he conducted his own research along more physiological lines. Hall's subsequent career shows that ultimately Wundt had little influence on him.

When Hall returned to the United States two year later he had no prospect of a job, yet within 10 years he became a figure of national importance. Hall recognized that the chance to satisfy his ambition lay in the application of psychology to education. In 1882 he gave a talk to a meeting of the National Education Association (NEA), urging that the psychological study of children be a major component of the teaching profession. He repeated this message at every opportunity. The president of Harvard invited him to deliver a series of Saturday morning talks on education. These speeches brought Hall much favorable publicity and an invitation to lecture part-time at Johns Hopkins University, which had been established in Baltimore five years earlier as the first graduate school in the United States.

Ferdinand Hamburger Jr. Archives, Johns Hopkins University

Hall's psychology laboratory at Johns Hopkins University is considered to be the first in the United States.

Hall's lectures were a great success, and he was offered a professorship at Hopkins. In 1883, he formally established what is usually considered to be the first American psychology laboratory, which he called his "laboratory of psychophysiology" (Pauly, 1986, p. 30). He taught a number of students who later became prominent psychologists, among them John Dewey and James McKeen Cattell.

In 1887, Hall founded the *American Journal of Psychology,* which was the first psychology journal in the United States and even today is considered an important publication. It provided a platform for theoretical and experimental ideas and a sense of solidarity and independence for American psychology. In a burst of enthusiasm, Hall printed an excessive number of copies of the first issue; it took him five years to pay back those initial costs.

The following year Hall became the first president of Clark University in Worcester, Massachusetts. Before taking the job, he embarked on an extended tour abroad to study European universities and to hire faculty for his new school. One writer, recording the first 100 years of Clark University's history, noted that Hall's trip served as a "paid vacation for labors not yet commenced. It included a number of stops wholly irrelevant to the task ahead, such as Russian military academies, ancient Greek historical sites, and [the] standard run of brothels, circuses, and curiosities" (Koelsch, 1987, p. 21).

Hall aspired to make Clark a graduate university along the lines of Johns Hopkins and the German universities, emphasizing research rather than teaching. He served as professor of psychology as well as president and taught in the graduate school. At his own expense Hall established the journal *Pedagogical Seminary* (now the *Journal of Genetic Psychology*) to serve as an outlet for research on child study and educational psychology. In 1915, he founded the *Journal of Applied Psychology,* bringing the number of American psychology journals to 16.

The APA was organized in 1892, largely through Hall's efforts. At his invitation, approximately a dozen psychologists met in his home to plan the organization, and they elected him the first president. By 1900 the group included 127 members.

Hall was one of the first American psychologists to become interested in Freudian psychoanalysis and was largely responsible for the early attention Sigmund Freud's system received in the United States. In 1909, to celebrate Clark University's twentieth anniversary, Hall invited Freud and Carl Jung to participate in the commemorative conferences, an invitation that was courageous because many scientists viewed psychoanalysis with suspicion. Hall had initially invited his former teacher, Wilhelm Wundt, but Wundt declined because of age and because he was scheduled to be the featured speaker at the five-hundredth anniversary of his university at Leipzig.

Psychology at Clark prospered under Hall. During his 36 years there, 81 doctorates were awarded in psychology. His students remember exhausting but exhilarating Monday evening seminars at Hall's home, when Hall and the faculty and other graduate students would quiz the doctoral candidates. After these meetings, which lasted up to four hours, a household servant would bring in a gigantic tub of ice cream.

Hall's comments on his students' papers could be devastating. Lewis Terman recalled:

*Hall would sum things up with an erudition and fertility of imagination that always amazed us and made us feel that his offhand insight into the problem went immeasurably beyond that of the student who had devoted months of slavish drudgery to it. [I] always went home dazed and intoxicated, took a hot bath to quiet my nerves, then lay awake for hours rehearsing the drama and formulating the clever things I should have said and did not. (Terman, 1930/1961, p. 316)*

Adept at nurturing intelligent students, as long as they were properly deferential, Hall was often generous and supportive. At one time it could be claimed that the majority of American psychologists had been associated with Hall either at Clark or at Johns Hopkins, although he was not the primary source of inspiration for all of them. His personal influence may be best reflected in the fact that one-third of his doctoral students eventually followed his path into college administration.

Hall made Clark University more receptive to women and minority students than most schools in the United States at that time. Although he shared the nationwide opposition to coeducation for undergraduates, he readily admitted women as graduate students and junior faculty. He took the unusual step of encouraging Japanese students to enroll at Clark and refused to restrict the hiring of Jewish faculty when most other universities would not hire them. Hall also encouraged blacks to become graduate students.

The first African American to earn a Ph.D. in psychology, Francis Cecil Sumner, studied with Hall. Sumner later became chair of the psychology department at Howard University in Washington, D.C., where he implemented a strong academic program to introduce blacks to psychology (Dewsbury & Pickren, 1992). In addition, Sumner translated several thousand articles from German, French, and Spanish journals and abstracted them for American psychology journals.

After Hall's retirement from Clark in 1920, he continued to write. He died four years later, a few months after he was elected to a second term as APA president. A survey of APA members on Hall's contributions to psychology showed that, of the 120 people who responded, 99 ranked Hall among the world's top 10 psychologists. Many praised his teaching ability, his efforts in promoting psychology, and his defiance of orthodoxy. However, they, and others who knew him, were critical of his personal qualities. Hall was described as difficult, untrustworthy, unscrupulous, devious, and aggressively self-promoting as well as "aloof and competitive to the point of arousing jealousy and unnecessarily antagonizing his colleagues" (Youniss, 2006, p. 225). William James, whose friendship with Hall had deteriorated in later years, called Hall the "queerest mixture of bigness and pettiness I ever knew" (quoted in Myers, 1986, p. 18). But even his critics had to agree with the survey's conclusion: "[Hall] has been the cause of more writing and research than any other three men in the field" (quoted in Koelsch, 1987, p. 52).

## Evolution and the Recapitulation Theory of Development

Although Hall was interested in many areas, his intellectual wanderings had a single theme: evolutionary theory. His work was governed by the conviction that the normal growth of the mind involved a series of evolutionary stages.

Hall is often called a genetic psychologist because of his concern with human and animal development and the related problems of adaptation. At Clark, Hall's genetic interests led him to the psychological study of childhood, which he made the core of his psychology. In a speech at the 1893 Chicago World's Fair, he said: "Hitherto we have gone to Europe for our psychology. Let us now take a child and place him in our midst and let America make her own psychology" (quoted in Siegel & White, 1982, p. 253). Hall intended to apply his psychology to the functioning of the child in the real world. A former student aptly recalled, "The child became, as it were, [Hall's] laboratory" (Averill, 1990, p. 127).

In conducting his research, Hall made extensive use of questionnaires, a procedure he had learned in Germany. Hall and his students developed and administered 194 questionnaires covering many topics (White, 1990). For a time the method came to be associated in the United States with Hall's name, even though the technique had been developed earlier in England by Francis Galton.

The early studies of children generated great public enthusiasm and led to the formalization of the child study movement. However, this approach disappeared in a few years because of poorly executed research. The subject samples were inadequate, the questionnaires unsound, the data collectors untrained, and the data poorly analyzed—an effort considered "very poor psychology, inaccurate, inconsistent and misguided" (Thorndike, quoted in Berliner, 1993, p. 54). Despite such deserved criticism, the child study movement promoted both the empirical study of the child and the concept of psychological development.

Hall's most influential work is the 1,300-page, two-volume *Adolescence: Its Psychology, and Its Relations to Physiology, Anthropology, Sociology, Sex, Crime, Religion, and Education* (1904). The result of some 10 years of research, this encyclopedia became Hall's "first (and only) major work in psychology [and inaugurated] the scientific study of adolescent psychology" (Arnett & Cravens, 2006, p. 165). It contains the most complete statement of Hall's **recapitulation theory** of psychological development. In essence, Hall asserted that children in their personal development repeat the life history of the human race, evolving from a near-savage state in infancy and childhood to a rational, civilized human being in adulthood.

The *Adolescence* book became controversial because of what some psychologists considered an excessive and enthusiastic focus on sex, and Hall was accused of having prurient interests. In a book review, the psychologist E. L. Thorndike wrote, "The acts and feelings, normal and morbid, resulting from sex are discussed in a way without precedent in English science." Thorndike was even harsher in a letter to a colleague, saying that Hall's book was "chock full of errors, masturbation and Jesus. He is a mad man" (quoted in Ross, 1972, p. 385). Hall had also scheduled a series of lectures at Clark on sex, an action considered scandalous even though he did not allow women to attend. He eventually stopped the talks because "too many outsiders got in and even listened surreptitiously at the door" (Koelsch, 1970, p. 119). "Is there no turning Hall away from this d——d sexual rut?" wrote Angell to Titchener. "I really think it is a bad thing morally and intellectually to harp so much on the sexual string" (quoted in Boakes, 1984, p. 163). Hall's psychologist colleagues need not have worried; the productive and energetic Hall soon turned to other interests.

As Hall grew older, he naturally became curious about the later stages of human development. At the age of 78 he published *Senescence* (1922), the first large-scale

**Recapitulation theory:** Hall's idea that the psychological development of children repeats the history of the human race.

survey of the psychological issues of old age. In his last few years he wrote two auto-biographies, *Recreations of a Psychologist* (1920) and *The Life and Confessions of a Psychologist* (1923).

## Comment

Hall was once introduced to an audience as the Darwin of the mind. The characterization evidently pleased him and expressed his aspirations and the attitude that permeated his work. He was introduced to another audience as the "greatest authority in the world on the study of the child," and reportedly said the praise was correct (Koelsch, 1987, p. 58). In his second autobiography he wrote, "All my active conscious life has been made up of a series of fads or crazes, some strong, some weak; some lasting long and others ephemeral" (1923, pp. 367–368). It was a perceptive observation. Hall was bold, versatile, and aggressive, often at odds with colleagues, but he was never dull.

# The Founding of Functionalism

The scholars associated with the founding of functionalism had no ambition to start a new school of thought. They protested against the restrictions and limitations of Wundt's version of psychology and of Titchener's structuralism, but they did not want to replace these with another formal "ism." The primary reason for this was personal, not ideological: none of the major proponents of the functionalist position claimed the ambition to establish a movement in the way Wundt and Titchener did. In time, functionalism did incorporate many of the characteristics of a school of thought, but that was not the goal of its leaders. They appeared content to modify the existing orthodoxy without actively striving to replace it.

Thus, functionalism was never as rigid or as formally differentiated a systematic position as Titchener's structuralism. There was not a single functional psychology, as there was a single structural psychology. Several functional psychologies coexisted, and although they differed somewhat, all shared an interest in studying the functions of consciousness. Further, as an outgrowth of this emphasis on mental functions, the functionalists became interested in the potential applications of psychology to everyday problems of how people function in, and adapt to, different environments. The rapid development of applied psychology in the United States may be considered the most important legacy of the functionalist movement (see Chapter 8).

Paradoxically, the formalization of this protest movement was imposed on it by the founder of structuralism: E. B. Titchener. He may have indirectly founded functional psychology when he adopted the word "structural" as opposed to "functional" in an article, "The Postulates of a Structural Psychology," published in the *Philosophical Review* in 1898. In this article, Titchener pointed out the differences between structural and functional psychology and argued that structuralism was the only proper study for psychology.

By establishing functionalism as an opponent, Titchener unwittingly gave it an identity and a status it might otherwise not have attained. "What Titchener was attacking was in fact nameless until he named it; hence he thrust the movement into high relief and did more than anyone else to get the term *functionalism* into psychological currency" (Harrison, 1963, p. 395).

# The Chicago School

Not all the credit for founding functionalism can go to Titchener, but those psychologists whom history has labeled the founders of functional psychology were reluctant founders, at best. Two psychologists who contributed directly to the founding of the functionalist school of thought were John Dewey and James Rowland Angell. In 1894 they arrived at the newly established University of Chicago; later, each appeared on the cover of *Time* magazine. None other than William James later announced that Dewey and Angell should be considered the founders of the new system, which James designated the "Chicago school" (see Backe, 2001, p. 328).

# John Dewey (1859–1952)

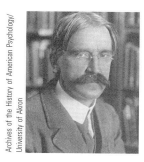

JOHN DEWEY

*Archives of the History of American Psychology/ University of Akron*

John Dewey had an undistinguished early life and showed little intellectual promise until his junior year at the University of Vermont. After graduation he taught high school for a few years and studied philosophy on his own, writing several scholarly articles. He enrolled in graduate school at Johns Hopkins University in Baltimore, received his Ph.D. in 1884, and taught at the universities of Michigan and Minnesota. In 1886, he published the first American textbook in the new psychology (titled, appropriately, *Psychology*), which became highly successful in the United States and Europe. It brought Dewey "instant fame, for it was the only available one suitable for instruction in American colleges" (Martin, 2002, p. 105). The book remained popular until it was eclipsed in 1890 by James's *The Principles of Psychology*.

Dewey spent 10 years at the University of Chicago. He established a laboratory school—a radical innovation in education—which became the cornerstone for the progressive education movement. Dewey and his wife were considered progressive parents; their children called them by their first names, and at home they practiced nudity to teach the children that there was nothing shameful about the human body.

In 1904 Dewey went to Columbia University in New York to continue his work applying psychology to educational and philosophical problems, thus providing another example of the practical orientation of many functional psychologists. Dewey was brilliant, but he was not a good teacher. One of his students recalled that he wore a green beret:

*He would come [to class], sit down at a desk, and he'd lay the green cap down in front of him, and then he would lecture to the green cap—in a monotone. If there was anything that would put students to sleep, it was that. But if you could pay attention to what that guy had to say, it was well worth it. (May, 1978, p. 655)*

He frequently kept his late afternoon class beyond its scheduled time because he was so intent on the subject matter. His wife would send one of their children to the classroom to remind him that it was time to go home. Often he would "simply sit the child on the [desk] while he finished his thought" (Martin, 2002, p. 259).

## The Reflex Arc

**Reflex arc:** The connection between sensory stimuli and motor responses.

Dewey's article, "The Reflex Arc Concept in Psychology," published in the *Psychological Review* (1896), was the point of departure for functional psychology. Indeed, one historian termed it the "opening shot" of the functionalist movement (Bergmann, 1956, p. 268). The article became so popular that it was voted the "most influential article published in the first 50 volumes of the *Psychological Review*" (Backe, 2001, p. 329).

In this important work, Dewey attacked the psychological molecularism, elementism, and reductionism of the **reflex arc** with its distinction between stimulus and response. In doing so, Dewey was arguing that neither behavior nor conscious experience could be reduced to elements, as Wundt and Titchener claimed to do. Thus, Dewey was attacking the core of their approaches to psychology. The proponents of the reflex arc argued that any unit of behavior ends with the response to a stimulus, such as when a child withdraws his or her hand from a flame. Dewey suggested that the reflex forms more of a circle than an arc because the child's perception of the flame changes, thus serving a different function.

Initially the flame attracted the child, but after feeling its effects the child is repelled by the flame. The response has altered the child's perception of the stimulus (the flame). Therefore, perception and movement (stimulus and response) must be considered as a unit and not as a composition of individual sensations and responses.

Thus, Dewey was arguing that the behavior involved in a reflexive response cannot be meaningfully reduced to basic sensorimotor elements any more than consciousness can be meaningfully analyzed into elementary component parts.

This type of artificial analysis and reduction causes behavior to lose all meaning, leaving only abstractions in the mind of the psychologist performing the exercise. Dewey noted that behavior should be treated not as an artificial scientific construct but rather in terms of its significance to the organism adapting to its environment. Dewey concluded that the proper subject matter for psychology had to be the study of the total organism as it functions in its environment.

### Comment

Dewey's ideas were strongly influenced by evolutionary theory. In the struggle for survival, both consciousness and behavior support the life of the organism; consciousness brings about the appropriate behavior that enables the organism to survive. It follows that a functional psychology will study the organism in use.

It is interesting that Dewey never called his psychology *functionalism*. He apparently did not believe structure and function could be meaningfully separated, despite his attack on structuralism's basic premise. It remained for Angell and other psychologists to proclaim that functionalism and structuralism were opposing forms of psychology.

Dewey's significance for psychology lies in his influence on psychologists and other scholars and his development of the philosophical framework for the new school of thought. When he left the University of Chicago in 1904, the leadership of the functionalist movement passed to Angell.

## James Rowland Angell (1869–1949)

James Rowland Angell molded the functionalist movement into a working school of thought. He made the psychology department at the University of Chicago the most influential of its day. It became the major training ground for functional psychologists.

### Angell's Life

Angell was born into an academic family in Vermont. His grandfather had been president of Brown University in Providence, Rhode Island, and his father was president of the University of Vermont and, later, the University of Michigan. Angell completed his undergraduate work at Michigan, where he studied under Dewey. He also read James's *The Principles of Psychology,* which he said influenced his thinking more than any other book he ever read. Angell worked with James for a year at Harvard and received his master's degree in 1892.

Angell went to Europe to continue his graduate studies at the universities in Halle and in Berlin, Germany. At Berlin he attended lectures by Ebbinghaus and Helmholtz. He hoped to go on to Leipzig, but Wundt would not accept any more students that year. Angell was unable to complete the work for his doctoral degree. His dissertation was accepted with the condition that he rewrite it in better German, but to do so he would have had to remain at Halle without any source of income. He decided to accept an appointment at the University of Minnesota, where the salary, though low, was better than nothing, particularly for a young man eager to end a four-year engagement by getting

JAMES ROWLAND
ANGELL

married. Although he never earned a Ph.D., Angell was instrumental in granting many doctorates, and in the course of his career he received 23 honorary degrees.

After a year at Minnesota, Angell accepted a position at the University of Chicago, where he remained for 25 years. Following in the family tradition, he became president of Yale University and helped to develop the Institute of Human Relations. In 1906, he was elected the fifteenth president of the APA. After retiring from academic life, he served on the board of the National Broadcasting Company (NBC).

Angell was described by *Time* magazine, and by others who knew him, as a "chipper, bouncy little man" and "the life of the party." His nickname at the University of Chicago was "Sunny Jim." It was also widely believed that it was unwise to walk or drive with him because of "his ineradicable habit of jaywalking across traffic-riddled streets. Stoplights mean nothing to him. With the same reckless assurance and incredible skill, he drives his car" (quotes from Dewsbury, 2003, pp. 66–69).

# The Province of Functional Psychology

Angell's textbook, *Psychology* (1904), embodies the functionalist approach. The book was so successful that it appeared in four editions in four years, indicating the appeal of the functionalist position. In it Angell noted that the function of consciousness is to improve the organism's adaptive abilities. The goal of psychology is to study how the mind assists the organism in adjusting to its environment.

In Angell's 1906 presidential address to the APA, published in the *Psychological Review,* he outlined what he called the "province" of functional psychology. We have noted previously that new movements gain vitality and momentum only with reference to, or in opposition to, the currently popular position. Angell drew the battle lines sharply but concluded with modesty, "I formally renounce any intention to strike out new plans; I am engaged in what is meant as a dispassionate summary of actual conditions" (Angell, 1907, p. 61).

Functional psychology, Angell said, was not at all new but had been a significant part of psychology from the earliest times. It was structural psychology that had set itself apart from the older and more truly pervasive functional form of psychology. Angell then described the three major themes of the functionalist movement:

1. Functional psychology is the psychology of mental operations, in contrast to structuralism, which is the psychology of mental elements. Titchener's elementistic approach still had its supporters, and Angell was promoting functionalism in direct opposition to it. The task of functionalism is to discover how a mental process operates, what it accomplishes, and under what conditions it occurs.

2. Functional psychology is the psychology of the fundamental utilities of consciousness. Thus, consciousness is viewed in a utilitarian spirit as it mediates between the needs of the organism and the demands of the environment. Structures and functions of the organism exist because they allow the organism to adapt to its environment and thus to survive. Angell suggested that because consciousness has survived, it must therefore perform some essential service for the organism. Functional psychologists needed to discover precisely what this service was, not only for consciousness but also for more specific mental processes, such as judging and willing.

3. Functional psychology is the psychology of psychophysical relations (mind-body relations) and is concerned with the total relationship of the organism to its environment. Functionalism encompasses all mind-body functions and recognizes no real distinction between mind and body. It considers them as belonging to the same order and assumes an easy transfer from one to the other.

## Comment

Angell's APA address was delivered at a time when the spirit of functionalism was already widely accepted. Angell shaped that spirit into a prominent, active enterprise with a laboratory, a body of research data, an enthusiastic staff of teachers, and a dedicated core of graduate students. In guiding functionalism to the status of a formal school, he gave it the focus and stature to make it effective. However, he continued to insist that functionalism did not really constitute a separate school of thought and should not become identified exclusively with the University of Chicago. Despite Angell's disclaimers, functionalism flourished and was often referred to as the "Chicago school," permanently associating it with the kind of psychology taught and practiced there.

# Harvey A. Carr (1873–1954)

HARVEY A. CARR

Harvey Carr majored in mathematics at DePauw University in Indiana and at the University of Colorado. He switched his interest to psychology apparently because he liked the professor. "I decided to turn Psychologist," Carr wrote, "although I knew practically nothing about the nature of the subject" (Carr, 1930/1961, p. 71). There was no psychology laboratory at Colorado, so Carr transferred to the University of Chicago, where his first course in experimental psychology was taught by the young assistant professor James Rowland Angell.

In Carr's second year at Chicago he served as a laboratory assistant. He worked with John B. Watson, who was then an instructor and later the founder of the behaviorist school of thought. Watson introduced Carr to animal psychology.

After Carr received his Ph.D. in 1905, he taught at a Texas high school and a state teachers college in Michigan. In 1908, he returned to Chicago to replace Watson, who had accepted a position at Johns Hopkins University. Carr eventually succeeded Angell as head of Chicago's psychology department. During Carr's tenure as chair (1919–1938), the psychology department awarded 150 doctoral degrees.

# Functionalism: The Final Form

Carr elaborated on Angell's theoretical position. His work represents functionalism when it no longer needed to crusade against structuralism. Functionalism had bested the opposition and become a recognized position in its own right. Under Carr, functionalism at Chicago reached its peak as a formal system. Carr maintained that functional psychology was *the* American psychology.

Because Carr's textbook, *Psychology* (1925), presents functionalism in its most refined form, it is important for us to consider two of its major points:

- *Carr defined the subject matter of psychology as mental activity—processes such as memory, perception, feeling, imagination, judgment, and will.*
- *The function of mental activity is to acquire, fixate, retain, organize, and evaluate experiences and to use these experiences to determine one's actions. Carr called the specific form of action in which mental activities appear "adaptive" or "adjustive" behavior.*

We see in Carr's ideas the familiar emphasis of functional psychology on mental processes rather than on the elements and content of consciousness. We also see a description of mental activity in terms of what it accomplishes in enabling the organism to adapt to its environment. It is significant that by 1925 these issues were accepted as fact, no longer as matters for dispute. By then, functionalism was mainstream psychology.

## Functionalism at Columbia University

We noted that there was not a single form of functional psychology, as there was a single structural psychology (Titchener's). Although the primary development and founding of the functionalist school of thought occurred at the University of Chicago, another approach was being shaped by Robert Woodworth at Columbia University. Columbia was also the academic base for two other psychologists with a functional orientation. One was James McKeen Cattell, whose work on mental tests embodied the American functionalist spirit (see Chapter 8), and the other was E. L. Thorndike, whose research on problems of animal learning reinforced the functionalist trend toward greater objectivity (see Chapter 9).

## Robert Sessions Woodworth (1869–1962)

Robert Woodworth did not belong formally to the functionalist school in the tradition of Angell and Carr. He disliked the constraints imposed by membership in any school of thought. Nevertheless, much of what Woodworth wrote about psychology was in the functionalist spirit of the Chicago school, and he added an important point of view.

### Woodworth's Life

Woodworth was active in psychology for more than 60 years as a researcher, beloved teacher, writer, and editor. After receiving his bachelor's degree from Amherst College in Massachusetts, he taught high school science and then mathematics at a small college. During that period, two experiences changed his life: first, he heard G. Stanley Hall give a talk; second, he read William James's *The Principles of Psychology*. He decided that he had to become a psychologist.

He enrolled at Harvard University, where he earned his master's degree, and he received his Ph.D. in 1899 from James McKeen Cattell at Columbia. Woodworth taught

Robert Sessions Woodworth.

Archives of the History of American Psychology/University of Akron physiology in New York City hospitals for three years and spent another year working in England with the physiologist Charles Scott Sherrington. He returned to Columbia in 1903, where he taught until his first retirement in 1945. He was so popular with the students that he continued to lecture to large classes until he retired a second time, at the age of 89.

A former student, Gardner Murphy, remembered Woodworth as the best teacher he ever had in a psychology course. As Murphy described it, Woodworth entered the classroom "in an unpressed, baggy old suit, and wearing army shoes." He would walk to the blackboard and "utter some inimitable word of insight or whimsy, which would go into our notebooks to be remembered in the decades that followed" (Murphy, 1963, p. 132).

Woodworth described his view of psychology in several journal articles and in two books, *Dynamic Psychology* (1918) and *Dynamics of Behavior* (1958). He wrote an introductory text, *Psychology* (1921), which appeared in five editions in 25 years and is said to have outsold every other psychology text of its time. His *Experimental Psychology* (1938, 1954) also became a classic textbook. In 1956, Woodworth received the first Gold Medal Award from the American Psychological Foundation for "unequaled contributions to shaping the destiny of scientific psychology" as an "integrator and organizer of psychological knowledge."

## Dynamic Psychology

Woodworth maintained that his approach to psychology was not really new but was the one that good psychologists followed even in the days before psychology became a science. Psychological knowledge must begin with an investigation of the nature of the stimulus and the response; that is, with objective, external events. But when psychologists consider only the stimulus and the response in attempting to explain behavior, they miss what may be the most important part of their study—the living organism itself. A stimulus is not the complete cause of a particular response. The organism, with its varying energy levels and its current and past experiences, also acts to determine the response.

Psychology must consider the organism as interpolated between the stimulus and the response. Therefore, Woodworth suggested, the subject matter for psychology must be both consciousness and behavior. (This position was adopted later by the humanistic psychologists and the social-learning theorists.)

The external stimulus as well as the organism's overt response may be observed objectively, but what occurs inside the organism can be known only through introspection. Thus, Woodworth accepted introspection as a useful tool for psychology, along with observational and experimental methods.

**Dynamic psychology:** Robert Woodworth's system of psychology, which was concerned with the influence of causal factors and motivations on feelings and behavior.

Woodworth introduced into functionalism a **dynamic psychology** that elaborated on the teachings of John Dewey and William James. (Dewey had used the word "dynamic" in this context as early as 1884; James in 1908.) A dynamic psychology is concerned with motivation; Woodworth's intention was to develop what he called a "motivology."

Although we can find similarities between Woodworth's position and that of the Chicago functionalists, Woodworth emphasized the physiological events that underlie behavior. His dynamic psychology focused on cause-and-effect relationships, and his primary interest was in the forces that drive or motivate human beings. He believed that psychology's goal should be to determine why people behave as they do.

Woodworth did not adhere to a single system, nor did he desire to develop his own school of thought. His viewpoint was constructed not out of protest but by extending, elaborating, and synthesizing what he considered to be appropriate features of other approaches.

# Criticisms of Functionalism

Attacks on the functionalist movement came quickly and vehemently from the structuralists. For the first time, at least in the United States, the new psychology was divided into warring factions: Titchener's laboratory at Cornell for the structuralist camp and the psychology department at Chicago for the functionalists. Accusations, charges, and countercharges flew back and forth between the enemies with the righteousness typical of those convinced they alone possess the truth.

Titchener and his followers argued that functionalism was not psychology at all. Why? Because functionalism did not adhere to structuralism's subject matter and methods! Thus, in Titchener's view, any approach to psychology that deviated from the introspective analysis of the mind into elements could not truly be called psychology. Of course, it was just this definition of psychology that the functionalists were questioning.

Structuralists also found fault with the functional psychologists' interest in practical concerns, thus reawakening the longstanding controversy between pure and applied science. The structuralists disdained any application of psychological knowledge to real-world problems, whereas the functionalists had no stake in maintaining psychology as a pure science and never apologized for their practical interests.

Carr and other functionalists argued that both pure and applied psychology could adhere to rigorous scientific procedures and that valid research could be performed in factories, offices, and classrooms as well as in university laboratories. It is the method and not the subject matter that determines the scientific worth of any field of inquiry. This ongoing dispute between pure and applied science is no longer as extreme in American psychology as it once was, largely because applied psychology has become so pervasive. This practical application of psychology to real-life problems is among functionalism's most important and lasting contributions.

# Contributions of Functionalism

Functionalism's vigorous opposition to structuralism had an immense impact on the development of psychology in the United States. The long-range consequences of the shift in emphasis from structure to function also were significant. One result was that research on animal behavior, which was not part of the structuralist approach, became a vital area of study for psychology.

The functionalists' broadly based psychology also incorporated studies of infants, children, and people with mental disabilities. Functional psychologists supplemented the introspective method with data obtained from other methods, such as physiological research, mental tests, questionnaires, and objective descriptions of behavior. These approaches, rejected by the structuralists, became respectable sources of information for psychology.

By the time of Wundt's death in 1920 and Titchener's in 1927, their approaches to psychology had been overshadowed in the United States. By 1930, the functionalist victory was virtually complete. As we see in Chapter 8, functionalism left its imprint on contemporary American psychology most significantly through its emphasis on the application of the methods and findings of psychology to the solution of practical problems.

# Discussion Questions

1. According to Angell, what were functionalism's three major themes? According to Carr, what is the proper subject matter of psychology?

2. According to James, what are the components of a person's sense of self? What role does clothing seem to play in our sense of self, in James's view?

3. Compare functionalism's contributions to psychology with the contributions of structuralism.

4. Describe Hollerith's approach to processing information by machine.

5. Describe Spencer's notion of social Darwinism.

6. Describe the variability hypothesis and its influence on the idea of male superiority. How did research by Woolley and Hollingworth refute these ideas?

7. Describe Woodworth's dynamic psychology and his views on introspection. Did Woodworth consider himself to be a functional psychologist? Why or why not?

8. How did James's view of consciousness differ from Wundt's view? According to James, what was the purpose of consciousness?

9. How did the prescribed cures for neurasthenia differ for men and for women?

10. How was the work of G. Stanley Hall influenced by Darwin's evolutionary theory? Describe Hall's recapitulation theory of development.

11. In what ways did Titchener and Dewey contribute to the founding of functional psychology? Why was there no single form of functionalism as there was a single structuralism?

12. What "firsts" in American psychology can be attributed to Hall? Why was he called a genetic psychologist?

13. What is neurasthenia? What segment of nineteenth-century American society was most likely to be afflicted with neurasthenia?

14. What methods did James consider appropriate for the study of consciousness? What was the value of pragmatism for the new psychology?

15. Who extended Darwin's ideas on evolution to machines? Describe this person's position on mechanical evolution.

16. Why did applied psychology develop under functionalism and not under structuralism?

17. Why was James considered to be the most important American psychologist? Describe his attitude toward laboratory work.

18. Why was the type of calculating machine developed by Babbage in the mid-nineteenth century no longer appropriate by the end of that century?

19. Why was the United States so receptive to Spencer's ideas about social Darwinism?

# Applied Psychology

## FDA Raid: Target Coca-Cola

During the evening of October 20, 1909, U.S. federal agents stopped a truck on the highway outside of Chattanooga, Tennessee. They were conducting a drug bust under the provisions of the recently enacted Federal Food and Drugs Act. Their target was a shipment of 40 barrels and 20 kegs containing a substance the government claimed was poisonous and habit-forming. The syrup in the kegs and barrels was the basis of Coca-Cola; the deadly, addictive ingredient was caffeine.

If found guilty, the management of the Coca-Cola Company would have been in serious trouble. They spared no expense preparing for the case that finally went to trial in 1911. As the court date grew closer, the corporate lawyers realized that they had no evidence to demonstrate that the amount of caffeine in the soft drink had no harmful effects on human behavior or thought processes. They needed to recruit a psychologist to conduct an impressive research program—and hope that the results would prove their point.

First they asked James McKeen Cattell, one of the most prominent psychologists in the United States, but he was not interested, nor were several others. But one man was eager to accept what he perceived as a great opportunity. His name was Harry Hollingworth.

"With me there was a double motive at work," he wrote. "I needed money, and here was a chance to accept employment at work for which I had been trained, with not only the cost of the investigation met but with a very satisfactory retaining fee and stipend for my time and services" (quoted in Benjamin, Rogers, & Rosenbaum, 1991, p. 43).

Hollingworth was then teaching at Barnard College in New York City, being paid little more than a subsistence wage. His wife, Leta Stetter, had been unable to secure a teaching job (because of her married status), and she had been unsuccessful in selling her short stories. She had hoped to go to graduate school, but the couple could not afford it. Thanks to the Coca-Cola case, however, she was appointed assistant director of the research program and together the Hollingworths earned enough money to pay her way through the graduate program.

Despite the financial gain, Harry Hollingworth insisted on the highest ethical standards. He would not be accused of providing only the answers the company desired. Coca-Cola agreed to his terms. He would be permitted to publish his results even if they proved harmful to the company; in turn, the company agreed not to use his findings in advertising, no matter how favorable they might turn out to be.

The intensive 40-day research program, as rigorous and sophisticated as any conducted in the best equipped laboratory of the finest university, involved approximately 64,000 individual measurements. Data were recorded on a wide range of motor and mental functions under conditions providing various dosages of caffeine. No harmful effects or significant declines in performance were found.

The Coca-Cola Company won the case, though the verdict was later overturned by the Supreme Court, and the effects on the Hollingworths, and on psychology as a whole, were profound. They demonstrated that sound experimental research could be funded by a major corporate entity without dictating or otherwise prejudicing the results. A more lasting effect was the knowledge that psychologists could have successful and financially rewarding careers in applied psychology without challenging their professional integrity.

# Toward a Practical Psychology

Evolutionary doctrine and the functional psychology that derived from it rapidly took hold in the United States toward the end of the nineteenth century. We have seen that American psychology was guided much more by the ideas of Darwin, Galton, and Spencer than by the work of Wundt. This was a curious, even paradoxical, historical phenomenon. Wundt trained many of the first generation of American psychologists in his form of psychology, yet they brought few of his ideas home with them. When these students of Wundt's—these new psychologists—returned to the United States, they set about establishing a psychology that bore little resemblance to what Wundt had taught them. Thus, the new science, not unlike a living species, was changing to adapt to its new environment.

Wundt's psychology and Titchener's structuralism could not long survive in their original form in the American intellectual climate—the American Zeitgeist—and so they evolved into functionalism. They were not practical kinds of psychology; they did not deal with the mind in use and could not be applied to everyday demands and problems. American culture was oriented toward the practical; people valued what worked. "We need a psychology that is usable," wrote G. Stanley Hall. "Wundtian thoughts can never be acclimated here, as they are antipathetic to the American spirit and temper" (Hall, 1912, p. 414).

The new American psychologists transformed the German species of psychology in aggressive American fashion. They began to study not what the mind is but what it does. While some American psychologists—notably James, Angell, and Dewey—were developing the functionalist approach in academic laboratories, others were applying it in settings outside the universities. This move toward a practical psychology was occurring at the same time that functionalism was being founded as a separate school of thought.

The applied psychologists took their psychology into the real world, into the schools, factories, advertising agencies, courthouses, child guidance clinics, and mental health centers. In doing so, they changed the nature of American psychology even more radically than had functionalism's academic founders. The professional literature reflects their impact. By around 1900, 25 percent of the research articles published in American psychology journals dealt with applied psychology and less than 3 percent involved introspection (O'Donnell, 1985). The approaches of Wundt and Titchener, themselves so recently the "new" psychology, were rapidly being overtaken by a newer psychology. Even Titchener, the great structural psychologist, recognized this sweeping change in American psychology. In 1910 he wrote, "If, then, one were asked to sum up, in a sentence, the trend of psychology during the past ten years, one's reply would be: Psychology has leaned, very definitely, toward application" (quoted in Evans, 1992, p. 74).

## The Growth of American Psychology

Psychology grew and prospered in the United States. The vibrant development of American psychology during the years 1880 to 1900 was a striking phenomenon in the history of science:

- *In 1880, there were no laboratories in the United States; by 1900 there were 41, and they were better equipped than laboratories in Germany.*
- *In 1880, there were no American psychology journals; by 1895 there were three.*

- *In 1880, Americans had to go to Germany to study psychology; by 1900, most chose to enter graduate programs at home; by then there were some 40 doctoral programs at U.S. universities.*
- *From 1892 to 1904, over 100 Ph.D.s were awarded in psychology, more than in any other science except chemistry, zoology, and physics.*
- *In 1910, more than 50 percent of all published articles in psychology were written in the German language; only 30 percent were in English. By 1933, 52 percent of the articles published were in English and only 14 percent in German (Wertheimer & King, 1994). By the end of the twentieth century, English had become the dominant language at international meetings and in the published literature; the APA journal* Psychological Abstracts *no longer covered publications in languages other than English (Draguns, 2001).*
- *The British publication* Who's Who in Science *for 1913 stated that the United States was predominant in psychology, having more of the world's leading psychologists (84) than Germany, England, and France combined (Benjamin, 2001; Jonçich, 1968; Wertheimer & King, 1994).*

In little more than 20 years after psychology began in Europe, then, American psychologists assumed undisputed leadership of the field. In his 1895 APA presidential address, James McKeen Cattell reported:

*[The] academic growth of psychology in America during the past five years is almost without precedent. Psychology is a required subject in the undergraduate curriculum … and among university courses psychology now rivals the other leading sciences in the number of students attracted and in the amount of original work accomplished. (Cattell, 1896, p. 134)*

Along with growing student interest in psychology, the number of psychology laboratories increased rapidly. The 41 laboratories in the United States in 1900 represented the majority of the research labs worldwide. The European countries counted no more than 10 (Benjamin, 2000a). Thus, psychology was advancing in the classroom, in the experimental laboratory, and in the real world.

*The general public took an immediate and avid interest in this fledgling discipline. Students began flocking to both undergraduate and graduate programs. Popular magazines devoted feature articles to the discipline's promising new discoveries … and anticipated exciting practical applications in education, industry, and medicine. (Fuller, 2006, p. 221)*

Psychology made its debut before an eager American public at the 1893 Chicago World's Fair. In a program similar to Galton's anthropometric laboratory in England, psychologists organized exhibits of research apparatus and a testing laboratory in which visitors could have their sensory capacities measured for a small fee. People were delighted:

*Magazines and newspaper reports on the fair applauded the psychological laboratory, which contained the largest collection of instruments and appliances ever brought together in America, as the exposition's greatest educational contribution. The fact that psychologists were given an official exhibit there for the first time at an international fair demonstrated that the discipline had finally conceded popular recognition. (Shore, 2001, pp. 72, 83)*

An even more extensive exhibition was mounted at the 1904 Louisiana Purchase Exposition in St. Louis, Missouri. This star-studded event featured talks by some of the leading psychologists of the day: E. B. Titchener, C. Lloyd Morgan, Pierre Janet, G. Stanley Hall, and John B. Watson. Such a popular display of psychology would not have found favor with Wundt, and of course nothing like it ever took place in Germany. The popularizing of psychology reflected the American temperament. It substantially remade Wundt's form of psychology into functional psychology and extended it far beyond the experimental laboratory.

Thus, America embraced psychology with enthusiasm and quickly welcomed it into college classrooms and everyday life. The scope of the field today is far broader than its founders ever thought possible, or even desirable. One current evaluation noted that "psychological research is dominated by Americans" who conduct more research than psychologists in all other countries, even though the United States accounts for less than 5 percent of the world's population (Arnett, 2008, p. 602).

## Economic Influences on Applied Psychology

Although the American Zeitgeist—the intellectual spirit and temper of the times—helped foster the emergence of applied psychology, other more practical contextual forces were also responsible for its development. In Chapter 1 we discussed the role of economic factors in shifting the focus of American psychology from pure research to application. While the number of psychology laboratories was increasing toward the end of the nineteenth century, the number of Americans with doctoral degrees in psychology was growing even faster. Many of these new Ph.D.s, particularly those without an independent source of income, were forced to look beyond the university for means of economic survival, as was the case with Harry Hollingworth and his work for Coca-Cola.

Hollingworth performed applied research for a number of companies; for example, determining the most effective advertisements for a firearms manufacturer and also for Wrigley's chewing gum. He reported that the act of chewing gum relaxed muscle tension and helped people feel at ease (Hollingworth, 1939). He once told a friend that he "never considered any of his investigations to lie in the field of applied psychology. He thought of them as straightforward efforts to discover the nature of certain facts and relationships" (see Poffenberger, 1957, p. 139).

Hollingworth was not alone in conducting research that could be applied to real-world problems. Other pioneers in applied psychology also acted out of economic necessity. This does not mean that they did not find challenge and stimulation in their practical work. Most did, and they also came to recognize that human behavior and cognitive activities could be studied in real-world settings as effectively as in academic laboratories. Also, some psychologists chose to work in applied areas out of a genuine desire to do so. Yet the fact remains that many of the first generation of applied psychologists in the United States were compelled to abandon their dreams of pure academic experimental research as the only way to escape a life of poverty.

The situation was more critical for psychologists teaching at less endowed state universities in the Midwest and West. By 1910, one-third of American psychologists held such positions, and as their numbers grew so did the pressure on them to deal with practical problems and thus prove to their college administrators and state legislators that the new field of psychology had some financial worth.

In 1912, C. A. Ruckmick surveyed psychologists in the United States and concluded that psychology was held in low esteem by administrators at colleges and universities, despite its popularity with students. The courses were under-funded and the laboratories poorly equipped, and there seemed to be little hope for improvement. It appeared that the only way to increase departmental budgets and faculty salaries was to demonstrate to college administrators and politicians that the science of psychology could help cure society's ills.

G. Stanley Hall advised a Midwestern colleague to make psychology's influence felt "outside the university, lest some irresponsible, sensational man or party criticize it in the legislature." Cattell urged colleagues to "make practical applications and develop a profession of applied psychology" (quoted in O'Donnell, 1985, pp. 215, 221).

The solution was obvious: make psychology more valuable by applying it. But applying it to what? Fortunately, the answer soon became clear. Public school enrollments were increasing dramatically. Between 1870 and 1915 they rose from 7 million to 20 million, and government spending on public education during that period grew from $63 million to $605 million (Siegel & White, 1982). Education had become a big business, and this development caught the attention of psychologists.

Hall proclaimed that the "one chief and immediate field of application for [psychology] was its application to education" (Hall, 1894, quoted in Leary, 1987, p. 323). Even William James, who could not be considered an applied psychologist, wrote a book called *Talks to Teachers,* about the uses of psychology in the classroom (James, 1899). By 1910 more than one-third of American psychologists expressed interest in applying psychology to problems in education, and three-fourths of those calling themselves applied psychologists were already working in that area. Psychology had begun to find a place in the real world.

We discuss in this chapter the careers and contributions of four applied psychologists who extended the new science into other areas, including industry, psychological testing, the criminal justice system, and mental health clinics. These psychologists were trained by Wundt at Leipzig to become academic psychologists, but they all moved away from Wundt's teachings when they began their careers in American universities. They provide striking examples of how American psychology came to be influenced more by Darwin and Galton than by Wundt, and how the Wundtian approach was refashioned when transplanted to American soil.

## Mental Testing

The functionalist spirit of American psychology was also well represented in the life and work of James McKeen Cattell, who promoted a practical, test-oriented approach to the study of mental processes. Cattell's psychology was concerned with human abilities rather than the content of consciousness, and in this respect he comes close to being a functionalist.

## James McKeen Cattell (1860–1944)

Cattell was born in Easton, Pennsylvania. He earned his bachelor's degree in 1880 at Lafayette College, where his father was president. Following the custom of going to Europe for graduate studies, Cattell went first to the University of Göttingen and then to Leipzig and Wilhelm Wundt.

A paper on philosophy won Cattell a fellowship to Johns Hopkins University in 1882. At the time his major interest was philosophy, and during his first semester at Hopkins no psychology courses were offered. Apparently Cattell became interested in psychology as a result of his own experiments with drugs. He tried a variety of substances—hashish, morphine, opium, caffeine, tobacco, and chocolate—and found the results to be of both personal and professional interest. Some drugs, notably hashish, cheered him considerably and reduced his depression. He recorded in a journal the effects of the drugs on his cognitive functioning.

"I felt myself making brilliant discoveries in science and philosophy. My only fear being that I could not remember them until morning." Later he wrote, "Reading has become uninteresting. I keep reading without paying much attention. It takes a long time to write a word. I'm rather confused" (quoted in Sokal, 1981, pp. 51, 52). Cattell was not so confused that he failed to recognize the psychological importance of the various drugs, however, and he observed his own behavior and mental state with increasing fascination. "I seemed to be two persons, one of whom could observe and even experiment on the other" (quoted in Sokal, 1987, p. 25).

JAMES MCKEEN
CATTELL

During Cattell's second semester at Hopkins, G. Stanley Hall began to teach classes in psychology, and Cattell enrolled in Hall's laboratory course. Cattell chose to conduct experiments on reaction time—the time required for different mental activities—and the results of this work reinforced his desire to become a psychologist.

Cattell's return to Wundt in Germany in 1883 is the subject of legends in the history of psychology, and these legends provide additional examples of how historical data can be distorted. Cattell said he appeared at the University of Leipzig and boldly announced to Wundt, "Herr Professor, you need an assistant, and I shall be your assistant" (Cattell, 1928, p. 545). Cattell made it clear to Wundt that he would choose his own research project on the psychology of individual differences, a topic that was not central to Wundtian psychology. Wundt was said to have characterized Cattell and his project as *ganz Amerikanisch* [typically American], which was a prophetic remark, if true. The interest in individual differences, a natural outcome of an evolutionary point of view, has since been a feature of American psychology, not German psychology.

In addition, Cattell supposedly gave Wundt his first typewriter, on which most of Wundt's many books were written. For this gift Cattell was teased by his colleagues for having "done a serious disservice ... for it had enabled Wundt to write twice as many books as would otherwise have been possible" (Cattell, 1928, p. 545).

Careful archival research on Cattell's letters and journals has questioned these stories (see Sokal, 1981). Cattell's accounts written many years later are not supported by his correspondence and journal entries written at the time the events occurred. Wundt thought highly of Cattell and appointed him laboratory assistant in 1886. There is no evidence that Cattell wanted to study individual differences at that time. Cattell showed Wundt how to use a typewriter but did not give him one.

Cattell did not lack self-confidence as Wundt's student, as typified in his letters to his parents. "I suppose you won't consider it egotistical when I say that I know a great deal more about [reaction time] than [Wundt] does.... I'm quite sure my work is worth more than all done by Wundt and his pupils.... Prof. Wundt seems to like me and to appreciate my phenomenal genius" (quoted in Benjamin, 2006a, pp. 64, 65).

After obtaining his doctoral degree in 1886 Cattell returned to the United States to teach psychology at Bryn Mawr College and the University of Pennsylvania. He went to England to lecture at Cambridge University, where he met Francis Galton. The two shared an interest in individual differences, and Galton, then at the peak of his fame, "provided [Cattell] with a scientific goal—the measurement of the psychological differences between people" (Sokal, 1987, p. 27).

Cattell admired Galton's breadth of interests and his emphasis on measurement and statistics. Under Galton's influence, Cattell became one of the first American psychologists to stress quantification, ranking, and ratings, even though personally he was "mathematically illiterate" and often made simple errors when adding and subtracting (Sokal, 1987, p. 37). Cattell developed the widely used order-of-merit ranking method (described later in this chapter) and was the first psychologist to teach the statistical analysis of experimental results.

Wundt did not favor statistical techniques, so it was Galton's influence on Cattell that was responsible for the emphasis on statistics that came to characterize the new American psychology. This emphasis also explains why American psychologists began to focus on studies of large groups of subjects, for which statistical comparisons could be made, rather than on individual subjects, as Wundt did.

The graphic display of data was used frequently by Galton, Ebbinghaus, Hall, and the American psychologist Thorndike in the closing decades of the nineteenth century. The British statistician Karl Pearson, who had proposed the formula for calculating the correlation coefficient, in 1900 devised the chi-square test. Both techniques were used more widely by American psychologists than by their counterparts in England. In 1907, John Edgar

Cover, a psychologist at Stanford University, was apparently the first to advocate the use of experimental and control groups (Dehue, 2000; Smith, Best, Cylke, & Stubbs, 2000).

In addition to statistics, Cattell was interested in Galton's work in eugenics (see Chapter 6). He argued for the sterilization of delinquents and so-called defective persons and for offering incentives to healthy, intelligent people if they would intermarry. He promised his seven children $1,000 each if they would marry sons or daughters of college professors (Sokal, 1971).

In 1888 Cattell became professor of psychology at the University of Pennsylvania, an appointment arranged by his father. Learning that an endowed chair in philosophy was to be established at the university, the elder Cattell lobbied the school's provost, an old friend, to secure the post for his son. The elder Cattell urged his son to publish more articles to enhance his professional reputation, and he even traveled to Leipzig to obtain Wundt's personal letter of recommendation. He told the provost that because the family was wealthy, the salary was unimportant, and thus Cattell was hired for extremely low pay (O'Donnell, 1985). Cattell would later claim, inaccurately, that his was the world's first psychology professorship, but his appointment was actually in philosophy. He stayed at the University of Pennsylvania only three years until he became the professor of psychology and department head at Columbia University, where he remained for 26 years.

Because of his dissatisfaction with Hall's *American Journal of Psychology,* Cattell began the *Psychological Review* in 1894 with J. Mark Baldwin. Cattell acquired from Alexander Graham Bell the weekly journal *Science,* which was about to cease publication for lack of funds. Five years later it became the official journal of the American Association for the Advancement of Science (AAAS). In 1906 Cattell instituted a series of reference books, including *American Men of Science* and *Leaders in Education.* He bought *Popular Science Monthly* in 1900; he sold the name in 1915 and continued to publish it as *Scientific Monthly.* Another weekly, *School and Society,* commenced in 1915. Although it was Cattell who began or purchased these publications, his wife Josephine served as the unacknowledged "managing editor" for the journals (Sokal, 2009, p. 99).

During Cattell's career at Columbia, more doctorates in psychology were awarded there than at any other graduate school in the United States. Cattell advocated independent work and gave his students considerable freedom to conduct their own research. He believed that a professor should maintain some distance from university concerns, so he made his home 40 miles from the campus. Reflecting his growing truculent attitude toward the university, he called his home "Fort Defiance" (Sokal, 2009, p. 99). Cattell established a laboratory and an editorial office at home and visited the campus only a few days each week.

This aloofness was one of several factors that strained relations between Cattell and the university administration. He urged greater faculty participation, arguing that faculty, not administrators, should be making many of the decisions about university governance. To this end, he helped found the American Association of University Professors (AAUP). He was not seen as tactful in his dealings with Columbia's administration and was described as "ungentlemanly, irretrievably nasty, and lacking in decency" (Gruber, 1972, p. 300).

Cattell's biographer wrote, he "often exhibited a self-righteous egotism that led him to expect others to defer to his view [and an] impatience with all groups of which he was not the center." he was also characterized as difficult, disagreeable, and sarcastic (Sokal, 2009, p. 90).

On three occasions between 1910 and 1917, the university trustees considered forcing Cattell to retire. The deciding blow fell during World War I, when Cattell wrote two letters to U.S. congressmen protesting the practice of sending draftees into combat. This was an unpopular position, but Cattell remained adamant. He was dismissed in 1917, charged with disloyalty to the United States. He sued the university for libel, and although he was awarded $40,000 (a large sum of money at that time), he was not reinstated.

Cattell isolated himself from his colleagues and wrote satirical pamphlets about the university administration. A bitter man to the end, Cattell made many enemies. He never returned to academic life, and instead he devoted himself to his publications and to the AAAS and other learned societies. Within psychology, his promotional efforts elevated the new science to a higher standing in the scientific community.

In 1921 Cattell realized one of his ambitions—promoting applied psychology as a business. He organized the Psychological Corporation, with stock purchased by members of the APA, to provide psychological services to industry, the psychological community, and the public. Initially the venture was a failure; in its first two years the company realized a profit of $51. As long as Cattell remained president, the situation did not improve. By 1969, however, the Psychological Corporation had generated $5 million in sales and was bought by publisher Harcourt Brace, which 10 years later reported $30 million in sales from the venture Cattell began.

## Mental Tests

**Mental tests:** Tests of motor skills and sensory capacities; intelligence tests use more complex measures of mental abilities.

In an article published in 1890, Cattell used the term **mental tests**, and while at the University of Pennsylvania he administered a series of such tests to his students. Cattell wrote: "Psychology cannot attain the certainty and exactness of the physical sciences unless it rests on a foundation of experiment and measurement. A step in this direction could be made by applying a series of mental tests and measurements to a large number of individuals" (Cattell, 1890, p. 373). This is precisely what Cattell was attempting to do. He continued the testing program at Columbia and collected data from several classes of entering students.

The kinds of tests Cattell used in trying to measure the range and variability of human capacities differed from the intelligence or cognitive ability tests psychologists developed later, which use more complex mental tasks. Cattell's tests, like Galton's, dealt primarily with elementary sensorimotor measurements, including dynamometer pressure, rate of movement (how quickly the hand can move 50 cm), two-point skin sensitivity threshold, amount of pressure on the forehead necessary to cause pain, just noticeable differences in judging weights, reaction time for sound, and time for naming colors.

By 1901 Cattell had amassed enough data to correlate the test scores with measures of the students' academic performance. The correlations proved disappointingly low, as did inter-correlations among individual tests. Because similar results had been obtained in Titchener's laboratory, Cattell concluded that tests of this type were not valid predictors of college achievement or, by assumption, of intellectual ability.

## Comment

Cattell's strongest influence on American psychology was through his work as an organizer, executive, and administrator of psychological science and practice, and as an articulate link between psychology and the greater scientific community. He became an ambassador of psychology, delivering lectures, editing journals, and promoting practical applications of the field.

Building on Galton's work, Cattell investigated the nature and origin of scientific ability, using his order-of-merit ranking method. Stimuli ranked by a number of judges were arranged in a final rank order by calculating the average rating given to each stimulus item. The method was applied to eminent American scientists by having competent people in each scientific field rank their outstanding colleagues. The source book *American Men of Science* emerged from this work. Despite the book's title, it also included American women of science. The 1910 edition lists 19 female psychologists, about 10 percent of the psychologists cited (O'Donnell, 1985).

A young boy uses an instrument to measure vital capacity, which is the maximum volume of air that is exhaled after deep inhalation. Vital capacity was believed to be related to intelligence.

Through his work on mental testing, the measurement of individual differences, and the promotion of applied psychology, Cattell energetically reinforced the functionalist movement in American psychology. When Cattell died, the historian E. G. Boring wrote to Cattell's children, "In my opinion your father did more than William James even to give American psychology its peculiar slant, to make it different from the German psychology from which it stemmed" (quoted in Bjork, 1983, p. 105).

# The Psychological Testing Movement
## Binet, Terman, and the IQ Test

Although Cattell coined the term *mental tests,* the first truly psychological test of mental ability was developed by Alfred Binet (1857–1911), who entered the field of psychology "quite by accident and who failed miserably, repeatedly, and publicly until he created the exams that are the foundation of intelligence tests today" (Murdoch, 2007, p. 29). Independently wealthy, Binet explored careers in law and medicine but did not like either. Recovering from a nervous breakdown at age 22, he discovered psychology, which he studied on his own. He went on to publish more than 200 books and articles, and he wrote four plays that were performed in Paris theaters. By using more complex measures than those selected by Cattell, Binet provided an effective measure of human cognitive abilities and thus initiated the era of modern intelligence testing. He also conducted research on issues in developmental, experimental, educational, and social psychology.

Binet disagreed with Galton and Cattell's approach, which used tests of sensorimotor processes to attempt to measure intelligence. He believed that assessing such cognitive functions as memory, attention, imagination, and comprehension would provide a more appropriate measure of intelligence. He reached this conclusion on the basis of research he conducted at home with his two young daughters as subjects. Initially he administered the same kinds of sensorimotor tests used by Galton and Cattell, but he found that his children performed just as well and as fast as adults did. It was then that

Archives of tthe History of American Psychology/University of Akron

Alfred Binet developed the first truly psychological test of mental ability, which has evolved into the widely used Stanford-Binet Intelligence Scale.

he turned to tests of cognitive ability; for these kinds of tasks, he did find significant differences between his daughters and adult subjects.

In 1904, in response to a practical need, the opportunity arose for Binet to prove his point. The French ministry of public instruction appointed a commission to study the learning abilities of children who were having difficulties in school. Binet and Théodore Simon (a psychiatrist) were appointed to the commission, and together they investigated the intellectual tasks that the majority of children could master at different ages. From their identification of these tasks they constructed an intelligence test consisting of 30 problems arranged in ascending order of difficulty. The test focused on three cognitive functions: judgment, comprehension, and reasoning.

Three years later they revised and expanded the test and introduced the concept of **mental age**, defined as the age at which children of average ability could perform specific tasks. If a child with a chronological age of four passed all the tests mastered by the sample of average five-year-old children, for example, then that four-year-old child was assigned a mental age of five.

**Mental age:** The age at which children of average ability can perform certain tasks.

A third revision of the test was prepared in 1911, but after Binet's death progress in intelligence testing shifted to the United States. Binet's work soon proved more popular in the United States than in France; large-scale intelligence testing efforts did not become widely accepted in France until the 1940s.

Binet's test was translated from French and presented to American psychologists in 1908 by Henry Goddard (1866–1957), who was the only undefeated head football coach at the University of Southern California (USC), a rare distinction for a psychologist

LEWIS TERMAN

**Intelligence quotient (IQ):** A number denoting a person's intelligence, determined by the following formula: mental age divided by chronological age, multiplied by 100.

(Benjamin, 2009b). Goddard then headed east and earned his Ph.D. from G. Stanley Hall at Clark University. He later worked at a school for children who had mental disabilities. Goddard called his translation of the intelligence test the *Binet-Simon Measuring Scale for Intelligence.* In his writings on intelligence testing he also introduced the word *moron,* derived from the Greek word for "slow."

In 1916 Lewis M. Terman, who had also studied with Hall, developed the version of the test that has since become the standard. Terman named it the *Stanford-Binet,* after the university with which he was affiliated, and adopted the concept of the **intelligence quotient (IQ).** The IQ measure—defined as the ratio between mental age and chronological age—had originally been developed by the German psychologist William Stern. The *Stanford-Binet* has undergone several revisions and continues to be widely used.

## World War I and Group Testing

On the day in 1917 that the United States entered World War I, a meeting of Titchener's Society of Experimental Psychologists was being held at Harvard University. The president of the APA, Robert Yerkes, urged the group to consider how psychology could aid the war effort. Titchener declined to participate, on the grounds that he was a British citizen. He actually picked up his chair and removed it, and himself, from the room in order to avoid being involved in any further talk of war. The more likely reason for Titchener's lack of enthusiasm is that he disliked the idea of applying psychology to practical problems, fearing that psychology would be trading "a science for a technology" (O'Donnell, 1979, p. 289).

As the American army mobilized, military leaders faced the problem of assessing the level of intelligence of great numbers of recruits, to classify them and assign them suitable tasks. The *Stanford-Binet* was an individual intelligence test and required a highly trained person to administer it properly. Obviously that test could not be used when so many people needed to be evaluated in a short time. The army needed a group test that was simple to administer.

With an army commission as a major, Yerkes assembled a staff of 40 psychologists to develop a group intelligence test. They examined a number of proposed tests, none of which was in general use, and selected as their basis the one prepared by Arthur S. Otis, who had studied with Terman. Otis's most important contribution to testing was the multiple-choice type of question. The Yerkes group then prepared the *Army Alpha* and *Army Beta.* (The *Beta* is a version for non-English-speaking and illiterate people; instead of oral or written directions, instructions are given by demonstration or pantomime.)

Work on the program proceeded slowly, and formal orders to actually begin testing the army recruits were not given until three months before the war ended. More than 1 million men were eventually tested, but by then the military no longer needed the information, which was fortunate because the results surprised the psychologists who had carried out the program. The data revealed that "far more Americans were illiterate than had been previously thought. One out of every four men who took the tests could not read or comprehend articles in a daily newspaper or even write letters home" (Murdoch, 2007, p. 86). Although the program had little direct effect on the war effort, it had a significant impact on the field of psychology. The publicity enhanced psychology's stature, and the army tests became prototypes for many that were devised later.

The psychologists' war work also spurred the development and application of group testing for personality characteristics. Previously, only limited attempts had been made to assess the human personality. At the end of the nineteenth century, the German psychiatrist Emil Kraepelin, once a student of Wundt's, had used what he called a "free association test," in which a patient responded to a stimulus word with the first word that came to mind (a technique originated by Galton). In 1910, Carl Jung developed a similar device, his word-association test, to determine personality complexes in his patients (see Chapter 14). Both of these approaches were individual personality tests. When the army expressed interest in separating out neurotic recruits, Robert Woodworth constructed the *Personal Data Sheet,* a self-report inventory on which respondents were instructed to check the nervous symptoms that applied to them. Like the *Army Alpha* and *Army Beta,* the *Personal Data Sheet* served as a prototype for future group tests.

Psychological testing won its own victory in the war—the success of public acceptance. Millions of employees, schoolchildren, and college applicants soon faced batteries of tests, the results of which would determine the course of their lives. In the early 1920s up to 4 million intelligence tests were being purchased every year, mostly for use in public schools. Terman's *Stanford-Binet* sold over a half million copies in 1923 alone. The public education system in the United States was reorganized around the concept of the intelligence quotient, and IQ scores became the most important criterion for student placement and advancement.

Eventually, many psychologists found gainful employment developing and applying psychological tests (Bottom, 2009). Some enterprising psychologists even hoped to use tests to identify potential baseball players. The great Babe Ruth agreed to be tested at Columbia University's psychology laboratory, where, in an effort to establish the characteristics that made him such an outstanding player, they measured his performance on tasks using sensory and motor skills. The tests were similar to those used by Galton and Cattell (Fuchs, 2009). The endeavor was unsuccessful, but as one historian noted:

> *The faith that psychology was a science capable of discovering the basis of extraordinary feats of hitting attests to the success of psychologists in establishing the public identity of the discipline and to the faith of the informed public in the ability of science to provide answers to their questions. (Fuchs, 1998, p. 153)*

An epidemic of testing swept the United States, but in the haste to answer the urgent call of business and education, it was inevitable that some poorly designed and inadequately researched tests would be promoted, leading to disappointing results. As a result, many organizations abandoned their use of psychological tests for a time.

## Ideas from Medicine and Engineering

To lend authority and scientific credibility to their fledgling enterprise, intelligence testers had adopted terminology from the older disciplines of medicine and engineering. Their purpose was to persuade people that psychology was just as legitimate, scientific, and essential as the more established sciences.

Psychologists described the people they tested not as subjects but as patients. Tests were said to be analogous to thermometers, which at that time were available only to physicians. No one who lacked proper training was permitted to use a thermometer, a claim also made for psychological tests. Tests were promoted as X-ray machines that enabled psychologists to see inside the mind and to dissect their patients' mental mechanisms. "The more [psychologists] sounded like doctors, the more willing the public was to accord them similar status" (Keiger, 1993, p. 49).

Metaphors from engineering also were cited. Schools were referred to as education factories, and tests as ways to measure a factory's products (the students' levels of intelligence). Society was likened to a bridge, and intelligence tests were the scientific tool preserving the strength of the bridge by detecting its weakest elements—its feebleminded citizens—who could then be removed from society and institutionalized.

## Racial Differences in Intelligence

The growth of the psychological testing movement became part of a social controversy that continues today. In 1912 Henry Goddard, who had translated the Binet test, visited Ellis Island in New York, the entry point for millions of European immigrants to the

HENRY GODDARD

United States. There was considerable public concern that the physicians at Ellis Island who were examining the new arrivals were "failing to prevent mentally retarded people from entering the country" (Richardson, 2003, p. 143). Goddard believed that the doctors were identifying no more than 10 percent of those people with mental retardation. He proposed that psychologists conduct the examinations instead by using his translation of the Binet intelligence test.

On his first visit to the Ellis Island processing facility Goddard selected a young man whom he thought looked mentally deficient and confirmed his diagnosis by administering the Binet test with the aid of an interpreter. Although the interpreter pointed out that he himself could not have answered the questions when he was a new arrival in the United States and that the test was unfair to people unfamiliar with the English language or American culture, Goddard disagreed (see Zenderland, 1998).

Later testing of immigrant populations (all of which had limited command of the English language that was used for the tests) revealed, according to Goddard's test results, that the majority—87 percent of Russians, 83 percent of Jews, 80 percent of Hungarians, and 79 percent of Italians—were feebleminded, with a mental age less than 12 (Cannato, 2009; Gould, 1981). This evidence from the tests was later used to support federal legislation restricting the immigration of racial and ethnic groups assumed to be inferior in intelligence.

The idea of racial differences in intelligence received additional support in 1921 when the results obtained from the World War I testing of the army recruits were made public. The data showed that blacks and immigrants from Mediterranean and Latin American countries had lower measured IQs than whites. Only northern European immigrants had IQs equal to those measured for whites. These findings raised questions among scientists, politicians, and journalists. How could any democratically elected government survive if its citizens were so stupid? Should groups with low IQs be allowed to vote? Should the government refuse entry to immigrants from low-IQ countries? How could the notion that people were created equal be meaningful?

Archives of the History of American Psychology/University of Akron

An immigrant's mental ability is being tested at Ellis Island. Three different examiners would administer the tests with the aid of an interpreter.

The concept of racial differences in intelligence had been advanced in the United States as early as the 1880s, and many calls had been made for quotas on immigration from Mediterranean and Latin American countries. The allegedly inferior intelligence of American blacks had also been widely accepted, even before the development of intelligence tests.

A vocal and articulate critic of this idea was Horace Mann Bond (1904–1972), an African-American scholar and president of Lincoln University in Pennsylvania. Bond, who earned a doctoral degree in education from the University of Chicago, published a number of books and articles in which he argued that any recorded differences in the IQ scores between blacks and whites were attributable to environmental rather than inherited factors. His research showed that blacks from northern states scored higher on intelligence tests than whites from southern states, a finding that severely damaged the charge that blacks were genetically inferior (Jackson, 2004).

Many psychologists had responded to this issue by charging that the tests were biased, but in time the controversy faded. It was revived in 1994 with the publication of *The Bell Curve* (Herrnstein & Murray, 1994), a book arguing that, based on intelligence test scores, blacks are inferior in intelligence to whites. A preponderance of evidence now shows that the more soundly researched intelligence tests are not culturally biased in any significant way (Rowe, Vazsonyi, & Flannery, 1994; Suzuki & Valencia, 1997). Further, 52 mainstream testing experts endorsed that conclusion as follows: "Intelligence tests are not culturally biased against American blacks or other native-born, English speaking peoples in the U.S. Rather, IQ scores predict equally accurately for all such Americans, regardless of race and social class" (Gottfredson, 1997, p. 14).

A report prepared by the APA's Board of Scientific Affairs agreed that today's cognitive ability tests did not seem to discriminate against minority groups but reflected, in quantitative terms, the discrimination that had been created by society over time (Neisser et al., 1996).

## Contributions of Women to the Testing Movement

We have seen that for much of psychology's history, women were effectively prohibited from seeking university positions. For that reason, many female psychologists found employment in the applied fields, particularly the helping professions such as clinical and counseling psychology, child guidance, and school psychology. Women have made significant contributions in those areas, notably in the development and application of psychological tests.

Florence L. Goodenough received her Ph.D. from Stanford University in 1924. She developed the *Draw-A-Man Test* (now the *Goodenough-Harris Drawing Test*), a widely used nonverbal intelligence test for children. A pioneer in test construction, Goodenough worked for more than 20 years at the Institute of Child Development at the University of Minnesota. She published a detailed review of the psychological testing movement (Goodenough, 1949) and wrote several works on child psychology.

Maude Merrill James, director of a psychological clinic for children in California, wrote with Lewis Terman the 1937 revision of the *Stanford-Binet Intelligence Test,* which became widely known as the Terman-Merrill test. Thelma Gwinn Thurstone (a 1927 Ph.D. from the University of Chicago) married psychologist L. L. Thurstone and, like many women who work with their husbands, found her contributions overlooked and uncredited. She helped develop the *Primary Mental Abilities* test battery, a group intelligence test, and was professor of education at the University of North Carolina and director of the psychometric laboratory. Her husband described her as a "genius in test construction" (Thurstone, 1952, p. 317).

Psyche Cattell (1893–1989) was the daughter of James McKeen Cattell, who refused to support her college education because he thought she was not smart enough.

Nevertheless, she earned her doctoral degree in education from Harvard University in 1927. Her contributions to the testing movement included extending the age range of the *Stanford-Binet* downward with the *Cattell Infant Intelligence Scale*. Her test could be used with infants as young as three months old.

The long career of Anne Anastasi (1908–2001) at Fordham University established her as an authority on psychological testing. She was successful from an early age, entering college at 15 and earning her doctoral degree at 21. She decided to become a psychologist because of the influence of one of her professors, Harry Hollingworth. Anastasi wrote more than 150 articles and books, including a popular textbook on psychological testing (Anastasi, 1988, 1993). In 1971, she served as APA president and received many professional honors, including the National Medal of Science. One survey named Anastasi the most prominent female psychologist in the English-speaking world (Gavin, 1987).

A year after Anastasi married, at the age of 25, she was diagnosed with cervical cancer. The treatment left her unable to bear children, yet she viewed the cancer as "one of the principle reasons for her success. Women of her generation frequently had to choose between motherhood and a career. That choice was taken from her, and she was free to concentrate on her career without conflict or guilt" (Hogan, 2003, p. 267).

Although some women became successful in areas such as testing, working in applied psychology put them at a professional disadvantage. Jobs in nonacademic institutions rarely provide the time, financial support, or graduate-student assistance required to conduct research and write scholarly articles, which are the primary vehicles for professional visibility. In an applied setting such as a business agency or a clinic, one's contributions often go unrecognized beyond the confines of that organization.

Thus, the tremendous growth of applied psychology in the United States—the legacy of the functionalist school of psychology—offered employment opportunities for women, but it also meant that they remained largely removed from mainstream academic psychology, where the theories, research, and schools of thought were being developed.

Many academic psychologists held a negative view of applied work, considering it menial and inferior. Applied areas such as counseling were belittled as "women's work." Published histories of psychology tended to undervalue applied psychology and the contributions of the many women pioneers who worked in hospitals, clinics, businesses, research institutes, and military and government agencies. It is interesting to note that no woman was elected president of the American Association for Applied Psychology, despite the fact that by 1941 one-third of its members were women (Rossiter, 1982). Also by that time, approximately half of all psychology jobs in educational and clinical organizations were held by women (Gilgen, Gilgen, Koltsova, & Oleinik, 1997).

## The Clinical Psychology Movement

While Cattell was changing forever the nature of American psychology by applying it to the measurement of mental abilities, a student of Cattell and Wundt was applying psychology to the assessment and treatment of abnormal behavior. Just 17 years after Wundt defined and founded the new science of psychology, we have yet another of his former students using psychology in a practical manner inconsistent with Wundt's intentions.

## Lightner Witmer (1867–1956)

Lightner Witmer taught psychology at the University of Pennsylvania, filling that position when Cattell left for Columbia University. Described as contentious, antisocial, and conceited (Landy, 1992), Witmer began the field he called clinical psychology. In 1896 he opened the world's first psychology clinic.

LIGHTNER WITMER

The kind of psychology Witmer practiced in his clinic was not clinical psychology as we know it today. Witmer did not practice psychotherapy, a technique he "detested" and knew little about (Taylor, 2000, p. 1029). Instead, he was interested in assessing and treating learning and behavioral problems in schoolchildren, an applied specialty area now called school psychology. Although Witmer was instrumental in developing clinical psychology and used the term freely, the field has become much broader than he ever envisioned.

Witmer offered the first college course on clinical psychology and started the first journal, *Psychological Clinic,* which he edited for 29 years. He was one of those pioneers of the functionalist approach to psychology who believed that the new science should be used to help people solve problems rather than to study the contents of their minds.

## Witmer's Life

Born in 1867 in Philadelphia, Witmer graduated from the University of Pennsylvania in 1884 and taught history and English at a Philadelphia private school before returning to the university for law courses. He apparently had no thought of a career in psychology at the time but changed his mind for a practical reason. He wanted a paid assistantship, and one of the few available was with Cattell in the psychology department. Here again we see the influence of economic forces. Witmer's biographer noted:

> Witmer's actual entry into psychology was occasioned in part by the very down-to-earth need for the additional income that would be provided by an assistantship. (McReynolds, 1997, p. 34)

Witmer began research studies on individual differences in reaction time and expected to earn his Ph.D. from Penn, but Cattell had other plans. He thought so highly of Witmer that he chose him as his successor. This was a remarkable opportunity for the young man, but Cattell placed one condition on the appointment: Witmer would have to go to Leipzig to earn his doctorate from Wundt. Because the prestige of a German Ph.D. was still paramount in the 1880s, Witmer agreed to go.

He studied with Wundt and with Külpe; Titchener was one of his classmates. Witmer was not impressed with Wundt's research methods, calling them slovenly. He described how Wundt once made Titchener repeat an observation "because the results obtained by Titchener were not such as he, Wundt, had anticipated" (quoted in O'Donnell, 1985, p. 35). Witmer participated as a subject in Wundt's reaction time studies, but his service did not last long because his reaction times "were the quickest ever recorded in Wundt's laboratory. This led to Wundt claiming that Witmer was not doing the task as a proper introspectionist should." Wundt refused to use Witmer's data; Witmer quickly came to doubt the usefulness of the introspective method (Benjafield, 2010, p. 56).

Witmer later said he got nothing out of his Leipzig experience but his degree. Wundt refused to allow Witmer to continue the reaction-time work he had begun with Cattell and restricted Witmer's studies to introspective research on the elements of consciousness.

Nevertheless, Witmer did receive his degree, and he returned to his new position at the University of Pennsylvania in the summer of 1892, the same year Titchener earned his degree and went to Cornell University. This also was the year another of Wundt's students, Hugo Münsterberg, was brought to Harvard University by William James, and the year Hall started the APA with Witmer as one of the charter members. Thus we see that the functional, applied spirit had begun to take hold of American psychology.

For two years Witmer worked as an experimental psychologist, conducting research and presenting papers on individual differences and on the psychology of pain. At the same time, he was searching for an opportunity to apply psychology to abnormal behavior. The chance came in March 1896, resulting from an incident that originated in the economic circumstances of the time: the growth in funding for public education.

Many state boards of education were establishing college-level departments of pedagogy to offer instruction in the principles and methods of teaching. Psychologists were being asked to offer courses to education majors and to public school teachers working for advanced degrees. Psychologists were urged to shift the focus of their laboratory research from experimental work to finding ways to train students to become educational psychologists. Psychology departments profited handsomely from this sudden influx of students because then, as now, departmental budgets were contingent on enrollments.

Witmer taught some of the courses established for public school teachers at the University of Pennsylvania. In 1896 one of these teachers, Margaret Maguire, consulted Witmer about a problem with a 14-year-old student who was having difficulty learning to spell, although he was progressing in some other subjects. Could psychology help? Witmer wrote, "It appeared to me that if psychology was worth anything to me or to others, it should be able to assist the efforts of a teacher in a retarded case of this kind" (quoted in McReynolds, 1997, p. 76).

Witmer organized a makeshift clinic and thus embarked on his lifelong work. Within a few months, Witmer was preparing courses on methods for treating mentally defective, blind, and disturbed children. He published an article in the journal *Pediatrics* titled "Practical Work in Psychology," recommending that psychology be applied to practical affairs:

> *The practical side of psychology deserves serious attention from professional psychologists. The practice of psychology may become as well defined a pursuit of a trained professional class as is the practice of medicine.* (quoted in McReynolds, 1997, p. 78)

He presented a paper on the topic at the annual APA meeting, using the term "clinical psychology" for the first time. In 1907 he founded the journal *Psychological Clinic*, the first and for many years the only journal in the field. In the first issue Witmer proposed the new profession of clinical psychology. The following year he established a boarding school for retarded and disturbed children, and in 1909 he expanded his university clinic as a separate administrative unit.

Witmer remained at the University of Pennsylvania, teaching, promoting, and practicing his clinical psychology. He retired from the university in 1937 and died in 1956 at the age of 89, the last of the small group of psychologists who had met in G. Stanley Hall's study in 1892 to found the APA.

## Clinics for Child Evaluation

As the world's first clinical psychologist, Witmer had no examples or precedents for his actions, so he developed diagnostic and treatment approaches as needed. "The absence of any principles to guide me made it necessary to apply myself directly to the study of these children, working out my methods as I went along" (Witmer, 1907/1996, p. 249).

Children who had been referred to Witmer's clinic showed a broad range of problems, some of which he identified as hyperactivity, learning disabilities, and poor speech and motor development. As his experience and confidence grew, he developed standard programs of assessment and treatment. In time he added physicians, social workers, and psychologists to the clinic's staff.

Witmer recognized that emotional and cognitive functioning could be affected by physical problems, so he had physicians examine the children to determine if malnutrition or visual and hearing deficits were contributing to a child's difficulties. The patients were then tested and interviewed by the psychologists, and social workers prepared case histories on their family background.

Initially Witmer believed genetic factors were largely responsible for behavioral and cognitive disturbances, but he later realized that environmental factors were more important. He foresaw the need to provide a variety of sensory experiences early in a child's life, anticipating a Head Start type of enrichment and intervention program. He believed in involving families and schools in the treatment of his patients, arguing that if home and school conditions were improved, a child's behavior might change for the better.

## Comment

Many psychologists soon followed Witmer's example. By 1914 almost 20 psychology clinics were operating in the United States, the majority patterned on Witmer's clinic. In addition, the students he trained spread his approach and taught new generations of students about clinical work. Witmer's influence spread to the area of special education. His student Morris Viteles extended Witmer's work by establishing a vocational guidance clinic, the first such facility in the United States. Other followers applied Witmer's clinical approach to adult patients.

# The Profession of Clinical Psychology

In addition to Witmer's efforts to apply psychology to the assessment and treatment of abnormal behavior, two books provided an impetus to the field. Clifford Beers, a former mental patient, wrote *A Mind That Found Itself* (1908), which became immensely popular and focused public attention on the need to deal humanely with mentally ill people. Hugo Münsterberg's *Psychotherapy* (1909), also widely read, described techniques for treating a variety of mental disorders. Münsterberg promoted clinical psychology by describing specific ways in which disturbed persons could be helped.

The first child guidance clinic was established in 1909 by a Chicago psychiatrist, William Healey. More such clinics followed. Their purpose was to treat childhood disorders early so that the problems would not develop into more serious disturbances in adulthood. These clinics used Witmer's team approach, in which physicians, psychologists, psychiatrists, and social workers combined to evaluate all aspects of a patient's problem.

The ideas of Sigmund Freud were crucial to the advancement of clinical psychology and moved the field far beyond its origins in Witmer's clinic. Freudian psychoanalysis both fascinated and outraged segments of the psychology establishment and the American public. Freud's ideas provided clinical psychologists with their initial psychological techniques of therapy.

Nevertheless, clinical psychology advanced slowly as a profession. As late as 1918, nine years after Freud's visit to the United States, there were still no graduate programs in clinical psychology. Even by 1940, clinical psychology remained only a minor part of psychology. Few treatment facilities existed for disturbed adults and, consequently, there were few job opportunities for clinical psychologists. Training programs for new clinical psychologists were limited. Job duties rarely extended beyond administering tests.

However, the situation changed when the United States entered World War II in 1941. Large numbers of draftees "showed up at induction centers with severe anxieties, depression, antisocial demeanors, uncontrolled anger, and generally unstable psychic presentations. They were bed-wetters, dropouts, and chronic misfits" (Engel, 2008, pp. 43-44). By the time the war ended in 1945, almost 2 million men had been rejected for military service for psychiatric reasons. Of those accepted, 1 million had to be hospitalized for treatment of mental disorders during their time on active duty, and another 500,000 were discharged for the same reason. The military leadership quickly concluded that a lot of men needed help and there were not enough psychologists or mental health counselors to do the job. That stimulus helped make clinical psychology the dynamic applied specialty area it has become. The army established training programs for hundreds of clinical psychologists so they could treat the emotional disturbances of military personnel.

After the war the need for clinical psychologists was even greater. The Veterans Administration (the VA, now the Department of Veterans Affairs) found itself responsible for more than 40,000 veterans diagnosed with psychiatric problems. More than 3 million others needed vocational and personal counseling to help them return comfortably to civilian life. Some 315,000 veterans expected assistance in adjusting to physical disabilities resulting from war wounds. The demand for mental health professionals was staggering and far exceeded the supply.

To help meet these needs, the VA funded university-level graduate programs and paid tuition for graduate students willing to work at VA hospitals and clinics. One outcome of these programs was that clinical psychologists would be dealing with a different type of patient. Prior to the war, most of their work had been with children who had delinquency and adjustment problems, but the veterans' postwar needs brought adult patients with more severe emotional problems. The Department of Veterans Affairs remains the largest employer of psychologists in the United States.

Today, clinical psychologists are employed in mental health centers, schools, businesses, and private practices. Clinical psychology is the largest of the applied specialty areas, with more than one-third of all graduate students enrolled in clinical programs.

# The Industrial-Organizational Psychology Movement

Another student of Wundt's at Leipzig, Walter Dill Scott, left the world of pure introspective psychology to apply the new science to advertising and business. Scott dedicated much of his adult life to make the marketplace and the workplace more efficient and to determine how business leaders could motivate employees and consumers.

# Walter Dill Scott (1869–1955)

Scott's work reflects the concern of the functionalist school of psychology with practical issues. One historian of psychology noted:

*Upon returning from Wundt's Leipzig to turn-of-the-century Chicago, Scott's publications shifted from Germanic theorizing to American usefulness. Instead of explaining motives and impulses in general, Scott described how to influence people, including consumers, lecture audiences, and workers. (Von Mayrhauser, 1989, p. 61)*

Scott compiled an impressive list of firsts. He was the first person to apply psychology to personnel selection, management, and advertising. He was the author of the first book in the field and the first to hold the title of professor of applied psychology. In addition, he was the founder of the first psychological consulting company, and the first psychologist to receive the Distinguished Service Medal from the U.S. Army.

### Scott's Life

Born on a farm near the town of Normal, Illinois, the young Scott was struck by the idea of workplace efficiency while he was plowing a field. Because his father was often ill, the 12-year-old boy bore much of the responsibility for the operation of the small family farm. One day he paused at the end of a plowed furrow to rest his two horses. Gazing in the distance at the campus buildings of Illinois State Normal University, he suddenly realized that if he were ever going to achieve anything in this world, he would have to stop wasting time. Here he was losing 10 minutes out of every hour's plowing to rest the horses! That added up to about an hour and a half every day, time he could use for studying. Scott decided to carry books with him and to spend every spare moment reading.

To earn his college tuition, he picked and canned blackberries, salvaged scrap metal to sell, and took on odd jobs. He saved some of the money and spent the rest on books. At age 19 he enrolled at Illinois State Normal University to begin his long journey away

WALTER DILL SCOTT

from the farm. Two years later he won a scholarship to Northwestern University in Evanston, Illinois, and took tutoring jobs to make extra money. He played varsity football and met Anna Marcy Miller, the woman he would marry.

He also chose his career; he decided to become a missionary to China, although it meant three more years of study. By the time Scott graduated from a Chicago theological seminary, prepared to depart for China, there were no vacancies for missionaries—China was full. It was then that his thoughts turned to psychology. He had taken a psychology course and liked it and had read a magazine article about Wundt's Leipzig laboratory. With his scholarships, tutoring, and frugal lifestyle, Scott had saved several thousand dollars, enough to pay for the passage to Germany and to get married.

On July 21, 1898, Scott and his bride departed. While he studied with Wundt, Anna Miller Scott worked on her Ph.D. in literature at the University of Halle, 20 miles away. Often they saw each other only on weekends. Both received doctoral degrees two years later. Scott joined the faculty of Northwestern University as instructor of psychology and pedagogy, showing he was already influenced by the trend toward applying psychology to problems in education.

A few years later his interests changed when an advertising executive asked him to attempt to apply psychology to make advertisements more effective. The idea intrigued him. In keeping with the spirit of American functionalism, Scott's path continued to diverge from Wundtian psychology as he found more ways to use psychology to deal with real-world concerns.

Scott wrote *The Theory and Practice of Advertising* (1903), the first book on the topic, and followed it with other books and magazine articles. His expertise, reputation, and contacts in the business community broadened quickly. He also directed his attention to problems of personnel selection and management. In 1905 he was promoted to professor, and in 1909 became professor of advertising at Northwestern's school of commerce. In 1916 he was appointed professor of applied psychology and director of the bureau of salesmanship research at Pittsburgh's Carnegie Technical University.

When the United States entered World War I in 1917, Scott offered his skills to the army to help select military personnel. At first Scott and his proposals were not well received, as not everyone was convinced of psychology's practical value. The army general with whom Scott dealt was outraged and voiced his suspicions of professors. "He said it was his function to see that college professors did not get in the way of progress, that we were at war with Germany and that we had no time to fool with experiments" (Scott, quoted in Von Mayrhauser, 1989, p. 65). Scott calmed the irate man, took him to lunch, and persuaded him of the value of his selection techniques. Apparently Scott proved his point; the army later awarded him its Distinguished Service Medal.

After the war, Scott formed his own company (called, imaginatively, The Scott Company) to provide consulting services to corporations that sought assistance with problems of personnel selection and worker efficiency. He also served as president of Northwestern University from 1920 to 1939. The university's Scott Hall is named for both Walter Dill Scott and Anna Miller Scott.

## Advertising and Human Suggestibility

The imprint of Scott's training in Wundt's physiologically oriented experimental psychology and his attempt to extend it into the realm of the practical are evident in his writings on advertising. For example, he noted that the human sense organs were the

> *… windows of the soul. The more sensations we receive from an object, the better we know it. The function of the nervous system is to make us aware of the sights, sounds, feelings, tastes, et cetera, of the objects in our environment.*

*Advertisements are sometimes spoken of as the nervous system of the business world. The advertisement of musical instruments which contains nothing to awaken images of sounds is a defective advertisement. As our nervous system is arranged to give us all the possible sensations from every object, so the advertisement which is comparable to the nervous system must awaken in the reader as many different kinds of images as the object itself can excite. (quoted in Jacobson, 1951, p. 75)*

Scott argued that because consumers often do not act rationally, they can be easily influenced. He cited emotion, sympathy, and sentimentality as factors that heighten consumer suggestibility. He also believed, as was common at the time, that women were more persuadable than were men. Applying his law of suggestibility, he recommended that companies use direct commands—such as *Use Pears Soap*—to sell products. He promoted the use of return coupons because they required consumers to take direct action, such as tearing the coupon out of the newspaper, filling in their name and address, and mailing it to the company to receive a free sample. These techniques were eagerly adopted by advertisers and by 1910 were widely used.

## Employee Selection

For selecting the best employees, especially among salespeople, business executives, and military personnel, Scott devised rating scales and group tests to measure the characteristics of people who were already successful in those occupations.

Like Witmer in clinical psychology, Scott had no prior work on which to base his approach. He questioned army officers and business managers, asking them to rank their subordinates on appearance, demeanor, sincerity, productivity, character, and value to the organization. He then ranked job applicants on the qualities found to be necessary for effective job performance, a procedure similar to that in use today.

Scott developed psychological tests to measure intelligence and other abilities, but instead of assessing individual applicants he constructed tests to administer to groups. When large numbers of candidates must be evaluated within a short period of time, it is more efficient and less expensive to test groups.

Scott's tests differed from those being developed by Cattell and other applied psychologists. Scott was not only measuring general intelligence but in addition was interested in determining how a person used his or her intelligence. In other words, he wanted to understand how people processed information and how intelligence operated in the everyday world. Scott defined intelligence not in terms of specific cognitive abilities but in practical terms such as judgment, quickness, and accuracy. The latter were the characteristics needed to perform well on a job. He compared applicants' test scores with the scores of successful employees and was unconcerned with what those test scores might signify about mental elements.

## Comment

Scott, like Witmer, received only passing attention in the history of psychology for many years. There are several reasons for this relative neglect. Like most applied psychologists, Scott formulated no theories, founded no school of thought, and trained no loyal core of students to continue his work. He conducted little experimental research and published rarely in the mainstream journals. His work for private corporations and for the military was strictly problem oriented. Many academic psychologists, particularly those in tenured positions with major universities and well-funded laboratories, discounted the work of applied psychologists, believing it contributed little to the advancement of psychology as a science.

Scott and other applied psychologists disputed this notion. They found no conflict between applying psychology and advancing it as a science. Applied psychologists argued that bringing psychology to the public's attention demonstrated its worth, which in turn increased the recognition of psychological research in the academic laboratories. Thus, the pioneers of applied psychology reflected the American functionalist spirit and the goal of making psychology useful.

## The Impact of the World Wars

World War I brought about a monumental increase in the scope, popularity, and growth of industrial-organizational psychology. We noted that Scott volunteered his services to the U.S. Army and developed a rating scale for selecting army captains based on his tests for rating business leaders. By the end of the war, he had evaluated the job qualifications of 3 million soldiers, and his work provided another highly publicized example of psychology's practical worth. After the war, business, industry, and government clamored for the services of industrial psychologists to reorganize their personnel procedures and to prepare psychological tests to help select the best employees.

World War II brought even more psychologists into war work for testing, screening, and classifying recruits. Also, by then the weapons of war (such as high-speed aircraft) had become increasingly complex, requiring more highly skilled people to operate them. The need to identify those military personnel who possessed the ability to learn the required skills led psychologists to refine their selection and training procedures. These necessities of war also spawned a new specialty within industrial psychology variously called engineering psychology, human engineering, human factors engineering, or ergonomics.

Engineering psychologists work closely with weapons systems engineers to supply information about human capacities and limitations. Their work directly influences the design of military equipment to make it more compatible with the abilities of the people who use it. Engineering psychologists today work not only on military hardware but also on consumer products such as computer keyboards and the display of information on computer monitors, office furniture, home appliances, and automobile dashboard displays.

## The Hawthorne Studies and Organizational Issues

The primary focus of industrial psychologists during the 1920s was the selection and placement of job applicants—matching the right person with the right job. In 1927, the scope of the field broadened considerably with an innovative research program conducted by the Western Electric Company at its Hawthorne plant in Illinois (Roethlisberger & Dickson, 1939). These studies extended the field beyond selection and placement to more complex problems of human relations, motivation, and morale.

The research began as a straightforward investigation of the effects of the physical work environment—such as conditions of lighting and temperature—on the efficiency of the employees. The results astonished the psychologists and the plant managers. They found that social and psychological aspects of the workplace were much more important than the physical conditions.

For example, researchers conducted

> *... 20,000 interviews of workers and found that it was not the substance of the interviews but the very fact of being interviewed (i.e., being given attention, scrutinized, surveyed, watched, listened to) that defused their griping and made them more docile and "better adjusted." (Lemov, 2005, p. 65)*

In other words, just the fact of being questioned or observed on the job as part of a research program persuaded many workers that management cared, that their boss was truly interested in them as individuals and not merely as interchangeable cogs in the great industrial machine.

Studies conducted during the 1920s and 1930s at the Hawthorne, Illinois, plant of the Western Electric Company led applied psychologists into the complex areas of human relations, leadership styles, and employee motivation and morale.

The Hawthorne studies led psychologists to explore the social-psychological work climate, including the behavior of leaders, informal work groups, employee attitudes, communication patterns between workers and managers, and other factors capable of influencing motivation, productivity, and satisfaction. Business leaders soon came to recognize and accept the impact of these forces on job performance. Psychologists today study different types of organizations, their communication and organizational styles, and their formal and informal social structures. Recognizing the importance of organizational variables, the APA's Division of Industrial Psychology was renamed the Society for Industrial and Organizational Psychology.

## Contributions of Women to Industrial-Organizational Psychology

Industrial-organizational psychology as a profession historically has provided career opportunities for women. The first person to receive a Ph.D. in the field was Lillian Moller Gilbreth (1878–1972), who earned her degree in 1915 from Brown University. With her husband, Frank Gilbreth, she promoted time-and-motion analysis as a technique to improve efficiency in job performance. However, many business leaders of the day refused to accept female psychologists in their offices or factories.

When Lillian and Frank wrote a book on industrial efficiency, the publisher refused to put her name on the cover, explaining that a woman's name would detract from the book's credibility. Her own book about the psychology of management was published only when she agreed to be named L. M. Gilbreth instead of Lillian Gilbreth; it was said that businessmen would never buy it if a woman's name was on it. She overcame these and other barriers to have a long, successful career (Kelly & Kelly, 1990; Lancaster, 2004). Her likeness even appeared on a U.S. postage stamp.

And Lillian Gilbreth did it all while raising 12 children. "Between 1905 and 1922, Lillian gave birth 13 times, at 15-month intervals; one child died at the age of 5" (Lepore, 2009, p. 88). She worked well into her nineties and was responsible for major changes in the way in which work is managed and the efficiency with which it is carried out both in organizations and in the home. For example, open your refrigerator and look at the shelves inside the door. That was Lillian Gilbreth's idea. As a result, refrigerators have a greater capacity and a more efficient design. For more about Lillian Gilbreth, go to www. webster.edu~woolflm/gilbreth2.html. Today, more than half of all Ph.D. candidates in industrial-organizational psychology are women.

# Hugo Münsterberg (1863–1916)

HUGO MÜNSTERBERG

Hugo Münsterberg, the stereotypical German professor, for a time was a phenomenal success in American psychology and much in the public eye. He wrote hundreds of popular magazine articles and almost two dozen books in such applied areas as clinical, industrial, and forensic psychology. He was a frequent visitor to the White House as the guest of presidents Theodore Roosevelt and William Howard Taft. Münsterberg was a powerful consultant to business and government leaders and counted among his acquaintances the rich and famous, including Germany's Kaiser Wilhelm, steel magnate Andrew Carnegie, philosopher Bertrand Russell, and assorted movie stars and intellectuals.

For a time Münsterberg was an honored professor at Harvard University. He was elected president of both the APA and the American Philosophical Association. A founder of applied psychology in the United States and Europe, he was also one of only two psychologists ever accused of being a spy.

Münsterberg has been described as a "prolific propagandizer for applied psychology" (O'Donnell, 1985, p. 225). According to his biographer, Münsterberg was also a successful publicist, "blessed with an uncanny flair for the sensational. [His] life can be read as a series of promotions—of himself, his science, and his [German] fatherland" (Hale, 1980, p. 3).

He was extremely self-centered and had a strong sense of self-importance. The philosopher George Santayana described him as "pompous" and "egotistical beyond endurance." Münsterberg once told Santayana, during a transatlantic crossing, that it was "surprising how many people are sailing on this ship simply because I am here" (quoted in Benjamin, 2006b, p. 419).

Toward the end of his life Münsterberg became a figure of scorn and ridicule, the subject of newspaper cartoons and caricatures, an embarrassment to the university he had served for many years, and "one of the most hated individuals in America" (Benjamin, 2000b, p. 113). When he died in 1916, there were few eulogies for the man who had once been a giant in American psychology.

## Münsterberg's Life

In 1882, at the age of 19, Münsterberg left his birthplace in Danzig, Germany (now Gdansk, Poland), and traveled to Leipzig, intending to study medicine at the university. When he took a psychology course with Wilhelm Wundt, however, his career plans changed. The new science excited him, promising opportunities that medical research and practice did not. He earned his Ph.D. from Wundt in 1885 and an M.D. from the University of Heidelberg two years later, expecting that both degrees would equip him better for a career in academic research. He accepted a teaching position at the University of Freiburg and set up a laboratory in his home, at his own expense, because the university lacked suitable facilities.

Münsterberg wrote articles about his experimental work in psychophysics, which Wundt criticized because the research dealt with the mind's cognitive contents rather than feeling states. But Münsterberg's work attracted followers, and soon students from throughout Europe were flocking to his laboratory. He seemed well on his way to securing a major professorship and a reputation as a respected scholar.

William James enticed Münsterberg from this career path in 1892, offering him the chance to become the highly paid director of Harvard's psychology laboratory. James resorted to flattery, writing to Münsterberg that Harvard was America's greatest university and needed a genius to run its laboratory. Münsterberg preferred to stay in Germany, but his ambition led him to accept James's offer.

The transition from Germany to the United States and from pure experimental psychology to applied psychology was difficult. At first Münsterberg disapproved of the spread of applied psychology specialties. In an article in the American magazine *Atlantic Monthly* (1898), he attacked colleagues who were applying psychological knowledge to education or who used questionnaires and other mental measurement techniques (Benjamin, 2006b). In so doing, he alienated many leading psychologists, including Cattell. He also criticized those American psychologists who wrote for the general public, gave paid lectures to business leaders, and offered their services for a fee. However, it was not long before Münsterberg was doing the same.

After a decade at Harvard, perhaps realizing that no university in Germany was ever going to offer him a professorship, he wrote his first book in English. *American Traits* (1902) was a psychological, social, and cultural analysis of American society. A rapid and gifted writer, Münsterberg was able to dictate to a secretary a 400-page book in less than a month. James remarked that Münsterberg's brain never seemed to get tired.

The enthusiastic response to Münsterberg's book encouraged him to direct subsequent writings to the general public rather than to colleagues, and soon his work was a staple in popular magazines instead of psychology journals. He abandoned psychophysical research on the mind's contents to deal with everyday problems that psychologists could solve. His articles covered courtroom trials and the criminal justice system, advertising for consumer products, vocational counseling, mental health and psychotherapy, education, issues in business and industry, and even the psychology of motion pictures. He prepared correspondence courses on learning and business and made films about mental tests that were shown in movie theaters nationwide.

Münsterberg never shied from controversy. During a sensational murder trial, he administered almost 100 mental tests to the confessed killer of 18 people who had accused a labor union leader of paying for the murders. On the basis of the test results, Münsterberg announced, even before the jury reached its verdict in the labor leader's trial, that the murderer's confession implicating the labor leader was true. When the jury acquitted the labor leader, the damage to Münsterberg's credibility was enormous; a newspaper dubbed him Professor Monster-work.

In 1908, Münsterberg became involved with Prohibition, the movement to ban the sale of alcoholic beverages. He argued against Prohibition, citing his expertise as a psychologist, and expressed the position that alcoholic beverages in moderation could be beneficial. German-American beer brewers, including Adolphus Busch and Gustave Pabst, were delighted to have Münsterberg's support and made sizable financial contributions to Münsterberg's efforts to bolster Germany's image in the United States. In an unfortunate and suspicious bit of timing, Busch donated $50,000 for Münsterberg's proposed Germanic Museum only a few weeks after Münsterberg published an article denouncing Prohibition. The coincidence received considerable attention in the news media.

Münsterberg's beliefs about women were also controversial. He was supportive of the education of several female graduate students at Harvard, including Mary Whiton Calkins (see Chapter 7), but in general he thought that graduate work was too demanding for women. He declared that women should not be trained for careers because that took them away from the home. Nor should women teach in the public schools because they were poor role models for boys. And women should not be allowed to serve on juries because they were incapable of rational deliberation; this last remark generated international newspaper headlines.

Harvard's president as well as many of Münsterberg's colleagues were not pleased with his sensational comments to the press on controversial issues, nor did they approve of his interest in applied psychology. Strained relations reached the breaking point over Münsterberg's vocal defense of his German homeland during World War I. American public opinion was decidedly anti-German. Germany was the aggressor in a war that had claimed millions of lives, but Münsterberg, still a German citizen, openly defended Germany.

Newspapers reported that Münsterberg was a secret agent, a spy, or a high-ranking German military officer, and clamored for his resignation from Harvard. A London newspaper called him one of the Kaiser's American agents. Neighbors suspected that the pigeons his daughter fed in the backyard of their house were carrying messages to other spies. A Harvard alumnus offered $10 million if the university would fire Münsterberg (Spillmann & Spillmann, 1993).

Colleagues snubbed him, and he received death threats in the mail. The ostracism and virulent public attacks broke his spirit. On December 16, 1916, the newspapers published speculations about peace talks in Europe. "By spring we shall have peace," he told his wife (Münsterberg, 1922, p. 302). He set off on foot through the deep snow to teach his morning class and was exhausted by the time he reached the lecture hall. Münsterberg entered the classroom and had lectured "for about a half hour when he appeared to hesitate and a moment later stretched his right hand toward the desk as though to steady himself" (*New York City Evening Mail,* December 16, 1916).[1] He fell to the floor without saying another word and died instantly of a massive stroke.

## Forensic Psychology and Eyewitness Testimony

Forensic psychology deals with psychology and the law. Münsterberg wrote magazine articles on such topics as crime prevention, using hypnosis to question suspects and administering mental tests to detect guilty persons and the questionable trustworthiness of eyewitness testimony. He was particularly interested in the latter—the fallibility of human perception in viewing a criminal event and subsequently describing it.

He conducted research on simulated crimes in which witnesses were asked immediately after seeing the crime to describe what had occurred. The subjects disagreed on the details, even though the scene was still fresh in their memory. Münsterberg asked how accurate such testimony could be in a courtroom when the event under discussion would have taken place many months earlier.

In 1908 he published *On the Witness Stand,* which described the psychological factors that can affect a trial's outcome. These include false confessions, the power of suggestion in the cross-examination of witnesses, and the use of physiological measurements (heart rate, blood pressure, and skin resistance) to detect heightened emotional states in suspects and defendants. The book was reprinted as recently as 1976, almost 70 years after its publication, because of a resurgence of interest in the issues he had raised (see Loftus, 1979; Loftus & Monahan, 1980). The American Psychology-Law Society was established at that time as a division of the APA to promote basic and applied research on forensic psychology.

## Psychotherapy

Münsterberg's 1909 book, *Psychotherapy,* focused on a different applied area. He treated patients in his laboratory rather than in a clinic, and he never charged a fee. He insisted that his position conveyed a certain authority that gave him the right to make direct suggestions to patients about how they could be cured. He believed mental illness was really a behavioral maladjustment problem, not something attributable to underlying unconscious conflicts, as Sigmund Freud claimed. "There is no subconscious," Münsterberg announced (quoted in Landy, 1992, p. 792). When Freud visited Clark University in 1909,

---

[1]We are grateful to Dr. Ludy T. Benjamin, Jr., for supplying this information based on his research on the Münsterberg papers in the Boston Public Library.

at the invitation of G. Stanley Hall, Münsterberg left the country to avoid a confrontation. He returned only after Freud went back to Europe.

Although Münsterberg's book on psychotherapy did much to bring the field of clinical psychology to public attention, it was not well received by Lightner Witmer, who had opened his clinic at the University of Pennsylvania several years before. Witmer had never achieved, nor had he desired, the popular acclaim Münsterberg thrived on. In an article in his journal, *Psychological Clinic,* Witmer complained that Münsterberg had "cheapened" the profession by hawking claims of cures in the marketplace. He referred to Münsterberg as little better than a faith healer because of the "jaunty way in which the professor of psychology at [Harvard] goes about the country, claiming to have treated in his psychological laboratory hundreds and hundreds of cases of this or that form of nervous disorder" (quoted in Hale, 1980, p. 110).

## Industrial Psychology

Münsterberg was also a promoter of industrial psychology. He embarked on this work in 1909 with an article titled "Psychology and the Market," which covered several areas to which psychology could contribute: vocational guidance, advertising, personnel management, mental testing, employee motivation, and the effects of fatigue and monotony on job performance.

He worked as a consultant for several companies and performed a great deal of practical research for them. He published his findings in *Psychology and Industrial Efficiency* (1913), written for the general public. The book made the best-seller list. Münsterberg argued that the best way to increase job efficiency, productivity, and satisfaction was to select workers for positions that matched their mental and emotional abilities. How? By

Archives of the History of American Psychology/University of Akron

Münsterberg designed the chronoscope to measure time intervals in units of hundredths of a second for his research on worker efficiency.

developing the proper psychological selection techniques, such as mental tests and job simulations, to assess the applicants' knowledge, skills, and abilities.

Münsterberg conducted research on such diverse occupations as ship captain, streetcar driver, telephone operator, and salesperson, to show how his selection techniques could improve job performance. His studies also showed that talking while working decreased efficiency. His solution was not to prohibit conversation among the workers, which would likely engender hostility, but to redesign the workplace to make it difficult for workers to talk to one another. He suggested increasing the distance between machine work stations in the factory or separating office workers' desks with partitions (a forerunner of today's office cubicles).

## Comment

Münsterberg formulated no theories, started no new school of thought, and conducted no academic research once he became an applied psychologist. His research served the purposes of business; it was functional research that was oriented toward helping people in some way. Although he had been trained by Wundt in the introspective method, he criticized colleagues who were unwilling to use other psychological methods and findings for the betterment of humanity. The overriding idea that characterized Münsterberg's colorful and controversial career was that psychology be useful. For all his Germanic temperament, he was the quintessential American functional psychologist, reflecting and displaying the spirit of his times.

# Applied Psychology in the United States: A National Mania

The contributions of psychologists during World War I put psychology "on the map and on the front page" (Cattell, quoted in O'Donnell, 1985, p. 239). Hall wrote that the war had "given applied psychology a tremendous impulse. This will, on the whole, do good for psychology; [we] must not try to be too pure" (Hall, 1919, p. 48). Some journals, such as the *Journal of Experimental Psychology,* ceased publication during the war years, but the *Journal of Applied Psychology* thrived. By the time the war ended in 1918, applied psychology had become far more respectable within the profession as a whole. "Applied psychology is scientific work," declared Thorndike. "Making psychology for business or industry or the army is harder than making psychology for other psychologists, and intrinsically requires higher talents" (quoted in Camfield, 1992, p. 113).

Academic psychology also benefited from the success of applied psychology during the war years. For the first time there were enough jobs and financial support for university psychologists. New psychology departments were established, new buildings and laboratories constructed, and more funds appropriated for faculty salaries. APA membership increased threefold, from 336 in 1917 to over 1,100 in 1930 (Camfield, 1992). Still, most academic psychologists disdained applied psychology. Lewis Terman, who developed the *Stanford-Binet* intelligence test, recalled that "many of the old-line psychologists regarded the whole test movement with scorn. I had the feeling that I hardly counted as a psychologist" (Terman, 1961, p. 324).

The APA, controlled by the academic branch of psychology, changed the membership requirements in 1919. Candidates for membership had to have published experimental research. In effect, this eliminated the possibility of membership for many applied psychologists and certainly for most female psychologists, whose employment opportunities were largely limited to applied work.

Despite this negative attitude toward applied psychology on the part of many university psychologists, its popularity skyrocketed and it became something of a "national mania"

(Dennis, 1984, p. 23). People came to believe that psychologists could fix everything—from marital disharmony to job dissatisfaction—and sell everything from automobiles to toothpaste. New magazines promoted the field. Among the most popular were *The Modern Psychologist* and a magazine with the even more promising-sounding title *Psychology: Health, Happiness, Success* (Benjamin & Bryant, 1997). A 1923 editorial in *The New York Times* noted that "the new psychology is making its way into one domain after another of human activity, and always proves its value" (quoted in Dennis, 2002, p. 377).

An increasing clamor for solutions to real-world problems drew more and more psychologists away from academic research and into applied areas. In the 1921 edition of Cattell's *American Men of Science,* more than 75 percent of the listed psychologists reported doing applied work; in 1910 the figure had been 50 percent (O'Donnell, 1985). The meetings of the APA's New York branch in the early 1920s show a substantial increase from prewar days in the number of papers dealing with applied issues (Benjamin, 1991).

However, by the 1930s, the decade of the worldwide economic depression, applied psychology came under attack for failing to live up to its promises. Business leaders complained that industrial psychologists were not curing all their corporate ills. For example, bad experiences with poorly designed selection tests had led them to hire unproductive workers.

Perhaps the expectations of psychologists and their clients had been too high, but whatever the reason, disenchantment with applied psychology set in. One vocal critic was Grace Adams, a student of Titchener's. In "The Decline of Psychology in America," an article in a popular magazine, Adams argued that psychology had "forsaken its scientific roots so that individual psychologists might achieve popularity and prosperity" (quoted in Benjamin, 1986, p. 944). *The New York Times* and other influential newspapers criticized psychologists for overstating their abilities and failing to ameliorate the malaise created by the economic depression. Public attention to psychology declined, and its image was not restored until 1941, when the United States entered World War II. Thus we see again that war has been a significant influence on psychology's development.

World War II (1941–1945) provided a different set of problems for psychology and revived and expanded its influence. Fully 25 percent of American psychologists were directly involved in the war effort, and many others made indirect contributions through research and writing. Women psychologists had few opportunities to participate in war work; some were advised to do community volunteer work. Of the 1,006 psychologists who served in the U.S. armed forces, only 33 were women (Gilgen et al., 1997). "World War II and the changed conditions of postwar American life resulted in exponential growth in every area of psychology and created the need for a greater number of professional psychologists than ever before in the nation's history" (Pickren, 2007, p. 279).

In the last half of the twentieth century, applied psychology outstripped the academic, research-oriented psychology that had dominated for so many years. No longer was it true that the majority of psychologists worked in universities conducting experimental research. Before World War II, almost 70 percent of the doctorates awarded in psychology were in experimental psychology. By 1984 that figure had dropped to 8 percent (Goodstein, 1988). Before the war, 75 percent of all psychologists with doctoral degrees worked in academic settings. By 1996, that number had fallen to 34 percent (Borman & Cox, 1996). Currently, nearly 65 percent of all psychologists work in applied areas.

One result has been a shift in power within the APA, where applied psychologists (particularly clinical psychologists) now assume a commanding position. In 1988 a group of academic and research-oriented members revolted and founded their own organization, the American Psychological Society (APS).

## Comment

The nature of American psychology changed immensely in the years since Hall, Cattell, Witmer, Scott, and Münsterberg studied with Wilhelm Wundt in Germany and brought that psychology to the United States. Psychology is no longer restricted to lecture halls, libraries, and laboratories but extends into many areas of everyday life. Today applied psychologists work in testing, educational and school psychology, clinical and counseling psychology, industrial-organizational psychology, forensic psychology, community psychology, consumer psychology, population and environmental psychology, health and rehabilitation psychology, family services, exercise and sports psychology, military psychology, media psychology, addictive behaviors, religion, culture, and concerns of minority groups.

None of these areas of application would have been possible had psychology remained focused on mental elements or the contents of conscious experience. The people, ideas, and events described in Chapters 6, 7, and 8 on the functionalist school of thought compelled American psychology to move far beyond the confines of Wundt's Leipzig laboratory.

Consider the following factors:

- *Darwin's notion of adaptation and function.*
- *Galton's measurement of individual differences.*
- *The American intellectual focus on the practical and the useful.*
- *The shift within academic research laboratories from content to function brought about by James, Angell, and Woodworth.*
- *Economic and social factors and the forces of war.*

All these forces intertwined to bring forth the active, assertive, engaging, and influential science of psychology that has changed our lives. This overall movement in American psychology toward the practical was reinforced by the next school of thought in psychology's evolution—the school known as behaviorism.

# Discussion Questions

1. Compare the approaches of Cattell and Binet to the development of mental tests.
2. Compare the growth and popularity of applied psychology in the 1920s, the 1930s, and the period since the end of World War II.
3. Define the concepts of *mental age* and *IQ*. How are they calculated?
4. Describe Münsterberg's contributions to forensic psychology.
5. Describe the impact of World War I on the testing movement.
6. Discuss the role of women in the testing movement. Why was their work at a professional disadvantage?
7. Discuss the roles of Scott and Münsterberg in the origin of industrial-organizational psychology.
8. How did Cattell's work alter the nature of American psychology? How did he promote psychology to the public?
9. How did economic forces influence the development of applied psychology? Do you think applied psychology would have developed when it did without these forces?
10. How did the work of Witmer and Münsterberg influence the growth of clinical psychology?
11. How did Witmer and Münsterberg differ in their views of clinical psychology?
12. How was industrial-organizational psychology affected by the Hawthorne studies and the wars?
13. How were tests used in the United States to support the notion of racial differences in intelligence and the alleged inferiority of immigrants?
14. In what ways did psychology grow and prosper in the United States in the period from 1880 to 1900? Give specific examples.
15. In your opinion, are intelligence tests biased against members of minority groups? Defend your answer.

16. What was the significance for psychology of the Coca-Cola trial and Hollingworth's research?
17. What role did women play in the development of industrial-organizational psychology?
18. Why did some organizations abandon the use of psychological tests in the 1920s despite their popularity?

19. Why did the approaches to psychology pursued by Wundt and by Titchener fail to survive in the United States?
20. Why were Münsterberg's outspoken views often unpopular with other psychologists? How did he come to be a despised figure among the general public?

## CHAPTER 9

# Behaviorism: Antecedent Influences

## Hans the Wonder Horse—Math Genius?

Clever Hans was the most famous horse in the entire history of psychology. Of course he was the *only* horse in the history of psychology, but that does not diminish his extraordinarily brilliant accomplishments. In the early 1900s nearly every person throughout Europe and the United States knew about Hans the Wonder Horse. He was the smartest horse in the world, and he was even reputed to be the most intelligent four-legged creature that had ever lived.

Clever Hans, who resided in Berlin, Germany, was clearly a celebrity. Advertisers used his name to sell their products. His achievements inspired songs, magazine articles, and books. His phenomenal knowledge was tested by eminent mathematicians, and he was judged to have numerical reasoning ability equivalent to that of a typical 14-year-old boy.

Hans could add and subtract, use fractions and decimals, read, identify coins, play card games, spell, recognize a variety of objects, and perform astonishing feats of memory. A writer for *the New York Times* claimed that Hans "forms little sentences, remembers them the next day, and discriminates 12 colors and shades" (August 14, 1904). The horse replied to the questions posed to him by tapping its hoof a specific number of times or by nodding its head in the direction of the appropriate object.

*"How many of the gentlemen present are wearing straw hats?"* the horse was asked.

*Clever Hans tapped the answer with his right foot, being careful to omit the straw hats worn by the ladies.*

*"What is the lady holding in her hand?"*

*The horse tapped out "Schirm," meaning parasol, indicating each of the letters by means of a special chart. He was invariably successful at distinguishing between canes and parasols and also between straw and felt hats.*

*More important, Hans could think for himself. When asked a completely novel question, such as how many corners in a circle, he shook his head from side to side to say there were none. (Fernald, 1984, p. 19)*

No wonder people were dazzled. No wonder Hans's owner, Wilhelm von Osten, a retired mathematics teacher, was pleased. He had spent several years teaching Hans the fundamentals of human intelligence (having tried previously, and unsuccessfully, to teach a cat and a bear).

Von Osten did not profit financially from Hans's performances. When he staged demonstrations of Hans's brilliance, in the courtyard of his apartment building, he never charged a fee. Nor did he benefit from the resulting publicity. The motivation for his painstaking efforts was purely scientific. His goal was to prove that Darwin was correct

Archives of the History of American Psychology/University of Akron

Clever Hans, the clever horse.

in suggesting that humans and animals have similar mental processes. Von Osten believed that the only reason horses and other animals appear to be less intelligent is because they have not been given sufficient education. He was convinced that with the right kind of training, the horse could show that it was an intelligent being. Because of his efforts, much of the Western world was convinced!

But there were some skeptics, some doubters, who questioned whether Hans or any other animal could really be so clever. There had to be trickery involved. Some thought it was the scandal of the century.

Do you believe it is possible to teach an animal to answer such questions correctly? Was the display of the animal's intelligence legitimate? And what does this all have to do with the history of psychology? We will see that it was a psychologist who finally solved the mystery.

## Toward a Science of Behavior

By the second decade of the twentieth century, fewer than 40 years after Wilhelm Wundt formally launched psychology, the science had undergone drastic revision. No longer did all psychologists agree on the value of introspection, the existence of mental elements, or the need for psychology to remain a pure science. The functional psychologists were rewriting the rules, using psychology in ways that were unacceptable at Leipzig and Cornell.

The movement toward functionalism was less revolutionary than evolutionary. The functionalists did not set out deliberately to destroy the establishment of Wundt and E. B. Titchener. Instead they modified it, adding a bit here and changing something there, so that over the years a new form of psychology emerged. It was more a chipping away from the inside than an attack from the outside.

The leaders of the functionalist movement were not eager to formalize their position. They saw their task not as breaking with the past but building on it. Thus, the situation in American psychology in the second decade of the twentieth century was that functionalism was maturing, while structuralism maintained a strong but no longer exclusive position.

The year 1913 brought a declaration of war, a deliberate break with both of these positions. A protest movement began that was intended to destroy the older points of view. Its leader wanted no modification of the past, and no compromise with it. This revolutionary movement was called behaviorism, and it was promoted by the 35-year-old American psychologist John B. Watson. Just 10 years earlier, Watson had received his Ph.D. from James Rowland Angell at the University of Chicago, when it was the center of functional psychology, one of the two movements Watson set out to smash.

The basic tenets of Watson's behaviorism were simple, direct, and bold. He called for a scientific psychology that dealt only with observable behavioral acts that could be described objectively in terms such as "stimulus" and "response." Further, Watson's psychology rejected all mentalistic concepts and terms. Words such as "image," "sensation," "mind," and "consciousness"—which had been carried over from the days of mental philosophy—were meaningless for a science of behavior, so far as Watson was concerned.

Watson was particularly vehement in rejecting the concept of consciousness. He believed that consciousness had absolutely no value for behavioral psychology. Further, he said that consciousness had "never been seen, touched, smelled, tasted, or moved. It is a plain assumption just as unprovable as the old concept of the soul" (Watson & McDougall, 1929, p. 14). Therefore, introspection, which assumed the existence of conscious processes, was irrelevant and of no use to a science of behavior.

These basic ideas of the behaviorist movement did not originate with Watson but had been developing for some time in psychology and in biology. Like all founders, Watson organized and promoted ideas and issues that already were acceptable to the intellectual Zeitgeist. Consider, then, the major forces Watson effectively brought together to form his system of behavioral psychology: the philosophical tradition of objectivism and mechanism, animal psychology, and functional psychology.

The recognition of the need for greater objectivity in psychology has a long history. It can be traced to Descartes, whose mechanistic explanations for the operations of the human body were among the initial steps toward an objective science. More important in the history of objectivism is the French philosopher Auguste Comte (see Chapter 2), founder of the movement known as positivism that emphasized positive knowledge (facts), the truth of which was not debatable. According to Comte, the only valid knowledge is that which is social in nature and objectively observable. These criteria rule out introspection, which depends on a private individual consciousness and cannot be objectively observed.

By the early years of the twentieth century, positivism had become part of the scientific Zeitgeist. In his writings, Watson rarely discussed positivism, nor did most American psychologists of the day; there was no need to do so. According to one historian, these psychologists "acted like positivists, even if they did not assume the label" (Logue, 1985, p. 149). Thus, by the time Watson set to work on his behaviorism, the objectivistic, mechanistic, and materialistic influences were so pervasive that they led inevitably to a new kind of psychology—one without consciousness, mind, or soul—one that focused on only what could be seen, heard, or touched. The result was a science of behavior that viewed human beings as machines.

# The Influence of Animal Psychology on Behaviorism

Watson offered a clear statement of the relationship between animal psychology and behaviorism: behaviorism is a direct outgrowth of studies in animal behavior during the first decade of the twentieth century (Watson, 1929, p. 327). Thus, we can say that the most important antecedent of Watson's program was animal psychology, which grew out of evolutionary theory and led to attempts to demonstrate the existence of mind in lower organisms and the continuity between animal and human minds.

We noted in Chapter 6 the work of George John Romanes and Conwy Lloyd Morgan, two pioneers in animal psychology. With Morgan's law of parsimony and his greater reliance on experimental instead of anecdotal techniques, animal psychology became more objective, although consciousness remained its focus. The methodology was becoming more objective, even though the subject matter was not.

In 1889, for example, Alfred Binet published *The Psychic Life of Micro-Organisms,* in which he proposed that single-cell protozoa possess the ability to perceive and discriminate between objects and to display behavior that has purpose. In 1908, Francis Darwin (son of Charles Darwin) discussed the role of consciousness in plants. In the early years of animal psychology in the United States, there was a continuing interest in the conscious processes of animals. The influence of Romanes and Morgan persisted for quite some time.

## Jacques Loeb (1859–1924)

**Tropism:** An involuntary forced movement.

A significant step toward greater objectivity in animal psychology can be credited to Jacques Loeb (1859–1924), a German physiologist and zoologist who liked to water his lawn whenever it rained. He worked at several institutions in the United States, including the University of Chicago. Reacting against the anthropomorphic tradition and the method of introspection by analogy, Loeb developed a theory of animal behavior based on the concept of **tropism**, an involuntary forced movement. Loeb believed that an animal's reaction to a stimulus is direct and automatic. Thus, the behavioral response is said to be forced by the stimulus and does not require any explanation in terms of the animal's alleged consciousness.

**Associative memory:** An association between stimulus and response, taken to indicate evidence of consciousness in animals.

Although Loeb's work represented the most objective and mechanistic approach to animal psychology of its time, Loeb had not been able to totally cast off the past. He did not reject consciousness in animals (e.g., humans) that were high on the evolutionary scale (Loeb, 1918). Loeb argued that animal consciousness was revealed by **associative memory**; that is, the animals had learned to react to certain stimuli in a desirable way. For example, when an animal responds to its name or reacts to a specific sound by going repeatedly to the place where it receives food, this is evidence of some mental connection, an associative memory. So even in Loeb's otherwise mechanistic approach, he still invoked the idea of consciousness.

Watson took courses with Loeb at the University of Chicago and hoped to do research under his direction, showing a curiosity about Loeb's mechanistic views. Angell, along with the neurologist H. H. Donaldson, talked Watson out of this plan. They argued that Loeb was unsafe, a word open to interpretation but perhaps indicating disapproval of Loeb's objectivism.

## Rats, Ants, and the Animal Mind

By the beginning of the twentieth century, experimental animal psychologists were hard at work. Robert Yerkes began animal studies in 1900 using a variety of animals, and his research strengthened the position and influence of comparative psychology.

Also in 1900, the rat maze was introduced by Willard S. Small at Clark University (see Figure 9.1), and the white rat and maze became a standard method for the study of learning. Yet consciousness continued to intrude in animal psychology, even with the white rat running the maze. In interpreting the rat's behavior, Small used mentalistic terms, writing about the rat's ideas and images.

Although Small's conclusions were more objective than those produced by Romanes's brand of anthropomorphizing, they, too, reflected a concern with mental processes and

ROBERT YERKES

**FIGURE 9.1** The rat maze. A hungry rat placed in the maze is allowed to wander freely until it finds food.

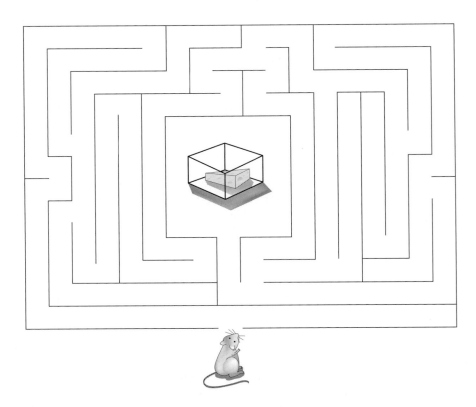

elements. Even Watson, early in his career, fell under that influence. His doctoral dissertation, completed in 1903, was titled "Animal Education: The *Psychical* Development of the White Rat" (italics added). As late as 1907 he was discussing the conscious experience of sensation in his rats.

In 1906, while a graduate student at the University of Chicago, Charles Henry Turner (1867–1923) published an article titled "A Preliminary Note on Ant Behavior." Watson reviewed the paper in the prestigious journal *Psychological Bulletin* and praised it highly. In his review, Watson used the word *behavior,* taken from Turner's title. This may have been the first time Watson used the word in print, although he had written it earlier in a grant application (Cadwallader, 1984, 1987).

Turner, an African American, received his Ph.D. magna cum laude in 1907 from the University of Chicago. Although his degree was in zoology, he published so much research on comparative and animal studies in psychology journals that some psychologists claim him as one of their own. Recall, however, that jobs for minority psychologists were scarce, so Turner's teaching opportunities were limited. "Yet working alone as a high school science teacher, he made important discoveries in the field of insect learning and behavior" (Abramson, 2009, p. 344).

By 1910, eight comparative psychology laboratories had been established; the earliest were at Clark, Harvard, and the University of Chicago. Many other universities offered courses in the field. Margaret Floy Washburn, who had been Titchener's first doctoral student (see Chapter 5), taught animal psychology at Cornell. Her book, *The Animal Mind* (1908), was the first comparative psychology textbook published in the United States.

Note the title of Washburn's book: *The Animal Mind.* In her work, the attribution of consciousness to animals persisted, as did the method of introspecting the animal mind by analogy with the human mind. Washburn noted:

*We are obliged to acknowledge that all psychic interpretation of animal behavior must be on the analogy of human experience. We must be anthropomorphic in the notions we form of what takes place in the mind of an animal. (1908, p. 88)*

Although Washburn's book was the most thorough treatment of animal psychology research of its day, it also marked the end of an era. After it, no other text would use the approach of inferring mental states from behavior:

*The questions that had interested [Herbert] Spencer, Lloyd Morgan, and Yerkes went out of fashion and mostly disappeared from the literature. Almost all subsequent textbooks in the field were behaviorist in orientation, and primarily concerned with the issues and problems of learning. (Demarest, 1987, p. 144)*

## On Becoming an Animal Psychologist

Whether dealing with mind or with behavior, it was not easy to be an animal psychologist. State legislators and university administrators, always concerned with funding, did not consider the field to have any practical value. Harvard's president saw "no future in Yerkes's brand of comparative psychology. It was smelly and expensive and seemed to have no relation to practical public service" (Reed, 1987a, p. 94). Yerkes wrote that he was

*gently and tactfully advised … that educational psychology offered a broader and more direct path to a professorship and to increased academic usefulness than did my special field of comparative psychology, and that I might well consider effecting a change. (1930/1961, pp. 390–391)*

The students Yerkes trained in his laboratory sought jobs in applied fields because they were unable to find employment in comparative psychology. Those who did secure university positions knew they were the most expendable members of their psychology departments. In times of financial hardship, animal psychologists were likely to be the first to be fired.

Watson himself faced problems early in his career. "I am very hampered in my research at present," he wrote to Yerkes. "We have absolutely no place to keep animals and no funds to run the 'menagerie' if we had the place" (Watson, 1904, quoted in O'Donnell, 1985, p. 190). In 1908 only six animal studies were published in psychology journals, which accounted for only 4 percent of all the psychological research that year. The following year, when Watson suggested to Yerkes that all the animal psychologists meet for dinner during the APA convention, he knew they could be seated at one table; there were only nine of them. In the 1910 edition of Cattell's *American Men of Science*, only six of the 218 psychologists listed claimed to be active in animal research. Career prospects were poor, yet the field expanded because of the dedication of the few who stayed with it.

In 1911, the *Journal of Animal Behavior* (later the *Journal of Comparative Psychology*) began publication. In 1906, a lecture by the Russian physiologist Ivan Pavlov was reprinted in the journal *Science,* introducing his work on animal psychology to the American audience. Yerkes and Sergius Morgulis, a Russian student, published a more detailed account of Pavlov's methodology and results in the *Psychological Bulletin* (1909).

Pavlov's research supported an objective psychology, and Watson's behaviorism in particular. Thus, animal psychology became established and grew increasingly objective in subject matter and methodology. That trend toward greater objectivity in the study of animal behavior was strongly supported by events in Germany in 1904. That was the year the government established a committee to examine Clever Hans's powers and determine whether any deception or trickery was involved. The group included a circus manager, a veterinarian, horse trainers, an aristocrat, the director of the Berlin Zoo, and psychologist Carl Stumpf from the University of Berlin.

## Was Hans Really Clever?

In September 1904, after a lengthy investigation, the committee concluded that Hans the Wonder Horse was not receiving intentional signals or cues from his owner. No fraud, no deceit. Stumpf was not completely satisfied, however. He was curious about how the horse was able to respond correctly to so many kinds of questions. He assigned the problem to a graduate student, Oskar Pfungst, who approached the task in the careful manner of an experimental psychologist.

The horse had demonstrated that it could answer questions even when the trainer was not present, so Pfungst designed an experiment to test this phenomenon. He formed two groups of questioners, one composed of people who knew the answers to the questions put to the horse, and another composed of people who did not know the answers. The results showed that the horse answered correctly only when the questioners themselves knew the answers. Obviously Hans was receiving information from whoever was questioning him, even when that person was a stranger.

After a series of well-controlled experiments, Pfungst concluded that Hans had been unintentionally conditioned by his owner, von Osten. The horse would begin tapping his hoof whenever he perceived the slightest downward movement of von Osten's head. When the correct number of taps had been made, von Osten's head automatically bobbed up and the horse would stop. Pfungst demonstrated that everyone—even people who had never before been near a horse—made the same barely perceptible head gestures when speaking to the animal.

Thus, the psychologist demonstrated that Hans did not have a storehouse of knowledge. He had simply been trained to start tapping his hoof or to incline his head toward an object whenever his questioner made a certain movement. And the horse had been conditioned to stop tapping in response to the questioner's opposite movement. Von Osten had reinforced Hans during the training period by giving him carrots and sugar lumps when he made a correct response. As the training progressed, von Osten found that he no longer had to reinforce every correct behavior, so he began to reward the horse only occasionally. The behavioral psychologist B. F. Skinner would later demonstrate the great effectiveness of such partial or intermittent reinforcement in the conditioning process:

> *What did von Osten think of Pfungst's report? The man was devastated! He felt abused, exploited, and physically ill. But he directed his anger not at Pfungst, but at Hans who, von Osten believed, had somehow deceived him. Von Osten said that the horse's deceitful behavior had made him sick. And he had become very sick indeed with what the physician diagnosed as cancer of the liver. (Candland, 1993, p. 135)*

Von Osten never forgave Hans for his treachery. He put a curse on the horse, vowing that the animal would spend the rest of its days pulling hearses. Von Osten died two years after Pfungst's revelations, still maintaining that the ungrateful horse's behavior was responsible for his illness. Clearly, he was still attributing intelligence to Hans.

Clever Hans's new owner, Hans Krall, a wealthy jeweler, put Hans and two other horses on display for popular performances in which the horses tapped out answers to questions. Their answers were always correct, and Krall called them the Wizard Horses. They amazed audiences with their powers; they could even calculate the square root of numbers, among other tricks (see Kressley-Mba, 2006). Apparently much of the public had not heard of or paid attention to Pfungst's research showing that Hans's alleged powers were no mystery but were simply learned responses.

The case of Clever Hans illustrates the value and necessity of an experimental approach to the study of animal behavior. It made psychologists more skeptical of claims of great feats of animal intelligence. However, it also showed that animals were capable of learning and that they could be conditioned to modify their behavior. The experimental study of animal learning came to be seen as a more useful approach to the problem than the earlier type of speculation about some alleged consciousness operating in an animal's mind. Pfungst's experimental report about Clever Hans was reviewed by John B. Watson for the *Journal of Comparative Neurology and Psychology,* and its conclusions influenced Watson's growing inclination to promote a psychology that would deal only with behavior, not with consciousness (Watson, 1908).

# Edward Lee Thorndike (1874–1949)

Archives of the History of American Psychology/ University of Akron

E. L. THORNDIKE

One of the most important researchers in the development of animal psychology, Thorndike fashioned a mechanistic, objective learning theory that focused on overt behavior. Thorndike believed that psychology must study behavior, not mental elements or conscious experiences, and thus he reinforced the trend toward greater objectivity begun by the functionalists. He did not interpret learning subjectively but rather in terms of concrete connections between stimuli and responses, although he did permit some reference to consciousness and mental processes.

The works of Thorndike and Ivan Pavlov provide an example of independent simultaneous discovery. Thorndike developed his law of effect in 1898, and Pavlov proposed a similar law of reinforcement in 1902.

## Thorndike's Life

Edward Lee Thorndike was one of the first American psychologists to receive all of his education in the United States. It is significant that this was possible—that he did not have to travel to Germany for graduate study—just two decades after the formal founding of psychology. His interest in psychology was awakened, as it was for so many others, when he read William James's *The Principles of Psychology* while an undergraduate at Wesleyan University in Middletown, Connecticut. Thorndike later studied under James at Harvard and began his investigation of learning.

He had planned to conduct his research with children as subjects, but this was forbidden. The university administration was still sensitive about a scandal involving charges that an anthropologist had loosened children's clothing to take their body measurements. When Thorndike learned that he could not study children, he chose chicks instead. He may have been inspired by the lectures given by Morgan describing his research with chicks.

Thorndike improvised mazes by stacking books on end and trained his chicks to run through them. The story is told that Thorndike had difficulty finding a place to house his chicks. His landlady refused to allow him to keep the birds in his bedroom, so he asked William James for advice. James was unsuccessful in finding space in the laboratory or the university museum, so he took Thorndike and the chicks into the basement of his home, to the delight of James's children.

Thorndike did not complete his education at Harvard. Believing that a certain young lady did not return his affection, he applied to James McKeen Cattell at Columbia University in order to get away from the Boston area. When Cattell offered him a fellowship, Thorndike went to New York, taking with him his two best-trained chicks. He continued his animal research at Columbia, working with cats and dogs in puzzle boxes of his own design. He was awarded his doctoral degree in 1898. His dissertation, "Animal Intelligence: An Experimental Study of the Associative Processes in Animals," was published in the *Psychological Review* and enjoys the distinction of being the first psychology doctoral dissertation to use animal subjects (Galef, 1998). Thorndike later published considerable subsequent research on associative learning in chicks, fish, cats, and monkeys.

Fiercely ambitious and competitive, Thorndike wrote to his fiancée, "I've decided to get to the top of the psychology heap in five years, teach ten more, and then quit" (quoted in Boakes, 1984, p. 72). He did not remain an animal psychologist for long. He admitted that he had no real interest in it but had stuck with it only to complete his degree and establish a reputation. Animal psychology was not the field for someone with an intense drive to succeed. As noted earlier, there were many more job opportunities in applied areas than in animal research.

Thorndike became an instructor in psychology at Teachers College of Columbia University. There he worked with human subjects on problems of learning, adapting his animal research techniques for children and young people (Beatty, 1998). He branched out to educational psychology and mental testing, wrote several textbooks, and in 1910 founded the *Journal of Educational Psychology*. He got to the top of the psychology heap in 1912 when he was elected president of the APA. Royalties from his tests and textbooks made him wealthy, and by 1924 he boasted an income of nearly $70,000 a year, a tremendous sum at that time (Boakes, 1984).

Thorndike's 50 years at Columbia are among the most productive ever recorded in the history of psychology. His bibliography lists 507 items. Although he retired in 1939, he continued to work until his death 10 years later.

## Connectionism

**Connectionism:** Thorndike's approach to learning that was based on connections between situations and responses.

Thorndike called his experimental approach to the study of association **connectionism**. He wrote that if he were to analyze the human mind he would find

> *connections of varying strength between (a) situations, elements of situations, and compounds of situations, and (b) responses, readinesses to respond, facilitations, inhibitions, and directions of responses. If all these could be completely inventoried, telling what the man would think and do and what would satisfy and annoy him, in every conceivable situation, it seems to me that nothing would be left out. … Learning is connecting. The mind is man's connection-system. (1931, p. 122)*

This position was a direct extension of the older philosophical notion of association (see Chapter 2), but with one significant difference. Instead of talking about associations or connections between ideas, Thorndike was dealing with connections between objectively verifiable situations and responses.

Although Thorndike developed his theory within a more objective frame of reference, he continued to invoke mental processes. He spoke of satisfaction, annoyance, and discomfort when discussing the behavior of his experimental animals, terms that are more mentalistic than behavioristic. Thus, Thorndike retained the influence of Romanes and Morgan. His objective analyses of animal behaviors often incorporated subjective judgments about the animal's alleged conscious experiences.

We note that Thorndike, like Jacques Loeb, was not freely granting high levels of consciousness and intelligence to animals as extravagantly as Romanes had. You can see a steady reduction in the importance of consciousness in animal psychology from its beginnings to Thorndike's time, along with an increasing use of the experimental method to study behavior.

In spite of the mentalistic tinge to Thorndike's work, his approach was indeed in the mechanistic tradition. He argued that behavior must be reduced to its simplest elements: the stimulus–response units. He shared with the structuralists and the British empiricists a mechanistic, analytical, and atomistic point of view. Stimulus–response units are the elements of behavior (not of consciousness) and are the building blocks from which more complex behaviors are compounded.

## The Puzzle Box

Thorndike designed and built crude puzzle boxes out of old crates and sticks, to be used for his research on animal learning (see Figure 9.2). To escape from the box, the animal had to learn to operate a latch. Thorndike traced his idea for the puzzle box as an apparatus for studying learning to the anecdotal reports of Romanes and Morgan that described the way cats and dogs opened latches on gates.

In one series of experiments, Thorndike placed a food-deprived cat in the slatted box. Food was left outside the box as a reward for escaping. The cat had to pull a lever or chain, and sometimes engage in several acts in succession, to unfasten the latches and open the door. At first the cat displayed random behaviors, poking, sniffing, and clawing to get at the food. Eventually the cat executed the correct behavior and unlatched the door. During the first trial, that behavior occurred by accident. On subsequent trials, the random behaviors were displayed less frequently until learning was complete. Then the cat would exhibit the appropriate behavior as soon as it was placed in the box.

To record his data, Thorndike used quantitative measures of learning. One technique was to log the number of wrong behaviors, the actions that did not lead to escape. Over a series of trials the number of these behaviors diminished. Another technique was to record the elapsed time from the moment the cat was placed in the box until it succeeded in escaping. As learning took place, this time period decreased.

Thorndike wrote about "stamping in" and "stamping out" a response tendency by its favorable or unfavorable consequences. Unsuccessful response tendencies that did nothing to get the cat out of the box tended to disappear, to be stamped out over a number of

**FIGURE 9.2** Thorndike's puzzle box.

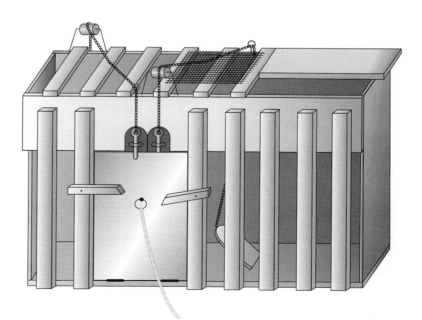

**Trial-and-error learning:** Learning based on the repetition of response tendencies that lead to success.

**Law of effect:** Acts that produce satisfaction in a given situation become associated with that situation; when the situation recurs, the act is likely to recur.

**Law of exercise:** The more an act or response is used in a given situation, the more strongly the act becomes associated with that situation.

trials. Response tendencies that led to success were stamped in after a number of trials. This kind of learning has come to be known as **trial-and-error learning**, although Thorndike preferred to call it trial-and-accidental success.

## Laws of Learning

Thorndike formally presented his ideas about the stamping in or stamping out of a response tendency as the **law of effect**:

> *Any act which in a given situation produces satisfaction becomes associated with that situation, so that when the situation recurs the act is more likely than before to recur also. Conversely, any act which in a given situation produces discomfort becomes disassociated from that situation, so that when the situation recurs the act is less likely than before to recur. (1905, p. 203)*

A companion law—the **law of exercise** or the **law of use and disuse**—states that any response made in a particular situation becomes associated with that situation. The more the response is used in the situation, the more strongly it becomes associated with it. Conversely, prolonged disuse of the response tends to weaken the association.

In other words, simply repeating a response in a given situation tends to strengthen that response. Further research persuaded Thorndike that the reward consequences of a response (a situation that produces satisfaction) are more effective than mere repetition of the response.

Through an extensive research program using human subjects, Thorndike later reexamined the law of effect. The results revealed that rewarding a response did indeed strengthen it, but punishing a response did not produce a comparable negative effect. He revised his views to place greater emphasis on reward than on punishment.

## Comment

Thorndike's investigations of human and animal learning are among the most significant research programs in the history of psychology. His work heralded the rise of learning theory to prominence in American psychology, and the objective spirit in which he conducted his research was an important contribution to behaviorism. Watson wrote that Thorndike's research laid the foundation for behaviorism. Ivan Pavlov also paid tribute to Thorndike:

> *Some years after the beginning of the work with our new method I learned that somewhat similar experiments had been performed in America, and indeed not by physiologists but by psychologists. I must acknowledge that the honor of having made the first steps along this path belongs to E.L. Thorndike. By two or three years his experiments preceded ours and his book must be considered a classic, both for its bold outlook on an immense task and for the accuracy of its results. (Pavlov, 1928, quoted in Jonçich, 1968, pp. 415–416)*

# Ivan Petrovitch Pavlov (1849–1936)

Ivan Pavlov's work on learning helped to shift associationism from its traditional emphasis on subjective ideas to objective and quantifiable physiological events such as glandular secretions and muscular movements. As a result, Pavlov's work provided Watson with a method for studying behavior and for attempting to control and modify it.

## Pavlov's Life

Ivan Pavlov was born in the town of Ryazan, in central Russia, the eldest of 11 children of a village priest. His position in such a large family required him to develop at an early

Archives of the History of American Psychology/ University of Akron

IVAN PAVLOV

age a sense of responsibility and the drive to work hard. He retained these characteristics all his life. He was unable to attend school for several years because of head injuries sustained in an accident at the age of seven, so his father tutored him at home. Pavlov entered the theological seminary intending to prepare for the priesthood, but he changed his mind after reading about Darwin's theory. He was so determined to attend the university at St. Petersburg to study animal physiology that he walked there, a distance of several hundred miles.

With his university training, Pavlov became part of the intelligentsia, an emerging class in Russian society that was distinct from the other classes: the aristocracy and the peasantry. One historian noted that Pavlov was

> *too well-educated and too intelligent for the peasantry from which he came, but too common and too poor for the aristocracy into which he could never rise. These social conditions often produced an especially dedicated intellectual, one whose entire life was centered on the intellectual pursuits that justified his existence. And so it was with Pavlov, whose almost fanatic devotion to pure science and to experimental research was supported by the energy and simplicity of a Russian peasant. (Miller, 1962, p. 177)*

Pavlov obtained his degree in 1875 and began medical training, not to practice as a physician but in the hope of pursuing a career in physiological research. He studied in Germany for two years, then returned to St. Petersburg to spend several years as a laboratory research assistant.

Pavlov was totally dedicated to his research. He refused to be distracted by practical matters such as salary, clothing, or living conditions. His wife, Sara, whom he married in 1881, devoted herself to protecting him from mundane matters. They made a pact early in their marriage, agreeing that she would take care of everyday concerns and allow nothing to interfere with his work. In return, Pavlov promised never to drink or play cards and to socialize only on Saturday and Sunday evenings. Otherwise he adhered to a rigorous schedule, working seven days a week from September to May and spending summers in the countryside.

His indifference to finances is illustrated by the story that Sara often had to remind him to collect his pay. She also said he could not be trusted to buy clothes for himself. Once, when he was in his seventies, Pavlov was riding the streetcar to his laboratory. Being impetuous, he jumped off before it stopped, fell, and broke his leg. "A woman standing near saw it and said, 'My, here is a man of genius, but he doesn't know how to get off a streetcar without breaking his leg'" (Gantt, 1979, p. 28).

The Pavlov family lived in poverty until 1890 when, at the age of 41, Pavlov received an appointment as professor of pharmacology at St. Petersburg's Military Medical Academy. A few years earlier, while he was preparing his doctoral dissertation, their first child was born. The doctor said that the frail infant would probably not survive unless mother and child could rest in the country. Pavlov was finally able to borrow enough money for the journey, but not in time, and the child died. When the next child arrived, the family lived with relatives while Pavlov slept on a cot in his laboratory because they could not afford an apartment.

A group of Pavlov's students, knowing of his financial difficulties, gave him money on the pretext of paying for lectures they asked him to present. Pavlov kept none of the money for himself, spending the funds instead on dogs for his laboratory. He never seemed bothered by these hardships. They reportedly caused him no concern.

Although laboratory research was Pavlov's overriding interest, he rarely conducted experiments himself. Instead, he usually supervised the efforts of others. From 1897 to 1936, nearly 150 researchers worked under Pavlov's direction, producing more than 500 scientific papers. One student wrote that the "entire laboratory worked like the mechanism of a watch" (Todes, 2002, p. 107).

*Pavlov incorporated [the researchers] into a factory-like system that essentially used them as his own hands and eyes: He assigned them a specific topic, provided them with a suitably equipped dog technology, supervised ... their research, interpreted their results, and closely edited their written products. (Todes, 1997, p. 948)*

Pavlov's temper was famous. He was given to explosive tirades at work, often directed at his research assistants. During the Bolshevik Revolution of 1917, he berated an assistant for being 10 minutes late. Gunfire in the streets was no excuse and should not be permitted to interfere with laboratory work. Usually these emotional outbursts were quickly forgotten. His researchers knew what was expected—because Pavlov never hesitated to tell them. He was honest and direct, if not always considerate, in dealing with other people. He was well aware of his volatile nature. One laboratory worker who could no longer tolerate the insults asked to be relieved of his duties. "Pavlov replied that his abusive behavior was just a habit ... it was not of itself a sufficient reason to quit the laboratory" (quoted in Windholz, 1990, p. 68). Any failure of an experiment would make Pavlov depressed, but a success brought such joy that he would congratulate not only his assistants but also the dogs.

He tried to be as humane as possible with the dogs and believed that the surgical procedures to which they were subjected were unfortunate but unavoidable in scientific research:

*We must painfully acknowledge that precisely because of its great intellectual development, the best of man's domesticated animals—the dog—most often becomes the victim of physiological experiments. The dog is irreplaceable; moreover, it is extremely touching. It is almost a participant in the experiments conducted upon it, greatly facilitating the success of the research by its understanding and compliance. (Pavlov, quoted in Todes, 2002, p. 123)*

A monument to a dog, an ornate fountain, was erected in 1935 on the grounds of Pavlov's research facility. "At the core is a pedestal with a large canine sitting on it with bas-reliefs of laboratory scenes and quotations from Pavlov. Around the top are busts of 8 canines, water pouring from their mouths as they salute in salivation" (Johnson, 2008, pp. 136–137).

Jersy Konorski, a psychologist from Poland who had worked at the laboratory, recalled that Pavlov's students treated him like royalty. Konorski wrote that there was

*clear jealousy among Pavlov's pupils about who was closest to him. People boasted when Pavlov spoke to them at some length ... the attitude of Pavlov toward an individual was the main factor determining the hierarchy within the group. (1974, p. 193)*

An American student, W. H. Gantt, who later translated Pavlov's works into the English language, wrote that when he first met Pavlov it was "a day he remembered all his life" (quoted in Kosmachevskaya & Gromova, 2007, p. 303).

Pavlov was one of the few Russian scientists to allow women and Jews to study in his laboratory. Any suggestion of anti-Semitism angered him. He had a good sense of humor and knew how to enjoy a joke, even when it was played on him. During the ceremony at which he received an honorary degree from Cambridge University, students sitting in the balcony lowered a toy dog on a rope, dropping it into Pavlov's lap. Pavlov kept the dog by his desk in his apartment.

E. R. Hilgard, then a Ph.D. candidate at Yale University, heard Pavlov speak in 1929 at the Ninth International Congress of Psychology in New Haven, Connecticut. Pavlov addressed the audience in Russian, pausing periodically to allow the translator to present

Pavlov's remarks in English. The translator later told Hilgard that "Pavlov would stop and say, 'You know all about this. You tell them about it. I'll go ahead and tell them something else'" (reported in Fowler, 1994, p. 3).

Pavlov's relations with the government of the Soviet Union were difficult. He was openly critical of the 1917 Russian Revolution and of the Soviet political and economic system. He wrote protest letters to Joseph Stalin, the tyrannical dictator who killed and exiled millions. Pavlov's refusal to attend Soviet scientific meetings demonstrated his disapproval of the regime. Not until 1933 did he acknowledge that the Soviets had achieved some success. Despite his attitude, Pavlov continued to receive generous research support from the government and was allowed to conduct his research free of official interference (see Zagrina, 2009).

Pavlov remained a scientist to the last. He was accustomed to practicing self-observation whenever he was ill, and the day of his death was no exception. Weak from pneumonia, he called in a physician and described his symptoms: "My brain is not working well, obsessive feelings and involuntary movements appear; mortification may be setting in." He discussed his condition with the doctor for a while and then fell asleep. When he awoke, Pavlov raised himself in bed and began to search for his clothes, with the same restless energy he had shown all his life. "It is time to get up," he exclaimed. "Help me, I must dress!" And with that, he fell back on the pillows and died (Gantt, 1941, p. 35).

## Conditioned Reflexes

During his distinguished career, Pavlov worked on three major problems. The first concerned the function of the nerves of the heart, and the second involved the primary digestive glands. His brilliant research on digestion won worldwide recognition and the 1904 Nobel Prize. His third research area, for which he occupies a prominent place in the history of psychology, was the study of **conditioned reflexes**.

The notion of conditioned reflexes originated, as so many scientific breakthroughs did, with an accidental discovery. In working on the digestive glands in dogs, Pavlov used the method of surgical exposure to permit digestive secretions to be collected outside the body where they could be observed, measured, and recorded (Pavlov, 1927/1960). One aspect of this work dealt with the function of saliva, which the dogs secreted involuntarily whenever food was placed in their mouths. Pavlov noticed that sometimes saliva flowed even before the food was given. The dogs salivated at the sight of the food or at the sound of the footsteps of the man who regularly fed them. The unlearned response of salivation somehow had become connected with, or conditioned to, stimuli previously associated with receiving food.

**Conditioned reflexes:** Reflexes that are conditional or dependent on the formation of an association or connection between stimulus and response.

*Psychic reflexes*   These psychic reflexes, as Pavlov first called them, were aroused in the laboratory dogs by stimuli other than the original one (i.e., the food). Pavlov reasoned that this reaction occurred because these other stimuli (such as the sight and sounds of the attendant) had so often been related to feeding.

In accordance with the prevailing Zeitgeist in animal psychology—and like Thorndike, Loeb, and others before him—Pavlov focused initially on the mentalistic experiences of his laboratory animals. We can see this viewpoint in the term "psychic reflexes," his original term for conditioned reflexes. He wrote about the animals' desires, judgment, and will, interpreting the animals' mental events in subjective and human terms. In time, Pavlov dropped such mentalistic references in favor of a more objective, descriptive approach:

*At first in our psychical experiments ... we conscientiously endeavored to explain our results by imagining the subjective state of the animal. But nothing came of this except sterile controversy and individual views that could not be reconciled. And so we could do nothing but conduct the research on a purely objective basis. (Pavlov, quoted in Cuny, 1965, p. 65)*

In the English translation of his classic book, *Conditioned Reflexes* (1927), Pavlov gave due credit to René Descartes for developing the idea of the reflex 300 years before. He noted that what Descartes called the nervous reflex was the starting point for his research program.

Pavlov's first experiments with dogs were simple. He held a piece of bread in his hand and showed it to the dog before giving it to the animal to eat. In time, the dog began to salivate as soon as it saw the bread. The dog's response of salivating when food is placed in its mouth is a natural reflexive response of the digestive system; no learning is necessary for it to occur. Pavlov called this an innate or unconditioned reflex.

Salivating at the sight of food, however, is not reflexive but must be learned. Pavlov now called this response a conditional reflex (instead of his earlier mentalistic term "psychic reflex") because it was conditional or dependent on the dog's forming an association or connection between the sight of the food and the subsequent eating of it.

In translating Pavlov's work from the Russian into the English language, W. H. Gantt, his American disciple, used the word "conditioned" instead of "conditional." Gantt later said he regretted making the change. Nevertheless, *conditioned reflex* remains the accepted term.

Pavlov and his assistants discovered that many stimuli would produce the conditional salivary response in laboratory animals as long as a stimulus was capable of attracting the animal's attention without arousing anger or fear. They tested buzzers, lights, whistles, tones, bubbling water, and ticking metronomes with the dogs and achieved similar results.

The thoroughness and precision of the research program are evident in the sophisticated equipment devised to collect saliva, which flowed through a rubber tube attached to a surgical opening in the dog's cheek. When each drop of saliva fell onto a platform resting on a sensitive spring, it activated a marker on a revolving drum. This arrangement, which made it possible to record the precise number of drops and the exact moment at which each fell, is but one example of Pavlov's painstaking efforts to follow the scientific method—to standardize experimental conditions, apply rigorous controls, and eliminate sources of error.

***The Tower of Silence***    Pavlov was so concerned about preventing outside influences from affecting the reliability of the research that he designed special cubicles, one for the experimental animal and another for the experimenter. The researcher could operate the various conditioning stimuli, collect saliva, and present food without being seen by the animal.

These precautions did not completely satisfy him. He worried that extraneous environmental stimuli might contaminate the results. Using funds supplied by a Russian businessman, Pavlov designed a three-story research building, known as the "Tower of Silence." The windows were covered with extra-thick glass and the rooms had double steel doors that formed an airtight seal when closed. Steel girders embedded in sand supported the floors. A straw-filled moat encircled the building. Vibration, noise, temperature extremes, odors, and drafts were eliminated. Pavlov wanted nothing to influence the experimental animals except the conditioning stimuli to which he exposed them.

***A conditioning experiment***    Let us follow a typical conditioning experiment in Pavlov's laboratory. The conditioned stimulus (a light, let us say) is presented; in this example, we will say that the light is switched on. Immediately, the experimenter presents the unconditioned stimulus—the food. After a number of pairings of the light and the food, the animal will salivate at the sight of the light alone. An association or bond has been formed between the light and the food, and the animal has become conditioned to respond to the conditioned stimulus. This conditioning or learning will not occur unless the light is followed by the food a sufficient number of times. Thus, **reinforcement** (actually being fed) is necessary for learning to take place.

**Reinforcement:**
Something that in-
creases the likelihood
of a response.

It is important to note that Pavlov's experimental program extended over a longer time period and involved more people than any research effort since Wundt. In the following excerpts from Pavlov's book, *Conditioned Reflexes*, we see how he built on the work of Descartes and how his approach was analytic, mechanistic, and atomistic. Also note how rigorous were the conditions under which he carried out his research.

## IN THEIR OWN WORDS

### Original Source Material from *Conditioned Reflexes* (1927)

**Ivan Pavlov**

Our starting point has been Descartes' idea of the nervous reflex. This is a genuine scientific conception, since it implies necessity. It may be summed up as follows: An external or internal stimulus falls on some one or other nervous receptor and gives rise to a nervous impulse; this nervous impulse is transmitted along nerve fibers to the central nervous system, and here, on account of existing nervous connections, it gives rise to a fresh impulse which passes along outgoing nerve fibers to the active organ, where it excites a special activity of the cellular structures. Thus a stimulus appears to be connected of necessity with a definite response, as cause with effect. It seems obvious that the whole activity of the organism should conform to definite laws....

Reflexes are the elemental units in the mechanism of perpetual equilibration. Physiologists have studied and are studying at the present time these numerous machine-like, inevitable reactions of the organism—reflexes existing from the very birth of the animal, and due therefore to the inherent organization of the nervous system.

Reflexes [are] like the driving-belts of machines of human design.... It was thought at the beginning of our research that it would be sufficient simply to isolate the experimenter in the research chamber with the dog on its stand, and to refuse admission to anyone else during the course of an experiment. But this precaution was found to be wholly inadequate, since the experimenter, however still he might try to be, was himself a constant source of a large number of stimuli. His slightest movements—blinking of the eyelids or movement of the eyes, posture, respiration, and so on—all acted as stimuli which, falling upon the dog, were sufficient to vitiate the experiments by making exact interpretation of the results extremely difficult.

In order to exclude this undue influence on the part of the experimenter as far as possible, he had to be stationed outside the room in which the dog was placed, and even this precaution proved unsuccessful in laboratories not specially designed for the study of these particular reflexes. The environment of the animal, even when shut up by itself in a room, is perpetually changing. Footfalls of a passer-by, chance conversations in neighboring rooms, slamming of a door or vibration from a passing van, street-cries, even shadows cast through the windows into the room, any of these casual uncontrolled stimuli falling upon the receptors of the dog set up a disturbance in the cerebral hemispheres and vitiate the experiments.

To get over all these disturbing factors a special laboratory was built at the Institute of Experimental Medicine in Petrograd, the funds being provided by a keen and public-spirited Moscow businessman. The primary task was the protection of the dogs from uncontrolled extraneous stimuli, and this was effected by surrounding the building with an isolating trench and employing other special structural devices. Inside the building all the research rooms (four to each floor) were isolated from one another by a cross-shaped corridor; the top and ground floors, where these rooms were situated, were separated by an intermediate floor. Each research room was carefully partitioned by the use of soundproof materials into two compartments—one for the animal, the other for the experimenter. For stimulating the animal, and for registering the corresponding reflex response, electrical methods or pneumatic transmission were used. By means of these arrangements it was possible to get something of that stability of environmental conditions so essential to the carrying out of a successful experiment.

## E. B. Twitmyer (1873–1943)

One historical sidelight involves another instance of independent simultaneous discovery. In 1904 a young American named Edwin Burket Twitmyer (1873–1943), a former student of Lightner Witmer's at the University of Pennsylvania, presented a paper at the annual convention of the APA based on his doctoral dissertation, which he had completed two years earlier. His work concerned the familiar knee-jerk reflex. Twitmyer had noticed that his subjects began to respond to stimuli other than the original stimulus, which was the tap of the hammer just below the knee. He described the subjects' reactions as a new and unusual kind of reflex and suggested that it be a topic for further study.

No one at the meeting expressed any interest in Twitmyer's report. There were no questions from the audience after he finished his presentation, and his research findings were ignored. Discouraged, he did not pursue the issue.

Historians have suggested several reasons for Twitmyer's continued obscurity. The Zeitgeist in American psychology may not have been ready to accept the notion of a conditioned reflex. Twitmyer may have been too young and inexperienced, or he may have lacked the skills and economic resources to persevere and publicize his ideas. Or perhaps it was simply a matter of bad timing that day. Twitmyer delivered his talk on reflexes just before lunch, as part of a series of papers in a session chaired by William James. The meeting was running late, and James (perhaps hungry, maybe bored) adjourned the meeting without allowing much time for comments on Twitmyer's report. An obituary written by a friend and colleague noted that "Twitmyer's own recollections of the occasion were always mingled with feelings of disappointment at the failure of his [audience] to express interest in his results" (Irwin, 1943, p. 452).

Periodically, historians revive this sad tale of a scientist who could have become famous for making one of the most important discoveries in all of psychology. "Surely Twitmyer must have wrestled with that realization most of his life—an awareness of what his legacy to psychology might have been" (Benjamin, 1987, p. 1119).

Another relatively unknown precursor of Pavlov's work was Alois Kreidl, an Austrian physiologist who demonstrated the basic principles of conditioning in 1896, predating Twitmyer's report by some eight years. Kreidl found that goldfish learned to anticipate feedings from the stimuli associated with the laboratory attendant walking toward their tank. Kreidl concluded that the fish saw the keeper approach, "then they became alert through the vibrations in the water produced by his [footsteps]" (quoted in Logan, 2002, p. 397). Kreidl's main interest, however, was the process of sensation, not conditioning or learning, and so these findings were not pursued within the scientific community.

## Comment

Pavlov demonstrated that higher mental processes in animal subjects could be described in physiological terms without any mention of consciousness. His conditioning methods have had broad practical applications in areas such as behavior therapy. Joseph Wolpe (1915–1997), the founder of behavior therapy, called Pavlov's conditioning principles essential to the development of his methods (Wolpe & Plaud, 1997). Pavlov's research also influenced psychology's shift toward greater objectivity in subject matter and method and reinforced the trend toward functional and practical applications.

Pavlov continued in the tradition of mechanism and atomism, views that shaped the new psychology from its beginnings. To Pavlov, all animals—whether his laboratory dogs or human beings—were machines. He admitted that they were complicated machines, but he believed, as one historian put it, that they were "just as submissive and obedient as any other machine" (Mazlish, 1993, p. 124).

Pavlov's conditioning techniques provided psychology with a basic element of behavior, a workable concrete unit to which complex human behavior could be reduced and experimented on under laboratory conditions. John B. Watson recognized this unit of behavior and made it the core of his program. Pavlov noted that he was pleased with Watson's work and that the growth of behaviorism in the United States represented a confirmation of his ideas and methods.

It is ironic that Pavlov's greatest influence was in psychology, a field toward which he was not altogether favorable. He was familiar with the structuralist and functionalist schools of thought. Also, he knew of William James's work and agreed with James that psychology might claim to be a science but had not yet achieved that status. Consequently, Pavlov excluded psychology from his own scientific work and even levied fines on laboratory assistants who used psychological terminology instead of physiological terminology. Pavlov later revised his attitude toward the field and occasionally referred to himself as an experimental psychologist. In any case, his initially negative view did not prevent psychologists from making effective use of his work.

# Vladimir M. Bekhterev (1857–1927)

Vladimir Bekhterev is another important figure in the development of animal psychology in that he helped lead the field away from subjective ideas toward objectively observed overt behavior. Although less well known than Ivan Pavlov, this Russian physiologist, neurologist, and psychiatrist was a pioneer in several research areas. He was a political radical openly critical of the czar and the Russian government. He accepted women and Jews as students and colleagues at a time when they were excluded from Russian universities.

Bekhterev received his degree from St. Petersburg's Military Medical Academy in 1881. He studied at the University of Leipzig with Wilhelm Wundt, took additional courses in Berlin and Paris, and returned to Russia to accept a professorship in mental diseases at the University of Kazan. In 1893 he was appointed chair of mental and nervous diseases at the Military Medical Academy, where he organized a mental hospital. In 1907 he founded the Psychoneurological Institute, which now bears his name.

Bekhterev and Pavlov became enemies after Pavlov published a negative review of one of Bekhterev's books:

> The enmity between Bekhterev and Pavlov was so pronounced that they would insult each other in the street. If they ran into each other at the same congress they would soon be embroiled in dispute. Forming cliques and slinging snide shots at each other, they were engaged in a constant struggle to expose one another's faults and weaknesses. No sooner had some pupil of Bekhterev made a public statement than it was parried by Pavlov's retort—which followed virtually as a conditioned reflex. (Ljunggren, 1990, p. 60)

In 1927, 10 years after the Bolshevik Revolution toppled the czar, Bekhterev was summoned to Moscow to treat Joseph Stalin, who was said to be suffering from depression. Bekhterev examined the dictator and told him the diagnosis was severe paranoia. Suspiciously, Bekhterev died that afternoon. No autopsy was permitted, and the body was quickly cremated. It was suggested that Stalin had Bekhterev poisoned as revenge for the psychiatric diagnosis. Stalin later ordered Bekhterev's research work suppressed and had his son executed (Lerner, Margolin, & Witztum, 2005; Ljunggren, 1990). In 1952, a year before Stalin died, the Soviet Union issued a postage stamp honoring Bekhterev.

### Associated Reflexes

**Associated reflexes:** Reflexes that can be elicited not only by unconditioned stimuli but also by stimuli that have become associated with the unconditioned stimuli.

Whereas Pavlov's conditioning research focused almost exclusively on glandular secretions, Bekhterev's interest was the motor conditioning response. In other words, he applied Pavlov's conditioning principles to the muscles. Bekhterev's basic discoveries were the **associated reflexes**, revealed through his study of motor responses. He found that reflexive movements—such as withdrawing one's finger from the source of an electric shock—could be elicited not only by the unconditioned stimulus (the electric shock), but also by the stimuli that had become associated with the original stimulus. For example, a buzzer sounded at the time of the shock soon brought about by itself the withdrawal of the finger.

The associationists explained such connections in terms of mental processes, but Bekhterev considered the reactions to be reflexive. He believed that higher-level behaviors of greater complexity could be explained in the same way; that is, as an accumulation or compounding of lower-level motor reflexes. Thought processes were similar in that they depended on inner actions of the speech musculature, an idea later adopted by Watson. Bekhterev argued for a completely objective approach to psychological phenomena and against the use of mentalistic terms and concepts.

He described his ideas in the book *Objective Psychology,* published in 1907. It was translated into German and French in 1913, and a third edition was published in English in 1932 as *General Principles of Human Reflexology.*

From the beginnings of animal psychology in the work of Romanes and Morgan, we can see a steady movement toward increased objectivity in subject matter and methodology. The initial work in the field invoked consciousness and mental processes and relied on subjective research methods. But by the early twentieth century, animal psychology was completely objective in subject matter and methods. Glandular secretions, conditional responses, acts, behaviors—these terms left no doubt that animal psychology had discarded its subjective past.

Animal psychology soon was to become a model for behaviorism, whose leader, Watson, preferred animal to human subjects for his psychological research. Watson made the findings and techniques of the animal psychologists the foundation of a science of behavior applicable to animals and humans alike.

# The Influence of Functional Psychology on Behaviorism

Another direct antecedent of behaviorism was functionalism. Although not a totally objective school of thought, functional psychology in Watson's day did represent greater objectivity than did its predecessors. Cattell and other functionalists emphasized behavior and objectivity and expressed dissatisfaction with introspection (see Chapter 8). Mark Arthur May (1891–1977), a graduate student at Columbia University in 1915, recalled Cattell's visit to his laboratory:

*May showed Cattell the equipment, which impressed him, but when May attempted to show Cattell the introspective reports obtained from the subjects, Cattell muttered "Not worth a damn!" and stormed out of the lab. (quoted in May, 1978, p. 655)*

Applied psychologists had little use for consciousness and introspection, and their various specialty areas essentially constituted an objective functional psychology. Even before Watson came on the scene, the functional psychologists had moved away from Wundt's and Titchener's pure psychology of conscious experience. In writings and lectures, some functional psychologists were quite specific in calling for an objective psychology, a psychology that would focus on behavior instead of consciousness.

Cattell, speaking at the 1904 World's Fair in St. Louis, Missouri, said:

*I am not convinced that psychology should be limited to the study of consciousness.... The rather widespread notion that there is no psychology apart from introspection is refuted by the brute argument of accomplished fact. It seems to me that most of the research work that has been done by me or in my laboratory is nearly as independent of introspection as work in physics or in zoology.... I see no reason why the application of systematized knowledge to the control of human nature may not in the course of the present century accomplish results commensurate with the nineteenth-century applications of physical science to the material world. (pp. 179–180, 186)*

Watson was in the audience for Cattell's speech. The similarity between Cattell's talk and Watson's later public position is striking. One historian suggested that if Watson is the father of behaviorism, Cattell should be called the grandfather (Burnham, 1968).

In the decade before Watson formally founded behaviorism, the intellectual climate in the United States favored the idea of an objective psychology. Indeed, the overall movement of American psychology was in a behavioristic direction. Robert Woodworth at Columbia University wrote that American psychologists were "slowly coming down with behaviorism … as more and more of them, from 1904 on, expressed a preference for defining psychology as the science of behavior rather than as an attempt to describe consciousness" (Woodworth, 1943, p. 28).

In 1911, Walter Pillsbury, who had studied with Titchener, defined psychology in his textbook as the science of behavior. He argued that it was possible to treat human beings as objectively as any other aspect of the physical universe. That same year Max Meyer published a book titled *The Fundamental Laws of Human Behavior*. William McDougall wrote *Psychology: The Study of Behavior* (1912), and Knight Dunlap, a psychologist at Johns Hopkins University, where Watson was teaching, proposed that introspection be banned from psychology.

Also that year, William Montague presented a paper—"Has Psychology Lost Its Mind?"—to the APA's New York branch. Montague spoke of moving to discard the "concept of mind or consciousness and to substitute the concept of behavior as the sufficient object of psychological study" (quoted in Benjamin, 1993, p. 77).

J. R. Angell at the University of Chicago, perhaps the most progressive of the functional psychologists, predicted that American psychology was ready for greater objectivity. In 1910, he commented that it seemed possible that the term "consciousness" would disappear from psychology, much as the term "soul" had disappeared. Three years later, shortly before the publication of Watson's behaviorist manifesto, Angell (1913) suggested that it would be profitable if consciousness were forgotten and animal and human behavior described objectively instead.

Thus, the notion that psychology should be the science of behavior was already gaining converts. Watson's greatness was not in being the first to propose the idea but in seeing, perhaps more clearly than anyone else, what the times were calling for. He responded boldly and articulately as the agent of a revolution whose inevitability and success were assured, because it was already under way.

# Discussion Questions

1. Compare Pavlov's concept of conditioned reflex with Bekhterev's associated reflex.
2. Describe the basic tenets of Watson's behaviorism and show how they differed from the positions of Wundt and Titchener.
3. Describe the development of animal psychology since the work of Romanes and Morgan. Why was it difficult to be an animal psychologist?
4. Describe Pavlov's initial focus on mentalistic experiences and his attempts to control outside influences on his research.
5. Describe Thorndike's puzzle-box research and the laws of learning suggested by the results.
6. Discuss the impact of the Clever Hans incident on animal psychology. What did Pfungst's experiments demonstrate?
7. Discuss the overall significance for the development of behaviorism of Thorndike's research on human and animal learning.
8. Discuss the Zeitgeist in American psychology in the second decade of the twentieth century with reference to ideas promoted by the structuralists and functionalists.
9. How did Pavlov's work influence Watson's behaviorism?
10. How did the functionalist school influence Watson's behaviorism?
11. How would you design an experiment to condition a rabbit to salivate to the ringing of a cell phone?
12. In what ways did Loeb, Washburn, Small, and Turner influence the new animal psychology?
13. In what ways had psychology changed by the second decade of the twentieth century?
14. Relate Thorndike's connectionism to the older philosophical notion of association.
15. What is Twitmyer's experience of interest to historians of psychology?
16. What role did positivism play in the scientific Zeitgeist of the twentieth century?
17. What were the three major forces Watson brought together to form his new psychology?
18. Why was Clever Hans considered such a sensation throughout the Western world?
19. Why was Watson so opposed to the study of consciousness and the method of introspection?

CHAPTER **10**

# The Beginnings of Behaviorism

## The Psychologist, the Baby, and the Hammer: Don't Try This at Home!

The beautiful young graduate student held the baby while the handsome, distinguished psychologist held the hammer. She waved her hand slowly in the air to hold the baby's attention so that he would fixate on it and not turn his head to look above or behind him. Thus distracted, the child did not notice the steel rod, four feet in length and three-fourths of an inch thick, hanging from the ceiling. He did not see the man who raised the hammer and sharply struck the metal bar.

The dry prose of their research report stated, "The child started violently, his breathing was checked and the arms were raised." When the psychologist struck the bar again, the child's lips "began to pucker and tremble" and with the third strike he "broke into a sudden crying fit" (Watson & Rayner, 1920, p. 2).

Have you guessed who these people are and what they were doing? The subject of this experiment became known as "Little Albert," the most famous baby in the history of psychology. The handsome psychologist was 42-year-old John B. Watson, the founder of the school of thought called *behaviorism*. His assistant was 21-year-old Rosalie Rayner, a graduate student who drove to the Johns Hopkins University campus in her Stutz Bearcat, the hottest and most expensive sports car of the time. Together they changed psychology and, in the process, ended Watson's brilliant academic career.

Albert (his surname remains unknown) was eight months old when the hammer struck the metal bar behind his head. A healthy, happy baby, he had been chosen by Watson to be the subject of his research precisely because he seemed so emotionally stable and not easily excited.

Two months before he was fated to be startled by the hammer strikes Albert had been shown a variety of stimuli, including a white rat, a rabbit, a dog, a monkey, burning newspapers, and an assortment of masks. He had not displayed any fear in response to those objects. In fact, neither Albert's mother nor anyone else had ever noticed the child displaying fear of any kind in any situation—until that day in the laboratory.

After Watson struck the bar initially, Albert reacted fearfully, apparently for the first time in his life. This gave Watson an *unconditioned* emotional response with which to work. He wanted to find out if he could produce in Albert a *conditioned* emotional response—such as fear of a white rat that he had not previously been afraid of—by pairing the sight of the rat with the loud, startling noise. In no more than seven pairings of the white rat with the noise, the child showed fear every time he spotted the rat, even when the bar had not been struck behind his head.

Thus Watson and Rayner established a response of fear to a previously neutral object, and they had done so easily and effectively. They then demonstrated that Albert's fear response could be generalized to other furry white things such as a rabbit, a dog, a fur coat, and a Santa Claus mask!

Watson concluded that our adult fears, anxieties, and phobias must therefore be simple conditioned emotional responses that were established in infancy and childhood and that stayed with us throughout our lives.

And what about Little Albert? Did he hide from furry white objects for the rest of his life? Did he have to undergo psychotherapy? Perhaps he became a psychologist. Attempts have been made to discover his real name and whereabouts, but so far they have been unsuccessful. (See, for example, Beck, Levinson, & Irons, 2009; Deangelis, 2010; Powell, 2010.) Although his identity remains unknown, there is no denying his contribution to the history of psychology and his role in the development of John B. Watson's behaviorism.

# John B. Watson (1878–1958)

We have discussed several trends that influenced John B. Watson in his attempt to construct the behaviorist school of thought for psychology. He recognized that founding is not the same as originating, and he described his efforts as a crystallization of the ideas already emerging within psychology. Like Wilhelm Wundt, psychology's first promoter-founder, Watson announced his goal of founding a new school. This deliberate intention clearly distinguishes him from others whom history now labels as precursors of behaviorism.

JOHN B. WATSON

Photo courtesy of James B. Watson

## Watson's Life

John B. Watson was born on a farm near Greenville, South Carolina, where his early education was conducted in a one-room schoolhouse. His mother was intensely religious, his father the opposite. The elder Watson drank heavily, was given to violence, and had several extramarital affairs. Because he rarely held any job for long, the family lived on the edge of poverty, subsisting on the output of their farm. Neighbors regarded them with pity and contempt. When Watson was 13 his father ran off with another woman, never to return, and Watson resented him all his life. Years later, when Watson was rich and famous, his father went to New York to see him, but Watson refused to meet him.

As a youth and teenager, Watson was something of a delinquent. He characterized himself as lazy and insubordinate, and he never earned better than passing grades in school. Teachers recalled him as indolent, argumentative, and sometimes uncontrollable. He got into fistfights and was twice arrested, once for shooting a gun within the city limits. Nevertheless, at age 16 he enrolled at Baptist-affiliated Furman University in Greenville, intending to become a minister, something he had promised his mother. He studied philosophy, mathematics, Latin, and Greek, expecting to enter Princeton Theological Seminary after graduating from Furman.

A curious thing allegedly occurred during Watson's senior year at Furman. The story is told that a professor warned the students that anyone who handed in the final examination with the pages in reverse order would receive a failing grade. Watson took up the challenge, turned in his exam backward, and failed; at least that is how Watson reported the story. Later examination of the pertinent historical data—in this case, Watson's grades—shows that he did not fail that particular course. His biographer suggests that the story Watson chose to tell reveals something of his personality, "his ambivalence toward success. Watson's constant striving for achievement and approval was often sabotaged by acts of sheer obstinacy and impulsiveness more characteristic of a flight from respectability" (Buckley, 1989, p. 11). Another of Watson's professors remembered him as a nonconformist, "a brilliant but somewhat lazy and insolent student—a bit heavy but handsome—who thought too highly of himself and was more interested in his own ideas than in people" (Brewer, 1991, p. 174).

Watson remained at Furman for another year, receiving his master's degree in 1899, but during that year his mother died, which released him from his vow to become a clergyman. Instead of the theological seminary, Watson went to the University of Chicago. His biographer noted that Watson was at this time "an ambitious, extremely status-conscious young man, anxious to make his mark upon the world but wholly unsettled as to his choice of profession and desperately insecure about his lack of means and social sophistication. He arrived on campus with fifty dollars to his name" (Buckley, 1989, p. 39).

He had chosen Chicago to pursue graduate work in philosophy with the great John Dewey but found Dewey's lectures incomprehensible. "I never knew what he was talking about then," Watson said, "and, unfortunately for me, I still don't know" (1936, p. 274). Not surprisingly, Watson's enthusiasm for philosophy diminished. Attracted to psychology by the work of James Rowland Angell, the functional psychologist, Watson also studied biology and physiology with Jacques Loeb, who acquainted him with the concept of mechanism.

Watson held several part-time jobs, working as a waiter in a boarding house, a rat caretaker, and an assistant janitor responsible for dusting Angell's desk. He began to have acute anxiety attacks toward the end of his graduate school years, and for a while he was unable to sleep without a light on in his room.

In 1903 Watson received his Ph.D. at age 25, the youngest person in the University of Chicago's history to earn a doctoral degree. Although he graduated with honors (magna cum laude and Phi Beta Kappa), he experienced profound feelings of inferiority when Angell and Dewey told him that his doctoral examination was not as good as that of Helen Bradford Thompson Woolley, who had graduated three years earlier (see Chapter 7). Watson wrote, "I wondered then if anybody could ever equal her record. That jealousy existed for years" (1936, p. 274).

That year Watson married one of his students, 19-year-old Mary Ickes, from a socially and politically prominent family. She had written a long love poem to Watson on one of her examination papers. It is not known what grade she got, but she did get Watson. Unfortunately, the marriage proved unsatisfactory for both (Buckley, 1989).

***Watson's academic career***   Watson stayed at the University of Chicago as an instructor until 1908. He published his dissertation on the neurological and psychological maturation of the white rat, research that showed his early preference for animal subjects:

> *I never wanted to use human subjects. I hated to serve as a subject. I didn't like the stuffy, artificial instructions given to subjects. I always was uncomfortable and acted unnaturally. With animals I was at home. I felt that, in studying them, I was keeping close to biology with my feet on the ground. More and more the thought presented itself: Can't I find out by watching their behavior everything that the other students are finding out by using [human observers]? (1936, p. 276)*

Watson's colleagues recall that he was not successful at introspection. Whatever talent or temperament was needed to pursue that technique, Watson did not have it. This lack may have helped to direct him toward an objective behavioral psychology. After all, if he was hopeless at practicing introspection, the primary research technique in his field, then career prospects were surely dim. He would have to develop another approach. Also, if he followed his inclination to see psychology as a science that studied only behavior—which, of course, could be done by experimenting on animals as well as humans—then he could help bring the professional interests of animal psychologists into the mainstream.

In 1908, Watson was offered a professorship at Johns Hopkins University in Baltimore. Although he was reluctant to leave Chicago, the promised promotion, substantial raise, and the chance to direct the laboratory left him little choice. As it turned out, Watson's 12 years at Hopkins were his most productive for psychology.

James Mark Baldwin (1861–1934), the psychologist who had offered Watson the job, was one of the founders (along with James McKeen Cattell) of the journal *Psychological Review*. A year after Watson arrived at Hopkins, Baldwin was forced to resign because of a scandal. He had been caught in a police raid on a house of prostitution, and his explanation was unacceptable to the university president. Baldwin said that he had "foolishly yielded to a suggestion, made after a dinner, to visit [the brothel] and see what was done there. I did not know before going that immoral women were harbored there" (quoted in Evans & Scott, 1978, p. 713). He did, however, give a false name to the police. Baldwin became an outcast from American psychology and spent his remaining years in England and in Mexico. He died in Paris in 1934 (Horley, 2001). Eleven years after Baldwin's dismissal, history would repeat itself. The same university president called for Watson's resignation because of another sex scandal.

When Baldwin resigned, Watson became chair of the psychology department and editor of the influential *Psychological Review*. Thus, at age 31, he suddenly had become a major figure in American psychology, in the right place at the right time. "The whole tenor of my life was changed," he wrote. "I tasted freedom in work without supervision. I was lost and happy in my work." Watson was less happy at home, however. "Two kids are enough," he wrote after his second son was born (quoted in Hulbert, 2003, p. 131). He began to pursue an active social life and developed a reputation as a womanizer, not unlike his father.

Watson was extremely popular with the Hopkins students. They dedicated their yearbook to him and voted him the handsomest professor, surely a unique accolade in the history of psychology. He remained ambitious and intense. Often fearful of losing control, he would drive himself to exhaustion.

## The Development of Behaviorism

Watson began to think seriously about a more objective psychology around 1903, and he expressed these ideas publicly in 1908 in a lecture at Yale University and in a paper presented at the annual meeting in Baltimore of the Southern Society for Philosophy and Psychology. Watson argued that psychic or mental concepts have no value for a science of psychology. In 1912, at Cattell's invitation, Watson delivered a series of lectures at Columbia University. The following year, he published his now famous article in the *Psychological Review* (Watson, 1913), and behaviorism was officially launched.

Watson's book, *Behavior: An Introduction to Comparative Psychology,* appeared in 1914. He argued for the acceptance of animal psychology and described the advantages of using animal subjects in psychological research. Many younger psychologists and graduate students found his proposals for a behavioral psychology appealing, insisting that Watson was cleansing psychology's muddled atmosphere by casting out longstanding mysteries carried over from philosophy.

Mary Cover Jones (1896–1987), then a graduate student and later president of the APA's Division of Developmental Psychology, recalled the excitement that greeted the publication of each of Watson's books. "[Watson's behaviorism] shook the foundations of traditional European-bred psychology, and we welcomed it…. It pointed the way from armchair psychology to action and reform and was therefore hailed as a panacea" (Jones, 1974, p. 582). Older psychologists usually were not so captivated by Watson's program. Indeed, most of them rejected his approach.

Only two years after the publication of the *Psychological Review* article, Watson was elected president of the APA. His election may not have represented an official endorsement of his position as much as it served as recognition of his visibility and the personal network he had established with many prominent psychologists.

He wanted his new behaviorism to be of practical value; his ideas were not only for the laboratory but for the real world as well. He promoted psychology's applied specialties and became a personnel consultant for a large insurance company. He also offered a course for business students at Hopkins on the psychology of advertising and started a program to train graduate students to work in industrial psychology.

During World War I, Watson served as a major in the U.S. Army, developing perceptual and motor ability tests to be used as selection devices for pilots. He also conducted research on how pilots are affected by the reduced oxygen at high altitudes. After the war, Watson and a physician established the Industrial Service Corporation to provide personnel selection and management consulting assistance to the business world (DiClemente & Hantula, 2000).

Despite his activities in these applied psychology areas, Watson's focus remained on developing his behaviorist approach to psychological thought. In 1919 he published *Psychology from the Standpoint of a Behaviorist,* which he dedicated to Cattell. In the book he presented a more complete statement of his behavioral psychology and argued that the methods and principles he had recommended for animal psychology were also appropriate for the study of humans.

***An affair to remember***   Meanwhile, Watson's marriage deteriorated; his many infidelities made his wife furious. He wrote to Angell that Mary no longer cared for him. "She instinctively loathes my touch. Haven't we made a mess of our lives?" (Watson, quoted in Buckley, 1994, p. 27). He was about to make an even greater mess.

Watson fell in love with Rosalie Rayner and wrote torrid, if somewhat scientifically worded, love letters, 15 of which his wife found. During the sensational divorce proceedings that followed, excerpts of the letters were printed in the *Baltimore Sun* newspaper:

> *Every cell I have is yours, individually and collectively. My total reactions are positive and toward you. So likewise each and every heart reaction. I can't be more yours than I am, even if a surgical operation made us one. (Watson, quoted in Pauly, 1979, p. 40)*

Thus ended Watson's promising university career. He was forced to resign from Johns Hopkins, an act that "almost certainly altered the history of American psychology" (Benjamin, Whitaker, Ramsey, & Zeve, 2007, p. 131). A biographer wrote, "Watson was stunned. Until the end, he had refused to believe that he would actually be fired. He had been convinced that his professional stature would have rendered him impervious to any censure of his private life" (Buckley, 1994, p. 31). Although he married Rosalie Rayner, he was never permitted to return to a full-time academic position. No university would have him because of the notoriety attached to his name, and he soon realized he would have to make a new life. "I can find a commercial job," he wrote, "but I frankly love my work. I feel that my work is important for psychology and that the tiny flame which I have tried to keep burning for the future of psychology will be snuffed out if I go" (quoted in Pauly, 1986, p. 39).

Many academic colleagues, including his mentor Angell at the University of Chicago, publicly criticized Watson. He was bitter about their lack of support, believing they were somehow disloyal. Ironically, considering their radically different temperaments and theoretical positions, it was E. B. Titchener at Cornell University who provided emotional sustenance for Watson during this personal crisis. "I am terribly sorry for the Watson children," Titchener wrote to Robert Yerkes. "Just as I am sorry for Watson himself; he will have to disappear for five or ten years, I am afraid, if he ever wants to return to psychology" (quoted in Leys & Evans, 1990, p. 105).

***Watson's business career***    Unemployed and ordered to pay two-thirds of his former salary in alimony and child support, Watson began a second professional career as an applied psychologist in the field of advertising. He joined the J. Walter Thompson advertising agency in 1921 for an annual salary of $25,000, four times his academic salary. He conducted house-to-house surveys, sold coffee, and clerked in Macy's department store to learn about the business world. Acting with his characteristic ingenuity and drive, he became a vice president within three years. He joined another advertising agency in 1936, where he remained until his retirement in 1945.

Watson believed that human behavior is not unlike that of machines. Therefore, the behavior of people as consumers of goods and services could be predicted and controlled, just like the behavior of other machines. To control a consumer, he said,

> *it is only necessary to confront him with either fundamental or conditional emotional stimuli. … tell him something that will tie up with fear, something that will stir up a mild rage, that will call out an affectionate or love response, or strike at a deep psychological or habit need. (quoted in Buckley, 1982, p. 212)*

He proposed laboratory studies of consumer behavior. He stressed that advertising messages should focus on style rather than substance and should convey the impression of a new and improved image. The purpose was to make consumers dissatisfied with the products they were using and to instill the desire for new goods.

For many years, Watson was credited with pioneering the use of celebrity endorsements of products and services and for devising techniques to manipulate our motives and emotions. Later research has shown that although he strongly promoted these techniques, they were already in use before he joined the advertising world (see Coon, 1994; Kreshel, 1990). Nevertheless, Watson's contributions to advertising were highly effective and soon brought him prominence and wealth.

After 1920, Watson had only indirect contact with academic psychology. Instead, he presented his ideas for a behavioral psychology to the general public through lectures, radio addresses, and articles in popular magazines, thus increasing his visibility—and, some would say, his notoriety. In one article written for popular consumption, for example, he predicted the end of the institution of marriage. "Monogamy is passing, I believe. The social mechanism has slipped its trolley. We are unfettered and unshackled and are romping and frolicking in our freedom" (quoted in Simpson, 2000, p. 64). If Watson was out to shock people, he was succeeding.

In his magazine articles, Watson also conveyed the more serious message of behaviorism to a wide audience. His writing style was clear, readable, and somewhat simplistic. In his autobiography he commented that although his work was no longer acceptable to the professional psychology journals, there was no reason why he should not "sell his wares" to the public (Watson, 1936). This attitude alienated him further from the academic community. "Those who were not particularly tolerant of the application of psychological principles more generally, or of the behaviorist doctrine itself, were even less tolerant of Watson's 'campaigns' to spread the doctrine" (Kreshel, 1990, p. 56).

A rare formal contact with academic psychology came through a series of lectures Watson delivered at New York's New School for Social Research, but his appointment there did not last long. He was dismissed because of alleged sexual misconduct, though the charges were never made public (Buckley, 1989).

Other outlets for Waston's views became available, however. The lectures at the New School formed the basis of his book, *Behaviorism*, which described his program for the improvement of society. The book was first published in 1925, and Watson later admitted that it had been hastily prepared. "My lectures were taken down in shorthand and then I looked over them and rushed them to [the publisher]" (quoted in Carpentero, 2004, p. 185). A more polished version was released in 1930. Both editions were immensely successful, and Watson's ideas reached and influenced a large number of people outside the realm of psychology.

***Child-rearing practices***   In 1928 Watson published *Psychological Care of the Infant and Child*, in which he severely criticized the child-rearing practices of the day. He charged that "parents today are incompetent. Most of them should be indicted for psychological murder" (quoted in Hulbert, 2003, p. 123). He proposed a regulatory rather than a permissive system of child rearing, in keeping with his strong environmentalist position. The book was full of stern advice on the behaviorist way to bring up children. According to Watson, parents should never

> *hug and kiss them, never let them sit on your lap. If you must, kiss them once on the forehead when they say goodnight. Shake hands with them in the morning. Give them a pat on the head if they have made an extraordinarily good job of a difficult task.... you will find how easy it is to be perfectly objective with your child and at the same time kindly. You will be utterly ashamed at the mawkish, sentimental way you have been handling it. (1928, pp. 81–82)*

This book also was extremely popular, and it transformed American child-rearing practices. A generation of children, including his own, was raised in accordance with these prescriptions. Watson's son James, a California businessman, recalled that his father was unable to show affection to him and his brother. He described Watson as

> *unresponsive, emotionally uncommunicative, unable to express and cope with any feelings or emotions of his own, and determined unwittingly to deprive, I think, my brother and me of any kind of emotional foundation. He deeply believed that any expression of tenderness or affection would have a harmful effect on us. He was very rigid in carrying out his fundamental philosophies as a behaviorist. We were never kissed or held as children; we were never shown any kind of emotional closeness. It was absolutely verboten in the family. When I went to bed at night, I recall shaking hands with my parents.... I never tried (nor did my brother Billy) to ever get close to our parents physically because we both knew it was taboo. (quoted in Hannush, 1987, pp. 137–138)*

Watson's wife, Rosalie, wrote an article for *Parents Magazine* titled "I Am the Mother of a Behaviorist's Sons," in which she publicly disagreed with his child-rearing practices. "In some respects," she wrote, "I bow to the great wisdom in the science of behaviorism, and in others I am rebellious. I secretly wish that on the score of [the children's] affections, they will be a little weak when they grow up, that they will have a tear in their eyes for the poetry and drama of life and a throb for romance.... I like being merry and gay and having the giggles. The behaviorists think giggling is a sign of maladjustment" (quoted in Simpson, 2000, p. 65). Rosalie also contended that she found it difficult to restrain completely her affection for her children and occasionally wanted to break the behaviorist rules. However, her son James could not recall that ever happening.

Both sons suffered from serious depression throughout adolescence and adulthood. One son committed suicide and the other had a mental collapse, fighting his own suicidal impulses. Although he survived, his own daughter took her life some years later. In addition, Watson's daughter by his first marriage made several suicide attempts.

"I've always been suicidal," she told her daughter. "The depression began during the [divorce] scandal in Baltimore" (quoted in Hartley & Commire, 1990, p. 273).

Her daughter (Watson's granddaughter), the actress Mariette Hartley, also suffered from depression, alcoholism, and suicidal thoughts. She noted that "there wasn't exactly a plethora of physical affection in our family" (quoted in Stimpert, 2010, p. 2) It appears that Watson's behavioral approach to child rearing was not exactly a success within his own family.

**Watson's later years**   Watson was intelligent, articulate, handsome, and charming, and it was these qualities that made him a celebrity. He was often in the public eye, courting and relishing the attention. His clothes were stylish, he raced speedboats, and he mingled easily with the cream of New York society. He considered himself a great lover and romantic adventurer, and he liked to take on all challengers in drinking bouts. He built a mansion in Connecticut and staffed it with servants, yet he enjoyed dressing in old clothes and doing his own yard work.

> [Watson was] very concerned with manly activities, for example, hunting, fishing, and other ways in which adults and children could demonstrate their courage and personal capabilities. In that way he had a Hemingway-like aura about him for he valued competency, bravery and manliness. (James Watson, quoted in Hannush, 1987, p. 138)

In 1935, Rosalie died at the age of 37. James Watson recalled that this was the only time he saw his father cry. For a brief moment, Watson hugged his sons for the only time they could recall. He then sent them off to boarding school and never spoke of Rosalie to them again.

When Myrtle McGraw, a psychologist in New York, ran into Watson not long afterward, he told her how unprepared he was to deal with Rosalie's death. Because he was 20 years older, he had always assumed he would die first. He talked to McGraw at some length, questioning how he would cope with his grief (McGraw, 1990). He soon became a recluse, shutting himself off from social contact and plunging into work. He sold the big house and moved to a wooden farmhouse that resembled his boyhood home.

In 1957, when Watson was 79, the APA awarded him a citation, praising his work as "one of the vital determinants of the form and substance of modern psychology ... the point of departure for continuing lines of fruitful research." A friend drove Watson to the New York hotel where the presentation was to be held,

> but at the last minute Watson refused to go inside and insisted that his eldest son attend in his stead. Watson was afraid that in that moment his emotions would overwhelm him, that the apostle of behavior control would break down and weep. (Buckley, 1989, p. 182)

Before Watson died the following year, he burned all of his letters, manuscripts, and notes, feeding them into the fireplace one by one, refusing to leave them to history.

The best way to begin our coverage of Watson's behaviorist school of thought is to read an excerpt from the article that launched the movement. In the following passage, Watson discusses the definition and goal of his new psychology and criticizes the structuralist and functionalist schools. He also explains his view that areas of applied psychology can be considered scientific because they seek general laws for the prediction and control of behavior.

# IN THEIR OWN WORDS

## Original Source Material on Behaviorism from *Psychology as the Behaviorist Views It* (1913)

John B. Watson[1]

Psychology as the behaviorist views it is a purely objective experimental branch of natural science. Its theoretical goal is the prediction and control of behavior. Introspection forms no essential part of its methods, nor is the scientific value of its data dependent upon the readiness with which they lend themselves to interpretation in terms of consciousness. The behaviorist, in his efforts to get a unitary scheme of animal response, recognizes no dividing line between man and brute. The behavior of man, with all of its refinement and complexity, forms only a part of the behaviorist's total scheme of investigation....

I do not wish unduly to criticize psychology. It has failed signally, I believe, during the fifty-odd years of its existence as an experimental discipline to make its place in the world as an undisputed natural science. Psychology, as it is generally thought of, has something esoteric in its methods. If you fail to reproduce my findings, it is not due to some fault in your apparatus or in the control of your stimulus, but it is due to the fact that your introspection is untrained. The attack is made upon the observer and not upon the experimental setting....

The time seems to have come when psychology must discard all reference to consciousness; when it need no longer delude itself into thinking that it is making mental states the object of observation. We have become so enmeshed in speculative questions concerning the elements of the mind, the nature of conscious content ... that I, as an experimental student, feel that something is wrong with our premises and the types of problems which develop from them....

I firmly believe that two hundred years from now, unless the introspective method is discarded, psychology will still be divided on the question as to whether auditory sensations have the quality of extension, whether intensity is an attribute which can be applied to color, whether there is a difference in texture between image and sensation, and upon many hundreds of other [questions] of like character....

My psychological quarrel is not with the systematic and structural psychologist alone. The last fifteen years have seen the growth of what is called functional psychology. This type of psychology decries the use of elements in the static sense of the structuralists. It throws emphasis upon the biological significance of conscious processes instead of upon the analysis of conscious states into introspectively isolable elements.

I have done my best to understand the difference between functional psychology and structural psychology. Instead of clarity, confusion grows upon me. The terms *sensation, perception, affection, emotion, volition* are used as much by the functionalist as by the structuralist.... Surely if these concepts are elusive when looked at from a content standpoint, they are still more deceptive when viewed from the angle of function, and especially so when function is obtained by the introspection method....

I was greatly surprised some time ago when I opened [Walter] Pillsbury's book and saw psychology defined as the "science of behavior." A still more recent text states that psychology is the "science of mental behavior." When I saw these promising statements I thought, now surely we will have texts based upon different lines. After a few pages the science of behavior is dropped and one finds the conventional treatment of sensation, perception, imagery, and so forth, along with certain shifts in emphasis and additional facts which serve to give the author's personal imprint.

---

[1]From "Psychology as the Behaviorist Views It," by J. B. Watson, 1913, *Psychological Review*, 20, 158–177. Copyright 1913 by the American Psychological Association. Reprinted by permission.

I believe we can write a psychology, define it as Pillsbury, and never go back upon our definition: never use the terms *consciousness, mental states, mind, content, introspectively verifiable, imagery,* and the like.... It can be done in terms of *stimulus* and *response,* in terms of *habit formation, habit integrations* and the like. Furthermore, I believe that it is really worthwhile to make this attempt now....

What gives me hope that the behaviorist's position is a defensible one is the fact that those branches of psychology which have already partially withdrawn from the parent, experimental psychology, and which are consequently less dependent upon introspection are today in a most flourishing condition. Experimental pedagogy, the psychology of drugs, the psychology of advertising, legal psychology, the psychology of tests, and psychopathology are all vigorous growths. These are sometimes wrongly called "practical" or "applied" psychology. Surely there was never a worse misnomer. In the future there may grow up vocational bureaus which really apply psychology. At present these fields are truly scientific and are in search of broad generalizations which will lead to the control of human behavior.

For example, we find out by experimentation whether a series of stanzas may be acquired more readily if the whole is learned at once, or whether it is more advantageous to learn each stanza separately and then pass to the succeeding. We do not attempt to apply our findings. The application of this principle is purely voluntary on the part of the teacher.

In the psychology of drugs we may show the effect upon behavior of certain doses of caffeine. We may reach the conclusion that caffeine has a good effect upon the speed and accuracy of work. But these are general principles. We leave it to the individual as to whether the results of our tests shall be applied or not.

Again, in legal testimony, we test the effects of recency upon the reliability of a witness's report. We test the accuracy of the report with respect to moving objects, stationary objects, color, and so forth. It depends upon the judicial machinery of the country to decide whether these facts are ever to be applied.

For a "pure" psychologist to say that he is not interested in the questions raised in these divisions of the science because they relate indirectly to the application of psychology shows, in the first place, that he fails to understand the scientific aim in such problems, and secondly, that he is not interested in a psychology which concerns itself with human life. The only fault I have to find with these disciplines is that much of their material is stated in terms of introspection, whereas a statement in terms of objective results would be far more valuable. There is no reason why appeal should ever be made to consciousness in any of them. Or why introspective data should ever be sought during the experimentation, or published in the results.

The plans which I most favor for psychology lead practically to the ignoring of consciousness in the sense that that term is used by psychologists today. I have virtually denied that this realm of psychics is open to experimental investigation. I don't wish to go further into the problem at present because it leads inevitably over into metaphysics. If you will grant the behaviorist the right to use consciousness in the same way that other natural scientists employ it—that is, without making consciousness a special object of observation—you have granted all that my thesis requires.

# The Reaction to Watson's Program

Watson's attack on the old psychology and his call for a new approach were stirring appeals for many psychologists. Let us reconsider his major points. Psychology was to be the science of behavior, not the introspective study of consciousness, and a purely objective, experimental natural science. Both human and animal behavior would be investigated, and psychologists would discard all mentalistic ideas and use only behavior concepts such as stimulus and response. Psychology's goal would be the prediction and control of behavior.

Despite its appeal to some, however, Watson's program was not embraced immediately or universally. At first, behaviorism received relatively little attention in the professional journals. Not until the publication of Watson's 1919 book, *Psychology from the Standpoint of a Behaviorist,* did the movement begin to have a significant impact.

One psychologist who disagreed with Watson was Mary Whiton Calkins. Questioning his rejection of introspection, she spoke for many psychologists who believed that certain psychological processes could be studied only by introspection. The arguments about introspection persisted for years; Margaret Washburn went so far as to call Watson an enemy of psychology.

Inevitably, support for Watson's movement grew, particularly among younger psychologists, and by the 1920s universities were offering courses in behaviorism and the term was becoming acceptable in the professional journals. Among the older psychologists, William McDougall issued a public warning against behaviorism's popularity, and E. B. Titchener complained that behaviorism had engulfed the country like a tidal wave. By 1930, however, Watson could proclaim proudly that behaviorism was so important that no university could avoid teaching it.

The behaviorism movement did succeed, of course, but the changes Watson called for in 1913 came about slowly. And when they finally arrived, his was not the only form of behavioral psychology being promoted.

## The Methods of Behaviorism

We have seen that when scientific psychology formally began, it was eager to ally itself with the older, well-established, and more respectable natural science of physics. The new psychology tried to adapt natural science methods to its own needs. This tendency is most obvious with behaviorism.

Watson insisted that psychology restrict itself to the data of the natural sciences, to what could be observed. To put it simply, psychology must restrict itself to the objective study of behavior. Only the most stringently objective methods of investigation were acceptable in the behaviorist's laboratory. To Watson, these methods included the following:

- *Observation with and without the use of instruments*
- *Testing methods*
- *The verbal report method*
- *The conditioned reflex method*

Observation is a necessary basis for the other methods. Objective testing methods were already in use, but Watson proposed that test results be treated as samples of behavior rather than indicators of mental qualities. To Watson, a test did not measure intelligence or personality; instead, it measured the subject's responses to the stimulus situation of taking the test, and nothing more.

Verbal report is more controversial. Because Watson so vocally opposed introspection, his use of verbal reporting in the laboratory left him open to criticism. Some psychologists considered it a weak compromise, saying that he let introspection sneak in the back door after throwing it out through the front.

Why did Watson allow verbal reports? Despite his aversion to introspection, he could not ignore the work of psychophysicists that used introspection. Therefore, he suggested that speech reactions, because they are objectively observable, are as meaningful for behaviorism as any other type of motor response. "Saying is doing—that is, behaving," Watson wrote. "Speaking overtly or to ourselves (thinking) is just as objective a type of behavior as baseball" (Watson, 1930, p. 6).

Nevertheless, the verbal report method in behaviorism was a concession widely challenged. Opponents contended that Watson was playing word games, offering merely a semantic change. Watson countered by agreeing that verbal reports could be imprecise and were not a satisfactory substitute for objective observation. He restricted their use to situations in which they could be verified, such as reporting differences between tones. Unverifiable verbal reports, such as imageless thoughts or accounts of feeling states, were ruled out.

The conditioned reflex method was adopted by Watson in 1915, two years after behaviorism's formal founding. Conditioning methods were already in limited use, but Watson was largely responsible for their widespread application in American psychological research. Watson told psychologist Ernest Hilgard that his interest in conditioned reflexes grew out of his study of Bekhterev's work, although he later gave credit to Pavlov as well (Hilgard, 1994).

Watson wrote to his student Karl Lashley in 1915 that the conditioned reflex "works so beautifully in place of introspection that it deserves to be driven home; we can work on the human being as we can on animals and from the same point of view" (quoted in Buckley, 1989, p. 86).

Watson described conditioning in terms of stimulus substitution. A response is conditioned when it becomes attached or connected to a stimulus other than the one that originally aroused it. (With Pavlov's dogs, salivation to the sound of a bell instead of to the sight of food is a conditioned response.) Watson chose this approach because it provided an objective method of analyzing behavior, of reducing it to its elementary units, the stimulus–response (S-R) bonds. Because all behavior could be reduced to these elements, the conditioned reflex method permitted psychologists to conduct laboratory investigations of complex human behaviors.

Watson was continuing in the atomistic and mechanistic tradition established by the British empiricists and adopted by the structural psychologists. He intended to study human behavior in the same way the physical scientists were studying the universe, by breaking it down into its component parts, into its atoms and elements.

This exclusive focus on objective methods, along with the elimination of introspection, meant a change in the nature and role of the human subject in the psychology laboratory. For Wundt and Titchener, subjects were both observer and observed because they observed their own conscious experience. Their role was clearly much more important than that of the experimenter.

In behaviorism, the subjects themselves became less important. They no longer observed; instead, they were observed by the experimenters. With this change in focus, the laboratory subjects who used to be called "observers" became commonly known as "subjects." The true observers were the experimenters, the research psychologists who established the experimental conditions and recorded the subjects' responses.

Thus, human subjects were demoted in status. They no longer actively observed their own characteristics. They merely behaved—and almost anyone can behave: infants, children, people with mental and emotional disorders, pigeons, or white laboratory rats. This viewpoint reinforced psychology's image of people as machines. As one historian noted, "You put a stimulus in one of the slots and out comes a packet of reactions" (Burt, 1962, p. 232).

## The Subject Matter of Behaviorism

The primary subject matter for Watson's behavioral psychology was the elements of behavior; that is, the body's muscular movements and glandular secretions. As the science of behavior, psychology would deal only with acts that could be described objectively, without using subjective or mentalistic terminology.

Despite their stated goal of reducing all behavior to S-R units, ultimately behaviorists must strive to understand the organism's total behavior. For example, although a response can be as simple as a knee jerk, it can also be more complex. Watson called these more complex responses "acts." He considered response acts to include such events as eating, writing, dancing, or constructing a house. In other words, an act involves the organism's movement in space. Apparently Watson conceived of response acts in terms of accomplishing some goal that affects one's environment, rather than as a simple linking of muscular elements. Nevertheless, behavioral acts, no matter how complex, were capable of being reduced to lower-level motor or glandular responses.

Responses can be either explicit or implicit. Explicit responses are overt and directly observable. Implicit responses, such as visceral movements, glandular secretions, and nerve impulses, occur inside the organism. Although not overt, they are still considered to be behavior. By including implicit responses, Watson was modifying his requirement that all of psychology's data be actually observable. He accepted that some items of behavior could be potentially observable. The movements or responses that occur within the organism are observable through the use of instruments.

Like the responses with which behaviorism deals, the stimuli may be simple or complex. Light waves striking the eye's retina are relatively simple stimuli, but stimuli can also be more complex. Just as the constellation of responses involved in an action can be reduced to component responses, so the stimulus situation can be resolved into specific component stimuli. Thus, Watson's behavioral psychology investigates the behavior of the whole organism in relation to its environment. Specific laws of behavior can be proposed by first analyzing the S-R complexes into their elementary S-R units.

Thus, in both methods and subject matter, Watson's behaviorism was an attempt to construct a science free of subjective notions and methods, a science as objective as physics. Let us consider how Watson treated three major topics: instincts, emotions, and thoughts. Like all systematic theorists, Watson developed his psychology in accordance with the underlying belief that all areas of behavior would be considered in objective S-R terms.

## Instincts

Initially Watson accepted the role of instincts in behavior. In his book *Behavior: An Introduction to Comparative Psychology* (1914), he described 11 instincts, including one dealing with random behaviors. He had studied instinctive behavior in terns, a species of aquatic bird, in the Dry Tortugas Islands off the Florida coast. Accompanying him was Karl Lashley, his student at Johns Hopkins University. Lashley claimed that the expedition was cut short when he and Watson ran out of cigarettes and whiskey.

By 1925 Watson revised his position and eliminated the concept of instinct altogether. He argued that behaviors that seem instinctive are really socially conditioned responses. By adopting the view that learning, or conditioning, is the key to understanding all human development, Watson became an extreme environmentalist. And then he went further. Not only did he deny instincts, he refused to admit to his system any inherited capacities, temperaments, or talents of any kind.

Behaviors that seemed inherited were traced to early childhood training. For example, he argued that children were not born with the ability to be great athletes or musicians but were slanted in that direction by parents or caregivers who encouraged and reinforced the appropriate behaviors. This emphasis on the overwhelming nurturing effect of the parental and social environment was one reason for Watson's phenomenal popularity. He concluded, simply and optimistically, that children could be trained to be whatever one wanted them to be. There were no limitations imposed by genetic factors.

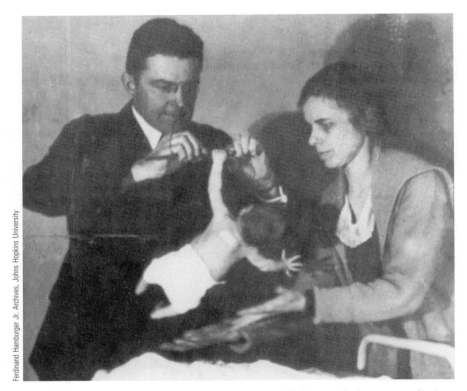

Ferdinand Hamburger Jr. Archives, Johns Hopkins University

Watson tests the grasping reflex of an infant. (From a still photo made from a 1919 film.)

Watson was not alone in suggesting that environmental influences were more important than any traits or potentials we might be born with. It was already becoming popular within psychology to minimize the role of instincts as behavioral determinants. Thus, Watson's position reflected a shift in viewpoint already in progress. In addition, his stand may have been influenced by the applied orientation of early twentieth-century American psychology. Psychology could not be applied in ways to alter behavior unless it was accepted that behavior was capable of being changed. Behaviors governed by forces such as instincts could not be modified, whereas behaviors dependent on learning or training could.

## Emotions

To Watson, emotions were merely physiological responses to specific stimuli. A stimulus (such as a person suddenly threatening you with bodily harm) produces internal physical changes such as rapid heart rate along with the appropriate learned overt responses. This explanation for emotions denies any conscious perception of the emotion or the sensations from the internal organs.

Each emotion involves a particular pattern of physiological changes. Although Watson noted that emotional responses do involve overt movements, he believed that the internal responses were predominant. Thus, emotion is a form of implicit behavior in which internal reactions are evident in physical manifestations, such as blushing, perspiration, or increased pulse rate.

Watson's theory of emotions is less complex than that of William James. In James's theory, the bodily changes immediately followed the perception of the stimulus, and the feeling of those bodily changes was the emotion. Watson criticized James's position.

Discarding the conscious process of perceiving the situation and the feeling state, Watson claimed that emotions could be described completely in terms of the objective stimulus situation, the overt bodily response, and the internal physiological changes.

In a now classic study, Watson investigated the stimuli that produce emotional responses in infants. He suggested that infants show three fundamental unlearned emotional response patterns: fear, rage, and love. Fear can be produced by loud noises and by sudden loss of support. Rage is produced by the restriction of bodily movements. Love is evoked by caressing the skin or by rocking and patting. Watson also found typical response patterns to these stimuli. Other emotional responses are compounded of these basic emotions through the conditioning process, and they may become attached to stimuli that were not originally capable of eliciting them.

## Albert, Peter, and the Rabbits

As we noted at the beginning of this chapter, Watson demonstrated his theory of conditioned emotional responses in his experimental studies of eight-month-old Albert, who was conditioned to fear a white rat, something he had not feared before the conditioning trials. From that research Watson concluded that all adult fears, aversions, and anxieties likewise are conditioned in early childhood. They do not arise, as Freud claimed, from unconscious conflicts. Watson rejected the whole notion of the unconscious because, like consciousness, it could not be objectively observed. Initially he was fascinated by many of Freud's concepts, but he eventually dismissed psychoanalysis as "voodooism" (quoted in Rilling, 2000, p. 302).

Watson described the Albert research as preliminary, a pilot study only. Nevertheless, it has never been successfully replicated. Although psychologists have since noted serious methodological flaws, the results of the Albert study have been accepted as scientific evidence and are cited in virtually every basic psychology textbook.

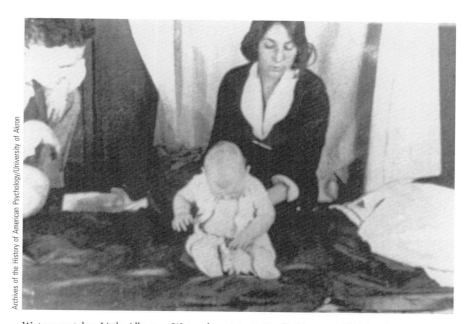

Watson watches Little Albert as Watson's assistant, Rosalie Rayner, holds the child in a sitting position. The child seems to be reaching for the white rat between his feet. Albert was conditioned to fear the rat and similar stimuli.

MARY COVER JONES

Although Albert had been conditioned to fear white rats, rabbits, and Santa Claus masks, he was no longer available when Watson wanted to try to eliminate those fears. Not long after starting this research program, Watson left academics. Later, when working in advertising in New York, he gave a talk about his research. In the audience was Mary Cover Jones (a college classmate of his wife, Rosalie). Watson's remarks sparked Jones's interest, and she wondered whether the conditioning technique could be used to remove children's fears. She asked Rosalie to introduce her to Watson, and then she undertook a study that has since become another classic in the history of psychology (Jones, 1924).

Her subject was three-year-old Peter, who already showed a fear of rabbits, although his fear had not been conditioned in the laboratory. While Peter was eating, a rabbit was brought into the room but kept at a distance great enough so as not to trigger a fearful response. Over a series of trials lasting several weeks, the rabbit was brought progressively closer, always while the child was eating. Eventually Peter got used to the rabbit and could touch it without showing fear. Generalized fear responses to similar objects were also eliminated by this procedure.

Jones's study has been described as a precursor of behavior therapy (the application of learning principles to change maladaptive behavior), almost 50 years before the technique became popular. Jones, long associated with the Institute of Child Welfare at the University of California, Berkeley, received the G. Stanley Hall award in 1968 for her outstanding contributions to developmental psychology.

## Thought Processes

The traditional view of thought processes was that they occurred in the brain "so faintly that no neural impulse passes out over the motor nerve to the muscle, hence no response takes place in the muscles and glands" (Watson, 1930, p. 239). According to this theory, because thought processes occur in the absence of muscular movements, they are not accessible to observation and experimentation. Thought was regarded as intangible, something exclusively mental that therefore had no physical reference points (see Bouton, 2009; Hall, 2009).

Watson's behaviorist system attempted to reduce thinking to implicit motor behavior. He argued that thought, like all other aspects of human functioning, was a type of sensorimotor behavior. He reasoned that the behavior of thinking must involve implicit speech reactions or movements. Thus, he reduced thinking to sub-vocal talking that relies on the same muscular habits we learn for overt speech. As we grow up, these muscular habits become inaudible and invisible because our parents and teachers frequently admonish us to stop talking aloud to ourselves. In this way, thinking becomes a way of talking silently.

Watson suggested that the focal points for much of this implicit behavior are the muscles of the tongue and the larynx (the so-called voice box). We also express thought through gestures such as frowns and shrugs, which are overt reactions to stimuli.

One obvious source of corroboration for Watson's theory is that most of us are aware that we do talk to ourselves while we are thinking. A study of college students' introspective reports found that 73 percent of the thoughts sampled involved talking to themselves while they were thinking (Farthing, 1992). This kind of evidence, however, is unacceptable to behaviorists precisely because it is introspective, and Watson could hardly depend on introspection to support his behavioral theory. Behaviorism required objective evidence of implicit speech movements, so he made experimental attempts to record tongue and larynx movements during thought.

These measurements revealed slight movements some of the time the subjects were thinking. Measurements from the fingers and hands of hearing-impaired people using sign language also revealed movements some of the time during thought. Despite his inability to secure more reliable supportive results, Watson remained convinced of the existence of implicit speech movements. He insisted that their demonstration awaited only the development of more sophisticated laboratory equipment.

## Behaviorism's Popular Appeal

Why did Watson's bold pronouncements win him such a large public following? Surely most people did not care that some psychologists pretended to be conscious while others proclaimed psychology had lost its mind, or that some said thinking took place in the head and others voted for the neck. These issues aroused considerable comment among psychologists, but they hardly concerned anyone else.

What stirred the public was Watson's call for a society based on scientifically shaped and controlled behavior, free of myths, customs, and conventional behaviors. His ideas offered hope to people disenchanted with old ideas. In fervor and faith, behaviorism took on aspects of a religion. Among the hundreds of articles and books written about Watson's behaviorism was *The Religion Called Behaviorism* (Berman, 1927), soon to be read by a 23-year-old man named B. F. Skinner, who wrote a review of the book and sent it to a popular literary magazine. "They did not publish [my review], but in writing it I was more or less defining myself for the first time as a behaviorist" (Skinner, 1976, p. 299). Skinner would go on to refine and extend Watson's work (see Chapter 11).

Some of the excitement generated by Watson's ideas is evident in the newspaper comments on his book *Behaviorism* (1925). The *New York Times* declared, "It marks an epoch in the intellectual history of man" (August 2, 1925). The *New York Herald Tribune* called it "the most important book ever written. One stands for an instant blinded with a great hope" (June 21, 1925).

The hope stemmed from Watson's emphasis on the nurturing effect of the childhood environment in determining behavior and from his minimization of the impact of inherited tendencies. The following paragraph from *Behaviorism* is frequently quoted to support his point:

> *Give me a dozen healthy infants, well-formed, and my own specified world to bring them up in, and I'll guarantee to take any one at random and train him to become any type of specialist I might select—doctor, lawyer, artist, merchant-chief, and, yes, even beggar-man and thief, regardless of his talents, penchants, tendencies, abilities, vocations, and race of his ancestors. (Watson, 1930, p. 104)*

Watson's conditioned reflex experiments, such as the Albert study, persuaded him that emotional disturbances in adulthood are caused by conditioned responses established in infancy, childhood, and adolescence. If adult disturbances are a function of faulty childhood conditioning, then a proper program of childhood conditioning should prevent the emergence of adult disorders. Watson believed this kind of practical control over childhood behavior (and hence over the later adult behavior) was not only possible but absolutely necessary. He developed a plan for improving society, a program of experimental ethics, based on the principles of behaviorism.

No one gave him a dozen healthy infants so he could test his claim, and he later admitted that in making it he was going beyond the facts. However, he noted that people who disagreed with him and believed the impact of heredity was greater than that of the environment had been stating their case for thousands of years and still had no real evidence for their view.

The following passage from *Behaviorism* shows the vitality with which Watson described his program for living under a behaviorist system. It may help you appreciate why so many people adopted behaviorism as a new faith.

*Behaviorism ought to be a science that prepares men and women for understanding the principles of their own behavior. It ought to make men and women eager to rearrange their own lives, and especially eager to prepare themselves to bring up their own children in a healthy way. I wish I could picture for you what a rich and wonderful individual we should make of every healthy child if only we could let it shape itself properly and then provide for it a universe in which it could exercise that organization—a universe unshackled by legendary folklore of happenings thousands of years ago; unhampered by disgraceful political history; free of foolish customs and conventions which have no significance in themselves, yet which hem the individual in like taut steel bands.*

*I am not asking here for revolution; I am not asking people to go out to some Godforsaken place, form a colony, go naked and live a communal life, nor am I asking for a change to a diet of roots and herbs. I am not asking for "free love." I am trying to dangle a stimulus in front of you, a verbal stimulus which, if acted upon, will gradually change this universe. For the universe will change if you bring up your children, not in the freedom of the libertine, but in behavioristic freedom—a freedom which we cannot even picture in words, so little do we know of it. Will not these children in turn, with their better ways of living and thinking, replace us as society and in turn bring up their children in a still more scientific way, until the world finally becomes a place fit for human habitation? (Watson, 1930, pp. 303–304)*

Watson's plan to replace religion-based ethics with his experimental ethics based on behaviorism remained only a hope and was never carried out. He outlined his program and left it as a framework for others. Years later, B. F. Skinner (see Chapter 11) conceived in greater detail a scientifically shaped utopia in the spirit of Watson's ideas.

## An Outbreak of Psychology

By the 1920s the field of psychology had captured and captivated the public's attention. Given Watson's charisma, personal charm, persuasiveness, and message of hope, Americans were enthralled by what one writer called an "outbreak" of psychology. Much of the public was convinced that psychology provided the path to health, happiness, and prosperity. Psychological advice columns sprouted up in the pages of the daily newspapers.

Psychologist Joseph Jastrow (1863–1944) was once called "the most prolific university-trained popular psychologist" in the United States during the 1920s and 1930s (Pettit, 2007, p. 162). He received his Ph.D. in 1886 from Johns Hopkins and pursued a lengthy academic career at the University of Wisconsin. He also wrote magazine articles about psychology, acting on his belief that the "popularization of psychology was essential to its public appreciation and official support" (Jastrow, 1930/1961, p. 150). Topics included curing the blues, the psychology of crooks, fears and worries, the meaning of IQ scores, inferiority complexes, family conflicts, and why we drink coffee. Obviously psychology had come a long way from the laboratory work of Wundt and Titchener.

Jastrow's newspaper column, "Keeping Mentally Fit," was syndicated in 150 papers, and he participated in radio programs such as "Herald of Sanity" and "Women's Radio Review." He wrote a pop psychology manual, *Piloting Your Life: The Psychologist as Helmsman,* not unlike the self-help books perpetually on today's best-seller lists. His articles on the usefulness of psychology in everyday life appeared frequently in popular magazines such as *Popular Science Monthly, Cosmopolitan,* and *Harper's* (Behrens, 2009; Hull, 1944).

Another promoter of psychology was Albert Wiggam. Although not a psychologist, he wrote a popular newspaper column called "Exploring Your Mind." Following is a sample of his views:

*Men and women never needed psychology so much as they need it today. Young men and women need it in order to measure their own mental traits and capacities with a view to choosing their careers early and wisely. Businessmen need it to help them select employees; parents and educators need it as an aid in rearing and educating children; all need it in order to secure the highest effectiveness and happiness.*

*You cannot achieve these things in the fullest measure without the new knowledge of your own mind and personality that the psychologists have given us. (Wiggam, 1928, quoted in Benjamin, 1986, p. 943)*

The Canadian humorist Stephen Butler Leacock noted that psychology had once been safely confined to college campuses, where it had no connection with reality and did no visible harm to anyone who studied it. By 1924, however, psychology was everywhere. Leacock wrote, "For almost every juncture of life we now call in the services of an expert psychologist as naturally as we send for an emergency plumber. In all our great cities there are already, or soon will be, signs that read 'Psychologist—Open Day and Night'" (quoted in Benjamin, 1986, p. 944).

Thus was psychology welcomed throughout the United States, and John B. Watson may have done more than any other individual to help it spread.

## Criticisms of Watson's Behaviorism

Any system that proposes sweeping revisions, blatantly attacks the existing order, and suggests that the earlier version of the truth be discarded is sure to be criticized. We know that American psychology was already moving toward greater objectivity when Watson founded behaviorism, but not all psychologists were ready to accept the extreme objectivity that Watson proposed. Many psychologists, including some who supported the principle of objectivity, believed that Watson's program omitted important components such as sensory and perceptual processes.

### Karl Lashley (1890–1958)

KARL LASHLEY

Lashley was a student of Watson's at Johns Hopkins, where he earned his Ph.D. His career as a physiological psychologist took him to the universities of Minnesota and Chicago, to Harvard, and finally to the Yerkes Laboratory of Primate Biology. He upheld the mechanistic tradition that had characterized psychology since its founding.

*Lashley revealed that as a boy he was as baffled by people as he was skillful with mechano sets [toys for making mechanical constructions such as buildings and bridges]. Psychology finally fell open to him, he said, when he recognized that human beings and machines had a great deal in common. (Murray, quoted in Robinson, 1992, p. 213)*

Lashley was an advocate of Watson's behaviorism, though his research on brain mechanisms in rats challenged one of Watson's basic points. Lashley summarized his findings in *Brain Mechanisms and Intelligence* (1929). He offered two now famous principles: the **law of mass action**, which states that the efficiency of learning is a function of the intact mass of the cortex (the more cortical tissue available, the better the learning), and the principle of **equipotentiality**, which states that one part of the cortex is essentially equal to another in terms of its contribution to learning.

Lashley expected his research to lead him to specific sensory and motor centers in the cerebral cortex as well as corresponding connections between sensory and motor

**Law of mass action:** The efficiency of learning is a function of the total mass of cortical tissue.

**Equipotentiality:** The idea that one part of the cerebral cortex is essentially equal to another in its contribution to learning.

apparatus. Such findings would have supported the primacy and simplicity of the reflex arc as an elemental unit of behavior. What happened, however, was that his results challenged Watson's idea of a simple point-to-point connection in reflexes, according to which the brain serves merely to switch incoming sensory nerve impulses into outgoing motor impulses. Lashley's findings suggested that the brain plays a more active role in learning than Watson could accept. Thus, Lashley contested Watson's assumption that behavior is compounded bit by bit solely through conditioned reflexes.

Although Lashley's work discredited a fundamental part of Watson's system, it did not weaken the behaviorist insistence on objective research methods. On the contrary, Lashley's work confirmed the value of objective methods in psychological research.

## William McDougall (1871–1938)

One of Watson's more forceful opponents was William McDougall, an English psychologist who came to the United States in 1920, first to Harvard and later to Duke University. McDougall is known for his instinct theory of behavior and for the impetus his book on social psychology gave to that area (McDougall, 1908).

McDougall, who contributed so much to social psychology, was not very social himself. He wrote:

*I have never fitted neatly into any social group, never been able to find myself wholly at one with any party or any system; and, though not insensible to the attractions of group life, group feeling and thinking, have always stood outside, critical and ill-content. (1930, p. 192)*

He was a supporter of unpopular causes such as free will, Nordic superiority, and psychic research, and he was frequently denounced by the American press for his views. McDougall was also vilified in the psychological community because he strongly criticized behaviorism in the 1920s, when most psychologists had accepted its influence. Indeed, McDougall and Watson had been "flaying each other in print for years" (Larson, 1972, p. 3).

McDougall wrote that he "suffered much in the way of loss of reputation, unpopularity, slanderous misrepresentation, and scornful hostility" (quoted in Innis, 2003, p. 102). One American psychologist went so far as to say publicly, when McDougall was seriously ill, that psychology would be better off if he died. On a more sympathetic note, Robert Yerkes referred to McDougall's life as "a major tragedy" (Innis, 2003, p. 91).

McDougall's instinct theory states that human behavior derives from innate tendencies to thought and action. Although this idea was initially well received, it rapidly lost ground to behaviorism. Watson rejected the notion of instincts, and on this issue and many others the two men clashed.

## The Watson–McDougall Debate

Watson and McDougall met to debate their differences on February 5, 1924, at the Psychology Club in Washington, D.C. The fact that Washington had a psychology club not affiliated with a university attests to the field's widespread popularity. One thousand people attended the proceedings. Only a few were psychologists; at the time there were only 464 APA members nationwide. Thus, the size of the crowd also reflects the popularity of Watson's behaviorism. The judges of the debate, however, voted McDougall the winner. The arguments were published jointly in *The Battle of Behaviorism* (1929).

McDougall began optimistically. "I have an initial advantage over Dr. Watson," he said, "an advantage which I feel to be so great as to be unfair; namely, all persons of common sense will of necessity be on my side from the outset" (Watson & McDougall,

WILLIAM McDOUGALL

1929, p. 40). McDougall agreed with Watson that the data of behavior are a proper focus for psychological research, but he argued that the data of consciousness are also indispensable. (This position was later upheld by humanistic psychologists and social-learning theorists.)

If psychologists do not use introspection, McDougall asked, how can they determine the meaning of a subject's response or the accuracy of speech behavior (what Watson called verbal report)? Without self-report, how can we know anything about daydreams and fantasies? How can we understand or appreciate aesthetic experiences? McDougall challenged Watson to explain how a behaviorist would account for the experience of enjoying a violin concert. McDougall said:

> *I come into this hall and see a man on this platform scraping the guts of a cat with hairs from the tail of a horse, and, sitting silently in attitudes of rapt attention, are a thousand persons, who presently break into wild applause. How will the behaviorist explain these strange incidents? How explain the fact that the vibrations emitted by the catgut stimulate all the thousands into absolute silence and quiescence, and the further fact that the cessation of the stimulus seems to be a stimulus to the most frantic activity?*
>
> *Common sense and psychology agree in accepting the explanation that the audience heard the music with keen pleasure, and vented their gratitude and admiration for the artist in shouts and handclappings. But the behaviorist knows nothing of pleasure and pain, of admiration and gratitude. He has relegated all such "metaphysical entities" to the dust heap, and must seek some other explanation. Let us leave him seeking it. The search will keep him harmlessly occupied for some centuries to come. (Watson & McDougall, 1929, pp. 62–63)*

Then McDougall questioned Watson's assumption that human behavior is fully determined, that everything we do is the direct result of past experience and can be predicted once these past events are known. Such a psychology leaves no room for free will or freedom of choice. If this determinist position were true—that humans have no free will and therefore cannot be held responsible for their actions—then there would be no human initiative, no creative effort, no desire to improve ourselves or society. No one would attempt to prevent war, alleviate injustice, or achieve any personal or social ideal. Why even bother trying, if every thought and behavior is totally determined by past experience?

Watson's use of the verbal report method came under fire. He was charged with being inconsistent, accepting it when it could be verified and rejecting it when it could not. Of course, that was Watson's point and the goal of the entire behaviorist movement: to use only data that could be verified.

The Watson–McDougall debate came 11 years after Watson formally founded the behaviorist school of thought. McDougall predicted that in a few more years Watson's position would disappear without a trace. Five years later McDougall wrote that his forecast had been too rosy, "founded upon a too generous estimate of the intelligence of the American public. Dr. Watson continues, as a prophet of much honor in his own country, to issue his pronouncements" (Watson & McDougall, 1929, pp. 86, 87).

## Contributions of Watson's Behaviorism

Watson's productive career in psychology lasted fewer than 20 years, but he profoundly affected the course of psychology's development for many years to come. He was an effective agent of the Zeitgeist, of the times that were changing not only in psychology but in general scientific attitudes as well. The nineteenth century had witnessed magnificent advances in every branch of science. The twentieth century promised even more marvels. It was thought then that scientists, if given enough time, would find solutions to every problem, answers to every question.

Watson made psychology more objective in methods and terminology. Although his positions on specific topics stimulated much research, his original formulations are no longer useful. As a distinct school of thought, Watsonian behaviorism was replaced by other forms of psychological objectivism that built on it, as we see in Chapter 11. The historian E. G. Boring said in 1929 that behaviorism was already past its prime. Because revolutionary movements depend on protest for their strength, it is an effective tribute to Watson's behaviorism that just 16 years after its introduction it no longer needed to protest. Indeed, there was nothing left to protest against.

Watson's behaviorism effectively overcame the earlier mainstream positions in psychology. A graduate student at the University of Wisconsin in 1926 reported that by then, few students had heard of Wundt and Titchener (Gengerelli, 1976). Objective methods and language became identified with American psychology, and so Watson's system died, as have other successful movements, by being absorbed into the main body of thought to provide a strong conceptual base for modern psychology.

Although Watson's program did not realize its ambitious goals, he is widely recognized for his founding role. The centennial of his birth was celebrated in April 1979, the same year as the centennial of the birth of psychology as a science. A symposium at Furman University, where the psychology laboratory is named for Watson, drew psychologists from throughout the United States. One speaker was B. F. Skinner, whose talk was titled "What J. B. Watson Meant to Me." Hometown residents remembered Watson somewhat less favorably. Many recalled him as "an upstart and an atheist who had turned his back on his Southern heritage and Baptist upbringing" (*Greenville News,* April 5, 1979). In 1984, a commemorative marker was placed on the highway near his birthplace.

To some degree, the acceptance of Watsonian behaviorism was a function of Watson's personality. A charismatic figure, he projected his ideas with enthusiasm, optimism, and self-confidence. He was a strong and appealing speaker who scorned tradition and rejected the current psychology. These personal qualities, plus the spirit of the times he so ably manipulated, define John B. Watson as one of psychology's pioneers.

# Discussion Questions

1. Describe Lashley's law of mass action and principle of equipotentiality.
2. Describe Watson's approach to child rearing. What were the results of that approach within his family?
3. Describe Watson's views on instinct and thought processes.
4. Discuss how Watson's subject matter and methodology continued the atomistic, mechanistic, empiricistic tradition.
5. Do you think Watson's behaviorism would have become so popular without the earlier work of the functional psychologists? Explain your answer.
6. Explain the reasons for behaviorism's popular appeal.
7. In Watson's 1913 article, what criticisms did he make of structuralism and functionalism? On what basis did he argue that applied psychology could be called scientific?
8. In what way did Lashley's research results discredit a portion of Watson's system?
9. On what grounds did McDougall criticize Watson's form of behaviorism?
10. How did the behaviorists' view of the role and task of human subjects differ from that of the introspectionists?
11. How did Watson distinguish between responses and acts? How did he distinguish between explicit and implicit responses?
12. How did Watson establish a conditioned emotional response in Albert? Did that response

generalize to other stimuli? If so, to what kind of stimuli?

**13.** How do the studies of Albert and Peter support Watson's ideas on the role of learning in emotion?

**14.** How were Watson's ideas received by the younger generation of psychologists?

**15.** Was Watson concerned about the practical value of behaviorism? If your answer is yes, to what areas of everyday life did he apply his findings?

**16.** What ethical and moral considerations do you think were involved in the Little Albert study?

**17.** What research methods did Watson accept for a scientific psychology?

**18.** Why was Watson's use of verbal reports considered to be controversial?

## CHAPTER 11

# Behaviorism: After the Founding

## The IQ Zoo

It was called the IQ Zoo, located in Hot Springs, Arkansas. It's closed now, but for 35 years thousands of people visited it to watch animals perform an amazing variety of tricks. At least they looked like tricks, but in reality every animal had been carefully trained. Nothing had been left to chance at the IQ Zoo. Each animal you saw—whether a pigeon or a chicken or a raccoon—had become another Clever Hans (see Bailey & Gillaspy, 2005).

Consider Priscilla the Fastidious Pig. If you have ever seen pigs in a barnyard you might not think they were capable of doing anything exciting enough to make you watch. Priscilla, however, was fascinating. She performed a routine about getting up in the morning. First she switched on a radio, then ate breakfast at a table, picked up an array of dirty clothes, stowed them in a hamper, and ran a vacuum cleaner around her room. Once she was ready to face her public, she proceeded to answer questions put to her by the audience by activating signs that lit up to indicate "yes" or "no."

Another star of the IQ Zoo was Bird Brain, a chicken who played Tic-Tac-Toe with people and would invariably win or tie every game. She never lost, not even when she played against the great psychologist B. F. Skinner, whose reaction to losing to a chicken went unrecorded. At one time there were hundreds of chickens like Bird Brain featured at exhibitions and casinos throughout the United States, and not one ever lost a game to a human opponent.

In addition to Bird Brain, a "hen played a 5-note tune on a small piano, another performed a 'tap dance' in costume and shoes, while a third 'laid' wooden eggs in a nest box; the eggs rolled down a trough into a basket. The audience could call out any number of eggs desired, up to eight, and the hen would lay that number, nonstop" (Breland & Breland, 1951, p. 202).

There were chickens that walked tightropes, played baseball and poker, and fired popguns. Rabbits drove little fire trucks around the grounds, sirens wailing. Ducks played pianos and drums, parrots rode bicycles, and raccoons played basketball. And who could forget the dancing goat, the hamsters swinging on the trapeze, and the kissing rabbits (Joyce & Baker, 2008; *Time*, February 28, 1955)?

The zoo was established in 1955 by Keller and Marian Breland, former graduate students in psychology who left the university to earn a living by applying psychological conditioning techniques to animal behavior. They met when Marian, whose family called her "Mouse" because of her diminutive stature, literally ran into Keller one day when she was rushing out of the psychology laboratory to seek medical treatment because she had been bitten by a lab rat.

A year later they married, and in 1943 they formed Animal Behavior Enterprise to train animals to perform at state fairs and tourist attractions. By the time they opened the IQ Zoo their work was well known, thanks to articles in the *Wall Street Journal, Time, Life,* and *Reader's Digest.* At the peak of their success the Brelands were running nearly 140 trained-animal shows at major tourist attractions and twice that many in traveling animal shows. They had also trained hundreds of animals for roles in movies, television programs, and commercials. Overall they trained more than 6,000 animals of some 150 species (Marr, 2002).

And they did it all through the use of the basic conditioning techniques they had learned from B. F. Skinner, the leading behaviorist of the twentieth century.

## Three Stages of Behaviorism

John B. Watson's intended revolution did not transform psychology overnight. It took more time than he expected. Yet by 1924, little more than a decade after he formally launched behaviorism, even Titchener, Watson's greatest opponent, conceded that behaviorism had engulfed American psychology. By 1930 Watson was able to proclaim with considerable justification that his victory was complete.

Watson's behaviorism was the first stage in the evolution of the behavioral school of thought. The second stage, neobehaviorism, dates from 1930 to about 1960 and includes the work of Tolman, Hull, and Skinner. These neobehaviorists agreed on several points, as follows:

- *The core of psychology is the study of learning.*
- *Most behavior, no matter how complex, can be accounted for by the laws of conditioning.*
- *Psychology must adopt the principle of operationism.*

The third stage in behaviorism's evolution, neo-neobehaviorism or sociobehaviorism, dates from about 1960 to about 1990. This stage includes the work of Bandura and Rotter and is distinguished by a return to the consideration of cognitive processes while maintaining a focus on the observation of overt behavior.

## Operationism

**Operationism:** The doctrine that a physical concept can be defined in precise terms related to the set of operations or procedures by which it is determined.

The purpose of **operationism**, which was a major characteristic of neobehaviorism, was to render the language and terminology of science more objective and precise and to rid science of "pseudoproblems"; that is, those problems that are not actually observable or physically demonstrable. Operationism holds that the validity of any scientific finding or theoretical construct depends on the validity of the operations used in arriving at that finding.

The operationist viewpoint was promoted by Percy W. Bridgman (1882–1961), a Nobel Prize-winning physicist at Harvard University. His book, *The Logic of Modern Physics* (1927), captured the attention of many psychologists (Feest, 2005). Bridgman insisted that physical concepts be defined precisely and that all concepts lacking physical referents be discarded.

*We may illustrate by considering the concept of length. What do we mean by the length of an object? We evidently know what we mean by length if we can tell what the length of any and every object is, and for the physicist nothing more is required. To find the length of an object, we have to perform certain physical operations. The concept of length is therefore fixed when the operations by which length is measured are fixed;*

*that is, the concept of length involves as much as and nothing more than a set of operations; the concept is synonymous with the corresponding set of operations. (Bridgman, 1927, p. 5)*

Thus, a physical concept is the same as the set of operations or procedures by which it is determined. Many psychologists believed this principle would be useful for their work and were eager to apply it.

Bridgman's insistence on discarding pseudo-problems—those questions that defy answer by any known objective test—was particularly appealing to behavioral psychologists. Propositions that cannot be put to experimental test, such as the existence and nature of the soul, are meaningless for science. What is the soul? How can it be observed in the laboratory? Can it be measured and manipulated under controlled conditions to determine its effects on behavior? If not, then the concept has no use or meaning or relevance for science.

Following this reasoning, the concept of individual or private conscious experience is also a pseudo-problem for the science of psychology. The existence or characteristics of consciousness cannot be determined or even investigated by objective methods. According to the operationist viewpoint, then, consciousness has no place in a scientific psychology.

Critics suggested that operationism was little more than a formal statement of principles already being applied by psychologists to define ideas and concepts in relation to their physical referents. There is little in Bridgman's book on operationism that cannot be traced to the works of the British empiricists. The long-term trend in American psychology was, as we have seen, toward greater objectivity in methodology and subject matter, so it can be said that the operationist approach to research and theory had already been accepted by many psychologists.

Since the days of Wilhelm Wundt in Germany, however, physics had been the paragon of scientific respectability for the newer psychology. When physicists proclaimed their acceptance of operationism as a formal doctrine, many psychologists felt compelled to follow this role model. Eventually, psychologists used operationism more extensively than did physicists. As a result, the generation of neobehaviorists that came of age in the late 1920s and 1930s, including B. F. Skinner, incorporated operationism in their approach to psychology (Moore, 2005).

Bridgman lived long enough to witness not only psychology's embrace of operationism but also the later discarding of his approach. At the age of 79, knowing he was terminally ill, Bridgman completed the index to a seven-volume edition of his collected writings, mailed it to the publisher, and shot himself. He had feared that if he waited any longer, he would become incapacitated and unable to take such action. In his suicide note he wrote, "Probably, this is the last day I will be able to do it myself" (quoted in Nuland, 1994, p. 152).

# Edward Chace Tolman (1886–1959)

EDWARD CHACE TOLMAN

One of the early converts to behaviorism, Edward Tolman studied engineering at the Massachusetts Institute of Technology. He switched to psychology and received his Ph.D. from Harvard in 1915. In the summer of 1912, Tolman studied in Germany with the Gestalt psychologist Kurt Koffka. In Tolman's final year of graduate school, he became acquainted with Watson's new behaviorism. Having been trained in the tradition of Titchener's structural psychology, Tolman was already questioning the scientific usefulness of introspection. In his autobiography, he recalled that Watson's behaviorism came as a "tremendous stimulus and relief" (1952, p. 326).

Tolman became an instructor at Northwestern University in Evanston, Illinois, and in 1918 he took a new position at the University of California at Berkeley. It was at Berkeley where he taught comparative psychology and conducted research on learning in rats, and soon afterwards he became dissatisfied with Watson's form of behaviorism and began to develop his own. During World War II, Tolman served with the Office of Strategic Services (the OSS, the forerunner of the Central Intelligence Agency). In the early 1950s, he helped lead faculty opposition to the California state loyalty oath.

## Purposive Behaviorism

**Purposive behaviorism:** Tolman's system combining the objective study of behavior with the consideration of purposiveness or goal orientation in behavior.

Tolman's approach to behaviorism is presented in his book, *Purposive Behavior in Animals and Men* (1932). His term **purposive behaviorism** may appear at first glance to be a curious amalgam of two contradictory ideas: purpose and behavior. Attributing purpose to an organism's behavior seems to imply consciousness, a mentalistic concept that has no place in a behavioral psychology. Tolman made it clear, however, that he was very much the behaviorist in subject matter and methodology. He was not urging psychology to accept consciousness. Like Watson, he rejected introspection and had no interest in presumed internal experiences that were not accessible to objective observation.

Tolman argued that purposiveness in behavior can be defined in objective behavioral terms without resorting to introspection or to reports about how one may feel about an experience. It seemed obvious to Tolman that all actions were goal-directed. For example, a cat tries to find its way out of the psychologist's experimental puzzle box, a rat tries to master the maze, and a child tries to learn to play the piano or to kick a soccer ball.

In other words, Tolman said, behavior "reeks" of purpose and is oriented toward achieving a goal or learning the means to an end. The rat persistently runs the maze, making fewer errors each time, to reach the goal faster. What is happening in this case is that the rat is learning, and the fact of learning, whether in animal subjects or humans, is objective behavioral evidence of purpose. Note that Tolman is dealing with the objective responses of the organism and that the measurements are stated in terms of changes in response behavior as a function of learning. These are measures that yield objective data.

Watsonian behaviorists were quick to criticize the attribution of purpose to behavior. They insisted that any reference to purposiveness implied recognition of conscious processes. Tolman responded that it made no difference to him whether the person or the animal was conscious. The conscious experience—if there was any—associated with purposive behavior did not influence the organism's behavioral responses. And Tolman was interested only in overt responses.

## Intervening Variables

As a behaviorist, Tolman believed that both the initiating causes of behavior and the final resulting behavior must be capable of objective observation and operational definition. He listed five independent variables as causes of behavior: environmental stimuli, physiological drives, heredity, previous training, and age. Behavior is a function of these five variables, an idea Tolman expressed in a mathematical equation.

**Intervening variables:** Unobserved and inferred factors within the organism that are the actual determinants of behavior.

Between these observable independent variables and the resulting response behavior (the observable dependent variable), Tolman inferred a set of unobservable factors, the **intervening variables**, which are the actual determinants of behavior. These factors are internal processes that connect the stimulus situation with the observed response. The behaviorists' S-R proposition (for stimulus-response) should read S-O-R, so far as Tolman was concerned. The intervening variable is whatever is going on within O (the organism) that brings about the behavioral response to a given stimulus situation. But because intervening variables cannot be objectively observed, they are of no use to psychology unless they can be directly related to the experimental (independent) variables and the behavior (dependent) variable.

The classic example of an intervening variable is hunger. We cannot actually see hunger in a person or a laboratory animal, but hunger can be precisely and objectively related to an experimental variable, such as the length of time since the organism last received food. Hunger can also be related to an objective response or behavior variable, such as the amount of food consumed or the speed with which it was eaten. Thus, the unobservable variable of hunger can be described precisely in relation to empirical variables and made amenable to quantification and experimental manipulation.

By specifying the independent and dependent variables, which are observable events, Tolman was able to provide operational definitions of unobservable, internal states. He initially referred to his approach, in general, as operational behaviorism before selecting the more precise term "intervening variable."

## Learning Theory

The problem of learning formed a major part of Tolman's purposive behaviorism. He rejected Thorndike's law of effect, saying that reward or reinforcement has little influence on learning. In its place, Tolman proposed a cognitive explanation for learning, suggesting that the repeated performance of a task strengthens the learned relationship between environmental cues and the organism's expectations. In this way, the organism gets to know its environment. Tolman called these learned relationships "sign Gestalts" and posited that they are built up by the continued performance of a task.

Let us watch a hungry rat in a maze. The rat moves about in the maze, exploring correct alleys and blind alleys. Eventually the rat discovers food. In subsequent trials in the maze, the goal (finding food) gives purpose and direction to the rat's behavior. Expectations are established at each choice point, and the rat comes to expect that certain cues associated with the choice point will or will not lead to the food.

When the rat's expectation is confirmed and it obtains food, the sign Gestalt (the cue expectancy associated with a particular choice point) is strengthened. For all the choice points in the maze, then, the animal establishes a cognitive map, which is a pattern of sign Gestalts. This pattern is what the animal learns—that is, the map of the maze, not merely a set of motor habits. The rat's brain forms a comprehensive picture of the maze or of any familiar environment, enabling it to go from one place to another without being restricted to a fixed series of bodily movements. Tolman concluded that the same phenomenon occurs with people familiar with their neighborhood or town. They can go from one point to another by several routes because of the cognitive map they have developed of the area.

## Comment

Tolman is recognized as a forerunner of contemporary cognitive psychology (see Chapter 15), and his work had a great impact, especially his research on problems of learning and his concept of the intervening variable. Because intervening variables are a way of operationally defining unobservable internal states, they made such states respectable subjects for scientific study. Intervening variables were used by neobehaviorists such as Hull and Skinner.

Another significant contribution was Tolman's wholehearted support for the rat as an appropriate subject for psychological study. At the start of his career, Tolman was not enthusiastic. He said about rats, "I don't like them. They make me feel creepy" (Tolman, 1919, quoted in Innis, 1992, p. 191).

By 1945, his attitude had changed:

*Let it be noted that rats live in cages; they do not go on binges the night before one has planned an experiment; they do not kill each other off in wars; they do not invent engines of destruction, and, if they did, they would not be so inept about controlling such engines; they do not go in for either class conflicts or race conflicts; they avoid politics, economics, and papers on psychology. They are marvelous, pure, and delightful. (Tolman, 1945, p. 166)*

Thanks to the work of Tolman and others, the white rat became the primary research subject for the neobehaviorists and learning theorists from 1930 until the 1960s. It was assumed that research on white rats would yield insights into the basic processes underlying the behavior not only of rats but also of other animals and humans as well. Tolman wrote that "everything important in psychology can be investigated in essence through the continued experimental and theoretical analysis of the determiners of rat behavior at a choice point in a maze" (quoted in Innis, 2000, p. 92). Who needed human subjects when so many white rats were available?

CLARK LEONARD HULL

# Clark Leonard Hull (1884–1952)

Clark Hull and his followers dominated American psychology from the 1940s until the 1960s. Perhaps no other psychologist was so devoted to the problems of the scientific method. Hull had a prodigious command of mathematics and formal logic, and he applied these disciplines to psychological theory in a way no one had done before. Hull's form of behaviorism was more sophisticated and complex than Watson's. Hull liked to tell his graduate students that "Watson is too naïve. His behaviorism is too simple and crude" (quoted in Gengerelli, 1976, p. 686).

## Hull's Life

Throughout his life, Hull was plagued by ill health and poor eyesight. As a boy he nearly died from typhoid, which left his memory impaired. When he was 24 he contracted polio; as a result of the disease he had a permanent disability in one leg, forcing him to wear an iron brace, which he designed himself. His family was poor, and Hull was forced to interrupt his education several times to take teaching jobs to earn money. His greatest asset was an intense motivation to succeed, and he persevered in the face of many obstacles.

In 1918, at the relatively advanced age of 34, Hull received his Ph.D. from the University of Wisconsin, where he studied mining engineering before changing to psychology. He remained on the Wisconsin faculty for 10 years. His early research interests foretold his lifelong emphasis on objective methods and functional laws. Hull investigated concept formation, the effects of tobacco on behavioral efficiency, and tests and measurements, and he published a textbook on aptitude testing (Hull, 1928). He developed methods of statistical analysis and invented a machine for calculating correlations, which has been exhibited at the museums of the Smithsonian Institution in Washington, D.C. He devoted 10 years to the study of hypnosis and suggestibility, publishing 32 papers and a book summarizing the research (Hull, 1933).

In 1929 Hull accepted a position as research professor at Yale University to pursue his interest in formulating a theory of behavior based on Pavlov's laws of conditioning. He had read Pavlov's work a few years earlier and had become intrigued by problems of conditioned reflexes and learning. Hull referred to Pavlov's *Conditioned Reflexes* as a "great book" and decided to use animal subjects for his research. He had not run rats before because he detested the odors associated with a rat lab, but at Yale he visited the meticulously clean rat colony maintained by E. R. Hilgard. Hull looked at the rats, "sniffed them and said that he guessed he could use rats after all" (Hilgard, 1987, p. 201).

In the 1930s, Hull published articles about conditioning, arguing that complex higher-order behaviors could be explained in terms of basic conditioning principles.

Hull's *Principles of Behavior* (1943) outlined a comprehensive theoretical framework to account for all behavior. Hull soon became the most frequently cited psychologist in the field. In the 1940s, up to 40 percent of all experimental articles and 70 percent of all articles on learning and motivation in the two leading American psychology journals cited Hull's work (Spence, 1952). Hull continually revised his system, incorporating the results of his extensive research that put his propositions to experimental test. The final form was published in 1952 in *A Behavior System.*

## The Spirit of Mechanism

Hull described his behaviorism and his image of human nature in mechanistic terms and regarded human behavior as automatic and capable of being reduced to the language of physics. According to Hull, behaviorists should regard their subjects as machines, and he subscribed to the view that machines would one day be constructed to think and display other human cognitive functions. In 1926 Hull wrote, "It has struck me many times that the human organism is one of the most extraordinary machines—and yet a machine. And it has struck me more than once that so far as the thinking processes go, a machine could be built which would do every essential thing that the body does" (quoted in Amsel & Rashotte, 1984, pp. 2–3). We can see that the seventeenth-century spirit of mechanism as represented by Europe's mechanical figures, clocks, and automata (such as the defecating duck) was faithfully incorporated into Hull's work.

## Objective Methodology and Quantification

Hull's mechanistic, reductionistic, and objective behaviorism provides a clear view of what his methods of study had to be. First, they would be objective. In addition, they would be quantitative, with the fundamental laws of behavior expressed in the precise language of mathematics.

Hull noted four methods he considered useful for scientific research. Three were already widely used: simple observation, systematic controlled observation, and the experimental testing of hypotheses. The fourth method Hull proposed was the **hypothetico-deductive method**, which uses deduction from a set of formulations that are determined *a priori.* This method involves establishing postulates from which experimentally testable conclusions can be deduced. These conclusions are submitted to experimental test, and they must be revised if they are not supported by experimental evidence. If they are supported and verified, then they may be incorporated into the body of science. Hull believed that if psychology were to become truly objective like the other natural sciences—a basic principle of the behaviorist program—then the only appropriate method would be the hypothetico-deductive one.

**Hypothetico-deductive method:** Hull's method for establishing postulates from which experimentally testable conclusions can be deduced.

## Drives

To Hull, the basis of motivation was a state of bodily need that arose from a deviation from optimal biological conditions. Rather than introducing the concept of biological need directly into his system, however, Hull postulated the intervening variable of "drive," a term that had already come into use in psychology. Drive was defined as a stimulus arising from a state of tissue need that arouses or activates behavior. In Hull's view, reduction or satisfaction of a drive is the sole basis for reinforcement. The strength of the drive can be empirically determined by the length of deprivation, or by the intensity, strength, and energy expenditure of the resulting behavior. Hull considered length of deprivation to be an imperfect measure and placed greater emphasis on response strength.

Hull postulated two kinds of drive. Primary drives are associated with innate biological need states and are vital to the organism's survival. Primary drives include food, water, air, temperature regulation, defecation, urination, sleep, activity, sexual inter-course, and pain relief. Hull recognized, however, that organisms might be motivated by forces other than primary drives. Accordingly, he proposed the learned or secondary drives, which relate to situations or environmental stimuli associated with the reduction of primary drives and so may become drives themselves. Thus, previously neutral stimuli may acquire the characteristics of a drive because they are capable of eliciting responses similar to the responses aroused by the primary drive or original need state.

A simple example involves touching a hot stove and getting burned. The painful burn, caused by actual physical damage to the body's tissues, produces a primary drive—the desire for relief from the pain. Other environmental stimuli associated with this primary drive, such as the sight of the stove, may in the future quickly lead to withdrawing the hand when this visual stimulus is perceived. In this way, the sight of the stove becomes the stimulus for the learned drive of fear. These secondary or learned drives that moti-vate our behavior develop from the primary drives.

## Learning

**Law of primary reinforcement:** When a stimulus-response re-lationship is followed by a reduction in a bodily need, the prob-ability increases that on subsequent occa-sions the same stimu-lus will evoke the same response.

Hull's learning theory focuses on the principle of reinforcement, which is essentially Thorndike's law of effect. Hull's **law of primary reinforcement** states that when a stimulus-response relationship is followed by a reduction in need, the probability in-creases that on subsequent occasions the same stimulus will evoke the same response. Reward or reinforcement is defined not in terms of Thorndike's notion of satisfaction but rather in terms of reducing a primary need. Thus, primary reinforcement (the reduc-tion of a primary drive) is fundamental to Hull's theory of learning.

Just as his system contains secondary or learned drives, it also deals with secondary reinforcement. If the intensity of the stimulus is reduced because of a secondary drive, then that drive will act as a secondary reinforcement.

*It follows that any stimulus consistently associated with a reinforcement situation will through that association acquire the power of evoking the conditioned inhibition, i.e., reduction in stimulus intensity, and so of itself producing the resulting reinforcement. Since this indirect power of reinforcement is acquired through learning, it is called secondary reinforcement.* (Hull, 1951, pp. 27–28)

**Habit strength:** The strength of the stimulus-response connection, which is a function of the number of reinforcements.

Stimulus-response connections are strengthened by the number of reinforcements that have occurred. Hull called the strength of the S-R connection **habit strength**. It is a function of reinforcement and refers to the persistence of the conditioning.

Learning cannot take place in the absence of reinforcement, which is necessary to bring about a reduction of the drive. This emphasis on reinforcement characterizes Hull's system as a need-reduction theory, as opposed to Tolman's cognitive theory.

## Comment

As a leading exponent of neobehaviorism, Hull was the target of the same attacks aimed at Watson and other behaviorists. Psychologists who opposed any behavioral approach to psychology included Hull in the enemy camp.

His system can be faulted for its lack of generalizability. In his attempt to define vari-ables precisely, in quantitative terms, Hull necessarily operated on a narrow plane. He often formulated postulates from results obtained in a single experiment. Opponents ar-gued that it is difficult to generalize to all behavior on the basis of specific experimental demonstrations such as "the most favorable interval for human eyelid conditioning (Postulate 2)" or "the weight in grams of food needed to condition a rat (Postulate 7)" (quoted in Hilgard, 1956, p. 181). Although quantification is commendable, Hull's extreme approach reduced the range of applicability of his research findings.

Nevertheless, Hull's influence on psychology was substantial. The sheer quantity of research inspired by his work, as well as the large number of psychologists he influenced, assures his stature in the history of psychology. Hull defended, extended, and expounded the objective behaviorist approach to psychology as no one else had ever done. One historian wrote, "It is not often in any field that a true theoretical genius comes along; of the very few to whom psychology can lay claim, Hull must surely rank among the foremost" (Lowry, 1982, p. 211).

# B. F. Skinner (1904–1990)

B. F. SKINNER

For decades, B. F. Skinner was the world's most influential psychologist. When Skinner died in 1990, the editor of the journal *American Psychologist* praised him as "one of the giants of our discipline" who "made a permanent mark on psychology" (Fowler, 1990, p. 1203). Skinner's obituary in the *Journal of the History of the Behavioral Sciences* described him as the "leading figure in behavior science of this century" (Keller, 1991, p. 3).

Beginning in the 1950s, Skinner was the major embodiment of American behavioral psychology. He attracted a large, loyal, and enthusiastic band of followers. He developed a program for the behavioral control of society, promoted behavior modification techniques, and invented an automated crib for tending infants. His novel, *Walden Two*, remained popular decades after its publication. His 1971 book *Beyond Freedom and Dignity* was a national best-seller, giving Skinner the opportunity to advance his views on television talk shows. He became a celebrity, his name as familiar to the general public as to other psychologists. In 1972, the magazine *Psychology Today* noted that, "For perhaps the first time in American history, a professor of psychology has acquired the celebrity of a movie or TV star" (quoted in Rutherford, 2000, p. 372).

## Skinner's Life

Skinner, born in Susquehanna, Pennsylvania, recalled his childhood environment as affectionate and stable. He attended the same small high school from which his parents had graduated; there were only seven other students in Skinner's graduating class. As a child he was interested in building things: wagons, rafts, model airplanes, and a steam cannon to shoot potato and carrot plugs over the roof. He spent years trying to develop a perpetual motion machine. He read about animals and kept an assortment of turtles, snakes, lizards, toads, and chipmunks. At a county fair he saw performing pigeons; years later he would train pigeons to perform tricks.

Skinner's system of psychology reflects his early life experiences. According to his view, life is a product of past reinforcements. He claimed that his life was just as predetermined and orderly as his system dictated all human lives would be. He believed that his experiences could be traced solely and directly to stimuli in his environment.

Skinner enrolled in Hamilton College in New York but was not happy there. He wrote:

> I never fitted into student life. I joined a fraternity without knowing what it was all about. I was not good at sports and suffered acutely as my shins were cracked in ice hockey or better players bounced basketballs off my cranium. … I complained that the college was pushing me around with unnecessary requirements (one of them daily chapel) and that almost no intellectual interest was shown by most of the students. (Skinner, 1967, p. 392)

Skinner played practical jokes that disrupted the college community, and he openly criticized the faculty and administration. He graduated with a degree in English, a Phi Beta Kappa key, and a desire to become a writer. At a summer writing workshop, the poet Robert Frost had commented favorably on Skinner's poems and stories. For two years after graduation he worked at writing, and then decided that he had nothing to say. Depressed by his lack of success as a writer, he thought about consulting a psychiatrist. He considered himself a failure, and his self-worth was shattered. He was also disappointed in love; at least half a dozen women had rejected him.

He read about the conditioning experiments of Watson and Pavlov, which awakened a scientific, rather than a literary, interest in human nature. In 1928, Skinner enrolled as a graduate student in psychology at Harvard University, though he had never taken a psychology course. He received his Ph.D. in three years, completed postdoctoral fellowships, and taught at the University of Minnesota (1936–1945) and Indiana University (1945–1947), after which he returned to Harvard.

His dissertation topic provides a hint of the position to which he adhered throughout his career. He proposed that a reflex is the correlation between a stimulus and a response, and nothing more. He noted the usefulness of the reflex concept in describing behavior and gave ample credit to Descartes.

Skinner's 1938 book, *The Behavior of Organisms,* describes the basic points of his system. The book sold just 80 copies in four years—a total of 500 copies in its first eight years—and it received largely negative reviews. Fifty years later, it was judged "one of the handful of books that changed the face of modern psychology" (Thompson, 1988, p. 397). What turned this book from an initial failure to an overwhelming success was its usefulness for applied areas such as educational and clinical psychology. Such widespread practical application of Skinner's ideas was appropriate because he was keenly interested in solving real-world problems. A later work, *Science and Human Behavior* (1953), became the basic textbook for Skinner's behavioral psychology.

Skinner remained productive until his death at the age of 86. In the basement of his home, he constructed his personal Skinner box, a controlled environment to provide positive reinforcement. He slept in a yellow plastic tank large enough to contain a mattress, a few bookshelves, and a small television set. He went to bed each night at 10 PM, slept for three hours, worked for an hour, slept three more hours, and arose at 5 AM in the morning to work three more hours. Then he walked to his office for more work and administered self-reinforcement every afternoon by listening to music.

He enjoyed writing and said that it provided considerable positive reinforcement. At age 78, he wrote a paper titled "Intellectual Self-Management in Old Age," citing his own experiences as a case study (Skinner, 1983). He described how necessary it is for the brain to work fewer hours each day, with rest periods between spurts of effort, to cope with failing memory and diminished intellectual abilities. He was pleased to learn that he had been cited in the psychological literature more frequently than Sigmund Freud. When a friend asked if that had been a goal of his writing, he said simply, "I thought I might make it" (quoted in Bjork, 1993, p. 214).

In 1989, Skinner was diagnosed with leukemia and given two months to live. In a radio interview, he described his feelings:

> *I'm not religious, so I don't worry about what will happen after I'm dead. And when I was told that I had this and would be dead in a few months, I didn't have any emotion of any kind at all. Not a bit of panic, or fear, or anxiety. … The only thing that touched me was, and really, my eyes watered when I thought of this, I will have to tell my wife and my daughters. … I've had a very good life. It would be very foolish of me to complain, in any way, about it. So I'm enjoying these last few months as well as I ever enjoyed life. (quoted in Catania, 1992, p. 1527)*

Eight days before he died, though frail, Skinner presented a paper at the 1990 APA convention in Boston. He vigorously attacked the growth of cognitive psychology, which was challenging his form of behaviorism. The evening before his death, he was working on his final article, "Can Psychology Be a Science of Mind?" (Skinner, 1990), which was another indictment of the cognitive movement that threatened to supplant his view of psychology.

## Skinner's Behaviorism

In several respects, Skinner's position represented a renewal of Watson's behaviorism. One historian wrote, "Watson's spirit is indestructible. Cleaned and purified, it breathes through the writings of B. F. Skinner" (MacLeod, 1959, p. 34). Although Hull is also considered a rigorous behaviorist, there are differences between Hull's and Skinner's views. Whereas Hull emphasized the importance of theory, Skinner advocated an empirical system with no theoretical framework within which to conduct research.

Skinner summarized his approach this way: "I never attacked a problem by constructing a hypothesis. I never deduced theorems or submitted them to experimental check. So far as I can see I had no preconceived model of behavior—certainly not a physiological or mentalistic one, and I believe not a conceptual one" (Skinner, 1956, p. 227). Nor did Skinner draw on the work of other psychologists, with the exception of the ideas of Watson and Pavlov. "I find it very difficult to incorporate anybody's thinking in psychology in my own. I almost never read any psychology" (quoted in Overskeid, 2007, p. 591).

Skinner's behaviorism was devoted to the study of responses. He was concerned with describing rather than explaining behavior. His research dealt only with observable behavior, and he believed that the task of scientific inquiry is to establish functional relationships between experimenter-controlled stimulus conditions and the organism's subsequent responses.

Skinner was not concerned with speculating about what might be occurring inside the organism. His program included no presumptions about internal entities, whether intervening variables, drives, or physiological processes. Whatever might happen between stimulus and response is not the sort of objective data the Skinnerian behaviorist dealt with. Thus, Skinner's purely descriptive behaviorism has been called, with good reason, the "empty organism" approach. Human organisms are controlled and operated by forces in the environment, the external world, and not by forces within themselves. Note that Skinner did not question the existence of internal physiological or even mental conditions. What he did deny was their usefulness for a scientific study of behavior. A biographer reiterated that Skinner's position was "not a denial of mental events, but a refusal to resort to them as explanatory entities" (Richelle, 1993, p. 10).

In contrast to many of his contemporaries, Skinner did not consider it necessary to use large numbers of subjects or to make statistical comparisons between the average responses of subject groups. His method was the comprehensive investigation of a single subject.

> *A prediction of what the average individual will do is often of little or no value in dealing with a particular individual. ... A science is helpful in dealing with the individual only insofar as its laws refer to individuals. A science of behavior which concerns only the behavior of groups is not likely to be of help in our understanding of the particular case. (Skinner, 1953, p. 19)*

In 1958, Skinnerian behaviorists established the *Journal of the Experimental Analysis of Behavior,* largely in response to the unwritten requirements of mainstream psychology journals concerning statistical analysis and the size of the subject sample. The *Journal of Applied Behavior Analysis* was started as an outlet for behavior modification research, an applied outgrowth of Skinner's psychology.

In the following passage from *Science and Human Behavior,* Skinner described how the work of Descartes and the mechanical figures of seventeenth-century Europe influenced his approach to psychology. Here we see a good example of the uses of history, a twentieth-century psychologist building on work done 300 years before. This excerpt also demonstrates the continuing evolution of machines; apparently they are becoming ever more lifelike.

# IN THEIR OWN WORDS

## Original Source Material from *Science and Human Behavior* (1953)

**B. F. Skinner**[1]

Behavior is a primary characteristic of living things. We almost identify it with life itself. Anything which moves is likely to be called alive—especially when the movement has direction or acts to alter the environment. Movement adds verisimilitude to any model of an organism. The puppet comes to life when it moves, and idols which move or breathe smoke are especially awe-inspiring. Robots and other mechanical creatures entertain us just because they move. And there is significance in the etymology of the *animated* cartoon.

Machines seem alive simply because they are in motion. The fascination of the steam shovel is legendary. Less familiar machines may actually be frightening. We may feel that it is only primitive people who mistake them for living creatures today, but at one time they were unfamiliar to everyone. When [the 19th-century poets William] Wordsworth and [Samuel Taylor] Coleridge once passed a steam engine, Wordsworth observed that it was scarcely possible to divest oneself of the impression that it had life and volition. "Yes," said Coleridge, "it is a giant with one idea."

A mechanical toy which imitated human behavior led to the theory of what we now call reflex action. In the first part of the seventeenth century certain moving figures were commonly installed in private and public gardens as sources of amusement. They were operated hydraulically. A young lady walking through a garden might step upon a small concealed platform. This would open a valve, water would flow into a piston, and a threatening figure would swing out from the bushes to frighten her. René Descartes knew how these figures worked, and he also knew how much they seemed like living creatures. He considered the possibility that the hydraulic system which explained the one might also explain the other. A muscle swells when it moves a limb—perhaps it is being inflated by a fluid coming along the nerves from the brain. The nerves which stretch from the surface of the body into the brain may be the strings which open the valves.

Descartes did not assert that the human organism always operates in this way. He favored the explanation in the case of animals, but he reserved a sphere of action for the "rational soul"—perhaps under religious pressure. It was not long before the additional step was taken, however, which produced the full-fledged doctrine of "man a machine." The doctrine did not owe its popularity to its plausibility—there was no reliable support for Descartes's theory—but rather to its shocking metaphysical and theoretical implications.

Since that time two things have happened: machines have become more lifelike, and living organisms have been found to be more like machines. Contemporary machines are not only more complex, they are deliberately designed to operate in ways which resemble human behavior. "Almost human" contrivances are a common part of our daily experience. Doors see us coming and open to receive us. Elevators remember our commands and stop at the correct floor. Mechanical hands lift imperfect items off a conveyor belt. Others write messages of fair legibility. Mechanical or electric calculators solve equations too difficult or too time-consuming for human mathematicians. Man has, in short, created the machine in his own image. And as a result, the living organism has lost some of its uniqueness. We are much less awed by machines than our ancestors were and less likely to endow the giant with even one idea. At the same time, we have discovered more about how the living organism works and are better able to see its machine-like properties.

## Operant Conditioning

**Operant conditioning:** A learning situation that involves behavior emitted by an organism rather than elicited by a detectable stimulus.

Generations of psychology students have studied Skinner's **operant conditioning** experiments and how they differ from the respondent behavior investigated by Pavlov. In the Pavlovian conditioning situation, a known stimulus is paired with a response under conditions of reinforcement. The behavioral response is elicited by a specific observable stimulus; Skinner called this behavioral response a respondent behavior.

Operant behavior occurs without any observable external antecedent stimulus, so that the organism's response appears to be spontaneous. This does not mean that there is no stimulus that elicits the response but rather that no stimulus is detected when the response occurs. From the experimenters' viewpoint, however, there is no stimulus because they have not applied a stimulus and cannot see one.

Another difference between respondent and operant behavior is that operant behavior operates on the organism's environment; respondent behavior does not. The harnessed dog in Pavlov's laboratory can do nothing but respond (salivate, in this case) when the experimenter presents the stimulus (the food). The dog cannot act on its own to secure the stimulus. However, the operant behavior of the rat in the "Skinner box" is instrumental in securing the stimulus (the food). Skinner disliked the label "Skinner box," a term first used by Clark Hull in 1933. Skinner referred to his experimental equipment as an "operant conditioning apparatus." However, Skinner box has become popular and accepted usage.

When the rat in the Skinner box presses the bar, it receives food, and it does not get any food until it does press the bar, which thus operates on the environment. Skinner believed that operant behavior better represents the typical learning situation. Because behavior is mostly of the operant type, it follows that the most effective approach to a science of behavior is to study the conditioning and extinguishing of these operant behaviors.

Skinner's classic experimental demonstration involved bar pressing in a Skinner box constructed to eliminate extraneous stimuli. A rat deprived of food was placed in the apparatus and allowed to explore. Eventually in the course of this exploration the rat would accidentally depress a lever or bar that activated a mechanism releasing a food pellet onto a tray. After receiving a few pellets (the reinforcers), conditioning was usually rapid. Note that the rat's behavior (pressing the lever) operated on the environment and thus was instrumental in securing food. The dependent variable is simple and direct: it is the rate of response.

**Law of acquisition:** The strength of an operant behavior is increased when it is followed by the presentation of a reinforcing stimulus.

From this basic experiment Skinner derived his **law of acquisition**, which states that the strength of an operant behavior increases when it is followed by the presentation of a reinforcing stimulus. Although practice is important in establishing a high rate of bar pressing, the key variable is reinforcement. Practice by itself will not increase the rate of responding; all it does is provide the opportunity for additional reinforcement to occur.

Skinner's law of acquisition differs from Thorndike's and Hull's positions on learning. Skinner did not deal with any pleasure/pain or satisfaction/dissatisfaction consequences of reinforcement as did Thorndike. Nor did Skinner make any attempt to interpret reinforcement in terms of reducing drives as did Hull. Whereas the systems of Thorndike and Hull are explanatory, Skinner's is descriptive.

## Schedules of Reinforcement

The initial research on bar pressing in the Skinner box demonstrated the role of reinforcement in operant behavior. The rat's behavior was reinforced for every bar press. In other words, the rat received food every time it made the correct response. In the real world, however, reinforcement is not always so consistent or continuous, yet learning occurs and behaviors persist even when reinforced intermittently. Skinner wrote:

> We do not always find good ice or snow when we go skating or skiing. ... We do not always get a good meal in a particular restaurant because cooks are not always predictable. We do not always get an answer when we telephone a friend because the friend is not always at home. ... The reinforcements characteristic of industry and education are almost always intermittent because it is not feasible to control behavior by reinforcing every response. (Skinner, 1953, p. 99)

Consider your own experience. Even if you study continuously, you may not get an A on every test. On the job, even if you work at maximum efficiency, you do not receive praise or pay raises every day. So Skinner wanted to know how behavior might be affected by variable reinforcement. Is one **reinforcement schedule** or pattern better than another in determining an organism's responses?

The impetus for the research came not from intellectual curiosity but expediency, and it shows that science sometimes operates contrary to the idealized picture presented in many textbooks. One Saturday afternoon, Skinner noticed that his supply of rat food pellets was running low. At that time—the 1930s—food pellets could not simply be purchased from a laboratory supply company. The experimenter (or graduate students) had to compound them by hand, a laborious and time-consuming process. Rather than spend his weekend making food pellets, Skinner asked himself what would happen if he reinforced his rats only once a minute regardless of the number of responses they made. That way, he would need far fewer food pellets for the weekend. He designed a series of experiments to test different rates and times of reinforcement (Ferster & Skinner, 1957; Skinner, 1969).

In one set of studies, Skinner compared the response rates of animals reinforced for every response with those reinforced after a specified time interval. The second condition is the fixed interval reinforcement schedule. A reinforcer could be given once a minute or once every four minutes. The important point is that the animal is reinforced only after the passage of a fixed period of time. A job in which salary is paid once a week or once a month provides reinforcement on a fixed interval schedule. Employees are paid not for the number of items they produce (the number of responses) but for the number of days or weeks that elapse. Skinner's research showed that the shorter the time interval between reinforcers, the more rapidly the animals responded. As the interval between reinforcers lengthened, the response rate declined.

Frequency of reinforcement also affects the extinction of a response. Behaviors are eliminated more quickly when they have been reinforced continuously and reinforcement is then stopped than when they have been reinforced intermittently. Some pigeons responded up to 10,000 times without reinforcement when they had originally been conditioned on an intermittent reinforcement basis.

In the fixed ratio schedule, the reinforcer is presented not after a certain time interval (as above) but after a predetermined number of responses. The animal's behavior determines how often it will receive reinforcement. It may be required to respond 10 times or

**Reinforcement schedules:** Conditions involving various rates and times of reinforcement.

20 times after receiving the initial reinforcer before it gets another one. Animals on a fixed ratio schedule respond much faster than do those on a fixed interval schedule. Rapid responding on fixed interval reinforcement will not bring additional reinforcement; the animal on a fixed interval schedule may press the bar five times or 50 times and will still be reinforced only when the stated time interval has passed. The higher response rate on the fixed ratio schedule worked for rats, pigeons, and humans. In a fixed ratio payment schedule in the workplace, an employee's pay or commission depends on the number of items produced or sold. This reinforcement schedule is effective as long as the ratio is not too high, requiring an impossible amount of work for each unit of pay, and the specific reinforcement offered is worth the effort.

## Successive Approximation: The Shaping of Behavior

In Skinner's original operant-conditioning experiment, the operant behavior (pressing the lever) is a simple behavior that a laboratory rat would be expected to display eventually in the course of exploring its environment. Thus, the chance is high that such a behavior will occur, assuming the experimenter has sufficient patience. It is obvious, however, that animals and humans demonstrate many more complex operant behaviors that have a much lower probability of occurrence in the normal course of events. Remember the complicated sequence of behaviors shown by Priscilla the Fastidious Pig, or the amazing feats of Bird Brain, that were on display at the IQ Zoo. How are such complex behaviors learned? How can a trainer or an experimenter or a parent reinforce and condition an animal or a child to perform behaviors that are not likely to occur spontaneously?

**Successive approximation:** An explanation for the acquisition of complex behavior. Behaviors such as learning to speak will be reinforced only as they come to approximate or approach the final desired behavior.

Skinner answered these questions with the method of **successive approximation**, or *shaping* (Skinner, 1953). He trained a pigeon in a very short time to peck at a specific spot in its cage. The probability that the pigeon on its own would peck at that precise spot was low. At first the pigeon was reinforced with food when it merely turned toward the designated spot. Then reinforcement was withheld until the pigeon made some movement, however slight, toward the spot. Next, reinforcement was given only for movements that brought the pigeon closer to the spot. After that, the pigeon was reinforced only when it thrust its head toward the spot. Finally, the pigeon was reinforced only when its beak touched the spot. Although this sounds time-consuming, Skinner conditioned pigeons in less than three minutes.

The experimental procedure itself explains the term "successive approximation." The organism is reinforced as its behavior comes in successive or consecutive stages to approximate the final behavior desired. Skinner suggested that this is how children learn the complex behavior of speaking. Infants spontaneously emit meaningless sounds, which parents reinforce by smiling, laughing, and talking. After a while parents reinforce this childish babbling in different ways, providing stronger reinforcers for sounds that approximate words. As the process continues, parental reinforcement becomes more restricted, given only for appropriate usage and pronunciation. Thus, the complex behavior of acquiring language skills is shaped by providing differential reinforcement in stages.

## Aircribs, Teaching Machines, and Pigeon-Guided Missiles

The operant conditioning apparatus brought Skinner prominence among psychologists, but it was the aircrib, a device to automate the care of infants, that brought him public notoriety (Benjamin & Nielsen-Gammon, 1999). When Skinner and his wife decided to have a second child, she said baby care through the first two years required too much menial labor, so Skinner invented a mechanized environment to relieve parents of routine tasks. Although the aircrib was made available commercially, it was not a successful product. Skinner's daughter, reared in the aircrib, apparently bore no ill effects from the experience.

Skinner first described the device in *Ladies Home Journal* magazine in 1945 and later in his autobiography. It was

> … *a crib-sized living space that we began to call the "baby-tender." It had sound-absorbing walls and a large picture window. Air entered through filters at the bottom and, after being warmed and moistened, moved upward through and around the edges of a tightly stretched canvas, which served as a mattress. A strip of sheeting ten yards long passed over the canvas, a clean section of which could be cranked into place in a few seconds. (Skinner, 1979, p. 275)*

Another piece of equipment Skinner promoted was the teaching machine, invented in the 1920s by Sidney Pressey. Unfortunately for Pressey, the device was ahead of its time then, and there was insufficient interest to continue marketing it (Pressey, 1967). Contextual forces may have been responsible for the lack of interest then as well as for the enthusiastic resurrection of the device some 30 years later (Benjamin, 1988). When Pressey introduced the machine, he promised it would teach students at a faster pace and require fewer classroom teachers. At the time, however, there was a surplus of teachers and no public pressure to improve the learning process. In the 1950s, when Skinner promoted a similar device, there was a shortage of teachers, an excess of students, and public pressure to improve education so the United States could compete with the Soviet Union in space exploration. Skinner summarized his work in this field in *The Technology of Teaching* (1968). He said that he had not known about Pressey's invention when he developed his own teaching machine, but he gave due credit to his predecessor once he learned of Pressey's work. Teaching machines were widely used in the 1950s and 1960s, until they were superseded by computer-assisted instructional methods.

During World War II, Skinner, with the assistance of the Brelands, developed a guidance system to steer bombs dropped from warplanes to specific targets on the ground. Pigeons housed in the nose-cones of the missiles were conditioned to peck at an image of the target. Their responses affected the angles of the missiles' fins so that they would be targeted correctly. Skinner demonstrated that his pigeons could achieve a high degree of accuracy. The U.S. military was apparently not impressed, however, when they opened the nose cone and saw three pigeons instead of the sophisticated electronic equipment they were expecting. They declined to add pigeons to their arsenal of weaponry (Skinner, 1960).

In the 1960s and 1970s, Keller and Marian Breland worked for the U.S. Department of Defense. They

> … *conditioned herring gulls to conduct 360-degree searches over lakes and oceans, taught pigeons to fly along a road to spot snipers, and conditioned ravens to perform long-distance complex tasks such as taking pictures with small cameras held in their beaks. It was notable that although they were able to escape from captivity, these animals consistently performed their tasks and returned. (Gillaspy & Bihm, 2002, p. 293)*

## *Walden Two*—A Behaviorist Society

Skinner mapped out a technology of behavior, an attempt to apply his laboratory findings to society as a whole. Whereas Watson spoke in general terms about constructing a foundation for saner living through conditioning, Skinner described in detail the operation of such a society. His novel, *Walden Two* (1948), follows life in a 1,000-member rural community in which behavior is controlled by positive reinforcement. The book was the outgrowth of Skinner's personal midlife crisis, a depression he suffered at age 41. He sought to resolve it by resuming his post-college identity as a writer, expressing his conflicts and despair through the story's main character, T. E. Frazier. Skinner wrote,

"Much of the life in *Walden Two* was my own at the time. I let Frazier say things I myself was not yet ready to say to anyone" (1979, pp. 297–298).

Three years passed before Skinner found a publisher for *Walden Two*. Many editors rejected the manuscript, claiming it was wordy, slow, overly long, and badly organized (Wiener, 1996). It was finally accepted when Skinner agreed to write an introductory textbook on behavioral psychology for the same publisher. That work became his highly popular *Science and Human Behavior* (1953). *Walden Two* went on to sell more than 3 million copies.

The society depicted in Skinner's novel is based on his assumption that human nature is machinelike. This idea reflects the line of thought we have traced from Galileo and Newton through the British empiricists to Watson and Skinner. Skinner's mechanistic, analytic, and deterministic natural science approach, reinforced by the results of his conditioning experiments, persuaded many behavioral psychologists that with an awareness of environmental conditions and the application of positive reinforcement, human behavior could be guided, modified, and shaped.

## Behavior Modification

**Behavior modification:**
The use of positive reinforcement to control or modify the behavior of individuals or groups.

Skinner's society that is based on positive reinforcement exists only in fictional terms, but the control or modification of human behavior, individually and in small groups, is widespread. **Behavior modification** through positive reinforcement is a frequently used clinical application in mental hospitals, factories, prisons, and schools to change undesirable behaviors to more acceptable ones. Behavior modification works with people the same way operant conditioning works to change the behavior of rats and pigeons; that is, by reinforcing the desired behavior and not reinforcing undesired behavior.

Think of the child who throws temper tantrums to get food or attention. When parents give in to the child's demands, they are reinforcing unpleasant behavior. In a behavior modification situation, behavior such as kicking and screaming would never be reinforced. Only more socially acceptable behaviors would be reinforced. After a time the child's behavior will change because the tantrums no longer work to bring rewards, whereas nicer behaviors will.

Operant conditioning and reinforcement have been applied in the workplace, where behavior modification programs have been used to reduce absenteeism, improve job performance, promote safe work practices, and teach job skills. Behavior modification has also been successful in altering the behavior of patients in mental hospitals. By rewarding patients for appropriate behavior with tokens that can be exchanged for goods or privileges, and by not reinforcing negative or disruptive behaviors, positive behavioral changes can be induced. Unlike traditional clinical techniques, the behavioral psychologist here is not concerned about whatever might be going on in the patient's mind, any more than the experimenter is concerned with any mental activities of the rat in the Skinner box. The focus is exclusively on overt behavior and positive reinforcement.

Research has shown that behavior modification programs are usually successful only within the organization or institution in which they are carried out. The effects rarely transfer to outside situations because the program of reinforcement would have to be continued, even intermittently, for the desired behavior changes to persist. For patients, this can be done if caregivers in the home, for example, are trained to reinforce desirable behaviors with smiles, praise, or other signs of affection and approval.

Punishment is not part of a behavior modification program. According to Skinner, people should not be punished for failing to behave in desirable ways. Instead, they are to be reinforced or rewarded when their behavior changes in positive ways. Skinner's position that positive reinforcement is more effective than punishment in altering behavior is supported by considerable human and animal research.

Skinner wrote that as a child he was never physically punished by his father and only once by his mother, when she washed out his mouth with soap and water for saying a naughty word (Skinner, 1976). He did not say whether the punishment was effective in changing his behavior.

## Criticisms of Skinner's Behaviorism

Criticism of Skinner's behaviorism has been directed toward his extreme positivism and opposition to theory. Opponents argue that it is impossible to eliminate all theorizing. Advance planning of the details of an experiment is evidence of theorizing, however simple. Also, Skinner's acceptance of basic conditioning principles as the framework for his research constitutes a degree of theorizing.

Skinner made confident assertions about economic, social, political, and religious issues that he derived from his system. In 1986, he wrote an article with the all-embracing title "What Is Wrong with Life in the Western World?" He stated that "human behavior in the West has grown weak, but it can be strengthened through the application of principles derived from an experimental analysis of behavior" (Skinner, 1986, p. 568). This willingness to extrapolate from the data, particularly for proposals about solutions to complex human problems, is inconsistent with an anti-theoretical stand and shows that Skinner went beyond observable data in presenting his blueprint for the redesign of society.

Skinner's position that all behaviors are learned was challenged by the animal-training work of his former students, Keller and Marian Breland. They found that pigs, chickens, hamsters, porpoises, whales, cows, and other animals demonstrated a tendency toward "instinctive drift." This means that animals tended to substitute instinctive behaviors for behaviors that had been reinforced, even when such instinctive behaviors interfered with obtaining food.

Using food as a reinforcer, pigs and raccoons were quickly conditioned to pick up a coin, carry it some distance, and drop it into a toy bank. After a while, however, the animals began performing unwanted behaviors.

*Pigs would stop on their way, bury the coin in the sand, and take it out with their snout; raccoons would spend a lot of time handling the coin, with their well-known washing-like movements. This was at first amusing, but eventually it became time-consuming and would make the whole show appear very imperfect to the spectator. Commercially, it was a disaster. (Richelle, 1993, p. 68)*

What was occurring was instinctive drift. The animals were reverting to innate behaviors that took precedence over learned behaviors, even though this caused a delay in receiving food. Clearly in these cases, reinforcement was not as all-powerful as Skinner claimed.

Skinner's explanation of how infants learn to speak has been contested. Critics insist that some behavior must be inherited. Infants do not learn language on a word-by-word basis because they receive reinforcement for the correct usage or pronunciation of each word. Instead, they master the grammatical rules necessary to produce sentences. The potential to construct those rules, so this argument runs, is inherited, not learned (Chomsky, 1959, 1972).

## Contributions of Skinner's Behaviorism

Despite these criticisms, Skinner remained the uncontested champion of behavioral psychology from the 1950s to the 1980s. During this period, American psychology was shaped more by his work than by the ideas of any other psychologist. In 1958, the

APA bestowed on Skinner the Distinguished Scientific Contribution Award, noting that "few American psychologists have had so profound an impact on the development of psychology and on promising younger psychologists."

In 1968, Skinner received the National Medal of Science, the highest accolade bestowed by the U.S. government for contributions to science. The American Psychological Foundation presented Skinner with its Gold Medal Award, and he appeared on the cover of *Time* magazine. In 1990, Skinner was awarded the APA's Presidential Citation for Lifetime Contribution to Psychology.

Skinner's overall goal was the betterment of human lives and society through the application of the principles of his form of behaviorism (see Rutherford, 2009). Despite the mechanistic nature of his system, he was a humanitarian, a quality apparent in his efforts to modify behavior in the real-world settings of homes, schools, businesses, and institutions. He expected his technology of behavior to relieve human suffering and felt increasingly frustrated that his ideas, though popular and influential, had not been applied more widely and wisely.

Although Skinner's brand of behaviorism continues to be applied in laboratory, clinical, organizational, and other real-world settings, it has been challenged by the work of the neo-neobehaviorists, including Albert Bandura and Julian Rotter, among others, who take a more sociobehavioral approach.

## Sociobehaviorism: The Cognitive Challenge

Bandura and Rotter and the followers of their sociobehavioral approach are primarily behaviorists themselves, but their form of behaviorism is quite unlike Skinner's. They question his total disavowal of mental or cognitive processes and propose instead a social learning or sociobehavioral approach, a reflection of the broader cognitive movement in psychology as a whole. Social learning theories mark the third stage (the neo-neobehaviorism stage) in the development of the behaviorist school of thought. We discuss the origins and impact of the cognitive movement as a whole in Chapter 15.

## Albert Bandura (1925– )

ALBERT BANDURA

Albert Bandura was born in Canada, in a town so small that his high school had only 20 students and two teachers. His parents were immigrants from Eastern Europe who had little formal education, but who placed a high value on it for their son. After Albert graduated from high school, he worked with construction crews in the Yukon Territory, filling potholes in the Alaska Highway. "Finding himself in the midst of a curious collection of characters, most of whom had fled creditors, alimony, and probation officers, [Bandura] quickly developed a keen appreciation for the psychopathology of everyday life, which seemed to blossom in the austere tundra" (Distinguished Scientific Contribution Award, 1981, p. 28).

Bandura enrolled at the University of British Columbia in Vancouver where, quite by accident, he discovered what he wanted to do with his life. "I was in a carpool with premeds and engineers who enrolled in classes at an unmercifully early hour. So while waiting for my English class, I flipped through a course catalogue that happened to have been left on a table in the library. I noticed an introductory psychology course that would be an early time filler. I enrolled in it and found my future profession" (Bandura, 2007, p. 46).

Thus he took his first course in psychology only because it was offered at a convenient time. He earned a Ph.D. from the University of Iowa in 1952 and went from there to a distinguished and highly productive career at Stanford University.

## Social Cognitive Theory

Bandura's social cognitive theory is a less extreme form of behaviorism than Skinner's, and it reflects the spirit of its times and the impact of psychology's renewed interest in cognitive factors. Bandura's viewpoint remained behaviorist, however. His research focus was to observe the behavior of human subjects in interaction. He did not use introspection, and he emphasized the importance of rewards or reinforcements in acquiring and modifying behavior.

In addition to being a behavioral theory, Bandura's system is cognitive. He stressed the influence on external reinforcement schedules of such thought processes as beliefs, expectations, and instructions. In Bandura's view, behavioral responses are not automatically triggered in humans by external stimuli, as with a machine or a robot. Instead, reactions to stimuli are self-activated, initiated by the person. When an external reinforcer alters behavior, it does so because the person is consciously aware of the response that is being reinforced and anticipates receiving the same reinforcer for behaving in the same way the next time the situation arises.

Although Bandura agreed with Skinner that human behavior can be changed through reinforcement, he also suggested, and demonstrated empirically, that individuals can learn virtually all kinds of behavior without experiencing reinforcement directly. We do not *always* have to be reinforced ourselves in order to learn something. We can also learn through what Bandura called **vicarious reinforcement**, by observing how other people behave and seeing the consequences of their behavior.

This ability to learn by example and vicarious reinforcement assumes that we have the capacity to anticipate and appreciate consequences we observe in others, even though we have not experienced them ourselves. We can regulate our behavior by visualizing the consequences of a particular behavior we have not personally experienced and then making a conscious decision to behave or not behave similarly. Bandura suggests that there is not a direct link between stimulus and response, or between behavior and reinforcement, as Skinner noted. Instead, a mediating mechanism is interposed between stimulus and response, and that mechanism is the person's cognitive processes.

Thus, cognitive processes came to play a powerful role in Bandura's social cognitive theory, and this distinguished his views from Skinner's. To Bandura, it is not the actual reinforcement schedule that is effective in changing a person's behavior but rather what the person thinks that schedule is. Rather than learning by experiencing reinforcement directly, we learn through "modeling," which involves observing other people and patterning our behavior on theirs. For Skinner, whoever controls the reinforcers controls behavior. For Bandura, whoever controls society's models controls behavior.

Bandura has conducted extensive research on the characteristics of the models that influence human behavior. We are much more likely to model our behavior after a person of the same sex and age, our peers, who have solved problems similar to our own. We also tend to be impressed by models high in status and prestige. The type of behavior involved affects the extent of our imitation. Simple behaviors are more likely to be imitated than highly complex behaviors. Hostile and aggressive behaviors tend to be strongly imitated, especially by children (Bandura, 1986). Thus, what we see in real life or in the media can often determine our behavior.

For example, research conducted in several countries has consistently found that children who watch a great deal of violence on television and in movies, or who spend time playing action-packed videogames, display far more violent and aggressive behavior as adolescents and young adults than do children who are exposed to less violence (Anderson et al., 2010; Rogoff, Paradise, Correa-Chavez, & Angelillo, 2003; Uhlmann & Swanson, 2004). Research has also shown that teenagers and young adults who listen

**Vicarious reinforcement:** Bandura's notion that learning can occur by observing the behavior of other people, and the consequences of their behavior, rather than by always experiencing reinforcement personally.

frequently to rap music tend to become more hostile and sexually aggressive than those who listen to less of this type of music (Chen, Miller, Grube, & Walters, 2006).

Bandura's approach is a *social* learning theory because it studies behavior as formed and modified in social situations. Bandura criticized Skinner for using only individual subjects (mostly rats and pigeons) instead of human subjects interacting with one another. Few people live in social isolation. Bandura charged that psychologists cannot expect research findings that ignore social interactions to be relevant to the modern world.

## Self-Efficacy

**Self-efficacy:** One's sense of self-esteem and competence in dealing with life's problems.

Bandura conducted considerable research on **self-efficacy**, described as our sense of self-esteem or self-worth and our feeling of adequacy, efficiency, and competence in dealing with problems (Bandura, 1982). His work has shown that people who have a great deal of self-efficacy believe they are capable of coping with the diverse events in their lives. They expect to be able to overcome obstacles. They seek challenges, persevere, and maintain a high level of confidence in their ability to succeed and to exert control over their lives. One researcher described self-efficacy simply as the "power of believing you can," adding that "believing that you can accomplish what you want to accomplish is one of the most important ingredients in the recipe for success" (Maddux, 2002, p. 277).

People low in self-efficacy feel helpless, even hopeless, about coping and think they have little chance to affect the situations they confront. When they encounter problems, they are likely to give up if their initial attempts at solutions fail. They believe nothing they can do will make a difference and that they have little or no control over their fate.

Bandura's research has shown that our belief in our level of self-efficacy influences many aspects of our lives. For example, people higher in self-efficacy tend to earn better grades, consider more career possibilities, have greater job success, set higher personal goals, and enjoy better physical and mental health than people lower in self-efficacy. In general, men have been found to be higher than women in self-efficacy. For both men and women, self-efficacy seems to peak in middle age and decline after age 60.

It seems obvious that a high degree of self-efficacy will lead to positive effects in many aspects of life. Research has shown that people high in self-efficacy feel better and healthier, and are less bothered by stress, more tolerant of physical pain, and likely to recover more quickly from illness or surgery than people low in self-efficacy. Self-efficacy also affects classroom and job performance. For example, employees high in self-efficacy have been found to be more satisfied with their work, committed to their organization, and motivated to perform well on the job and in training programs than are employees low in self-efficacy (Salas & Cannon-Bowers, 2001). Also, people high in social self-efficacy feel confident about their ability to initiate social contact and develop new friendships. They score high on measures of emotional well-being and are less likely to become addicted to Internet use than are those who score low in social self-efficacy (Herman & Betz, 2006; Iskender & Akin, 2010).

Bandura's research showed that groups develop collective efficacy levels that influence their performance of various tasks. Research on such diverse units as sports teams, corporate departments, military outfits, urban neighborhoods, and political action groups found that "the stronger the perceived collective efficacy, the higher the group's aspirations and motivational investment in their undertakings, the stronger their staying power in the face of impediments and setbacks, the higher their morale and resilience to stressors, and the greater their performance accomplishments" (Bandura, 2001, p. 14).

## Behavior Modification

Bandura's purpose in developing a social cognitive approach to behaviorism was to change or modify those behaviors society considers abnormal or undesirable. He reasoned that if all behaviors are learned by observing other people and modeling our behavior on theirs, then undesirable behaviors can be altered or relearned in the same way. Like Skinner, Bandura focused on externals, on the behavior itself and not on any presumed internal conscious or unconscious conflict. To Bandura, treating the symptom means treating the disorder, because symptom and disorder are the same.

Modeling techniques are used to change behavior by having subjects observe a model in a situation that usually causes them some anxiety. For example, children who are afraid of dogs watch a child their age approach and touch a dog. Observing from a safe distance, the fearful children see the model make progressively closer and bolder movements toward the dog. The model pets the dog through the bars of a playpen, then enters the pen to play with the dog. As a result of this observational learning situation, the children's fear of dogs can be reduced. In a variation of this technique, subjects watch models play with the feared object, such as a snake, and then the subjects themselves make progressively closer movements toward the object until they are actually able to handle it.

Bandura's form of behavior therapy is widely used in clinical, business, and classroom situations and has been supported by hundreds of experimental studies. It has been effective in eliminating phobias about snakes, closed spaces, open spaces, and heights. It is also useful in treating obsessive-compulsive disorders, sexual dysfunctions, and some forms of anxiety, and it can be used to enhance self-efficacy.

Bandura's work has been adapted for radio and television programs designed to present models for appropriate behavior in addressing social and national problems such as preventing unwanted pregnancies, controlling the spread of AIDS, promoting literacy, raising the status of women, and adopting family-planning strategies. These programs rely on fictional characters who act as models for listeners and viewers to emulate in changing their behavior. Research conducted on these radio and television dramas reports significant increases in desirable behaviors such as safe-sex practices, family planning, and enhancing the status of women (Bandura, 2007, 2009; Smith, 2002a).

## Comment

As you would expect, traditional behaviorists criticized Bandura's social cognitive behaviorism, arguing that cognitive processes such as belief and anticipation have no causal effect on behavior. Bandura responded by saying that "it is amusing to see radical behaviorists, who contend that thoughts have no causal influence, devoting considerable time to speeches, articles, and books in an effort to convert people's beliefs to their way of thinking" (quoted in Evans, 1989, p. 83).

Social cognitive theory has been widely accepted in psychology as an effective way to study behavior in the laboratory and to modify it in clinical settings. In addition, Bandura's contributions have been widely recognized by his peers. He was president of the APA in 1974, and in 1980 he received the APA's Distinguished Scientific Contribution Award. In 2004 he received the APA's Outstanding Contribution to Psychology Award, and in 2006 he was the recipient of the American Psychological Foundation's Gold Medal Award for Life Achievement in the Science of Psychology.

Bandura's theory and the modeling therapy derived from it fit the functional, practical cast of American psychology. His approach is objective and amenable to precise laboratory methods. It is responsive to the current intellectual climate that focuses on internal cognitive variables and is applicable to real-world issues.

# Julian Rotter (1916– )

Julian Rotter grew up in Brooklyn, New York. The family lived comfortably until his father lost his business at the beginning of the Great Depression in 1929. This unfortunate change in economic circumstances was a turning point for the 13-year-old Rotter. He wrote, "It began in me a lifelong concern with social injustice and provided me with a powerful lesson on how personality and behavior were affected by situational conditions" (Rotter, 1993, p. 274).

During high school he discovered books on psychoanalysis by Sigmund Freud and Alfred Adler. As a game he started interpreting the dreams of his friends and decided he wanted to become a psychologist. Disappointed to learn that there were few jobs for psychologists, Rotter chose to major in chemistry at Brooklyn College. Once there, however, he happened to meet Adler and switched to psychology after all, even though he knew it was impractical. He hoped to pursue an academic career, but prejudice against Jews thwarted that goal. "At Brooklyn College and again in graduate school I had been warned that Jews simply could not get academic jobs, regardless of their credentials. The warnings seemed justified" (Rotter, 1982, p. 346).

After Rotter received his Ph.D. from Indiana University in 1941, he accepted a job at a state mental hospital in Connecticut. He served as a psychologist with the U.S. Army during World War II, taught at Ohio State University until 1963, and moved to the University of Connecticut. In 1988, he received the APA's Distinguished Scientific Contribution Award.

## Cognitive Processes

Rotter was the first psychologist to use the term "social learning theory" (Rotter, 1947). He developed a cognitive form of behaviorism, which, like Bandura's, includes reference to internal subjective experiences. Thus his behaviorism, like Bandura's, is less radical than Skinner's.

Rotter criticized Skinner for studying individual subjects in isolation, arguing that we learn behavior primarily through social experiences. Rotter's laboratory research was rigorous and well controlled, typical of the behaviorist movement. He studied only human subjects in social interaction.

Rotter emphasized cognitive processes to a greater extent than Bandura. Rotter believed that we perceive ourselves as conscious beings capable of influencing the experiences that affect our lives. Our behavior is determined by external stimuli and by the reinforcement they provide, but the relative influence of these two factors is mediated by our cognitive processes. Rotter delineated the following four principles that govern behavioral outcomes (Rotter, 1982):

- *We form subjective expectations of the outcomes or results of our behavior in terms of the amount and kind of reinforcement likely to follow it.*
- *We estimate the likelihood that behaving in a certain way leads to a specific reinforcement and adjust our behavior accordingly.*
- *We place different values on different reinforcers and assess their relative worth for different situations.*
- *Because each of us functions in a psychological environment that is unique to us as individuals, the same reinforcement can have different values for different people.*

Thus, to Rotter, our subjective expectations and values, which are internal cognitive states, determine the effects that different external experiences (different external stimuli and reinforcers) will have on us.

## Locus of Control

**Locus of control:** Rotter's idea about the perceived source of reinforcement. Internal locus of control is the belief that reinforcement depends on one's own behavior; external locus of control is the belief that reinforcement depends on outside forces.

Rotter focused considerable research on our beliefs about the source of our reinforcers. Some people believe reinforcement depends on their own behavior; these people are said to have an **internal locus of control**. Other people believe reinforcement depends on outside forces such as fate, luck, or the actions of other people; they are said to have an **external locus of control** (Rotter, 1966).

Obviously, these perceptions about the source of control exert different influences on behavior. To people with an external locus of control, their own abilities and actions make little difference in the reinforcers they receive. Convinced they are powerless with respect to outside forces, they make minimal attempts to change or improve their situation. But people with an internal locus of control expect to be in charge of their lives and behave accordingly.

Rotter's research has shown that people with an internal locus of control tend to be physically and mentally healthier than those with an external locus of control. In general, internals have lower blood pressure, fewer heart attacks, less anxiety and depression, and are better able to cope with stress. They receive better grades in school and believe they have greater freedom of choice. They are more popular and socially skilled and rank higher in self-esteem. In addition, Rotter's work suggests that locus of control is learned in childhood from the behavior of parents or caregivers. Parents of adults who have an internal locus of control tend to be supportive, generous with praise for achievement (positive reinforcement), consistent in their discipline, and not authoritarian in their attitudes.

Rotter developed a test to measure locus of control. The test consists of 23 forced-choice alternatives; subjects select the one in each pair that best describes their beliefs (see Table 11.1).

---

### TABLE 11.1 SAMPLE ITEMS FROM THE I-E SCALE

**1.** Many of the unhappy things in people's lives are partly due to bad luck.
People's misfortunes result from the mistakes they make.

**2.** One of the major reasons why we have wars is because people don't take enough interest in politics.
There will always be wars, no matter how hard people try to prevent them.

**3.** In the long run, people get the respect they deserve in this world.
Unfortunately, an individual's worth often passes unrecognized no matter how hard he or she tries.

**4.** The idea that teachers are unfair to students is nonsense.
Most students don't realize the extent to which their grades are influenced by accidental happenings.

**5.** Without the right breaks, one cannot be an effective leader.
Capable people who fail to become leaders have not taken advantage of their opportunities.

**6.** No matter how hard you try, some people just don't like you.
People who can't get others to like them don't understand how to get along with others.

**Note:** From "Generalized Expectancies for Internal Versus External Control of Reinforcement," by J. B. Rotter, 1966, *Psychological Monographs, 80,* p. 11.

---

***A chance discovery*** We saw that Skinner's accidental discovery of reinforcement schedules was the result of expedience, of not wanting to spend the weekend in the laboratory making food pellets for his rats. We noted that science does not always advance in the rational, systematic fashion described in many textbooks. Random or accidental factors intrude to shape the development of a field of study. For Rotter's concept of locus of control, which he considered his most significant discovery, the impetus was a chance remark made by a colleague.

Rotter was conducting an experiment in which subjects working with sets of cards were instructed to guess whether the reverse side of the cards showed a square or a circle. They were told that they were being rated on their powers of extrasensory perception (ESP). After they had finished with one set of cards, they were asked to estimate how successful they believed they would be with the second set of cards.

Some subjects reported they would do worse because they thought that their successful guesses on the first trial were simply a matter of luck. Other subjects said they would do better because they believed that their successful guesses the first time were based on their ESP skills, which they expected would improve with practice.

At the time Rotter was conducting this research, he was also supervising the clinical training of E. Jerry Phares. Phares spoke to Rotter about a patient who was upset about his lack of social life. At Phares's urging the man went to a party and danced with several women, but even with that apparent social success his outlook did not change. He told Phares that he had just been lucky: "It would never happen again."

When Rotter heard the story, he realized that

> … there were always some subjects in our experiments whose expectancies, like this patient's, never went up even after successes. My graduate students and I had run various experiments in which we rigged the volunteers' success or failure…. Some volunteers, whether we told them they were right or wrong most of the time, didn't change their expectations that they'd get most of them wrong on the next set. Others, whatever we told them, thought they'd do better the next time.
>
> At that point I put together the two sides of my work—as practitioner and as scientist—and hypothesized that some people feel that what happens to them is governed by external forces of one kind or another, while others feel that what happens to them is governed largely by their own efforts and skills. (Rotter, quoted in Hunt, 1993, p. 334)

We are left to wonder whether Rotter would have developed the idea of locus of control had Phares's patient revised his outlook about his own popularity after going to the dance.

### Comment

Rotter's social learning theory has attracted many followers who are primarily experimentally oriented and who agree on the importance of cognitive variables in influencing behavior. His research is as rigorous and controlled as the subject matter allows, and he defined his concepts with the precision that makes them amenable to experimental testing. A large number of research studies, particularly on internal-external locus of control, support his approach. Rotter claimed that locus of control was "one of the most studied variables in psychology and the other social sciences" (Rotter, 1990, p. 489).

## The Fate of Behaviorism

Although the cognitive challenge to behaviorism from within succeeded in modifying the behaviorist movement we have followed from Watson through Skinner, it is important to remember that Bandura, Rotter, and the other neo-neobehaviorists who support the cognitive approach still consider themselves behaviorists. We may call them *methodological* behaviorists because they invoke internal cognitive processes as part of psychology's subject matter, whereas *radical* behaviorists believe psychology must study only overt behavior and environmental stimuli, not any presumed internal states. Watson and Skinner were radical behaviorists. Hull, Tolman, Bandura, and Rotter can be classified as methodological behaviorists.

The dominance of Skinner's brand of behaviorism peaked in the 1980s and declined after Skinner's death in 1990. Even the famous Harvard pigeon laboratory, begun by Skinner in 1948, was closed in 1998 (Azar, 2002). Skinner conceded before his death that his form of behaviorism was losing ground and that the impact of the cognitive approach was growing. Other scholars agree, noting that "fewer scholars at major universities now call themselves behaviorists in the traditional sense. In fact, 'behaviorism' is often referred to in the past tense" (Baars, 1986, p. 1).

The behaviorism that remains vital in contemporary psychology, especially within applied psychology, is a different behaviorism from that which flourished in the decades between Watson's 1913 manifesto and Skinner's death. As with all evolutionary movements in science and in nature, species will continue to evolve. In that sense, behaviorism survives in the spirit of its founder's intent, which was to develop a technology that could be used to change behavior for the better.

# Discussion Questions

1. Define Hull's concepts of primary and secondary drives and primary and secondary reinforcement.
2. Describe the three stages in the evolution of the behaviorist school of thought.
3. Describe Skinner's views on theorizing, the mechanistic spirit, intervening variables, and the use of statistics.
4. Distinguish between operant and respondent conditioning. How is operant conditioning used to modify behavior?
5. Distinguish between self-efficacy and locus of control in terms of their effects on behavior.
6. Give an example of an intervening variable. Describe how it can be defined operationally.
7. How did Hull's behaviorism differ from the views of Watson and Tolman?
8. How do Bandura's and Rotter's views on cognitive factors differ from Skinner's views?
9. How do people high in self-efficacy differ from people low in self-efficacy?
10. How is modeling used to change behavior? Give an example.
11. How would you apply the method of successive approximation to train a dog to walk in a circle?

12. On what grounds has Skinner's system been criticized?
13. What are pseudo-problems? Why was the notion of pseudo-problems so appealing to behaviorists?
14. What did Tolman mean by purposive behaviorism?
15. What does Priscilla the Fastidious Pig have to do with the history of psychology? By what techniques was this animal trained?
16. What is Skinner's law of acquisition? How did it differ from Thorndike's and Hull's positions on learning?
17. What is the difference between fixed-interval and fixed-ratio reinforcement schedules? Give a few examples of each.
18. What is the hypothetico-deductive method? List some criticisms of Hull's system.
19. What role did the spirit of mechanism play in Hull's approach to behaviorism?
20. What was operationism and how did it influence the neobehaviorists of the 1920s and 1930s?
21. Which psychologists can be classified as neobehaviorists? On what major points did they agree?

## CHAPTER 12
# Gestalt Psychology

## A Sudden Insight

Tenerife, located 200 miles off the coast of Africa, is the most famous island in the history of psychology; perhaps it is the only island in the history of psychology. Nevertheless, the work of a German psychologist living there in the second decade of the twentieth century is without question a significant part of the history of the field.

Wolfgang Köhler studied apes on Tenerife. No, this is not another Clever Hans or Priscilla the Fastidious Pig tale. Those animals had been trained, or conditioned, to behave in certain ways. But until Köhler went to Tenerife, it was thought that the only way animals could learn was through trial and error; that is, by accidentally stumbling on the correct response—the one that brought food as reinforcement. Most of the animal research we have cited in earlier chapters involved animals taught to behave in whatever way the experimenter, or trainer, wanted them to.

Köhler had no interest in training the apes he found living on the island. His goal was to observe them to see how they solved problems. He believed they were more intelligent than people thought and that they were capable of solving problems in much the same way humans did. So he put his apes in large cages, gave them implements that they could use to obtain the food that was placed in plain view, and sat back to watch what they did.

One female ape, Nueva, picked up a stick that Köhler had placed in her cage. She scraped the ground with it for a short time, then lost interest and dropped it. Ten minutes later some fruit was placed outside the cage. She stretched one arm through the bars toward the fruit but could not reach it. She began to whimper, then moan, and she threw herself on the ground in "a gesture most eloquent of despair," Köhler wrote.

Several minutes later she looked at the stick, stopped whining, and suddenly grabbed it. She stretched the stick through the bars of the cage and dragged the fruit close enough so that she could grasp it with her hand.

An hour later Köhler repeated the experiment. This time Nueva showed little hesitation. She picked up the stick and used it as a tool more adroitly than the first time, thus obtaining the food more quickly. The third time she went for the stick immediately, reacting even faster.

It was clear to Köhler that Nueva had not fumbled around, using the trial-and-error method of learning, until she happened in the course of random movements to touch the food with the stick. In contrast, her movements were goal-oriented, purposeful, and deliberate. This was different from the behavior of Thorndike's cats in the puzzle box or rats in a maze.

Nueva, and the rest of the chimps studied on Tenerife, exhibited a different way of learning, and their actions helped to bring about another revolution in psychology, another way of approaching the study of mind and behavior.

# The Gestalt Revolt

We have traced the development of psychology from the initial ideas of Wundt and their elaboration by Titchener, through the functionalist school of thought and the applied areas of psychology, to the behaviorism of Watson and Skinner and the cognitive challenge within that movement. At approximately the same time the behaviorist revolution was gathering strength in the United States, the Gestalt revolution was taking hold of German psychology. This was yet another protest against Wundtian psychology—further testimony to the importance of Wundt's ideas as an inspiration for new viewpoints and a basis for launching new systems of psychology.

In its attack on the psychology establishment, Gestalt psychology focused primarily on the elementistic nature of Wundt's work. Recall that sensory elements were the foundation of Wundt's psychology; Gestalt psychologists made this the target of their opposition. Wolfgang Köhler, a founder of Gestalt psychology, wrote, "We had been shocked by the thesis that all psychological facts consist of unrelated inert atoms and that almost the only factors which combine these atoms and thus introduce action are associations" (Köhler, 1959, p. 728).

To understand the Gestalt protest, let us recall what psychology was like in 1912. Watson's behaviorism was beginning its attack on Wundt and Titchener and on functionalism. Animal research from Thorndike's and Pavlov's laboratories was exerting a significant impact. Sigmund Freud's psychoanalysis (see Chapter 13) was already a decade old. Although the Gestalt psychologists' movement against Wundt's position paralleled the rise of behaviorism in the United States, they were independent of one another. Although both schools of thought started by opposing the same ideas—Wundt's focus on sensory elements—eventually they would come to oppose each other.

The differences between Gestalt psychology and behaviorism were soon evident. Gestalt psychologists accepted the value of consciousness while criticizing the attempt to reduce it to atoms or elements. Behavioral psychologists refused to acknowledge the usefulness of the concept of consciousness for a scientific psychology.

Gestalt psychologists referred to Wundt's approach (as they understood it) as brick-and-mortar psychology, implying that the elements (the bricks) were held together by the mortar of the association process. They argued that when we look out a window we really see trees and sky, not individual sensory elements such as brightness and hue that may be somehow connected to constitute our perception of trees and sky.

Further, the Gestalt psychologists maintained that when sensory elements are combined, the elements form a new pattern or configuration. If you assemble a group of individual musical notes (musical elements), for example, a melody or tune emerges from their combination, something new that did not exist in any of the individual elementary notes. The popular way to state this notion is that the whole is different from the sum of its parts. In fairness to Wundt, it should be noted that he recognized this point with his doctrine of creative synthesis.

## More to Perception than Meets the Eye

To illustrate the basic difference between the Gestalt and the Wundtian approaches to perception, imagine you are a student in a Wundtian-style German psychology laboratory in the early part of the twentieth century. The psychologist in charge asks you to describe a certain object that you see on a table. You say:

*"A book."*

*"Yes, of course, it is a book," he agrees, "but what do you really see?"*

*"What do you mean, 'What do I really see?' " you ask, puzzled. "I told you that I see a book. It is a small book with a red cover."*

*The psychologist is persistent. "What is your perception really?" he insists. "Describe it to me as precisely as you can."*

*"You mean it isn't a book? What is this, some kind of trick?"*

*There is a hint of impatience. "Yes, it is a book. There is no trickery involved. I just want you to describe to me exactly what you can see, no more and no less."*

*You are growing very suspicious now. "Well," you say, "from this angle the cover of the book looks like a dark red parallelogram."*

*"Yes," he says, pleased. "Yes, you see a patch of dark red in the shape of a parallelogram. What else?"*

*"There is a grayish white edge below it and another thin line of the same dark red below that. Under it I see the table—" He winces. "Around it I see a somewhat mottled brown with wavering streaks of lighter brown running roughly parallel to one another."*

*"Fine, fine." He thanks you for your cooperation.*

*As you stand there looking at the book on the table you are a little embarrassed that this persistent fellow was able to drive you to such an analysis. He made you so cautious that you were not sure any longer what you really saw and what you only thought you saw.... In your caution you began talking about what you saw in terms of sensations, where just a moment earlier you were quite certain that you perceived a book on a table.*

*Your reverie is interrupted suddenly by the appearance of a psychologist who looks vaguely like Wilhelm Wundt. "Thank you, for helping to confirm once more my theory of perception. You have proved," he says, "that the book you see is nothing but a compound of elementary sensations. When you were trying to be precise and say accurately what it was you really saw, you had to speak in terms of color patches, not objects. It is the color sensations that are primary, and every visual object is reducible to them. Your perception of the book is constructed from sensations just as a molecule is constructed from atoms."*

*This little speech is apparently a signal for battle to begin. "Nonsense!" shouts a voice from the opposite end of the hall. "Nonsense! Any fool knows that the book is the primary, immediate, direct, compelling, perceptual fact!" The psychologist who charges down upon you now bears a faint resemblance to William James, but he seems to have a German accent, and his face is so flushed with anger that you cannot be sure. "This reduction of a perception into sensations that you keep talking about is nothing but an intellectual game. An object is not just a bundle of sensations. Any man who goes about seeing patches of dark redness where he ought to see books is sick!"*

*As the fight begins to gather momentum you close the door softly and slip away. You have what you came for, an illustration that there are two different attitudes, two different ways to talk about the information that our senses provide. (Miller, 1962, pp. 103–105)[1]*

Gestalt psychologists believe that there is more to perception than meets the eye. In other words, our perception goes beyond the sensory elements, the basic physical data provided to the sense organs.

## Antecedent Influences on Gestalt Psychology

As with all movements, the ideas of the Gestalt protest have their roots in earlier ideas. The basis of the Gestalt position, its focus on the wholeness of perception, can be found in the work of the German philosopher Immanuel Kant (1724–1804), who wrote his

---

[1]From *Psychology: The Science of Mental Life* (pp. 103–105), by G. A. Miller, 1962, New York: Harper & Row. Copyright 1962 by George A. Miller. Reprinted by permission of Harper & Row, Publishers, Inc.

books while dressed in bathrobe and slippers. Kant argued that when we perceive what we call objects, we encounter mental states that appear to be composed of bits and pieces. These are like the sensory elements proposed by the English empiricists and associationists we discussed in Chapter 2. To Kant, however, these elements are organized meaningfully not through some mechanical process of association. Instead, the mind in the process of perceiving will form or create a whole experience. Thus, perception is not a passive impression and combination of sensory elements, as the empiricists and associationists said, but an active organizing of elements into a coherent experience. In this way the mind gives shape and form to the raw data of perception.

Franz Brentano (see Chapter 4) at the University of Vienna, who opposed Wundt's focus on the elements of conscious experience, proposed that psychology study the act of experiencing. He considered Wundt's introspection to be artificial and favored a less rigid and more direct observation of experience as it occurred. Brentano's approach was much like the later methods of the Gestalt psychologists.

Ernst Mach (1838–1916), a physics professor at the University of Prague, exerted a more direct influence on Gestalt thinking with *The Analysis of Sensations* (1885). In this book, Mach discussed spatial patterns such as geometric figures and temporal patterns such as melodies, and he considered them to be sensations. These space-form and time-form sensations were independent of their individual elements. For example, the space-form of a circle might be white or black, large or small, and still retain its elemental quality of circularity.

Mach argued that our perception of an object does not change, even if we change our orientation to it. A table remains a table to us whether we look at it from the side or the top or from an angle. Similarly, a tune remains the same in our perception even when its time-form is changed; that is, when it is played faster or slower.

Christian von Ehrenfels (1859–1932) elaborated on Mach's ideas and proposed qualities of experience that cannot be explained as combinations of sensory elements. He called these qualities *Gestalt qualitäten* (form qualities), which are perceptions based on something greater than a merging of individual sensations. A melody is a form quality because it sounds the same even when transposed to a different key. The melody is independent of the sensations of which it is composed. To Ehrenfels and his followers, form itself was an element created by the mind operating on the sensory elements. Thus, the mind was able to create form out of elementary sensations. Max Wertheimer, one of the three principal founders of Gestalt psychology, studied with Ehrenfels at Prague and noted that the greatest stimulus for the Gestalt movement came from Ehrenfels's work.

William James, who opposed the trend toward elementism in psychology, is also a precursor of the Gestalt school of psychology. James regarded elements of consciousness as artificial abstractions. He stated that people see objects as wholes, not as bundles of sensations. The other major founders of Gestalt psychology, Kurt Koffka and Wolfgang Köhler, learned of James's work when they were students of Carl Stumpf.

Another early influence is the movement in German philosophy and psychology known as **phenomenology**, a doctrine based on an unbiased description of immediate experience just as it occurs. The experience is not analyzed or reduced to elements or otherwise artificially abstracted. It involves the almost naïve experience of common sense rather than experience reported by a trained introspector with a systematic bias or orientation.

**Phenomenology:** An approach to knowledge based on an unbiased description of immediate experience as it occurs, not analyzed or reduced to elements.

# The Changing Zeitgeist in Physics

A significant influence on the development of Gestalt psychology was the Zeitgeist, especially the intellectual climate in physics. In the closing decades of the nineteenth century, ideas in physics were becoming less atomistic with the recognition and acceptance of

**Fields of force:** Regions or spaces traversed by lines of force, such as of a magnet or electric current.

**fields of force**, those regions or spaces crossed by lines of force such as from an electric current.

The classic example is magnetism, a property difficult to understand in traditional Galilean-Newtonian terms. For example, when iron filings are shaken onto a sheet of paper that rests on a magnet, the filings arrange themselves in a characteristic pattern. Although the iron filings do not touch the magnet, they are obviously affected by the field of force around the magnet. Light and electricity were believed to operate similarly. These force fields were considered new structural entities, not summations of the effects of individual elements or particles.

Thus, the atomism or elementism so influential in the establishment of the much newer science of psychology was being reconsidered in physics. Physicists were describing fields and organic wholes, thus providing ammunition and support for the Gestalt psychologists' revolutionary ways of looking at perception. The ideas offered by the Gestalt psychologists were reflecting the new physics. Once again, psychologists were striving to emulate the established natural sciences.

The impact of the new physics on Gestalt psychology had a personal connection. Köhler had studied with Max Planck, one of the architects of modern physics. Köhler wrote that because of Planck's influence he perceived a connection between field physics and the Gestalt concept of wholes. Köhler saw firsthand in physics the increasing reluctance to deal with atoms and the replacement of this idea with a focus on the larger concept of fields. Köhler wrote, "Gestalt psychology has since become a kind of application of field physics to essential parts of psychology" (1969, p. 77).

In contrast, Watson apparently had no training in the new physics. His behaviorist school of thought continued the reductionistic approach by emphasizing elements, the elements of behavior. This view is compatible with the older atomistic approach in physics.

## The Phi Phenomenon: A Challenge to Wundtian Psychology

Gestalt psychology grew out of a research study conducted in 1910 by Max Wertheimer. While riding on a train through Germany during his vacation, Wertheimer got an idea for an experiment about seeing motion when no actual motion occurred. Abandoning his travel plans, he left the train at Frankfurt, purchased a toy stroboscope, and verified his insight in a preliminary way in his hotel room. (The stroboscope, a forerunner of the motion picture camera, rapidly projects a series of different pictures on the eye, producing apparent motion.) Wertheimer later carried out a more extensive research program at the University of Frankfurt, joined by two other psychologists, Koffka and Köhler.

Wertheimer's research problem, for which Koffka and Köhler served as subjects, involved perceiving apparent movement, that is, the perception of motion when no actual physical movement has taken place. Wertheimer referred to it as the "impression" of movement. Using the tachistoscope, he projected light through two slits, one vertical and the other 20 or 30 degrees from the vertical. If light was shown first through one slit and then the other, with a relatively long interval between (more than 200 milliseconds), the subjects saw what appeared to be two successive lights, first at one slit and then at the other. When the interval between the lights was shorter, the subjects saw what seemed to be two lights on continuously. With an optimal time interval between the lights, about 60 milliseconds, the subjects saw a single line of light that appeared to move from one slit to the other and back again.

These findings may seem unremarkable to you. Scientists had been aware of the phenomenon for years, and movies, or motion pictures, had at that time already been popular for a decade. Why, then, was apparent movement considered to be such a breakthrough? Because according to the prevailing position in psychology, still dominated by Wundt's point of view, all conscious experience could be analyzed or broken down into its sensory elements. Yet how could the perception of apparent movement be explained in terms of a summation of individual elements when the elements were simply two stationary slits of light? Could one stationary stimulus be added to the other to produce a sensation of movement? It could not, and this was precisely the point of Wertheimer's brilliantly simple demonstration. It defied explanation by the Wundtian system.

Wertheimer believed that the phenomenon he verified in his laboratory was in its way as elementary as a sensation yet obviously was different from a sensation or a series of sensations. He gave it the name **phi phenomenon**. And how did Wertheimer explain the phi phenomenon when the psychology of the day could not? His answer was as ingenious as his research. Apparent movement did not need explaining. It existed as it was perceived and could not be reduced to anything simpler.

**Phi phenomenon:** The illusion that two stationary flashing lights are moving from one place to another.

According to Wundt, introspection of the stimulus would produce two successive lines of light and nothing more. However, no matter how rigorously an observer introspected the two exposures of light, the experience of a single line in motion persisted. Any further attempt at analysis failed. The whole experience—the apparent movement of the line from one slit to another—differed from the sum of its parts (the two stationary lines). Thus, the elementistic, associationistic psychology had been challenged, and the challenge could not be met.

Wertheimer published the results of his research in 1912 as "Experimental Studies of the Perception of Movement," an article considered to mark the formal beginning of the Gestalt psychology school of thought.

## Max Wertheimer (1880–1943)

Max Wertheimer was born in Prague and attended local schools until age 18. He studied law at the University of Prague, changed his major to philosophy, attended lectures by Ehrenfels, and then went to the University of Berlin to pursue work in philosophy and psychology. He earned his doctoral degree in 1904 at the University of Würzburg under Oswald Külpe. He settled at the University of Frankfurt to lecture and conduct research, receiving a professorship in 1929. During World War I, he did military research on listening devices for submarines and harbor fortifications.

During the 1920s at the University of Berlin, Wertheimer carried out some of his most productive work for the development of Gestalt psychology. One student recalled that the walls of Wertheimer's office were painted bright red. Wertheimer apparently found bright colors stimulating. He felt that "if the walls of a room are gray or light green or some kind of dull color, one does not work as well as if they are painted in an exciting color such as red" (King & Wertheimer, 2005, p. 188).

Wertheimer's lecture style was also stimulating, and his imagery quite vivid. Some students found this easy to understand, but others thought it unclear and confusing. Another student, captivated by the professor's passion, zeal, and convictions, believed at first that few of them knew what Wertheimer was talking about. "It took me about a half a year going to his lectures two or three times a week until I caught on. When we did catch on, we were delighted! Our whole lives changed, our whole outlook on life changed. All of a sudden, everything became colorful and lively and had meaning" (King & Wertheimer, 2005, p. 171).

That particular student's life changed significantly. At the age of 22 she married her 43-year-old professor, despite his warning about his obsession with his work. "You must

Archives of the History of American Psychology/University of Akron

Max Wertheimer with apparatus for visual imagery experiments.

always remember," he told her, "I will always be at my desk. I will always work. I must create Gestalt theory" (King & Wertheimer, 2005, p. 172). He was not exaggerating.

In 1921 Wertheimer, Koffka, and Köhler, assisted by Kurt Goldstein and Hans Gruhle, founded the journal *Psychological Research,* which became the official publication of the Gestalt psychology school of thought. The Nazi government suspended its printing in 1938, but publication resumed after the war in 1949.

Wertheimer was among the first group of refugee scholars to flee Nazi Germany for the United States, arriving in New York City in 1933. He became associated with the New School for Social Research, where he remained until his death 10 years later. Although his years in America were productive, he had difficulty adapting to a new language and culture.

In 1994, more than 60 years after the Gestalt psychologists fled Germany, the University of Frankfurt established the Max Wertheimer Lecture Series. His son Michael, a prominent psychologist, delivered a lecture to honor his father in the same hall where his father had taught so many years before (see King & Wertheimer, 2005).

Max Wertheimer made a strong impression on the young psychologist Abraham Maslow, who was so in awe that he began to study Wertheimer's personal characteristics. From these observations of Wertheimer and others, Maslow developed the concept of self-actualization and later promoted the humanistic psychology school of thought (see Chapter 14).

# Kurt Koffka (1886–1941)

Kurt Koffka, born in Berlin, was the most inventive of Gestalt psychology's founders. Interested in science and philosophy, he received his education at the University of Berlin. He studied psychology with Carl Stumpf, earning his Ph.D. in 1909. The following year he began his long, fruitful association with Wertheimer and Köhler at the University of Frankfurt. Koffka wrote:

> *We liked each other personally, had the same kind of enthusiasms, the same kind of backgrounds, and saw each other daily discussing everything under the sun.... [I could] still feel the thrill of the experience when it dawned upon me what [the phi phenomenon] really meant.... now at last form had become a subject that could be handled, it [had] made its final entry into the system of psychology. (quoted in Ash, 1995, pp. 120, 131)*

In 1911, Koffka accepted a position at the University of Giessen, 40 miles from Frankfurt, where he remained until 1924. During World War I, he worked with brain-damaged and aphasic patients at the psychiatric clinic.

After the war, perceiving that American psychologists were becoming aware of developments in Gestalt psychology in Germany, Koffka wrote an article for the American journal *Psychological Bulletin* titled "Perception: An Introduction to the Gestalt-Theorie" (Koffka, 1922). He presented the basic concepts of Gestalt psychology along with the results and implications of considerable research.

Kurt Koffka (left) and Wolfgang Köhler (right).

Although the article was important as the first comprehensive explanation of the Gestalt movement for psychologists in the United States, it may have done more harm than good. The word *perception* in the title created the lingering misunderstanding that Gestalt psychologists dealt exclusively with perception and that the movement had no relevance for other areas of psychology. Max Wertheimer wrote in 1925 that the belief that Gestalt psychology was concerned only with perception was a "widespread misunderstanding [that was] objectively and historically false" (quoted in King, Wertheimer, Keller, & Crochetiere, 1994, pp. 1–2). In reality, Gestalt psychology was more broadly concerned with cognitive processes, with problems of thinking, learning, and other aspects of conscious experience. Michael Wertheimer explained the initial Gestalt focus on perception as follows:

> *The main reason why the early Gestalt psychologists concentrated their systematic publications on perception was because of the Zeitgeist: Wundt's psychology, against which the Gestaltists rebelled, had obtained most of its support from studies of sensation and perception, so the Gestalt psychologists chose perception as the arena in order to attack Wundt in his own stronghold. (Michael Wertheimer, 1979, p. 134)*

In 1921 Koffka published *The Growth of the Mind*, a book about developmental child psychology that became successful in Germany and in the United States. Koffka taught as a visiting professor at Cornell University and the University of Wisconsin, and in 1927 he was appointed professor at Smith College in Northampton, Massachusetts, where he remained until his death in 1941. In 1935 he published *Principles of Gestalt Psychology*, a difficult book that did not become the definitive treatment of Gestalt psychology he had intended it to be.

# Wolfgang Köhler (1887–1967)

Wolfgang Köhler has been called the most prolific promoter of the Gestalt movement (see Mandler, 2007). His books, written with care and precision, became standard works on Gestalt psychology. Köhler's training in physics with Max Planck persuaded him that psychology must ally itself with physics and that *Gestalten* (forms or patterns) occur not only in physics but in psychology as well.

Born in Estonia, Köhler was five years old when his family moved to northern Germany. His university education was at Tübingen, Bonn, and Berlin, and he received his doctorate from Stumpf at the University of Berlin in 1909. He went to the University of Frankfurt, arriving just ahead of Wertheimer and his toy stroboscope.

In 1913, at the invitation of the Prussian Academy of Science, Köhler journeyed to Tenerife in the Canary Islands off Africa's northwest coast, to study chimpanzees. Six months after his arrival, World War I started, and Köhler reported that he was unable to leave. (Other German citizens did manage to return home during the war years.)

One psychologist has suggested, based on his own interpretation of historical data, that Köhler may have been a German spy and that his research facility was a cover for espionage activities (Ley, 1990). It was also charged that a powerful radio transmitter was concealed on the top floor of his house, which Köhler used to broadcast information about Allied ship movements. In 2006 an American psychologist visited the house and observed that it was "situated on a cliff overlooking the ocean [and] did have a good view of an important segment of the Atlantic. If Kohler were operating a secret transmitter, this would have been an ideal place to do so" (Johnson, 2007, p. 907). However, the evidence to support these intriguing claims remains circumstantial and has been challenged by Köhler's followers and by historians (see Lück, 1990).

Whether a spy or a scientist marooned by war, Köhler spent the next seven years studying the behavior of chimpanzees. He recorded his work in the now-classic volume *The Mentality of Apes* (1917), which appeared in a second edition in 1924 and was translated into English and French. Although Köhler initially found the chimp research interesting, he soon became bored working with animals. He wrote, "Two years of apes every day; one becomes chimpanzoid oneself and no longer notices something about the animals as easily" (cited in Ash, 1995, p. 167).

In 1920 Köhler returned to Germany. He sold the chimps to the Berlin Zoo, but they did not survive long, unable to cope with the change in climate. Two years later Köhler succeeded Stumpf as professor of psychology at the University of Berlin. The most likely reason for this prestigious appointment was the publication of *Static and Stationary Physical Gestalts* (1920), a book that won considerable praise for its high level of scholarship. Köhler suggested that Gestalt theory was a general law of nature that should be extended to all the sciences.

In the mid-1920s, Köhler divorced his wife, married a wealthy young Swedish student, and thereafter cut off all contact with the four children of his first marriage. Some 60 years later his second wife told an interviewer that Köhler opposed marriage in principle, looking upon it as an "imposition on his freedom," and disliked family life. He thought "everyone should be free" (quoted in Ley, 1990, p. 201). Not long after that, Köhler developed a tremor in his hands, which became more noticeable when he was annoyed. His laboratory assistants would watch his shaking hands every morning to gauge his mood.

During the 1925–1926 academic year, Köhler lectured at Harvard University and at Clark University, where he also taught the graduate students how to dance the tango. In 1929 he published *Gestalt Psychology*, a comprehensive account of the Gestalt movement.

He left Nazi Germany in 1935 because of conflicts with the government. After he criticized the regime in his lectures, a gang of Nazi thugs invaded his classroom. The threats did not stop him from taking risks that could easily have led to a death sentence. He wrote a courageous anti-Nazi letter to a Berlin newspaper, incensed by the dismissal of Jewish professors from German universities. On the evening the letter was published, he and some friends waited at his home, expecting the Gestapo to arrest him, but the dreaded knock on the door never came.

Köhler was the only non-Jewish psychologist in Germany to protest publicly the dismissals of Jewish scholars (Geuter, 1987). The majority of faculty and students supported the Nazi government enthusiastically from its earliest days. One faculty member called the dictator Adolf Hitler a "great psychologist," and another praised him as "far-seeing, bold and emotionally deep" (quoted in Ash, 1995, p. 342). The leaders of the German Psychological Society gave their immediate support to the Nazi regime, dismissed Jewish journal editors from their positions even before it was required by law, and paid public tribute to Hitler. At society meetings, they trumpeted the "evil influence" of the Jews (Mandler, 2002b, p. 197).

After Köhler immigrated to the United States, he taught at Swarthmore College in Pennsylvania, published several books, and edited the Gestalt journal *Psychological Research*. In 1956 he received the Distinguished Scientific Contribution Award from the APA, and in 1959 he was elected president of the APA.

# The Nature of the Gestalt Revolt

The ideas of the Gestalt psychologists contradicted much of the academic tradition of German psychology. In the United States, behaviorism was a less immediate revolt against Wundtian psychology and against Titchener's structuralism because functionalism had already brought about fundamental changes in American psychology. No such tempering effects paved the way for the Gestalt revolution in Germany. The pronouncements of the Gestalt psychologists were nothing less than heresy.

Like most intellectual revolutionaries, the Gestalt leaders demanded a complete revision of the old order. Köhler wrote:

> *We were excited by what we found, and even more by the prospect of finding further revealing facts. It was not only the stimulating newness of our enterprise which inspired us. There was also a great wave of relief—as though we were escaping from a prison. The prison was psychology as taught at the universities when we still were students. (Köhler, 1959, p. 728)*

**Perceptual constancy:**
A quality of wholeness or completeness in perceptual experience that does not vary even when the sensory elements change.

After Wertheimer initiated the studies on the perception of apparent movement, Gestalt psychologists seized on other perceptual phenomena. The experience of **perceptual constancies** afforded additional support for their views. For example, when we stand in front of a window, a rectangular image is projected onto the retina of the eye, but when we stand to one side, the retinal image becomes a trapezoid, although of course we continue to perceive the window as a rectangle. Our perception of the window remains constant, even though the sensory data (the images projected on the retina) change.

Similarly, with brightness and size constancy the sensory elements may change but perception does not. In these cases, as with apparent movement, the perceptual experience has a quality of wholeness or completeness that is not to be found in any of the component parts. Thus, there exists a difference between the character of the sensory stimulation and the character of the actual resulting perception. The perception cannot be explained simply as a collection of elements or the sum of the parts.

The perception is a whole, a *Gestalt*, and any attempt to analyze or reduce it to elements will destroy it.

> *To begin with elements is to begin at the wrong end; for elements are products of reflection and abstraction, remotely derived from the immediate experience they are invoked to explain. Gestalt psychology attempts to get back to naïve perception, to immediate experience, and it insists that it finds there not assemblages of elements, but unified wholes; not masses of sensations, but trees, clouds, and sky. And this assertion it invites any one to verify simply by opening his eyes and looking at the world about him in his ordinary everyday way. (Heidbreder, 1933, p. 331)*

The word *Gestalt* has caused problems. Unlike functionalism or behaviorism, the term does not clearly denote what the movement stands for. Also, it has no precise English-language counterpart, although by now it has become part of the everyday language of psychology. Commonly used equivalents are "form," "shape," and "configuration."

In *Gestalt Psychology* (1929), Köhler noted that the word was used in two ways in German. One usage denotes shape or form as a property of objects. In this sense, *Gestalt* refers to general properties that can be expressed in such terms as angular or symmetrical and describes characteristics such as triangularity in geometric figures or tempos in a melody. The second usage denotes a whole or concrete entity that has as one of its attributes a specific shape or form. In this sense, the word may refer to triangles, let us say, rather than to the notion of triangularity.

Thus, *Gestalt* can be used to refer to objects as well as to their characteristic forms. Also, the term is not restricted to the visual or even the total sensory field. It may encompass learning, thinking, emotions, and behavior (Köhler, 1947). It is in this general, functional sense of the word that the Gestalt psychologists attempted to deal with the entire province of psychology.

# Gestalt Principles of Perceptual Organization

Wertheimer presented the principles of perceptual organization of the Gestalt school of psychology in a paper published in 1923. He asserted that we perceive objects in the same way we perceive apparent motion, as unified wholes rather than clusters of individual sensations. These Gestalt principles are essentially rules by which we organize our perceptual world.

One underlying premise is that perceptual organization occurs instantly whenever we sense various shapes or patterns. The discrete parts of the perceptual field connect, uniting to form structures distinct from their background. Perceptual organization is spontaneous and inevitable whenever we look or listen. Typically, we do not have to learn to form patterns, as the associationists claimed, although some higher-level perception, such as labeling objects by name, does depend on learning.

According to Gestalt theory, the brain is a dynamic system in which all elements active at a given time interact. The visual area of the brain does not respond separately to individual elements of visual input, connecting these elements by some mechanical process of association. Rather, the elements that are similar or close together tend to combine, and elements that are dissimilar or farther apart tend not to combine.

Several perceptual organization principles are listed as follows and are illustrated in Figure 12.1.

1. *Proximity.* Parts that are close together in time or space appear to belong together and tend to be perceived together. In Figure 12.1(a), you see the circles in three double columns rather than as one large collection.
2. *Continuity.* There is a tendency in our perception to follow a direction, to connect the elements in a way that makes them seem continuous or flowing in a particular direction. In Figure 12.1(a), you tend to follow the columns of small circles from top to bottom.

**FIGURE 12.1**

Examples of perceptual organization.

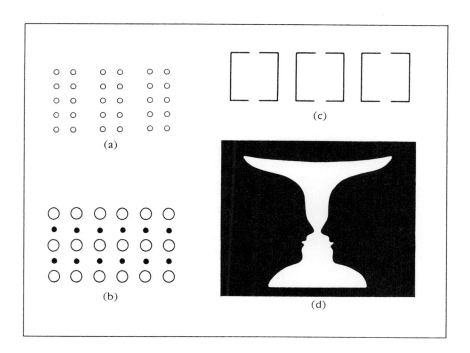

3. *Similarity.* Similar parts tend to be seen together as forming a group. In Figure 12.1(b), the circles and the dots each appear to belong together, and you tend to perceive rows of circles and rows of dots instead of columns.

4. *Closure.* There is a tendency in our perception to complete incomplete figures, to fill in gaps. In Figure 12.1(c), you perceive three squares even though the figures are incomplete.

5. *Simplicity.* We tend to see a figure as being as good as possible under the stimulus conditions; the Gestalt psychologists called this *prägnanz*, or good form. A good Gestalt is symmetrical, simple, and stable and cannot be made simpler or more orderly. The squares in Figure 12.1(c) are good Gestalts because they are clearly perceived as complete and organized.

6. *Figure/ground.* We tend to organize perceptions into the object being looked at (the figure) and the background against which it appears (the ground). The figure seems to be more substantial and to stand out from its background. In Figure 12.1(d), the figure and the ground are reversible; you may see two faces or you may see a vase, depending on how your perception is organized.

These organizing principles do not depend on higher mental processes or past experiences but are present in the stimuli themselves. Wertheimer called them peripheral factors, but he also recognized that central factors within the organism influence perception. For example, we know that the higher mental processes of familiarity and attitude can affect perception. In general, however, the Gestalt psychologists focused more on the peripheral factors of perceptual organization than on the effects of learning or experience.

## Gestalt Studies of Learning: Insight and the Mentality of Apes

We mentioned Köhler's prolonged visit to Tenerife (1913–1920), where he investigated the intelligence of chimpanzees as demonstrated in their problem-solving abilities. These studies were conducted in and around the animals' cages and involved simple props such as the bars of the cages (used to block access), bananas, sticks for drawing bananas into cages, and boxes on which to climb to reach fruit suspended from the ceiling. Consistent with the Gestalt view of perception, Köhler interpreted the results of his animal research in terms of the whole situation and the relationships among the stimuli. He considered problem solving to be a matter of restructuring the perceptual field.

In one study a banana was placed outside the cage, and a string attached to the banana led into the cage. The ape grasped the string and pulled the banana into the cage with little hesitation. Köhler concluded that in this situation the problem as a whole was easy for the animal to perceive. If several strings led from the cage in the general direction of the fruit, however, the ape would not recognize instantly which string to pull to get the banana. This indicated to Köhler that the total problem could not be envisioned clearly.

In another study, a piece of fruit was placed outside the cage just beyond the chimp's reach. If a stick was put near the bars of the cage in front of the fruit, the stick and the food would be perceived as part of the same situation, and the animal would quickly use the stick to bring the fruit into the cage. If the stick was placed at the rear of the cage, however, then the two objects (the stick and the banana) were less readily seen as part of the same problem. In this case, a restructuring of the perceptual field was necessary for the chimp to solve the problem.

Another experiment involved positioning a banana outside the cage beyond reach and placing two hollow bamboo sticks inside the cage. Each stick by itself was too short to retrieve the fruit. To reach the banana, the animal had to push the sticks together (inserting the end of one into the end of the other) to make a stick of sufficient length. Thus, to solve the problem, the animal had to visualize a new relationship between the two sticks.

The following passages from Köhler's book describe other studies and observations on learning in chimpanzees. Köhler discusses the efforts of his chimps to learn to use implements to retrieve food. These experiments show how the animals used boxes to reach the stimulus object, typically a banana suspended from the roof of the cage. Note the non-technical language Köhler used to describe his work. He focused on the personalities of his chimps and their individual differences. He used no formal experimental design or measurement, no rigorous experimental treatment, control group, or statistical analysis. Instead, Köhler described his observations of the animals' reactions to the situations he created.

## IN THEIR OWN WORDS

### Original Source Material on Gestalt Psychology from *The Mentality of Apes* (1927)

Wolfgang Köhler[2]

The chimpanzee is not simply provided for life with any special disposition which will help him to attain objects placed high up, by heaping up any building material, and yet he can accomplish this much by his own efforts, when circumstances require it, and when the material is available.

Adult human beings are inclined to overlook the chimpanzee's real difficulty in such construction, because they assume that adding a second piece of building material to the first is only a repetition of the placing of the first one on the ground (underneath the objective); that when the first box is standing on the ground, its surface is the same thing as a piece of level ground, and that, therefore, in the building-up process the only new factor is the actual lifting up. So the only questions seem to be, whether the animals proceed at all tidily in their work, whether they handle the boxes very clumsily, and so forth....

That another special difficulty exists, however, should become obvious from the further details of Sultan's first attempt at building: When Sultan [considered the most intelligent chimp] for the first time fetches a second box and lifts it, he waves it about enigmatically above the first, and does not put it on the other. The second time he places it upright on the bottom one, seemingly without any hesitation, but the construction is still too low, as the objective has accidentally been hung too high up.

The experiment is continued at once, the objective hung about two meters to one side at a lower spot in the roof, and Sultan's construction is left in its old place, but Sultan's failure seems to have a disturbing aftereffect; for a long time he pays no attention at all to the boxes, quite contrary to other cases, where a new solution was found and usually repeated readily....

Further on in the experiment a curious incident occurs: the animal reverts to older methods, wants to lead the keeper by his hand to the objective, is shaken off, attempts the same thing with me, and is again turned away. The keeper is then told that if Sultan tries to fetch him again, he is apparently to give in, but, as soon as the animal climbs on his shoulders, he is to kneel down very low.

Soon this actually happens: Sultan climbs onto the man's shoulders, after he has dragged him underneath the objective, and the keeper quickly bends down. The animal gets off, complaining, takes hold of the keeper by his seat with both hands, and tries with all his might to push him up. A surprising way to try to improve the human implement!

When Sultan now takes no further notice of the box, since he once discovered the solution by himself, it seems justifiable to remove the cause of his failure. I put the boxes

[2]From *The Mentality of Apes* (pp. 135–172), by W. Köhler, 1927, London: Routledge & Kegan Paul.

on top of each other for Sultan, underneath the objective, exactly as he had himself done the first time, and let him pull down the objective.

As to Sultan's effort to push the keeper into an erect position, I should like at the very beginning to rebut the reproach of misunderstanding, of "reading into the animal"; the procedure has merely been described, and there is no possibility at all of its being misunderstood. But lest suspicions should arise, this case being an isolated one (an unjustifiable suspicion in any case, considering that Sultan tries to utilize both the keeper and me, not once, but over and over again, as a footstool), I shall briefly add a description of similar cases:

Sultan cannot solve a problem, in which the objective is outside the bars beyond reach; I am near him inside. After vain attempts of all sorts, the animal comes up to me, seizes me by the arm, pulls me toward the bars, at the same time pulling my arm with all his might down to himself, and then pushes it through the bars toward the objective. As I do not seize it, he goes to the keeper, and tries the same thing with him.

Later he repeats this proceeding, with the only difference that he first has to call me with plaintive pleading to the bars, as this time I am standing outside. In this case, as in the first, I offered so much resistance that the animal could barely overcome it, and he did not release me until my hand was actually on the objective; but I did not do him the favor (in the interests of future experiments) of bringing it in.

I must mention further, that one hot day the animals had had to wait longer than usual for their water course, so that finally they simply grabbed hold of the keeper's hand, foot, or knee, and pushed him with all their strength toward the door, behind which the water jug usually stood. This became their custom for some time; if the man tried to continue feeding them on bananas, Chica would calmly snatch them out of his hand, put them aside, and pull him toward the door (Chica is always thirsty).

It would be erroneous to consider the chimpanzee unenlightened and stupid in these matters. I must add that the animals understand the human body particularly easily in its local costume of shirt and trousers without any coat. If anything puzzles them, they will investigate it on occasion, and any large change in the manner of dressing or appearance (for example, a beard) will make Grande and Chica undertake an immediate and very interested examination.

After the encouraging assistance to Sultan, the boxes are again put aside. A new objective is hung in the same place on the roof. Sultan immediately builds up both boxes, but at the place where the objective had been hung at the very beginning of the experiment and where his own first construction had stood. In about a hundred cases of using boxes for building, this is the only one in which a stupidity of this kind was committed. Sultan is quite confused while doing this, and is probably quite exhausted, as the experiment has lasted over an hour in this hot place.[3] As Sultan keeps on pushing the boxes to and fro quite aimlessly, they are once more put on top of each other underneath the objective; Sultan reaches it, and is allowed to go. Only on one occasion did I see him similarly confused and disturbed.

The next day it is clear that a particular difficulty must lie in the problem itself. Sultan carries one box underneath the objective, but does not bring the second one; finally it is built up for him and he attains the goal. The new one immediately replacing it (the construction was again destroyed) does not induce him to work at all; he keeps on trying to use the observer as a footstool; so once more the construction is made for him. Underneath the third objective Sultan places a box, pulls the other one up beside it, but stops at the critical moment, his behavior betraying complete perplexity; he keeps on looking up at the objective, and meanwhile fumbling about with the second box. Then, quite suddenly, he seizes it firmly, and with a decided movement places it on the first. His long uncertainty is in the sharpest contrast to this sudden solution.

Two days later the experiment is repeated; the objective is again hung at a new spot. Sultan places a box a little aslant underneath the objective, brings the second one up, and has begun to lift it, when, all the while looking at the objective, he lets it drop again. After several other actions (climbing along the roof, pulling the observer up) he again starts to build; he carefully stands the first box upright underneath the objective, and now takes great pains to get the second one on top of it; in the turning and twisting, it

---

[3]I only noticed later that I used to strain the animals a little too much during the first months; only with time did I develop the slowness of procedure adequate to the apes and to the climate.

gets stuck on the lower one, with its open side caught on one of the corners. Sultan gets up on it, and straightaway tumbles with the whole thing to the floor.

Quite exhausted, he remains lying in one corner of the room, and from here gazes at both box and objective. Only after a considerable time does he resume work; he stands one box upright and tries to reach his goal thus; jumps down, seizes the second, and finally, with tenacious zeal, succeeds in making it stand upright also, on the first one; but it is pushed so far to one side that, at every attempt to climb up, it begins to topple. Only after a long attempt, during which the animal obviously acts quite blindly, letting everything depend on the success or failure of planless movements, the upper box attains a more secure position, and the objective is attained.

After this attempt Sultan always used the second box at once and, above all, was never uncertain as to where he had to put it.

## Comment

**Insight:** Immediate apprehension or cognition.

Köhler interpreted these and similar studies as providing evidence of **insight**, the apparently spontaneous apprehension or understanding of relationships. Sultan finally achieved insight into the problem after many trials by grasping the relationship between the boxes and the banana that was suspended overhead. Köhler's word in German to describe this phenomenon was *Einsicht,* which translates into English as insight or understanding. "There is no underlying conditioning taking place" he wrote, "rather, from a certain point on, the animal *realizes* what it is all about, and from this moment on the resultant behavior is of course perfect" (quoted in Ley, 1990, p. 182). In another example of independent, simultaneous discovery, the American animal psychologist Robert Yerkes found evidence in orangutans to support the concept of insight, which he called "ideational learning."

In the 1930s, Ivan Pavlov replicated some of Köhler's research studies in which an ape needed to place one box atop another to reach food suspended from the ceiling. He found that it took the animals several months to solve the problem. He questioned Köhler's suggestion that the apes developed insight into the situation and called the

Yerkes Primate Research Center

A chimpanzee uses sticks of different lengths to reach a piece of fruit.

animals' alleged problem-solving behavior "chaotic." Pavlov said their responses were not so different from the trial-and-error learning in Thorndike's research (Windholz, 1997).

In 1974 the keeper of Köhler's chimps, Manuel Gonzalez y Garcia, described the research to an interviewer. He told many stories about the animals, particularly Sultan, who used to help him feed the other apes. Gonzalez would give Sultan bunches of bananas to hold. "On the oral command, 'two each,' Sultan would walk about the compound and dole out two bananas to each of the other apes" (quoted in Ley, 1990, pp. 12–13).

One day, Sultan watched the keeper painting a door. When the keeper left, Sultan picked up the paintbrush and began to imitate the behavior he had observed. On another occasion, Köhler's young son Claus sat in front of a cage, trying unsuccessfully to pull a banana out between the bars. Sultan, inside the cage and apparently not hungry, turned the banana 90 degrees so it would fit between the bars, whereupon Köhler told his son that Sultan was smarter than he was.

Once Sultan encouraged Claus to climb to the top of a tree, and the boy refused to come down despite his angry father's commands. When Claus finally came down, Köhler grabbed him, pulled down his shorts, and spanked him. Not long after that, Sultan snuck up on Köhler himself and pulled down his pants from behind. Some 70 years later Claus recounted that story for an interviewer, his eyes "twinkling with impish delight" (Ley, 1990, p. 240).

Köhler believed that the insight and problem-solving abilities demonstrated by his chimps differed from the trial-and-error learning described by Thorndike. Köhler criticized Thorndike's work, arguing that its experimental conditions were artificial and allowed the research animals to display only random behaviors. Köhler said that the cats in Thorndike's puzzle boxes could not survey the entire release mechanism (all the elements pertaining to the whole situation), and thus could make only trial-and-error responses.

Similarly, an animal in a maze could not see the overall pattern or design but only each alley as it was encountered. Therefore, the animals could do little but try one path at a time. In the Gestalt view, the organism must be able to perceive the relationships among the various parts of the problem before insight learning can occur.

These studies of insight supported the Gestalt psychologists' molar or global conception of behavior, as opposed to the molecular or atomistic view promoted by the behaviorists. The research also reinforced the Gestalt idea that learning involves a reorganization or restructuring of one's psychological environment.

# Productive Thinking in Humans

Wertheimer's book on productive thinking (Wertheimer, 1945), published post-humously, applied Gestalt principles of learning to creative thinking in humans. He proposed that thinking is done in terms of wholes. The learner regards the situation as a whole, and the teacher must present the situation as a whole. You can see the differences from the trial-and-error method in which a solution to a problem is hidden, in a sense, and the learner may make mistakes before hitting on the correct answer.

The cases presented in Wertheimer's book range from children's thought processes in solving geometric problems to the complex cognitive processes of the physicist Albert Einstein developing his theory of relativity. At different ages and at various levels of difficulty, Wertheimer found evidence to support the idea that the whole problem must dominate the parts. He believed that the details of a problem should be considered only in relation to the total situation. Further, problem solving should proceed from the whole problem downward to the parts, not the reverse.

In a classroom setting, for example, if a teacher arranges or organizes the elements of word or number exercises into meaningful wholes, then students will more easily display insight and grasp the problems and solutions. Wertheimer showed that once the basic principle of a solution had been understood, that principle could be transferred or applied to other situations.

He challenged traditional educational practices, such as mechanical drill and rote learning, which derive from the associationist approach to learning. He found repetition to be rarely productive and cited as evidence a student's inability to solve a variation of a problem when the solution had been learned by rote rather than grasped by insight. He agreed, however, that facts such as names and dates should be learned by rote, through association strengthened by repetition. Thus he conceded that repetition was useful for some purposes, but he maintained that repetition could lead to mechanical performance rather than to understanding or to creative or productive thinking.

## Isomorphism

Having established to their satisfaction that humans perceive organized wholes rather than collections of sensory elements, Gestalt psychologists shifted their focus to the brain mechanisms involved in perception. They attempted to develop a theory about underlying neurological correlates of perceived Gestalts. The cerebral cortex was depicted as a dynamic system, in which the elements active at a given time interact. This idea contrasts with the machinelike conception that compares neural activity to a telephone switchboard mechanically linking sensory inputs according to the principles of association. In this associationist view, the brain operates passively, incapable of actively organizing or modifying the sensory elements it receives. This latter theory also implies a direct correspondence between the perception and its neurological counterpart.

From his research on apparent movement, Wertheimer suggested that brain activity is a configural, whole process. Because apparent motion and actual motion are experienced identically, the cortical processes for apparent and actual motion must be similar. It follows that corresponding brain processes must be operating.

In other words, to account for the phi phenomenon, there must be a correspondence between the psychological or conscious experience and the underlying brain experience. This idea is called **isomorphism**, a principle already accepted in biology and chemistry. Gestalt psychologists likened a perception to a map, in that it is identical ("iso") in form or shape ("morph") to what it represents, without being a literal copy of the terrain. However, the perception does serve as a reliable guide to the perceived real world.

**Isomorphism:** The doctrine that there is a correspondence between psychological or conscious experience and the underlying brain experience.

Köhler extended Wertheimer's position in *Static and Stationary Physical Gestalts* (1920), in which Köhler considered cortical processes to behave similarly to fields of force. He suggested that like the behavior of an electromagnetic force field around a magnet, neuronal activity fields are established by electromechanical processes in the brain in response to sensory impulses.

## The Spread of Gestalt Psychology

By the mid-1920s, the Gestalt movement was a coherent, dominant, and forceful school of thought in Germany. Centered at the Psychological Institute of the University of Berlin, the movement was attracting large numbers of students (nearly half of whom were women) from many countries. The institute was housed in a wing of the former Imperial Palace and boasted one of the world's largest laboratories, equipped for the investigation of a variety of psychological issues from the Gestalt point of view. The Gestalt journal *Psychological Research* was widely read and respected.

After the Nazis seized power in Germany in 1933, their anti-intellectualism, anti-Semitism, and repressive actions forced many scholars, including the founders of the Gestalt school, to leave the country. The core of Gestalt psychology shifted to the United States, spreading through personal contacts as well as published works. Even before the school's formal founding, many American psychologists had studied with its future leaders, absorbing their ideas.

A few books by Koffka and Köhler had been translated from German into English and reviewed in American psychology journals. A series of articles by the American psychologist Harry Helson, published in the *American Journal of Psychology*, also helped spread Gestalt theory in the United States (Helson, 1925, 1926). Koffka and Köhler visited the United States to lecture at universities and conferences. Koffka gave 30 talks in three years, and in 1929 Köhler was a keynote speaker at the Ninth International Congress of Psychology at Yale University. (The other keynote speaker was Ivan Pavlov, who was spat on by one of Robert Yerkes's chimps.)

So Gestalt psychology was attracting attention in the United States, but for several reasons its acceptance as a school of thought came slowly. First, behaviorism was at the peak of its popularity. Second, there was the language barrier. The major Gestalt publications were in German, and the need for translation delayed full and accurate dissemination of the Gestalt viewpoint. Third, as noted previously many psychologists incorrectly believed that Gestalt psychology dealt only with perception. Fourth, the founders Wertheimer, Koffka, and Köhler settled at small colleges in the United States that did not have graduate programs, so it was difficult for them to attract disciples to carry on their ideas.

Fifth, and most important, was that American psychology had advanced far beyond the ideas of Wundt and Titchener, which the Gestalt psychologists were opposing. Behaviorism was already the second stage of American opposition. Hence, American psychology was much further removed from Wundt's elementistic position than was German psychology. American psychologists believed that Gestalt psychologists were fighting an enemy they had already beaten. The Gestalt psychologists had come to America protesting something that was no longer of any concern.

This situation was hazardous for the survival of the Gestalt school. We have seen continuing evidence throughout history that revolutionary movements need something to oppose, something to push against if they expect to be successful in promoting their ideas. But initially, the Gestalt psychologists arriving in the United States found little to oppose.

## The Battle with Behaviorism

When Gestalt psychologists became aware of the trends within American psychology, they readily spied their new target. If it were pointless to protest Wundtian psychology, already vanquished from American psychology, then they could attack the reductionistic qualities typical of the behaviorist school of thought. So the Gestalt psychologists argued that behaviorism, like Wundt's psychology, also dealt with artificial abstractions. It made little difference to them whether analysis was in terms of introspective reduction to mental elements (Wundt) or objective reduction to conditioned stimulus-response units (Watson). The result was the same: a molecular instead of a molar approach. Gestalt psychologists also disputed the behaviorists' denial of the validity of introspection and their discarding of any recognition of consciousness. Koffka charged that it was senseless to develop a psychology without consciousness, as behaviorists had done, because that meant psychology would be restricted to little more than a collection of animal research studies.

The battles between Gestalt and behavioral psychologists grew emotional and personal. When Clark Hull, E. C. Tolman, Wolfgang Köhler, and several other psychologists went out for a few beers after a scientific meeting in Philadelphia in 1941, Köhler said he had been told that Hull used the insulting phrase "those goddamned Gestalters" in his classroom lectures. Embarrassed by this revelation, Hull said he hoped that scientific disagreements would not be turned into personal attacks.

Köhler replied that he was "willing to discuss most things in a logical and scientific manner, but when people try to make man out to be a kind of slot machine, then he would fight." He slammed his fist on the table "with a resounding smack" to emphasize his point (quoted in Amsel & Rashotte, 1984, p. 23).

### Gestalt Psychology in Nazi Germany

Although the founders of the Gestalt psychology school of thought fled wartime Germany, some of their disciples remained there through the Nazi era, which ended with Germany's defeat by the Allies in 1945. These adherents to the Gestalt position continued to conduct research, focusing on studies in vision and depth perception. Köhler's Psychological Institute remained in operation at the University of Berlin, though, like all German universities at the time, it no longer was characterized by openness of inquiry and academic freedom. An American visitor to the institute in 1936 commented on the "utter barrenness of the intellectual climate of this former stronghold of the Gestalt school" (quoted in Ash, 1995, p. 340). The research activities of most German psychologists during World War II were directed toward the war effort, primarily the assessment of military personnel. Practical and applied research took precedence over pure science and theory construction.

## Field Theory: Kurt Lewin (1890–1947)

We noted the trend in late nineteenth-century science to think in terms of field relationships rather than within an atomistic and elementistic framework. Gestalt psychology reflected this trend. Field theory arose within psychology as a counterpart to the concept of force fields in physics. In psychology today the term **field theory** usually refers to the ideas of Kurt Lewin. Lewin's work is Gestalt in orientation but extends beyond the orthodox Gestalt position to include human needs, personality, and social influences on behavior.

**Field theory:** Lewin's system using the concept of fields of force to explain behavior in terms of one's field of social influences.

### Lewin's Life

Kurt Lewin was born in Mogilno, Germany, and studied at universities in Freiburg, Munich, and Berlin. He received his Ph.D. in psychology from Carl Stumpf at Berlin in 1914, where he also trained in mathematics and physics. During World War I, Lewin served in the German army, was wounded in action, and received Germany's Iron Cross decoration. He returned to the University of Berlin and pursued Gestalt research interests in association and motivation so enthusiastically that he was often considered a colleague of the three Gestalt founders. He presented a version of his field theory to American psychologists at the 1929 International Congress of Psychology at Yale.

Thus, Lewin was already known in the United States when he became visiting professor at Stanford in 1932. The following year, he decided to leave Germany because of the Nazi menace. He wrote to Köhler, "I now believe there is no other choice for me but to emigrate, even though it will tear my life apart" (quoted in Benjamin, 1993, pp. 158, 160).[4] He spent two years at Cornell University and then went to the University of Iowa. His research on the social psychology of the child led to an invitation to develop the new Research Center for Group Dynamics at the Massachusetts Institute of Technology. Although he died within a few years of accepting the position, his program was so effective that the research center, now located at the University of Michigan, remains active today.

---

[4]Lewin's mother and sister died in Nazi concentration camps.

Kurt Lewin uses life-space drawings to illustrate a person's psychological field.

## The Life Space

Throughout a career of 30 years, Lewin devoted himself to the broadly defined area of human motivation, describing human behavior within its total physical and social context (Lewin, 1936, 1939). His overall conception of psychology was practical, focusing on social issues that affect how we live and work. He sought to humanize the factories of the day so that work would become a source of personal satisfaction instead of solely a way to earn a living.

Lewin's knowledge of field theory in physics led him to consider that a person's psychological activities occur within a kind of psychological field, which he called the life space. The life space encompasses all past, present, and future events that may affect us. From a psychological standpoint, each of these events determines behavior in a given situation. Thus, the life space consists of the person's needs in interaction with the psychological environment.

A life space shows varying degrees of development as a function of the amount and kind of experience we have accumulated. Because an infant lacks experiences, it has few differentiated regions in its life space. A highly educated, sophisticated adult has a complex and well differentiated life space showing a variety of experiences.

Lewin sought a mathematical model to represent his theoretical conception of psychological processes. Because he was interested in the individual person (the single case) rather than groups or average performance, statistical analysis was not useful for his purpose. He chose topology, a form of geometry, to diagram the life space, showing at any given moment a person's possible goals and the paths leading to them.

Within his topological maps, which he used to diagram all forms of behavior and psychological phenomena, Lewin used arrows (vectors) to represent the direction of a person's movement toward a goal. He added the notion of weighting these choices (valences) to refer to the positive or negative value of objects within the life space. Objects that are attractive or that satisfy human needs have a positive valence; objects that are threatening have a negative valence. His diagrams were sometimes referred to as a "blackboard psychology."

**FIGURE 12.2** A simplified example of a life space.

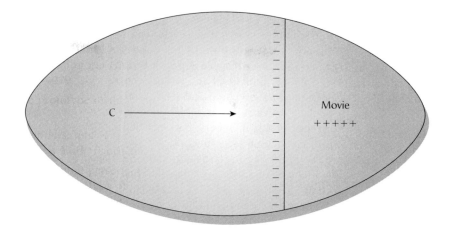

In the simple example presented in Figure 12.2, a child wants to go to the movies but is forbidden to do so by his or her parents. The ellipse represents the life space; C represents the child. The arrow is the vector indicating that C is motivated toward the goal of going to the movie, which has a positive value. The vertical line is the barrier to the goal, established by the parents, and it has a negative valence.

## Motivation and the Zeigarnik Effect

Lewin proposed a basic state of balance or equilibrium between the person and the environment. Any disturbance of this equilibrium leads to tension, which in turn leads to some action in an effort to relieve the tension and restore the balance. Thus, to explain human motivation, Lewin believed that behavior involves a cycle of tension-states or need-states followed by activity and relief.

An early experiment to test this proposition was performed by Bluma Zeigarnik in 1927 under Lewin's supervision. Subjects were given a series of tasks and allowed to finish some but were interrupted before they could complete others. Lewin made the following predictions:

1. A tension-system develops when subjects are given a task to perform.
2. When the task is completed, the tension is dissipated.
3. If the task is not completed, the persistence of tension results in a greater likelihood that the subjects will recall the task.

Zeigarnik's results confirmed the predictions. The subjects remembered the uncompleted tasks more readily than they recalled the completed tasks. This effect has since become known as the **Zeigarnik effect**.

Lewin's inspiration for this research on motivation came from observing a waiter in a café across the street from the Psychological Institute in Berlin. One evening, while meeting at the café with some of his graduate students,

> ... *someone expressed amazement at the café waiter's apparent ability to remember what everyone had ordered without writing anything down. Some time after they had paid, Lewin called the waiter and asked what they had ordered. He replied indignantly that he no longer knew. (Ash, 1995, p. 271)*

Once the waiter's customers had paid, his task was complete and the tension had dissipated. He no longer needed to remember what everyone had ordered.

**Zeigarnik effect:** The tendency to recall uncompleted tasks more easily than completed tasks.

## Social Psychology

Lewin's interest in social psychology began in the 1930s. His pioneering efforts in this field are sufficient to justify his stature within the history of psychology. The outstanding feature of Lewin's social psychology is group dynamics, the application of psychological concepts to individual and group behavior. Just as the individual and his or her environment form a psychological field, so the group and its environment form a social field. Social behaviors occur within and result from coexisting social entities such as subgroups, group members, barriers, and channels of communication. Group behavior at any given time is a function of the total field situation. Lewin conducted studies on behavior in various social situations. A classic experiment involved authoritarian, democratic, and laissez-faire leadership styles among groups of boys (Lewin, Lippitt, & White, 1939). The results showed that boys in the authoritarian group became very aggressive. Those in the democratic group were friendly toward one another and completed more tasks than those in the other two groups. Lewin's research initiated new areas of social research and spurred the growth of social psychology.

In addition, he emphasized social action research, the study of relevant social problems with a view to introducing change. Reflecting a personal concern about racial problems, he conducted community studies on integrated housing, equal employment opportunities, and the development and prevention of prejudice in childhood. His work transformed these controversial issues into controlled research studies, applying the rigor of the experimental method without the artificiality of the academic laboratory.

Lewin promoted sensitivity training for educators and business leaders to reduce intergroup conflict and develop individual potential. His sensitivity training groups (T-groups) were forerunners of the encounter groups popular in the 1960s and 1970s.

In general, Lewin's experimental programs and research findings are more acceptable to psychologists than many of his theoretical views. His influence on social and child psychology is considerable, and many of his concepts and techniques are still used in studies of personality and motivation.

# Criticisms of Gestalt Psychology

Critics of the Gestalt psychology school of thought charged that the organization of perceptual processes, as in the phi phenomenon, was not approached as a scientific problem to be investigated but treated instead as a phenomenon whose existence was simply accepted. This was like denying there was a problem at all.

Further, experimental psychologists asserted that the Gestalt position was vague and that basic concepts were not defined with sufficient rigor to be scientifically meaningful. Gestalt psychologists countered these charges by insisting that in a young science, attempts at explanation and definition may be incomplete, but being incomplete was not the same as being vague.

Other psychologists alleged that Gestalt proponents were too occupied with theory at the expense of research and empirical data. Although the Gestalt school assuredly has been theoretically oriented, it also emphasized experimentation and provided a considerable amount of research.

Related to this point is the suggestion that Gestalt experimental work was inferior to behavioral psychology research because it lacked adequate controls and its unquantified data were not amenable to statistical analysis. Gestalt psychologists held that because qualitative results took precedence in their system, much of their research was deliberately less quantitative than other schools considered necessary. Much Gestalt research was exploratory, investigating psychological problems within a different framework.

Köhler's notion of insight has also been questioned. Attempts to replicate the two-stick experiment with chimps have provided little support for the role of insight in learning. These later studies suggested that problem solving does not occur suddenly and may depend on prior learning or experience (see, for example, Windholz & Lamal, 1985).

Also, some psychologists considered Gestalt psychologists to be using poorly defined physiological assumptions. Gestalt researchers admitted that their theorizing in this area was tentative, but they believed their speculations were a useful adjunct to their system.

# Contributions of Gestalt Psychology

The Gestalt movement left an indelible imprint on psychology and influenced work on perception, learning, thinking, personality, social psychology, and motivation. Unlike its chief competitor at the time—behaviorism—Gestalt psychology retained a separate identity. Its major tenets were not fully absorbed into mainstream psychological thought. It continued to foster interest in conscious experience as a legitimate problem for psychology during the years when behaviorism was dominant.

The Gestalt focus on conscious experience was not like the approach of Wundt and Titchener but centered instead on a modern version of phenomenology. Contemporary adherents of the Gestalt position believe that conscious experience does occur and is a legitimate subject for study. They recognize, however, that it cannot be investigated with the same precision and objectivity as overt behavior. A phenomenological approach to psychology is more widely accepted by European psychologists than it is in the United States, but its influence can be seen in the American humanistic psychology movement (see Chapter 14). Many aspects of contemporary cognitive psychology also owe their origins to Gestalt psychology.

# Discussion Questions

1. Describe Lewin's concept of a field theory and tell how it was influenced by physics.
2. Describe some of the principles of perceptual organization.
3. Describe the antecedent influences on Gestalt psychology.
4. Explain the differences between the Gestalt and behaviorist revolts against Wundtian psychology.
5. Give an example of Köhler's research on insight on the island of Tenerife.
6. How did the Zeitgeist in physics change toward the end of the nineteenth century? How did that change influence Gestalt psychology?
7. How did Wertheimer apply Gestalt principles of learning to creative thinking in humans?
8. How does field theory deal with motivation and with social psychology? What is social action research?
9. How does insight learning differ from the trial-and-error learning described by Thorndike?
10. How does isomorphism relate perception to underlying neurological correlates?
11. How do studies of perceptual constancies support the Gestalt viewpoint?
12. If you looked at a book on a table and said, "I see a book on the table," what error would you be committing, according to Titchener?
13. In what ways did Gestalt psychology affect psychology as a whole?
14. On what grounds did Gestalt psychologists criticize behaviorism?
15. On what grounds has Gestalt psychology been criticized?
16. What did the Gestalt psychologists mean by the expressions "the whole is different from the sum of its parts" and "there is more to perception than meets the eye?"
17. What factors impeded the acceptance of Gestalt psychology in the United States?
18. What is the phi phenomenon? How is it produced? Why couldn't the phi phenomenon be explained by Wundt's psychology?
19. Why did some people mistakenly assume that Gestalt psychology dealt only with perception?
20. Why has the word *Gestalt* caused problems for the movement?

## CHAPTER 13

# The Beginnings of Psychoanalysis

## Was It Only a Dream?

The little boy stared in horror as his mother was carried into the room. It was a sight he never forgot. He gazed at her face; she was so young and beautiful but he was puzzled, frightened even, by its peaceful expression. Was she merely asleep, or was she dead? His gaze shifted to the people who were carrying her, only they did not look like people. They did not seem human at all. They were extremely tall and dressed in strange clothing, but it was the faces that frightened him most of all. They appeared to be some kind of bird-like creatures with very long beaks. Suddenly he awoke from his dream, his nightmare, screaming and crying. He jumped out of bed and ran to his parents' bedroom. Only when he saw for himself that his mother was alive was he able to calm down and sleep.

Thirty years later that dream was still a highly emotional experience for Sigmund Freud, and when he applied his own techniques for analyzing dreams he finally understood why. The superficial meaning was obvious; a little boy afraid of losing his mother. There was nothing unusual or suspicious in that. But the more Freud thought about the dream, the more he realized that it revealed a more subtle, sinister, even shocking meaning.

Freud focused on the dream's most bizarre aspect, the long-beaked and bird-like figures. What could they signify? What could they reveal about the unconscious longings of a seven-year-old boy? Then he recalled a childhood friend, a youngster who was much more worldly than Freud had been. That boy liked to talk about sex, a forbidden topic, and had introduced Freud to the German slang expression for sexual intercourse. The word was *Vögeln*.

As an adult Freud knew the word and was aware that it was derived from the German word for bird. The creatures in his nightmare had faces like birds. As soon as he made the connection, he knew the true meaning of his dream. It symbolized the sexual longing of a seven-year-old boy for his mother. In his unconscious, he wanted to make love to her.

If the child is the father to the man, as the saying goes—and as Freud believed—then we can see the similarity to the child who dreamed of losing and loving his mother, and the middle-aged physician who unraveled the dream's thread and, in the process, sparked another revolution in psychology.

## The Development of Psychoanalysis

The term "psychoanalysis" and the name Sigmund Freud are recognized throughout the modern world. Whereas other prominent people in the history of psychology, such as Fechner, Wundt, and Titchener, are little known outside of psychology, Freud has maintained a high level of visibility among the general public. He appeared on the cover of *Time* magazine three times, the last appearance occurring some 60 years after his death. On the 150th anniversary of his birth, in 2006, his picture appeared on the cover of *Newsweek* and he was lionized in a lengthy editorial column in the *Wall Street Journal*. The *Newsweek* writer described him as "an inescapable force [who] captivates us even now" (Adler, 2006, p. 43). Without a doubt, Sigmund Freud was one of a handful of individuals pivotal in the history of civilization who altered the way humans think about themselves.

Freud himself suggested that in all recorded history, there have been three great shocks to the collective human ego (Freud, 1917). The first was when Copernicus (1473–1543), the Polish astronomer, showed us that the earth was not the center of the universe but merely one of many planets revolving around the sun. The second revelation came in the nineteenth century when Charles Darwin demonstrated that we are not a unique and separate species with a privileged place in creation but only a higher form of animal species that evolved from lower forms of animal life. Freud administered the third shock by proclaiming that we are not the rational rulers of our lives but are under the influence of unconscious forces of which we are unaware and over which we have little, if any, control.

Chronologically, psychoanalysis overlaps psychology's other schools of thought. Consider the situation in 1895, the year Freud published his first book marking the formal beginning of his new movement. In that year, Wundt was 63 years old. The 28-year-old Titchener had been at Cornell for only two years and was just beginning to develop his structural psychology. The spirit of functionalism was starting to flourish in the United States. Neither behaviorism nor Gestalt psychology had yet been proposed; Watson was then 17 years old and Wertheimer was 15.

Yet by the time of Freud's death in 1939, the entire psychological world had changed radically. Wundtian psychology, Titchenerian structuralism, and functional psychology were history. Gestalt psychology was being transplanted from Germany to the United States, and behaviorism was the dominant form of American psychology.

Despite their fundamental disagreements, the schools of psychological thought we have discussed thus far shared an academic heritage and owed much of their inspiration and form to Wilhelm Wundt. Their concepts and scientific methods were refined in laboratories, libraries, and lecture halls, and all dealt with topics such as sensation, perception, and learning. In contrast, psychoanalysis was neither a product of the universities nor a pure science, but arose within the traditions of medicine and psychiatry from attempts to treat persons labeled by society as mentally ill. Thus, psychoanalysis was not (and still is not) a school of thought directly comparable with the others we have studied.

From its beginnings, psychoanalysis was distinct from mainstream psychological thought in goals, subject matter, and methods. Its subject matter is psychopathology, or abnormal behavior, relatively neglected by other schools of thought. Its primary method is clinical observation rather than controlled laboratory experimentation. In addition, psychoanalysis deals with the unconscious, a topic virtually ignored by other systems of thought.

Wundt and Titchener did not accept the idea of unconscious forces in their systems because it is impossible to apply the method of introspection to the unconscious. Therefore, since the unconscious cannot be introspected, it cannot be reduced to sensory elements. The functional psychologists, with their exclusive focus on consciousness, had no use for the unconscious mind, although James did admit to the notion of unconscious processes. Angell's 1904 textbook devotes no more than two pages at the end to the unconscious. Woodworth's 1921 textbook had little more to say, covering the topic as an afterthought. Of course, Watson had no more room in his system of behaviorism for the unconscious than he did for consciousness. He referred dismissively to the unconscious as that which the individual has not yet verbalized. It was Freud who brought the notion of the unconscious to psychology.

# Antecedent Influences on Psychoanalysis

Three major sources of influence on the psychoanalytic movement were as follows:

1. Philosophical speculations about unconscious psychological phenomena
2. Early ideas about psychopathology
3. Evolutionary theory

### Theories of the Unconscious Mind

**Monadology:** Leibnitz's theory of psychic entities, called monads, which are similar to perceptions.

Early in the eighteenth century, the German philosopher and mathematician Gottfried Wilhelm Leibnitz (1646–1716) developed an idea he called **monadology**. Monads were not physical atoms but were nevertheless considered to be the individual elements of all reality. Thus, they were not composed wholly of matter in the sense that physicists used the word. Each monad was an unextended psychic entity, mental in nature, which nevertheless had some properties of physical matter. When enough monads were grouped together, they created an extension.

Monads can be likened to perceptions. Leibnitz believed that mental events (which are composed of the activity of monads) had different degrees of consciousness ranging from completely unconscious to clearly conscious. Lesser degrees of consciousness were called *petites perceptions;* the conscious realization of these was described as apperception. For example, the sound of waves breaking on the shore is an apperception, but it is composed of individual falling drops of water (the *petites perceptions*). We do not consciously perceive each drop of water, but when enough of them collect they summate to produce an apperception.

A century later, the German philosopher Johann Friedrich Herbart (1776–1841) refined Leibnitz's notion of the unconscious into the concept of threshold of consciousness. Reflecting the impact of the mechanistic Zeitgeist, Herbart argued that ideas below the proposed threshold are unconscious. When an idea rises to a conscious level of awareness, it is apperceived (to use Leibnitz's term). In order for an idea to rise into consciousness, however, it must be compatible with the ideas already in consciousness. Incongruous ideas cannot exist in consciousness at the same time, and irrelevant ideas are forced out of consciousness to become inhibited ideas. Inhibited ideas (similar to Leibnitz's *petites perceptions*) exist below the threshold of consciousness. According to Herbart, conflict develops among ideas as they struggle for conscious realization.

Fechner also speculated about the unconscious. Although he used the notion of threshold, it was his suggestion that the mind is analogous to an iceberg that had a greater impact on Freud. Fechner suggested that like the greater portion of the iceberg, much of the mind lies hidden below the surface where it is influenced by unobservable forces.

It is interesting that Fechner's work, to which experimental psychology owes so much, also had an influence on psychoanalysis. Freud quoted from Fechner's *Elements of Psychophysics* in several of his books and derived some major concepts (such as the pleasure principle, psychic energy, and aggression) from Fechner's writings. Freud's letters to a boyhood friend tell that in his late teens and early twenties he liked to read the satirical essays of one Dr. Mises, the pen name Fechner used to lampoon trends in science and medicine (see Boehlich, 1990).

Discussion of the unconscious was very much part of the European intellectual Zeitgeist of the 1880s when Freud was beginning his clinical practice. And it was not only of interest to professionals; the issue was also a fashionable topic of conversation among the educated public. A book titled *Philosophy of the Unconscious* became so popular that it appeared in nine editions (Hartmann, 1869/1884). In the 1870s, at least a half dozen other books published in Germany included the word "unconscious" in their titles.

The notion that unconscious forces may overtake and dominate a person's more rational being soon appeared in the popular literature. In Robert Louis Stevenson's novel, *Dr. Jekyll and Mr. Hyde,* published in 1889, the good doctor drinks a mysterious potion that releases a different side of his character, one addicted to all forms of vice. This lower self, this demanding amoral presence, gradually consumes the moral, upstanding, rational self.

Thus we see that Freud was not the first to discuss seriously the unconscious human mind. He conceded that writers and philosophers before him had dealt with it extensively but he claimed that he had discovered a scientific way to study it.

## Early Ideas about Psychopathology

As we have noted, a new movement requires something to revolt against in order to gain momentum. Because psychoanalysis did not develop within academic psychology, the movement it opposed was not Wundt's form of psychology or any other then-current school of psychological thought. To understand what Freud opposed, we must consider the prevailing trends in the area in which he worked: the treatment of mental disorders.

The history of the treatment of mental illness is both fascinating and depressing. Recognition of mental disturbance dates to 2000 BC. The Babylonians believed that the cause of mental illness was possession by demons, a condition they treated humanely with a combination of magic and prayer. Ancient Hebrew cultures regarded mental illness as punishment for sin and relied on magic and prayer to cure it. Greek philosophers—notably Socrates, Plato, and Aristotle—argued that mental illness arose from disordered thought processes. They prescribed the persuasive, healing power of words.

When Christianity became established in the fourth century, mental illness was once again blamed on evil spirits. The treatment mandated by the church for over 1,000 years involved torture and execution for those thought to be possessed by the devil. Beginning in the fifteenth century, and continuing for 300 years, the Inquisition carried on by the church pursued heresy and witchcraft, relentlessly identifying symptoms of mental disorders, for which severe punishment was the only cure.

By the eighteenth century, mental illness came to be viewed as irrational behavior, and mentally ill persons were confined in institutions similar to jails. Although they were no longer tortured or put to death, no treatment was offered. Sometimes patients were displayed publicly like animals in a zoo. Some were chained to their beds for years or had arms and legs pinioned by iron bars. Others had iron rings riveted around their neck, fastened by chains to a hook on the wall, not unlike dogs on a leash. These prisons came to be known as lunatic asylums, described as "cemeteries for the still breathing" (Scull, MacKenzie, & Hervey, 1996, p. 118).

***More humane treatments***   Juan Luis Vives (1492–1540), a Spanish scholar, was among the first to urge that mentally disturbed persons be treated sensitively and humanely. Because of barriers of language and geography, however, his pleas for lenient treatment were unknown outside of Spain. It was not until the end of the eighteenth century that his ideas took root elsewhere.

Philippe Pinel (1745–1826), a French physician, considered mental illness to be a natural phenomenon treatable by the methods of natural science. He released patients from their chains and treated them decently, taking time to listen to their complaints. He maintained precise case-history files and data on cure rates.

*The mentally sick, far from being guilty people deserving punishment, are sick people whose miserable state deserves all the consideration that is due to suffering humanity. One should try with the most simple methods to restore their reason. (Pinel, quoted in Wade, 1995, p. 25)*

Under Pinel's direction, the number of patients pronounced cured rose dramatically. Following his example, chains were struck from patients in Europe and the United States, and the scientific study of mental illness became widespread. "Scientific enlightenment resulted in the treatment of human beings as machines that, when broken, needed to be fixed. This repair was to take place in insane asylums equipped with gadgets and apparatuses reflective of the industrial inventions of the industrial revolution" (Brems, Thevenin, & Routh, 1991, p. 12).

In the United States, the most influential reformer of insane asylums was Dorothea Dix (1802–1887), a deeply religious person who suffered from depression. Impressed by what Pinel had accomplished with his patients, she applied her considerable energies and persuasive abilities to duplicating his success. She traveled throughout the United States, petitioning state legislators to mandate humanitarian treatment for the mentally ill. During the American Civil War she crusaded to improve conditions for wounded Union soldiers; her activism brought her an appointment as superintendent of women nurses for the army.

The first psychiatrist to open a formal practice in the United States was Benjamin Rush (1745–1813), who had been a signer of the Declaration of Independence. Rush established the first hospital that was devoted solely for the treatment of emotional disturbances. Working within the familiar mechanistic tradition, Rush stated that everything in the universe "including man's mind and morality, could be explained in terms of physical laws and fitted within a scientific, rational structure" (Gamwell & Tomes, 1995, p. 19). For example, Rush believed that some irrational behaviors were caused by too much or too little blood. His remedy was simple: drain blood from his patients or pump more blood into them.

Rush developed a rotating chair that would spin the unfortunate patient at high speed, a procedure that often led to fainting. In an early form of shock treatment, Rush dunked patients in icy water. He is also credited with the first sedating technique. A patient was strapped in a tranquilizing chair and restrained around the chest, wrists, and ankles; pressure was applied to the patient's head by large wooden blocks gripped in a vise.

Although these techniques sound cruel to us today, remember that Rush was trying to help people with mental disorders instead of dumping them in institutions where their needs would be ignored. He recognized that his patients were sick, not possessed by evil spirits.

During the nineteenth century, psychiatrists were divided into two camps: the somatic and the psychic. The somatic approach held that abnormal behavior had physical causes such as brain lesions, under-stimulated nerves, or overly tight nerves. The psychic school subscribed to emotional or psychological explanations for abnormal behavior. In general, the somatic viewpoint dominated and was supported by the ideas of the German philosopher Immanuel Kant, who ridiculed the view that emotional problems somehow led to mental illness.

Psychoanalysis developed as a revolt against the somatic orientation. As the treatment of mental illness advanced, some scientists became convinced that emotional factors were of far greater importance than brain lesions or other physical causes.

### The Emmanuel Movement

The trend toward the psychic approach to mental illness was fostered in the United States by the amazingly successful Emmanuel Church Healing Movement, which argued for the use of psychotherapy. By focusing on the benefits of talk therapy, its promoters made the public and the medical community aware of the importance of psychological factors as potential causes of mental illness (Caplan, 1998; Gifford, 1997). The movement was begun by Elwood Worcester, rector of the Emmanuel Church in Boston, Massachusetts, and was most influential from about 1906 to 1910. The Reverend Worcester was an unusual clergyman in that he had earned a Ph.D. in philosophy and psychology from the University of Leipzig, Germany, where he studied under Wilhelm Wundt. Thus, Worcester became another of Wundt's American students who went astray, who left the confines of Wundt's approach to experimental psychology and began to apply it to problems of the real world.

> *The movement began in 1906 when Worcester announced in a public lecture for his parishioners that he would be willing to meet the next morning with anyone who had moral or psychological problems they wanted to discuss. He expected that a few might show up but was astounded when nearly 200 appeared. (Benjamin & Baker, 2004, p. 49)*

Clearly there was a need for what Worcester wanted to offer.

The talk therapy sessions, for individuals and groups, were conducted by religious leaders of several denominations. They relied heavily on the power of suggestion and the moral authority of the clergymen in urging the proper course of behavior for the patients. The therapy quickly became popular throughout the United States and was soon supplemented by a series of articles in *Good Housekeeping* magazine, which ran for nearly two years. A 1908 book by Worcester and two colleagues, *Religion and Medicine: The Moral Control of Nervous Disorders,* was hailed by the press as the most important book published dealing with "scientific psychotherapy" (Caplan, 1998, p. 297).

In 1909, a journal titled *Psychotherapy* was published; it called for "sound psychology, sound medicine, and sound religion" (Zaretsky, 2004, p. 80). Not so incidentally, as we shall see, 1909 was also the year Freud made his only visit to the United States.

Although the movement was embraced enthusiastically by the public, the medical community and clinical psychologists such as Witmer and Münsterberg strongly opposed the idea of ministers acting as psychotherapists. However, it was primarily due to the popularity of the Emmanuel Movement that Freud and his psychoanalysis were warmly welcomed in the United States when he brought his message in person in 1909. The notion of a talk therapy was already part of the national consciousness.

**Hypnosis**   Interest in the phenomenon of hypnosis also helped foster the growing focus on psychic causes of mental illness. The application of hypnosis to the treatment of emotional disturbances originated in a mysterious, murky force called "animal magnetism," introduced by Franz Anton Mesmer (1734–1815), a Viennese physician who was part scientist, part showman.

Mesmer believed that the human body contained a magnetic force that operated like the magnets used by physicists. This animal magnetism was capable of penetrating objects and acting on them from a distance. Animal magnetism could also cure nervous disorders by restoring the equilibrium between the patient's magnetic levels and the levels prevalent in the environment.

At first, Mesmer claimed to reverse mental illness by having patients clutch magnetized iron bars. Later, Mesmer decided that all he needed to do was touch or stroke the patients' hands and his own magnetic force would be transmitted into the sufferers' bodies. Not surprisingly, Vienna's medical community considered him a quack.

Mesmer became enormously successful in Paris, where he led group therapy sessions in a dimly lit room with soft music and the scent of orange blossoms in the background. Attired in lilac-colored robes, he orchestrated dramatic results. The patients, attached to one another by cords, perched around a tub filled with magnetized fluid and grasped the iron rods that protruded from it. Mesmer and his assistant magnetizers passed among the patients, laying hands on the bodies of the disturbed persons. Patients often experienced convulsions or trances before returning to conscious awareness, miraculously cured (Wade, 1995). "Mesmer made a fortune running several clinics and attending private parties, often of upper-class women. The ladies would convulse, scream, and faint as Mesmer waved his hands over them or touched them" (Dingfelder, 2010, p. 30).

When an investigating commission reported unfavorably on Mesmer's so-called cures—that he was not really curing people at all—he fled to Switzerland. However, the popularity of mesmerism spread, particularly in the United States. A cultural historian of the period wrote that by the mid-nineteenth century,

> ... there were between twenty and thirty thousand mesmerists lecturing in the Northeast alone. Many of them used their ... force to control the behavior and attitudes of their mesmerized subjects, to the wonder of audiences that often reached two or three thousand. (Reynolds, 1995, p. 260)

In England, mesmerism was given a new name and greater credibility when the physician and surgeon James Braid (1795–1860) called the trancelike state *neurohypnology*, from which the term *hypnosis* was eventually derived. Braid's careful work and disdain for exaggerated claims earned for hypnosis some scientific respectability (see Schmit, 2005).

Hypnosis achieved greater professional recognition in medical circles with the work of the French physician Jean Martin Charcot (1825–1893), head of a neurological clinic at Salpêtrière, a Paris hospital for insane women. Charcot had some success treating hysterical patients by means of hypnosis. More important, he described the symptoms of hysteria and the use of hypnosis in medical terminology, making them more acceptable to the French Academy of Science. Charcot's work was primarily neurological, however, emphasizing physical disturbances such as paralysis. Most doctors continued to ascribe hysteria to somatic or physical causes until 1889, when Charcot's student, Pierre Janet (1859–1947), became director of the psychological laboratory at Salpêtrière. Charcot also made substantial contributions to medicine, helping map centers in the brain as well as the structure of the lungs, liver, and kidneys. He made the recording of a patient's body temperature standard hospital practice.

Janet rejected the opinion that hysteria was a physical problem and conceived of it as a mental disorder caused by memory impairments, fixed ideas, and unconscious forces. He chose hypnosis as the method of treatment. Thus, during the early years of Sigmund Freud's career, the medical establishment was paying increasing attention to hypnosis and the psychological causes of mental illness. As we will see, Janet's work anticipated many of Freud's ideas.

The work of Charcot and Janet in treating mental disturbances helped change psychiatrists' ideas from the somatic (physical) to the psychic (mental) point of view. Physicians began to think in terms of curing emotional disturbances by treating the mind instead of the body. By the time Freud started to publish his ideas, the term "psychotherapy" was already in widespread use in the United States and in Europe as well.

## The Influence of Charles Darwin

In 1979, Frank J. Sulloway, a distinguished historian of science, published *Freud: Biologist of the Mind*, in which he argued that Freud's thinking had been strongly influenced by Darwin's writings. Sulloway based his conclusions on a new interpretation of the data of history. He examined data that had existed for years but that no one else had viewed in the same way. What Sulloway did was to check the books in Freud's personal library, where he found copies of Darwin's works. Freud had read them all and had written notes in the margins. He had praised them to colleagues and in his own publications. Sulloway wrote that Darwin "probably did more than any other individual to pave the way for Sigmund Freud and the psychoanalytic revolution" (Sulloway, 1979, p. 238). More recent research supports Darwin's impact on Freud's psychoanalytic theory. Later in his life, Freud insisted that the study of Darwin's theory of evolution was an essential part of the training program for psychoanalysts (Ritvo, 1990).

Darwin discussed several ideas that Freud later made central issues in psychoanalysis, including unconscious mental processes and conflicts, the significance of dreams, the hidden symbolism of certain behaviors, and the importance of sexual arousal. Overall, Darwin focused, as Freud did later, on the nonrational aspects of thought and behavior.

Darwin's theories also affected Freud's ideas about childhood development. Darwin had given his notes and unpublished materials to Romanes (see Chapter 6), who later wrote two books based on Darwin's material about mental evolution in humans and animals. Sulloway found copies of Romanes's books on Freud's library shelves, with Freud's handwritten comments in the margins. Romanes elaborated on Darwin's notion of a continuous progression in emotional behavior from childhood to adulthood and on the suggestion that evidence of a sex drive appears in infants as young as seven weeks. Both themes became central to Freudian psychoanalysis.

Further, Darwin insisted that humans were driven by the biological forces of love and hunger, which he believed were the foundation of all behavior. Less than a decade later, the German psychiatrist Richard von Krafft-Ebing expressed a similar view, that sexual gratification and self-preservation were the only instincts in human physiology. Thus, respected scientists were following Darwin's lead and recognizing sex as a basic human motivation.

## Additional Influences

During Freud's university training he was exposed to the idea of mechanism, as represented by the physiologists, including Helmholtz, who had been students of Johannes Müller (see Chapter 3). They had united to take the position that there are no forces active within the organism other than the common physical and chemical ones. Freud was influenced by this mechanistic orientation promoted by Ernst Brücke, his major professor, and when he later formulated his theory of human behavior it was a deterministic one. Indeed, he referred to it as psychic determinism.

Another aspect of the Zeitgeist reflected in Freud's work was the attitude toward sex in late nineteenth-century Vienna, where Freud lived and worked. It has been popularly but wrongly assumed that because society in Freud's day was so repressive, his open discussion of sexual matters was perceived as shocking. Although sexual inhibitions may have been typical of Freud, and of the neurotic upper-middle-class women who became his patients, this was assuredly not the attitude of the culture as a whole. Vienna at the time was a permissive society. (Even Victorian England and Puritan America were not really as prudish and inhibited as we usually think.) The 1880s and 1890s were characterized by a breakdown of the Victorian sublimation of sexuality. Passion, prostitution, and pornography flourished.

Interest in sex was apparent in everyday life as well as in scientific literature. In the last decade of the nineteenth century, the scientific study of sexuality had become popular both in Europe and the United States. Researchers, called "sexologists," were expected to "bring a naturalist's cold eye to matters long thought indecent, immoral, disgusting, and sinful. Sexologists were encouraged to study varieties of human sexual experience not as vices, sins, or crimes, but as an integral part of the natural world" (Makari, 2008, p. 93).

As a result, in the years before Freud advanced his sex-based theory, research had been published on such topics as sexual pathologies, infantile sexuality, and the suppression of sexual impulses and its consequences for mental and physical health.

In 1845, the German physician Adolf Patze argued that the sex drive could be detected in children as young as three years old, a point reiterated in 1867 by Henry Maudsley, a British psychiatrist. In 1886, Krafft-Ebing published his sensational book, *Psychopathia Sexualis,* and in 1897 a Viennese physician, Albert Moll, wrote about childhood sexuality and the child's love for the parent of the opposite sex, anticipating Freud's Oedipus complex.

A colleague of Freud's in Vienna, the neurologist Moritz Benedikt, achieved dramatic cures with hysterical women by getting them to talk about their sex lives. The French psychologist Alfred Binet published work on sexual perversions. Even the word "libido," which would assume great significance in Freudian psychoanalysis, was already in use with much the same meaning that Freud intended. Thus, the sexual component of Freud's work had been anticipated in one form or another. Largely because the professional and the public Zeitgeists were already receptive, Freud's ideas would receive a great deal of attention.

**Catharsis:** The process of reducing or eliminating a complex by recalling it to conscious awareness and allowing it to be expressed.

The concept of **catharsis** was also popular before Freud published his work. In 1880, a year before Freud received his medical degree, an uncle of Freud's future wife wrote about Aristotle's concept of catharsis, a way of treating emotional difficulties by having the patient recall and describe unconscious conflicts. Catharsis soon became a popular topic of conversation among the elite. By 1890, there were more than 140 publications in German about catharsis (Sulloway, 1979).

Many of Freud's ideas about dream symbolism had been anticipated in philosophy and physiology as far back as the seventeenth century. Although Freud claimed he was the only scientist to show an interest in dreams, the facts of history tell a different story. The study of dreams had become "a well-established arena for empirically studying the undercurrents of mental life" (Makari, 2008, p. 76). By the end of the nineteenth century more than a dozen works on dreams were being published annually. Even Wilhelm Wundt and the psychophysicists were conducting research on dreams, specifically on how external stimuli were able to invade consciousness during sleep.

Three of Freud's contemporaries were already working on dreams. Charcot proposed that the psychological trauma associated with hysteria was revealed in the patient's dreams. Janet said the causes of hysteria were contained in dreams, and he used dream analysis as a therapeutic tool. And Krafft-Ebing argued that unconscious sexual wishes could be found in dreams (Sand, 1992).

Although there were many diverse influences on Freud's thinking, let us not lose sight of his genius, and that of all founders. It lies in their ability to draw together the threads of various ideas and trends to weave a coherent system. Freud himself acknowledged his anticipators. In 1924, he wrote that psychoanalysis "did not drop from the skies ready-made. It had its starting point in older ideas, which it developed further; it sprang from earlier suggestions, which it elaborated" (quoted in Grubrich-Simitis, 1993, p. 265).

## Sigmund Freud (1856–1939) and the Development of Psychoanalysis

Sigmund Freud was born on May 6, 1856, in Freiberg, Moravia (now Pribor, Czech Republic). Freud's father was a wool merchant. When his business failed in Moravia, he moved the family to Leipzig and later, when Freud was four years old, to Vienna. Freud remained in Vienna for nearly 80 years. Freud's father, 20 years older than Freud's mother, who was the elder Freud's third wife, was strict and authoritarian. As a boy,

Library of Congress

SIGMUND FREUD

Freud felt both fear and love toward his father. Freud's mother was protective and loving; toward her, young Freud felt a passionate attachment. This fear of the father and sexual attraction to the mother is what Freud later called the Oedipus complex. We will see that much of Freud's theory is autobiographical, deriving from his childhood experiences and recollections.

Freud's mother took immense pride in her firstborn, providing constant attention and support. She was totally convinced of his future greatness. It is noteworthy that the house in which Freud was born has been restored and maintained as a museum, and the town of Pribor renamed its Stalin Square as Freud Square.

Among Freud's adult personality characteristics were self-confidence, ambition, desire for achievement, and dreams of glory and fame. He wrote, "A man who has been the indisputable favorite of his mother keeps for life the feeling of a conqueror, that confidence of success that often induces real success" (quoted in Jones, 1953, p. 5).

One of eight children, Freud demonstrated considerable intellectual ability, which the family tried to encourage. His was the only room to have an oil lamp, providing better light for study than the candles used by the other children. Freud's brothers and sisters were not allowed to play musical instruments, lest their practicing disturb the young scholar. Despite this special treatment, Freud seemed to resent his siblings.

Freud entered high school a year earlier than normal and was considered a brilliant student, graduating with distinction at age 17. He spoke German and Hebrew at home, and in school he learned Latin, Greek, French, and English. In addition, he taught himself Italian and Spanish. His exposure to Darwin's theory of evolution awakened an interest in the scientific approach to knowledge, and he decided to study medicine. He felt no pull to be a practicing physician but hoped that a medical degree would lead to a career in scientific research.

He began his studies in 1873 at the University of Vienna. Because he insisted on taking courses, such as philosophy, that were not part of the medical curriculum, he spent eight years earning his degree. He concentrated on biology, dissecting more than 400 male eels to determine the structure of the testicles. His findings were inconclusive, but it is interesting that his first research problem involved sex. He moved on to physiology and worked on the spinal cord of fish, spending six years hunched over a microscope in the physiological institute.

During these university years Freud experimented with the drug cocaine, which at that time was not an illegal substance. He used cocaine himself, made it available to his fiancée, sisters, and friends, and introduced it into medical practice. He was enthusiastic about the substance and claimed it eased his depression and chronic indigestion. Convinced that in cocaine he had discovered a miracle drug to cure everything from sciatica to seasickness, he expected his discoveries to win him the recognition he craved. This was not to be. Carl Koller, one of Freud's medical colleagues, after overhearing Freud's casual conversation about the drug, conducted his own experiments and found that cocaine could be used to anesthetize the human eye, facilitating the use of surgical procedures for treating eye disorders. Thus, Koller achieved the fame that Freud desired.

In 1996, a German historian reviewing Koller's papers at the Library of Congress in Washington, D.C., found a small envelope containing white powder. Written on the envelope: "Remainder of the 1st dose of cocaine, which I used in my first cocaine experiments in August 1884." The powder was quickly removed by surprised library officials.

Freud published a paper on cocaine's benefits, which was later held partly responsible for the epidemic of cocaine use in Europe and the United States that lasted well into the 1920s. Freud was criticized severely for advocating the use of cocaine for purposes other than eye surgery and for unleashing this plague upon the world. For the rest of his life he tried to erase the memories of his endorsement of cocaine and omitted any reference to these publications in his own bibliography. It was widely believed that Freud stopped his personal use of cocaine after medical school, but a later examination of his letters (more recently uncovered data of history) revealed that he used the drug for at least 10 more years, well into middle age (Masson, 1985).

Freud hoped to continue his scientific research at an academic laboratory, but Ernst Brücke, the medical school professor who directed the physiological institute where Freud worked, discouraged him for economic reasons. Freud was too poor to support himself during the many years it would take to secure one of the few university professorships that might become available. Knowing that Brücke was right, Freud decided to take his medical examinations and enter private practice in the hope of improving his financial situation. He received his M.D. in 1881 and established his practice as a clinical neurologist. He did not find this career to be any more attractive than he had anticipated, but the money won out. He had become engaged to Martha Bernays, but the couple postponed their marriage several times until they could afford it, though even then he had to borrow money and pawn their watches.

During their four-year courtship, Freud displayed extreme jealousy toward anyone who claimed Martha's attention or affection, even members of her own family. He wrote to her:

*From now on you are but a guest in your family. I will not leave you to anyone. If you can't be fond enough of me to renounce for my sake your family, then you must lose me and wreck your life. I do have a tyrannical streak. (quoted in Appignanesi & Forrester, 1992, pp. 30, 31)*

Freud's long working hours prevented him from spending a great deal of time with his wife and children, of whom there were eventually six. He took vacations alone or with his sister-in-law Minna because Martha could not keep up the pace of hiking and sightseeing.

## The Case of Anna O.

The physician Josef Breuer (1842–1925), who had gained fame for his study of respiration and of the functioning of the semicircular canals in the ears, befriended the young Freud. The successful, sophisticated Breuer offered Freud advice, lent him money, and apparently viewed him as a precocious younger brother. To Freud, Breuer was a father figure. The two men frequently discussed Breuer's patients, including the 21-year-old Anna O., whose case became pivotal in the development of psychoanalysis.

An intelligent and attractive woman, Anna O. suffered from severe hysterical complaints that including paralysis, memory loss, mental deterioration, nausea, and disturbances of vision and speech. The symptoms first appeared when she was nursing her dying father, who had always pampered her. It was said that she felt for him a kind of passionate love (Ellenberger, 1972, p. 274).

Breuer began Anna's treatment by using hypnosis. He found that while hypnotized she would recall specific experiences that seemed to have given rise to certain symptoms. Talking about the experiences under hypnosis often relieved the symptoms. For more than a year Breuer saw Anna every day. She would recount the day's disturbing incidents, and after they talked she sometimes reported that her symptoms had been eased. She referred to their conversations as chimney sweeping or the talking cure. As their sessions continued, Breuer realized (so he told Freud) that the incidents Anna remembered involved thoughts or events she found repulsive. Reliving the disturbing experiences under hypnosis reduced or eliminated the symptoms.

Breuer's wife grew jealous of the close emotional relationship developing between Breuer and Anna O. The young patient was exhibiting what later became known as

**Transference:** The process by which a patient responds to the therapist as if the therapist were a significant person (such as a parent) in the patient's life.

positive **transference** toward Breuer. In other words, she was transferring the love she felt for her father to her therapist. This transference was aided by the physical resemblance between her father and Breuer. Also, it may have happened that Breuer was experiencing an emotional attachment to his patient. One historian noted, "her youthful attractions, her charming helplessness, and her very name [the same as his mother's] reawakened in Breuer his dormant Oedipal longings for his own mother" (Gay, 1988, p. 68). Breuer finally perceived the situation as a threat and told Anna he could no longer treat her. Within hours, Anna was stricken by the pains of hysterical childbirth. Breuer terminated this condition through hypnosis. Then, according to legend, he took his wife to Venice on a kind of second honeymoon, during which she became pregnant.

This tale turns out to be a myth perpetuated by several generations of psychoanalysts and historians. It provides us with yet another example of distorted data of history. In this case, the story persisted nearly 100 years. Breuer and his wife may indeed have gone to Venice, but the birth dates of their children reveal that none could have been conceived at that time (Ellenberger, 1972).

Further examination of historical records revealed that Anna O. (whose real name was Bertha Pappenheim) was not cured by Breuer's cathartic treatments. Two weeks after Breuer stopped seeing her, she was institutionalized and spent hours sitting beneath a portrait of her father, talking of visiting his grave. She experienced hallucinations and convulsions, facial neuralgia, and recurring language difficulties. She became addicted to morphine, which Breuer had prescribed for facial pain. "To live with a syringe [of morphine] always at the ready is not a situation to be envied," she wrote (quoted in Ramos, 2003, p. 239).

However, more recent data of history provide an alternate version. According to this account, Breuer's treatment had been successful and Anna O.'s later symptoms were very mild. This writer also suggests that the source of the information critical of Breuer, suggesting that Anna O. had not been cured, was none other than Sigmund Freud himself (Miller, 2009).

Bertha Pappenheim became a social worker and feminist, endorsing education for women. She published short stories and a play about women's rights and was honored on a German postage stamp (Shepherd, 1993). She died in 1936, not long after a strenuous interrogation by the Gestapo regarding an anti-Nazi remark she had allegedly made. In 1992, her life was the subject of a Broadway play, "The Mystery of Anna O."

Breuer's case report on Anna O. is significant in the development of psychoanalysis because it introduced Freud to the cathartic method, the so-called talking cure, that later figured so prominently in his work.

## The Sexual Basis of Neurosis

In 1885, Freud received a small postgraduate grant that enabled him to spend several months in Paris studying with Charcot. He observed Charcot's use of hypnosis to treat hysteria and soon came to regard the man as another father figure, imagining how advantageous it would be for his career if he were married to Charcot's daughter. Freud even wrote to Martha to describe how attractive Charcot's daughter was (Gelfand, 1992).

Charcot alerted Freud to the role of sex in hysterical behavior. At a party, Freud overheard Charcot say that a particular patient's difficulties had a sexual basis: "In this sort of case it's always a question of the genitals—always, always, always" (quoted in Freud, 1914, p. 14). Freud observed that while Charcot was discussing sex he "crossed his hands in his lap and jumped up and down several times. For a moment I was almost paralyzed with astonishment" (quoted in Prochnik, 2006, p. 135).

After Freud returned to Vienna, he was again reminded of the possible sexual basis of emotional disturbance. Rudolph Chrobak, an eminent gynecologist, asked Freud to take the case of a woman suffering anxiety attacks that were relieved only when she knew the whereabouts of her physician at every moment. Chrobak told Freud that the basis of the anxiety was the impotence of the patient's husband. After 18 years their marriage had not been consummated. Freud wrote that Chrobak told him, "The sole prescription for such a malady is familiar enough to us, but we cannot order it. It runs: *Rx Penis normalis dosim repetatur!*" (Freud, 1914). Chrobak later denied making the remark (Ritvo, 1990, p. 75).

Freud had adopted Breuer's methods of hypnosis and catharsis to treat his patients, but he was growing dissatisfied with hypnosis and soon abandoned it. Although the technique was apparently successful in relieving or eliminating some symptoms, it was rarely able to effect a long-term cure. Many patients returned with new complaints. Also, Freud had found that some neurotic patients could not be easily or deeply hypnotized. He retained catharsis as a treatment method and developed from it the technique of **free association**. (Recall that in Chapter 1 we noted that Freud's intended meaning was free intrusion or invasion, not free association.)

**Free association:** A psychotherapeutic technique in which the patient says whatever comes to mind.

In free association, the patient lies on a couch and is encouraged to talk openly and spontaneously, giving complete expression to every idea, no matter how embarrassing, unimportant, or foolish it may seem. Freud's goal in his system of psychoanalysis was to bring into conscious awareness repressed memories or thoughts, which were assumed to be the source of the patient's abnormal behavior. Freud believed there was nothing random about the material that invaded the patient's mind, to be revealed during the free-association sessions. The experiences thus recounted were predetermined and could not be censored by the patient's conscious choice. The nature of the patient's conflict forced this material to intrude on the patient's consciousness so that it had to be expressed to the therapist.

Through the free-association technique, Freud found that his patients' memories reached back to childhood, and that many of the repressed experiences they recalled concerned sexual issues. Already sensitive to sexual factors as potential causes of emotional distress and aware of current writings on sexual pathology, Freud began to pay increasing attention to the sexual material revealed in his patients' narratives. By 1898, he was convinced that "the most immediate and, for practical purposes, the most significant causes of neurotic illness are to be found in factors arising from sexual life" (quoted in Breger, 2000, p. 117).

## Studies on Hysteria

In 1895, Freud and Breuer published *Studies on Hysteria,* the book considered to mark the formal beginning of psychoanalysis, although Freud did not use the word "psychoanalysis" until a year later (Rosenzweig, 1992). The book contained papers by both authors and several case histories, including that of Anna O. It received some negative reviews but was largely praised in scientific and literary journals throughout Europe as a valuable contribution to the field. It was a firm but modest beginning of the recognition Freud desired, even though the book sold only 626 copies over the next 13 years (Makari, 2008).

Breuer had been reluctant to publish, as they had argued about Freud's conviction that sex was the sole cause of neurotic behavior. Breuer agreed that sexual factors were important, but he was not persuaded that they were the only explanation. He told Freud there was not enough evidence on which to base that conclusion. Although they decided to proceed with publication, the controversy led to a rift in their friendship.

Freud believed that he was right and that there was no need for him to accumulate additional data to support his position. One reason why he was unwilling to wait for more research support, however, was that the delay might allow someone else to publish the idea and claim priority. Freud's ambition for success may have taken precedence over scientific caution about rushing into print based on insufficient evidence.

Breuer found Freud's dogmatic attitude about his work disturbing, and within a few years the break between them was complete. Freud was embittered. He did, however, later give Breuer credit in print for his pioneering work on the treatment of hysteria, and by the time Breuer died in 1925, more than two decades later, Freud had mellowed. He wrote a sensitive obituary, acknowledging his mentor's accomplishments. He also sent a letter of condolence to Breuer's son, noting the "magnificent part played by your late father in the creation of our new science" (quoted in Hirschmüller, 1989, p. 321).

## The Childhood Seduction Controversy

As we have seen, Freud had no doubt that sex played the determining role in neurosis. He had observed that most of his women patients reported traumatic sexual experiences in childhood, often involving family members. He also came to believe that neurotic conditions could not arise in a person who led a normal sex life.

In a paper presented to the Viennese Society of Psychiatry and Neurology in 1896, Freud reported that, using material uncovered in his free-association technique, his patients revealed childhood seductions, with the seducer usually being an older relative, often the father. Further, Freud asserted that these seduction traumas were the cause of adult neurotic behavior. His patients were hesitant about describing details of the seduction experience, as though the events were somehow unreal or had never really occurred. Patients spoke haltingly, suggesting they could not fully recall the experiences.

The group received Freud's paper with skepticism. Krafft-Ebing, the society's president, said it sounded like a "scientific fairy tale" (quoted in Jones, 1953, p. 263). Freud said his critics were asses and could go to hell. It has generally been thought that the negative response to Freud's paper was based on the audience's shock and anger at his contention that sexual abuse in childhood occurred so frequently. A contemporary Freud scholar has argued otherwise, that the "opposition to the seduction theory claim was based either on a belief in the predominantly constitutional [somatic] bases of nervous disorder or, more often, on the grounds that findings obtained by means of Freud's clinical procedures were unreliable" (Esterson, 2002, pp. 117–118). Whatever the most valid explanation may be, the fact remains that the paper was far from a success for the ambitious Freud.

About a year later, Freud reversed his position. At that point he claimed that in most cases the childhood seduction experiences his patients described were not real; they had not actually happened. At first the awareness that his patients were reporting fantasies instead of facts came as a shock to Freud because his theory of neurosis was based on his belief that the patients had experienced childhood sexual trauma that accounted for their irrational behavior as adults. On reflection, however, Freud decided that the patients' fantasies were quite real to them. Because the fantasies focused on sex, then sex remained the root of the problem. By this reasoning, Freud preserved the basic idea of sex as the cause of neurosis.

Nearly a century later, in 1984, a psychoanalyst who had briefly been director of the Freud Archives, Jeffrey Masson, asserted that Freud lied about the reality of his patients' childhood sexual experiences. Masson claimed that the sexual abuses reported by Freud's patients had indeed occurred, and that Freud deliberately decided to call these seductions fantasies to make his system more acceptable to colleagues and to the public (Masson, 1984). Most reputable scholars denounced Masson's charges, arguing that his evidence was unconvincing (see Gay, 1988; Krüll, 1986; Malcolm, 1984), and the dispute received nationwide media coverage.

In a *Washington Post* newspaper interview (February 19, 1984), the eminent Freud scholars Paul Roazen and Peter Gay described Masson's theory as a hoax and a slander, "a severe distortion of the history of psychoanalysis." We must note that Freud never abandoned his belief that childhood sexual abuse sometimes happened; what he revised was his view that the experiences reported by his patients had *always* happened. It was, Freud wrote, "hardly credible that perverted acts against children were so general" (Freud, 1954, pp. 215–216).

Later evidence indicates that childhood sexual abuse is far more common than Freud may have been prepared to accept. One writer noted that the "actual occurrence of father-daughter incest is higher than the professional literature has been generally willing to acknowledge" (Lerman, 1986, p. 65). This awareness led some psychoanalysts to suggest that Freud's original conception of the seduction theory as an explanation for neurosis may have been correct. We do not know whether Freud actively suppressed the truth, as Masson claimed, or whether he genuinely came to believe his patients were reporting fantasies.

In the 1930s, Sandor Ferenczi, a disciple of Freud, decided that symptoms of the Oedipus complex reported by his patients resulted from real acts of sexual abuse and not from fantasies. When he described his findings at a psychoanalytic congress in 1932, Freud tried to prevent him from speaking. When that failed, Freud led the opposition to Ferenczi's position.

Another reason why Freud may have come to oppose the original seduction theory was that if it were true, then all fathers, including his own, could be judged guilty of perverse acts against their children (Krüll, 1986).

## Freud's Sex Life

Regardless of the ultimate judgment on the seduction theory, Freud himself held a negative attitude toward sex and experienced personal sexual difficulties. He wrote of the dangers of sexuality (even among people who were not neurotic) and argued that people should strive to rise above this "common animal need." He considered the sex act degrading, arguing that it contaminated mind and body. At the age of 41, he gave up sex. "Sexual excitation is of no more use to a person like me" (Freud, 1954, p. 227). He had occasionally experienced impotence and sometimes abstained from sex because he disliked condoms and coitus interruptus, the standard birth control methods.

Freud blamed his wife for ending their sex life, and he interpreted some of his dreams as depicting his resentment toward her for forcing him to give up sex. A biographer wrote, "He felt resentful because she became pregnant so easily, because she often became ill during her pregnancies, and because she refused to engage in any kind of sexual activity beyond [procreative acts]" (Elms, 1994, p. 45). Freud's conflicts about sex apparently led to an attraction to and fascination with beautiful women, who seemed to gravitate to his circle of disciples. A friend commented that among Freud's students "there were so many attractive women that it began to look like more than a matter of chance" (Roazen, 1993, p. 138).

Freud soon became a textbook example of his theory. His sexual frustrations surfaced in the form of neuroses. He described a major neurotic episode that occurred the year he gave up sex as involving "odd states of mind not intelligible to consciousness—cloudy thoughts and veiled doubts, with barely here and there a ray of light.... I do not know what has been happening to me" (Freud, 1954, pp. 210–212). His troubling physical symptoms included migraine headaches, urinary problems, and spastic colon. He worried about dying, feared for his heart, and became anxious about travel and open spaces.

His self-diagnosis was anxiety neurosis and neurasthenia resulting from the accumulation of sexual tension. He had previously concluded that male neurasthenia resulted from masturbation and that anxiety neurosis was linked to abnormal practices such as *coitus interruptus* and abstinence. By so labeling his symptoms, "his personal life was thus deeply involved in this particular theory, since with its help he was trying to interpret and solve his own problems. ... Freud's theory of actual neurosis is thus a theory of his own neurotic symptoms" (Krüll, 1986, pp. 14, 20). Recognizing that he needed psychoanalysis, Freud proceeded to analyze himself. The method he chose was the analysis of his dreams.

## Dream Analysis

**Dream analysis:** A psychotherapeutic technique involving the interpretation of dreams to uncover unconscious conflicts.

Freud had learned that a patient's dreams could be a rich source of significant emotional material and could contain clues to the underlying causes of a disturbance. Because of his positivist belief that everything had a cause, he assumed that dream events could not be completely without meaning and that they most likely result from something in the patient's unconscious mind. Freud realized that he could not analyze himself with the free-association technique, being patient and therapist at the same time, so he decided to analyze his dreams. On awakening each morning, he conducted a personal **dream analysis**. He wrote down the dream stories from the night before and then free-associated to the material.

Through dream exploration, Freud realized the considerable hostility he felt toward his father. He recalled for the first time his childhood sexual longings for his mother and dreamed of sexual wishes toward his eldest daughter. This intense exploration of his unconscious became the basis of his theory. Thus, much of his psychoanalytic system was formulated from analyzing his own neurotic episodes and childhood experiences. He perceptively observed, "The most important patient for me was my own person" (quoted in Gay, 1988, p. 96).

Freud's self-analysis continued for about two years, culminating in the publication of *The Interpretation of Dreams* (1900), now considered his major work. He later said that the book contained "the most valuable of all the discoveries it has been my good fortune to make" (quoted in Forrester, 1998). He outlined for the first time the Oedipus complex, drawing largely on his childhood experiences. Although not universally praised, the book drew much favorable comment. Professional journals reviewed it, as did magazines and newspapers in Vienna, Berlin, and other European cities. In Zurich, Carl Jung read it and became a convert to psychoanalysis.

Freud adopted dream analysis as a standard psychoanalytic technique and devoted the last half-hour of each day to analyzing his dreams. It is interesting that of the more than 40 of his own dreams Freud described in the book, few had any sexual content, despite his assertion that dreams typically involve infantile sexual wishes. The significant theme in Freud's dreams was ambition, a personal trait he denied (Welsh, 1994).

## The Pinnacle of Success

Freud continued to write and publish his ideas.

> From 1900 on, he turned out a major essay or book-length work at the rate of at least one a year. It is hard to be ignored when one is so prolific, when one applies a comprehensive theory to subject matter as diverse as human sexuality, creativity, destructiveness, loss, guilt, anxiety, and the tendency to repeat traumatic experiences. (Messer & McWilliams, 2003, p. 76)

**Freudian slip:** An act of forgetting or a lapse in speech that reflects unconscious motives or anxieties.

In 1901, he published *The Psychopathology of Everyday Life,* which contains a description of the famous **Freudian slip**. Freud's term in German was *Fehlleistung,* which means a blunder or a faulty performance. The term "Freudian slip" did not become popular until the 1950s (Erard, 207).

Freud suggested that in everyday behavior, unconscious ideas struggling for expression affect our thoughts and actions. What might seem a casual slip of the tongue or act of forgetting is actually a reflection of real, though unacknowledged, motives.

*Three Essays on the Theory of Sexuality* appeared in 1905. Three years earlier, some students had urged Freud to conduct a weekly discussion group on psychoanalysis. It has been reported that the topic of their first meeting was the psychology of cigar making (Kerr, 1993). These early disciples included Jung and Adler, who later developed important systems in opposition to Freud, but most were considered "marginal neurotics" (Gardner, 1993, p. 51). Anna Freud called them "the odd ones, the dreamers, and those who knew neurotic suffering from their own experience" (quoted in Coles, 1998, p. 144). One of the group's members, Herbert Nunberg, recalled that "they discussed not only the problems of others, but also their own difficulties; they revealed their inner conflicts, confessed their masturbation, their fantasies and reminiscences concerning their parents, friends, wives, and children" (quoted in Breger, 2000, p. 178).

As with the breakdown of the relationship between Freud and Breuer, Freud tolerated no disagreement about the role of sexuality in his theory. Disciples or students who would not accept this premise or sought to change it were excommunicated. Freud wrote, "Psychoanalysis is my creation; for ten years I was the only person who concerned himself with it. No one can know better than I do what psychoanalysis is" (Freud, 1914, p. 7). Even a loyal and devoted follower noted that "Freud was not merely the father of psychoanalysis, but also its tyrant!" (Sadger, 2005, p. 40).

During the years from 1900 to 1910, Freud's status improved. His private practice was thriving, and colleagues paid attention to his pronouncements. In 1909, he and Jung were invited by G. Stanley Hall to speak at the twentieth anniversary of Clark University in Massachusetts. Freud delivered lectures and received an honorary doctorate in psychology. "Perhaps the person most profoundly affected by Freud's lectures was Freud himself. Here, to an audience far, far superior to any he had ever commanded in Europe, he proposed himself as a scientist and a therapist who had made important empirical discoveries, and they responded with adulation" (Kerr, 1993, pp. 243–244).

Freud met prominent American psychologists such as James, Titchener, and Cattell. Freud's lectures were published in the *American Journal of Psychology* and translated into several languages (Freud, 1909/1910). The American Psychoanalytic Association (APA) discussed his work at its annual convention. The APA was founded in 1911, followed by psychoanalytic societies in New York, Boston, Chicago, and Washington, D.C.

Freud's concept of the unconscious mind also received an enthusiastic reception from the American public. People were already interested in the idea, thanks to the writings of Canadian psychologist H. Addington Bruce. Between 1903 and 1917, Bruce wrote 63 magazine articles and seven books about the unconscious, helping to stimulate public interest (Dennis, 1991).

Although Freud was widely welcomed and honored on the trip, he retained many unfavorable impressions. He criticized the quality of American cooking, the scarcity of public toilets, the difficulty of the language, and the informality of manners. He was offended when a tour guide at Niagara Falls referred to him as "the old fellow." He told a biographer, "America is a mistake; a gigantic mistake, it is true, but nonetheless a mistake" (Jones, 1955, p. 60). The passage of time did not modify his opinion. Fourteen years after his visit to the United States, he was asked why he seemed to hate it. He said, "I don't hate America. I regret it! I regret that Columbus ever discovered it!" (quoted in Rabkin, 1990, p. 34). In fairness let us note that Freud also claimed to dislike Vienna, where he lived for nearly 80 years.

The official psychoanalytic family soon became torn as discord and dissension arose about certain of Freud's ideas. The situation frequently led to defections. Freud's break with Adler came in 1911 and three years later with Jung, whom Freud once considered his spiritual son and heir to psychoanalysis. Freud was furious. At a family dinner party he complained of their disloyalty. His aunt remarked, "The trouble with you, Sigi, is that you just don't understand people" (quoted in Hilgard, 1987, p. 641).

At Clark University, 1909. Seated, from left: Sigmund Freud, G. Stanley Hall, Carl Jung. Standing, from left: A. A. Brill, Ernest Jones, Sandor Ferenczi.

In 1923, at the peak of his fame, Freud's mouth cancer was diagnosed. Over the next 16 years he suffered continuous pain and underwent 33 operations to remove portions of his palate and upper jaw. He received X-ray and radium treatments and had a vasectomy, which physicians believed would reverse the tumor's growth. The artificial device made necessary by his mouth surgery affected his speech so that it was often difficult to understand him. Although he continued to see patients and disciples, he shunned other personal contacts. He did not stop his habit of smoking 20 cigars a day, however, even after the illness was diagnosed.

After Hitler came to power in Germany, the official Nazi position on psychoanalysis was made clear: Freud's books were publicly burned at a Berlin rally in May 1933. As the volumes were flung onto the bonfire, a Nazi leader shouted, "Against the soul-destroying overestimation of the sex life—and on behalf of the nobility of the human soul—I offer to the flames the writings of one Sigmund Freud!" (quoted in Schur, 1972, p. 446). Freud commented, "What progress we are making. In the Middle Ages they would have burnt me; nowadays they are content with burning my books" (quoted in Jones, 1957, p. 182).

By 1934, the more farsighted Jewish psychologists and psychoanalysts had emigrated. The Nazi campaign to eradicate psychoanalysis in Germany was effective; knowledge of Freud, once so widespread, was almost obliterated. A student at the Institute for Psychological Research and Psychotherapy, established by the Nazis in Berlin, recalled that "Freud's name was never mentioned, and his books were kept in a locked bookcase" (*The New York Times,* July 3, 1984). Many important psychoanalytic books remain unavailable in the German language.

Despite the dangers, Freud insisted on remaining in Vienna. In March 1938, German troops were welcomed into Austria, and shortly thereafter a gang of Nazis invaded his home. A week later, his daughter Anna was arrested and detained. This last act finally persuaded Freud to leave the country for his own safety. Partly through the intervention of the U.S. government, the Nazis agreed to let Freud go to England (see Cohen, 2010). Four of his sisters remained in Vienna and died in Nazi concentration camps.

To secure an exit visa, Freud had to sign a document attesting to his considerate, respectful treatment by the Gestapo (the secret police). He signed the form and supposedly added the sarcastic comment, "I can heartily recommend the Gestapo to anyone" (quoted in Jones, 1957, p. 226). So noted Ernest Jones, Freud's friend and biographer, who presumably related the incident as Freud told it. More recently discovered data of history—the original document that Freud signed—reveal no such comment (Decker, 1991). Nevertheless, the original, now discredited, version continues to appear in print.

Although Freud was welcomed in England, his health was deteriorating and he was unable to enjoy his last year. In his diary and in letters to friends, he wrote about the pain from the spreading cancer. "I had to cancel my work for twelve days, and I lay with pain and hot-water bottles on the couch which is meant for others" (Freud, 1939/1992, p. 229). Nevertheless, he remained mentally alert and worked almost to the end.

Some years before, when he had selected Max Schur as his personal physician, Freud had made Schur promise not to let him suffer unnecessarily. On September 21, 1939, Freud reminded Schur of his vow. "You promised me then not to forsake me when my time comes. Now it's nothing but torture and makes no sense anymore" (quoted in Schur, 1972, p. 529). Schur wrote that he administered an overdose of morphine over a 24-hour period, thus bringing to an end Freud's many years of suffering.

In yet another example of the dynamic, ever-changing nature of history, this account of Freud's death, written by his personal physician, has been challenged. Intensive archival research has revealed that Schur was not present at Freud's death and that the final (and fatal) dose of morphine was administered by Josephine Stross, a retired physician and long-time friend of Anna Freud (Lacoursiere, 2008).

# IN THEIR OWN WORDS

### Original Source Material on Hysteria from Sigmund Freud's First Lecture at Clark University, September 9, 1909[1]

*In this excerpt from Freud's initial lecture at Clark University, he discusses the case of Anna O.*

————

Ladies and Gentlemen: It is a new and somewhat embarrassing experience for me to appear as lecturer before students of the New World. I assume that I owe this honor to the association of my name with the theme of psychoanalysis, and, consequently, it is of psychoanalysis that I shall aim to speak. I shall attempt to give you, in very brief form, an historical survey of the origin and further development of this new method of research and cure.

Granted that it is a merit to have created psychoanalysis, it is not my merit. I was a student, busy with the passing of my last examinations, when another physician of Vienna, Dr. Joseph Breuer, made the first application of this method to the case of an hysterical girl (1880–1882). We must now examine the history of this case and its treatment, which can be found in detail in *Studies on Hysteria,* later published by Dr. Breuer and myself....

Dr. Breuer's patient was a girl of 21, of a high degree of intelligence. She had developed, in the course of her two years' illness, a series of physical and mental disturbances which well deserved to be taken seriously. She had a severe paralysis of both right extremities, with anaesthesia, and at times the same affection of the members of the left side of the body; disturbance of eye-movements and much impairment of vision; difficulty in maintaining the position of the head; an intense *Tussis nervosa* [uncontrollable cough]; nausea when she attempted to take nourishment; and at one time, for several weeks, a loss of the power to drink in spite of tormenting thirst. Her power of speech was also diminished, and this progressed so far that she could neither speak nor understand her mother tongue; and, finally, she was subject to states of "absence," of confusion, delirium, alteration of her whole personality. These states will later claim our attention.

When one hears of such a case, one does not need to be a physician to incline to the opinion that we are concerned here with a serious injury, probably of the brain, for which there is little hope of cure and which will probably lead to the early death of the patient. The doctors will tell us, however, that in one type of case with just as unfavorable symptoms, another, far more favorable, opinion is justified. When one finds such a series of symptoms in the case of a young girl, whose vital organs (heart, kidneys) are shown by objective tests to be normal, but who has suffered from strong emotional disturbances, and when the symptoms differ in certain finer characteristics from what one might logically expect, in a case like this the doctors are not too much disturbed. They consider that there is present no organic lesion of the brain, but that enigmatical state, known since the time of the Greek physicians as *hysteria,* which can simulate a whole series of symptoms of various diseases. They consider, in such a case, that the life of the patient is not in danger and that a restoration to health will probably come about of itself.

The differentiation of such an hysteria from a severe organic lesion is not always very easy. But we do not need to know how a differential diagnosis of this kind is made; you may be sure that the case of Breuer's patient was such that no skillful physician could fail to diagnose an hysteria. We may also add a word here from the history of the case. The illness first appeared while the patient was caring for her father, whom she tenderly loved, during the severe illness which led to his death, a task which she was compelled to abandon because she herself fell ill....

It had been noticed that the patient, in her states of absence, of psychic alteration, usually mumbled several words to herself. These seemed to spring from associations with which her thoughts were busy. The doctor, who was able to get these words, put her in a sort of hypnosis and repeated them to her over and over, in order to bring up any associations that they might have. The patient yielded to his suggestion and reproduced for him those psychic creations which controlled her thoughts during her absences, and which betrayed themselves in these single spoken words. These were fancies [fantasies], deeply sad, often poetically beautiful—daydreams, we might call them—which commonly took as their starting point the situation of a girl beside the sickbed of her father. Whenever she had related a number of such fancies, she was, as it were, freed and restored to her normal mental life. This state of health would last for several hours, and then give place on the next day to a new absence, which was removed in the same way by relating the newly created fancies.

It was impossible not to get the impression that the psychic alteration which was expressed in the absence was a consequence of the excitations originating from these intensely emotional fancy-images. The patient herself, who at this time of her illness strangely enough understood and spoke only English, gave this new kind of treatment the name "talking cure," or jokingly designated it as "chimney sweeping."

The doctor soon hit upon the fact that, through such cleansing of the soul, more could be accomplished than a temporary removal of the constantly recurring mental clouds. Symptoms of the disease would disappear when in hypnosis the patient could be made to remember the situations, and the associative connections under which they first appeared, provided free vent was given to the emotions which they aroused.

There was in the summer a time of intense heat, and the patient had suffered very much from thirst, for, without any apparent reason, she had suddenly become unable to drink. She would take a glass of water in her hand, but as soon as it touched her lips, she would push it away, as though suffering from hydrophobia. Obviously for these few seconds she was in her absent state. She ate only fruit, melons and the like, in order to relieve this tormenting thirst. When this had been going on about six weeks, she was talking one day in hypnosis about her English governess, which she disliked, and finally told, with every sign of disgust, how she had come into the room of the governess, and how that lady's little dog, that she abhorred, had drunk out of a glass. Out of respect for the conventions, the patient had remained silent. Now, after she had given energetic expression to her restrained anger, she asked for a drink, drank a large quantity of water without trouble, and woke from hypnosis with the glass at her lips. The symptom there-upon vanished permanently.

Permit me to dwell for a moment on this experience. No one had ever cured an hysterical symptom by such means before, or had come so near understanding its cause. This would be a discovery [of great consequence] if the expectation could be confirmed that still other, perhaps the majority, of symptoms originated in this way and could be removed by the same method. Breuer spared no pains to convince himself of this and investigated the path-ogenesis of the other, more serious, symptoms in a more orderly way.

Such was indeed the case; almost all the symptoms originated in exactly this way, as remnants, as precipitates, if you like, of affectively toned experience, which for that rea-son we later call *psychic traumata*. The nature of the symptoms became clear through their relation to the scene which caused them. They were, to use the technical term, "de-termined" by the scene whose memory traces they embodied, and so could no longer be described as arbitrary or enigmatical functions of the neurosis.

Only one variation from what might be expected must be mentioned. It was not always a single experience which occasioned the symptom, but usually several; perhaps many similar repeated traumata cooperated in this effect. It was necessary to repeat the whole series of pathogenic memories in chronological sequence, and of course in reverse order, the last first, and the first last. It was quite impossible to reach the first and often most es-sential trauma directly, without first clearing away those coming later.

You will, of course, want to hear me speak of other examples of the causation of hysterical symptoms besides this inability to drink on account of the disgust caused by the dog drinking from the glass. I must, however, if I hold to my program, limit myself to very few examples. Breuer relates, for instance, that his patient's visual disturbances could be traced back to exter-nal causes in the following way: The patient, with tears in her eyes, was sitting by the sickbed when her father suddenly asked her what time it was. She could not see distinctly, strained her eyes to see, brought the watch near her eyes so that the dial seemed very large, or else she tried hard to suppress her tears so that the sick man might not see them.

All the pathogenic impressions sprang from the time when she shared in the care of her sick father. Once she was watching at night, in the greatest anxiety for the patient who was in a high fever, and in suspense, for a surgeon was expected from Vienna to operate on the patient. Her mother had gone out for a little while, and Anna sat by the sickbed, her right arm hanging over the back of her chair. She fell into a reverie and saw a black snake emerge, as it were, from the wall, and approach the sick man as though to bite him. (It is very probable that several snakes had actually been seen in the meadow behind the house, that she had already been frightened by them, and that these former experiences furnished the material for the hallucination.)

She tried to drive off the creature but was as though paralyzed. Her right arm, which was hanging over the back of the chair, had "gone to sleep," become anaesthetic and paretic [numb and tingling], and as she was looking at it, the fingers changed into little snakes with death's heads [the fingernails]. Probably she attempted to drive away the snake with her paralyzed right hand, and so the anaesthesia and paralysis of this mem-ber formed associations with the snake hallucination. When this had vanished, she tried in her anguish to speak, but could not. She could not express herself in any language, until finally she thought of the words of an English nursery song, and thereafter she could think and speak only in this language. When the memory of this scene was revived in hypnosis, the paralysis of the right arm, which had existed since the beginning of the illness, was cured, and the treatment ended.

When, a number of years later, I began to use Breuer's researches and treatment on my own patients, my experiences completely coincided with his. . . .

Ladies and Gentlemen: If you will permit me to generalize, as is indispensable in so brief a presentation, we may express our results up to this point in the formula: *Our hys-terical patients suffer from reminiscences.* Their symptoms are the remnants and the memory-symbols of certain traumatic experiences.

# Psychoanalysis as a Method of Treatment

Freud found that the free-association method did not always operate freely. Sooner or later patients reached a point in their recollections where they were unable or unwilling to continue. Freud thought these **resistances** indicated that patients had brought into conscious awareness memories that were too shameful to be faced. Thus, the resistance was a kind of protection against the emotional pain. The mere presence of the pain, however, indicated that the analytic process was closing in on the source of the problem and that the analyst should continue to probe that line of thought.

Freud's discovery of his patients' resistances led him to formulate the fundamental principle of **repression**, which he described as the process of ejecting or excluding from consciousness any unacceptable ideas, memories, and desires, leaving them to operate instead in the unconscious. He wrote that the "essence of repression lies simply in turning something away, and keeping it at a distance, from the conscious." Further, he regarded repression as "the cornerstone on which the whole structure of psychoanalysis rests" (quoted in Boag, 2006, p. 74). Not only are unpleasant ideas or impulses pushed out of consciousness, but they are forcefully kept out. The therapist must help patients bring this repressed material back into awareness so that it can be confronted and dealt with.

Freud recognized that the effective treatment of neurotic patients depended on developing an intimate, personal relationship between patient and therapist. We noted earlier how Anna O.'s transference toward Breuer so disturbed him that he ended her therapy. To Freud, transference was a necessary part of the therapeutic process. A goal of therapy was to wean patients from this childlike dependency on the therapist and help them assume a more adult role in their own lives.

Another important treatment method in Freudian psychoanalysis is dream analysis. Freud believed that dreams represented the disguised satisfaction of repressed desires. The essence of a dream is the fulfillment of one's wishes. Dream events occur on two levels. The dream's manifest content is the patient's actual story, recalling the events of the dream. The dream's true significance lies in the latent content, the dream's hidden or symbolic meaning.

Freud believed that when patients describe dreams they are expressing their forbidden desires (the latent dream content) in symbolic form. Although many dream symbols can be linked only to the person reporting the dream, other symbols are believed to be common to all of us (see Table 13.1). Despite the apparent universality of these dream symbols, however, interpreting a particular dream for therapeutic purposes requires knowledge of the patient's specific conflicts.

Not all dreams are caused by emotional conflicts. Some dream stories arise from simpler stimuli such as the temperature of the bedroom, contact with one's partner, or overeating before bedtime. Recent research also indicates that dream content can be affected by exposure to electronic media such as the Internet, television, and videogames (Gackenbach, 2009). Therefore, not all dreams will contain repressed or symbolic material.

Despite the growing popularity of psychoanalysis for therapy, Freud had little personal interest in the potential treatment value of his system. His primary concern was not to cure people but to explain the dynamics of human behavior. He identified himself more as scientist than therapist and viewed the free-association and dream-analysis methods as research tools for collecting data for his case studies. To Freud, the fact that these techniques also had therapeutic application was secondary to their scientific use.

**Resistance:** A blockage or refusal to disclose painful memories during a free-association session.

**Repression:** The process of barring unacceptable ideas, memories, or desires from conscious awareness, leaving them to operate in the unconscious mind.

**TABLE 13.1 DREAM SYMBOLS OR EVENTS AND THEIR LATENT PSYCHOANALYTIC MEANING**

| SYMBOL | INTERPRETATION |
|---|---|
| Smooth-fronted house | Male body |
| House with ledges, balconies | Female body |
| King and queen | Parents |
| Small animals | Children |
| Children | Genital organs |
| Playing with children | Masturbation |
| Baldness, tooth extraction | Castration |
| Elongated objects (e.g., tree trunks, umbrellas, neckties, snakes, candles) | Male genitals |
| Enclosed spaces (e.g., boxes, ovens, closets, caves, pockets) | Female genitals |
| Climbing stairs or ladders; driving cars; riding horses; crossing bridges | Sexual intercourse |
| Bathing | Birth |
| Beginning a journey | Dying |
| Being naked in a crowd | Desiring to be noticed |
| Flying | Desiring to be admired |
| Falling | Desiring to return to a state (such as childhood) where one is satisfied and protected |

Perhaps because of his relative lack of interest in treating patients, Freud has been described as an impersonal, even indifferent, therapist. He placed his chair at the head of the psychoanalytic couch because he did not want patients to stare at him. Sometimes he fell asleep during analytic sessions. He admitted, "I lack that passion for helping" (quoted in Jones, 1955, p. 446). His passion was for the research on which he built his theory to explain the functioning of the human personality.

One of Freud's American patients recalled that Freud's dog, a chow named Jofi, participated in his therapy sessions. When Jofi scratched at the door to be let out, Freud would say, "Jofi doesn't approve of what you're saying." When Jofi later scratched at the door to be let back in, Freud would say, "Jofi wanted to give you another chance." Once when the patient became very emotional, Jofi jumped on him. Freud said, "You see? Jofi is so excited that you've been able to discover the source of your anxiety" (quoted in Grinker, 2001, p. 39).

Freud's system differed greatly in content and methodology from the traditional experimental psychology of his time. Despite his scientific training, we have seen that Freud did not use experimental research methods, relying on free association, dream analysis, and the compilation of case histories. He did not collect data from controlled experiments or use statistics to analyze his results. Although he had little faith in the formal experimental approach, he insisted that his work was scientific and that case histories and his self-analysis provided ample support for his conclusions. Freud wrote:

*When I set myself the task of bringing to light what human beings keep hidden within them, not by the compelling power of hypnosis, but by observing what they say and what they show, I thought the task was a harder one than it really is. He that has eyes to see and ears to hear may convince himself that no mortal can keep a secret. If the lips are silent, he chatters with his fingertips; betrayal oozes out of him at every pore. And thus the task of making conscious the most hidden recesses of the mind is one which it is quite possible to accomplish. (Freud, 1901, pp. 77–78)*

Freud formulated, revised, and extended his ideas in terms of the evidence as he alone interpreted it. His own critical abilities were his most important guide in the construction of his theory. He insisted that only psychoanalysts who used his methods were qualified to judge the scientific worth of his work. He ignored criticism from others, particularly from those unsympathetic to psychoanalysis. Psychoanalysis was his system, and his alone.

# Psychoanalysis as a System of Personality

Freud's system did not deal with all those topics typically included in the psychology textbooks of his time, but he did explore areas other psychologists tended to ignore: unconscious motivating forces, conflicts among those forces, and the effects of the conflicts on behavior.

## Instincts

**Instincts:** To Freud, mental representations of internal stimuli (such as hunger) that motivate personality and behavior.

**Instincts** are the propelling or motivating forces of the personality, the biological forces that release mental energy. Although the word "instinct" has become accepted usage in the English language, it does not convey Freud's intention. He did not use the German equivalent, *Instinkt,* when referring to the human personality, only when describing innate drives in animals. Freud's term for human motivating forces was *Trieb,* best translated as impulse or driving force (Bettelheim, 1982). Freudian instincts are not inherited predispositions—the usual meaning of *instinct*—but rather refer to sources of stimulation within the body. The goal of instincts is to remove or reduce that stimulation through some behavior, such as eating, drinking, or sexual activity.

Freud did not attempt to offer a detailed list of every possible human instinct, but he grouped them in two general categories: the life instincts and the death instinct. Life instincts include hunger, thirst, and sex. They are concerned with self-preservation and the survival of the species and thus are the creative forces that sustain life. The form of energy through which life instincts are manifested is called **libido**. The death instinct is a destructive force that can be directed inward, as in masochism or suicide, or outward, as in hatred and aggression. As Freud grew older, he became convinced that aggression could be as powerful a motivator for human behavior as could sex.

**Libido:** To Freud, the psychic energy that drives a person toward pleasurable thoughts and behaviors.

He was aware of an aggressive tendency within himself. Colleagues described him as a good hater, and some of his writings indicate a high level of aggressiveness. The tendency can also be detected in the bitterness and finality of his breaks with dissenters within the psychoanalytic movement.

The concept of aggression as a motivator has been far better received by psychoanalysts than the suggestion of a death instinct. One analyst wrote that the death instinct should be "relegated to the dustbin of history" (Becker, 1973, p. 99). Another suggested that if Freud was a genius, then the death instinct was an instance of genius having a bad day (Eissler, 1971).

## Levels of Personality

In his early work Freud suggested that mental life consisted of two parts: conscious and unconscious. The conscious portion, like the visible part of an iceberg, is small and insignificant. It presents only the surface; that is, only a superficial glimpse of the total personality. The vast and powerful unconscious—like the portion of the iceberg that exists beneath the water's surface—contains the instincts, those driving forces for all human behavior.

**Id:** The source of psychic energy and the aspect of personality allied with the instincts.

In later writings, Freud revised this simple conscious-unconscious distinction and proposed the id, ego, and superego. The **id**, which corresponds roughly to Freud's earlier notion of unconscious, is the most primitive and least accessible part of the personality. The id's powerful forces include the sex and aggressive instincts. Freud wrote, "We call it a cauldron full of seething excitations. [The id] knows no judgments of value, no good and evil, no morality" (Freud, 1933, p. 74). Id forces seek immediate satisfaction without regard for the circumstances of reality. They operate according to the pleasure principle, concerned with reducing tension by seeking pleasure and avoiding pain. Freud's word in German for the id was *es,* meaning "it," a term suggested by the psychoanalyst Georg Groddeck, who had sent Freud the manuscript of his book called *The Book of It* (Isbister, 1985).

The id contains our basic psychic energy, or libido, and is expressed through the reduction of tension. Increases in libidinal energy result in increased tension. And we then act in an attempt to reduce this tension to a more tolerable level. However, we must interact with the real world in order to satisfy our needs and maintain a comfortable level of tension. For example, people who are hungry must act to find food if they expect to discharge the tension induced by hunger. Therefore, some functional link between the id's demands and reality must be established.

**Ego:** The rational aspect of personality responsible for controlling the instincts.

The **ego** serves as the mediator between the id and the circumstances of the external world to facilitate their interaction. The ego represents reason or rationality, in contrast to the unthinking, insistent passions of the id. Freud called the ego *ich,* which translates into English as "I." He did not like the word *ego* and rarely used it. Whereas the id craves blindly and is unaware of reality, the ego is aware of reality, manipulates it, and regulates the id accordingly. The ego follows the reality principle, holding off the id's pleasure-seeking demands until an appropriate object can be found to satisfy the need and reduce the tension.

The ego does not exist independently of the id; indeed, the ego derives its power from the id. The ego exists to help the id and is constantly striving to bring about satisfaction of the id's instincts. Freud compared the interaction of ego and id to a rider on a horse. The horse supplies the energy to move the rider along the trail, but the horse's power must be guided or reined in or else the horse may balk and throw the rider. Similarly, the id must be guided and checked or it will overthrow the rational ego.

**Superego:** The moral aspect of personality derived from internalizing parental and societal values and standards.

The third part of Freud's structure of personality, the **superego**, develops early in life when the child assimilates the rules of conduct taught by parents or caregivers through a system of rewards and punishments. Behaviors that are wrong and bring punishment become part of the child's conscience, one part of the superego. Behaviors that are acceptable to the parents or social group and that bring rewards become part of the ego-ideal, the other part of the superego. Thus, childhood behavior is initially controlled by parental actions, but once the superego has formed behavior is determined by self-control. At that point, the person administers his or her own rewards and punishments. Freud's term for the superego was a word he coined, *über-ich,* meaning, literally, "above I."

The superego represents morality. Freud described it as the "advocate of a striving toward perfection—it is, in short, as much as we have been able to grasp psychologically of what is described as the higher side of human life" (Freud, 1933, p. 67). You can see that obviously the superego will be in conflict with the id. Unlike the ego, which attempts to postpone id satisfaction to more appropriate times and places, the superego will attempt to inhibit id satisfaction completely.

Thus, Freud envisioned a continuous struggle within the personality as the ego is pressured by insistent and opposing forces. The ego must try to delay the id's sexual and aggressive urges, perceive and manipulate reality to relieve the resulting tension, and cope with the superego's demands for perfection. The ego is thus pressured on three sides, threatened by persistent dangers from the id, reality, and the superego. When the ego becomes too severely stressed, the inevitable result is the development of anxiety.

## Anxiety

Anxiety functions as a warning that the ego is being threatened. Freud described three types of anxiety. Objective anxiety arises from fear of actual dangers in the real world. Neurotic anxiety and moral anxiety, the other two types, derive from objective anxiety.

Neurotic anxiety comes from recognizing the potential dangers inherent in gratifying the id instincts; it is not fear of the instincts themselves but fear of the punishment likely to follow any indiscriminate, id-dominated behavior. In other words, neurotic anxiety is a fear of being punished for expressing impulsive desires.

Moral anxiety arises from fear of one's conscience. When we perform, or even think of performing, some action contrary to our conscience's moral values, we are likely to experience guilt or shame. Our resulting level of moral anxiety depends on how well developed our conscience is. Less virtuous people experience less moral anxiety.

Anxiety induces tension, which motivates the individual to take some action to reduce it. According to Freud's theory, the ego develops protective defenses—the so-called **defense mechanisms**—which are unconscious denials or distortions of reality. Some of these defense mechanisms are described in Table 13.2.

**Defense mechanisms:** Behaviors that represent unconscious denials or distortions of reality but which are adopted to protect the ego against anxiety.

## Psychosexual Stages of Personality Development

Freud was convinced that his patients' neurotic disturbances originated in their childhood experiences. Thus, he became one of the first theorists to emphasize the importance of child development. He believed that the adult personality was formed almost completely by age five.

### TABLE 13.2 FREUDIAN DEFENSE MECHANISMS

**Denial**

Denying the existence of an external threat or traumatic event; for example, a person living with a terminal illness may deny the imminence of death.

**Displacement**

Shifting id impulses from a threatening or unavailable object to an object that is available, such as replacing hostility toward one's boss with hostility toward one's child.

**Projection**

Attributing a disturbing impulse to someone else, such as saying you do not really hate your professor but that he or she hates you.

**Rationalization**

Reinterpreting behavior to make it more acceptable and less threatening, such as saying the job from which you were fired was not really a good job anyway.

**Reaction formation**

Expressing an id impulse that is the opposite of the one that is driving the person. For example, someone disturbed by sexual longings may become a crusader against pornography.

**Regression**

Retreating to an earlier, less frustrating period of life and displaying the childish and dependent behaviors characteristic of that more secure time.

**Repression**

Denying the existence of something that causes anxiety, such as involuntarily removing from consciousness some memory or perception that brings discomfort.

**Sublimation**

Altering or displacing id impulses by diverting instinctual energy into socially acceptable behaviors, such as diverting sexual energy into artistically creative behaviors.

**Psychosexual stages:**
In psychoanalytic theory, the developmental stages of childhood centering on erogenous zones.

According to his psychoanalytic theory of development, children pass through a series of **psychosexual stages**. During this time, children are considered to be autoerotic; that is, they derive sensual pleasure from stimulating the body's erogenous zones or being stimulated by parents in normal caregiving activities. Each developmental stage centers on a specific erogenous zone.

The oral stage lasts from birth into the second year of life. During this stage, stimulation of the mouth, such as sucking, biting, and swallowing, is the primary source of sensual satisfaction. Inadequate satisfaction (too little or too much) may produce an oral personality type, a person preoccupied with mouth habits such as smoking, kissing, and eating. Freud believed that a wide range of adult behaviors, from excessive optimism to sarcasm and cynicism, could be attributed to events of the oral stage of development.

In the anal stage, gratification shifts from the mouth to the anus, and children derive pleasure from the anal area of the body. This stage coincides with toilet training. Children may expel or withhold feces. Either situation shows a defiance of parental wishes. Conflicts during this period can produce an anal-expulsive adult, who is dirty, wasteful, and extravagant, or an anal-retentive adult, who is excessively neat, clean, and compulsive.

**Oedipus complex:** At ages four to five, the unconscious desire of a boy for his mother and the desire to replace or destroy his father.

During the phallic stage, which occurs around age four, erotic satisfaction involves sexual fantasies and fondling and exhibiting of the genitals. The **Oedipus complex** occurs during this stage. Freud named the complex after the Greek legend in which Oedipus unknowingly kills his father and marries his mother. Freud suggested that children become sexually attracted to the parent of the opposite sex and fearful of the parent of the same sex, who is perceived as a rival. His childhood experiences supported this idea. He wrote, "I have found love of the mother and jealousy of the father in my own case too" (Freud, 1954, p. 223).

Usually, children overcome the Oedipus complex by identifying with the parent of the same sex. In addition, they replace their sexual longing for the parent of the opposite sex with a more socially acceptable kind of affection. However, the attitudes toward the opposite sex that develop during this stage will persist, influencing adult relationships with members of the opposite sex. One outcome of identifying with the parent of the same sex is in terms of the superego's development. By adopting the mannerisms and attitudes of the same-sex parent, children assume the parent's superego standards.

Children who outlast the struggles of these early stages enter a period of latency from about age five to age 12, when the onset of puberty signals the beginning of the genital stage. At that time heterosexual behavior becomes important and the person begins to prepare for marriage and parenthood.

## Mechanism and Determinism in Freud's System

We saw that the structural psychologists, and later the behaviorists, considered humans to be like machines. First the human mind and then human behavior were reduced to their most elemental components. It may come as a surprise to learn that Freud, who approached human nature from such a different perspective, was also influenced by mechanistic ideas. No less vigorously than the experimental psychologists, Freud believed that all mental events, even dreams, are predetermined; nothing occurs by chance or free will. Every action has a conscious or unconscious motive or cause. Further, Freud accepted the doctrine that all phenomena could be reduced to the principles of the natural sciences. By adopting the word "analysis" as part of his system of psychoanalysis, Freud was acknowledging the analytical methods then used in physics and chemistry (Haynal, 1993).

In 1895, Freud decided to develop his conception of a scientific psychology, attempting to show that psychology must be rooted in the principles of physics and that mental

Freud works in his Vienna study in 1937. He is surrounded by his collection of Greek, Roman, and Egyptian antiquities.

phenomena exhibit many of the characteristics of the neurophysiological processes on which they are based. Psychology's aim would be to "represent [mental] processes as quantitatively determined states of specifiable material particles" (Freud, 1895, p. 359). He never completed the project, but we see in his later writings the ideas and terminology he adopted from physics, especially mechanics, electricity, and hydraulics. His writings along these lines provide another instance of data lost to history because they were not uncovered for more than 50 years. Until then, no one knew Freud had considered such an approach to psychology.

Although Freud modified his intention to model psychology after physics when he found that his chosen subject matter—the human personality—could not be treated by physical and chemical techniques, he remained true to the positivism and determinism that nurtured experimental psychology. In addition, although Freud was influenced by this view, he was not constrained by it. He altered or discarded the philosophy in areas where he saw it would not fit. In the end, he demonstrated how restricting a mechanistic conception of human nature could be.

## Relations Between Psychoanalysis and Psychology

Psychoanalysis developed outside of mainstream academic psychology and remained so for many years. "Academic psychology largely closed its doors to psychoanalytic doctrine. An unsigned editorial in a 1924 issue of the *Journal of Abnormal Psychology* bemoaned the endless stream of writings on the unconscious by European psychologists" (Fuller, 1986, p. 123). The editorial dismissed those writings as essentially worthless. Following that strong statement, few articles on psychoanalysis were accepted for professional publication, a prohibition that continued for at least 20 years.

Many academic psychologists offered forceful criticisms of psychoanalysis. In 1916, when virtually everything German was considered suspect because of Germany's wartime aggression, Christine Ladd-Franklin wrote that psychoanalysis was a product of the "undeveloped German mind." Robert Woodworth, at Columbia University, called psychoanalysis an "uncanny religion" that led rational people to draw absurd conclusions. John B. Watson called it "voodooism" (all quoted in Hornstein, 1992, pp. 255, 256). James McKeen Cattell, who was vehemently opposed to psychoanalysis, described Freud as a man who "lives in the fairyland of dreams among the ogres of perverted sex" (quoted in Fancher, 2000, p. 1027).

Despite these and other scathing attacks by the leaders of American psychology, some of Freud's ideas made their way into American psychology textbooks. By the 1920s, defense mechanisms were being discussed seriously, along with the concept of the unconscious mind and the manifest and latent contents of dreams (Popplestone & McPherson, 1994). Still, behaviorism remained the dominant school of thought in psychology, and psychoanalysis was generally ignored.

But by the 1930s and 1940s, psychoanalysis had captured public attention. The combination of sex, violence, and hidden motives, and the promise to cure a variety of emotional problems, proved almost irresistible to the general public. The academic psychology establishment, however, was furious! People were confusing psychoanalysis and psychology, making the assumption that the two fields were the same. Psychologists hated the thought that sex, dreams, and neuroses were all that psychology was about. Historians noted, "It had become clear to psychologists by the 1930s that psychoanalysis was not a passing craze but a serious competitor which threatened the foundations of scientific psychology, at least in the minds of the public" (Morawski & Hornstein, 1991, p. 114).

To deal with this threat, psychologists resolved to apply the experimental method to test psychoanalysis in order to determine its scientific legitimacy. Hundreds of studies later, psychologists declared that psychoanalysis was inferior to a psychology based on experimentation, at least in the eyes of the experimental psychologists. Although the design of many of these studies was questionable, psychologists believed that the results restored their position of primacy. In addition, their research showed that academic psychology could be relevant to the public interest because it was studying the same things as the psychoanalysts (Hornstein, 1992).

The 1950s and 1960s found behaviorists translating psychoanalytic terminology into the language of behavior. Watson set the pace earlier when he defined emotions as merely sets of habits and described neurotic behavior as the result of faulty conditioning. Skinner recast the Freudian defense mechanisms in the language of operant conditioning.

Eventually psychology incorporated many Freudian concepts and made them part of the mainstream. The role of the unconscious, the importance of childhood experiences, and the operation of the defense mechanisms are a few examples of psychoanalytic ideas that are firmly part of contemporary psychology.

## The Scientific Validation of Psychoanalytic Concepts

As we noted, in the 1930s and 1940s many Freudian concepts were submitted to experimental tests with questionable results. In later years, research of greater validity was performed. An analysis of 2,500 studies from psychiatry, psychology, anthropology, and other disciplines examined the scientific credibility of Freud's formulations (Fisher & Greenberg, 1977, 1996).

Although some concepts resisted attempts at scientific validation (id, ego, superego, death wish, libido, and anxiety), others were found to be amenable to scientific testing. The analysis showed that published studies provide some support for the following:

**1.** Some characteristics of the oral and anal personality types
**2.** Castration anxiety

3. The notion that dreams reflect emotional concerns
4. Aspects of the Oedipus complex in boys (rivalry with the father and sexual fantasies about the mother)

Freudian concepts that were tested but *not* supported by the experimental results include the following:

1. Dreams satisfy symbolically repressed wishes and desires.
2. In resolving the Oedipus complex, boys identify with the father and accept his superego standards out of fear.
3. Women have an inferior conception of their bodies, have less severe superego standards than men, and find it more difficult to achieve an identity.
4. Personality is formed by age five and changes little after that.

More recent research shows strong support for the influence of unconscious processes on thoughts, emotions, and behavior, suggesting that unconscious influences may be more pervasive than Freud claimed (see, for example, Bornstein & Masling, 1998; Custers & Aarts, 2010; Scott & Dienes, 2010; Winkielman, Berridge, & Wilbarger, 2005). As one researcher noted, "today there is agreement that much [psychological] functioning occurs in opposition to what is consciously desired" (Pervin, 2003, p. 225). We shall see in Chapter 15 that cognitive psychology has readmitted the study of unconscious mental processes.

Research also supports the defense mechanisms of repression, denial, identification, projection, and displacement. Experiments on the so-called Freudian slip have shown that at least some of these verbal misstatements appear to be just what Freud said they were: unconscious conflicts and anxieties revealing themselves in embarrassing ways.

The most important point about scientific attempts to analyze Freudian principles is the finding that at least some psychoanalytic concepts can be reduced to propositions that can be tested by the methods of science.

## Criticisms of Psychoanalysis

Freud's methods of collecting data have been the target of considerable criticism. He drew insights and conclusions from the responses of his patients while they were undergoing analysis. Consider the deficiencies of this approach when compared with the experimental method of systematic data collection under controlled conditions of observation used by the other schools of thought.

First, the conditions under which Freud collected data were unsystematic and uncontrolled. He did not make a verbatim transcript of each patient's words but worked from notes made several hours after seeing the patient. "I write them down from memory in the evening after work is done" (quoted in Grubrich-Simitis, 1993, p. 20). Some original data (the patient's words) were surely lost in the time that elapsed because of the vagaries of memory and the possibility of distortions and omissions. Thus, the data consist of only what Freud remembered.

Second, while recalling his patients' words Freud may have reinterpreted them, guided by a desire to find supportive material. He may have recalled and recorded only what he wanted to hear. Of course it is also possible that Freud's notes were accurate, but the important point is that we cannot be certain because the original data have not survived.

Third, Freud may have inferred, rather than actually heard, the stories of sexual seduction in childhood based on his evaluation of the patient's symptoms. One writer suggested that although Freud claimed that almost all his female patients said they had been seduced by their fathers,

*... examination of the actual cases referred to by Freud reveals not a single instance in which this was the case. There is no evidence that any patient ever* told *Freud she had been seduced by her father. This is nothing more than an inference on Freud's part. (Kihlstrom, 1994, p. 683)*

Other critics contend that Freud may have used suggestion, or more coercive procedures, to elicit or implant such memories when no actual seduction had occurred (Powell & Boer, 1994; Showalter, 1997). Freud even acknowledged that seduction recollections may have been "fantasies which my patients had made up or which I myself had perhaps forced on them" (quoted in Webster, 1995, p. 210).

Fourth, Freud's research was based on a small and unrepresentative sample of people, limited to himself and those who chose to undergo psychoanalysis with him. No more than a dozen or so cases have been detailed in Freud's writings, and most of those patients were young, unmarried, educated, upper-class women. It is difficult to generalize from this limited sample to the general population.

Fifth, there are discrepancies between Freud's notes on the therapy sessions and the published case histories supposedly based on those notes. Researchers have found differences involving the length of the analysis and the sequence of events disclosed during analysis as well as unsubstantiated claims of cures (Eagle, 1988; Mahony, 1986). There is no way to determine whether Freud made these statements deliberately to provide support for his position or whether they resulted from forces in his own unconscious. Historians cannot attempt to trace errors in Freud's unpublished case studies because he destroyed most of the patient files. Also, Freud published only six case histories after his break with Breuer, and none provides compelling supportive evidence for psychoanalysis. A biographer concluded:

*Some of the cases present such dubious evidence in favor of psychoanalytic theory that one may seriously wonder why Freud even bothered to publish them. Two of the cases were incomplete and the therapy ineffective. A third case was not actually treated by Freud. (Sulloway, 1992, p. 160)*

Sixth, even if an accurate, word-for-word record of the therapy sessions had been kept, it would not always have been possible to confirm the accuracy of the patients' reports. Freud made limited attempts to verify his patients' reported accounts of their childhood experiences. Critics argue that he should have questioned relatives and friends about the events described. In summary, then, we must describe the first step in scientific theory building, that of data collection, as incomplete, imperfect, and inaccurate.

As for the next step, drawing inferences and generalizations from the data, we cannot assess how this was done because Freud never explained his reasoning. Because his data could not be quantified or analyzed statistically, historians cannot determine their reliability or statistical significance.

Scholars have challenged Freud's assumptions about women. He suggested that women have poorly developed superegos and inferiority feelings about their bodies because they lack a penis. The analyst Karen Horney (see Chapter 14) left Freud's psychoanalytic circle because of this issue and developed her own system, disagreeing that women have penis envy. She suggested instead that men have womb envy. Most analysts today believe Freud's ideas about female psychosexual development are unproven and incorrect. Chapter 14 describes the work of other theorists who disagreed with Freud's emphasis on biological forces, particularly sex, as determinants of personality. These theorists considered the impact of social forces on personality development.

Other neo-Freudians challenged Freud's denial of free will and his focus on past behavior while excluding future hopes and goals as motivating forces. Some criticized Freud for developing a personality theory based only on neurotics and ignoring the traits of emotionally healthy persons. All of these points were used to build competing views of the human personality. The rise of these alternative theories soon led to divisiveness within the psychoanalytic family and to the formalization of derivative analytic schools of thought, some of which are explored in Chapter 14.

## Contributions of Psychoanalysis

Why has psychoanalysis survived so long with all these strikes against it? To some extent all theories of behavior can be criticized on the grounds of scientific acceptability. Psychologists in search of a theory must sometimes select it on the basis of criteria other than formal scientific precision, and those who choose psychoanalysis do not do so in the absence of supporting evidence. Psychoanalysis does offer evidence, although not the kind usually accepted by science. Acceptance of psychoanalysis is based instead on an intuitive appearance of plausibility.

Freud, who had little confidence in traditional experimental methods, argued that his work *was* scientific and that he had amassed ample proof to support his conclusions. He also believed that the only people qualified to judge the scientific merit of his ideas were psychoanalysts like himself. He wrote that his system was based on "an incalculable number of observations and experiences, and only someone who has repeated those observations on himself and on others is in a position to arrive at a judgment of his own upon it" (Freud, 1940, p. 144).

Regardless of the scientific credibility of Freud's work, there is no denying the tremendous impact it has had on American academic psychology. Interest in Freud's ideas remains high. However, the popularity of psychoanalysis as therapy has declined when measured by the number of clients and by the number of people training to become analysts, even though some research supports the contention that psychodynamic psychotherapy, derived from Freudian ideas, can be successful (Engel, 2008; Shedler, 2010).

Expensive, long-term Freudian therapy has been superseded by briefer and less expensive psychotherapies (some of which derive from psychoanalysis) and by behavioral and cognitive therapies. This trend has been reinforced by the cost-cutting measures instituted by managed health care programs. It is far less expensive to prescribe a psychoactive drug in a single doctor's visit than a course of psychotherapy lasting several months. The number and variety of prescription antidepressant and antipsychotic medications have increased dramatically over the last 25 years (Carlat, 2010; Mojtabai & Olfson, 2010).

The development of various drug regimens has reduced the need for psychotherapies for certain types of mental disorders. The success of many drug therapies has led some psychiatrists and clinical psychologists to revise their thinking about the contributing factors to mental illness, away from the psychic school of thought and back to the somatic.

The somatic or biochemical approach holds that mental disorders result from chemical imbalances in the brain. Why prescribe expensive, time-consuming psychotherapies when the patient can pop a pill and feel better? Drug treatment, however, is not appropriate for all conditions or all patients. It is interesting that Freud long ago predicted this development in the treatment of mental disorders.

Freud's influence on American popular culture and consciousness has been enormous and was evident immediately after his 1909 visit to Clark University. Newspapers featured many stories about Freud, and by 1920 more than 200 books had been published on psychoanalysis (Abma, 2004). Magazines such as *Ladies Home Journal, The Nation,* and *The New Republic* ran feature stories. Dr. Benjamin Spock's phenomenally successful baby and child care books were based on Freud's teachings. A major movie studio, MGM, offered Freud $100,000 to collaborate on a film about love, but he refused. In October 1924, Freud appeared on the cover of *Time* magazine, and his work on dreams had become so well known by that time that a popular song was written about it. One line was "Don't tell me what you dream'd last night/For I've been reading Freud!" (quoted in Fancher, 2000, p. 1026).

In 2005, the British Broadcasting Company produced a four-hour television documentary about Freud's influence in Western society. "The Century of the Self" showed how his theories affected marketing and advertising, political campaigning, and public relations, particularly as developed in the United States by his nephew, Edward Bernays (Held, 2009; Stevens, 2005). As noted, this public enthusiasm for Freud's ideas occurred much sooner than his acceptance by academic psychology.

The twentieth century saw a loosening of sexual restraints in behavior, the arts, literature, and entertainment. It has become widely believed that inhibiting or repressing sexual impulses can be harmful. But it is ironic that Freud's message about sex has been so misinterpreted. He never argued for weakening sexual codes of conduct or for increased sexual freedom. Rather, his view was that inhibiting the sex drive was necessary for the survival of civilization. Despite his intention, however, the degree of sexual liberation that marked much of the twentieth century was partly a result of Freud's work because his emphasis on sex helped popularize his ideas. Even in scientific journals, articles about sex attract attention. The 1998 Library of Congress exhibition, "Sigmund Freud: Conflict and Culture," reinforced the impact of his work on popular culture.

We must conclude, then, that despite its lack of scientific rigor and its methodological weaknesses, Freudian psychoanalysis became a vital force in modern psychology. Freud remains the most frequently cited individual in the psychology research literature, according to published citation indexes (see, for example, Fancher, 2000; Haagbloom et al., 2002). The Division of Psychoanalysis (Division 39) is the sixth largest of all the APA's divisions.

"When *Time* magazine put Freud on its cover in April 1956 [for the second time], the psychoanalytic movement in America had arrived, and for the next several decades psychoanalysts largely dominated the mental health field" (Stossel, 2008, p. 16). Now, well into the twenty-first century, Freud's influence even beyond psychology remains vital and strong. In 2008, an American psychologist surveyed the textbooks used in college-level American history courses and found that all of them mentioned Freud's visit to the United States 100 years before (Burnham, 2009).

In 1929, E. G. Boring wrote in his textbook, *A History of Experimental Psychology,* that psychology had no truly great proponent of the stature of Darwin or Helmholtz. In his second edition, published 21 years later, Boring revised his opinion. Reflecting the developments in psychology during the intervening decades, he wrote of Freud with admiration:

> *Now he is seen as the greatest originator of all, the agent of the Zeitgeist who accomplished the invasion of psychology by the principle of the unconscious process.... It is not likely that the history of psychology can be written in the next three centuries without mention of Freud's name and still claim to be a general history of psychology. And there you have the best criterion of greatness: posthumous fame. (Boring, 1950, pp. 743, 707)*

# Discussion Questions

1. According to Freud, what were the three great shocks in history that were delivered to the collective human ego?
2. Define repression, instinct, id, ego, and superego. What are the life instincts and the death instinct?
3. Describe the historical development of psychoanalysis relative to the other schools of thought in psychology.
4. Describe the psychosexual stages of development.
5. Describe the results of attempts to test Freudian concepts experimentally.
6. Describe the theories of the unconscious developed by Leibnitz and Herbart.
7. Discuss the influences of evolutionary theory and of the notion of mechanism on the development of psychoanalysis.
8. Discuss two major sources of influence on the psychoanalytic movement.
9. Do you believe that Freud was correct when he included himself in the list of the three people who changed the world?
10. How did Freud attempt to explain mental processes in mechanistic and deterministic terms?
11. How were mentally ill persons dealt with before the time of Freud?

12. In what ways do Freud's proposed levels of personality differ from one another? Why are they so often in conflict?

13. In what ways was Freud influenced by Mesmer and by Charcot?

14. In what ways was psychoanalysis influenced by Freud's own childhood experiences and by his own views on sexuality?

15. What criticisms have been made of Freud's methods for collecting data? How did Freud believe his concepts should be tested?

16. What, in general, has been the impact of psychoanalysis on psychology and on popular culture?

17. What is the relationship between psychoanalysis and mainstream academic psychology?

18. What is the therapeutic significance of free association, of resistances, and of repression?

19. What was the controversy about Freud's view of childhood seduction experiences?

20. What was the Emmanuel Movement? How did it influence the acceptance of psychoanalysis in the United States?

21. What was the role of the unconscious in structuralism, functionalism, and behaviorism?

22. Why was the case of Anna O. of such importance in Freud's thinking?

CHAPTER **14**

# Psychoanalysis: After the Founding

## When Life Hands You Lemons...

The lonely little boy saw two stray kittens and gathered them up in his arms. He needed something to love, something to feel close to. He brought them home, but his mother snatched them from him. She smashed them against a wall, head first, repeatedly, until they were dead. He should have known she would do something like that.

Abraham Maslow never loved his mother, certainly not the way Freud said all little boys did. There was no Oedipus complex in store for him. On the contrary, his passionate, deep-seated hatred for his mother helped determine the direction of his life's work.

As one of seven children born to poor Russian immigrant parents living in a Brooklyn, New York, tenement apartment, Maslow had a nightmarish childhood. He later told an interviewer, "With my childhood, it's a wonder I'm not psychotic" (quoted in Hall, 1968, p. 37). "My family was a miserable family and my mother was a horrible creature" (quoted in Hoffman, 1996, p. 2).

He grew up isolated, unloved, and unwanted. He had no friends, and his father was of little help. Distant and aloof, Maslow's father frequently abandoned the family and was known for drinking, fighting, and womanizing. Maslow described feelings of anger and hostility toward his father, but his relationship with his mother was far worse. She openly rejected him in favor of his younger brothers and sisters. She frequently punished him harshly for the slightest misdeed, warning that God would also punish him for his behavior. He never forgave her for the way she treated him. When she died, he refused to attend the funeral.

The relationship with his mother affected not only his emotional life but also his work in psychology. "The whole thrust of my life-philosophy," he told a biographer, "and all my research and theorizing, has its roots in a hatred for and revulsion against everything she stood for" (quoted in Hoffman, 1988, p. 9).

As a teenager he faced other problems. Convinced he was ugly because of a prominent nose, he also felt inferior because of his scrawny build. His parents taunted him about his appearance and frequently remarked on how unattractive and awkward he was. "I was all alone in the world. I felt peculiar. This was really in my blood, a very profound feeling that somehow I was wrong. Never any feelings that I was superior. Just one big aching inferiority complex" (quoted in Milton, 2002, p. 42).

Maslow hoped to compensate for his feelings of inferiority by becoming an athlete, thinking this might bring recognition and acceptance. When he failed at sports, however, he turned to books. The local library became his solitary playground, and reading and education provided the path that would take him out of his isolation.

His years of study brought him in contact with the major schools of psychological thought, from Titchener to Freud, and out of these differing definitions of psychology Maslow fashioned his own way of studying human nature. In maturity, his ideas brought him the acceptance, admiration, and adulation he had lacked as a child.

# Competing Factions

As with Wundt and his experimental psychology, Freud did not long enjoy a monopoly on his new system of psychoanalysis. Barely 20 years after he founded the movement, it splintered into competing factions led by analysts who disagreed on basic points. Freud did not react well to these dissenters. Analysts who espoused new positions were scorned. No matter how close they may have been to Freud personally and professionally, once they abandoned his teachings, he cast them out and never spoke to them again.

We begin with two analysts who did not disagree totally with Freud's basic views; they built upon and expanded his work. These include his daughter Anna and the object relations theorist Melanie Klein. We then discuss the three most prominent dissenters, who developed their own theories during Freud's lifetime: Carl Jung, Alfred Adler, and Karen Horney. Next we describe the humanistic psychology movement that developed in the 1960s, many years after Freud's death. Two major theorists, Abraham Maslow and Carl Rogers, aspired to replace psychoanalysis (as well as behaviorism) with their own views of human nature. A contemporary derivative and expansion of humanistic psychology is today's positive psychology, which applies the experimental method to the study of human strengths. Keep in mind that no matter how far these and other theorists diverged from Freud's teachings, they all derived their ideas from his work, either by elaborating on it or opposing it.

# The Neo-Freudians and Ego Psychology

As we noted, not all theorists and practitioners who followed Freud in the psychoanalytic tradition felt the need to abandon or overthrow his system. There remained a sizable group of neo-Freudian analysts who adhered to the central premises of psychoanalysis but nevertheless modified the system. The major change these loyalists introduced was an expansion of the concept of the ego. Rather than being the servant of the id, the ego was seen as having a more extensive role.

Ego psychology included the ideas that the ego was more independent of the id, possessed its own energy not derived from the id, and had functions separate from the id. Neo-Freudian analysts also suggested that the ego was free of the conflict produced when id impulses pressed for satisfaction. In Freud's view, the ego was forever responsive to the id, never free of its demands. In the revised view, the ego could function independently of the id, which was a significant departure from orthodox Freudian thought.

Another change introduced by neo-Freudians was to place less emphasis on biological forces as influences on personality. Instead, more credit was given to the impact of social and psychological forces. Neo-Freudians also minimized the importance of infantile sexuality and the Oedipus complex, suggesting that personality development was determined primarily by psychosocial rather than psychosexual forces. Thus, social interactions in childhood assumed greater importance than real or imagined sexual interactions.

# Anna Freud (1895–1982)

Sigmund Freud's daughter Anna was a leader of neo-Freudian ego psychology. The youngest of six children, Anna Freud wrote that she would never have been born if a safe form of contraception had been available to her parents. Her father announced the birth with more resignation than enthusiasm in a letter to a friend, commenting that had the infant been a boy, he would have sent the news by telegram (Young-Bruehl, 1988). Yet the year of Anna's birth (1895) was symbolic, perhaps prophetic, because it coincided with the birth of psychoanalysis. Anna would be the only Freud child to follow her father's path and become an analyst.

ANNA FREUD

As the least-favored girl in the family, Anna had an unhappy childhood. She recalled feeling bored and lonely and being left out of activities by the older ones. She was jealous of her sister Sophie, their mother's pet. Anna became her father's favorite; he became "as addicted to his youngest daughter as he was to his cigars" (Appignanesi & Forrester, 1992, p. 277).

At the age of 14 she became interested in Sigmund Freud's work. She would sit unobtrusively in a corner at meetings of the Vienna Psychoanalytic Society, absorbing everything that was said. At 22, driven by the emotional attachment to her father and concern about her sexuality, Anna entered into analysis with him. She reported violent dreams involving shooting, killing, dying, and defending him from enemies. The analysis, which was long kept secret, lasted four years, with sessions six nights a week beginning at 10 PM. Freud was later criticized for attempting to analyze his daughter.

The situation was called "impossible and incestuous," "a momentous and bizarre event," and an "Oedipal acting-in at both ends of the couch" (quoted in Mahony, 1992, p. 307). At the time, however, there seemed to them no other course to take. One historian wrote, "No one else would presume to undertake the task, for Anna's analysis would inevitably call into question Freud's role as her father" (Donaldson, 1996, p. 167). For another analyst to hear intimate details about life with the father of psychoanalysis was unthinkable.

In 1924 Anna read her first scholarly paper to the Vienna Psychoanalytic Society. Titled "Beating Fantasies and Daydreams," it was allegedly based on a patient's case history but was actually about her own fantasies. She described dreams involving beating, masturbation, and an incestuous father-daughter love relationship. The paper was well received by Freud and his colleagues and earned her admission into the society.

Freud was ambivalent about Anna becoming a psychoanalyst, and she experienced an identity crisis about the situation that lasted some six years. At age 30, having rejected offers of courtship from several of her father's younger disciples and family friends, she finally made the decision to become an analyst. She also settled into a long-term friendship with an American heiress, Dorothy Tiffany Burlingham, and became like a second mother to Dorothy's children.

Freud was reported to have been "troubled to learn that Anna had finally decided against getting married and having her own children, and furthermore that she was developing an intense emotional relationship with a woman" (Elms, 2001, p. 88). However, Anna Freud's biographer argued persuasively that the relationship was strictly emotional, not sexual (see Young-Bruehl, 1988).

Anna Freud devoted her life to the development and extension of psychoanalytic theory and its application to the treatment of emotionally disturbed children. Her only other focus was the care of her father during his long illness. When he died, she kept his overcoat in her closet. Several years after he died she reported a series of dreams about him. She wrote:

> *He is here again. All of these recent dreams have the same character: the main role is played not by my longing for him but rather his longing for me. In the first dream of this kind, he openly said: "I have always longed for you so" (quoted in Zaretsky, 2004, p. 263).*

More than 40 years later, as Anna was near death herself, a friend accompanied her to the park and watched as "the diminutive figure of Anna Freud, now as small as a schoolgirl, sat [in her wheelchair] wrapped inside her father's big wool coat" (Webster, 1995, p. 434).

## Child Analysis

In 1927, Anna Freud published *Introduction to the Technique of Child Analysis,* which foretold the direction of her interests. She developed an approach to psychoanalytic therapy with children that took into account their relative immaturity and the level of their verbal skills. Although Sigmund Freud had not treated children in his private practice, he took pride in Anna's work. He wrote, "Anna's views on child analysis are independent of mine; I share her views, but she has developed them out of her own independent experience" (quoted in Viner, 1996, p. 9).

Her innovations included the use of play materials and the observation of the child in the home setting. Most of her observations were carried out in London, where the Freud family settled in 1938 after fleeing Vienna and the Nazis. She opened a clinic next door to her father's house and there established a treatment center and psychoanalytic training institute that attracted clinical psychologists from throughout the world. The Anna Freud Centre in London continues her work today. Her studies were reported in annual volumes of *The Psychoanalytic Study of the Child*, which began publication in 1945. Her collected works were cumulated in eight volumes published between 1965 and 1981.

Anna Freud revised orthodox psychoanalytic theory to expand the role of the ego functioning independently of the id. In *The Ego and the Mechanisms of Defense* (1936), she clarified the defense mechanisms as they operate to protect the ego from anxiety. The standard list of Freudian defense mechanisms (see Table 13.2 in Chapter 13) was substantially her work. She gave the mechanisms more precise definition and contributed examples from her analyses of children.

### Comment

Ego psychology, as developed by Anna Freud and others, became the primary American form of psychoanalysis from the 1940s to the early 1970s. One goal of the neo-Freudians was to make psychoanalysis an accepted part of scientific psychology. "They did so by translating, simplifying, and operationally defining Freudian notions, by encouraging the experimental investigation of psychoanalytic hypotheses, and by modifying psychoanalytic psychotherapy" (Steele, 1985, p. 222). In the process, the neo-Freudians fostered a more conciliatory relationship between psychoanalysis and academic experimental psychology.

## Object Relations Theories: Melanie Klein (1882–1960)

Freud used the word "object" to refer to any person, object, or activity that can satisfy an instinct. In his view, the first object in an infant's life that can gratify an instinct is the mother's breast. Later, the mother as a person becomes an instinct-gratifying object. As the child grows, other people also become instinct-gratifying objects.

Object relations theories focus on the interpersonal relationships with these objects, whereas Freud focused more on the instinctual drives themselves. Thus, object relations theorists emphasize the social and environmental influences on personality, particularly within the mother-child interaction. They also believe that personality is formed in infancy by the nature of that relationship, at an earlier age than Freud proposed.

Object relations theorists argue that the most crucial issues in personality development are the increasing ability and need of the child, over time, to break free from the primary object (the mother) in order to establish a strong sense of self and to develop relations with other objects (people). We briefly consider the work of object relations theorist Melanie Klein.

Melanie Klein knew the importance of parent-child relations from her own experiences as a child and a parent. An unwanted child, she suffered from lifelong depression because of her feeling that her parents had rejected her. She became estranged from her own adult daughter (who later became an analyst). The daughter accused Klein of interfering in her life and maintained that her brother, who died while mountain climbing, had actually committed suicide because of his poor relationship with their mother.

Klein's object relations theory focused on the intense emotional bond between mother and child, particularly during the first six months of a child's life. She described the connection between infant and mother in social and cognitive terms rather than sexual terms. Klein suggested that the mother's breast is the first part-object for a baby, who judges it as either good or bad, depending on whether it has satisfied an id instinct. Thus, the infant's environment, as defined and represented by this good or bad part-object, is perceived as either satisfying or hostile. As the infant's world expands, he or she relates to whole objects (the mother as a person, for example), instead of part-objects, and defines those whole objects the same way he or she had defined the breast; that is, as satisfying or hostile. The initial social interaction between infant and mother generalizes to all objects (people) in the child's life, and in this manner the adult personality is rooted in the nature of the relationship of the first six months of life.

# Carl Jung (1875–1961)

Freud once regarded Carl Jung as a surrogate son and heir to the psychoanalytic movement, calling him "my successor and crown prince" (quoted in McGuire, 1974, p. 218). After their friendship disintegrated in 1914, Jung developed his **analytical psychology**, which opposed much of Freud's work.

### Jung's Life

Jung grew up in a small village in northern Switzerland near the famous Rhine Falls. By his own account, his childhood was lonely, isolated, and unhappy (see Jung, 1961). His father, a clergyman who had apparently lost his faith, was moody, irritable, and given to loud rages. "Carl heard everything," a biographer noted, "as his father's anger resonated throughout the house" (Bair, 2003, p. 20). His mother suffered from emotional disorders. Her behavior was erratic, and she could change in an instant from a happy housewife to a mumbling, incoherent demon. Another biographer suggested that the "whole maternal side of the family appeared to be tainted with insanity" (Ellenberger, 1978, p. 149).

Jung learned at an early age not to trust or confide in either parent and, by extension, not to trust the rest of the world. He turned away from the conscious world of reason and ventured inward to the world of his dreams, visions, and fantasies, the world of his unconscious. This became his guide in childhood and remained so through his adult life. More than 50 years later a neighbor of the Jung family, recalling the first time he had met the boy Carl, wrote, "I had never come across such an asocial monster before" (quoted in Bair, 2003, p. 23).

At critical times Jung resolved problems and made decisions based on what his unconscious told him through his dreams. When he was ready to enter college, his major field was revealed in a dream. He saw himself unearthing bones of prehistoric animals deep beneath the earth's surface. He interpreted this to mean he should study nature and science. A memory from age three, when he dreamed he was in an underground cavern, foretold his future study of personality. Jung would focus on the unconscious forces that lie beneath the surface of the mind.

Jung attended the University of Basel, Switzerland, and graduated in 1900 with a medical degree. He was interested in psychiatry, and his first professional appointment was at a mental hospital in Zurich. The director was Eugen Bleuler, a psychiatrist noted for work on schizophrenia. In 1905 Jung was appointed lecturer in psychiatry at the University of Zurich. Several years later, after marrying the second wealthiest heiress in

CARL JUNG

**Analytical psychology:**
Jung's theory of personality.

all of Switzerland, he was able to resign from the university to devote time to writing, research, and private practice.

In his work with patients, Jung did not adopt Freud's habit of asking them to lie on a couch; he said he had no wish to put his patients to bed. Jung and the patient sat opposite each other in comfortable chairs. Occasionally he held therapy sessions aboard his sailboat, happily racing across the lake in a high wind. Sometimes he sang to his patients. At other times he was deliberately rude. When one patient appeared at the appointed time, Jung said, "Oh no. I can't stand the sight of another one. Just go home and cure yourself today" (quoted in Brome, 1981, p. 185).

Jung became interested in Freud's work in 1900 when he read *The Interpretation of Dreams*, which he considered a masterpiece. By 1906 the two men had begun to correspond, and a year later Jung traveled to Vienna to visit Freud. Their initial meeting lasted 13 hours, an exciting beginning for what would become an intimate, father-son relationship. (Freud was almost 20 years older than Jung.)

Their closeness may have contained elements of the Oedipus complex, as proposed by Freud in his psychoanalytic theory, with the inevitable desire of the son to destroy the father. Another complicating factor that may have doomed the relationship was a sexual experience Jung reported having had at age 18. A family friend, whom Jung saw as a father figure, had made unwanted sexual advances. Jung was repelled and immediately ended that relationship. Years later, when Freud attempted to ensure that Jung would carry on the psychoanalytic movement as Freud envisioned it, Jung rebelled against the burden, perhaps feeling once again that an older man was trying to dominate him. In both instances, Jung was disappointed in his chosen father figure. Perhaps because of the earlier incident, he was unable to sustain the close emotional relationship Freud desired (Alexander, 1994; Elms, 1994).

Unlike most of the psychoanalytic disciples, Jung had already established a professional reputation before becoming associated with Freud. He was the best known of the early converts to psychoanalysis. As a result, he may have been less impressionable and suggestible than younger analysts who joined Freud's psychoanalytic family, many of whom were still in medical school or graduate school and unsure of their professional identity.

Although for a time Jung identified himself as a disciple of Freud's, he was never an uncritical one. Early in their relationship, he did attempt to suppress his doubts and objections. While writing *The Psychology of the Unconscious* (1912), he reported that he was troubled, realizing that when the book was published, publicly setting forth his own position that differed significantly from orthodox psychoanalysis, it would damage his standing with Freud. For months Jung was unable to proceed with the project, so disturbed was he about Freud's potential reaction. Of course he did eventually publish and the inevitable occurred.

In 1911, at Freud's insistence and despite opposition from the Viennese members, Jung became the first president of the International Psychoanalytic Association. Freud believed that anti-Semitism would impede the growth of psychoanalysis if the group's president was Jewish. The Viennese analysts, almost all of whom were Jewish, resented and distrusted the Swiss-born Jung, who so obviously was Freud's favorite. They not only had seniority in the movement but they also believed that Jung held anti-Semitic views. Shortly thereafter, Jung's friendship with Freud began to show signs of strain, and by 1912 they had terminated their personal correspondence. In 1914, Jung resigned and withdrew from the association.

When Jung was 38 years old he was stricken with intense emotional problems that persisted for three years; Freud had experienced a similar period of turmoil at the same stage of life. Believing he was going insane, Jung felt unable to do any intellectual work or even read a scientific book. He considered suicide and kept a gun next to his bed "in case he felt he had passed beyond the point of no return" (Noll, 1994, p. 207).

During those years he was haunted by visions of a bloody apocalypse and wide-spread carnage and desolation. He meticulously recorded these dreams in calligraphy and elaborate drawings in some 200 pages of what became known as *The Red Book.* This journal was kept secret in a Swiss bank vault and was not published until 2009, nearly 50 years after his death (see Harrison, 2009). Jung's visions came to him in a seemingly endless stream, which he described as a feeling like rocks tumbling down on his head. "I often had to cling to the table," he said, "so as not to fall apart" (quoted in Corbett, 2009, p. 36). It is interesting, however, that during this crisis Jung did not stop treating his patients.

He resolved his dilemma in essentially the same way Freud did, by confronting his unconscious mind. Although he did not analyze his dreams systematically, as Freud had done, Jung followed his unconscious impulses as revealed in dreams and fantasies. As with Freud, this period became a time of immense creativity for Jung and led him to formulate his personality theory. He wrote, "The years when I was pursuing my inner images were the most important in my life—in them everything essential was decided" (Jung, 1961, p. 199). He concluded, based on this experience, that the most important stage in personality development was not childhood, as Freud believed, but middle age, the time of his own crisis.

Even though Jung's personal crisis was apparently resolved by his confrontation with his unconscious, some aspects of his behavior remained unusual. Each morning he would speak to his kitchen utensils: "Greetings to you" he would say to frying pans, or "Good morning to you" to the coffee pot (Bair, 2003, p. 568). He hid large amounts of cash inside books and stuffed in jars that he buried in the garden, and he promptly forgot the secret codes he had devised to remind him where the jars were hidden. Nevertheless, Jung remained highly productive and continued to write and develop his system for most of his 86 years.

## Analytical Psychology

Jung's life experiences undoubtedly influenced his analytical psychology. We mentioned that his acceptance of the forces of his own unconscious mind foretold his later professional interests. Autobiographical evidence is also strong with regard to his views on sex. Jung's theory had no place for an Oedipus complex; it simply was not relevant to his childhood. He thought his mother was fat and unattractive, and he never understood Freud's insistence that little boys develop sexual longings for their mothers.

Jung developed no adult insecurities, inhibitions, or anxieties about sex, as Freud surely did. Further, Jung made no attempt to limit his sexual activities, as Freud had. Jung preferred the company of women to men and surrounded himself with adoring female patients and disciples. When they inevitably developed a crush, he did not hesitate to begin a sexual liaison, some of which endured for years. He even warned his female disciples that sooner or later they would fall in love with him (Noll, 1997). An analysis of the ill-fated relationship between Freud and Jung noted, "To Jung, who freely and frequently satisfied his sexual needs, sex played a minimal role in human motivation. To Freud, beset by frustrations and anxious about his thwarted desires, sex played the central role" (Schultz, 1990, p. 148).

As a child, Jung isolated himself from the company of other children, preferring a solitary existence. This choice is also reflected in his theory and in its focus on inner growth instead of social relationships. In contrast, Freud's theory is more concerned with interpersonal relationships; Freud did not have such an isolated and introverted childhood.

Another point of difference between Jung's analytical psychology and Freud's psychoanalysis concerns libido. Whereas Freud defined libido largely in sexual terms, Jung regarded it as a generalized life energy of which sex was only a part. For Jung, basic libidinal energy expressed itself in growth, reproduction, and other activities, depending on what was crucial for an individual at any given time.

Still another difference between the work of Jung and Freud is the direction of the forces that affect personality. Freud described people as victims of childhood events; Jung believed we are shaped not only by the past but also by our goals, hopes, and aspirations. To Jung, personality was not fully determined by experiences during the first five years of childhood but could be changed throughout one's lifetime.

Also, Jung attempted to probe more deeply than Freud into the unconscious mind. He added a new dimension, the collective unconscious, which he described as the inherited experiences of the human species and their animal ancestors.

## The Collective Unconscious

Jung described two levels of the unconscious mind. Beneath our conscious awareness is the **personal unconscious**, which contains memories, impulses, wishes, faint perceptions, and other experiences in a person's life that have been suppressed or forgotten. This level of unconsciousness is not very deep. Incidents from the personal unconscious can easily be recalled to conscious awareness.

The experiences in the personal unconscious are grouped into complexes, which are patterns of emotions and memories with common themes. A person will manifest a complex by a preoccupation with some idea (such as power or inferiority) that then influences his or her behavior. Thus, a complex is essentially a smaller personality within the total personality. At a level below the personal unconscious is the **collective unconscious**, unknown to the individual. It contains the cumulated experiences of previous generations, including our animal ancestors. These universal, evolutionary experiences form the basis of personality.

Remember that the experiences within the collective unconscious are unconscious. We are not aware of them, nor do we remember or have images of them, as we do of experiences within the personal unconscious.

## Archetypes

Inherited tendencies called **archetypes** within the collective unconscious are innate determinants of mental life that dispose a person to behave not unlike ancestors who confronted similar situations. We typically experience archetypes in the form of emotions associated with significant life events such as birth, adolescence, marriage, and death or with reactions to extreme danger. Jung referred to archetypes as the "gods" of the unconscious (Noll, 1997).

When Jung investigated the mythical and artistic creations of ancient civilizations, he discovered common archetypal symbols, even in cultures so widely separated in time and place that there was no possibility of direct influence. He also found what he considered traces of these symbols in dreams reported by his patients. All of this material supported his conception of the collective unconscious. The archetypes that occur most frequently are the persona, the anima and animus, the shadow, and the self.

The *persona* is the mask each of us wears when we come in contact with other people; the mask represents us as we want to appear to society. As such, the persona may not correspond to an individual's true personality. The notion of the persona is similar to the sociological concept of role-playing, in which we act as we think other people expect us to act in different situations.

The *anima* and *animus* archetypes reflect the idea that each person exhibits some of the characteristics of the other sex. The "anima" refers to feminine characteristics in man; the "animus" denotes masculine characteristics in woman. As with other archetypes, these

---

**Personal unconscious:** The reservoir of material that once was conscious but has been forgotten or suppressed.

**Collective unconscious:** The deepest level of the psyche; it contains inherited experiences of human and pre-human species.

**Archetypes:** Inherited tendencies within the collective unconscious that dispose a person to behave similarly to ancestors who confronted similar situations.

arise from the primitive past of the human species when men and women adopted behavioral and emotional tendencies of the other sex.

Our darker self, represented by the *shadow* archetype, is the animalistic part of personality. Jung considered it to be inherited from lower forms of life. The shadow contains immoral, passionate, and unacceptable desires and activities. The shadow urges us to do things we ordinarily would not allow ourselves to do. Once having done them, we are likely to insist that something came over us. That something is the shadow, the primitive part of our nature. There is also a positive side to the shadow, as it serves as a wellspring of spontaneity, creativity, insight, and deep emotion, all of which are necessary for complete human development.

Jung considered the *self* to be the most important archetype. Integrating and balancing all aspects of the unconscious, the self provides the personality with unity and stability. Jung likened it to a drive toward self-actualization, by which he meant harmony, completeness, and the full development of our abilities. However, he believed that self-actualization could not be attained until middle age (30–40), years he believed were crucial to personality development. This is a natural time of transition when the personality undergoes necessary and beneficial changes. Here we see another autobiographical element in Jung's theory; his middle years were when he achieved self-integration following the resolution of his neurotic crisis. As we noted, to Jung the significant stage in personality development was not childhood (as in Freud's life and system) but one's thirties and forties, the time of his own personal change.

## Introversion and Extraversion

Jung's concepts of introversion and extraversion are well known. The extravert directs libido (life energy) outside the self to external events and people. This type of person is strongly influenced by forces in the environment and is sociable and self-confident in a variety of situations. In contrast, the libido of the introvert is directed inward. Such a person is contemplative, introspective, and resistant to external influences. The introvert is likely to be less confident than the extravert in dealing with other people and situations.

These opposing attitudes exist in everyone to some degree, but one attitude is usually stronger than the other. No one is a complete extravert or introvert. The dominant attitude at any given time can be determined by circumstances. Frequently, introverted people become sociable and outgoing in situations that hold their interest.

## Psychological Types: The Functions and Attitudes

In Jung's theory, personality differences are expressed not only by the introversion or extraversion attitudes but also through four functions: thinking, feeling, sensing, and intuiting. These functions are ways in which we orient ourselves to the objective external world as well as to our subjective internal world.

- *Thinking is a conceptual process that provides meaning and understanding.*
- *Feeling is a subjective process of weighing and valuing.*
- *Sensing is the conscious perception of physical objects.*
- *Intuiting involves perceiving in an unconscious way.*

Jung labeled thinking and feeling as the rational modes of responding because they involve the cognitive processes of reason and judgment. Sensing and intuiting are considered non-rational because they do not involve the use of reason. Within each pair of functions, only one is dominant at a given time. The dominant functions combine with the dominant attitude of extraversion or introversion to produce the eight psychological types, such as the extraverted thinking type or the introverted intuiting type.

## Comment

Jung's ideas have influenced such diverse fields as religion, history, art, and literature. Historians, theologians, and writers acknowledge him as a source of inspiration. However, scientific psychology in general has ignored much of his analytical psychology. Many of his books were not translated into English until the 1960s, and his convoluted writing style and unsystematic organization impede the full understanding of his work.

Jung's disdain for traditional scientific methods repels many experimental psychologists, for whom Jung's mystical, religion-based theories hold even less appeal than Freud's. Further, the criticisms we noted about supporting evidence for Freudian psychoanalysis apply to Jung's work. Jung, too, relied on clinical observation and interpretation rather than controlled laboratory investigation.

However, some of Jung's work has had a lasting and continuing influence on psychology. The word-association test, for example, which Jung developed in the early 1900s, is now a standard laboratory and clinical tool in psychology. Jung's version of the test used a list of 100 stimulus words that he believed were capable of eliciting emotions. He measured the time it took for a patient to respond to each word as well as the person's physiological reactions to determine the emotional intensity of the stimulus words.

Jung's eight psychological types have stimulated considerable research. Noteworthy is the Myers-Briggs Type Indicator, a personality test designed to measure the psychological types. Constructed in the 1920s by Katharine Briggs and Isabel Briggs Myers, the test is widely used for research and applied purposes, especially employee selection and counseling. The introversion-extraversion formulation inspired English psychologist Hans Eysenck to develop the Maudsley Personality Inventory, a test to measure the two attitudes. Research using these tests has provided empirical support for these concepts and demonstrated that at least some Jungian notions are amenable to experimental testing. Indeed, Jung's concepts of introversion and extraversion are widely accepted in psychology today.

As with Freud's work, however, broader aspects of Jung's theory (i.e., complexes, archetypes, and the collective unconscious) resist attempts at scientific validation. The concept of self-actualization anticipated the work of Abraham Maslow and the humanistic psychologists. The notion of a midlife crisis has been embraced by Maslow and others and is accepted by many as a necessary stage of personality development. Its existence is supported by considerable research.

Formal training in Jungian analysis is available in a number of cities in Europe and the United States, including New York, San Francisco, and Los Angeles. The Society of Analytical Psychology publishes the Jungian *Journal of Analytical Psychology*.

# Social Psychological Theories: The Zeitgeist Strikes Again

We noted that Freud was influenced by the mechanistic and positivistic outlook of nineteenth-century science. Toward the end of that century, new disciplines were suggesting other ways to view human nature, ways that exceeded the boundaries of biology and physics. Research in anthropology, sociology, and social psychology supported the proposition that people are products of social forces and institutions and therefore should be studied in social rather than strictly biological terms. As anthropologists publicized their studies of various cultures, it became clear that some of the neurotic symptoms and taboos Freud described were not universal, as he proposed. For example, not all cultures had prohibitions against incest. Further, sociologists and social psychologists had learned that much human behavior stems from social conditioning rather than from actions taken to satisfy biological needs.

Thus, the Zeitgeist was calling for a revised conception of human nature, but Freud, to the dismay of some of his followers, clung to biological determinants of personality. Younger analysts, less constrained by tradition, drifted away from orthodox psychoanalysis to reshape Freudian theory in line with the then-current social science thought. Their focus, that personality is more a product of environment than of biological instincts, was compatible with American culture and thought and offered a more optimistic scenario than Freud's deterministic position.

We will discuss Alfred Adler and Karen Horney, two dissenters who believed that human behavior is determined not by biological forces but by the interpersonal relationships to which the person is exposed, particularly in childhood.

# Alfred Adler (1870–1937)

Because he broke with Freud in 1911, Adler is usually considered the first proponent of the social psychological approach to psychoanalysis. He developed a theory in which social interest plays a major role, and he is the only psychologist to have a string quartet named for him.

## Adler's Life

ALFRED ADLER

Adler was born to wealthy parents in a suburb of Vienna, Austria. His childhood was marked by illness, jealousy of an older brother, and rejection by his mother. He thought of himself as puny and unattractive. Adler felt closer to his father than to his mother. He later rejected the Freudian definition of the Oedipus complex perhaps because, as was true for Jung, it did not reflect his own childhood experiences. The young Adler worked intently to become popular with his peers and eventually achieved the self-esteem and acceptance he had not found within his family.

Initially Adler was a poor student, so inept that a teacher told his father that the only job the boy was fit for was shoemaker's apprentice. Through persistence and dedication Adler rose from the bottom to the top of his class. He strove academically and socially to overcome his handicaps and inferiorities, thus becoming an early example of his later theory of the necessity of compensating for one's weaknesses. Inferiority feelings, at the core of his system, are a direct reflection of his childhood, a debt Adler acknowledged. "Those who are familiar with my life work," he wrote, "will clearly see the accord existing between the facts of my childhood and the views I expressed" (quoted in Bottome, 1939, p. 9).

Adler recalled that at age four, recovering from a near-fatal bout of pneumonia, he resolved to become a physician. He pursued this goal, and in 1895 he received his medical degree from the University of Vienna. He specialized in ophthalmology and practiced general medicine. When he became interested in psychiatry in 1902, he joined Sigmund Freud's weekly discussion group on psychoanalysis, one of four charter members. Although he worked closely with Freud, their relationship was not personal. (Freud once said Adler bored him.)

Over the next several years Adler developed a personality theory that differed in several ways from Freud's, especially with regard to Freud's emphasis on sexual factors. In 1910, Freud named Adler president of the Vienna Psychoanalytic Society in an attempt to reconcile their growing rift, but by 1911 the inevitable split was complete. Their parting was bitter. Adler described Freud as a swindler and psychoanalysis as "filth" (Roazen, 1975, p. 210). Freud referred to Adler as "abnormal" and "driven mad by ambition," as well as paranoid, jealous, sadistic, and short (Gay, 1988, p. 223).

During World War I (1914–1918), Adler served as a physician in the Austrian army. He later organized child guidance clinics for the Vienna school system. During the 1920s

**Individual psychology:** Adler's theory of personality; it incorporates social as well as biological factors.

his social psychological system, which he called **individual psychology**, attracted many followers. He frequently visited the United States to lecture and was appointed professor of medical psychology at New York's Long Island College of Medicine.

His talks and his writings in America were immensely popular. A biographer noted that Adler's personal qualities, his "geniality, optimism, and warmth coupled with an intensely ambitious drive," made it easy for people to accord him celebrity status and accept him as an expert on human nature (Hoffman, 1994, p. 160). Adler died in Aberdeen, Scotland, while on a strenuous speaking tour.

Freud, replying to a letter from a friend expressing sadness at Adler's death, revealed his lingering bitterness over Adler's defection from his own point of view when he wrote:

> *I don't understand your sympathy for Adler. For a Jewish boy out of a Viennese suburb a death in Aberdeen is an unheard-of career in itself and a proof of how far he had got on. The world really rewarded him richly for his service in having contradicted psychoanalysis. (quoted in Scarf, 1971, p. 47)*

## Individual Psychology

Adler believed that human behavior is determined largely by social forces, not biological instincts. He proposed the concept of **social interest**, defined as an innate potential to cooperate with others to achieve personal and societal goals. Our social interest develops in infancy through learning experiences. In contrast to Freud, Adler minimized the influence of sex in the shaping of one's personality. Also, Adler focused on conscious rather than unconscious determinants of behavior. Whereas Freud associated present behavior with past experiences, Adler believed we are more strongly affected by our plans for the future. Striving for goals or anticipating coming events can influence present behavior. For example, a person who fears eternal damnation after death is likely to behave differently from a person with a different expectation.

Whereas Freud divided personality into separate parts (i.e., id, ego, and superego), Adler emphasized the unity and consistency of personality. He posited an innate, dynamic force that channels the personality's resources toward an overriding goal. This goal, for all of us, is superiority (in the sense of perfection), and it represents the complete development and fulfillment of the self.

Another crucial difference between Adler and Freud was their views on women. Adler argued that there was no biological reason, such as Freud's concept of penis envy, for any alleged sense of inferiority women might feel. Adler charged that this was a myth invented by men to bolster their own alleged sense of superiority. Any inferiority women might feel resulted from social forces such as sex-role stereotypes. Adler believed in equality for the sexes and supported the women's emancipation movements of the day.

**Social interest:** Adler's conception of an innate potential to cooperate with other people to achieve personal and societal goals.

## Inferiority Feelings

Adler proposed a generalized feeling of inferiority as a motivating force in behavior, as it was in his own life. Initially Adler related this feeling of inferiority to physical defects. The child with a hereditary organic weakness will attempt to compensate, to overemphasize the deficient function. A child who stutters may, through conscientious speech therapy, become a great orator; a child with weak limbs may, through intensive exercise, excel as an athlete or dancer. Adler later broadened this concept to include any physical, mental, or social handicap, real or imagined.

In infancy, the child's helplessness and dependence on other people awaken this sense of inferiority. Thus, it is a feeling experienced by everyone. Consciously aware of the need to overcome it, the child at the same time is driven by the innate striving for the betterment of the self. This pushing and pulling process continues throughout life, propelling us toward greater accomplishments.

Inferiority feelings operate to the advantage of the individual and the society because they lead to continuous improvement. If in childhood these feelings are met with pampering or with rejection, however, the result can be abnormal compensatory behaviors. Failure to compensate adequately for inferiority feelings can lead to the development of an **inferiority complex**, which renders the person incapable of coping with life's problems.

**Inferiority complex:** A condition that develops when a person is unable to compensate for normal inferiority feelings.

## Style of Life

According to Adler, the drive for superiority or perfection is universal, but each of us behaves in a different way to try to reach that goal. We demonstrate our striving in a unique or characteristic mode of responding by developing a style of life. This style of life involves the behaviors by which we compensate for real or imagined inferiority. In the example of the physically weak child, the style of life may include exercise or sports that will increase stamina and strength.

The style of life is fixed at the age of four or five and becomes difficult to change thereafter. It provides the framework within which all later experiences are dealt with. Again we see that Adler recognized the importance of the early years of life, but he differed from Freud in believing that we can consciously create a lifestyle for ourselves.

## The Creative Power of the Self

Adler's concept of the creative power of the self suggests that we have the capacity to determine our own personality in accordance with our unique style of life. This active, creative human power may be likened to the theological notion of the soul. Certain abilities and experiences come to us through heredity and environment, but the way we actively use and interpret these experiences provides the basis for our personality, our attitude toward life. Adler meant that each of us is consciously involved in shaping our personality and destiny. We can determine our fate rather than have it determined by past experience and by unconscious forces.

## Birth Order

In examining his patients' childhood years, Adler became interested in the relationship between personality and birth order. He found that the oldest, middle, and youngest children, because of their positions in the family, have varying social experiences that result in different attitudes toward life and different ways of coping.

The oldest child receives a great deal of attention until dethroned by the birth of the second child. The first-born may then become insecure and hostile, authoritarian and conservative, manifesting a strong interest in maintaining order. Adler suggested that criminals, neurotics, and perverts are often first-born children. He also suggested that Freud was a typical eldest son.

Adler found the second child to be ambitious, rebellious, and jealous, constantly striving to surpass the first-born. Adler himself was a second-born and had a lifelong competitive relationship with his older brother, whose name, coincidentally, was Sigmund. Even when Adler had achieved an international reputation for his work, he continued to feel overshadowed by his brother, then a wealthy businessman. Adler referred to Sigmund as a "good, industrious fellow [who] was always ahead of me—and is *still* ahead of me" (quoted in Hoffman, 1994, p. 11).

Nevertheless, Adler believed that the second-born child is better adjusted than the first-born or the youngest child. He said that the youngest child in the family was likely to be spoiled and predisposed toward behavioral problems in childhood and adulthood.

In addition, an only child may experience difficulties in adjusting to the world outside the family, where he or she is not the center of attention.

## Comment

Adler's theories were warmly received by scholars dissatisfied with Freud's image of a human personality dominated by sexual forces and governed by childhood experiences. It is, after all, more pleasant and hopeful to think that we are able to consciously direct our own development and strive to better ourselves regardless of genetic limitations and childhood events. Adler presented a far more satisfying and optimistic view of human nature.

Individual psychology did not lack critics, however. Many psychologists claimed that Adler's theories were superficial and relied on commonsense observations from everyday life; others considered his ideas shrewd and insightful. Freud said Adler's system was too simple. It could take two years to learn psychoanalysis because of its complexity, but Adler could be mastered in a few weeks "because with Adler there is so little to know" (Freud, quoted in Sterba, 1982, p. 156). Adler said that was precisely his point. It had taken him 40 years to make his psychology simple.

The objections of experimental psychologists to the work of Freud and Jung also apply to Adler. His observations of patients cannot be repeated or verified, nor were they obtained in controlled and systematic fashion. He did not attempt to confirm the accuracy of his patients' reports and did not explain the procedures by which he analyzed his data and reached his conclusions.

Although many of Adler's concepts resist attempts at scientific validation, the notion of birth order has been the subject of considerable research. Studies show that first-borns are high in intelligence and the need to achieve, and they tend to experience anxiety when a second child becomes part of the family. First-borns are also more likely than later-borns to complete more years of formal education, to work in more prestigious occupations, and to achieve greater eminence in their careers (see Herrera, Zajonc, Weiczorkowska, & Cichomski, 2003; Kristensen & Bjerkedal, 2007). These results support Adler's views.

In general, research does not support Adler's contention that second-borns are more competitive and ambitious than their siblings. However, some interesting recent studies are raising questions. One study of 700 brothers who played major league baseball found that younger brothers were 10 times more likely to steal bases than their older brothers and were also superior in overall batting success. This and other studies also showed that younger siblings were far more likely to participate in high-risk activities such as skydiving (Sulloway & Zweigenhaft, 2010).

Research does not support Adler's view that only children are more selfish and have difficulty adjusting to the real world. Some research shows that only-borns tend to be higher in achievement, intelligence, initiative, industriousness, and self-esteem (Falbo & Polit, 1986; Mellor, 1990).

Adler's influence on post-Freudian psychoanalysis has been substantial (see Olt, 2009). The work of the ego psychologists, which focuses more on rational, conscious processes than on the unconscious, follows Adler's lead. His emphasis on social forces in personality is seen in the work of Karen Horney. The creative power to shape one's style of life influenced Abraham Maslow, who wrote, "Alfred Adler becomes more and more correct year by year. As the facts come in, they give stronger and stronger support to his image of man" (Maslow, 1970, p. 13).

Adler's focus on social variables can be seen in the work of the neo-neobehavioral social learning theorist Julian Rotter, who wrote nearly 50 years after Adler's death that he continues to be "impressed by Adler's insights into human nature" (Rotter, 1982, pp. 1–2). Adler may have been ahead of his time in recognizing social and cognitive variables;

these ideas are more compatible with contemporary psychology than they were with the psychology of his day.

Although many of Adler's ideas have become widely accepted, his public acclaim declined after his death and he has received relatively little credit for his contributions. Many concepts have been borrowed from his theory without proper acknowledgment. For example, in the (London) *Times* obituary for Sigmund Freud, Freud was named as the originator of the term *inferiority complex*. When Carl Jung died, *The New York Times* reported that *he* had coined the term! Neither paper mentioned Adler.

Adler's followers claim that individual psychology remains influential among psychologists, psychiatrists, social workers, and educators. *Individual Psychology: The Journal of Adlerian Theory, Research and Practice* is published quarterly in the United States, and other Adlerian journals are published in Germany, Italy, and France. There are at present Adlerian training institutes operating in New York, San Francisco, and Chicago.

# Karen Horney (1885–1952)

An early feminist, Karen Horney was trained as a Freudian psychoanalyst in Berlin. She described her work as an extension of Freud's system rather than an effort to supplant it.

KAREN HORNEY

### Horney's Life

Horney was born in Hamburg, Germany. Her father was a devout, morose ship's captain many years older than her mother, who was a liberal and vivacious woman. Her mother made it clear to Karen that she wished her husband dead; she had married him out of fear of remaining a spinster. Her mother rejected Karen in favor of the first-born brother, whom Karen envied simply for being a boy, and her father belittled her appearance and intelligence. As a result, she felt inferior, worthless, and hostile (Sayers, 1991). "Why is everything beautiful on earth given to me," she wrote in her diary at age 16, "only not the highest thing, not love! I have a heart so needing love" (Horney, 1980, p. 30).

This lack of parental love fostered what Horney later called "basic anxiety" and provides another instance of the impact of personal experience on a theorist's views. A biographer wrote, "In all her psychoanalytic writings, Karen Horney was struggling to make sense of herself and to obtain relief from her own difficulties" (Paris, 1994, p. xxii).

As an adolescent Horney developed emotional crushes as part of her search for the love and acceptance she lacked at home. She began a newsletter she called a "virginal organ for super-virgins" and took to walking streets known to be frequented by prostitutes. In her diary she wrote, "In my imagination there is no spot on me that has not been kissed by a burning mouth. In my imagination there is no depravity I have not tasted, to the dregs" (Horney, 1980, p. 64).

Ignoring the opposition from her father, Horney entered medical school at the University of Berlin and in 1913 received her degree. She married, gave birth to three daughters (two of whom would later be analyzed by Melanie Klein to help them deal with their conflicts with their mother), and became increasingly depressed. She described a long period of unhappiness and oppression as well as marital difficulties. She complained of crying spells, stomach pains, chronic fatigue, compulsive behaviors, an inability to work, and thoughts of suicide.

After several affairs, she divorced her husband to continue her restless quest for acceptance the rest of her life. Her most enduring affair was with the psychoanalyst Erich Fromm. When the relationship ended, she was devastated. She chose to undergo psychoanalysis to deal with her depression and sexual problems. Her Freudian analyst told her that her search for love and her attraction to forceful men reflected childhood Oedipal longings for her powerful father (Sayers, 1991).

When Horney realized that Freudian analysis was not helping her, she turned to self-analysis, a practice she continued throughout her life. Sensitive to Adler's observation that physical unattractiveness caused inferiority feelings, she concluded that by studying medicine and engaging in promiscuous sexual behavior, she was acting more like a man than like a woman. This helped her feel superior, but she never stopped her search for love. As she aged, however, she singled out younger and younger men, many of whom were analysts whose training she was supervising. Her attitude toward them became casual and detached. Telling a friend about one of these young men, she said that she did not know whether to marry him or to get a cocker spaniel. She chose the dog (Paris, 1994).

From 1914 to 1918, Horney took orthodox psychoanalytic training at the Berlin Psychoanalytic Institute. Later she became a faculty member there and began a private practice. She wrote journal articles about problems of the female personality, outlining her disagreement with certain Freudian concepts. In 1932 she went to the United States as associate director of the Chicago Institute for Psychoanalysis. She also taught at the New York Psychoanalytic Institute and continued to see patients. Her growing disaffection with Freudian theory soon led her to break with this group. She founded the American Institute of Psychoanalysis and remained its head until her death.

## Disagreements with Freud

Horney disputed Freud's view that personality depends on unchanging biological forces. She denied the preeminence of sexual factors, challenged the validity of the Oedipal theory, and discarded the concepts of libido and the three-part structure of personality. However, she did accept unconscious motivation and the existence of emotional, non-rational motives.

Counter to Freud's belief that women are motivated by penis envy, Horney argued that men are motivated by womb envy; that is, jealousy of women for their ability to give birth. She believed that men manifest womb envy and its accompanying resentment unconsciously, through behaviors designed to harass and belittle women. By denying women equal rights, limiting their opportunities, and downgrading their efforts to achieve, men attempt to retain an alleged natural superiority. To Horney, the fundamental reason for such masculine behavior is a sense of inferiority resulting from womb envy.

Horney and Freud also differed in their views of human nature. Horney wrote:

*Freud's pessimism as regards neuroses and their treatment arose from the depths of his disbelief in human goodness and human growth. Man, he postulated, is doomed to suffer or to destroy. My own belief is that man has the capacity as well as the desire to develop his potentialities and become a decent human being. I believe that man can change and go on changing as long as he lives. (Horney, 1945, p. 19)*

## Basic Anxiety

**Basic anxiety:**
Horney's conception of pervasive loneliness and helplessness, feelings that are the foundation of neuroses.

**Basic anxiety** is the fundamental concept in Horney's system. She defined it as "the feeling a child has of being isolated and helpless in a potentially hostile world" (Horney, 1945, p. 41). This definition characterized her own childhood feelings. Basic anxiety results from parental actions such as dominance, lack of protection and love, and erratic behavior. Anything that disrupts a secure relationship between child and parents can produce basic anxiety. Thus, the condition is not innate but results from social forces and interactions in the child's environment. Instead of accepting Freudian instincts as motivating forces, Horney proposed that the helpless infant was driven by the need to seek security, safety, and freedom from fear in a threatening world.

Horney shared with Freud a belief that personality develops in the early childhood years, but she insisted that personality continues to change throughout life. Whereas Freud detailed psychosexual stages of development, Horney focused on how the growing child is treated by parents and caregivers. She denied universal developmental phases, such as an oral or anal stage. She suggested that if a child developed tendencies toward an oral or anal personality, these tendencies were a result of parental behaviors. Nothing in a child's development was universal; everything depended on social, cultural, and environmental factors.

## Neurotic Needs

To Horney, then, basic anxiety arises from the parent-child relationship. When this socially produced anxiety becomes evident, the child develops behavioral strategies in response to parental behavior as a way of coping with the accompanying feelings of helplessness and insecurity. If any one of the child's behavioral strategies becomes a fixed part of the personality, it is called a neurotic need, which is a way of defending against the anxiety.

Initially Horney listed 10 neurotic needs, including affection, achievement, and self-sufficiency. In later writings she grouped the neurotic needs into three trends (Horney, 1945):

- *The compliant personality—one who needs to move toward other people, expressing needs for approval, affection, and a dominant partner*
- *The detached personality—one who needs to move away from people, expressing needs for independence, perfection, and withdrawal*
- *The aggressive personality—one who needs to move against people, expressing needs for power, exploitation, prestige, admiration, and achievement*

Movement toward people implies accepting one's feelings of helplessness and acting to win the affection of others, the only way the person can feel secure with other people. Movement away from people involves withdrawing, behaving so as to appear self-sufficient and avoid dependency. Movement against people involves hostility, rebellion, and aggression. None of the neurotic needs or trends is a realistic way of dealing with anxiety. Because they are incompatible, they can lead to conflicts. Once we establish a behavioral strategy for coping with basic anxiety, this pattern ceases to be flexible enough to permit alternative behaviors.

When a fixed behavior proves inappropriate for a particular situation, we are unable to change in response to the demands of the situation. These entrenched behaviors intensify our difficulties because they affect the total personality, our relations with other people, with ourselves, and with life as a whole.

## The Idealized Self-Image

The idealized self-image provides the person with a false picture of the personality or self. It is an imperfect, misleading mask that prevents neurotic persons from understanding and accepting their true selves. In donning the mask, they deny the existence of their inner conflicts. They believe that the idealized self-image is genuine, and that belief, in turn, enables them to think they are superior to the sort of person they really are.

Horney did not suggest that such neurotic conflicts were innate or inevitable. Although they arose from undesirable situations in childhood, they could be prevented if warmth, understanding, security, and love characterized the child's home life.

## Comment

Horney's optimism about the possibility of avoiding neuroses was welcomed by psychologists and psychiatrists as a relief from Freud's pessimism. Her work is also noteworthy because she described personality development in terms of social forces, attributing little influence to innate factors.

The evidence to support Horney's theory, like that cited by Freud, Jung, and Adler, is taken from clinical observations of patients and thus subject to the same questions of scientific credibility. Little research has been conducted on the concepts in her system. Freud did not comment directly on her work but once said of her, "she is able but malicious" (quoted in Blanton, 1971, p. 65). Elsewhere, in a thinly disguised allusion to Horney's work, Freud wrote, "We shall not be greatly surprised if a woman analyst, who has not been sufficiently convinced of the intensity of her own wish for a penis, also fails to attach proper importance to that factor in her patients" (1940, p. 65). Horney was described as "bitter" over Freud's failure to recognize the legitimacy of her views (Paris, 1994).

Although Horney did not have disciples or a journal to disseminate her ideas, her work has had considerable impact. The Karen Horney Psychoanalytic Center remains active in New York. With the rise of the feminist movement beginning in the 1960s, her books enjoyed renewed popularity. Today, her writings on feminine psychology are considered her major contribution. Many of her feminist positions, stated more than 80 years ago, have a strong contemporary ring. She began work on feminine psychology in 1922 and was the first woman to present a paper on the topic at an international psychoanalytic congress. That meeting, in Berlin, was chaired by Sigmund Freud. Writing in the 1930s, Horney drew a distinction between the traditional woman, seeking self-identity through marriage and motherhood, and the modern woman, seeking identity through a career. This conflict between love and work, as Horney saw it, characterized her own life. She chose to focus on work, which brought enormous satisfaction, but she continued to search for love throughout her life.

Her dilemma remains as relevant in the twenty-first century as it was to her in the 1930s, and she fought for women to have the right to make their own decisions in the face of restrictions imposed by a male-dominated society.

# The Evolution of Personality Theory: Humanistic Psychology

Freudian psychoanalytic theory did not long remain the sole approach to explaining the human personality. We have seen that during Freud's lifetime, alternatives were offered by Jung and the social psychological theorists and by neo-Freudian loyalists. The study of personality, both theory and research, has grown immensely, splintering the field with conflicting viewpoints. Contemporary textbooks typically discuss 15 to 20 theories. Although these systems differ in specifics as well as generalities, they have a common heritage in that they all owe their origin and form, to some degree, to the founding efforts of Sigmund Freud.

Freud served the same purpose on the psychoanalytic side of psychology's history that Wundt served on the experimental side, and that is as a source of inspiration as well as a force to oppose. Every structure, whether actual or theoretical, depends on the soundness of its foundation. Like Wundt, Freud provided a solid and challenging base on which to build. As examples of the evolution in personality theory since Freud's time, we describe the work of Abraham Maslow and Carl Rogers and their humanistic psychology movement.

In the early 1960s, less than two decades before the 100th anniversary of the formal founding of psychology, a so-called third force developed within American psychology. This humanistic psychology was not intended to be a revision or adaptation of any current school of thought, as was the case with some neo-Freudian positions. Instead, humanistic psychologists expected to supplant both of psychology's two main forces: behaviorism and psychoanalysis.

Humanistic psychology emphasized human strengths and positive aspirations, conscious experience, free will (rather than determinism), the fulfillment of human potential, and a belief in the wholeness of human nature. You can readily see that these themes are quite different from those of behaviorism or psychoanalysis.

## Antecedent Influences on Humanistic Psychology

As with all ideas, anticipations of humanistic psychology can be found in the works of earlier psychologists. Consider Brentano, an opponent of Wundt's and an anticipator of Gestalt psychology. Brentano had criticized the mechanistic, reductionistic, natural-science approach to psychology and favored the study of consciousness as a molar quality rather than a molecular content.

Külpe demonstrated that not all conscious experience could be reduced to elementary form or explained in terms of responses to stimuli. And James argued against the mechanistic approach and urged a focus on consciousness and the whole individual. Gestalt psychologists believed psychology should take a "wholes" approach to consciousness. In defiance of behaviorism's dominance, Gestalt psychologists continued to insist that conscious experience was a legitimate and fruitful area of study.

Roots of the humanistic position can also be found in psychoanalysis. Adler, Horney, and other personality theorists disagreed with Freud's notion that our lives are governed by unconscious forces. These dissenters from orthodox psychoanalysis believed that we are conscious beings who possess spontaneity and free will and who are influenced by the present and future as well as by the past. These theorists credit the personality with the creative power to shape itself.

The Zeitgeist is always influential in organizing precedents and trends into a cohesive viewpoint. Humanistic psychology reflected the disaffection of the 1960s that was voiced against mechanistic and materialistic aspects of Western culture. The counterculture of the time was composed of so-called hippies, primarily college students and dropouts, some of whom relied on hallucinogenic drugs to stimulate and expand their conscious experiences. As a group they shared ideals consistent with the humanistic approach to psychology: a focus on personal fulfillment, a belief in human perfectibility, an emphasis on the present and on hedonism (satisfying one's pleasure-seeking instincts), the tendency to self-disclose (to speak one's mind freely), and the valuing of feelings over reason and intellect.

## The Nature of Humanistic Psychology

To humanistic psychologists, behavioral psychology was a narrow, artificial, and sterile approach to human nature. They believed that the focus on overt behavior was dehumanizing and reduced human beings to the status of mere animals and machines. They disputed the contention that we function in a predetermined fashion in response to stimulus events in our lives. Further, humanistic psychologists argued that humans are more complex than laboratory rats or robots and cannot be objectified, quantified, and reduced to stimulus-response units.

Behaviorism was not the humanistic psychologists' sole target. They also opposed the deterministic tendencies of Freudian psychoanalysis and the way it minimized the role of consciousness. They also criticized Freudians for studying only neurotic and psychotic individuals.

If psychologists concentrated only on mental dysfunction, how could they learn anything about emotional health and other positive human qualities? By disregarding joy, contentment, ecstasy, kindness, and generosity, for example, to deal instead with the darker side of the human personality, psychology was ignoring unique human strengths and virtues.

Thus, in response to the perceived limitations of both behaviorism and psychoanalysis, humanistic psychologists advanced what they hoped would be the third force within psychology. As a serious study of neglected aspects of human nature, humanistic psychology is best expressed in the works of Abraham Maslow and Carl Rogers.

# Abraham Maslow (1908–1970)

ABRAHAM MASLOW

Maslow has been called the spiritual father of humanistic psychology and probably did more than anyone else to spark the movement and confer on it some degree of academic respectability. He was driven to understand the greatest achievements of which we are capable, and so he studied a small sample of psychologically outstanding people to determine how they differed from those of average or normal mental health.

## Maslow's Life

We described earlier Maslow's unhappy childhood and how he turned to books and to study to escape his feelings of loneliness and inferiority. When he went to college, at Cornell University, his first experience with the field of psychology alienated him almost completely. The course in which he enrolled, taught by E. B. Titchener, was "awful and bloodless and had nothing to do with people, so I shuddered and turned away from it" (quoted in Hoffman, 1988, p. 26). Maslow transferred to the University of Wisconsin, where he found a different approach to psychology, and received his Ph.D. in 1934.

Maslow became an enthusiastic Watsonian behaviorist, convinced that the mechanistic natural-science approach provided answers to all the world's problems. Then a series of personal experiences persuaded him that behaviorism was too limited to be relevant to enduring human issues. He was deeply affected by the birth of his child and by his reading of philosophy, Gestalt psychology, and psychoanalysis. Maslow was also influenced by his contact with European psychologists who had fled Nazi Germany and settled in the United States—Adler, Horney, Koffka, and Wertheimer. His feelings of awe toward Gestalt psychologist Max Wertheimer and the anthropologist Ruth Benedict led to his first study of the characteristics of psychologically healthy self-actualizing persons. Wertheimer and Benedict were Maslow's models of the best of human nature.

Maslow was also deeply affected by a parade he witnessed shortly after the surprise attack by Japan on the U.S. fleet at Pearl Harbor, Hawaii, on December 7, 1941, which forced America into World War II. "That moment changed my whole life," he wrote, "and determined what I have done ever since" (quoted in Hall, 1968, p. 54). He resolved to devote himself to developing a psychology that would deal with the highest human ideals. He would work to improve the human personality and show that people are capable of more noble behaviors than hatred, prejudice, and war.

At that time Maslow was teaching at Brooklyn College, where his early attempts to humanize psychology had negative personal consequences. The predominant behaviorist psychology community ostracized him. Although students thought his ideas were interesting, faculty colleagues avoided him. He was considered too unorthodox and too far out of step with behaviorism, the mainstream psychology of the day. Editors of the major journals refused to publish his work. It was at Brandeis University, during the years 1951 to 1969, that Maslow developed and refined his theory and presented it in a series of popular books. He supported the sensitivity group movement, and in 1967 he was elected president of the APA.

In the 1960s Maslow became a celebrity, a hero to the counterculture movement, and finally achieved the adulation he had craved since his youth. "Younger people found Maslow's work especially appealing, and for many he became a guru-like figure"

(Nicholson, 2001, p. 86). Maslow had successfully compensated, in Adlerian terms, for the inferiorities of his childhood.

## Self-Actualization

**Self-actualization:** The full development of one's abilities and the realization of one's potential.

In Maslow's view, each person possesses an innate tendency toward **self-actualization** (Maslow, 1970). This state, which is the highest of the human needs, involves the active use of all our qualities and abilities, the development and fulfillment of our potential. To become self-actualizing, we must first satisfy needs that stand lower in an innate hierarchy. Each need must be satisfied in turn before the next need can motivate us.

The needs Maslow proposed, in the order in which they must be satisfied, are the physiological, safety, belonging and love, esteem, and self-actualization needs (see Figure 14.1).

Maslow's research sought to identify characteristics of people who satisfied the self-actualization need and therefore could be considered psychologically healthy. By his definition, these people are free of neuroses. They are almost always middle-aged or older and account for less than 1 percent of the population. Among the several dozen self-actualizers Maslow studied by analyzing biographies and other written records were the physicist Albert Einstein, the writer and social activist Eleanor Roosevelt, the African-American scientist George Washington Carver, and the Gestalt psychologist Max Wertheimer.

Self-actualizers share the following tendencies:

1. An objective perception of reality
2. A full acceptance of their own nature
3. A commitment and dedication to some kind of work
4. Simplicity and naturalness of behavior
5. A need for autonomy, privacy, and independence
6. Intense mystical or peak experiences
7. Empathy with and affection for all humanity
8. Resistance to conformity
9. A democratic character structure
10. An attitude of creativeness
11. A high degree of what Adler termed "social interest"

Maslow believed that prerequisites for self-actualization are sufficient love in childhood and the satisfaction of the physiological and safety needs within the first two years of life. If children are made to feel secure and confident in their early years (which Maslow certainly was not), then they will remain so as adults. Without adequate parental

**FIGURE 14.1**
Maslow's hierarchy of needs.

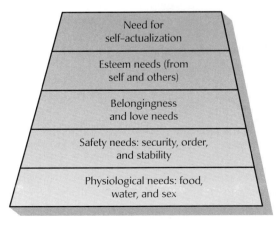

love, security, and esteem in childhood, it will be difficult for the adult to attain self-actualization.

In this excerpt from Maslow's book, *Motivation and Personality*, he describes three of the characteristics previously listed that he found in his study of self-actualizers. Note the relatively simple, non-technical language and the way in which he drew on the work of William James and Alfred Adler to support his views.

# IN THEIR OWN WORDS

## Original Source Material on Humanistic Psychology from *Motivation and Personality* (1970)

Abraham Maslow[1]

### Continued Freshness of Appreciation

Self-actualizing people have the wonderful capacity to appreciate again and again, freshly and naively, the basic goods of life, with awe, pleasure, wonder, and even ecstasy, however stale these experiences may have become to others. ... Thus for such a person, any sunset may be as beautiful as the first one, any flower may be of breathtaking loveliness, even after he has seen a million flowers. The thousandth baby he sees is just as miraculous a product as the first one he saw. He remains as convinced of his luck in marriage thirty years after his marriage and is as surprised by his wife's beauty when she is sixty as he was forty years before. For such people, even the casual workaday, moment-to-moment business of living can be thrilling, exciting, and ecstatic. These intense feelings do not come all the time; they come occasionally rather than usually, but at the most unexpected moments. The person may cross the river on the ferry ten times and at the eleventh crossing have a strong recurrence of the same feelings, reaction of beauty, and excitement as when he rode the ferry for the first time.

There are some differences in choice of beautiful objects. Some subjects go primarily to nature. For others it is primarily children, and for a few subjects it has been primarily great music; but it may certainly be said that they derive ecstasy, inspiration, and strength from the basic experiences of life. No one of them, for instance, will get this same sort of reaction from going to a nightclub or getting a lot of money or having a good time at a party.

### The Peak (Mystic) Experience

Those subjective expressions that have been called the mystic experience and described so well by William James are a fairly common experience for our subjects though not for all. The strong emotions described in the previous section sometimes get strong enough, chaotic, and widespread enough to be called mystic experiences.

My interest and attention in this subject was first enlisted by several of my subjects who described their sexual orgasms in vaguely familiar terms which later I remembered had been used by various writers to describe what *they* called the mystic experience. There were the same feelings of limitless horizons opening up to the vision, the feeling of being simultaneously more powerful and also more helpless than one ever was before, the feeling of great ecstasy and wonder and awe, the loss of placing in time and space with, finally, the conviction that something extremely important and valuable had happened, so that the subject is to some extent transformed and strengthened even in his daily life by such experiences.

It is quite important to dissociate this experience from any theological or supernatural reference, even though for thousands of years they have been linked. Because this experience is a natural experience, well within the jurisdiction of science, I call it the peak experience.

We may also learn from our subjects that such experiences can occur in a lesser degree of intensity. The theological literature has generally assumed an absolute, qualitative difference between the mystic experience and all others. As soon as it is divorced from supernatural reference and studied as a natural phenomenon, it becomes possible to place the mystic experience on a quantitative continuum from intense to mild. We discover then that the mild mystic experience occurs in many, perhaps even most individuals, and that in the favored individual it occurs often, perhaps even daily.

Apparently the acute mystic or peak experience is a tremendous intensification of any of the experiences in which there is loss of self or transcendence of it, e.g., problem centering, intense concentration, intense sensuous experience, self-forgetful and intense enjoyment of music or art.

### Social Interest (*Gemeinschaftsgefuehl*)

This word, invented by Alfred Adler, is the only one available that describes well the flavor of the feelings for mankind expressed by self-actualizing subjects. They have for human beings in general a deep feeling of identification, sympathy, and affection in spite of the occasional anger, impatience, or disgust described below. Because of this they have a genuine desire to help the human race. It is as if they were all members of a single family. One's feelings toward his brothers would be on the whole affectionate, even if these brothers were foolish, weak, or even if they were sometimes nasty. They would still be more easily forgiven than strangers.

If one's view is not general enough and if it is not spread over a long period of time, then one may not see this feeling of identification with mankind. The self-actualizing person is after all very different from other people in thought, impulse, behavior, emotion. When it comes down to it, in certain basic ways he is like an alien in a strange land. Very few really understand him, however much they may like him.

He is often saddened, exasperated, and even enraged by the shortcomings of the average person, and while they are to him ordinarily no more than a nuisance, they sometimes become bitter tragedy. However far apart he is from them at times, he nevertheless feels a basic underlying kinship with these creatures whom he must regard with, if not condescension, at least the knowledge that he can do many things better than they can, that he can see things that they cannot see, that the truth that is so clear to him is for most people veiled and hidden. This is what Adler called the older-brotherly attitude.

### Comment

Maslow's data and research methodology have been faulted because the subject sample was considered too small to permit the kinds of generalizations he made. Also, his subjects were selected according to his subjective criteria of psychological health, and his terms are defined ambiguously and inconsistently. Maslow agreed that his investigations did not meet the rigors of scientific research but argued that there was no other way to study self-actualization. He referred to his work as "preliminary" and remained convinced that his conclusions would one day be confirmed.

Later studies have provided some support for the characteristics of self-actualizers and the order of needs in the hierarchy Maslow advanced. For example, researchers have found that people highest in satisfaction of the needs for safety, belongingness, and esteem were far less likely to display neurotic behaviors than were people who failed to satisfy these needs. Also, people who scored high in self-esteem also scored high on measures of self-worth, self-confidence, and competence.

Despite limited empirical support for Maslow's ideas, his goal of dealing with the highest human ideals won a large following among those disenchanted with both behaviorism and psychoanalysis. His theories have had a broad impact beyond psychology. Teachers, counselors, business and government leaders, health care professionals, and others trying to cope with the problems of modern life have found Maslow's views compatible with their needs and useful in helping to solve everyday problems.

Some of the themes of his approach to psychology can be found in the contemporary positive psychology movement. Some promoters of this approach credit Maslow as a forerunner (see, for example, Diener, Oishi, & Lucas, 2003). Thus, Maslow's legacy has endured over several decades, from one century into the next.

# Carl Rogers (1902–1987)

Doug Land, photographer

CARL ROGERS

Carl Rogers is best known for a popular approach to psychotherapy called person-centered therapy. Rogers also advanced a personality theory based on a single motivational factor similar to Maslow's concept of self-actualization. Unlike Maslow, however, Rogers's ideas did not derive from the study of emotionally healthy people but from applying his person-centered therapy to those treated at his university counseling centers.

The name of Rogers's therapy indicates his view of the human personality. By placing the responsibility for improvement on the person or client rather than on the therapist (as in orthodox psychoanalysis), Rogers assumed that people can consciously and rationally change their thoughts and behaviors from undesirable to desirable. He did not believe that we are permanently restrained by unconscious forces or childhood experiences. Personality is shaped by the present and how we consciously perceive it.

## Rogers's Life

Carl Rogers was born in Oak Park, Illinois, a suburb of Chicago. His parents espoused strict fundamentalist views that, as Rogers put it, held him like a vise throughout childhood and adolescence. Their religious beliefs, and the suppression of any display of emotion, forced him to live by a code that was not his own. He said later that these restrictions gave him something to revolt against, although the rebellion would be long in coming.

He was a solitary child who read incessantly. He believed that his older brother was his parents' favorite; as a result, Rogers felt he was always in competition with his brother. He grew up with "bitter memories of being the inevitable butt of his brother's jokes, even as he was starved of joy by his mother" (Milton, 2002, p. 128).

Loneliness led Rogers to rely on his own experiences, and he turned to books as an escape. He read everything he could find, even a dictionary and an encyclopedia. His solitude forced him to depend on his own resources and his own personal view of the world, a characteristic that was to become the foundation of his approach to the understanding of the human personality:

> As I look back, I realize that my interest in interviewing and in therapy certainly grew out of my early loneliness. Here was a socially approved way of getting really close to individuals and thus filling some of the hunger I undoubtedly felt. (Rogers, 1980, p. 34)

Rogers's physical health as a child was poor, and his family considered him overly sensitive and nervous. "This sometimes led to a teasing banter that could verge on cruelty and exacerbated a tendency on Carl's part to retreat into his own fantasy world" (Rogers & Russell, 2002, p. 2).

When Rogers was 12, the family moved to a farm where he developed a strong interest in nature. He read about agricultural experiments and the scientific approach to solving problems. Although this reading helped focus his intellectual life, his emotional life was in turmoil. He wrote, "My fantasies during this period were definitely bizarre and probably would be classified as schizoid by a diagnostician, but fortunately I never came in contact with a psychologist" (Rogers, 1980, p. 30).

At age 22, while attending a Christian student conference in China, he finally freed himself from his parents' fundamentalist code and adopted a more liberal philosophy of life. He became convinced that people must choose to guide their lives by their own interpretation of events rather than relying on the views of others. He was also persuaded that we must strive actively to improve ourselves. These concepts became cornerstones of his personality theory.

Breaking with his parents' religious view, while liberating for Rogers, was also physically and emotionally debilitating. Not long after his return from China he was hospitalized with an ulcer, which may have been induced by stress. He stayed at home for a year to recuperate before returning to college.

Rogers received his Ph.D. in clinical and educational psychology in 1931 from Teachers College of Columbia University. He spent nine years at the Society for the Prevention of Cruelty to Children, working with delinquent and disadvantaged youngsters. In 1940 he began his academic career, teaching at Ohio State University, the University of Chicago, and the University of Wisconsin. During those years, he developed and refined his theory and his method of psychotherapy.

At one point during his academic career he succumbed to what was then called a nervous breakdown, triggered when he failed to help a severely disturbed patient. His self-confidence shattered, Rogers wrote that he felt "deeply certain of my complete inadequacy as a therapist, my worthlessness as a person, and my lack of any future in the field of psychology" (1967, p. 367). Fortunately, he turned out to be incorrect on all three points.

It is important to remember that Rogers's clinical experience during the time he was developing his theory was undertaken mostly with college students in the counseling center. Thus, the type of person he treated was primarily young, intelligent, and highly verbal. Their problems, in general, were adjustment issues rather than severe emotional disorders. This was a vastly different subject population than those seen by Freudian or other clinical psychologists in private practice.

## Self-Actualization

The greatest motivating force in personality is the drive to actualize the self (Rogers, 1961). Although this urge toward self-actualization is innate, it can be helped or hindered by childhood experiences and by learning. Rogers emphasized the importance of the mother-child relationship as it affects the child's growing sense of self. If the mother satisfies the infant's need for love, which Rogers called **positive regard**, then the infant will tend to become a healthy personality.

**Positive regard:** The unconditional love of a mother for her infant.

If the mother's love for her child is conditional on proper behavior (conditional positive regard), then the child will internalize the mother's attitude and develop conditions of worth. In that event, the child feels worthy only under certain conditions and will try to avoid behaviors that bring disapproval. As a result, the child's self is not allowed to develop fully. The child cannot express all aspects of the self because he or she has learned that some of those behaviors bring rejection.

Thus, the primary requisite for the development of psychological health is unconditional positive regard in childhood. Ideally, the mother will demonstrate love and acceptance of the child regardless of the child's behavior. The child who receives unconditional positive regard will not develop conditions of worth and therefore will not have to repress any part of the emerging self. Only in this way can a person eventually achieve self-actualization.

Self-actualization is the highest level of psychological health. Rogers's conception, by his own admission, is similar in principle to Maslow's, although they differ somewhat on the characteristics of psychologically healthy people.

To Rogers, psychologically healthy or fully functioning persons have the following qualities:

- *An openness to, and a freshness of appreciation of, all experience*
- *A tendency to live fully in every moment*
- *The ability to be guided by their instincts rather than by reason or the opinions of others*
- *A sense of freedom in thought and action*
- *A high degree of creativity*
- *The continual need to maximize their potential*

Rogers described fully functioning persons as actualiz*ing* rather than actualiz*ed*, to indicate that the development of the self is always a work in progress. This emphasis on spontaneity, flexibility, and our continued ability to grow is neatly captured in the title of Rogers's most popular book: *On Becoming a Person* (1961).

## Comment

Rogers's unique person-centered psychotherapy has had a major impact on psychology. Its rapid acceptance was fostered in part by the social circumstances in the United States in 1945 at the end of World War II. A huge number of veterans returning from active duty overseas needed help adjusting to civilian life. The result was a demand for psychologists and for an effective counseling technique that could be learned quickly. Training in traditional psychoanalysis required a medical degree and several years of specialization. In contrast, Rogers's person-centered therapy was far simpler and required much less preparation for the therapist. It perfectly suited the needs of the time.

Rogers's approach remains influential in counseling and psychotherapy (see Kirschenbaum & Jourdan, 2005; Patterson & Joseph, 2007). In the business world it is used as a training technique for managers. In the helping professions it is applied to train clinical psychologists, social workers, and counselors. More than 50 professional journals and some 200 organizations worldwide are dedicated to promoting some version of person-centered therapy.

Rogers was influential in the human potential movement of the 1960s and part of the overall trend toward humanizing psychology. He was elected APA president in 1946 and received the Distinguished Scientific Contribution Award and Distinguished Professional Contribution Award.

# The Fate of Humanistic Psychology

The humanistic psychology movement became formalized with its own journal, association, and division of the APA. The *Journal of Humanistic Psychology* began in 1961, the American Association for Humanistic Psychology in 1962, and the Division of Humanistic Psychology of the APA in 1971. *The Humanistic Psychologist* became the division's official journal in 1989, and in 1986 the humanistic psychology archive was established at the University of California at Santa Barbara. Thus the distinguishing traits of a cohesive school of thought were evident. Humanistic psychologists offered a definition of psychology distinct from the other two forces in the field (behaviorism and psychoanalysis), and they possessed what every other school of thought boasted in its early days—a passionate conviction that theirs was the best path for psychology.

Despite these attributes of a school of thought, humanistic psychology did not actually become one. That was the judgment of humanistic psychologists themselves more than 20 years after the movement evolved. One wrote that "humanistic psychology was a great experiment, but it is basically a failed experiment in that there is no humanistic school of thought in psychology, no theory that would be recognized as a philosophy of science" (Cunningham, 1985, p. 18). Carl Rogers agreed: "Humanistic psychology has not had a significant impact on mainstream psychology. We are perceived as having relatively little importance" (quoted in Cunningham, 1985, p. 16). Even 10 years after Rogers's harsh judgment on humanistic psychology's fate, a psychologist evaluating mainstream psychology described it as "surprisingly unaffected" by the concerns of humanistic psychology, noting its exclusion from publications, research grants, college courses, and licensing and accreditation standards (Aanstoos, 1994, p. 2).

In the twenty-first century, humanistic psychology remains isolated outside the mainstream of psychology (Giorgi, 2005). One sympathetic observer wrote, "compared to its heyday in the 1960s and early 1970s, humanistic psychology has relatively little power or influence in American psychology" (Elkins, 2009, p. 268).

Why did humanistic psychology remain separate from the accepted body of psychological thought? One reason is that most humanistic psychologists were in clinical practice and not at universities. Unlike academic psychologists, humanistic psychologists in private practice could not to the same extent conduct research, publish papers, or train new generations of graduate students to carry on their tradition.

Another reason for its lack of impact relates to the timing of the humanistic psychology protest. At its peak—the 1960s and early 1970s—humanistic psychologists were attacking positions no longer influential in psychology. Freud's psychoanalysis and Skinner's behaviorism had already been weakened by internal divisiveness, and both were already beginning to change in the way urged by the humanistic psychologists. As a result, the humanistic protest was fighting movements that were no longer dominant in their original form.

Although humanistic psychology did not transform psychology, it can be credited with strengthening the idea within psychoanalysis that people can consciously and freely shape their lives. Humanistic psychology also indirectly helped restore the study of consciousness to academic experimental psychology because it arose contemporaneously with the cognitive psychology movement and became part of the Zeitgeist.

One of the founders of cognitive psychology said he was "much moved by the spirit of humanistic psychologists [and] saw the cognitive approach as a more humanistic view of the human organism" (Neisser, quoted in Baars, 1986, p. 273). Overall, humanistic psychology helped ratify changes already occurring in the field, and from that standpoint it may be called successful. In addition, it was to have an impact four decades later on contemporary psychology (see Nicholson, 2007).

# Positive Psychology

The theme of humanistic psychology, the idea that psychologists should study the best of human attributes as well as the worst, the positive characteristics as well as the negative, was reprised in 1998 by APA president Martin Seligman. Speaking at a symposium on the science of optimism and hope, Seligman noted that the field's "relentless focus on the negative has left psychology blind to the many instances of growth, mastery, drive and insight that develop out of undesirable, painful life-events" (Seligman, 1998, p. 1). Sounding not unlike Maslow 30 years earlier, Seligman added:

> *How has it happened that the social sciences view the human strengths and virtues—altruism, courage, honesty, duty, joy, health, responsibility and good cheer—as derivative, defensive or downright illusions, while weakness and negative motivations—anxiety, lust, selfishness, paranoia, anger, disorder and sadness—are viewed as authentic? (Seligman, 1998, p. 1)*

His goal was to persuade psychologists to develop a more positive conception of human nature and human potential that would build on the pioneering work of Maslow and Rogers (see Seligman, Steen, Park, & Peterson, 2005).

Seligman's call for a positive psychology received a highly enthusiastic response. Research studies, articles, and books began to pour forth. By 2001 studies of subjective well-being, of dealing with the correlates and causes of happiness and other positive emotions, had shown the "strongest increase in number of publications over the past 40 years" (Staudinger, 2001, p. 552). In 2000 the *American Psychologist,* a leading APA journal, devoted a special issue of nearly 200 pages to positive psychology. The issue focused on happiness, excellence, and optimal human functioning, concepts rarely found in the works of Freud and other psychoanalysts (see Seligman & Csikszentmihalyi, 2000). Also in 2000 the *Journal of Happiness Studies* began publication, the first such journal in the field. The following year an issue of *American Psychologist* included four articles on positive psychology. The introduction to this group of articles was titled "Why Positive Psychology Is Necessary" (Sheldon & King, 2001).

In 2002 Seligman published a popular book titled *Authentic Happiness: Using the New Positive Psychology to Realize Your Potential for Lasting Fulfillment.* The book was the topic of a laudatory article in *Newsweek,* which also described the positive psychology movement as a "whole new age in research psychology" (Cowley, 2002, p. 49). In 2005 *Time* magazine published a 40-page special issue devoted to the work of Seligman and his colleagues in this exciting new field. The following year the *Journal of Positive Psychology* was started. At Harvard University that year the most popular undergraduate course, with an enrollment of 855 students, was "Positive Psychology." No other course came close.

Thus, in less than 10 years since Seligman issued his initial call for a positive psychology the field became phenomenally successful. Hundreds of research studies are produced every year; seminars are held, books published, and popular magazines and television talk shows are praising its goals. Today's textbooks on positive psychology typically cover topics such as subjective well-being, the science of happiness, love and life satisfaction, interventions for enhanced well-being, leisure, peak performance, positive affectivity, emotional creativity, optimism, hope theory, goal-setting for life and happiness, and positive psychology on the job (see, for example, Compton, 2006).

What are the characteristics of a happy personality? What accounts for the state of subjective well-being? Did you guess "money?" Well, yes and no; that may depend on how you phrase the question. One survey of 136,000 people in 132 countries found that life satisfaction varied with income. Those who earned more money said they were more satisfied with their lives than those who earned less (Diener, Ng, Harter, & Arora, 2010). However, positive feelings such as joy, happiness, and subjective well-being were less dependent on money and more dependent on such factors as feeling respected, being in control of one's life, and having close friends and family. The primary researcher in that survey said in an interview that money "makes you more satisfied than it makes you feel good. Positive feelings are less affected by money and more affected by the things people are doing day to day" (quoted in Stein, 2010, p. 1).

These findings seem to support the old adage that money alone does not buy happiness. However, a lack of financial resources and economic insecurity can lead to unhappiness. Even winning a multimillion-dollar lottery results in only a temporary increase in subjective well-being, after which most winners revert to their previous level of happiness.

This idea has been given formal expression as the "hedonic treadmill" model of happiness, for which there is strong research support. *Hedonic* refers to that which is characterized by pleasure. This theory states that both positive and negative events will affect our level of happiness only temporarily, after which we revert to our normal level of hedonic neutrality.

> *Thus, happiness and unhappiness are merely short-lived reactions to changes in people's circumstances. People continue to pursue happiness because they incorrectly believe that greater happiness lies just around the corner. (Diener, Lucas, & Scollon, 2006, p. 305)*

So, if you think all you need is a bigger house or a more expensive car, think again. Surveys of adults show that more and showier possessions do not equate with greater happiness. One researcher concluded that "the more people endorse materialistic goals, the less happy and satisfied they are with life" (Van Boven, 2005, p. 133). Other research has found that high-income people tend to be more tense and tend to devote less of their time to relaxation and leisure activities. "The activities that higher-income individuals spend relatively more of their time engaged in are associated with no greater happiness, on average, but with slightly higher tension and stress" (Kahneman, Krueger, Schkade, Schwartz, & Stone, 2006, p. 1908).

Similar to the relationship between money and well-being, having good health does not guarantee happiness either. Poor health, however, like a low income, can diminish overall life satisfaction. No gender differences have been found between men and women on measures of happiness for the factors we have discussed.

The relationship between age and happiness seems clear. Studies show that subjective well-being improves with age, except among people with serious health problems or physical limitations in old age (Kunzmann, Little, & Smith, 2000). A study comparing two groups of adults (average age 31 and average age 68) reported that happiness increases with age (Lacey, Smith, & Ubel, 2006). A survey of 340,000 Americans ages 18 to 85 found that subjective well-being and life satisfaction were high at 18, fell progressively until about age 50, and increased to the point where 85-year-olds were more satisfied than they were at 18 (Stone, Schwartz, Broderick, & Deaton, 2010).

A study of nearly 7,000 Americans over a 28-year period found that subjective well-being, positive feelings, and life satisfaction were all related to longevity. In other words, happier people lived longer (Xu & Roberts, 2010). Research on older people in Spain found that exercise or other physical activity was strongly and positively related to feelings of happiness and subjective well-being (Garatachea, Molinero, Martinez-Garcia, Jimenez-Jiminez, Gonzales-Gallego, & Marquez, 2009).

It has also been found that marriage and personality variables relate to a positive approach to life. Research evidence shows that married people report higher levels of happiness than do people who have never married or who are divorced or widowed. People who score high on measures of subjective well-being are also high in self-efficacy, internal locus of control, a strong desire for control over one's life, self-esteem, self-acceptance, self-determination, extraversion, and conscientiousness. They also score low in neuroticism (see, for example, Roberts, Walton, & Bogg, 2005; Ryan & Deci, 2001; Seligman & Csikszentmihalyi, 2000; Snyder & Lopez, 2001; Staudinger, Fleeson, & Baltes, 1999).

What other factors influence happiness? With regard to racial and ethnic variables, studies show that African-American college students as well as older African Americans who experienced discrimination had lower levels of happiness than did those who had not experienced discrimination (Prelow, Mosher, & Bowman, 2006; Utsey, Payne, Jackson, & Jones, 2002). Black college students who reported a strong sense of identification with, and acceptance by, the black community had higher levels of subjective well-being than did those who felt less of an identity with the black community (Postmes & Branscombe, 2002).

You may be surprised to learn that a very low correlation has been found between physical attractiveness and happiness. In addition, a comparison of 90 countries showed that people who lived in highly developed, urbanized, and industrialized nations were happier and lived longer than those living in less well-developed nations (Veenhoven, 2005).

Are happy people more likely to be successful just because they are happy? Or are they happy because they are successful? Research indicates that happiness comes first and leads to the kinds of behaviors that can result in success (Oishi, Diener, & Lucas, 2007). "People high in subjective well-being are more likely to secure job interviews, to be evaluated more positively by supervisors once they obtain a job, to show superior performance and productivity, and to handle managerial jobs better" (Lyubomirsky, King, & Diener, 2005, p. 803).

## Comment

The research and theorizing on positive psychology have captured the interest of a growing number of psychologists and may represent the most enduring legacy of the humanistic psychology movement.

There is an important difference between positive psychology and humanistic psychology, however, as well as between positive psychology and the psychoanalytically derived approaches we described in earlier chapters. Instead of using highly subjective case histories, like the self-actualization work of Maslow, positive psychology relies solely on rigorous experimental research. It has "carefully avoided the antiscientific streak that spelled the downfall of humanistic psychology" (Simonton & Baumeister, 2005, p. 99).

As for the future development of positive psychology as a formal movement or school of thought, Seligman and other positive psychology pioneers have a less-structured goal. "We see Positive Psychology as a mere change in focus for psychology," Seligman wrote, "from the study of some of the worst things in life to the study of what makes life worth living. We do not see Positive Psychology as a replacement for what has gone before, but just as a supplement and extension of it" (Seligman, 2002, pp. 266–267).

Others agree with Seligman's early assessments. Two researchers wrote that the "range of topics is now so great that positive psychology can truly be considered a *general* psychology" (Simonton & Baumeister, 2005, p. 100). A similar judgment was offered by others: "The future of positive psychology? Just plain psychology" (Gable & Haidt, 2005, p. 108).

Whatever the eventual status of positive psychology, it is clearly taking a vastly different approach to human nature than that proposed by Sigmund Freud, who began the study of personality more than a century ago.

## The Psychoanalytic Tradition in History

We have described some of the diversity that arose within the psychoanalytic school during and after Freud's lifetime. Some contemporary positions bear little resemblance to his views and can be labeled "psychoanalytic" only by default to distinguish them from the behavioral-experimental tradition within psychology. Psychoanalysis was more divided by its revisionist theorists than was behaviorism. Despite the changes introduced by neo-behaviorists, they shared Watson's belief that behavior should remain the focus of study. In contrast, few of Freud's followers agreed that the focus of study should remain on unconscious biological forces or that people are motivated by sex and aggression.

The result has been many more sub-schools of psychoanalysis than of behaviorism. This multitude of viewpoints may be considered a sign of vitality or of weakness. The developments are too recent to judge. They are still history in the making, more than a hundred years after Freud began his monumental work.

# Discussion Questions

1. Compare the views of Maslow and Rogers on self-actualization and the characteristics of the psychologically healthy person.

2. Describe Anna Freud's relationship with her father. What changes did she introduce into psychoanalysis?

3. Describe the Jungian concepts of the collective unconscious and the archetypes.

4. Explain Horney's concepts of basic anxiety, neurotic needs, and idealized self-image.

5. Explain what Adler meant by "style of life." According to Adler's theory, how do inferiority feelings develop?

6. For what reasons did humanistic psychology fail to reach its goal of transforming psychology?

7. How did Jung's analytical psychology differ from Freudian psychoanalysis?

8. How did the approaches of Melanie Klein and Heinz Kohut differ from each other, and from Freudian psychoanalysis?

9. How did the changing Zeitgeist in social science influence the later development of psychoanalysis?

10. How were Horney's views of personality influenced by her childhood experiences?

11. In what ways did Freud and Horney differ in their views of feminine psychology?

12. In what ways did Jung's life experiences influence his analytical psychology?

13. In what ways did the neo-Freudians change Freudian psychoanalysis?

14. In your opinion, will the positive psychology movement have a more lasting influence on the field than the humanistic psychology movement did? Why or why not?

15. On what grounds did the humanistic psychologists criticize behaviorism and psychoanalysis?

16. On what grounds have the theories of Maslow and Rogers been criticized?

17. On what issues did Adler and Freud disagree?

18. To what does the word *object* refer in *object relations theory*?

19. What factors have been shown to affect subjective well-being? What factors can you list that influence your own happiness?

20. What lasting contributions to psychology have been made by Jung and by Adler?

21. What personal experiences influenced Maslow's approach to psychology?

CHAPTER **15**
# Contemporary Developments

## Schools of Thought in Perspective

We have seen how each of the schools of thought in psychology developed, prospered for a time, and then—with the exception of psychoanalysis—became part of mainstream contemporary psychological thought. We have also seen that each movement drew strength from its opposition to an earlier school. And when there was no longer a need to protest, when the new school had ousted its opposition, it ceased to be a revolutionary movement and became the established order, at least for a while.

Each school made substantial contributions to psychology's evolution. This is true even for structuralism, although it has left little direct imprint on psychology as we know it today. There are no longer structuralists of Titchener's sort in modern psychology, nor have there been for more than a century. Yet structuralism was an enormous success in promoting the enterprise Wundt began, the establishment of an independent science of psychology free of the strictures of philosophy. That structuralism failed to dominate psychology more than a short time does not detract from its revolutionary achievement as the first school of thought of a new science and a vital source of opposition for the systems that followed.

Consider the success of functionalism, which also has not endured as a separate school. As an attitude or viewpoint, however, which is all its advocates hoped it would be, functionalism permeated American psychological thought. To the extent that American psychology today is as much profession as science and applies its findings to virtually every aspect of modern life, the functional, utilitarian attitude has indeed changed the nature of psychology.

What of Gestalt psychology? It, too, on a more modest scale, accomplished its mission. The opposition to elementism, the support of a "wholes" approach, and the interest in consciousness have influenced psychologists in clinical psychology, learning, perception, social psychology, and thinking. Although the Gestalt school did not transform psychology the way its founders expected, it had considerable impact and can therefore be described as a success.

As noteworthy as the accomplishments of structuralism, functionalism, and Gestalt psychology are, they take second place to the phenomenal impact of behaviorism and psychoanalysis. The effects of these movements have been profound, and they have maintained their identities as separate and unique schools of thought.

We saw how behaviorism and psychoanalysis splintered into various positions after the days of their founders, Watson and Freud. No single form of behaviorism or of psychoanalysis has won allegiance from all members of either school. The emergence of sub-schools divided the systems into competing factions, each with its own map of the path to truth. Despite this internal diversity, however, behaviorists and psychoanalysts stand firmly opposed to each other in their approaches to psychology. For example, Skinnerian behaviorists have more in common with sociobehaviorist followers of Bandura and Rotter than they do with followers of Jung's or Horney's psychoanalysis. The vitality of these two schools of thought is evident in their continuing evolution.

We have seen that Skinner's psychology was not the last stage in the development of behaviorism any more than Adler's individual psychology was the final stage of psychoanalysis. We also saw that humanistic psychology, although failing to make an impact as a separate school of thought, nevertheless influenced contemporary psychology through the growth of the positive psychology movement.

By the 1960s and 1970s, two other movements arose within American psychology, and each attempted to shape a new definition for the field. These movements are cognitive psychology and evolutionary psychology.

# The Cognitive Movement in Psychology

In Watson's behaviorist manifesto in 1913, he insisted that psychology drop all references to mind, consciousness, or conscious processes. Indeed, the psychologists who followed Watson's dictates eliminated mention of these concepts and banished all mentalistic terminology. For decades, introductory psychology textbooks described the functioning of the brain but refused to discuss any conception of the mind. People joked that psychology had "lost consciousness" or "lost its mind," seemingly forever.

Then suddenly (though the trend actually had been building for some time) psychology regained consciousness. Words that once were politically incorrect were being uttered at meetings and appearing in print. In 1979, the *American Psychologist* published an article titled "Behaviorism and the Mind: A (Limited) Call for a Return to Introspection" (Lieberman, 1979), invoking not only mind but also the suspect technique of introspection. A few months earlier, the journal had published an article with the simple title "Consciousness." "After decades of deliberate neglect," its author wrote, "consciousness is again coming under scientific scrutiny, with discussions of the topic appearing at entirely respectable locations in psychology's literature" (Natsoulas, 1978, p. 906).

In 1976, in his annual address, the APA president told the assembled audience that psychology was changing and that the new conception included a refocus on consciousness. Psychology's image of human nature was becoming "human rather than mechanical" (McKeachie, 1976, p. 831). When an officer of the APA and a prestigious journal discuss consciousness so openly and optimistically, it seems obvious that a revolution—another new movement—is under way.

Revisions in introductory textbooks followed, redefining psychology as the science of behavior and mental processes instead of only behavior, a science seeking to explain overt behavior and its relationship to mental processes. Thus it became clear that psychology had progressed far beyond the desires and designs of Watson and Skinner. A new school of thought was taking hold.

## Antecedent Influences on Cognitive Psychology

Like all revolutionary movements in psychology, cognitive psychology did not spring up overnight. Many of its features had been anticipated. Interest in consciousness was evident in the earliest days of psychology before it became a formal science. The writings of the Greek philosophers Plato and Aristotle deal with thought processes, as do the theories of the British empiricists and associationists.

When Wundt founded psychology as a separate scientific discipline, his work centered on consciousness. He may be considered a forerunner of contemporary cognitive psychology because of his emphasis on the mind's creative activity. The structuralist and functionalist schools of thought dealt with consciousness, studying its elements and functions. Behaviorism, however, brought fundamental change, dismissing consciousness for nearly 50 years.

The return to consciousness, and the formal beginning of the cognitive psychology movement, can be traced to the 1950s, although signs were apparent as early as the 1930s. The behaviorist E. R. Guthrie, toward the end of his career, deplored the mechanistic model and argued that stimuli cannot always be reduced to physical terms. He suggested that psychologists describe stimuli in perceptual or cognitive terms so that they will be meaningful for the responding organism (Guthrie, 1959). The concept of meaning cannot be described solely in behaviorist terms because it is a mentalistic or cognitive process.

The purposive behaviorism of E. C. Tolman (Chapter 11) was another precursor of the cognitive movement. His form of behaviorism recognized the importance of cognitive variables and contributed to the decline of the stimulus-response approach. Tolman proposed cognitive maps, attributed purposive behavior to animals, and emphasized intervening variables as a way to operationally define internal unobservable states.

Gestalt psychology influenced the cognitive movement with its focus on "organization, structure, relationships, the active role of the subject, and the important part played by perception in learning and memory" (Hearst, 1979, p. 32). The Gestalt school of thought helped keep alive at least a token interest in consciousness during the years that behaviorism dominated American psychology.

Another anticipator of cognitive psychology is the Swiss psychologist Jean Piaget (1896–1980), who liked hiking in the mountains to hunt for snails. As a taste treat he enjoyed stale bread covered with mayonnaise and garlic. Piaget wrote his first scientific paper at age 10 and later studied with Carl Jung. Piaget also worked with Théodore Simon who, with Alfred Binet, developed the first psychological test of mental abilities (see Chapter 8).

Piaget assisted in administering the tests to children. He later became important for his work on child development, not in psychosexual stages as proposed by Freud but in cognitive stages. Piaget's clinical method of interviewing children and his insistence on highly detailed note-taking during the interviews were seen as a major inspiration for the famous Hawthorne studies of industrial workers in the 1920s, which we described in Chapter 8 (see Hsueh, 2004).

However, Piaget's work on cognitive development, which was published in the 1920s and 1930s, although highly influential in Europe, was not so widely accepted in the United States because of its incompatibility with the behaviorist position. The early cognitive theorists, however, welcomed Piaget's emphasis on cognitive factors. As the ideas of the cognitive psychologists took hold in American psychology, the relevance of Piaget's ideas became clearer. In 1969, he became the first European psychologist to receive the APA's Distinguished Scientific Contribution Award. Because his work focused on children, it helped broaden the range of behavior to which cognitive psychology would be applied.

## The Changing Zeitgeist in Physics

When we find a major shift in the evolution of a science, we know it is reflecting changes that are already part of its intellectual Zeitgeist. We have seen that a science, like a living species, adapts to the conditions and demands of its environment. What intellectual climate fostered the cognitive movement and moderated behaviorist ideas by readmitting consciousness? Once again we look to the Zeitgeist in physics, long psychology's role model, for it has influenced the field since its beginnings as a science.

Early in the twentieth century, a viewpoint developed within physics arising from the work of Albert Einstein, Niels Bohr, and Werner Heisenberg. They rejected the mechanistic model of the universe stemming from the days of Galileo and Newton, the prototype for the mechanistic, reductionistic, and deterministic view of human nature embraced by psychologists from Wundt to Skinner. The new look in physics discarded the requirement of total objectivity and the complete separation of the external world from the observer.

Physicists recognized that any observation we make of the natural world is likely to disturb it. They would have to attempt to bridge the artificial gap between observer and observed, between inner world and outer world, between mental and material. Thus, scientific investigation shifted from an independent and objectively knowable universe to one's observation of that universe. Modern scientists would no longer be so detached from the focus of their observation. In a sense, they would become "participant-observers."

As a result, the ideal of a totally objective reality was no longer considered attainable. Physics came to be characterized by the belief that what was once thought to be objective knowledge is actually subjective, that is, dependent on the observer. This idea that all knowledge is personal sounds suspiciously like what Berkeley proposed 300 years ago: Knowledge is subjective because it depends on the nature of the person perceiving it. One writer noted that our picture of the world, "far from being a genuine photographic reproduction of an independent reality 'out there,' [is] rather more on the order of a painting: a subjective creation of the mind which can convey a likeness but can never produce a replica" (Matson, 1964, p. 137).

The physicists' rejection of an objective, mechanistic subject matter and their concurrent recognition of subjectivity restored the vital role of conscious experience as a way of obtaining information about our world. This revolution in physics was an effective argument for again making consciousness a legitimate part of psychology's subject matter. Although the scientific psychology establishment resisted the new physics for a half century, clinging to an outdated model by stubbornly defining itself as an objective science of behavior, it eventually responded to the Zeitgeist and modified itself sufficiently to readmit cognitive processes.

## The Founding of Cognitive Psychology

A retrospective look at the cognitive movement gives the impression of a rapid transition that undermined psychology's behaviorist foundations in a few short years. At the time, of course, this transition was not at all apparent. The change that now seems so dramatic came about slowly and quietly, with no beating drums and no fanfare. One psychologist wrote, "the term 'revolution' is probably inappropriate. There were no cataclysmic events; the change occurred slowly in different subfields over some 10 to 15 years; there was no identifiable flashpoint or leader" (Mandler, 2002a, p. 339).

Often, the progression of history is clear only after the event. The founding of cognitive psychology did not occur overnight, nor could it be attributed to the charisma of one individual who, like Watson, changed the field almost single-handedly. Like functional psychology, the cognitive movement claims no solitary founder, perhaps because none of the psychologists working in the area had the personal ambition to lead a new movement. Their interest was pragmatic: simply getting on with the work of redefining psychology.

In retrospect, history identifies two scholars who are not founders in the formal sense but who contributed groundbreaking work in the form of a research center and books now considered milestones in the development of cognitive psychology. They are George Miller and Ulric Neisser. Their stories highlight some of the personal factors involved in shaping new schools of thought.

# George Miller (1920– )

GEORGE MILLER

George Miller majored in English and speech at the University of Alabama, where he received his master's degree in speech in 1941. While there, he expressed an interest in psychology and was offered an instructorship to teach 16 sections of introductory psychology, even though he had never taken a course in the field. He said that after teaching the same material 16 times a week, he began to believe in it.

Miller went on to Harvard University, where he worked in the psychoacoustic laboratory on problems in vocal communication. In 1946, he received his Ph.D. Five years later he published a landmark book on psycholinguistics, *Language and Communication* (1951). Miller initially accepted the behaviorist school of thought, noting that he had little choice because behaviorists held the leadership positions in major universities and professional associations.

> *The power, the honors, the authority, the textbooks, the money, everything in psychology was owned by the behavioristic school. … those of us who wanted to be scientific psychologists couldn't really oppose it. You just wouldn't get a job. (Miller, quoted in Baars, 1986, p. 203)*

By the mid-1950s, after investigating statistical learning theory, information theory, and computer-based models of the mind, Miller concluded that behaviorism was not, as he put it, "going to work out." The similarities between computers and the operation of the human mind impressed him, and his view of psychology became more cognitively oriented. At the same time, he developed an annoying allergy to animal hair and dander, so he could no longer conduct research with laboratory rats. Working only with human subjects was a disadvantage in the world of the behaviorists.

Miller's shift toward a cognitive psychology was also helped by his rebellious nature, so typical of many of his generation of psychologists. They were primed to revolt against the psychology then being taught and practiced, ready to offer their new approach, their focus on cognitive rather than behavioral factors. But as Miller wrote some 50 years later, "At the time it was happening, I did not realize that I was, in fact, a revolutionary" (2003, p. 141).

In 1956 Miller published an article, which has since become a classic, titled "The Magical Number Seven, Plus or Minus Two: Some Limits on our Capacity for Processing Information." In this work, Miller demonstrated that our conscious capacity for short-term memory of numbers (or, similarly, for words or colors) is limited to approximately seven "chunks" of information. That is all we are able to process at any given point. The importance, and impact, of this finding lies in the fact that it deals with a conscious, or cognitive, experience at a time when behaviorism still dominated psychological thought. In addition, Miller's use of the phrase "processing information" indicated the influence of a computer-based model of the human mind.

## The Center for Cognitive Studies

With Jerome Bruner (1915–), his colleague at Harvard, Miller established a research center to investigate the human mind. Miller and Bruner asked the university president for space, and in 1960 they were given the house in which William James had once lived. This was considered an appropriate site because James had dealt so exquisitely in his *Principles* book with the nature of mental life. Choosing a name for the new enterprise was not a trivial matter. Being associated with Harvard, the center had the potential to exert an enormous influence on psychology. They selected the word "cognition" to denote their subject matter and decided to call the facility the Center for Cognitive Studies:

> *In using the word "cognition" we were setting ourselves off from behaviorism. We wanted something that was* mental—*but "mental psychology" seemed terribly redundant.*

*"Common-sense psychology" would have suggested some sort of anthropological investiga-*
*tion, and "folk psychology" would have suggested Wundt's social psychology. What word*
*do you use to label this set of views? We chose cognition. (Miller, quoted in Baars,*
*1986, p. 210)*

Two students at the center later recalled that no one could tell them what cognition
really meant at that time or what ideas they were supposed to be promoting. The center
"was not set up to be for anything in particular; it was set up to be against things. What
was important was what it was not" (Norman & Levelt, 1988, p. 101).

It was not behaviorism. It was not the ruling authority, the establishment, or the
psychology of the present. In defining the center, its founders were demonstrating
how greatly they differed from behaviorism. As we have seen, every new movement
proclaims that its position or attitude differs from the current school of thought; this
is a necessary preliminary stage to defining what they are about and what changes they
propose. Miller, however, gave due credit to the Zeitgeist. "Neither of us should take
too much credit for the Center's success. It was an idea whose time had come" (Miller,
1989, p. 412).

Miller did not consider cognitive psychology to be a true revolution, despite its differences from behaviorism. He called it an "accretion," a change by slow growth or accumulation. He saw the movement as more evolutionary than revolutionary and believed it
was a return to a commonsense psychology that recognized and affirmed psychology's
concern with mental life as well as behavior.

Researchers at the center investigated a wide range of topics: language, memory, perception, concept formation, thinking, and developmental psychology. Most of these areas
had been eliminated from the behaviorists' vocabulary. Miller later established a program
for cognitive sciences at Princeton University.

Miller became president of the APA in 1969 and received the Distinguished Scientific
Contribution Award and the American Psychological Foundation's Gold Medal Award
for Life Achievement in the Application of Psychology. In 1991 he was awarded the
National Medal of Science. In 2003 he was given the APA's Outstanding Lifetime Contribution to Psychology Award. Additional acknowledgment of the significance of his work
includes the number of cognitive psychology laboratories modeled on his center and the
rapid development and formalization of the approach he did so much to define.

# Ulric Neisser (1928– )

ULRIC NEISSER

Born in Kiel, Germany, Ulric Neisser was brought to the United States by his parents at
the age of three. Describing his childhood, Neisser wrote, "I was afraid of girls, poor at
sports, and incompetent even in shop. I thought of myself as an outsider and of my few
friends as weird. Maybe I was weird, too" (2007, p. 272).

He began his college studies at Harvard, majoring in physics. Impressed with a young
psychology professor by the name of George Miller, Neisser decided that physics did not
excite him. He switched to psychology and took an honors course with Miller on the
psychology of communications and information theory. He reports also being influenced
by Koffka's book, *Principles of Gestalt Psychology*. After receiving his bachelor's degree
from Harvard in 1950, Neisser earned his master's degree at Swarthmore College, studying under Gestalt psychologist Wolfgang Köhler. Neisser returned to Harvard for his
Ph.D., which he completed in 1956.

Despite his growing attraction to a cognitive approach to psychology, Neisser saw no
escape from behaviorism if he wanted an academic career. "It was what you had to learn.

That was the age when it was supposed that no psychological phenomenon was real unless you could demonstrate it in a rat" (quoted in Baars, 1986, p. 275). It was fortunate for Neisser that his first academic job was at Brandeis University, where the psychology department chair was Abraham Maslow. At the time, Maslow was moving away from his own behaviorist training to develop the humanistic approach to the field. Maslow was not successful in turning Neisser into a humanistic psychologist, or in turning humanistic psychology into psychology's third force, but he provided the opportunity for Neisser to pursue his interest in cognitive issues. (Neisser later claimed that cognitive psychology, not humanistic psychology, was the third force.)

In 1967 Neisser published *Cognitive Psychology*. He reported that the book was a personal one, an attempt to define himself and the kind of psychologist he wanted to be. The book was also a landmark in the history of psychology, an attempt to define a new approach to the field. It became extremely popular, and Neisser was embarrassed to find himself designated the "father" of cognitive psychology.

"In the blink of an eye," Neisser wrote 40 years later, "there were cognitive journals, courses on cognition, training programs in cognitive psychology, and conferences of every kind. I myself was a star, now introduced everywhere as 'the father of cognitive psychology.' It was a heady experience for a young man not yet 40 years old" (2007, p. 284).

But he soon grew disillusioned with what he had created. Just nine years later, Neisser published *Cognition and Reality* (1976), which expressed his deepening dissatisfaction with what he saw as the narrowing of the cognitive position and its reliance on laboratory situations instead of real-world settings from which to collect data. He insisted that the results of psychological research should have ecological validity. By that he meant that they should be generalizable to situations beyond the confines of the laboratory.

In addition, Neisser insisted that cognitive psychologists should be able to apply their findings to practical problems, helping people deal with the everyday issues in their work and in their lives. Thus, Neisser concluded that the cognitive psychology movement had little to contribute to psychology's understanding of how people cope. And so this major figure in the founding of cognitive psychology became an outspoken critic, challenging the movement as he had earlier challenged behaviorism.

After 17 years at Cornell University, where his office was not far from where Titchener's pickled brain was housed, Neisser moved to Emory University in Atlanta. He returned to Cornell in 1996.

## The Computer Metaphor

Clocks and automata were the seventeenth-century metaphors for the mechanical view of the universe and, by extension, for the human mind. Those machines were widespread, easily understood models of how the mind was believed to work. Today, the mechanical model of the universe and the behavioral psychology that derived from it have been superseded by other viewpoints, such as the acceptance of subjectivity in physics and the cognitive movement in psychology.

As a result, the clock is no longer a useful example for the modern view of the mind. A twentieth-century machine, the computer, has emerged to serve as our model, as a new metaphor for the functioning of the mind. One historian of science wrote, "The vehicle for the reintroduction of mind, and a vital agent of behaviorism's overthrow, was the idea that the brain is a computer. This assertion has become a commonplace one in the historical literature on the 'cognitive revolution'" (Crowther-Heyck, 1999, p. 37). Psychologists invoke the operations of the computer to explain cognitive phenomena.

Computers, said to display artificial intelligence, are often described in human terms. The storage capacity is its memory, programming codes are languages, and new generations of computers are said to be evolving.

Computer programs, essentially sets of instructions for dealing with symbols, may be seen to function similarly to the human mind. Both the computer and the mind receive from the environment and process large amounts of information (sensory stimuli or data). They digest this information, manipulating, storing, and retrieving it, and acting on it in various ways. Thus, computer programming has become the basis for the cognitive view of human information processing, reasoning, and problem solving.

Cognitive psychologists are interested in the sequence of symbol manipulation that underlies human thought processes. In other words, they are concerned with how the mind processes information. Their goal is to discover the programs each of us has stored in our memory, those patterns of thinking that allow us to understand and articulate ideas, to remember and recall events and concepts, and to grasp and solve new problems. In more than 125 years of history, psychology has progressed from simple clocks to sophisticated computers as the models for its subject matter, but it is significant that both are mechanical. This demonstrates the historical continuity in psychology's evolution from older to newer schools of thought. We can also see a historical continuity in the evolution of computers themselves.

## The Development of the Modern Computer

We have already discussed the work of Charles Babbage and Henry Hollerith to develop machines that would "think" like humans. However, it was a practical problem during the early days of World War II that led to the beginning of the modern age of computers. In 1942 the U.S. Army desperately needed to find a faster way to make the rapid calculations required to fire artillery pieces. To aim a cannon accurately so that the shell hits its target was (and still is) a difficult process, far more complex than a soldier aiming a rifle and squeezing the trigger. Here is one description: "To aim a cannon, a gunner had to adjust the gun to several settings. That required [mathematical] tables to account for all the variables that affect the trajectory of an artillery shell; wind speed and direction, humidity, temperature, elevation, even the temperature of the gunpowder" (Keiger, 1999, p. 40).

The book of settings for each type of artillery piece contained hundreds, even thousands, of tables of settings. A single trajectory required 12 hours of continuous and complicated calculations (see Friedel, 2007). This work was being done by women, newly employed during wartime, using mechanical calculating machines. (The women holding these jobs were called "computers.") Within a year, however, they had fallen behind; they could not keep up with the demand. The situation was so critical that some cannons had to be withdrawn from combat because there were no firing tables available.

This need spurred the development of the first giant computer, Electronic Numerical Integrator and Calculator (ENIAC). Completed in 1943, the horseshoe-shaped machine took up three walls of a huge room with "arms 80 feet long. It would stand eight feet tall and weigh 30 tons. It would contain 17,468 vacuum tubes as well as 10,000 capacitors, 70,000 resistors, 1,500 relays, and 6,000 manual switches—an array of electronics so vast that large blowers would be required to dissipate the heat it produced" (Waldrop, 2001, p. 45).

Machines that can perform mental operations have come a long way from Babbage's calculating engine. You need only to compare the size and capacity of your laptop or smartphone to realize how primitive ENIAC was. The evolution of machines to perform mental functions continues at a rapid pace, which leads, inevitably, to the question of whether these machines truly demonstrate intelligence.

# Artificial Intelligence

We noted that cognitive psychologists accepted computers as a model for human cognitive functioning, suggesting that the machines display artificial intelligence and process information similarly to the way people do. Does it follow that the computer's intelligence is the same as human intelligence? Can computers think? In the seventeenth century, automata simulated human movements and speech. In the future, will new generations of computers simulate human thought?

Initially computer scientists and cognitive psychologists enthusiastically embraced the notion of artificial intelligence. As early as 1949, when computers were relatively primitive, the author of a book titled *Giant Brains* declared, "a machine can handle information; it can calculate, conclude, and choose; it can perform reasonable operations with information. A machine, therefore, can think" (quoted in Dyson, 1997, p. 108).

In 1950 the British computer genius Alan Turing (1912–1954) proposed a way to examine the proposition that computers can think. Called the Turing Test, it involved persuading a subject that the computer with which he or she is communicating is really another person, not a machine. If the subject cannot distinguish the computer's responses from human responses, then the computer must be displaying intelligence at a human level. The Turing Test works as follows:

> *The interrogator [the subject] has two different "conversations" with an interactive computer program. The goal of the interrogator is to figure out which of the two parties is a person communicating through the computer and which is the computer itself. The interrogator can ask the two parties any questions at all. However, the computer will try to fool the interrogator into believing that it is human, whereas the human will be trying to show the interrogator that she or he truly is human. The computer passes the Turing Test if an interrogator is unable to distinguish the computer from the human. (Sternberg, 1996, pp. 481–482)*

Not everyone agreed with the premise of the Turing Test. One of the most effective objections was offered by John Searle (1932– ), an American philosopher who advanced the Chinese Room problem (Searle, 1980). Imagine you are sitting at a desk. In the wall in front of you are two slots. Slips of paper appear one at a time from the slot on the left. Each paper contains a group of Chinese characters. Your job is to match by shape the set of symbols with those in a book. When you find the matching set, you are directed to copy another set of symbols from the book onto a piece of paper and feed the paper through the slot on the right.

What is happening here? You are receiving inputs from the left slot and writing outputs for the right slot, following the instructions (the program) you have been given. If you are like most subjects in the United States, you would not be expected to read or understand Chinese. All you are doing is mechanically following your instructions.

However, if a Chinese psychologist were on the far side of the wall containing the slots, he or she would not know you were unfamiliar with the Chinese language. Communications are going to you in Chinese and you are responding with appropriate answers in Chinese, copied from your book. But no matter how many messages you receive and respond to, you still do not know Chinese. You are not thinking; you are merely following instructions. You are not displaying intelligence but simply following orders.

Searle argued that computer programs that may appear to comprehend different kinds of inputs and respond to them in an intelligent manner are operating like the subject in the Chinese Room puzzle. A computer no more understands the messages it receives than you may have understood Chinese. In these instances, both you and the computer are operating strictly in accordance with a set of programmed rules.

Many cognitive psychologists came to agree that computers may pass the Turing Test and simulate intelligence without actually *being* intelligent. So far, however, none had been able to pass the Turing Test. Every year since 1990 a competition for the Loebner prize gold medal has been held to find a computer program that will persuade judges that they are communicating with a person and not a computer. As of 2009, no one had won the prize, although in 2009 a program won the bronze medal for convincing 3 of the 12 judges that it was an actual human (Floridi, Taddeo, & Turilli, 2009; Pavia, 2008).

# The Nature of Cognitive Psychology

In Chapter 11 we noted how the inclusion of cognitive factors in the social learning theories of Albert Bandura and Julian Rotter altered American behaviorism. Today it is not only in behavioral psychology that the cognitive movement has an impact. Cognitive factors are considered by researchers in virtually all areas: attribution theory in social psychology, cognitive dissonance theory, motivation and emotion, personality, learning, memory, perception, problem solving, creativity, and information processing in human intelligence and in artificial intelligence. Applied areas such as clinical, community, school, and industrial-organizational psychology have also seen an emphasis on cognitive factors.

Cognitive psychology differs from behaviorism on several points. First, cognitive psychologists focus on the process of knowing rather than merely responding to stimuli. The important factors are mental processes and events, not stimulus-response connections; the emphasis is on the mind, not behavior. This does not mean that cognitive psychologists ignore behavior, but behavioral responses are not the sole focus of their research. Behavioral responses are sources for making inferences and drawing conclusions about the mental processes accompanying them.

Second, cognitive psychologists are interested in how the mind structures or organizes experience. Gestalt psychologists, as well as Piaget, argued in favor of an innate tendency to organize conscious experience (sensations and perceptions) into meaningful wholes and patterns. The mind gives form and coherence to mental experience; this process is the subject matter of cognitive psychology. British empiricists and associationists and their twentieth-century derivatives, the Skinnerian behaviorists, insisted that the mind did not possess inherent organizational abilities.

Third, cognitive psychologists believe that the individual actively and creatively arranges the stimuli received from the environment. We are capable of participating in the acquisition and application of knowledge, deliberately attending to some events and choosing to commit them to memory. We are not, as the behaviorists claimed, passive responders to external forces or blank slates on which sensory experience will write.

## Cognitive Neuroscience

Research on mapping brain functions dates from the eighteenth and nineteenth centuries and the work of Hall, Flourens, and Broca (see Chapter 3). Using methods such as extirpation and electrical stimulation, early physiologists attempted to determine the specific parts of the brain that controlled various cognitive functions.

That quest continues today in the discipline called cognitive neuroscience, a hybrid of cognitive psychology and the neurosciences (see Spear, 2007). The goals of this field are to determine "how brain functions give rise to mental activity" and to "correlate specific aspects of information processing with specific brain regions" (Sarter, Bernston, & Cacioppo, 1996, p. 13).

Researchers in cognitive neuroscience have made striking advances in mapping the brain, largely due to the development and application of sophisticated imaging techniques. For example, the electroencephalogram (EEG) records variations in electrical activity in selected parts of the brain. Computerized axial tomography (CAT) scans reveal detailed cross sections of the brain. Magnetic resonance imagery (MRI) scans produce three-dimensional pictures of the brain. Whereas these techniques produce still images, positron emission tomography (PET) scans provide live pictures of various cognitive activities as they occur. These and other imaging techniques are providing scientists with a degree of precision and detail that was not previously attainable.

Cognitive neuroscientists have demonstrated that the human brain can exert control over a computer. Thought can be translated into movement by electrical impulses alone. The first subject for a demonstration of this kind was a 25-year-old man who had been totally paralyzed for the last three years. Electronic sensors, implanted in the motor cortex of his brain, were interfaced with a computer allowing him to control not only the computer but also a television set and a robot—all by using only his thoughts.

Within minutes he had learned to move the computer's cursor, allowing him to open e-mail, move objects using a robotic arm, play a simple videogame, and draw a crude circle on the screen. He exercised this control by thinking about—that is, by willing or intending to make—such movements. He could not, of course, move any control with his hands.

This application of cognitive neuroscience, called neuroprosthetics, offers the hope that people with these types of disabilities could one day be able to interact with and exercise control over objects in their environment (Hochberg et al., 2006; Isa, Fetz, & Muller, 2009; Pollack, 2006).

## The Role of Introspection

Cognitive psychologists' acceptance of conscious experiences led them to reconsider scientific psychology's first research approach, the introspective method introduced by Wundt more than a century ago. In a statement that could have been uttered by Wundt or Titchener, a psychologist writing in the late twentieth century noted the obvious fact that "if we are to study consciousness we must use introspection and introspective reports" (Farthing, 1992, p. 61). Much more recently, another psychologist affirmed that "introspection is indispensable to psychology" (Locke, 2009, p. 24).

Psychologists have attempted to quantify introspective reports to render them more objective and amenable to statistical analyses. One approach, retrospective phenomenological assessment, involves asking subjects to rate the intensity of their subjective experiences while responding to a previous stimulus situation. In other words, subjects retrospectively evaluate the subjective experiences that occurred during an earlier period when they were asked to respond to a given stimulus.

A leading cognitive psychologist noted that not only is introspection widely used but that the conscious states revealed by introspection are "often good predictors of people's behavior" (Wilson, 2003, p. 131).

Although some form of introspection constitutes the most frequently used research method in contemporary psychology, even its most ardent adherents recognize the limitations to its validity. For example, some subjects may give socially desirable introspective reports by telling researchers what they think the researchers want to hear in an effort to please them. Another problem with introspection is that subjects may not be able to access some of their thoughts or feelings because these reside deep in the unconscious, a topic to which psychologists are devoting increasing attention.

## Unconscious Cognition

The study of conscious mental processes sparked a renewed interest in unconscious cognitive activities. "After 100 years of neglect, suspicion, and frustration, unconscious processes have now taken a firm hold on the collective mind of psychologists" (Kihlstrom, Barnhardt, & Tataryn, 1992, p. 788). Increasingly, cognitive psychologists agree that the unconscious is able to accomplish many functions that were once thought to require deliberation, intention, and conscious awareness. Research suggests that much of our thinking and information processing takes place first in the unconscious, which may operate more quickly and efficiently than does the conscious mind (see Bargh & Morsella, 2008; Hassin, Uleman, & Margh, 2005; Wilson, 2002).

However, this is not the unconscious mind of which Freud spoke, overflowing with repressed desires and memories brought into conscious awareness only through psychoanalysis. The new unconscious is more rational than emotional and is involved in the first stage of cognition in responding to a stimulus. Thus, unconscious processes form an integral part of learning and can be studied experimentally.

To distinguish the modern version of the cognitive unconscious from the psychoanalytic version (and from the physical states of being unaware, asleep, or comatose), some cognitive psychologists prefer the term "nonconscious." In general, cognitive researchers agree that most human mental processing occurs at a nonconscious level. "It now appears that the unconscious is 'smarter' than first thought, capable of processing complex verbal and visual information and even anticipating (and planning for) future events. ... No longer simply a repository for drives and impulses, the unconscious appears to play a role in problem solving, hypothesis testing, and creativity" (Bornstein & Masling, 1998, p. xx).

In both laboratory experiments and observational studies of consumer purchasing behavior, researchers have found that unconscious thought (called here "deliberation-without-attention") was more creative and diverse and led to purchases with which people were more satisfied than when the laboratory responses and purchasing behavior were directed by conscious thought (Dijksterhuis, Bos, Nordgren, & van Baaren, 2006; Dijksterhuis & Meurs, 2006).

A popular approach to studying nonconscious processing involves subliminal perception (or subliminal activation), in which stimuli are presented below the subjects' levels of conscious awareness. Despite the subjects' inability to perceive those stimuli, the stimuli activate the subjects' conscious processes and behavior. Thus, this type of research shows that we can be influenced by stimuli we cannot see or hear. These and similar findings have persuaded cognitive psychologists that the process of acquiring knowledge (in or out of the laboratory setting) takes place at both conscious and nonconscious levels, but that most of the mental work involved in learning occurs at the nonconscious level.

## Animal Cognition

The cognitive movement restored consciousness not only to humans but to animals as well. Indeed, animal psychology and comparative psychology have come full circle, from observations of animal mental life reported by Romanes and Morgan in the 1880s and 1890s, through the mechanical stimulus-response conditioning research of Skinnerian behaviorists in the 1950s and 1960s, to the contemporary restoration of consciousness by cognitive psychologists.

Since the 1970s, animal psychologists have attempted to demonstrate how animals "encode, transform, compute, and manipulate symbolic representations of the real world's spatial, temporal, and causal textures for the purposes of adaptively organizing their behavior" (Cook, 1993, p. 174). In other words, the same computer-like information processing system believed to be operating in humans is being studied in animals.

Animal memory has been shown to be complex and flexible, and at least some cognitive processes may operate similarly in animals and humans. Laboratory animals are capable of learning diverse and sophisticated concepts. They display mental processes such as coding and organizing symbols, the ability to form abstractions about space, time, and number and to perceive cause-and-effect relationships. In addition, their use of tools and other implements and their ability to modify tools to operate in different situations imply a basic sense of reasoning (Bania, Harris, Kinsley, & Boysen, 2009; Wynne, 2001).

Studies of animals ranging from insects to mammals (including bees, pigs, rats, pigeons, chimps, parrots, dolphin, and crows) suggest that animals can perform a variety of cognitive functions. They can form cognitive maps, sense the motives of others, plan by taking into account past experiences, understand the concept of numbers, and solve problems through the use of reason (see, for example, Emery & Clayton, 2005; Pennisi, 2006).

A variety of studies have shown that parrots and dogs can function intellectually at levels comparable to those of a two-to-five-year-old human. Pigs can play videogames with joysticks and use mirrors to find food that is located behind them. Honeybees can learn to distinguish human faces (see Avargues-Weber, Portelli, Benard, Dyer, & Giorfa, 2010; Broom, Sena, & Moynihan, 2009; Jayson, 2009; Pepperberg, 2008).

As you might expect, however, the idea of animal cognition is still controversial. Some animal psychologists maintain that the research to date does not sufficiently support the generalization that animal cognition operates similarly to human cognition. The gap between human and animal functioning proposed by Descartes in the seventeenth century retains its appeal.

Behavioral psychologists still reject the notion of consciousness, in animals as well as humans. One behaviorist wrote about cognitive animal psychologists, "They are the George Romaneses of today. Speculating about memory, reasoning, and consciousness in animals is no less ridiculous today than it was a hundred years ago" (Baum, 1994, p. 138). A noted historian offered a contradictory view:

*Do animals show all the observable aspects of consciousness? The biological evidence points to a clear yes. Are they then likely to have the subjective side as well? Given the long and growing list of similarities, the weight of evidence, it seems to me, is inexorably moving toward yes. My sense is that the scientific community has now swung decisively in its favor. The basic facts have come home at last. We are not the only conscious beings on earth. (Baars, 1997, p. 33)*

If animals are conscious beings and can perform cognitive functions similar to humans, is it reasonable to ask whether they also display common personality characteristics? A growing number of psychologists believe the answer is yes.

## Animal Personality

In the early 1990s two psychologists decided to study the 44 red octopuses at the aquarium in Seattle, Washington, where staff scientists and keepers had often noticed what they thought were differing personalities among their charges. Indeed, they had given the creatures names to match their natures. A shy female octopus was called Emily Dickinson, after the poet. Another was so aggressive and destructive she was called Lucretia McEvil (Siebert, 2006).

The psychologists observed the behavior of the octopuses in three experimental situations and found that they differed on three factors: activity, reactivity, and avoidance. Their answer to the question, "Do octopuses have personalities?" was a qualified yes (Mather & Anderson, 1993).

Since the time of that research, studies have documented personality characteristics in a variety of animals, including fish, spiders, farm animals, hyenas, chimps, and dogs. For example, hyenas in a zoo were observed by their keepers to have such distinct human-like characteristics as excitability, sociability, curiosity, and assertiveness. Sheep were judged to differ markedly in shyness versus boldness, and this characteristic affected their behavior. Mice showed some degree of empathy for other mice in pain, as did chimps, elephants, and dolphin. Orangutans that rated high in extraversion and agreeableness and low in neuroticism were also rated high in subjective well-being. In addition, personality traits exhibited by dogs have been measured as accurately as those in humans (see Gosling, Kwan, & John, 2003; Hirayoshi & Nakajima, 2009; Miller, 2006; Sibbald, Erhard, McLeod, & Hooper, 2009; Siebert, 2006; Weiss, King, & Perkins, 2006).

"With the emergence of animal personality studies, we are gaining an even fuller appreciation not only of the distinctiveness of birds and beasts and their behaviors but also of their deep resemblances to us and our own behaviors" (Siebert, 2006, p. 51). If animals are so similar to humans in cognitive processing, temperament, and personality, does this lend additional support to the importance of evolution in all living creatures? As we shall see, the relatively new field of evolutionary psychology is dedicated to investigating this question.

## Current Status of Cognitive Psychology

With the cognitive movement in experimental psychology and the emphasis on consciousness within humanistic psychology and post-Freudian psychoanalysis, we can see that consciousness has reclaimed the central position it held when the field formally began. An analysis of 95 APA presidential addresses shows that the dominant view of psychology's subject matter has swung from subjective to objective and back again to subjective events. Consciousness has made a substantial and vigorous return.

As a school of thought, cognitive psychology boasts all the trappings of success. Within the decade of the 1970s, the movement had so many adherents that it could support its own journals: *Cognitive Psychology* (first published in 1970), *Cognition* (1971), *Cognitive Science* (1977), *Cognitive Therapy and Research* (1977), *Journal of Mental Imagery* (1977), and *Memory and Cognition* (1983). *Consciousness and Cognition* began publication in 1992 and the *Journal of Consciousness Studies* in 1994. By 2010 there were more than 40 journals dealing with various aspects of cognitive psychology.

Jerome Bruner once described cognitive psychology as "a revolution whose limits we still cannot fathom" (Bruner, 1983, p. 274). Nobel Prize–winning scientist Roger Sperry commented that compared to the behaviorist and psychoanalytic revolutions in psychology, the cognitive or consciousness revolution is the "most radical turnaround; the most revisionary and transformative" (Sperry, 1995, p. 35).

The impact of cognitive psychology has been felt in most areas of interest to psychologists. Further, cognitive psychologists have attempted to extend and consolidate the work of several major disciplines in a unified study of how the mind acquires knowledge. This perspective, dubbed *cognitive science,* is an amalgam of cognitive psychology, linguistics, anthropology, philosophy, computer sciences, artificial intelligence, and the neurosciences.

Although George Miller has questioned just how united such disparate fields of study could become (cognitive sciences, he suggested, rather than cognitive science), there is no denying the growth of the multidisciplinary approach. Cognitive science laboratories and institutes have been established at universities throughout the United States; some psychology departments have been renamed cognitive science departments. By whatever name, the cognitive approach to the study of mental phenomena and mental processes has come to dominate psychology and allied disciplines.

Perhaps the only feature it shares with its predecessor, behaviorism, is the use of the experimental method. "The methods used by cognitive psychologists to study the mind are the same as those used by behaviorists to study behavior, while ignoring (or denying) the mind" (Marken, 2009, p. 137).

A recent extension of cognitive psychology called *embedded cognition* recognizes that there are physical aspects of cognition revealed in brain activity and in sensation and perception. It follows, then, that perceptual and motor response systems affect, direct, and often determine the cognitive processes that occur in the mind. Thus "the mind must be understood in the context of its relationship to a physical body that interacts with the world" (Wilson, 2002, p. 625).

For example, studies have shown that situations as simple as holding a hot or a cold cup of coffee can affect how we judge or evaluate the personality of another person. Those people who were touching the hot cups gave different evaluations of other people than did those holding the cold cups. In another study, carrying light versus heavy clipboards affected how college students evaluated the worth of a foreign currency. Those who carried the heavier clipboards judged the currency to be far more valuable than those who carried the lighter clipboards. Thus, the physical cues gave context to the situation and influenced thought processes, which supports the suggestion that how we process information involves not only the mind but also the body (Jostmann, Lakens, & Schubert, 2009; Miles, Nind, & Macrae, 2010).

Another important topic in cognitive psychology is *cognitive overload*, which deals with that familiar activity known as multitasking. Research has shown that college students who were exposed to a variety of electronic images and tasks performed poorly. They were not able to focus nearly as well as non-multitaskers. The multitaskers were more easily distracted and had difficulty organizing information and shifting from one task to another (Ophir, Nass, & Wagner, 2009). "Multitaskers were just lousy at everything," one of the researchers said (Pennebaker, 2009).

No revolution, however successful, lacks critics. For example, most Skinnerian behaviorists oppose the cognitive movement. Even those who support it point out weaknesses and limitations, noting that there are few concepts that the majority of cognitive psychologists agree upon or consider important, and there remains considerable confusion about terminology and definitions.

Another criticism is directed at an overemphasis on cognition at the expense of other influences on thought and behavior, such as motivation and emotion. The professional literature on motivation and emotion has declined over the last few decades, whereas publications on cognition have increased. Ulric Neisser suggested that the result is a narrow, sterile approach to the field. "Human thinking is passionate and emotional, people operate from complex motives. A computer program, by contrast, has no emotion and is monomaniacal in its single-mindedness" (Neisser, quoted in Goleman, 1983, p. 57). He sensed a danger that cognitive psychology was fixated on thought processes to the same extreme that behaviorism focused only on overt behavior.

Jerome Bruner warned that cognitive science was becoming more restricted to increasingly narrow, even trivial, concerns (Bruner, 1990). A harsher judgment deals with the failure to unify the disparate fields of study concerned with cognitive functioning. One critic noted that there is, as yet, "no common view of the mind" (Erneling, 1997, p. 381).

Cognitive psychology is not finished. Because it is still developing, still history in the making, it is too soon to judge its ultimate contribution. It has the characteristics of a school of thought: its own journals, laboratories, meetings, jargon, and convictions, as well as the zeal of righteous believers. We may speak of cognitiv*ism,* as we do of functionalism and behaviorism. Cognitive psychology has already become what other schools of thought became in their time, part of psychology's mainstream. That, as we have seen, is the natural progression of revolutions when they become successful.

# Evolutionary Psychology

The most recent approach to psychology, evolutionary psychology, argues that people are biological creatures that have been wired or programmed by evolution to behave, think, feel, and learn in ways that have fostered survival over many past generations. This approach is based on the assumption that people with certain behavioral, cognitive, and affective tendencies were more likely to survive and bear and raise children.

As one evolutionary psychologist commented, "Humans who defended territory, nurtured children, and strove for domination were more likely to successfully reproduce than humans who did not do these things, with the result that their ultimate descendants—members of the present generation—generally have all of these behavioral tendencies" (Funder, 2001, p. 209). The genes for those behaviors that facilitate survival were "passed on through the generations because they were adaptive, enhancing survival or reproductive success, and eventually, they spread widely and became standard equipment" (Goode, 2000, p. D9).

Thus, we are shaped as much, if not more, by biology than by learning. While not denying that social and cultural forces can influence our behavior through learning, evolutionary psychologists proclaim that we are predisposed at birth to certain ways of behaving as shaped by evolution.

Evolutionary psychology deals with four fundamental propositions:

1. *All psychological mechanisms at some basic level originate from, and owe their existence to, evolutionary processes.*
2. *Darwin's theories of natural and sexual selection are the most important evolutionary processes responsible for creating evolved psychological mechanisms.*
3. *Evolved psychological mechanisms can be described as information-processing devices.*
4. *Evolved psychological mechanisms are functional; they function to solve recurrent adaptive problems that confronted our ancestors. (quoted from David Buss interview in Barker, 2006, pp. 69–70)*

Evolutionary psychology is a broad field that makes use of research findings from other disciplines, including animal behavior, biology, genetics, neuropsychology, and evolutionary theory. It applies these findings (to) areas of psychology such as intelligence, personality and individual differences, social psychology, and risk-taking behavior (see Buss, 2009; Kanazawa, 2010; Pawlowski, Atwal, & Dunbar, 2008; Webster, 2007).

We noted in Chapter 1 that psychology today is fragmented into varying approaches to its subject matter, and that there has been no single unifying theme to bring these factions together into a single psychology. Proponents of evolutionary psychology claim that their definition can unite this disparate field.

A founder of evolutionary psychology, David Buss, wrote that it "represents a true scientific revolution, a profound paradigm shift in the field of psychology" (2005, p. xxiv). In an interview the following year he called evolutionary psychology "one of the most important scientific revolutions we've ever had in the history of psychology" (Barker, 2006, p. 73).

## Antecedent Influences on Evolutionary Psychology

Any movement that calls itself evolutionary psychology owes a debt to Charles Darwin. The idea that only those with certain characteristics will survive and reproduce others with the same characteristics is the cornerstone of evolutionary psychology, as it was for Darwin. "The emergence of evolutionary psychology and related disciplines signals the fulfillment of Darwin's vision" (Buss, 2009b, p. 140).

In 1890, 31 years after Darwin published his monumental work on evolution, William James used the term "evolutionary psychology" in his book, *The Principles of Psychology.* James predicted that one day psychology would be based upon evolutionary theory. He also proposed that much of human behavior is programmed at birth by genetic predispositions he called instincts. These instinctive behaviors could be modified by experience or learning, but initially they are formed independently of experience.

James believed that a wide range of behaviors were instinctive, including fears of specific objects such as snakes, strange animals, and heights, all of which have obvious survival value. Other instinctive behaviors James discussed were parenting skills, love, sociability, and pugnacity (the tendency to quarrel and fight). James argued that instinctive behaviors evolved through natural selection and were adaptations designed to cope with specific problems of survival and reproduction.

During the reign of behaviorism, from 1913 to about 1960, the notion that any behavior might be determined genetically was anathema. All behavior was learned, said the behaviorists, but even during their years of supremacy and effective domination of psychology, there were scattered reports of genetic influences and inherited tendencies taking precedence over conditioned responses.

For example, in Chapter 11 we discussed the work of Skinner's students, the Brelands, who trained animals to perform for the IQ Zoo, television commercials, and state fairs. You will recall that some of their animals demonstrated a tendency toward instinctive drift. The animals sometimes substituted instinctive behaviors for those that had been reinforced with food, even when the instinctive behaviors interfered with obtaining food, a clear violation of the basic behavioristic principle that reinforcement rules all.

You are probably familiar with the monkey-mother love research of psychologist Harry Harlow (Harlow, 1971). Harlow raised baby monkeys with artificial mothers of two types. Both were constructed of wire mesh, but one was covered in soft, cuddly terry cloth while the other was hard, uncovered, and contained a nipple for dispensing milk. To Skinnerians it was obvious that reinforcement would be associated only with the hard mother that supplied the reward of milk. When the monkeys were frightened, however, they clung to the terry cloth mother, not the one that had always supplied reinforcement. It would seem that some other guiding force was at work that could not be explained by operant conditioning and reinforcement.

Research conducted by Martin Seligman, the initiator of positive psychology (discussed in Chapter 14), showed that it was easy to condition people to fear snakes, insects, dogs, heights, and tunnels. It was harder, however, to condition them to fear a more neutral or less threatening object such as a car or screwdriver (Seligman, 1971).

A fear of snakes has always been useful for survival in evolution, and so presumably we are born wired with this predisposing tendency. Fearing a neutral object, on the other hand, has had no survival value over the generations and so has not been passed on. Seligman called this phenomenon *biological preparedness.* This idea suggests that "phobias are indeed learned through classical conditioning but that certain fears that may have served some adaptive purpose in ancestral environments are more readily conditionable" (Siegert & Ward, 2002, p. 244).

The cognitive revolution was also a precursor of evolutionary psychology. The cognitive movement likened the human mind to a computer that could process whatever information it received. Part of the computer metaphor of the mind is the realization that the mind, like a computer, must be programmed to perform its multitude of tasks.

Thus, evolutionary psychology both draws on the cognitive revolution and expands its importance as a necessary framework within which to understand human and animal nature. It focuses on the importance of consciousness as it has evolved over time, and it places a greater emphasis on the notion of the computer as a metaphor for all conscious processes. Two leading evolutionary psychologists wrote:

> *The programs comprising the human mind were designed by natural selection to solve the adaptive problems regularly faced by our hunter-gatherer ancestors—problems such as finding a mate, cooperating with others, hunting, gathering, protecting children, navigating, avoiding predators, avoiding exploitation, and so on. The brain's evolved function is to extract information from the environment and use that information to generate behavior and regulate physiology. Hence, the brain is not just like a computer. It is a computer—that is, a physical system that was designed to process information. (Tooby & Cosmides, 2005, p. 5).*

## The Influence of Sociobiology

Another impetus for evolutionary psychology occurred in 1975 when Edward O. Wilson, a biologist, published a groundbreaking book titled *Sociobiology: A New Synthesis* (Wilson, 1975). The book was both hailed and reviled. Two years later it was featured on the cover of *Time* magazine. That same year Wilson was awarded the National Medal of Science and had a pitcher of ice water poured over his head at the annual meeting of the American Association for the Advancement of Science, an organization not noted for physical violence.

Wilson's bold and simple thesis was an affront to many people because it challenged their cherished belief that everyone is created equal, and that environmental and social forces alone can foster or limit human development. Wilson angered people by appearing to argue that genetic influences may be more important than cultural ones. If all behavior is determined genetically, then there is no hope of changing it through child-rearing practices, education, or any other way. That was not Wilson's central point, however, though he did take a strong hereditarian position at a time when such a view was anathema. Wilson wrote:

> *Human beings inherit a propensity to acquire behavior and social structures, a propensity that is shared by enough people to be called human nature. The defining traits include division of labor between the sexes, bonding between parents and children, heightened altruism toward closest kin, incest avoidance, other forms of ethical behavior, suspicion of strangers, tribalism, dominance orders within groups, male dominance overall, and territorial aggression over limiting resources. Although people have free will and the choice to turn in many directions, the channels of their psychological development are nevertheless—however much we might wish otherwise—cut more deeply by genes in certain directions than others. (Wilson, 1994, pp. 332–333)*

As a result of the outcry over Wilson's book, the word *sociobiology* developed such a negative connotation that it was dropped from use. In 1989, when a group of American scientists decided to form a professional association to study the field Wilson began, they called it the Human Behavior and Evolution Society and tried not to use the word *sociobiology* at their meetings.

The field of study Wilson started became incorporated into the changing views of a number of American psychologists who called their work *evolutionary psychology*. Under that more acceptable name, the field has become immensely popular (B. Webster, 2007).

## Current Status of Evolutionary Psychology

Evolutionary psychology deals with evolved psychological mechanisms that are wired or programmed into human cognition and behavior because they have been successful in solving specific problems of survival and reproduction in the organism's evolutionary history. The approach has become highly successful and influential and is occupying a central role in cognitive neuroscience (Confer, et al., 2010; C. Webster, 2007).

Despite the popularity of evolutionary psychology, it has generated considerable criticism, as every new movement does. As mentioned earlier, people who believe that humans are solely, or at least primarily, the products of learning oppose any discussion of biological determinants of behavior. If human nature is determined by genetic endowment alone, then there is no possibility of positive social and cultural forces changing behavior for the better, or for people to try to exercise free will.

The evolutionary psychologists' response to this criticism is to note, as Wilson did earlier, that they do not claim that all behavior is immutably determined by our genes. Human behavior is changeable; we remain free to choose. Social and cultural forces are influential and sometimes override or alter inherited programming to respond in certain ways.

Opponents argue that the breadth of the field "makes the theory difficult to test in any convincing way. The ability of evolutionary psychology to explain nearly everything is not an absolute virtue" (Funder, 2001, p. 210). Critics also question how it is possible to clearly identify a history of adaptation in a particular behavior, through hundreds of generations, to primitive peoples where the survival value of the behavior presumably originated.

### Comment

We have seen throughout this book that all approaches to psychology, all attempts to define the field, have had critics and points of apparent vulnerability. As with cognitive psychology, it is too early in the development of evolutionary psychology to judge its ultimate value. It, too, is history in the making. One advocate of the evolutionary psychology movement summed up the current status of the field in these terms: "We now have a powerful principle that will eventually provide a foundation for a deeper and richer psychology. But we have a lot of work to do" (Nesse, quoted in Goode, 2000, p. D9).

And so the search for the truly definitive approach to psychology, for the ultimate school of thought that might characterize the field for more than a few decades, continues. Will evolutionary psychology or cognitive psychology become that final arbiter of what psychology ought to be and do? Based on what we have seen so far, probably not.

All we can say with certainty is that if the history of psychology as we have recounted it tells us anything, it is that when a movement becomes formalized into a school it gains momentum that can be stopped only by its success in overthrowing the established position. When that happens, the unobstructed arteries of the once vigorous youthful movement begin to harden. Flexibility turns to rigidity, revolutionary passion turns to protection of position, and eyes and minds begin to close to new ideas. In this way a new establishment is born. So it is in the progress of any science, an evolutionary building to higher levels of development. There is no completion, no finish, just a never-ending process of growth, as newer species evolve from older ones and attempt to adapt to an ever-changing environment.

# Discussion Questions

1. Describe cognitive neuroscience and the techniques used to map the brain.
2. Describe the accomplishments, failures, and ultimate fates of the major schools of thought in psychology.
3. Describe the current view of animal cognition.
4. Describe the relationship between evolutionary psychology and cognitive psychology. Which one draws upon the other?
5. Describe what is meant by the terms "embedded cognition" and "cognitive overload."

6. Discuss the shift from clocks to computers as metaphors for the mind.

7. Discuss three ways in which cognitive psychology differs from behaviorism.

8. How are the Turing Test and the Chinese Room problem used to examine the proposition that computers can think?

9. How did the changing Zeitgeist in physics influence cognitive psychology?

10. How does cognitive neuroscience relate to earlier attempts to explain brain functioning?

11. How does evidence favoring the existence of personality in animals support Darwin's notion of evolution and the field of evolutionary psychology?

12. In what ways did cognitive psychology differ from behavioral psychology?

13. In what ways does the current version of the cognitive unconscious differ from the Freudian view of the unconscious?

14. In your opinion, are animals capable of cognitive activities, or are we attributing human functions to them that they do not really possess?

15. In your opinion, has psychology reached the stage of a unified paradigm that unites all the different approaches to psychology? Do you think evolutionary psychology is likely to be the final stage in the fractious and fragmented history of the field?

16. What are the limitations to the use of introspection in cognitive psychology?

17. What does the term "ecological validity" mean?

18. What is neuroprosthetics and how does it involve cognitive neuroscience?

19. What is the present status of cognitive psychology?

20. What personal factors motivated Miller and Neisser?

21. What practical need in World War II led to the development of the modern computer? What was ENIAC?

22. What were the early signs of a cognitive revolution in psychology?

23. What were the precursors of cognitive psychology?

# Recommended Resources

## Chapter 1

Cadwallader, T. C. (1975). Unique values of archival research. *Journal of the History of the Behavioral Sciences, 11,* 27–33.

Discusses the use of archival materials (unpublished documents, diaries, correspondence, and notebooks) to trace a theory's evolution in reverse, from its published form back through earlier versions, to uncover the impact of a theorist's personal context on his or her ideas.

Chabris, C., & Simons, D. (2010). *The invisible gorilla and other ways our intuitions deceive us.* New York: Crown.

Discusses the illusions and limitations of our attention and memory processes with both historical and contemporary examples.

Dewsbury, D. (2009). Is psychology losing its foundations? *Review of General Psychology, 13,* 281–289.

Examines the growing anti-intellectualism in society, in universities, and within the discipline of psychology and suggests some remedies.

Hilgard, E. R. (Ed.). (1978). *American psychology in historical perspective: Addresses of the presidents of the American Psychological Association, 1892–1977.* Washington, DC: American Psychological Association.

Biographical notes and selections from presidential addresses reflecting the growth of American psychology as a science and profession.

Hyman, I., Boss, S., Wise, B., McKenzie, K., & Caggiano, J. (2009). Did you see the unicycling clown: Blindness while walking and talking on a cell phone. *Applied Cognitive Psychology, 24,* 597–607.

The research on multi-tasking and divided attention that we cited at the beginning of this chapter. Presents a new twist on an old problem.

Karabel, J. (2005). *The chosen: The hidden history of admission and exclusion at Harvard, Yale, and Princeton.* Boston: Houghton Mifflin.

A former college admissions counselor describes cultural factors in discrimination against African-American, Jewish, and female college applicants, and explores the concept of ethnic diversity.

Philogene, G. (Ed.). (2004). *Racial identity in context: The legacy of Kenneth B. Clark.* Washington, DC: American Psychological Association.

Describes the life and work of Clark; explores the creation of racial identity and the effects of negative racial images.

Popplestone, J. A., & McPherson, M. W. (1998). *An illustrated history of American psychology.* Akron, OH: University of Akron Press.

A compilation of photographs and other illustrations providing a visual history of psychology from its origins in 19th-century Europe to the late 20th century in the United States.

**www.cengagebrain.com**

Check the publisher's web site and enter SCHULTZ HISTORY for find companion materials for this text.

**www.uakron.edu/ahap**

The Archives of the History of American Psychology holds an outstanding collection of documents and artifacts, including the professional papers of prominent psychologists, laboratory equipment, posters, slides, and films.

**www.apa.org/about/archives/index.aspx**

This link to the historical archives of the APA will help you locate APA-relevant historical material held by the Library of Congress in Washington, DC, as well as oral histories, photos, biographies, and obituaries.

**www.psychclassics.uorku.ca**

This amazing site maintained by psychologist Christopher Green at York University in Toronto, Canada includes the complete text of books, chapters, and important articles on the history of psychology. Google *York University History and Theory of Psychology Question & Answer Forum* to post questions about the history of psychology, answer questions others have submitted, or browse to learn what people are blogging. Green also does a weekly podcast, *This Week in the History of Psychology*, at www.yorku.ca/christo/podcasts.

**www.historyofpsychology.org/**

The web site for the Society for the History of Psychology (Division 26 of the American Psychological Association) offers student resources, online books and journals, and posters, T-shirts, coffee mugs, baseball caps, and more featuring great men and women from psychology's past. See also their Facebook page: **www.facebook.com/pages/Society-for-the-History-of-Psychology/86715677509?ref=mf**

# Chapter 2

Babbage, C. (1961). *On the principles and development of the calculator, and other seminal writings.* (P. Morrison & E. Morrison, Eds.). New York: Dover Publications.

Selections from Babbage's wide-ranging work on computing machines and other mechanical devices. Includes a biographical sketch.

Capaldi, N. (2004). *John Stuart Mill: A biography.* Cambridge, England: Cambridge University Press.

Recounts the personal, social, and environmental influences on Mill and his relationships with the other major thinkers of the day.

Clarke, D. (2006). *Descartes: A biography.* Cambridge, England: Cambridge University Press.

Emphasizes Descartes' unique contribution to the history of ideas in promoting a philosophy that accommodated the needs of the newly emerging scientific disciplines, thus earning the hostility of the established church.

Green, C., Shore, M., & Teo, T. (Eds.). (2001). *The transformation of psychology: Influences of 19th-century philosophy, technology, and natural science.* Washington, DC: American Psychological Association.

Reviews nineteenth-century social, intellectual, technological, and institutional ideas and practices as they influenced the development of the new psychology.

Johnson, G. (2008). *The ten most beautiful experiments.* New York: Knopf.

Describes historic experiments whose simplicity and hands-on research methodology yielded significant results that changed not only the scientific world but also our everyday lives.

Landes, D. S. (1983). *Revolution in time: Clocks and the making of the modern world.* Cambridge, MA: Belknap Press of Harvard University Press.

Recounts the invention of the mechanical clock and the refinement of precision timekeeping devices. Assesses their impact on the development of science and society.

Newton, R. (2004). *Galileo's pendulum: From the rhythm of time to the making of matter.* Cambridge, MA: Harvard University Press.

Covers basic issues in the history of science and deals extensively with the construction of clocks and the conceptualization of calendars.

Reeves, R. (2008). *John Stuart Mill: Victorian firebrand.* New York: Overlook.

A well-written biography setting Mill's ideas in the context of his era and assessing the lasting impact of his views.

Teresi, D. (2002). *Lost discoveries: The ancient roots of modern science—from the Babylonians to the Maya.* New York: Simon & Schuster.

Shows how outstanding human achievements in Western science (mathematics, astronomy, physics, chemistry, geology, and technology) were anticipated by the overlooked contributions of Indians, Chinese, Arabs, Polynesians, Mayans, Aztecs, among others.

Watson, R. (2002). *Cogito, ergo sum: The life of Rene Descartes.* Boston: Godine.

An engrossing narrative of Descartes' life emphasizing his importance to the modern world.

Wood, G. (2002). *Edison's Eve: A magical history of the quest for mechanical life.* New York: Knopf.

An account of the development of automata, including the mechanical toys and amusements of Europe as well as a so-called talking doll invented by Thomas Edison.

## Chapter 3

Burrell, B. (2004). *Postcards from the Brain Museum: The improbable search for meaning in the matter of famous minds.* New York: Broadway Books.

Offers a tour of brain collections held in various museums and explores scientific attempts (both the credible and the fantastic) to explain brain structures and functions.

Cahan, D. (Ed.). (1993). *Hermann von Helmholtz and the foundations of nineteenth-century science.* Berkeley: University of California Press.

Presents and assesses popular lectures Helmholtz delivered between 1853 and 1892. These cover the nature and purpose of scientific research, the optimum intellectual and social conditions for scientific advances, and the impact of science on society.

Dobson, V., & Bruce, D. (1972). The German university and the development of experimental psychology. *Journal of the History of the Behavioral Sciences, 8,* 204–207.

Describes the climate of academic freedom in German universities as a necessary condition for the growth of modern psychology.

Heidelberger, M. (2004). Nature from within: Gustav Theodor Fechner and his psychophysical worldview. Pittsburgh: University of Pittsburgh Press.

An excellent and informative introduction to Fechner's life and work discussing the originality and influence of his ideas.

Zimmer, C. (2004). *Soul made flesh: The discovery of the brain and how it changed the world.* New York: Free Press.

Examines 200 years of evolving scientific thought about the soul, the brain, and consciousness.

## Chapter 4

Baldwin, B. T. (1921). In memory of Wilhelm Wundt by his American students. *Psychological Review, 28,* 153–158.

Reminiscences of Wundt's American students.

Danziger, K. (1980). A history of introspection reconsidered. *Journal of the History of the Behavioral Sciences, 16,* 241–262.

Describes how Wundtian introspection was limited to simple responses to sensory stimuli, and how the method was expanded by other psychologists to include subjective responses to the experimenter's questions.

Langfeld, H. S. (1937). Stumpf's "Introduction to Psychology." *American Journal of Psychology, 50,* 33–56.

Describes Stumpf's 1906–1907 introductory psychology courses at the University of Berlin.

Lindenfeld, D. (1978). Oswald Külpe and the Würzburg School. *Journal of the History of the Behavioral Sciences, 14,* 132–141.

Describes the impact of Külpe's philosophical views on his conception of psychology and assesses his importance in the development of the field.

Ogden, R. M. (1951). Oswald Külpe and the Würzburg school. *American Journal of Psychology, 64,* 4–19.

Another perspective on Külpe's contributions to the development of modern psychology.

Postman, L. (1968). Hermann Ebbinghaus. *American Psychologist, 23,* 149–157.

Describes Ebbinghaus's contributions to the experimental study of memory.

Wong, W. (2009). Retracing the footsteps of Wilhelm Wundt. *History of Psychology, 12,* 229–265.

Offers observations on the continuing relevance of Wundt's ideas, goals, and methods in light of contemporary developments in psychology.

## Chapter 5

Angell, F. (1928). Titchener at Leipzig. *Journal of General Psychology, 1,* 195–198.

A fellow student describes Titchener's personal qualities and research interests while at Leipzig.

Boring, E. G. (1953). A history of introspection. *Psychological Bulletin, 50,* 169–189.

Details the practice of Titchener's form of introspection and describes the use of introspective reports in later schools of thought.

Danziger, K. (1980). The history of introspection reconsidered. *Journal of the History of the Behavioral Sciences, 16,* 241–262.

Reviews various views on the theory and practice of introspection from British, German, and American systems of psychology.

Hindeland, M. J. (1971). Edward Bradford Titchener: A pioneer in perception. *Journal of the History of the Behavioral Sciences, 7,* 23–28.

Discusses Titchener's experimental approach to the topics of sensation and perception.

Lieberman, D. A. (1979). Behaviorism and the mind: A (limited) call for a return to introspection. *American Psychologist, 34,* 319–333.

Reviews historical arguments against introspection, concludes that most are invalid or no longer appropriate, and advocates a wider application of introspective methods to problems in modern psychology.

## Chapter 6

Angell, J. R. (1909). The influence of Darwin on psychology. *Psychological Review, 16,* 152–169.

Discusses Darwin's ideas on evolution and their impact on the development of functional psychology.

Aydon, C. (2002). *Charles Darwin: The naturalist who started a scientific revolution.* New York: Carroll & Graf.

An engaging, highly readable account of Darwin's family life and career; includes photographs and an essay on the wide-ranging influence of his ideas over a span of more than 100 years.

Browne, J. (2002). *Charles Darwin: The power of place.* New York: Knopf.

This is the second volume of a major biography of Darwin. It covers Darwin's response to the work of Alfred Russel Wallace, the publication of *The Origin of Species,* and the impact of Darwin's ideas on the science of the Victorian era. The first volume, *Charles Darwin: Voyaging,* was published in 1996.

Costall, A. (1993). How Lloyd Morgan's Canon backfired. *Journal of the History of the Behavioral Sciences, 29,* 113–122.

Discusses the approaches of Morgan and Romanes to the study of animal behavior.

Diamond, S. (1977). Francis Galton and American psychology. *Annals of the New York Academy of Sciences, 291,* 47–55.

Describes the influence of Galton on American pioneers of functional psychology.

Fancher, R. (2009). Scientific cousins: The relationship between Charles Darwin and Francis Galton. *American Psychologist, 64,* 84–92.

Describes the personal and scientific relationship between these two great scientists as well as their agreements and disagreements on intellectual and philosophical issues.

Gribbin, J., & Gribbin, M. (2004). *Fitzroy: The remarkable story of Darwin's captain and the invention of the weather forecast.* New Haven, CT: Yale University Press.

Fitzroy, captain of the *Beagle* for Darwin's famous trip, had a distinguished career in both meteorology and government service.

Eldredge, N. (2005). *Darwin: Discovering the tree of life.* New York: Norton.

A museum curator assembling the exhibition for the 200th anniversary of Darwin's birth reconstructs Darwin's notebooks and follows his analytical processes, showing how Darwin organized his ideas, accepting some and discarding others.

Keynes, R. (2002). *Darwin, his daughter, and human evolution.* New York: Riverhead Books.

Discusses the impact of the death of Darwin's 10-year-old daughter on the development of his ideas about the role of human suffering.

Morgan, C. L. (1961). Autobiography. In C. Murchison (Ed.), *A history of psychology in autobiography* (Vol. 2, pp. 237–264). New York: Russell & Russell. (Original work published 1930)

Conwy Lloyd Morgan describes his life and work on animal psychology.

Shermer, M. (2002). *In Darwin's shadow: The life and science of Alfred Russel Wallace.* New York: Oxford University Press.

This "biographical study on the psychology of history" shows how Wallace, the co-discoverer of evolutionary theory, was a fascinating character, largely self-trained, breaking the mold of scientific orthodoxy.

Slotten, R. (2004). *The heretic in Darwin's court: The life of Alfred Russel Wallace.* New York: Columbia University Press.

Recounts the critical moment when Wallace and Darwin separately conceptualized the role of natural selection. Describes Wallace's other interests such as social justice, land reform, and spiritualism.

**www.victorianweb.org**

A web site maintained by a professor of English at Brown University that provides information and resources on all aspects of the Victorian age including political and social history, philosophy, science, and technology. See for material on Babbage, Darwin, Galton, Huxley, Lyell, Wallace, and others.

## Chapter 7

Appignanesi, L. (2008). *Mad, bad and sad: Women and the mind doctors.* New York: Norton.

An account of how women's creative lives throughout history have been limited by cultural and political norms, and how deviations or rebellions have often been labeled as mental instability.

Campbell-Kelley, M., & Aspray, W. (1996). *Computer: A history of the information machine.* New York: Basic Books.

Traces the development of the computer from the work of Hollerith and his punch card tabulator for the 1890 census.

Carr, H. A. (1961). Autobiography. In C. Murchison (Ed.), *A history of psychology in autobiography* (Vol. 3, pp. 69–82). New York: Russell & Russell. (Original work published 1930).

Harvey Carr's reminiscences of his career.

Furumoto, L. (1991). From "paired associates" to a psychology of self: The intellectual odyssey of Mary Whiton Calkins. In G. A. Kimble, M. Wertheimer, & C. White (Eds.), *Portraits of pioneers in psychology* (pp. 57–72). Washington, DC: American Psychological Association.

Describes Calkins's approach to experimental psychology research within the academic context of a women's college (Wellesley, 1887–1930).

Klein, A. (2002). *A forgotten voice: A biography of Leta Stetter Hollingworth.* Scottsdale, AZ: Great Potential Press.

Describes her extraordinary life, her struggle to take advantage of the opportunities open to women of the times, and her contributions to psychology and education, especially for gifted children.

Lewis, R. W. B. (1991). *The Jameses: A family narrative.* New York: Farrar, Straus and Giroux.

An account of the James family including William (psychologist), Henry (novelist), and Alice (political radical). For another family biography of the Jameses see P. Fisher, *House of Wits* (New York: Holt, 2008).

Lutz, T. (1991). *American nervousness, 1903: An anecdotal history.* Ithaca, NY: Cornell University Press.

Discusses neurasthenia, the prevalent cultural malady of the United States in the early 20th century, and speculates about its effect on William James, among others.

Martin, J. (2002). *The education of John Dewey: A biography.* New York: Columbia University Press.

A highly readable account of Dewey's personal life and the implementation of his ideas on progressive education.

McKinney, F. (1978). Functionalism at Chicago—memories of a graduate student: 1929–1931. *Journal of the History of the Behavioral Sciences, 14,* 142–148.

Describes the faculty, students, course work, and intellectual climate of the University of Chicago psychology department.

Richardson, R. D. (2006). *William James: In the maelstrom of American modernism.* Boston: Houghton Mifflin.

An outstanding biography of the personal and intellectual life of William James.

Simon, L. (1996). *William James remembered.* Lincoln: University of Nebraska Press.

Brings together reminiscences of James by family members, friends, and intellectual leaders of James's time.

Thorne, F. C. (1976). Reflections on the Golden Age of Columbia's psychology. *Journal of the History of the Behavioral Sciences, 12,* 159–165.

Describes the faculty and research interests of the Columbia University psychology department (1920–1940).

Werth, B. (2009). *Banquet at Delmonico's: Great minds, the Gilded Age, and the triumph of evolution in America.* New York: Random House.

Examines how evolutionary theory brought a challenge to 19th-century American science and society, with its subsequent influence on business, theology, and government.

White, S. H. (1990). Child study at Clark University: 1894–1904. *Journal of the History of the Behavioral Sciences, 26,* 131–150.

Describes questionnaire studies of child development initiated by Hall.

## Chapter 8

Engel, J. (2008). *American therapy: The rise of psychotherapy in the United States.* New York: Gotham.

A comprehensive survey of American health-care practices. Traces the rise and fall of psychoanalysis and the growth of more target therapies as well as medications.

Fuchs, A. H. (1998). Psychology and "The Babe." *Journal of the History of the Behavioral Sciences, 34,* 153–165.

Describes an instance of psychology's application to sports; baseball's greatest player, Babe Ruth, was tested at Columbia University's psychological laboratory to assess his batting skills in the hope that these quantitative measures would lead to tests for identifying potential outstanding players.

Kunda, D. P. (1976). The concept of suggestion in the early history of advertising psychology. *Journal of the History of the Behavioral Sciences, 12,* 347–353.

Discusses early psychological theories of advertising and suggestibility proposed by Walter Dill Scott and others.

Lancaster, J. (2004). *Making time: Lillian Moller Gilbreth: A life beyond "Cheaper by the Dozen."* Boston: Northeastern University Press.

An engaging biography of the psychologist and engineer who emphasized the human component of the work environment and challenged women's traditional roles.

Landy, F. J. (1992). Hugo Münsterberg: Victim or visionary? *American Psychologist, 47,* 787–802.

Examines Münsterberg's contributions to applied psychology.

McReynolds, P. (1997). *Lightner Witmer: His life and times.* Washington, DC: American Psychological Association.

Describes Witmer's life and career and the development of his clinic at the University of Pennsylvania.

Murdoch, S. (2007). *IQ: A smart history of a failed idea.* New York: Wiley.

Traces efforts to measure intelligence from Binet's first tests to more complex assessment instruments. Examines issues of racial discrimination, the misuse of test results to justify questionable procedures, and the dangers of an over-reliance on standardized testing.

Sokal, M. M. (Ed.). (1991). The origins of The Psychological Corporation. *Journal of the History of the Behavioral Sciences, 17,* 54–67.

Traces the development of The Psychological Corporation as a major undertaking for American applied psychology.

Spillmann, J., & Spillmann, L. (1993). The rise and fall of Hugo Münsterberg. *Journal of the History of the Behavioral Sciences, 29,* 322–338.

Describes Münsterberg's life, his psychological laboratory at Harvard, and his contributions to forensic and industrial psychology.

Von Mayrhauser, R. T. (1989). Making intelligence functional: Walter Dill Scott and applied psychological testing in World War I. *Journal of the History of the Behavioral Sciences, 25,* 60–72.

Describes the efforts of Scott, Thorndike, and others in constructing group intelligence tests.

Zenderland, L. (1998). *Measuring minds: Henry Herbert Goddard and the origins of American intelligence testing.* New York: Cambridge University Press.

Reviews Goddard's contributions to the intelligence testing movement and its widespread applications in the United States.

## Chapter 9

Bitterman, M. E. (1969). Thorndike and the problem of animal intelligence. *American Psychologist, 24,* 444–453.

Discusses Thorndike's career at Columbia University and his puzzle-box experiments on animal learning.

Dewsbury, D. A. (1990). Early interaction between animal psychologists and animal activists and the founding of the APA Committee on Precautions in Animal Experimentation. *American Psychologist, 45,* 315–327.

Reviews the conflict between comparative psychology and the animal rights movement; recounts media attacks on animal researchers such as Hall, Pavlov, Thorndike, and Watson.

Fernald, D. (1984). *The Hans legacy: A story of science.* Hillsdale, NJ: Erlbaum.

Recounts the Clever Hans story and its implications for scientific inquiry.

Todes, D. (2001). *Pavlov's physiology factory: Experiment, interpretation, laboratory enterprise.* Baltimore: Johns Hopkins University Press.

A thought-provoking, scholarly work portraying Pavlov as scientific entrepreneur.

Windholz, G. (1990). Pavlov and the Pavlovians in the laboratory. *Journal of the History of the Behavioral Sciences, 26,* 64–74.

Describes the daily routine in Pavlov's laboratory and his influence on associates and students.

Yerkes, R. M. (1961). Autobiography. In C. Murchison (Ed.), *A history of psychology in autobiography* (Vol. *2,* pp. 381–407). New York: Russell & Russell. (Original work published 1930).

Yerkes's account of his career in comparative psychology.

Zagrina, N. (2009). Ivan Petrovich Pavlov and the authorities. *Neuroscience and Behavioral Physiology, 39,* 383–385.

Cites recently released and translated documents from Russian scientific sources to describe Pavlov's contentious relationship with the government.

## Chapter 10

Brewer, C. L. (1991). Perspectives on John B. Watson. In G. A. Kimble, M. Wertheimer, & C. White (Eds.), *Portraits of pioneers in psychology* (pp. 171–186). Washington, DC: American Psychological Association.

Reviews Watson's life and his contributions to psychology and notes Furman University's efforts to acknowledge Watson's importance.

Buckley, K. W. (1989). *Mechanical man: John Broadus Watson and the beginnings of behaviorism.* New York: Guilford.

Describes Watson's academic and business careers and his role as a popularizer of psychology.

Duke, C., Fried, S., Pliley, W., & Walker, D. (1989). Rosalie Rayner Watson: The mother of a behaviorist's sons. *Psychological Reports, 65,* 163–169.

Describes Watson's wife, who coauthored the study of conditioned emotional reactions and assisted in the preparation of Watson's book on child care.

Hannush, M. J. (1987). John B. Watson remembered: An interview with James B. Watson. *Journal of the History of the Behavioral Sciences, 23,* 137–152.

An interview with the son of John B. Watson and Rosalie Rayner Watson, in an effort to link the psychologist's life with the theory he promoted.

Jastrow, J. (1961). Autobiography. In C. Murchison (Ed.), *A history of psychology in autobiography* (Vol. *1,* pp. 135–162). New York: Russell & Russell. (Original work published 1930)

Includes Jastrow's views on the popularization of psychology.

Samelson, F. (1981). Struggle for scientific authority: The reception of Watson's behaviorism, 1913–1920. *Journal of the History of the Behavioral Sciences, 17,* 399–425.

Reports the impact of Watson's ideas after the publication of his behaviorist manifesto.

## Chapter 11

Bandura, A. (1976). Albert Bandura. In R. I. Evans (Ed.), *The making of psychology: Discussions with creative contributors.* New York: Knopf.

Interviews with Bandura about his life and work.

Freeman, J. (2010). *The tyranny of e-mail.* New York: Scribner.

Proposes that the "variable reinforcement schedule" of receiving messages in our e-mail in-box has the effect of conditioning our behavior.

Kuhlmann, H. (2005). *Living Walden Two: B. F. Skinner's behaviorist utopia and experimental communities.* Champaign, IL: University of Illinois Press.

Describes the founding and functioning of several communities established on the basis of Skinner's principles of behaviorism and reinforcement.

Pressey, S. L. (1967). Autobiography. In E. G. Boring & G. Lindzey (Eds.), *A history of psychology in autobiography* (Vol. *5,* pp. 313–339). New York: Appleton-Century-Crofts.

Sidney Pressey's account of his work, including his development of the teaching machine.

Rutherfod, A. (2009). *Beyond the box: Skinner's technology of behavior from laboratory to life.* Toronto: University of Toronto Press.

Traces developments in behavior analysis since Skinner's work and shows the evolution of his ideas from laboratory experiments to a variety of applied situations.

Skinner, B. F. (1953). *Science and human behavior.* New York: Free Press.

Skinner's approach to the scientific analysis of human behavior.

Smith, L. D., & Woodward, W. R. (Eds.). (1996). *B. F. Skinner and behaviorism in American culture.* Bethlehem, PA: Lehigh University Press.

Offers analyses of Skinner's social philosophy and technological viewpoint and assesses his impact on American society. Includes biographical and autobiographical material.

Tolman, E. C. (1922). A new formula for behaviorism. *Psychological Review, 29,* 44–53.

Discusses the idea that a less physiologically based conception of behaviorism would allow psychologists to deal more comprehensively with the topics of motivation and emotion.

Tolman, E. C. (1952). Autobiography. In E. G. Boring, H. S. Langfeld, H. Werner, & R. M. Yerkes (Eds.), *A history of psychology in autobiography* (Vol. 4, pp. 323–339). Worcester, MA: Clark University Press.

Tolman's account of his career in psychology.

Walter, M. (1990). *Science and cultural crisis: An intellectual biography of Percy Williams Bridgman (1882–1961).* Stanford, CA: Stanford University Press.

Presents Bridgman's life and work and describes how he reluctantly became a major figure in the philosophy of science with his doctrine of operationism.

Wiener, D. N. (1996). *B. F. Skinner: Benign anarchist.* Boston: Allyn & Bacon.

A psychological and intellectual portrait of Skinner based on extensive interviews with the subject, colleagues, and students.

## Chapter 12

Arnheim, R. (1998). Wolfgang Köhler and Gestalt theory. *History of Psychology, 1,* 21–26.

An English-language translation of Köhler's introduction to his book on physical Gestalts, which also illustrates the process by which he developed and evaluated his ideas.

Ash, M. G. (1995). *Gestalt psychology in German culture, 1890–1967: Holism and the quest for objectivity.* Cambridge, England: Cambridge University Press.

Describes the development and reception of Gestalt psychology in Germany and provides colorful life histories of the movement's major proponents.

Cole, J. (2009). *The great American university.* New York: Public Affairs.

Cites the positive impact of immigrant scholars on American intellectual life. Includes, among many examples, the leaders of the Gestalt psychology movement.

Helson, H. (1925, 1926). The psychology of Gestalt. *American Journal of Psychology, 36,* 342–370, 494–526; *37,* 25–62, 189–223.

The series of articles that introduced the Gestalt psychology viewpoint to American psychologists.

Henle, M. (1978). One man against the Nazis— Wolfgang Köhler. *American Psychologist, 33,* 939–944.

Describes Köhler's last years in Berlin and his struggle to save the Psychological Institute from Nazi repression.

Henle, M. (1987). Koffka's *Principles* after fifty years. *Journal of the History of the Behavioral Sciences, 23,* 14–21.

Evaluates the impact of Koffka's book, *Principles of Gestalt Psychology.*

King, D. B., & Wertheimer, M. (2005). *Max Wertheimer and Gestalt theory.* Brunswick, NJ: Transaction Publishers.

Michael Wertheimer's carefully crafted biography of his father intertwined with the development of the Gestalt psychology school of thought.

Köhler, W. (1959). Gestalt psychology today. *American Psychologist, 14,* 727–734.

Describes differences between Gestalt psychology and the then-prevalent behavioral psychology.

Sokal, M. M. (1984). The Gestalt psychologists in behaviorist America. *American Historical Review, 89,* 1240–1263.

Describes the spread of the Gestalt psychology movement in the United States.

## Chapter 13

Decker, H. S. (1991). *Freud, Dora, and Vienna 1900.* New York: Free Press.

Describes Freud's treatment of 18-year-old Dora, who expressed her emotional disturbances through a nervous cough and loss of voice.

Drinka, G. F. (1984). *The birth of neurosis: Myth, malady, and the Victorians.* New York: Simon and Schuster.

Examines social and cultural influences on early theories of neurosis.

Ellenberger, H. F. (1972). The story of "Anna O.": A critical review with new data. *Journal of the History of the Behavioral Sciences, 8,* 267–279.

Assesses Anna O.'s case as the prototype of the cathartic cure.

Erard, M. (2007). *Um … Slips, stumbles, and verbal blunders, and what they mean.* New York: Pantheon.

Suggests that much can be learned about personality and language acquisition through an analysis of human speech. Outlines verbal blunder studies including the so-called Freudian slip, bloopers, malapropisms, and the verbal missteps of public figures.

Evans, R. B., & Koelsch, W. A. (1985). Psychoanalysis arrives in America: The 1909 psychology conference at Clark University. *American Psychologist, 40,* 942–948.

Describes the meeting that introduced Freud, Jung, and psychoanalysis to an American academic audience.

Freeman, L., & Strean, H. S. (1987). *Freud and women.* New York: Continuum.

Explores Freud's relationships with his mother, sisters, wife, daughters, and female colleagues and patients.

Hale, N. G., Jr. (1995). *The rise and crisis of psychoanalysis in the United States: Freud and the Americans, 1917–1985.* New York: Oxford University Press.

Provides an overview of the history of psychoanalysis in the United States. Deals with the disputes between orthodox and revisionist psychoanalysts and covers the treatment of psychoanalytic concepts by the American media.

Makari, G. (2008). *Revolution in mind: The creation of psychoanalysis.* New York: HarperCollins.

A comprehensive history of psychoanalysis from 1895 to 1946 showing the shifts in Freud's thinking about the nature of the psyche. Assesses the members of Freud's inner circle and the development of intellectual disputes among them.

Roazen, P. (1975). *Freud and his followers.* New York: Knopf.

Recounts Freud's life and his relationships with disciples including those who broke away to promote their own ideas about personality and psychotherapy.

Showalter, E. (1997). *Hystories: Hysterical epidemics and modern culture.* New York: Columbia University Press.

Reviews the literature on hysteria, which Freud viewed as a pathological disorder in the psychosexual development of women. Notes the anti-female biases of the times.

Zaretsky, E. (2004). *Secrets of the soul: A social and cultural history of psychoanalysis.* New York: Knopf.

Traces over several decades the rise, fall, and widespread incorporation of Freudian ideas in the general culture.

# Chapter 14

Bair, D. (2003). *Jung: A biography.* Boston: Little, Brown.

Balanced coverage of Jung's ambition, arrogance, and rivalries as well as with his originality as a theorist. Assesses the lasting impact of his ideas.

Elkins, D. (2009). Why humanistic psychology lost its power and influence in American psychology. *Journal of Humanistic Psychology, 49,* 267–291.

Attributes the waning popularity of humanistic psychology to forces within American psychology as well as conservative ideologies in the larger culture.

Ellenberger, H. F. (1970). *The discovery of the unconscious: The history and evolution of dynamic psychiatry.* New York: Basic Books.

Traces ideas about the unconscious from anthropological studies of primitive and ancient peoples to Freudian psychoanalysis and its derivatives (chapter 8 discusses Adler; chapter 9 discusses Jung).

Jung, C. G. (2009). *The red book.* New York: Norton.

Jung's compilation of writings about his dreams and visions, along with calligraphy and paintings, carefully amassed over a period of 15 years while he was actively developing his theory.

McLynn, F. (1997). *Carl Gustav Jung.* New York: St. Martin's Press.

A comprehensive biography of Jung, presenting him as a somewhat infuriating character with traits of genius.

Paris, B. J. (1994). *Karen Horney: A psychoanalyst's search for self-understanding.* New Haven, CT: Yale University Press.

Describes Horney's life and her impressive contributions to the understanding of neurosis and the self.

Rogers, C. R., & Russell, D. E. (2002). *Carl Rogers, the quiet revolutionary: An oral history*. Roseville, CA: Penmarin Books.

In-depth interviews with Rogers about his personal and professional life. Covers his work on education, counseling, psychotherapy, and conflict resolution.

Sayers, J. (1991). *Mothers of psychoanalysis: Helene Deutsch, Karen Horney, Anna Freud, Melanie Klein*. New York: Norton.

Discusses how these analysts helped redefine Freud's psychoanalysis by shifting the emphasis from a patriarchal to a matriarchal viewpoint.

Young-Bruehl, E. (1988). *Anna Freud: A biography*. New York: Summit Books.

Presents the life and work of Freud's daughter Anna, who developed a system of child analysis and served as her father's confidante.

## Chapter 15

Baars, B. J. (1986). *The cognitive revolution in psychology*. New York: Guilford.

Describes the transition from post-Watsonian behaviorism to cognitive psychology. Includes interviews with Miller, Neisser, and other cognitive psychologists.

Confer, J., Easton, J., Fleischman, D., Goetz, C., Lewis, D., Perilloux, C., & Buss, D. (2010). Evolutionary psychology. *American Psychologist, 65*, 110–126.

Discusses controversies, limitations, and prospects for the growing field of evolutionary psychology.

Leavitt, D. (2006). *The man who knew too much: Alan Turing and the invention of the computer*. New York: Norton.

A highly readable biography of this groundbreaking thinker and originator of the ideas that led to the invention of the computer. Recounts his tragic personal life at a time when homosexuality in England was considered indecent and illegal.

Miller, G. A. (1989). Autobiography. In G. Lindzey (Ed.), *A history of psychology in autobiography* (Vol. 8, pp. 391–418). Stanford, CA: Stanford University Press.

Includes Miller's recollections of the teachers who influenced his career in psychology.

Neisser, U. (2007). Autobiography. In A history of psychology in autobiography (Vol. 9, pp. 269–301). Washington, DC: American Psychological Association.

Describes his early years, his brief interest in parapsychology, his college years, and his outstanding career as a psychologist.

Pinker, S. (2002). *The blank slate: The modern denial of human nature*. New York: Viking.

Illustrates the common evolutionary themes in human nature over disparate cultures and argues for acceptance of our genetic heritage. Evaluates popular past conceptions of human nature such as the "blank slate," the "noble savage," and the "ghost in the machine."

Rychlak, J. F. (1997). *In defense of human consciousness*. Washington, DC: American Psychological Association.

See especially chapter 7 on computers and consciousness, with machines as the metaphor for human mental functions.

Skinner, B. F. (1987). Whatever happened to psychology as the science of behavior? *American Psychologist, 42*, 780–786.

Presents Skinner's view that humanistic psychology and cognitive psychology are obstacles in the way of psychology's acceptance of his program for the experimental analysis of behavior.

# Glossary

**Absolute threshold:**   The point of sensitivity below which no sensations can be detected and above which sensations can be experienced.

**Act psychology:**   Brentano's system of psychology, which focused on mental activities (e.g., seeing) rather than on mental contents (e.g., that which is seen).

**Analytical psychology:**   Jung's theory of personality.

**Anecdotal method:**   The use of observational reports about animal behavior.

**Apperception:**   The process by which mental elements are organized.

**Archetypes:**   Inherited tendencies within the collective unconscious that dispose a person to behave similarly to ancestors who confronted similar situations.

**Associated reflexes:**   Reflexes that can be elicited not only by unconditioned stimuli but also by stimuli that have become associated with the unconditioned stimuli.

**Association:**   The notion that knowledge results from linking or associating simple ideas to form complex ideas.

**Associative memory:**   An association between stimulus and response, taken to indicate evidence of consciousness in animals.

**Basic anxiety:**   Horney's conception of pervasive loneliness and helplessness, feelings that are the foundation of neuroses.

**Behavior modification:**   The use of positive reinforcement to control or modify the behavior of individuals or groups.

**Behaviorism:**   Watson's science of behavior, which dealt solely with observable behavioral acts that could be described in objective terms.

**Catharsis:**   The process of reducing or eliminating a complex by recalling it to conscious awareness and allowing it to be expressed.

**Clinical method:**   Posthumous examination of brain structures to detect damaged areas assumed to be responsible for behavioral conditions that existed before the person died.

**Cognitive psychology:**   A system of psychology that focuses on the process of knowing, on how the mind actively organizes experiences.

**Collective unconscious:**   The deepest level of the psyche; it contains inherited experiences of human and prehuman species.

**Conditioned reflexes:**   Reflexes that are conditional or dependent on the formation of an association or connection between stimulus and response.

**Connectionism:**   Thorndike's approach to learning that was based on connections between situations and responses.

**Creative synthesis:**   The notion that complex ideas formed from simple ideas take on new qualities; the combination of the mental elements creates something greater than or different from the sum of the original elements.

**Defense mechanisms:**   Behaviors that represent unconscious denials or distortions of reality but which are adopted to protect the ego against anxiety.

**Derived and innate ideas:** Derived ideas are produced by the direct application of an external stimulus; innate ideas arise from the mind or consciousness, independent of sensory experiences or external stimuli.

**Determinism:** The doctrine that acts are determined by past events.

**Differential threshold:** The point of sensitivity at which the least amount of change in a stimulus gives rise to a change in sensation.

**Dream analysis:** A psychotherapeutic technique involving the interpretation of dreams to uncover unconscious conflicts.

**Dynamic psychology:** Robert Woodworth's system of psychology, which was concerned with the influence of causal factors and motivations on feelings and behavior.

**Ego:** The rational aspect of personality responsible for controlling the instincts.

**Electrical stimulation:** A technique for exploring the cerebral cortex with weak electric current to observe motor responses.

**Empiricism:** The pursuit of knowledge through the observation of nature and the attribution of all knowledge to experience.

**Equipotentiality:** The idea that one part of the cerebral cortex is essentially equal to another in its contribution to learning.

**Extirpation:** A technique for determining the function of a given part of an animal's brain by removing or destroying it and observing the resulting behavior changes.

**Field theory:** Lewin's system using the concept of fields of force to explain behavior in terms of one's field of social influences.

**Fields of force:** Regions or spaces traversed by lines of force, such as of a magnet or electric current.

**Free association:** A psychotherapeutic technique in which the patient says whatever comes to mind.

**Freudian slip:** An act of forgetting or a lapse in speech that reflects unconscious motives or anxieties.

**Functionalism:** A system of psychology concerned with the mind as it is used in an organism's adaptation to its environment.

**Gestalt psychology:** A system of psychology that focuses largely on learning and perception, suggesting that combining sensory elements produces new patterns with properties that did not exist in the individual elements.

**Habit strength:** The strength of the stimulus-response connection, which is a function of the number of reinforcements.

**Historiography:** The principles, methods, and philosophical issues of historical research.

**Humanistic psychology:** A system of psychology that emphasizes the study of conscious experience and the wholeness of human nature.

**Hypothetico-deductive method:** Hull's method for establishing postulates from which experimentally testable conclusions can be deduced.

**Id:** The source of psychic energy and the aspect of personality allied with the instincts.

**Imageless thought:** Külpe's idea that meaning in thought can occur without any sensory or imaginal component.

**Individual psychology:** Adler's theory of personality; it incorporates social as well as biological factors.

**Inferiority complex:** A condition that develops when a person is unable to compensate for normal inferiority feelings.

**Insight:** Immediate apprehension or cognition.

**Instincts:** To Freud, mental representations of internal stimuli (such as hunger) that motivate personality and behavior.

**Intervening variables:** Unobserved and inferred factors within the organism that are the actual determinants of behavior.

**Introspection by analogy:** A technique for studying animal behavior by assuming that the same mental processes that occur in the observer's mind also occur in the animal's mind.

**Introspection:** Examination of one's own mind to inspect and report on personal thoughts or feelings.

**Isomorphism:** The doctrine that there is a correspondence between psychological or conscious experience and the underlying brain experience.

**Just noticeable difference:**    The smallest difference that can be detected between two physical stimuli.

**Law of acquisition:**    The strength of an operant behavior is increased when it is followed by the presentation of a reinforcing stimulus.

**Law of effect:**    Acts that produce satisfaction in a given situation become associated with that situation; when the situation recurs, the act is likely to recur.

**Law of exercise:**    The more an act or response is used in a given situation, the more strongly the act becomes associated with that situation.

**Law of mass action:**    The efficiency of learning is a function of the total mass of cortical tissue.

**Law of parsimony:**    (Lloyd Morgan's Canon): The notion that animal behavior must not be attributed to a higher mental process when it can be explained in terms of a lower mental process.

**Law of primary reinforcement:**    When a stimulus-response relationship is followed by a reduction in a bodily need, the probability increases that on subsequent occasions the same stimulus will evoke the same response.

**Libido:**    To Freud, the psychic energy that drives a person toward pleasurable thoughts and behaviors.

**Locus of control:**    Rotter's idea about the perceived source of reinforcement. Internal locus of control is the belief that reinforcement depends on one's own behavior; external locus of control is the belief that reinforcement depends on outside forces.

**Materialism:**    The doctrine that considers the facts of the universe to be sufficiently explained in physical terms by the existence and nature of matter.

**Mechanism:**    The doctrine that natural processes are mechanically determined and capable of explanation by the laws of physics and chemistry.

**Mediate and immediate experience:**    Mediate experience provides information about something other than the elements of that experience; immediate experience is unbiased by interpretation.

**Mental age:**    The age at which children of average ability can perform certain tasks.

**Mental tests:**    Tests of motor skills and sensory capacities; intelligence tests use more complex measures of mental abilities.

**Mentalism:**    The doctrine that all knowledge is a function of mental phenomena and dependent on the perceiving or experiencing person.

**Mind-body problem:**    The question of the distinction between mental and physical qualities.

**Monadology:**    Leibnitz's theory of psychic entities, called monads, which are similar to perceptions.

**Naturalistic theory:**    The view that progress and change in scientific history are attributable to the Zeitgeist, which makes a culture receptive to some ideas but not to others.

**Nonsense syllables:**    Syllables presented in a meaningless series to study memory processes.

**Oedipus complex:**    At ages four to five, the unconscious desire of a boy for his mother and the desire to replace or destroy his father.

**Operant conditioning:**    A learning situation that involves behavior emitted by an organism rather than elicited by a detectable stimulus.

**Operationism:**    The doctrine that a physical concept can be defined in precise terms related to the set of operations or procedures by which it is determined.

**Perceptual constancy:**    A quality of wholeness or completeness in perceptual experience that does not vary even when the sensory elements change.

**Personal unconscious:**    The reservoir of material that once was conscious but has been forgotten or suppressed.

**Personalistic theory:**    The view that progress and change in scientific history are attributable to the ideas of unique individuals.

**Phenomenology:**    Stumpf's introspective method that examined experience as it occurred and did not try to reduce experience to elementary components. Also, an approach to knowledge based on an unbiased description of immediate experience as it occurs, not analyzed or reduced to elements.

**Phi phenomenon:**    The illusion that two stationary flashing lights are moving from one place to another.

**Positive regard:**    The unconditional love of a mother for her infant.

**Positivism:**    The doctrine that recognizes only natural phenomena or facts that are objectively observable.

**Pragmatism:**   The doctrine that the validity of ideas is measured by their practical consequences.

**Primary and secondary qualities:**   Primary qualities are characteristics such as size and shape that exist in an object whether or not we perceive them; secondary qualities are characteristics such as color and odor that exist in our perception of the object.

**Psychoanalysis:**   Sigmund Freud's theory of personality and system of psychotherapy.

**Psychophysics:**   The scientific study of the relations between mental and physical processes.

**Psychosexual stages:**   In psychoanalytic theory, the developmental stages of childhood centering on erogenous zones.

**Purposive behaviorism:**   Tolman's system combining the objective study of behavior with the consideration of purposiveness or goal orientation in behavior.

**Recapitulation theory:**   Hall's idea that the psychological development of children repeats the history of the human race.

**Reductionism:**   The doctrine that explains phenomena on one level (such as complex ideas) in terms of phenomena on another level (such as simple ideas).

**Reflex action theory:**   The idea that an external object (a stimulus) can bring about an involuntary response.

**Reflex arc:**   The connection between sensory stimuli and motor responses.

**Reinforcement schedules:**   Conditions involving various rates and times of reinforcement.

**Reinforcement:**   Something that increases the likelihood of a response.

**Repetition:**   The notion that the more frequently two ideas occur together, the more readily they will be associated.

**Repression:**   The process of barring unacceptable ideas, memories, or desires from conscious awareness, leaving them to operate in the unconscious mind.

**Resistance:**   A blockage or refusal to disclose painful memories during a freeassociation session.

**Self-actualization:**   The full development of one's abilities and the realization of one's potential.

**Self-efficacy:**   One's sense of self-esteem and competence in dealing with life's problems.

**Simple and complex ideas:**   Simple ideas are elemental ideas that arise from sensation and reflection; complex ideas are derived ideas that are compounded of simple ideas and thus can be analyzed or reduced to their simpler components.

**Social interest:**   Adler's conception of an innate potential to cooperate with other people to achieve personal and societal goals.

**Stimulus error:**   Confusing the mental process under study with the stimulus or object being observed.

**Stream of consciousness:**   William James's idea that consciousness is a continuous flowing process and that any attempt to reduce it to elements will distort it.

**Structuralism:**   E. B. Titchener's system of psychology, which dealt with conscious experience as dependent on experiencing persons.

**Successive approximation:**   An explanation for the acquisition of complex behavior. Behaviors such as learning to speak will be reinforced only as they come to approximate or approach the final desired behavior.

**Superego:**   The moral aspect of personality derived from internalizing parental and societal values and standards.

**Synthetic philosophy:**   Herbert Spencer's idea that knowledge and experience can be explained in terms of evolutionary principles.

**Systematic experimental introspection:**   Külpe's introspective method that used retrospective reports of subjects' cognitive processes after they had completed an experimental task.

**Transference:**   The process by which a patient responds to the therapist as if the therapist were a significant person (such as a parent) in the patient's life.

**Trial-and-error learning:**   Learning based on the repetition of response tendencies that lead to success.

**Tridimensional theory of feelings:**   Wundt's explanation for feeling states based on three dimensions: pleasure/displeasure, tension/relaxation, and excitement/depression.

**Tropism:**   An involuntary forced movement.

**Two-point threshold:**   The threshold at which two points of stimulation can be distinguished as such.

**Variability hypothesis:** The notion that men show a wider range and variation of physical and mental development than women; the abilities of women are seen as more average.

**Vicarious reinforcement:** Bandura's notion that learning can occur by observing the behavior of other people, and the consequences of their behavior, rather than by always experiencing reinforcement personally.

**Voluntarism:** The idea that the mind has the capacity to organize mental contents into higher-level thought processes.

**Zeigarnik effect:** The tendency to recall uncompleted tasks more easily than completed tasks.

**Zeitgeist:** The intellectual and cultural climate or spirit of the times.

# References

Abramson, C. (2009). A study in inspiration: Charles Henry Turner (1867-1923) and the investigation of insect behavior. *Annual Review of Entomology, 54,* 343–359.

Aanstoos, C. M. (1994). Mainstream psychology and the humanistic alternative. In F. Wertz (Ed.), *The humanistic movement: Recovering the person in psychology* (pp. 1–12). Lake Worth, FL: Gardner Press.

Abma, R. (2004). Madness and mental health. In J. Jansz & P. Van Drunen (Eds.), *A social history of psychology* (pp. 93–128). Malden, MA: Blackwell.

Adelman, K. (1996, June). Examined lives. *Washingtonian Magazine,* 27–32.

Adler, J. (2006, March 27). Freud is not dead. *Newsweek,* pp. 43–49.

Agassiz, G. R. (Ed.). (1922). *Meade's headquarters, 1863–1865: Letters of Colonel Theodore Lyman from the Wilderness to Appomattox.* Boston: Atlantic Monthly Press.

Alexander, I. E. (1994). C. G. Jung: The man and his work, then and now. In G. A. Kimble, M. Wertheimer, & C. White (Eds.), *Portraits of pioneers in psychology* (pp. 153–169). Washington, DC: American Psychological Association.

Allen, G. W. (1967). *William James.* New York: Viking Press.

Amsel, A., & Rashotte, M. E. (Eds.). (1984). *Mechanisms of adaptive behavior: Clark L. Hull's theoretical papers with commentary.* New York: Columbia University Press.

Anastasi, A. (1988). *Psychological testing* (6th ed.). New York: Macmillan.

Anastasi, A. (1993). A century of psychological testing. In T. K. Fagan & G. R. VandenBos (Eds.), *Exploring applied psychology* (pp. 9–36). Washington, DC: American Psychological Association.

Anderson, C., Shibuya, A., Ihori, N., Swing, E., Bushman, B., Sakamoto, A., Rothstein, H., & Saleem, M. (2010). Violent video game effects on aggression, empathy, and prosocial behavior in Eastern and Western countries: A meta-analytic review. *Psychological Bulletin, 136,* 151–173.

Angell, J. R. (1904). *Psychology: An introductory study of the structure and function of human consciousness.* New York: Holt.

Angell, J. R. (1907). The province of functional psychology. *Psychological Review, 14,* 61–91.

Appignanesi, L. (2008). *Mad, bad, & sad: Women and the mind doctors.* New York: Norton.

Appignanesi, L., & Forrester, J. (1992). *Freud's women.* New York: Basic Books.

Ash, M. G. (1995). *Gestalt psychology in German culture, 1890–1967: Holism and the quest for objectivity.* Cambridge, England: Cambridge University Press.

Arnett, J. (2008). The neglected 95%: Why American psychology needs to become less American. *American Psychologist, 63,* 602–614.

Arnett, J., & Cravens, H. (2006). G. Stanley Hall's *Adolescence*: A centennial reappraisal introduction. *History of Psychology, 9,* 165–171.

Avargues-Weber, A., Portelli, G., Benard, J., Dyer, A., & Giorfa, M. (2010). Configural processing enables discrimination and categorization of face-like stimuli in honeybees. *Journal of Experimental Biology, 213,* 593–601.

Averill, L. A. (1990). Recollections of Clark's G. Stanley Hall. *Journal of the History of the Behavioral Sciences, 26,* 125–130.

Aydon, C. (2002). *Charles Darwin: The naturalist who started a scientific revolution*. New York: Carroll & Graf.

Azar, B. (2002). Saying goodbye to the Harvard Pigeon Lab. *Monitor on Psychology, 33*(9), 44.

Baars, B. J. (1986). *The cognitive revolution in psychology*. New York: Guilford.

Baars, B. J. (1997). *In the theater of consciousness: The workspace of the mind*. New York: Oxford University Press.

Backe, A. (2001). John Dewey and early Chicago functionalism. *History of Psychology, 4*, 323–340.

Bailey, R., & Gillaspy, J. (2005). Operant psychology goes to the fair: Marian and Keller Breland in the popular press, 1947-1966. *The Behavior Analyst, 28*, 143–159.

Bair, D. (2003). *Jung: A biography*. Boston: Little, Brown.

Balance, W. D. G., & Bringmann, W. G. (1987). Fechner's mysterious malady. *History of Psychology Newsletter, 19*(1/2), 36–47.

Baldwin, B. T. (Ed.). (1980). In memory of Wilhelm Wundt. In W. G. Bringmann & R. D. Tweney (Eds.), *Wundt studies: A centennial collection* (pp. 280–308). Toronto: C. J. Hogrefe. (Original work published 1921).

Bandura, A. (1982). Self-efficacy mechanism in human agency. *American Psychologist, 37*, 122–147.

Bandura, A. (1986). *Social foundations of thought and action: A social cognitive theory*. Englewood Cliffs, NJ: Prentice-Hall.

Bandura, A. (2001). Social cognitive theory: An agentic perspective. *Annual Review of Psychology, 52*, 1–26.

Bandura, A. (2007). Albert Bandura. In G. Lindzey & W. Runyan (Eds.), *History of psychology in autobiography* (vol. 9). Washington, DC: APA.

Bandura, A. (2009). Social cognitive theory goes global. *The Psychologist, 22*, 504–506.

Bania, A., Harris, S., Kinsley, H., & Boysen, S. (2009). Constructive and deconstructive tool modification by chimpanzees. *Animal Cognition, 12*, 85–95.

Bargh, J., & Morsella, E. (2008). The unconscious mind. *Perspectives on psychological science, 3*, 73–79.

Barker, L. (2006). Teaching evolutionary psychology: An interview with David M. Buss. *Teaching of Psychology, 33*(1), 69–76.

Baum, W. M. (1994). John B. Watson and behavior analysis. In J. T. Todd & E. K. Morris (Eds.), *Modern perspectives on John B. Watson and classical behaviorism* (pp. 133–140). Westport, CT: Greenwood Press.

Baumgartner, E. (2005). Book review of *Karl Pearson: The scientific life in a statistical age* by T. M. Porter. *Journal of the History of the Behavioral Sciences, 41*, 84–85.

Beck, H., Levinson, S., & Irons, G. (2009). Finding Little Albert: A journey to John B. Watson's infant laboratory. *American Psychologist, 64*, 605–614.

Becker, E. (1973). *The denial of death*. New York: Free Press.

Behrens, P. (2009). War, sanity, and the Nazi mind: the last passion of Joseph Jastrow. *History of Psychology, 12*, 266–284.

Bekhterev, V. M. (1932). *General principles of human reflexology*. New York: International Publishers.

Benjafield, J. (2010). The golden section and American psychology, 1892–1938. *Journal of the History of the Behavioral Sciences, 46*, 62–71.

Benjamin, L. T., Jr. (1975). The pioneering work of Leta Hollingworth in the psychology of women. *Nebraska History, 56*, 493–505.

Benjamin, L. T., Jr. (1986). Why don't they understand us? A history of psychology's public image. *American Psychologist, 41*, 941–946.

Benjamin, L. T., Jr. (1987). Knee jerks, Twitmyer, and the Eastern Psychological Association. *American Psychologist, 42*, 1118–1120.

Benjamin, L. T., Jr. (1988). A history of teaching machines. *American Psychologist, 43*, 703–712.

Benjamin, L. T., Jr. (1991). A history of the New York branch of the American Psychological Association: 1903–1935. *American Psychologist, 46*, 1003–1011.

Benjamin, L. T., Jr. (1993). *A history of psychology in letters*. Dubuque, IA: Brown & Benchmark.

Benjamin, L. T., Jr. (2000a). The psychology laboratory at the turn of the 20th century. *American Psychologist, 55*, 318–321.

Benjamin, L. T., Jr. (2000b). Hugo Münsterberg: Portrait of an applied psychologist. In G. A. Kimble & M. Wertheimer (Eds.), *Portraits of pioneers in psychology* (Vol. 4, pp. 113–129). Washington, DC: American Psychological Association.

Benjamin, L. T., Jr. (2001). American psychology's struggles with its curriculum: Should a thousand flowers bloom? *American Psychologist, 56*, 735–742.

Benjamin, L. T., Jr. (2003). Behavioral science and the Nobel Prize: A history. *American Psychologist, 58*, 731–741.

Benjamin, L. T., Jr. (2006a). *A history of psychology in letters*. Malden, MA: Blackwell.

Benjamin, L. T., Jr. (2006b). Hugo Münsterberg's attack on the application of scientific psychology. *Journal of Applied Psychology, 91*, 414–425.

Benjamin, L. T., Jr. (2008). America's first black female psychologist. *Monitor on Psychology, 39*(10), 20–21.

Benjamin, L. T., Jr. (2009a). Where's psychology's museum? *Monitor on Psychology, 40*(5), 22–33.

Benjamin, L. T., Jr. (2009b). The birth of American intelligence testing. *Monitor on Psychology, 40*(1), 20–21.

Benjamin, L. T., Jr., & Baker, D. (2004). *From séance to science: The history of the profession of psychology in America.* Belmont, CA: Thomson/Wadsworth.

Benjamin, L. T., Jr., & Bryant, W. H. M. (1997). A history of popular psychology magazines in America. In W. Bringmann et al. (Eds.), *A pictorial history of psychology* (pp. 585–593). Carol Stream, IL: Quintessence.

Benjamin, L. T., Jr., & Nielsen-Gammon, E. (1999). B. F. Skinner and psychotechnology: The case of the heir conditioner. *Review of General Psychology, 3,* 155–167.

Benjamin, L. T., Jr., & Shields, S. (1990). Leta Stetter Hollingworth (1886–1939). In A. N. O'Connell & N. F. Russo (Eds.), *Women in psychology: A bio-bibliographic sourcebook* (pp. 173–183). New York: Greenwood Press.

Benjamin, L. T., Jr., Bryant, W. H. M., Campbell, C., Luttrell, J., & Holtz, C. (1997). Between psoriasis and ptarmigan: American encyclopedia portrayals of psychology, 1880–1940. *Review of General Psychology, 1* (1), 5–18.

Benjamin, L. T., Jr., Durkin, M., Link, M., Vestal, M., & Acord, J. (1992). Wundt's American doctoral students. *American Psychologist, 47,* 123–131.

Benjamin, L. T., Jr., Rogers, A. M., & Rosenbaum, A. (1991). Coca-Cola, caffeine, and mental deficiency: Harry Hollingworth and the Chattanooga trial of 1911. *Journal of the History of the Behavioral Sciences, 27,* 42–55.

Benjamin, L. T., Jr., Whitaker, J., Ramsey, R., & Zeve, D. (2007). John B. Watson's alleged sex research: An appraisal of the evidence. *American Psychologist, 62,* 131–139.

Berkeley, G. (1957a). An essay towards a new theory of vision. In M. W. Calkins (Ed.), *Berkeley: Essay, principles, dialogues* (pp. 1–98). New York: Scribners. (Original work published 1709).

Berkeley, G. (1957b). A treatise concerning the principles of human knowledge. In M. W. Calkins (Ed.), *Berkeley: Essay, principles, dialogues* (pp. 99–216) New York: Scribners. (Original work published 1710).

Berliner, D. C. (1993). The 100-year journey of educational psychology. In T. K. Fagan & G. R. VandenBos (Eds.), *Exploring applied psychology: Origins and critical analyses* (pp. 37–78). Washington, DC: American Psychological Association.

Berman, L. (1927). *The religion called Behaviorism.* New York: Boni & Liveright.

Berscheid, E. (2003). Lessons in "greatness" from Kurt Lewin's life and work. In R. Sternberg (Ed.), *The anatomy of impact: What makes the great works of psychology great* (pp, 109–123). Washington, DC: American Psychological Association.

Bettelheim, B. (1982). *Freud and man's soul.* New York: Knopf.

Binet, A. (1971). *The psychic life of micro-organisms.* West Orange, NJ: Saifer. (Original work published 1889).

Bjork, D. W. (1983). *The compromised scientist: William James in the development of American psychology.* New York: Columbia University Press.

Bjork, D. W. (1993). *B. F. Skinner.* New York: Basic Books.

Blanton, S. (1971). *Diary of my analysis with Sigmund Freud.* New York: Hawthorn Books.

Blumenthal, A. (1980). Wilhelm Wundt and early American psychology. In R. Rieber (Ed.), *Wilhelm Wundt and the making of a scientific psychology* (pp. 117–135). New York: Plenum Press.

Blumenthal, A. (1985). Wilhelm Wundt: Psychology as the propaedeutic science. In C. E. Buxton (Ed.), *Points of view in the modern history of psychology* (pp. 19–50). Orlando, FL: Academic Press.

Boag, S. (2006). Freudian repression, the common view, and pathological science. *Review of General Psychology, 10,* 74–86.

Boakes, R. (1984). *From Darwin to behaviourism: Psychology and the minds of animals.* Cambridge, England: Cambridge University Press.

Boas, M. (1961). *The scientific renaissance: 1450–1630.* London: Collins.

Boehlich, W. (1990). *The letters of Sigmund Freud to Eduard Silberstein, 1871–1881.* Cambridge, MA: Harvard University Press.

Bogeart, A. (2003). Number of older brothers and social orientation: New tests and the attraction/behavior distinction in two national probability samples. *Journal of Personality and Social Psychology, 84,* 644–652.

Boorstin, D. J. (1983). *The discoverers.* New York: Random House.

Boring, E. G. (1927). Edward Bradford Titchener. *American Journal of Psychology, 38,* 489–506.

Boring, E. G. (1929). *A history of experimental psychology.* New York: Appleton.

Boring, E. G. (1950). *A history of experimental psychology* (2nd ed.). New York: Appleton-Century-Crofts.

Boring, E. G. (1952). Autobiography. In H. S. Langfeld, H. Werner, & R. M. Yerkes (Eds.), *A history of psychology in autobiography* (Vol. 4, pp. 27–52). Worcester, MA: Clark University Press.

Boring, E. G. (1967). Titchener's experimentalists. *Journal of the History of the Behavioral Sciences, 3,* 315–325.

Borman, W. C., & Cox, G. L. (1996). Who's doing what: Patterns in the practice of I/O psychology. *The Industrial-organizational Psychologist, 33*(4), 21.

Bornstein, R. F., & Masling, J. M. (1998). Introduction: The psychoanalytic unconscious. In R. F. Bornstein & J. M. Masling (Eds.), *Empirical perspectives on the psychoanalytic unconscious* (pp. xiii–xxvii). Washington, DC: American Psychological Association.

Bornstein, R. F., & Pittman, T. S. (1992). *Perception without awareness: Cognitive, clinical, and social perspectives.* New York: Guilford.

Bottom, W. (2009). Organizing intelligence: Development of behavioral science and the research based model of business education. *Journal of the History of the Behavioral Sciences, 45,* 253–283.

Bottome, P. (1939). *Alfred Adler: A biography.* New York: Putnam.

Bouton, M. (2009). Behaviorism, thoughts, and actions. *British Journal of Psychology, 100,* 181–183.

Breger, L. (2000). Freud: Darkness in the midst of vision. New York: Wiley.

Breland, K., & Breland, M. (1951). A field of applied animal psychology. *American Psychologist, 6,* 202–204.

Breland, K., & Breland, M. (1961). The misbehavior of organisms. *American Psychologist, 16,* 681–684.

Brems, C., Thevenin, D. M., & Routh, D. K. (1991). The history of clinical psychology. In C. E. Walker (Ed.), *Clinical psychology: Historical and research foundations* (pp. 3–35). New York: Plenum Press.

Brentano, F. (1874). *Psychology from an empirical standpoint.* Leipzig: Duncker & Humblot.

Breuer, J., & Freud, S. (1895). Studies on hysteria. In *Standard edition* (Vol. 2). London: Hogarth Press.

Brewer, C. L. (1991). Perspectives on John B. Watson. In G. A. Kimble, M. Wertheimer, & C. White (Eds.), *Portraits of pioneers in psychology* (pp. 171–186). Washington, DC: American Psychological Association.

Brewer, W., & Schommer-Aikins, M. (2006). Scientists are not deficient in mental imagery: Galton revised. *Review of General Psychology, 10,* 130–146.

Bridgman, P. W. (1927). *The logic of modern physics.* New York: Macmillan.

Bringmann, W. G., & Balk, M. M. (1992). Another look at Wilhelm Wundt's publication record. *History of Psychology Newsletter, 24*(3/4), 50–66.

Brock, A. (2006). Rediscovering the history of psychology: Interview with Kurt Danziger. *History of Psychology, 9,* 1–16.

Brome, V. (1981). *Jung: Man and myth.* New York: Atheneum.

Brookes, M. (2004). *Extreme measures: The dark visions and bright ideas of Francis Galton.* New York: Bloomsbury.

Broom, D., Sena, H., & Moynihan, K. (2009). Pigs learn what a mirror image represents and use it to obtain information. *Animal Behaviour, 78,* 1037–1041.

Browne, J. (2002). *Charles Darwin: The power of place.* New York: Knopf.

Brozek, J. (1980). The echoes of Wundt's work in the United States, 1887–1977: A quantitative citation analysis. *Psychological Research, 42,* 103–107.

Bruner, J. S. (1983). *In search of mind: Essays in autobiography.* New York: Harper & Row.

Bruner, J. S. (1990). *Acts of meaning.* Cambridge, MA: Harvard University Press.

Buckley, K. W. (1982). The selling of a psychologist: John Broadus Watson and the application of behavioral techniques to advertising. *Journal of the History of the Behavioral Sciences, 18,* 207–221.

Buckley, K. W. (1989). *Mechanical man: John Broadus Watson and the beginnings of behaviorism.* New York: Guilford.

Buckley, K. W. (1994). Misbehaviorism: The case of John B. Watson's dismissal from Johns Hopkins University. In J. T. Todd & E. K. Morris (Eds.), *Modern perspectives on John B. Watson and classical behaviorism* (pp. 19–36). Westport, CT: Greenwood Press.

Buckley, V. (2004). *Christina, Queen of Sweden: The restless life of a European eccentric.* New York: Harper Perennial.

Burghardt, G. (2009). Darwin's legacy to comparative psychology and ethology. *American Psychologist, 64,* 102–110.

Burnham, J. (1968). On the origins of behaviorism. *Journal of the History of the Behavioral Sciences, 4,* 143–151.

Burnham, J. (2009). What happened "after Freud left"? *The General Psychologist, 44,* 15–17.

Burt, C. (1962). The concept of consciousness. *British Journal of Psychology, 53,* 229–242.

Buss, D. (1999). *Evolutionary psychology: The new science of the mind.* Boston: Allyn & Bacon.

Buss, D. (2005). Introduction: The emergency of evolutionary psychology. In D. Buss (Ed.), *The handbook of evolutionary psychology* (pp. xiii–xxv). New York: Wiley.

Buss, D. (2009a). How can evolutionary psychology successfully explain personality and individual differences? *Perspectives on Psychological Science, 4,* 359–366.

Buss, D. (2009b). The great struggles of life: Darwin and the emergence of evolutionary psychology. *American Psychologist, 64,* 140–148.

Cadwallader, T. C. (1984). Neglected aspects of the evolution of American comparative and animal psychology. In G. Greenberg & E. Tobach (Eds.), *Behavioral evolution and integrative levels* (pp. 15–48). Hillsdale, NJ: Erlbaum.

Cadwallader, T. C. (1987). Early zoological input to comparative and animal psychology at the University of Chicago. In E. Tobach (Ed.), *Historical perspectives and the international status of comparative psychology* (pp. 37–59). Hillsdale, NJ: Erlbaum.

Cahan, D. (1993). Helmholtz and the civilizing power of science. In D. Cahan (Ed.), *Hermann von Helmholtz and the foundations of nineteenth century science* (pp. 559–601). Berkeley, CA: University of California Press.

Camfield, T. M. (1992). The American Psychological Association and World War I: 1914 to 1919. In R. B. Evans, V. S. Sexton, & T. C. Cadwallader (Eds.), *The American Psychological Association: A historical perspective* (pp. 91–118). Washington, DC: American Psychological Association.

Campbell-Kelly, M., & Aspray, W. (1996). *Computer: A history of the information machine.* New York: Basic Books.

Candland, D. K. (1993). *Feral children and clever animals: Reflections on human nature.* New York: Oxford University Press.

Cannato, V. (2009). American passage: *The history of Ellis Island.* New York: Harper.

Capaldi, N. (2004). *John Stuart Mill: A biography.* Cambridge, England: Cambridge University Press.

Caplan, E. (1998). Popularizing American psychotherapy: The Emmanuel Movement, 1906–1910. *History of Psychology, 1,* 289–314.

Capshaw, J. H. (1999). *Psychologists on the march: Science, practice, and professional identity in America, 1929–1969.* Cambridge, England: Cambridge University Press.

Carlat, D. (2010, April 25). Mind over meds: How I decided my psychiatry patients needed more from me than prescriptions. *New York Times.*

Carpentero, H. (2004). Watson's *Behaviorism*: A comparison of two editions (1925 and 1930). *History of Psychology, 7,* 183–202.

Carr, H. A. (1925). *Psychology.* New York: Longmans, Green.

Carr, H. A. (1930). Functionalism. In C. Murchison (Ed.), *Psychologies of 1930* (pp. 59–78). Worcester, MA: Clark University Press.

Carr, H. A. (1961). Autobiography. In C. Murchison (Ed.), *A history of psychology in autobiography* (Vol. 3, pp. 69–82). New York: Russell & Russell. (Original work published 1930).

Catania, A. C. (1992). B. F. Skinner, organism. *American Psychologist, 47,* 1521–1530.

Caton, H. (2007). Getting our history right: Six errors about Darwin and his influence. *Evolutionary Psychology, 5,* 52–69.

Cattell, J. M. (1890). Mental tests and measurements. *Mind, 15,* 373–381.

Cattell, J. M. (1896). Address of the president before the American Psychological Association, 1895. *Psychological Review, 3,* 134–148.

Cattell, J. M. (1904). The conceptions and methods of psychology. *Popular Science Monthly, 66,* 176–186.

Cattell, J. M. (1928). Early psychological laboratories. *Science, 67,* 543–548.

Cautin, R. (2009). The founding of the Association for Psychological Science. *Perspectives on Psychological Science, 4,* 211–223.

Chamberlin, J. (2010). Don't know much about history. *Monitor on Psychology, 41*(2), 44–47.

Cherry, F. (2004). Kenneth B. Clark and social psychology's other history. In G. Philogene (Ed.), *Racial identity in context: The legacy of Kenneth B. Clark* (pp. 17–33). Washington, DC: American Psychological Association.

Chomsky, N. (1959). [Review of *Verbal Behavior* by B. F. Skinner.] *Language, 35,* 26–58.

Chomsky, N. (1972). *Language and mind.* New York: Harcourt Brace.

Clark, K. B. (1978). Kenneth B. Clark: Social psychologist. In T. C. Hunter (Ed.), *Beginnings* (pp. 76–84). New York: Crowell.

Clarke, E. H. (1873). *Sex and education.* Boston: Osgood.

Clay, R. (2002). A renaissance for humanistic psychology. *Monitor on Psychology, 33*(8), 42–43.

Cohen, D. (2010). *The escape of Sigmund Freud.* London: J. R. Books Ltd.

Cohen, I. B. (2005). *The triumph of numbers: How counting shaped modern life.* New York: W. W. Norton.

Cohen, P. (2010, February 25). Descartes letter found, therefore it is. *New York Times.*

Cole, J. (2009). *The great American university: Its rise to preeminence, its indispensable national role, why it must be protected.* New York: Public Affairs Press.

Comte, A. (1896). *The positive philosophy of Comte.* London: Bell. (Original work published 1830).

Confer, J., Easton, J., Fleischman, D., Goetz, C., Lewis, D., Perilloux, C., & Buss, D. (2010). Evolutionary psychology: Controversies, questions, prospects, and limitations. *American Psychologist, 65,* 110–126.

Cook, R. C. (1993). The experimental analysis of cognition in animals. *Psychological Science, 4,* 174–178.

Coon, D. J. (1994). "Not a creature of reason": The alleged impact of Watsonian behaviorism on advertising in the 1920s. In J. T. Todd & E. K. Morris (Eds.), *Modern perspectives on John B. Watson and classical behaviorism* (pp. 37–63). Westport, CT: Greenwood Press.

Corbett, S. (2009, September 20). The holy grail of the unconscious. *New York Times Magazine.*

Cowley, G. (2002, Sept. 16). The science of happiness. *Newsweek, 49*.

Croarken, M. (2003). Astronomical labourers: Maskelyne's assistants at the Royal Observatory, Greenwich, 1765-1811. *Notes and Records of the Royal Society, 57*, 285–298.

Croce, P. J. (1999). Physiology as the antechamber to metaphysics: The young William James's hope for a philosophical psychology. *History of Psychology, 2*, 302–323.

Cromie, W. (2006, July 24). How Darwin's finches got their beaks. *Harvard University Gazette*.

Crosby, A. W. (1997). *The measure of reality: Quantification and western society, 1250–1600*. Cambridge, England: Cambridge University Press.

Crowther-Heyck, H. (1999). George A. Miller, language, and the computer metaphor of mind. *History of Psychology, 2*, 37–64.

Cunningham, S. (1985, May). Humanists celebrate gains, goals. *APA Monitor, 16*, 18.

Cuny, H. (1965). *Ivan Pavlov: The man and his theories*. New York: Eriksson.

Custers, R., & Aarts, H. (2010). The unconscious will: How the pursuit of goals operates outside of conscious awareness. *Science, 329*, 47–50.

Dallenbach, K. (1967). Autobiography. In E. G. Boring & G. Lindzey (Eds.), *A history of psychology in autobiography* (Vol. 5, pp. 57–93). New York: Appleton-Century-Crofts.

Danziger, K. (1980). A history of introspection reconsidered. *Journal of the History of the Behavioral Sciences, 16*, 241–262.

Darwin, C. (1859). *On the origin of species by means of natural selection*. London: Murray.

Darwin, C. (1871). *The descent of man*. London: Murray.

Darwin, C. (1872). *The expression of the emotions in man and animals*. London: Murray.

Darwin, C. (1877). A biographical sketch of an infant. *Mind, 2*, 285–294.

DeAngelis, T. (2010). Little Albert regains his identity. *Monitor on Psychology, 41*(1), 10.

Decker, H. S. (1991). *Freud, Dora, and Vienna 1900*. New York: Free Press.

Dehue, T. (2000). From deception trials to control reagents: The introduction of the control group about a century ago. *American Psychologist, 55*, 264–268.

Demarest, J. (1987). Two comparative psychologies. In E. Tobach (Ed.), *Historical perspectives and the international status of comparative psychology* (pp. 127–155). Hillsdale, NJ: Erlbaum.

Denmark, F. L., & Fernandez, L. C. (1992). Women: Their influence and their impact on the teaching of psychology. In A. E. Puente, J. R. Matthews, & C. L. Brewer (Eds.), *Teaching psychology in America: A history* (pp. 171–188). Washington, DC: American Psychological Association.

Dennis, P. M. (1984). The Edison questionnaire. *Journal of the History of the Behavioral Sciences, 20*, 23–37.

Dennis, P. M. (1991). Psychology's first publicist: H. Addington Bruce and the popularization of the subconscious and the power of suggestion before World War I. *Psychological Reports, 68*, 755–765.

Dennis, P. M. (2002). Psychology's public image in "Topics of the Times": Commentary from the editorial page of *The New York Times* between 1904 and 1947. *Journal of the History of the Behavioral Sciences, 38*, 371–392.

Descartes, R. (1912). *A discourse on method*. London: Dent. (Original work published 1637).

Desmond, A., & Moore, J. (1991). *Darwin*. New York: Warner Books.

Desmond, J. (1997). *Huxley: From devil's disciple to evolution's high priest*. Reading, MA: Addison-Wesley.

Dewey, J. (1886). *Psychology*. New York: Harper.

Dewey, J. (1896). The reflex arc concept in psychology. *Psychological Review, 3*, 357–370.

Dewsbury, D. (2003). James Rowland Angell: Born administrator. In G. Kimble & M. Wertheimer (Eds.), *Portraits of Pioneers in Psychology* (vol. 5, pp. 57–71). Washington, DC: American Psychological Association.

Dewsbury, D. (2009a). Charles Darwin and psychology at the bicentennial and sesquicentennial. *American Psychologist, 64*, 67–74.

Dewsbury, D. (2009b). Is psychology losing its foundations? *Review of General Psychology, 13*, 281–289.

Dewsbury, D., & Pickren, W. E. (1992). Psychologists as teachers: Sketches toward a history of teaching during 100 years of American psychology. In A. E. Puente, J. R. Matthews, & C. L. Brewer (Eds.), *Teaching psychology in America: A history* (pp. 127–151). Washington, DC: American Psychological Association.

Diamond, S. (1974). Francis Galton and American psychology. *Annals of the New York Academy of Sciences, 291*, 47–55.

Diamond, S. (1980a). A plea for historical accuracy [Letter to the editor]. *Contemporary Psychology, 25*, 84–85.

Diamond, S. (1980b). Wundt before Leipzig. In R. Rieber (Ed.), *Wilhelm Wundt and the making of a scientific psychology* (pp. 3–70). New York: Plenum Press.

DiClemente, D. F., & Hantula, D. A. (2000). John Broadus Watson, I/O psychologist. *The Industrial-organizational Psychologist, 37*(4), 47–55.

Diehl, L. A. (1986). The paradox of G. Stanley Hall: Foe of coeducation and educator of women. *American Psychologist, 41*, 868–878.

Diener, E., Lucas, R., & Scollon, C. (2006). Beyond the hedonic treadmill: Revising the adaptation theory of well-being. *American Psychologist, 61*, 305–314.

Diener, E., Ng, W., Harter, J., & Arora, R. (2010). Wealth and happiness across the world: Material prosperity predicts life evaluation, whereas psychosocial prosperity predicts positive feeling. *Journal of Personality and Social Psychology, 99*, 52–60.

Diener, E., Oishi, S., & Lucas, R. (2003). Personality, culture, and subjective well-being: Emotional and cognitive evaluations of life. *Annual Review of Psychology, 54*, 403–425.

Dijksterhuis, A., & Meurs, T. (2006). Where creativity resides: The generative power of unconscious thought. *Consciousness and Cognition: An International Journal, 15*, 135–146.

Dijksterhuis, A., Bos, M., Nordgren, L., & van Baaren, R. (2006). On making the right choice: The deliberation-without-attention effect. *Science, 311*(5763), 1005–1007.

Dingfelder, S. (2010). The first modern psychology study: Or how Benjamin Franklin unmasked a fraud and demonstrated the power of the mind. *Monitor on Psychology, 41*(7), 30–31.

Distinguished Scientific Contribution Award [Bandura]. (1981). *American Psychologist, 36*, 27–42.

Donaldson, G. (1996). Between practice and theory: Melanie Klein, Anna Freud, and the development of child analysis. *Journal of the History of the Behavioral Sciences, 32*, 160–176.

Donnelly, M. E. (Ed.). (1992). *Reinterpreting the legacy of William James*. Washington, DC: American Psychological Association.

Draguns, J. G. (2001). Toward a truly international psychology: Beyond English only. *American Psychologist, 56*, 1019–1030.

Dyson, G. B. (1997). *Darwin among the machines: The evolution of global intelligence*. Reading, MA: Addison-Wesley.

Eagle, M. N. (1988). How accurate were Freud's case histories? [Book review of *Freud and the Rat Man*]. *Contemporary Psychology, 33*, 205–206.

Ebbinghaus, H. (1885). *On memory*. Leipzig: Duncker & Humblot.

Ebbinghaus, H. (1902). *The principles of psychology*. Leipzig: Veit.

Ebbinghaus, H. (1908). *A summary of psychology*. Leipzig: Veit.

Eissler, K. R. (1971). *Talent and genius: The fictitious case of Tausk contra Freud*. New York: Quadrangle.

Elkins, D. (2009). Why humanistic psychology lost its power and influence in American psychology. *Journal of Humanistic Psychology, 49*, 267–291.

Ellenberger, H. F. (1972). The story of "Anna O.": A critical review with new data. *Journal of the History of the Behavioral Sciences, 8*, 267–279.

Ellenberger, H. F. (1978). Carl Gustav Jung: His historical setting. In H. Reise (Ed.), *Historical explanations in medicine and psychiatry* (pp. 142–150). New York: Springer.

Elms, A. (1994). *Uncovering lives: The uneasy alliance of biography and psychology*. New York: Oxford University Press.

Elms, A. (2001). Apocryphal Freud: Sigmund Freud's most famous "quotations" and their actual sources. In J. Winer & W. Anderson (Eds.), *Sigmund Freud and his impact on the modern world.* (pp. 83–104). Hillsdale, NJ: The Analytic Press.

Emery, N., & Clayton, N. (2005). Animal cognition. In J. Bolhuis & L. Giraldeau (Eds.), *The behavior of animals: Mechanisms, function, and evolution* (pp. 170–196). Malden, MA: Blackwell.

Engel, J. (2008). *American therapy: The rise of psychotherapy in the United States*. New York: Gotham Books.

Equine prodigy knows music and arithmetic. (1904, August 14). *The New York Times*.

Erard, M. (2007). *Um: Slips, stumbles, and verbal blunders, and what they mean*. New York: Pantheon.

Erneling, C. E. (1997). Cognitive science and the future of psychology. In D. M. Johnson & C. E. Erneling (Eds.), *The future of the cognitive revolution* (pp. 376–382). New York: Oxford University Press.

Esterson, A. (2002). The myth of Freud's ostracism by the medical community in 1896–1905: Jeffrey Masson's assault on truth. *History of Psychology, 5*, 115–134.

Evans, R. B. (1972). E. B. Titchener and his lost system. *Journal of the History of the Behavioral Sciences, 8*, 168–180.

Evans, R. B. (1991). E. B. Titchener on scientific psychology and technology. In G. A. Kimble, M. Wertheimer, & C. White (Eds.), *Portraits of pioneers in psychology* (pp. 89–103). Hillsdale, NJ: Erlbaum.

Evans, R. B. (1992). Growing pains: The American Psychological Association from 1903 to 1920. In R. B. Evans, V. S. Sexton, & T. C. Cadwallader (Eds.), *The American Psychological Association: A historical perspective* (pp. 73–90). Washington, DC: American Psychological Association.

Evans, R. B., & Scott, F. J. D. (1978). The 1913 International Congress of Psychology: The American congress that wasn't. *American Psychologist, 33*, 711–723.

Evans, R. I. (1989). *Albert Bandura: The man and his ideas*. New York: Praeger.

Falbo, T., & Polit, D. F. (1986). Quantitative review of the only child literature: Research evidence and theory development. *Psychological Bulletin, 100,* 176–189.

Fancher, R. (2000). Snapshots of Freud in America, 1899–1999. *American Psychologist, 55,* 1025–1028.

Fancher, R. (2009). Scientific cousins: The relationship between Charles Darwin and Francis Galton. *American Psychologist, 64,* 84–92.

Farthing, G. W. (1992). *The psychology of consciousness.* Englewood Cliffs, NJ: Prentice-Hall.

Fechner, G. (1966). *Elements of psychophysics.* New York: Holt, Rinehart and Winston. (Original work published 1860).

Feest, U. (2005). Operationism in psychology: What the debate is about, what the debate should be about. *Journal of the History of the Behavioral Sciences, 41,* 131–149.

Fernald, D. (1984). *The Hans legacy: A story of science.* Hillsdale, NJ: Erlbaum.

Ferster, C. B., & Skinner, B. F. (1957). *Schedules of reinforcement.* New York: Appleton-Century-Crofts.

Fisher, P. (2008). *House of wits: An intimate portrait of the James family.* New York: Holt.

Fisher, S. P., & Greenberg, R. P. (1977). *The scientific credibility of Freud's theories and therapy.* New York: Basic Books.

Fisher, S. P., & Greenberg, R. P. (1996). *Freud scientifically reappraised: Testing the theories and therapy.* New York: Wiley.

Floridi, L., Taddeo, M., & Turilli, M. (2009). Turing's imitation game: Still an impossible challenge for all machines and some judges; an evaluation of the 2008 Loebner contest. *Minds and Machines, 19,* 145–150.

Fowler, R. D. (1990). In memoriam: Burrhus Frederic Skinner, 1904–1990. *American Psychologist, 45,* 1203.

Fowler, R. D. (1994, Aug.). Convention wisdom from a true veteran [E. R. Hilgard]. *APA Monitor, 3.*

Francis, M. (2007). *Herbert Spencer and the invention of modern life.* Durham, England: Acumen Publishing.

Freeman, J. (2009). *The tyranny of email: The 4000-year journey to your inbox.* New York: Scribners.

Freud, A. (1936). *The ego and the mechanisms of defense.* London: Hogarth Press.

Freud, A. (1966). Introduction to the technique of child analysis. In *The writings of Anna Freud* (Vol. *1,* pp. 3–69). New York: International Universities Press. (Original work published as "Four lectures on child analysis," 1927)

Freud, S. (1895). On the origins of psychoanalysis. In J. Strachey (Ed. & Trans.), *The standard edition of the complete psychological works of Sigmund Freud* (Vol. *1*). London: Hogarth Press.

Freud, S. (1900). The interpretation of dreams. In *Standard edition* (Vols. *4, 5*). London: Hogarth Press.

Freud, S. (1901). The psychopathology of everyday life. In *Standard edition* (Vol. *6*). London: Hogarth Press.

Freud, S. (1905). Three essays on the theory of sexuality. In *Standard edition* (Vol. *7,* pp. 125–243). London: Hogarth Press.

Freud, S. (1910). Five lectures on psychoanalysis. In *Standard edition* (Vol. *11,* pp. 3–55). London: Hogarth Press. (Original work published 1909).

Freud, S. (1914). On the history of the psychoanalytic movement. In *Standard edition* (Vol. *14,* pp. 3–66). London: Hogarth Press.

Freud, S. (1917). A difficulty in the path of psychoanalysis. In *Standard edition* (Vol. *17,* pp. 136–144). London: Hogarth Press.

Freud, S. (1933). New introductory lectures on psychoanalysis. In *Standard edition* (Vol. *22,* pp. 3–182). London: Hogarth Press.

Freud, S. (1940). An outline of psychoanalysis. In *Standard edition* (Vol. *23,* pp. 141–207). London: Hogarth Press.

Freud, S. (1954). *The origins of psychoanalysis: Letters to Wilhelm Fliess, drafts and notes: 1887–1902.* New York: Basic Books.

Freud, S. (1964). *The letters of Sigmund Freud.* New York: McGraw-Hill. (Original letter published 1883)

Freud, S. (1992). *The diary of Sigmund Freud, 1929–1939: A record of the final decade.* New York: Charles Scribner's Sons. (Original work published 1939).

Friedel, R. (2007). *A culture of improvement: Technology and the Western millennium.* Cambridge: MIT Press.

Friend, T. (2009). *Cheerful money: Me, my family, and the last days of WASP splendor.* New York: Little, Brown.

Fuchs, A. (2009). Babe Ruth sees a psychologist. *Monitor on Psychology, 40*(10), 20–22.

Fuchs, A. H. (1998). Psychology and "The Babe." *Journal of the History of the Behavioral Sciences, 34,* 153–165.

Fuller, R. (1986). *Americans and the unconscious.* New York: Oxford University Press.

Fuller, R. (2006). American psychology and the religious imagination. *Journal of the History of the Behavioral Sciences, 42,* 221–235.

Funder, D. C. (2001). Personality. *Annual Review of Psychology, 52,* 197–221.

Furumoto, L. (1987). On the margins: Women and the professionalization of psychology in the United States, 1890–1940. In M. G. Ash & W. R. Woodward (Eds.), *Psychology in twentieth-century thought and society* (pp. 93–113). Cambridge, England: Cambridge University Press.

Furumoto, L. (1990). Mary Whiton Calkins (1863–1930). In A. N. O'Connell & N. F. Russo (Eds.),

*Women in psychology: A bio-bibliographic sourcebook* (pp. 57–65). New York: Greenwood Press.

Furumoto, L. (1998). Obituary: Lucy May Boring (1886–1996). *American Psychologist*, 53, 59.

Gable, S., & Haidt, J. (2005). What (and why) is positive psychology? *Review of General Psychology*, 9, 103–110.

Gackenbach, J. (2009). Electronic media and lucid-control dreams: Morning- after reports. *Dreaming*, 19, 1–6.

Galef, B. G. (1998). Edward Thorndike: Revolutionary psychologist, ambitious biologist. *American Psychologist*, 53, 1128–1134.

Galton, F. (1869). *Hereditary genius: An inquiry into its laws and consequences.* London: Macmillan.

Galton, F. (1874). *English men of science: Their nature and nurture.* London: Macmillan.

Galton, F. (1889). *Natural inheritance.* London: Macmillan.

Gamwell, L., & Tomes, N. (1995). *Madness in America: Cultural and medical perceptions of mental illness before 1914.* Ithaca, NY: Cornell University Press.

Gantt, W. H. (1941). Introduction. In I. P. Pavlov, *Lectures on conditioned reflexes.* New York: International Publishers.

Gantt, W. H. (1979, Feb.). Interview with Professor Emeritus W. Horsley Gantt. *Johns Hopkins Magazine*, 26–32.

Garatachea, N., Molinero, O., Martinez-Garcia, R., Jimenez-Jiminez, R., Gonzales-Gallego, J., & Marquez, S. (2009). Feelings of well-being in elderlypeople: Relationship to physical activity and physical function. *Archives of Gerontology and Geriatrics*, 48, 306–312.

Gardner, H. (1993). *Creating minds.* New York: Basic Books.

Gaukroger, S. (1995). *Descartes: An intellectual biography.* Oxford, England: Clarendon Press.

Gavin, E. (1987). Prominent women in psychology, determined by ratings of distinguished peers. *Psychotherapy in Private Practice*, 5, 53–68.

Gay, P. (1988). *Freud: A life for our time.* New York: Norton.

Gazzaniga, M. S. (1988). Life with George: The birth of the Cognitive Neuroscience Institute. In W. Hirst (Ed.), *The making of cognitive science: Essays in honor of George A. Miller* (pp. 230–241). Cambridge, England: Cambridge University Press.

Gelder, L. V. (2006, Feb. 10). Manuscript sheds light on early science. *The New York Times*, p. 1.

Gelfand, T. (1992). Sigmund-sur-Seine: Fathers and brothers in Charcot's Paris. In T. Gelfand & J. Kerr (Eds.), *Freud and the history of psychoanalysis* (pp. 29–57). Hillsdale, NJ: Analytic Press.

Gengerelli, J. A. (1976). Graduate school reminiscences: Hull and Koffka. *American Psychologist*, 31, 685–688.

Geuter, U. (1987). German psychology during the Nazi period. In M. G. Ash & W. R. Woodward (Eds.), *Psychology in twentieth-century thought and society* (pp. 165–187). Cambridge, England: Cambridge University Press.

Gibson, J. J. (1967). Autobiography. In E. G. Boring & G. Lindzey (Eds.), *A history of psychology in autobiography* (Vol. 5, pp. 127–143). New York: Appleton-Century-Crofts.

Gifford, S. (1997). *The Emmanuel Movement: The origins of group treatment and the assault on lay psychotherapy.* Boston: Countway Library of Medicine.

Gilgen, A. R., Gilgen, C. K., Koltsova, V. A., & Oleinik, Y. N. (1997). *Soviet and American psychology during World War II.* Westport, CT: Greenwood Press.

Gillaspy, J. A., & Bihm, E. M. (2002). Marian Breland Bailey, 1920 –2001. *American Psychologist*, 57, 292–293.

Gillham, N. W. (2001). *A life of Sir Francis Galton: From African exploration to the birth of eugenics.* Oxford, England: Oxford University Press.

Giorgi, A. (2005). Remaining challenges for humanistic psychology. *Journal of Humanistic Psychology*, 45, 204–216.

Gladwell, M. (2008, May 12). Who says big ideas are rare? *New Yorker*.

Goleman, D. (1983, May). A conversation with Ulric Neisser. *Psychology Today*, 54–62.

Goode, E. (2000, Mar. 4). Human nature: Born or made? Evolutionary theorists provoke an uproar. *The New York Times*.

Goodenough, F. L. (1949). *Mental testing: Its history, principles, and applications.* New York: Rinehart.

Goodstein, L. D. (1988). The growth of the American Psychological Association. *American Psychologist*, 43, 491–498.

Goodwin, C. (2005). Recognizing the experimentalists: The origins of the Society of Experimental Psychologists. *History of Psychology*, 8, 347–361.

Gopnik, A. (2008, October 6). Right again: The passions of John Stuart Mill. *New Yorker*.

Gorlick, A. (2009). Media multitaskers pay mental price, Stanford study shows. *news.stanford.edu/news/2009/August24/multitask-research-study-082409.html?vie*

Gosling, S., Kwan, V., & John, O. (2003). A dog's got personality: A cross-species comparative approach to personality judgments in dogs and humans. *Journal of Personality and Social Psychology*, 85, 1161–1169.

Gottfredson, L. S. (1997). Mainstream science on intelligence: An editorial with 52 signatories, history, and bibliography. *Intelligence*, 24, 13–23.

Gould, S. J. (1981). *The mismeasure of man.* New York: Norton.

Grant, P., & Grant, B. (2006). Evolution of character displacement in Darwin's finches. *Science, 313*(5784), 224–226.

Green, C. (2001). Charles Babbage, the analytic engine, and the possibility of a 19th-century cognitive science. In C. Green, M. Shore, & T. Teo (Eds.), *The transformation of psychology: Influences of 19th-century philosophy, technology, and natural science* (pp. 133–152). Washington, DC: American Psychological Association.

Green, C. (2005). Was Babbage's analytical engine intended to be a mechanical model of the mind? *History of Psychology, 8,* 35–45.

Green, C. (2009). Darwinian theory, functionalism, and the first American psychological revolution. *American Psychologist, 64,* 75–83.

Greenwood, J. (2008). Mechanism, purpose and progress: Darwin and early American psychology. *History of the Human Sciences, 21,* 103–126.

Gribbin, J. (2002). *The scientists: A history of science told through the lives of its greatest inventors.* New York: Random House.

Gribbin, J., & Gribbin, M. (2004). *Fitzroy: The remarkable story of Darwin's captain and the invention of the weather forecast.* New Haven, CT: Yale University Press.

Grinker, R., Jr. (2001). My father's analysis with Sigmund Freud. In J. Winer & J. Anderson (Eds.), *Sigmund Freud and his impact on the modern world* (pp. 35–47). Hillsdale, NJ: The Analytic Press.

Gruber, C. (1972). Academic freedom at Columbia University, 1917–1918: The case of James McKeen Cattell. *American Association of University Professors Bulletin, 58*(3), 297–305.

Grubrich-Simitis, I. (1993). *Back to Freud's texts: Making silent documents speak.* New Haven, CT: Yale University Press.

Gundlach, H. U. K. (1986). Ebbinghaus, nonsense syllables, and three-letter words [Book review]. *Contemporary Psychology, 31,* 469–470.

Guthrie, E. R. (1959). Association by contiguity. In S. Koch (Ed.), *Psychology: A study of a science* (Vol. 2, pp. 158–195). New York: McGraw-Hill.

Guthrie, R. V. (1976). *Even the rat was white: A historical view of psychology.* New York: Harper & Row.

Guthrie, R. V. (1990). Mamie Phipps Clark (1917–1983). In A. N. O'Connell & N. F. Russo (Eds.), *Women in psychology: A bio-bibliographic sourcebook* (pp. 66–74). New York: Greenwood Press.

Haagbloom, S. J., Warnick, R., Warnick, J. E., Jones, V. K., Yarbrough, G. L., Russell, T. M., et al. (2002). The 100 most eminent psychologists of the 20th century. *Review of General Psychology, 6,* 139–152.

Hale, M., Jr. (1980). *Human science and social order: Hugo Münsterberg and the origins of applied psychology.* Philadelphia: Temple University Press.

Hall, G. (2009). Watson: The thinking man's behaviorist. *British Journal of Psychology, 100,* 185–187.

Hall, G. S. (1904). *Adolescence: Its psychology, and its relations to physiology, anthropology, sociology, sex, crime, religion, and education.* New York: Appleton.

Hall, G. S. (1912). *Founders of modern psychology.* New York: Appleton.

Hall, G. S. (1919). Some possible effects of the war on American psychology. *Psychological Bulletin, 16,* 48–49.

Hall, G. S. (1920). *Recreations of a psychologist.* New York: Appleton.

Hall, G. S. (1922). *Senescence.* New York: Appleton.

Hall, G. S. (1923). *The life and confessions of a psychologist.* New York: Appleton.

Hall, M. (1968, July). A conversation with Abraham H. Maslow. *Psychology Today,* pp. 35–37, 54–57.

Ham, J., van den Bos, K., & van Doorn, E. (2009). Lady Justice thinks unconsciously: Unconsicous thought can lead to more accurate justice judgments. *Social Cognition, 27,* 509–521.

Hannush, M. J. (1987). John B. Watson remembered: An interview with James B. Watson. *Journal of the History of the Behavioral Sciences, 23,* 137–152.

Harlow, H. F. (1971). *Learning to love.* San Francisco: Albion.

Harris, B. (2009). Jewish quotas in clinical psychology?: The *Journal of Clinical Psychology* and the scandal of 1945. *Review of General Psychology, 13,* 252–261.

Harrison, R. (1963). Functionalism and its historical significance. *Genetic Psychology Monographs, 68,* 387–423.

Harrison, K. (2009, December 6). The symbologist: After he broke with Freud, Jung came to believe that myth and archetype were the unconscious mind's language. *New York Times Book Review.*

Hartley, D. (1749). *Observations on man, his frame, his duty, and his expectations.* London: Leake & Frederick.

Hartley, M., & Commire, A. (1990). *Breaking the silence.* New York: G.P. Putnam's Sons.

Hartmann, E. (1884). *Philosophy of the unconscious.* London: Trübner. (Original work published 1869)

Hassin, R., Uleman, J., & Margh, J. (2005). *The new unconscious.* New York: Oxford University Press.

Haynal, A. (1993). *Psychoanalysis and the sciences: Epistemology—history.* Berkeley: University of California Press.

Hearnshaw, L. S. (1987). *The shaping of modern psychology.* London: Routledge & Kegan Paul.

Hearst, E. (Ed.). (1979). *The first century of experimental psychology.* Hillsdale, NJ: Erlbaum.

Heidbreder, E. (1933). *Seven psychologies*. New York: Appleton.

Held, L. (2009). Psychoanalysis shapes consumer culture. *Monitor on Psychology, 40*(11), 32–34.

Helmholtz, H. (1856 –1866). *Handbook of physiological optics*. Leipzig: Voss.

Helmholtz, H. (1954). *On the sensations of tone*. New York: Dover. (Original work published 1863).

Helson, H. (1925, 1926). The psychology of Gestalt. *American Journal of Psychology, 36*, 342–370, 494–526; *37*, 25–62, 189–223.

Henle, M. (1974). E. B. Titchener and the case of the missing element. *Journal of the History of the Behavioral Sciences, 10*, 227–237.

Herman, K., & Betz, N. (2006). Path models of the relationships of instrumentality, social self-efficacy, and self-esteem to depression and loneliness. *Journal of Social and Clinical Psychology, 25*, 1086–1106.

Herrera, N., Zajonc, R., Wieczorkowska, G., & Cichomski, B. (2003). Beliefs about birth rank and their reflection in reality. *Journal of Personality and Social Psychology, 85*, 142–150.

Herrnstein, R. J., & Murray, C. (1994). *The bell curve: Intelligence and class structure in American life*. New York: Free Press.

Hess, U., & Thibault, P. (2009). Darwin and emotional expression. *American Psychologist, 64*, 120–128.

Hilgard, E. R. (1956). *Theories of learning* (2nd ed.). New York: Appleton-Century-Crofts.

Hilgard, E. R. (1987). *Psychology in America: A historical survey*. San Diego: Harcourt Brace Jovanovich.

Hilgard, E. R. (1994). Foreword. In J. T. Todd & E. K. Morris (Eds.), *Modern perspectives on John B. Watson and classical behaviorism* (pp. vx–vxii). Westport, CT: Greenwood Press.

Hirayoshi, S., & Nakajima, S. (2009). Analysis of personality trait structure of dogs with personality trait descriptors. *Japanese Journal of Animal Psychology, 59*, 57–75.

Hirschmüller, A. (1989). *The life and work of Josef Breuer: Physiology and psychoanalysis*. New York: New York University Press.

Hochberg, L., Serruya, M., Friehs, g., Mukand, J., Branner, A., Chen, D., Penn, R., & Donoghue, J. (2006, 13 July). Neuronal ensemble control of prosthetic devices by a human with tetraplegia. *Nature, 442*, 164–171.

Hoffman, E. (1988). *The right to be human: A biography of Abraham Maslow*. Los Angeles: Tarcher.

Hoffman, E. (1994). *The drive for self: Alfred Adler and the founding of individual psychology*. Reading, MA: Addison-Wesley.

Hoffman, E. (Ed.) (1996). *Future vision: The unpublished papers of Abraham Maslow*. Thousand Oaks, CA: Sage.

Hofstadter, R. (1992). *Social Darwinism in American thought*. Boston: Beacon Press.

Hogan, J. (2003). Anne Anastasi: Master of differential psychology and psychometrics. In G. Kimble & M. Wertheimer (Eds.), *Portraits of pioneers in psychology* (vol. 5, pp. 263–277). Mahwah, NJ: Lawrence Erlbaum.

Hollingworth, H. (1939). Chewing gum as a technique of relaxation. *Science, 90*, 385–387.

Hollingworth, H. L. (1943). *Leta Stetter Hollingworth*. Lincoln: University of Nebraska Press.

Horley, J. (2001). After the Baltimore affair: James Mark Baldwin's life and work, 1908 –1934. *History of Psychology, 4*, 24–33.

Horney, K. (1945). *Our inner conflicts*. New York: Norton.

Horney, K. (1980). *The adolescent diaries of Karen Horney, 1899–1911*. New York: Basic Books.

Hornstein, G. A. (1992). The return of the repressed: Psychology's problematic relations with psychoanalysis, 1909–1960. *American Psychologist, 47*, 254–263.

Hosking, S., Young, K., & Regan, M. (2009). The effects of text messaging on young drivers. *Human Factors, 51*, 582–592.

Howse, D. (1989). *Nevil Maskelyne: The seaman's astronomer*. Cambridge, England: Cambridge University Press.

Hsueh, Y. (2004). He sees the development of children's concepts upon a background of sociology: Jean Piaget's honorary degree at Harvard University in 1936. *History of Psychology, 7*, 20–44.

Hulbert, A. (2003). *Raising America: Experts, parents, and a century of advice about children*. New York: Alfred A. Knopf.

Hull, C. L. (1928). *Aptitude testing*. Yonkers, NY: World.

Hull, C. L. (1933). *Hypnosis and suggestibility*. New York: Appleton.

Hull, C. L. (1943). *Principles of behavior*. New York: Appleton.

Hull, C. L. (1944). Joseph Jastrow: 1863-1944. *American Journal of Psychology, 57*, 581–585.

Hull, C. L. (1951). *Essentials of behavior*. New Haven, CT: Yale University Press.

Hull, C. L. (1952). *A behavior system*. New Haven, CT: Yale University Press.

Hume, D. (1739). *A treatise of human nature*. London: Noon.

Hunt, H. (2005). Why psychology is/is not traditional science: The self-referential bases of psychological research and theory. *Review of General Psycholgoy, 9*, 358–374.

Hunt, M. (1993). *The story of psychology*. Garden City, NY: Doubleday.

Hyman, I., Boss, S., Wise, B., McKenzie, K., & Caggiano, J. (2010). Did you see the unicycling clown: Inattentional blindness while walking and talking on a cell phone. *Applied Cognitive Psychology, 24,* 597–607.

Innis, N. (1992). Tolman and Tryon: Early research on the inheritance of the ability to learn. *American Psychologist, 47,* 190–197.

Innis, N. (2000). Edward Chace Tolman. In A. Kazdin (Ed.), *Encyclopedia of psychology* (vol. 8). New York: Oxford University Press.

Innis, N. (2003). William McDougall: A major tragedy? In G. Kimble & M. Wertheimer (Eds.), *Portraits of pioneers in psychology* (vol. 5, pp. 91–108). Washington, DC: American Psychological Association.

I.Q. Zoo. (1955, February 28). *Time.*

Irwin, F. (1943). Edwin Burket Twitmyer: 1973-1943. *American Journal of Psychology, 56,* 451–453.

Isa, T., Fetz, E., & Muller, K. (2009). Recent advances in brain-machine interfaces. *Neural Networks, 22,* 1201–1202.

Isbister, J. N. (1985). *Freud: An introduction to his life and work.* Cambridge, England: Polity Press.

Iskender, M., & Akin, A. (2010). Social self-efficacy, academic locus of control, and Internet addiction. *Computers and Education, 54,* 1101–1106.

Jackson, J. (2004). Racially stuffed shirts and other enemies of mankind: Horace Mann Bond's parody of segregationist psychology in the 1950s. In A. Winston (Ed.), *Defining difference: Race and racism in the history of psychology* (pp. 261–283). Washington, DC: American Psychological Association.

Jacobson, J. Z. (1951). *Scott of Northwestern: The life story of a pioneer in psychology and education.* Chicago: Mariano.

Jahoda, G. (2005). Theodor Lipps and the shift from sympathy to empathy. *Journal of the History of the Behavioral Sciences, 41,* 151–163.

James, E. M. (1994). Sowing the seeds of the psychology of women: Helen Bradford Thompson Woolley and the mental traits of sex. Unpublished manuscript.

James, W. (1890). *The principles of psychology.* New York: Holt. (Reprinted 1950, Dover Publications).

James, W. (1892). *Psychology: Briefer course.* New York: Holt.

James, W. (1899). *Talks to teachers.* New York: Holt.

James, W. (1902). *The varieties of religious experience.* New York: Longmans, Green.

James, W. (1907). *Pragmatism.* New York: Longmans, Green.

Jardine, L. (1999). *Ingenious pursuits: Building the scientific revolution.* New York: Doubleday.

Jastrow, J. (1961). Autobiography. In C. Murchison (Ed.), *A history of psychology in autobiography* (Vol. 1, pp. 135–162). New York: Russell & Russell. (Original work published 1930)

Jaynes, J. (1970). The problem of animate motion in the seventeenth century. *Journal of the History of Ideas, 31,* 219–234.

Jayson, S. (2009, August 8). New tests shed light on how dogs think; smartest breeds. *USA Today.*

Jeshmaridian, S. (2007). Edward Bradford Titchener's life and work: A source of international psychology. *International Psychology Bulletin, 11*(2), 20–22.

Johnson, G. (2008). *The ten most beautiful experiments.* New York: Knopf.

Johnson, M. G., & Henley, T. B. (Eds.). (1990). *Reflections on the principles of psychology: William James after a century.* Hillsdale, NJ: Erlbaum.

Johnson, R. (2007). Searching for Kohler's Casa Amarilla. *The General Psychologist, 31,* 1–3.

Johnson, R., McClearn, G. E., Yuen, S., Nagoshi, C. T., Ahern, F. M., & Cole, R. E. (1985). Galton's data a century later. *American Psychologist, 40,* 875–892.

Jonçich, G. (1968). *The sane positivist: A biography of Edward L. Thorndike.* Middletown, CT: Wesleyan University Press.

Jones, E. (1953, 1955, 1957). *The life and work of Sigmund Freud* (3 vols.). New York: Basic Books.

Jones, M. C. (1924). A laboratory study of fear: The case of Peter. *Pedagogical Seminary, 31,* 308–315.

Jones, M. C. (1974). Albert, Peter, and John B. Watson. *American Psychologist, 29,* 581–583.

Jostmann, N., Lakens, D., & Schubert, T. (2009). Weight as an embodiment of importance. *Psychological Science, 9,* 1169–1174.

Joyce, N., & Baker, D. (2008a). Time capsule: Applying technology to phrenology. *Monitor on Psychology, 39*(6), 22.

Joyce, N., & Baker, D. (2008b). The IQ zoo: Early psychologists used animals to educate and entertain. *Monitor on Psychology, 39*(8), 24–25.

Judd, C. H. (1961). Autobiography. In C. Murchison (Ed.), *A history of psychology in autobiography* (Vol. 2, pp. 207–235). New York: Russell & Russell. (Original work published 1930).

Jung, C. G. (1912). *The psychology of the unconscious.* Leipzig: Franz Deuticke.

Jung, C. G. (1961). *Memories, dreams, reflections.* New York: Random House.

Kahneman, D., Krueger, A., Schkade, D., Schwartz, N., & Stone, A. (2006). Perspective: Would you be happier if you were richer? A focusing illusion. *Science, 312* (5782), 1908–1910.

Kamm, J. (1977). *John Stuart Mill in love.* London: Gordon & Cremonesi.

Kanazawa, S. (2010). Evolutionary psychology and intelligence research. *American Psychologist, 65,* 279–289.

Karabel, J. (2005). *The chosen: The hidden history of admission and exclusion at Harvard, Yale, and Princeton.* Boston: Houghton Mifflin.

Kasparov, G. (2010, February 11). The chess master and the computer [Review of *Chess Metaphors: Artificial Intelligence and the Human Mind,* by D. Raskin-Gutman, Cambridge: MIT Press, 2009.] *New York Review of Books.*

Keiger, D. (1993, Mar.). A profession built through metaphor. *Johns Hopkins Magazine,* 48–49.

Keiger, D. (1999, Nov.). The story that doesn't compute. *Johns Hopkins Magazine,* 40–45.

Keller, F. (1991). Burrhus Frederic Skinner, 1904–1990. *Journal of the History of the Behavioral Sciences, 27,* 3–6.

Kelly, R. M., & Kelly, V. P. (1990). Lillian Moller Gilbreth (1878 –1972). In A. N. O'Connell & N. F. Russo (Eds.), *Women in psychology: A bio-bibliographic sourcebook* (pp. 117–124). New York: Greenwood Press.

Kerr, J. (1993). *A most dangerous method: The story of Jung, Freud, and Sabina Spielrein.* New York: Knopf.

Keynes, R. (2002). *Darwin, his daughter, and human evolution.* New York: Riverhead Books.

Kiesow, F. (1961). Autobiography. In C. Murchison (Ed.), *A history of psychology in autobiography* (Vol. *1,* pp. 163–190). New York: Russell & Russell. (Original work published 1930)

Kihlstrom, J. F. (1994). Psychodynamics and social cognition: Notes on the fusion of psychoanalysis and psychology. *Journal of Personality, 62,* 681–696.

Kihlstrom, J. F., Barnhardt, M., & Tataryn, D. J. (1992). The psychological unconscious: Found, lost, and regained. *American Psychologist, 47,* 788–791.

King, D., & Wertheimer, M. (2005). *Max Wertheimer and Gestalt theory.* New Brunswick, NJ: Transaction Publishers.

King, D., Wertheimer, M., Keller, H., & Crochetiere, K. (1994). The legacy of Max Wertheimer and Gestalt psychology: 60th anniversary, 1934-1994. *Social Research, 61,* 907–935.

Kirschenbaum, H., & Jourdan, A. (2005). The current status of Carl Rogers and the person-centered approach. *Psychotherapy: Theory, Research, Practice, Training, 42,* 37–51.

Klein, A. (2002). *A forgotten voice: A biography of Leta Stetter Hollingworth.* Scottsdale, AZ: Great Potential Press.

Koelsch, W. A. (1970). Freud discovers America. *Virginia Quarterly Review, 46,* 115–132.

Koelsch, W. A. (1987). *Clark University: 1887–1987.* Worcester, MA: Clark University Press.

Koenigsberger, L. (1965). *Hermann von Helmholtz.* New York: Dover.

Koffka, K. (1921). *The growth of the mind.* New York: Harcourt.

Koffka, K. (1922). Perception: An introduction to the Gestalt-theorie. *Psychological Bulletin, 19,* 531–585.

Koffka, K. (1935). *Principles of Gestalt psychology.* New York: Harcourt.

Köhler, W. (1917, 1924, 1927). *The mentality of apes.* Berlin: Royal Academy of Sciences; New York: Harcourt Brace.

Köhler, W. (1920). *Static and stationary physical Gestalts.* Braunschweig: Vieweg.

Köhler, W. (1929). *Gestalt psychology.* New York: Liveright.

Köhler, W. (1959). Gestalt psychology today. *American Psychologist, 14,* 727–734.

Köhler, W. (1969). Gestalt psychology. In D. Krantz (Ed.), *Schools of psychology* (pp. 69–85). New York: Appleton-Century-Crofts.

Köhler, W. (1947). *Gestalt psychology: An introduction to new concepts in modern psychology.* New York: Liveright.

Konorski, J. (1974). Autobiography. In G. Lindzey (Ed.), *A history of psychology in autobiography* (Vol. 6, pp. 183–217). Englewood Cliffs, NJ: Prentice-Hall.

Korn, J. H., Davis, R., & Davis, S. F. (1991). Historians' and chairpersons' judgments of eminence among psychologists. *American Psychologist, 46,* 789–792.

Kosmachevskaya, E., & Gromova, L. (2007). Ivan Petrovich Pavlov and William [Horsley] Gantt: A meeting of generations, unknown photographs. *Neuroscience and Behavioral Physiology, 37,* 303–309.

Krech, D. (1974). Autobiography. In G. Lindzey (Ed.), *A history of psychology in autobiography* (Vol. 6, pp. 221–250). Englewood Cliffs, NJ: Prentice-Hall.

Kreshel, P. J. (1990). John B. Watson at J. Walter Thompson: The legitimation of "science" in advertising. *Journal of Advertising, 19*(2), 49–59.

Kressley-Mba, R. (2006). On the failed institutionalization of German comparative psychology prior to 1940. *History of Psychology, 9,* 55–74.

Kristensen, P., & Bjerkedal, T. (2007). Explaining the relation between birth order and intelligence. *Science, 316,* 1717.

Krüll, M. (1986). *Freud and his father.* New York: Norton.

Kuhn, T. S. (1970). *The structure of scientific revolutions* (2nd ed.). Chicago: University of Chicago Press.

Külpe, O. (1893). *Outline of psychology.* Leipzig: Engelmann.

Kunzmann, U., Little, T., & Smith, J. (2000). Is age-related stability of subjective well-being a paradox? Cross-sectional and longitudinal evidence from the Berlin Aging Study. *Psychology an Aging, 15,* 511–526.

Lacey, H., Smith, D., & Ubel, P. (2006). Hope I die before I get old: Mispredicting happiness across the adult lifespan. *Journal of Happiness Studies, 7,* 167–182.

Lacoursiere, R. (2008). Freud's death: Historical truth and biographical fictions. *American Imago, 66,* 107–128.

Lancaster, J. (2004). *Making time: Lillian Moller Gilbreth—a life beyond "Cheaper by the Dozen."* Boston: Northeastern University Press.

Landy, F. J. (1992). Hugo Münsterberg: Victim or visionary? *American Psychologist, 47,* 787–802.

Lange, L. (2005). Sleeping beauties in psychology: Comparison of hits and missed signals in psychological journals. *History of Psychology, 8,* 194–217.

Larson, C. (1979). The Watson-McDougall debate: "The debate of the century." *Monitor on Psychology, 10*(11), 3.

Lashley, K. (1929). *Brain mechanisms and intelligence.* Chicago: University of Chicago Press.

Lears, T. J. J. (1987, Autumn). William James. *Wilson Quarterly,* 84–95.

Leary, D. (1987). Telling likely stories: The rhetoric of the new psychology, 1880 –1920. *Journal of the History of the Behavioral Sciences, 23,* 315–331.

Leary, D. (2003). A profound and radical change: How William James inspired the reshaping of American psychology. In R. Sternberg (Ed.), *The anatomy of impact: What makes the great works of psychology great* (pp. 19–42). Washington, DC: American Psychological Association.

Leary, D. (2009). Between Peirce (1878) and James (1898): G. Stanley Hall, the origins of pragmatism, and the history of psychology. *Journal of the History of the Behavioral Sciences, 45,* 5–20.

Lehrer, J. (2010, February 28). Depression's upside: Is there an evolutionary purpose to feeling really sad? *New York Times Magazine.*

Lemov, R. (2005). *World as laboratory: Experiments with mice, mazes, and men.* New York: Hill & Wang.

Lepore, J. (2009, October 12). Not so fast: Scientific management started as a way to work. How did it become a way of life? *The New Yorker.*

Lerman, H. (1986). *A mote in Freud's eye: From psychoanalysis to the psychology of women.* New York: Springer-Verlag.

Lerner, V., Margolin, J., & Witztum, E. (2005). Vladimir Bekhterev: His life, his work and the mystery of his death. *History of Psychology, 16,* 217–227.

Leroy, H., & Kimble, G. (2003). Harry Frederick Harlow: And one thing led to another. In G. Kimble & M. Wertheimer (Eds.), *Portraits of pioneers in psychology* (vol. 5, pp. 279–297). Mahwah, NJ: Lawrence Erlbaum.

Levy, D. (2010). Jessica Riskin: Historian of science looks at automata and the quest for artificial life. *news.stanford.edu/pr/01/riskinprofile/024.html*

Lewin, K. (1936). *Principles of topological psychology.* New York: McGraw-Hill.

Lewin, K. (1939). Field theory and experiment in social psychology: Concept and methods. *American Journal of Sociology, 44,* 868–896.

Lewin, K., Lippitt, R., & White, R. (1939). Patterns of aggressive behavior in experimentally created social climates. *Journal of Social Psychology, 10,* 271–299.

Lewis, J. (2009). Ada Lovelace: Mathematician, computer pioneer. *womenshistory.about.com/ sciencemath1/a/bio_lovelace.htm?P=1*

Lewis, R. W. B. (1991). *The Jameses: A family narrative.* New York: Farrar, Straus and Giroux.

Ley, R. (1990). *A whisper of espionage: Wolfgang Köhler and the apes of Tenerife.* Garden City Park, NY: Avery Publishing Group.

Leys, R., & Evans, R. B. (1990). *Defining American psychology: The correspondence between Adolf Meyer and Edward Bradford Titchener.* Baltimore: Johns Hopkins University Press.

Lieberman, D. A. (1979). Behaviorism and the mind: A (limited) call for a return to introspection. *American Psychologist, 34,* 319–333.

Lin, L. (2009). Breadth-biased versus focused cognitive control in media multitasking behaviors. *Proceedings of the National Academy of Sciences, 106,* 15521-15522.

Ljunggren, B. (1990). *Great men with sick brains and other essays.* Park Ridge, IL: American Association of Neurological Surgeons.

Locke, E. (2009). It's time we brought introspection out of the closet. *Perspectives on Psychological Science, 4*(1), 24–25.

Locke, J. (1959). *An essay concerning human understanding.* New York: Dover. (Original work published 1690)

Loeb, J. (1918). *Forced movements, tropisms, and animal conduct.* Philadelphia: Lippincott.

Loehlin, J. C., Perloff, R., Sternberg, R. J., & Urbina, S. (1996). Intelligence: Knowns and unknowns. *American Psychologist, 51,* 77–101.

Loftus, E. (1979). *Eyewitness testimony.* Cambridge, MA: Harvard University Press.

Loftus, E., & Monahan, J. (1980). Trial by data: Psychological research as legal evidence. *American Psychologist, 35,* 270–283.

Logan, C. A. (2002). When scientific knowledge becomes scientific discovery: The disappearance of classical conditioning before Pavlov. *Journal of the History of the Behavioral Sciences, 38,* 393–403.

Logue, A. W. (1985). The origins of behaviorism: Antecedents and proclamation. In C. E. Buxton (Ed.), *Points of view in the modern history of psychology* (pp. 141–167). Orlando, FL: Academic Press.

Lowry, R. (1982). *The evolution of psychological theory: A critical history of concepts and presuppositions* (2nd ed.). Hawthorne, NY: Aldine.

Lück, H. E. (1990). Story or history: What did Wolfgang Köhler really do on Tenerife? *History of Psychology Newsletter, 22,* 80–82.

Lutz, T. (1991). *American nervousness, 1903: An anecdotal history.* Ithaca, NY: Cornell University Press.

Lyubomirsky, S., King, L., & Diener, E. (2005). The benefits of frequent positive affect: Does happiness lead to success? *Psychological Bulletin, 131,* 803–855.

Mach, E. (1914). *The analysis of sensations.* Chicago: Open Court. (Original work published 1885)

Mackenzie, B. (1977). *Behaviourism and the limits of scientific method.* Atlantic Highlands, NJ: Humanities Press.

MacLeod, R. B. (1959). Review of *Cumulative record* by B. F. Skinner. *Science, 130,* 34–35.

MacLeod, R. B. (Ed.). (1969). *William James: Unfinished business.* Washington, DC: American Psychological Association.

Maddux, J. (2002). The power of believing you can. In C. Snyder & S. Lopez (Eds.), *Handbook of positive psychology* (pp. 277–287). New York: Oxford University Press.

Madigan, S., & O'Hara, R. (1992). Short-term memory at the turn of the century: Mary Whiton Calkins's memory research. *American Psychologist, 47,* 170–174.

Mahony, P. (1986). *Freud and the Rat Man.* New Haven, CT: Yale University Press.

Mahony, P. (1992). Freud as family therapist: Reflections. In T. Gelfand & J. Kerr (Eds.), *Freud and the history of psychoanalysis* (pp. 307–317). Hillsdale, NJ: Analytic Press.

Makari, G. (2008). *Revolution in mind: The creation of psychoanalysis.* New York: Harper.

Malcolm, J. (1984). *In the Freud archives.* New York: Knopf.

Malthus, T. (1914). *Essay on the principle of population.* New York: Dutton. (Original work published 1789)

Mandler, G. (2002a). Origins of the cognitive revolution. *Journal of the History of the Behavioral Sciences, 38,* 339–353.

Mandler, G. (2002b). Psychologists and the National Socialist access to power. *History of Psychology, 5,* 190–200.

Mandler, G. (2007). *A history of modern experimental psychology.* Cambridge: MIT Press.

Marcus, G. (1998, Jan. 26). Where are the elixirs of yesteryear when we hurt? *The New York Times.*

Marken, R. (2009). You say you had a revolution: Methodological foundations of closed-loop psychology. *Review of General Psychology, 13,* 137–145.

Marr, J. (2002). Marian Breland Bailey: The mouse who reinforced. *Arkansas Historical Quarterly, 61,* 59–79.

Martin, J. (2002). *The education of John Dewey: A biography.* New York: Columbia University Press.

Marx, M. H., & Cronan-Hillix, W. A. (1987). *Systems and theories in psychology* (4th ed.). New York: McGraw-Hill.

Maslow, A. H. (1970). *Motivation and personality* (2nd ed.). New York: Harper & Row.

Masson, J. M. (1984). *The assault on truth: Freud's suppression of the seduction theory.* New York: Farrar Straus Giroux.

Masson, J. M. (Ed.). (1985). *The complete letters of Sigmund Freud to Wilhelm Fliess, 1887–1904.* Cambridge, MA: Harvard University Press.

Mather, J., & Anderson, R. (1993). Personalities of octopuses. *Journal of Comparative Psychology, 107,* 336–340.

Matson, F. W. (1964). *The broken image.* New York: Braziller.

May, W. W. (1978). A psychologist of many hats: A tribute to Mark Arthur May. *American Psychologist, 33,* 653–663.

Mazlish, B. (1993). *The fourth discontinuity: The co-evolution of humans and machines.* New Haven, CT: Yale University Press.

McDougall, W. (1908). *Introduction to social psychology.* London: Methuen.

McDougall, W. (1912). *Psychology: The study of behavior.* London: Oxford University Press.

McDougall, W. (1930). Autobiography. In C. Murchison (Ed.), *A history of psychology in autobiography* (Vol. 1, pp. 191–223). Worcester, MA: Clark University Press.

McGraw, M. B. (1990). Memories, deliberate recall, and speculations. *American Psychologist, 45,* 934–937.

McGuire, W. (Ed.). (1974). *The Freud/Jung letters.* Princeton, NJ: Princeton University Press.

McKeachie, W. J. (1976). Psychology in America's bicentennial year. *American Psychologist, 31,* 819–833.

McReynolds, P. (1997). *Lightner Witmer: His life and times.* Washington, DC: American Psychological Association.

Mellor, S. (1990). How do only children differ from other children? *Journal of Genetic Psychology, 151,* 221–230.

Merton, R. (1957). Priorities in scientific discovery. *American Sociological Review, 22,* 635–659.

Messer, S., & McWilliams, N. (2003). The impact of Sigmund Freud and *The Interpretation of Dreams.* In R. Sternberg (Ed.), *The anatomy of impact: What makes the great works of psychology great* (pp. 71–107). Washington, DC: American Psychological Association.

Milar, K. (2010). Overcoming "sentimental rot": One of the first female psychologists tried to bring gender research out of the Dark Ages. *Monitor on Psychology, 41*(2), 26–27.

Miles, L., Nind, L., & Macrae, C. (2010). Moving through time. *Psychological Science, 21*, 222–223.

Mill, J. (1829). *Analysis of the phenomena of the human mind.* London: Baldwin & Cradock.

Mill, J. S. (1909). Autobiography. In *The Harvard Classics.* New York: Collier. (Original work published 1873)

Miller, G. A. (1951). *Language and communication.* New York: McGraw-Hill.

Miller, G. A. (1956). The magical number seven, plus or minus two: Some limits on our capacity for processing information. *Psychological Review, 63*, 81–97.

Miller, G. A. (1962). *Psychology: The science of mental life.* New York: Harper & Row.

Miller, G. A. (1985). The constitutive problem of psychology. In S. Koch & D. Leary (Eds.), *A century of psychology as science* (pp. 40– 45). New York: McGraw-Hill.

Miller, G. A. (1989). Autobiography. In G. Lindzey (Ed.), *A history of psychology in autobiography* (Vol. 8, pp. 391–418). Stanford, CA: Stanford University Press.

Miller, G. A. (2003). The cognitive revolution: A historical perspective. *Trends in Cognitive Science, 7*, 141–144.

Miller, G. A. (2006). Animal behavior: Signs of empathy seen in mice. *Science, 312*(5782), 1860–1861.

Miller, G. A. (2009). Book review of R. A. Skues, *Sigmund Freud and the history of Anna O. History of Psychiatry, 20*, 509–510.

Miller, G. A., & Buckhout, R. (1973). *Psychology: The science of mental life* (2nd ed.). New York: Harper & Row.

Miller, M. V. (1991, July 7). Anybody who was anybody was neurasthenic. *The New York Times.*

Milton, J. (2002). *The road to malpsychia: Humanistic psychology and our discontents.* San Francisco: Encounter Books.

Moore, J. (2005). Some historical and conceptual background to the development of B. F. Skinner's "radical behaviorism." *Journal of Mind and Behavior, 26*, 85–124.

Morawski, J. G., & Hornstein, G. A. (1991). Quandary of the quacks: The struggle for expert knowledge in American psychology, 1890–1940. In J. Brown & D. K. van Keuren (Eds.), *The estate of social knowledge* (pp. 106–133). Baltimore: Johns Hopkins University Press.

Morgan, C. L. (1961). Autobiography. In C. Murchison (Ed.), *A history of psychology in autobiography* (Vol. 2, pp. 237–264). New York: Russell & Russell. (Original work published 1930)

Motjabai, R., & Olfson, M. (2010). National trends in psychotropic medication polypharmacy in office-based psychiatry. *Archives of General Psychiatry, 67*, 26–36.

Mullberger, A. (2008). Spanish experience with German psychology prior to World War I. *Journal of the History of the Behavioral Sciences, 44*, 161–179.

Müller, J. (1833–1840). *Handbook of the physiology of mankind* (3 vols.). Coblenz: Hölscher.

Münsterberg, H. (1909). *Psychotherapy.* New York: Moffat Yard.

Münsterberg, H. (1913). *Psychology and industrial efficiency.* Boston: Houghton Mifflin.

Münsterberg, M. (1922). *Hugo Münsterberg: His life and work.* New York: Appleton.

Murdoch, S. (2007). *IQ: A smart history of a failed idea.* New York: Wiley.

Murphy, G. (1963). Robert Sessions Woodworth, 1869–1962. *American Psychologist, 18*, 131–133.

Myers, G. E. (1986). *William James: His life and thought.* New Haven, CT: Yale University Press.

Natsoulas, T. (1978). Consciousness. *American Psychologist, 33*, 904–916.

Neisser, U. (1967). *Cognitive psychology.* New York: Appleton-Century-Crofts.

Neisser, U. (1976). *Cognition and reality.* San Francisco: W. H. Freeman.

Neisser, U. (2007). Ulric Neisser. In G. Lindzey & W. Runyan (Eds.), *A history of psychology in autobiography* (vol. 9). Washington, DC: American Psychological Association.

Neisser, U., Boodoo, G., Bouchard, T. J., Jr., Boykin, A. W., Brody, N., Ceci, S. J., Halpern, D. F., Nesse, R., & Ellsworth, P. (2009). Evolution, emotions, and emotional disorders. *American Psychologist, 64*, 129–139.

Newton, R. (2004). *Galileo's pendulum: From the rhythm of time to the making of matter.* Cambridge, MA: Harvard University Press.

Nichols, P. (2003). *Evolution's captain: The dark fate of the man who sailed Charles Darwin around the world.* New York: HarperCollins.

Nicholson, I. (2007). Review of Maslow, *Toward a psychology of being. The General Psychologist, 42*(2), 25–26.

Nicholson, I. A. M. (2001). Giving up maleness: Abraham Maslow, masculinity, and the boundaries of psychology. *History of Psychology, 4*, 79–91.

Noll, R. (1994). *The Jung cult: Origins of a charismatic movement.* Princeton, NJ: Princeton University Press.

Noll, R. (1997). *The Aryan Christ: The secret life of Carl Jung.* New York: Random House.

Norman, D. A., & Levelt, W. J. M. (1988). Life at the Center. In W. Hirst (Ed.), *The making of cognitive science: Essays in honor of George A. Miller* (pp. 100–109). Cambridge, England: Cambridge University Press.

Nuland, S. (1994). *How we die.* New York: Alfred A. Knopf.

Nyman, L. (2010). Documenting history: An interview with Kenneth Bancroft Clark. *History of Psychology, 13,* 74–88.

O'Donnell, J. M. (1979). The crisis of experimentalism in the 1920s: E. G. Boring and his uses of history. *American Psychologist, 34,* 289–295.

O'Donnell, J. M. (1985). *The origins of behaviorism: American psychology, 1870–1920.* New York: New York University Press.

Ogburn, W. F., & Thomas, D. S. (1922). Are inventions inevitable? *Political Science Quarterly, 37,* 83–100.

Ogden, R. M. (1951). Oswald Külpe and the Würzburg school. *American Journal of Psychology, 64,* 4–19.

Oishi, S., Diener, E., & Lucas, R. (2007). The optimum level of well-being. *Perspectives on Psychological Science, 2,* 346–360.

Olt, R. (2009). Members of the APA adherence to the classical views of Alfred Adler. *Dissertation Abstracts International* (section B: The sciences and engineering), 70.

Ophir, E., Nass, C., & Wagner, A. (2009). Cognitive control in media multitaskers. *Proceedings of the National Academy of Sciences, 106,* 15583–15587.

Overskeid, G. (2007). Looking for Skinner and finding Freud. *American Psychologist, 62,* 590–595.

Padilla, A. M. (1980). Note on the history of Hispanic psychology. *Hispanic Journal of Behavioral Science, 2*(2), 109–128.

Paris, B. J. (1994). *Karen Horney: A psychoanalyst's search for self-understanding.* New Haven, CT: Yale University Press.

Parker-Pope, T. (2009, October 22). What clown on a unicycle? Studying cellphone distraction. *New York Times.*

Pate, J. L., & Wertheimer, M. (1993). Preface. In J. L. Pate & M. Wertheimer (Eds.), *No small part: A history of regional organizations in American psychology* (pp. xv–xvii). Washington, DC: American Psychological Association.

Patterson, T., & Joseph, S. (2007). Person-centered personality theory: Support from self-determination theory and positive psychology. *Journal of Humanistic Psychology, 47,* 117–139.

Pauly, P. J. (1979, Dec.). Psychology at Hopkins: Its rise and fall and rise and fall and …. *Johns Hopkins Magazine,* 36–41.

Pauly, P. J. (1986). G. Stanley Hall and his successors: A history of the first half-century of psychology at Johns Hopkins. In S. H. Hulse & B. F. Green, Jr. (Eds.), *One hundred years of psychological research in America: G. Stanley Hall and the Johns Hopkins tradition* (pp. 21–51). Baltimore: Johns Hopkins University Press.

Pavia, W. (2008, October 13). Machine takes on man at mass Turing Test. *New York Times Online.*

Pavlov, I. P. (1897). *Work of the principal digestive glands.* St. Petersburg, Russia: Kushneroff.

Pavlov, I. P. (1960). *Conditioned reflexes: An investigation of the physiological activity of the cerebral cortex.* New York: Dover Publications. (Original work published 1927)

Pawlowski, B., Atral, R., & Dunbar, R. (2008). Sex differences in everyday risk-taking behavior in humans. *Evolutionary Psychology, 6,* 29–42.

Pennebaker, R. (2009, August 30). The mediocre multitaskers. *The New York Times.*

Pennisi, E. (2006). Animal cognition: Social animals prove their smarts. *Science, 312*(5871), 1734–1738.

Pepperberg, I. (2008). *Alex and me: How a scientist and a parrot uncovered a hiddel world of animal intelligence and formed a deep bond in the process.* New York: Collins.

Pervin, L. (2003). *The science of personality* (2nd ed.). New York: Oxford University Press.

Pettit, M. (2007). Joseph Jastrow, the psychology of deception, and the racial economy of observation. *Journal of the History of the Behavioral Sciences, 43,* 159–175.

Phillips, L. (2000). Recontextualizing Kenneth B. Clark: An Afrocentric perspective on the paradoxical legacy of a model psychologist-activist. *History of Psychology, 3,* 142–167.

Philogene, G. (Ed.). (2004). *Racial identity in context. The legacy of Kenneth B. Clark.* Washington, DC: American Psychological Association.

Pickering, G. (1974). *Creative malady.* New York: Oxford University Press.

Pickering, M. (1993). *Auguste Comte: An intellectual biography* (Vol. 1). Cambridge, England: Cambridge University Press.

Pickren, W. (2007). Tension and opportunity in post-World War II American psychology. *History of Psychology, 10,* 279–299.

Pillsbury, W. (1911). *Essentials of psychology.* New York: Macmillan.

Planck, M. (1949). *Scientific autobiography.* New York: Philosophical Library.

Poffenberger, A. (1957). Harry Levi Hollingworth: 1880-1956. *American Journal of Psychology, 70,* 136–140.

Pollack, A. (2006, July 13). Man uses chip to control robot with thoughts. *The New York Times.*

Popplestone, J. A., & McPherson, M. W. (1994). *An illustrated history of American psychology.* Dubuque, IA: Brown & Benchmark.

Postmes, T., & Branscombe, N. (2002). Influence of long-term racial environmental composition on subjective well-being in African-Americans. *Journal of Personality and Social Psychology, 83,* 735–751.

Powell, R. (2010). The Little Albert mystery isn't solved. *Monitor on Psychology, 41*(4), 4.

Powell, R., & Boer, D. P. (1994). Did Freud mislead patients to confabulate memories of abuse? *Psychological Reports, 74,* 1283–1298.

Prelow, H., Mosher, C., & Bowman, M. (2006). Perceived racial discrimination, social support, and psychological adjustment among African-American college students. *Journal of Black Psychology, 32,* 442–454.

Pressey, S. L. (1967). Autobiography. In E. G. Boring & G. Lindzey (Eds.), *A history of psychology in autobiography* (Vol. 5, pp. 313–339). New York: Appleton-Century-Crofts.

Prochnik, G. (2006). *Putnam Camp: Sigmund Freud, James Jackson Putnam, and the purpose of American psychology.* New York: Other Press.

Quinn, S. (1987). *A mind of her own: The life of Karen Horney.* New York: Summit Books.

Rabkin, L. Y. (1994). Psychotherapy for the masses: Dr. Joseph Jastrow and his self-help newspaper columns. *History of Psychology Newsletter, 26,* 52–60.

Raby, P. (2001). *Alfred Russel Wallace: A life.* Princeton, NJ: Princeton University Press.

Ramos, S. (2003). Revisiting Anna O.: A case of chemical dependence. *History of Psychology, 6,* 239–250.

Reed, E. S. (1997). *From soul to mind: The emergence of psychology from Erasmus Darwin to William James.* New Haven, CT: Yale University Press.

Reed, J. (1987a). Robert M. Yerkes and the comparative method. In E. Tobach (Ed.), *Historical perspectives and the international status of comparative psychology* (pp. 91–101). Hillsdale, NJ: Erlbaum.

Reed, J. (1987b). Robert M. Yerkes and the mental testing movement. In M. M. Sokal (Ed.), *Psychological testing and American society, 1890–1930* (pp. 75–94). New Brunswick, NJ: Rutgers University Press.

Reeves, R. (2009). *John Stuart Mill: Victorian firebrand.* New York: The Overlook Press.

Reynolds, D. S. (1995). *Walt Whitman's America: A cultural biography.* New York: Alfred A. Knopf.

Richards, R. J. (1980). Wundt's early theories of unconscious inference and cognitive evolution in their relation to Darwinian biopsychology. In W. G. Bringmann & R. D. Tweney (Eds.), *Wundt studies: A centennial collection* (pp. 42–70). Toronto: Hogrefe.

Richards, R. J. (1987). *Darwin and the emergence of evolutionary theories of mind and behavior.* Chicago: University of Chicago Press.

Richardson, J. (2003). Howard Andrew Knox and the origins of performance testing on Ellis Island, 1912-1916. *History of Psychology, 6,* 143–170.

Richardson, R. (2006). *William James: In the maelstrom of American modernism.* Boston: Houghton Mifflin.

Richelle, M. N. (1993). *B. F. Skinner: A reappraisal.* Hove, England: Erlbaum.

Richtel, M. (2010, January 17). Forget gum; walking and using phone is risky. *The New York Times.*

Ridley, M. (2003). *Nature via nurture: Genes, experience, and what makes us human.* New York: HarperCollins.

Rilling, M. (2000). John Watson's paradoxical struggle to explain Freud. *American Psychologist, 55,* 301–312.

Riskin, J. (2003). The defecating duck, or the ambiguous origins of artificial life. *Critical Inquiry, 29,* 599–633.

Ritvo, L. B. (1990). *Darwin's influence on Freud: A tale of two sciences.* New Haven, CT: Yale University Press.

Roazen, P. (1975). *Freud and his followers.* New York: Knopf.

Roazen, P. (1993). *Meeting Freud's family.* Amherst: University of Massachusetts Press.

Roback, A. A. (1952). *History of American psychology.* New York: Library Publishers.

Roberts, B., Walton, K., & Bogg, T. (2005). Conscientiousness and health across the life course. *Review of General Psychology, 9,* 156–168.

Robinson, D. (1981). *An intellectual history of psychology* (Rev. ed.). New York: Macmillan.

Robinson, D. (2003). Impact as substance and as fashion. In R. Sternberg (Ed.), *The anatomy of impact: What makes the great works of psychology great* (pp. 197–212). Washington, DC: American Psychological Association.

Robinson, F. G. (1992). *Love's story told: A life of Henry A. Murray.* Cambridge, MA: Harvard University Press.

Rodis-Lewis, G. (1998). *Descartes: His life and thought.* Ithaca, NY: Cornell University Press.

Roethlisberger, F. J., & Dickson, W. J. (1939). *Management and the worker: An account of a research program conducted by the Western Electric Company, Chicago.* Cambridge, MA: Harvard University Press.

Rogers, C. R. (1961). *On becoming a person.* Boston: Houghton Mifflin.

Rogers, C. R. (1967). Autobiography. In E. G. Boring & G. Lindzey (Eds.), *A history of psychology in autobiography* (vol. 5, pp. 341–384). New York: Appleton-Century-Crofts.

Rogers, C. R. (1980). *A way of being.* Boston: Houghton Mifflin.

Rogers, C. R., & Russell, D. (2002). *Carl Rogers: The quiet revolutionary, an oral history.* Roseville, CA: Penmarin Books.

Rogoff, B., Paradise, R., Arauz, R., Correa-chavez, M., & Angelillo, C. (2003). First-hand learning through intent participation. *Annual Review of Psychology, 54,* 175–203.

Romanes, G. J. (1883). *Animal intelligence.* London: Routledge & Kegan Paul.

Rose, P. (1983). *Parallel lives: Five Victorian marriages.* New York: Knopf.

Rosen, J. (2007, February 12). Missing link: Alfred Russel Wallace, Charles Darwin's neglected double. *The New Yorker.*

Rosenzweig, S. (1992). *Freud, Jung, and Hall the kingmaker: The historic expedition to America (1909).* Seattle: Hogrefe & Huber.

Ross, B. (1991). William James: Spoiled child of American psychology. In G. A. Kimble, M. Wertheimer, & C. White (Eds.), *Portraits of pioneers in psychology* (pp. 13–25). Washington, DC: American Psychological Association.

Ross, D. (1972). *Granville Stanley Hall: The psychologist as prophet.* Chicago: University of Chicago Press.

Rossiter, M. W. (1982). *Women scientists in America: Struggles and strategies to 1940.* Baltimore: Johns Hopkins University Press.

Rotter, J. B. (1966). Generalized expectancies for internal versus external control of reinforcement. *Psychological Monographs, 80* (Whole No. 609).

Rotter, J. B. (1982). *The development and applications of social learning theory: Selected papers.* New York: Praeger.

Rotter, J. B. (1990). Internal versus external control of reinforcement: A case history of a variable. *American Psychologist, 45,* 489–493.

Rotter, J. B. (1993). Expectancies. In C. E. Walker (Ed.), *History of clinical psychology in autobiography* (Vol. 2, pp. 273–284). Pacific Grove, CA: Brooks/Cole.

Rowe, D. C., Vazsonyi, A. T., & Flannery, D. J. (1994). No more than skin deep: Ethnic and racial similarity in developmental process. *Psychological Review, 101,* 396–413.

Rowe, F. B. (1983). Whatever became of poor Kinnebrook? *American Psychologist, 38,* 851–852.

Ruckmick, C. A. (1913). The use of the term "function" in English textbooks of psychology. *American Journal of Psychology, 24,* 99–123.

Russo, N. F., & Denmark, F. L. (1987). Contributions of women to psychology. *Annual Review of Psychology, 38,* 279–298.

Rutherford, A. (2000). Radical behaviorism and psychology's public: B. F. Skinner in the popular press, 1934–1990. *History of Psychology, 3,* 371–395.

Rutherford, A. (2009). *Beyond the box: B. F. Skinner's technology of behavior from laboratory to life.* Toronto: University of Toronto Press.

Ryan, R. M., & Deci, E. L. (2001). On happiness and human potentials: A review of research on hedonic and eudaimonic well-being. *Annual Review of Psychology, 52,* 141–166.

Sadger, I. (2005). *Recollecting Freud.* Madison, WI: University of Wisconsin Press.

Salas, E., & Cannon-Bowers, J. A. (2001). The science of training: A decade of progress. *Annual Review of Psychology, 52,* 471–499.

Sample, I. (2006, Feb. 19). Eureka! Lost manuscript found in cupboard. www.guardian.co.uk

Sand, R. (1992). Pre-Freudian discovery of dream meaning. In T. Gelfand & J. Kerr (Ed.), *Freud and the history of psychoanalysis* (pp. 215–229). Hillsdale, NJ: Analytic Press.

Sanua, V. D. (1993). Wundt's American students reminisce: "We like thee not Professor Wundt!" *History of Psychology Newsletter, 25*(4), 54–61.

Sarter, M., Bernston, G. G., & Cacioppo, J. T. (1996). Brain imaging and cognitive neuroscience. *American Psychologist, 51,* 13–21.

Sawyer, T. F. (2000). Francis Cecil Sumner: His views and influence on African American higher education. *History of Psychology, 3,* 122–141.

Sayers, J. (1991). *Mothers of psychoanalysis: Helene Deutsch, Karen Horney, Anna Freud, Melanie Klein.* New York: Norton.

Scarborough, E., & Furumoto, L. (1987). *Untold lives: The first generation of American women psychologists.* New York: Columbia University Press.

Scarf, M. (1971, Feb. 28). The man who gave us "inferiority complex," "compensation," "aggressive drive" and "style of life." *The New York Times Magazine,* 10ff.

Scarr, S. (1987, May). Twenty years of growing up. *Psychology Today,* 24–28.

Schmit, D. (2005). Revisioning antebellum American psychology: The dissemination of Mesmerism, 1836-1854. *History of Psychology, 8,* 403–434.

Schultz, D. P. (1990). *Intimate friends, dangerous rivals: The turbulent relationship between Freud and Jung.* Los Angeles: Tarcher.

Schur, M. (1972). *Freud: Living and dying.* New York: International Universities Press.

Scott, R., & Dienes, Z. (2010). Knowledge applied to new domains: The unconscious succeeds where the conscious fails. *Consciousness and Cognition, 19,* 391–398.

Scott, W. D. (1903). *The theory and practice of advertising: A simple exposition of the principles of psychology in their relation to successful advertising.* Boston: Small, Maynard.

Scull, A., MacKenzie, C., & Hervey, N. (1996). *Masters of bedlam: The transformation of the mad-doctoring trade.* Princeton, NJ: Princeton University Press.

Seabrook, J. (2007, May 14). Fragmentary knowledge: Was the *antikythera* mechanism the world's first computer? *New Yorker*.

Searle, J. R. (1980). Minds, brains, and programs. *Behavioral and Brain Sciences, 3*, 417–424.

Seligman, M. E. P. (1971). Phobias and preparedness. *Behavior Therapy, 2*, 307–320.

Seligman, M. E. P. (1998, Apr.). Positive social science. *APA Monitor*, 1.

Seligman, M. E. P. (2002). *Authentic happiness: Using the new positive psychology to realize your potential*. New York: Free Press.

Seligman, M. E. P., & Csikszentmihalyi, M. (Eds.). (2000). Positive psychology [special issue]. *American Psychologist, 55*(1).

Seligman, M. E. P., Steen, T., Park, N., & Peterson, C. (2005). Positive psychology progress: Empirical validation of intervention. *American Psychologist, 60*, 410–421.

Severo, R. (2005, May 2). Kenneth Clark, who helped end segregation, dies. *The New York Times*, pp. 1, 23.

Shapin, S. (2007, August 13). Man with a plan: Herbert Spencer's theory of everything. *The New Yorker*.

Shedler, J. (2010). The efficacy of psychodynamic psychotherapy. *American Psychologist, 65*, 98–109.

Sheehan, W., Meller, W., & Thurber, S. (2010). More on Darwin's illness: Comment on the final diagnosis of Charles Darwin. *Notes and Records of the Royal Society, 62*, 205–209.

Sheldon, K., & King, L. (2001). Why positive psychology is necessary. *American Psychologist, 56*, 216–217.

Shellenarger, S. (2003, February 27). Multitasking makes you stupid. *The Wall Street Journal*.

Shepherd, N. (1993). *A price below rubies: Jewish women as rebels and radicals*. Cambridge, MA: Harvard University Press.

Shields, S. (1975). Ms. Pilgrim's progress: The contributions of Leta Stetter Hollingworth to the psychology of women. *American Psychologist, 30*, 852–857.

Shields, S. (1982). The variability hypothesis: The history of a biological model of sex differences in intelligence. *Signs: Journal of Women in Culture and Society, 7*, 769–797.

Shields, S. (2007). Passionate men, emotional women: Psychology constructs gender differences in the late 19th century. *History of Psychology, 10*, 92–110.

Shields, S., & Bhatia, S. (2009). Darwin on race, gender, and culture. *American Psychologist, 64*, 111–119.

Shore, M. (2001). Psychology and memory in the midst of change: The social concerns of late 19th-century North American psychologists. In C. Green, M. Shore, & T. Teo (Eds.), *The transformation of psychology: Influences of 19th-century philosophy, technology, and natural science* (pp. 63–86). Washington, DC: American Psychological Association.

Shorto, R. (2008). *Descartes' bones: A skeletal history of the conflict between faith and reason*. New York: Doubleday.

Showalter, E. (1997). *Hystories: Hysterical epidemics and modern culture*. New York: Columbia University Press.

Sibbald, D. A., Erhard, W., McLeod, J., & Hooper, R. (2009). Individual personality and the spatial distribution of groups of grazing animals: An example with sheep. *Behavioural Processes, 82*, 319–326.

Siebert, C. (2006, Jan. 22). The animal self. *The New York Times*.

Siegel, A., & White, S. H. (1982). The child study movement. In H. W. Reese (Ed.), *Advances in child development and behavior* (Vol. *17*, pp. 233–285). New York: Academic Press.

Siegert, R., & Ward, T. (2002). Clinical psychology and evolutionary psychology: Toward a dialogue. *Review of General Psychology, 6*(3), 235–259.

Simon, L. (1998). *Genuine reality: A life of William James*. New York: Harcourt Brace.

Simonton, D., & Baumeister, R. (2005). Positive psychology at the summit. *Review of General Psychology, 9*, 99–102.

Simpson, J. C. (2000, Apr.). It's all in the upbringing: Doctor, lawyer, artist, thief? *Johns Hopkins Magazine*, 62–65.

Singer, P. W. (2009). *Wired for war: The robotics revolution and conflict in the 21st century*. New York: Penguin Press.

Skinner, B. F. (1938). *The behavior of organisms*. New York: Appleton.

Skinner, B. F. (1945, Oct.). Baby in a box. *Ladies Home Journal*, 30ff.

Skinner, B. F. (1948). *Walden Two*. New York: Macmillan.

Skinner, B. F. (1953). *Science and human behavior*. New York: Free Press.

Skinner, B. F. (1956). A case history of scientific method. *American Psychologist, 11*, 221–233.

Skinner, B. F. (1957). *Verbal behavior*. New York: Appleton.

Skinner, B. F. (1960). Pigeons in a pelican. *American Psychologist, 15*, 28–37.

Skinner, B. F. (1967). Autobiography. In E. G. Boring & G. Lindzey (Eds.), *A history of psychology in autobiography* (Vol. 5, pp. 387–413). New York: Appleton-Century-Crofts.

Skinner, B. F. (1968). *The technology of teaching*. New York: Appleton-Century-Crofts.

Skinner, B. F. (1969). *Contingencies of reinforcement*. New York: Appleton-Century-Crofts.

Skinner, B. F. (1971). *Beyond freedom and dignity*. New York: Knopf.

Skinner, B. F. (1976). *Particulars of my life*. New York: Knopf.

Skinner, B. F. (1979). *The shaping of a behaviorist*. New York: Knopf.

Skinner, B. F. (1983). Intellectual self-management in old age. *American Psychologist, 38*, 239–244.

Skinner, B. F. (1986). What is wrong with daily life in the Western world? *American Psychologist, 41*, 568–574.

Skinner, B. F. (1990). Can psychology be a science of mind? *American Psychologist, 45*, 1206–1210.

Slotten, R. (2004). *The heretic in Darwin's court: The life of Alfred Russel Wallace*. New York: Columbia University Press.

Smith, D. (2002). The theory heard 'round the world. *Monitor on Psychology, 33*(9), 30–32.

Smith, L. D., Best, L. A., Cylke, V. A., & Stubbs, D. A. (2000). Psychology without *p* values: Data analysis at the turn of the 19th century. *American Psychologist, 55*, 260–263.

Smith, M. (2010, June 8). Thinking man's mystery: Stolen Descartes letter returned. *Yahoo! News*.

Snyder, C. R., & Lopez, S. J. (Eds.). (2001). *Handbook of positive psychology*. New York: Oxford University Press.

Sokal, M. (2009). James McKeen Cattell, Nicholas Murray Butler, and academic freedom at Columbia University, 1902-1923. *History of Psychology, 12*, 87–122.

Sokal, M. M. (1971). The unpublished autobiography of James McKeen Cattell. *American Psychologist, 26*, 626–635.

Sokal, M. M. (1981). *An education in psychology: James Mc- Keen Cattell's journal and letters from Germany and England, 1880–1888*. Cambridge, MA: MIT Press.

Sokal, M. M. (1987). James McKeen Cattell and mental anthropometry: Nineteenth-century science and reform and the origins of psychological testing. In M. M. Sokal (Ed.), *Psychological testing and American society, 1890–1930* (pp. 21–45). New Brunswick, NJ: Rutgers University Press.

Sokal, M. M. (1992). Origins and early years of the American Psychological Association, 1890–1906. *American Psychologist, 47*, 111–122.

Sokal, M. M. (2001). Practical phrenology as psychological counseling in the 19th-century United States. In C. Green, M. Shore, & T. Teo (Eds.), *The transformation of psychology: Influences of 19th-century philosophy, technology, and natural science* (pp. 21–44). Washington, DC: American Psychological Association.

Spear, J. (2007). Prominent schools or other active specialties? A fresh look at some trends in psychology. *Review of General Psychology, 11*, 363–380.

Spence, K. W. (1952). Clark Leonard Hull: 1884–1952. *American Journal of Psychology, 65*, 639–646.

Spencer, H. (1855). *The principles of psychology*. London: Smith & Elder. (See also *www2.pfeiffer.edu/~iridener/dss/spencer/spencep2.html*)

Sperry, R. W. (1995). The impact and promise of the cognitive revolution. In R. L. Solso & D. W. Massaro (Eds.), *The science of the mind: 2001 and beyond* (pp. 35–49). New York: Oxford University Press.

Spillmann, J., & Spillmann, L. (1993). The rise and fall of Hugo Münsterberg. *Journal of the History of the Behavioral Sciences, 29*, 322–338.

Standage, T. (2002). *The Turk: The life and times of the famous 18th-century chess-playing machine*. New York: Walker.

Stanley, J., & Brody, L. (2004). The founder of gifted-child education [review of Klein's *A forgotten voice: A biography of Leta Stetter Hollingworth*]. *Contemporary Psychology, 49*, 729–731.

Staudinger, U. M. (2001). More than pleasure? Toward a psychology of growth and strength? [Review of the book *Well-being: The foundations of hedonic psychology*]. *Contemporary Psychology, 46*, 552–554.

Staudinger, U. M., Fleeson, W., & Baltes, P. B. (1999). Predictors of subjective physical health and global wellbeing. *Journal of Personality and Social Psychology, 76*, 305–319.

Steele, R. S. (1985). Paradigm lost: Psychoanalysis after Freud. In C. E. Buxton (Ed.), *Points of view in the modern history of psychology* (pp. 221–257). Orlando, FL: Academic Press.

Stein, B. (2010, July 1). Money can buy one form of happiness, massive global study finds. *Washington Post*.

Steinman, R., Pizlo, Z., & Pizlo, F. (2000). Phi is not beta, and why Wertheimer's discovery launched the Gestalt revolution. *Vision Research, 40*, 2257–2264.

Sterba, R. F. (1982). *Reminiscences of a Viennese psychoanalyst*. Detroit: Wayne State University Press.

Sternberg, R. J. (1996). *Cognitive psychology*. Fort Worth, TX: Harcourt Brace.

Stevens, D. (2005, Aug. 12). On every box of cake mix, evidence of Freud's theories. *The New York Times*.

Stimpert, J. (2001, January 22). John Broadus Watson: The father of behavioral psychology. *JHU Gazette*.

Stoloff, M., McCarthy, M., Keller, L., Varfglomeeva, V., Lynch, J., Makara, K., Simmons, S., & Smiley, W. (2010). The undergraduate psychology major: An examination of structure and sequence. *Teaching of Psychology, 37*(1), 4–15.

Stone, A., Schwartz, J., Broderick, J., & Deaton, R. (2010). A snapshot of the age distribution of psychological well-being in the United States. *Proceedings of the National Academy of Sciences* (online edition, May 17).

Stossel, S. (2008, December 21). Book review: Still crazy after all these years: A history and analysis of psychotherapy from Freud's couch to the present. *New York Times Book Review.*

Stumpf, C. (1883, 1890). *Psychology of tone.* Leipzig: Hirzel.

Stumpf, C. (1961). Autobiography. In C. Murchison (Ed.), *A history of psychology in autobiography* (Vol. *1*, pp. 389–441). New York: Russell & Russell. (Original work published 1930)

Sturm, T. (2006). Is there a problem with mathematical psychology in the 18th century? A fresh look at Kant's old argument. *Journal of the History of the Behavioral Sciences, 42*, 353–357.

Sulloway, F. J. (1979). *Freud: Biologist of the mind.* New York: Basic Books.

Sulloway, F. J. (1992). Reassessing Freud's case histories: The social construction of psychoanalysis. In T. Gelfand & J. Kerr (Eds.), *Freud and the history of psychoanalysis* (pp. 153–192). Hillsdale, NJ: Analytic Press.

Sulloway, F., & Zweigenhaft, R. (2010). Birth order and risk taking in athletes: A meta-analysis and study of major league baseball. *Personality and Social Psychology Review* (online edition, April 30), 1–13.

Suzuki, L. A., & Valencia, R. R. (1997). Race-ethnicity and measured intelligence: Educational implications. *American Psychologist, 52*, 1103–1114.

Swade, D. (2000). *The difference engine: Charles Babbage and the quest to build the first computer.* New York: Viking.

Taylor, E. (2000). Psychotherapeutics and the problematic origins of clinical psychology in America. *American Psychologist, 55*, 1029–1033.

Terman, L. (1961). Autobiography. In C. Murchison (Ed.), *A history of psychology in autobiography* (Vol. *2*, pp. 297–331). New York: Russell & Russell. (Original work published 1930.)

Thomas, R. (2000). George John Romanes. In A. Kazdin (Ed.), *Encyclopedia of psychology* (vol. *7*), 113–115.

Thompson, H. (1903). *The mental traits of sex: An experimental investigation of the normal mind in men and women.* Chicago: University of Chicago Press.

Thompson, T. (1988). *Benedictus* behavior analysis: B. F. Skinner's magnum opus at fifty [Book review of *The behavior of organisms: An experimental analysis*]. *Contemporary Psychology, 33*, 397–402.

Thorndike, E. L. (1898). Animal intelligence: An experimental study of the associative processes in animals (monograph supplement no. 8). *Psychological Review, 5*, 68–72.

Thorndike, E. L. (1905). *The elements of psychology.* New York: Seiler.

Thorndike, E. L. (1931). *Human learning.* New York: Appleton.

Thurstone, L. L. (1952). Autobiography. In E. G. Boring, H. S. Langfeld, H. Werner, & R. M. Yerkes (Eds.), *A history of psychology in autobiography* (Vol. 4, pp. 295–321). Worcester, MA: Clark University Press.

Titchener, E. B. (1896). *An outline of psychology.* New York: Macmillan.

Titchener, E. B. (1898a). The postulates of a structural psychology. *Philosophical Review, 7*, 449–465.

Titchener, E. B. (1898b). *Primer of psychology.* New York: Macmillan.

Titchener, E. B. (1901–1905). *Experimental psychology: A manual of laboratory practice.* New York: Macmillan.

Titchener, E. B. (1909). *A textbook of psychology.* New York: Macmillan.

Titchener, E. B. (1910). The method and scope of psychology. In L. Benjamin (Ed.). *A history of psychology: Original sources and contemporary research* (2nd ed.). New York: McGraw-Hill.

Titchener, E. B. (1912a). Prolegomena to a study of introspection. *American Journal of Psychology, 23*, 427–448.

Titchener, E. B. (1912b). The schema of introspection. *American Journal of Psychology, 23*, 485–508.

Titchener, E. B. (1921). Wilhelm Wundt. *American Journal of Psychology, 32*, 161–178.

Todes, D. P. (1997). From the machine to the ghost within: Pavlov's transition from digestive physiology to conditional reflexes. *American Psychologist, 52*, 947–955.

Todes, D. P. (2002). *Pavlov's physiology factory: Experiment, interpretation, laboratory enterprise.* Baltimore, MD: Johns Hopkins University Press.

Tolman, E. C. (1932). *Purposive behavior in animals and men.* New York: Appleton.

Tolman, E. C. (1945). A stimulus-expectancy needcathexis psychology. *Science, 101*, 160–166.

Tolman, E. C. (1952). Autobiography. In E. G. Boring, H. S. Langfeld, H. Werner, & R. M. Yerkes (Eds.), *A history of psychology in autobiography* (Vol. 4, pp. 323–339). Worcester, MA: Clark University Press.

Tooby, J., & Cosmides, L. (2005). Conceptual foundations of evolutionary psychology. In D. Buss (Ed.), *Handbook of evolutionary psychology.* New York: John Wiley.

Townsend, K. (1996). *Manhood at Harvard: William James and others.* New York: W. W. Norton.

Turner, C. H. (1906). A preliminary note on ant behavior. *Biological Bulletin, 12*, 31–36.

Turner, F. J. (1947). *The significance of the frontier in American history.* New York: Holt.

Turner, M. (1967). *Philosophy and the science of behavior.* New York: Appleton-Century-Crofts.

Turner, R. S. (1982). Helmholtz, sensory physiology, and the disciplinary development of German psychology. In W. R. Woodward & M. G. Ash (Eds.), *The problematic science: Psychology in nineteenth-century thought* (pp. 147–166). New York: Praeger.

Twitmyer, E. B. (1905). Knee-jerks without stimulation of the patellar tendon. *Psychological Bulletin, 2,* 43–44.

Uhlmann, E., & Swanson, J. (2004). Exposure to violent video games increases automatic aggressiveness. *Journal of Adolescence, 27,* 41–52.

Urban, W. J. (1989). The black scholar and intelligence testing: The case of Horace Mann Bond. *Journal of the History of the Behavioral Sciences, 25,* 323–334.

Utsey, S., Payne, Y., Jackson, E., & Jones, A. (2002). Race-related stress, quality of life indicators, and life satisfaction among elderly African Americans. *Cultural Diversity and Ethnic Minority Psychology, 8,* 7–17.

Van Boven, L. (2005). Experientialism, materialism, and the pursuit of happiness. *Review of General Psychology, 9,* 132–142.

Vande Kemp, H. (1992). G. Stanley Hall and the Clark school of religious psychology. *American Psychologist, 47,* 290–298.

Veenhoven, R. (2005). Is life getting better? How long and happily do people live in modern society? *European Psychologist, 10,* 330–343.

Vicedo, M. (2009). Mothers, machines, and morals: Harry Harlow's work on primate love from lab to legend. *Journal of the History of the Behavioral Sciences, 45,* 193–218.

Viner, R. (1996). Melanie Klein and Anna Freud: The discourse of the early dispute. *Journal of the History of the Behavioral Sciences, 32,* 4–15.

Viteles, M. S. (1967). Autobiography. In E. G. Boring & G. Lindzey (Eds.), *A history of psychology in autobiography* (Vol. 5, pp. 417–449). New York: Appleton-Century-Crofts.

Von Mayrhauser, R. T. (1989). Making intelligence functional: Walter Dill Scott and applied psychological testing in World War I. *Journal of the History of the Behavioral Sciences, 25,* 60–72.

Wade, N. (1995). *Psychologists in word and image.* Cambridge, MA: MIT Press.

Waldrop, M. M. (2001). *The dream machine: J. C. R. Licklider and the revolution that made computing personal.* New York: Viking.

Washburn, M. F. (1908). *The animal mind: A textbook of comparative psychology.* New York: Macmillan.

Washburn, M. F. (1932). Autobiography. In C. Murchison (Ed.), *A history of psychology in autobiography* (Vol. 2, pp. 333–358). Worcester, MA: Clark University Press.

Watson, C. (2004). The sartorial self: William James's philosophy of dress. *History of Psychology, 7,* 211–224.

Watson, J. B. (1903). *Animal education.* Chicago: University of Chicago.

Watson, J. B. (1907). [Review of C. H. Turner, "A preliminary note on ant behavior"]. *Psychological Bulletin, 4,* 296–297.

Watson, J. B. (1908). [Review of Pfungst's *Das Pferd des Herrn Von Osten*]. *Journal of Comparative Neurology and Psychology, 18,* 329–331.

Watson, J. B. (1913). Psychology as the behaviorist views it. *Psychological Review, 20,* 158–177.

Watson, J. B. (1914). *Behavior: An introduction to comparative psychology.* New York: Holt.

Watson, J. B. (1919). *Psychology from the standpoint of a behaviorist.* Philadelphia: Lippincott.

Watson, J. B. (1925). *Behaviorism.* New York: Norton.

Watson, J. B. (1928). *Psychological care of the infant and child.* New York: Norton.

Watson, J. B. (1929). Behaviorism. *Encyclopaedia Britannica* (Vol. 3, pp. 327–329).

Watson, J. B. (1930). *Behaviorism* (Rev. ed.). New York: Norton.

Watson, J. B. (1936). Autobiography. In C. Murchison (Ed.), *A history of psychology in autobiography* (Vol. 3, pp. 271–281). Worcester, MA: Clark University Press.

Watson, J. B., & McDougall, W. (1929). *The battle of behaviorism.* New York: Norton.

Watson, J. B., & Rayner, R. (1920). Conditioned emotional reactions. *Journal of Experimental Psychology, 3,* 1–14.

Watson, P. (2010). *The German genius: Europe's third renaissance, the second scientific revolution, and the twentieth century.* New York: HarperCollins.

Watson, R. (1978). *The great psychologists* (4th ed.). Philadelphia: Lippincott.

Watson, R. (2002). *Cogito, ergo sum: The life of Rene Descartes.* Boston: Godine.

Waugh, A. (2008). *The house of Wittgenstein: A family at war.* New York: Doubleday.

Webster, G. (2007a). Evolutionary theory's increasing role in personality and social psychology. *Evolutionary Psychology, 5,* 84–91.

Webster, G. (2007b). What's in a name: Is "evolutionary psychology" eclipsing "sociobiology" in the scientific literature? *Evolutionary Psychology, 5,* 683–695.

Webster, G. (2007c). Evolutionary theory in cognitive neuroscience: A 20-year quantitative review of publication trends. *Evolutionary Psychology, 5,* 520–530.

Webster, R. (1995). *Why Freud was wrong: Sin, science, and psychoanalysis.* New York: Basic Books.

Weiner, J. (1994). *The beak of the finch: A story of evolution in our time.* New York: Alfred A. Knopf.

Weiss, A., King, J., & Perkins, L. (2006). Personality and subjective well-being in orangutans. *Journal of Personality and Social Psychology, 90,* 501–511.

Weizmann, F., & Weiss, D. (2005). Obituary: David Bakan, 1921-2004. *History of Psychology, 8,* 317–320.

Welsh, A. (1994). *Freud's wishful dream book.* Princeton, NJ: Princeton University Press.

Werth, B. (2009). *Banquet at Delmonico's: Great minds, the Gilded Age, and the triumph of evolution in America.* New York: Random House.

Wertheimer, Max (1945). *Productive thinking.* New York: Harper.

Wertheimer, Michael (1979). *A brief history of psychology* (2nd ed.). New York: Holt, Rinehart and Winston.

Wertheimer, Michael, & King, D. B. (1994). Max Wertheimer's American sojourn, 1933–1943. *History of Psychology Newsletter, 26*(1), 3–15.

White, A. D. (1965). *A history of the warfare of science with theology in Christendom.* New York: Free Press. (Original work published 1896)

White, S. H. (1990). Child study at Clark University, 1884–1904. *Journal of the History of the Behavioral Sciences, 26,* 131–150.

White, S. H. (1994). G. Stanley Hall: From philosophy to developmental psychology. In R. D. Parke, P. A. Ornstein, J. J. Rieser, and C. Zahn-Waxler (Eds.), *A century of developmental psychology* (pp. 103–125). Washington, DC: American Psychological Association.

Wiener, D. N. (1996). *B. F. Skinner: Benign anarchist.* Boston: Allyn & Bacon.

Will, G. (2009, December 31). Out of catastrophe, renewal. *St. Petersburg (FL) Times.*

Wilson, E. O. (1975). *Sociobiology: A new synthesis.* Cambridge, MA: Harvard University Press.

Wilson, E. O. (1994). *Naturalist.* Washington, DC: Island Press/Shearwater Books.

Wilson, F. (1991). Mill and Comte on the method of introspection. *Journal of the History of the Behavioral Sciences, 27,* 107–129.

Wilson, M. (2002). Six views of embedded cognition. *Psychonomic Bulletin & Review, 9,* 625–636.

Wilson, T. (2002). *Strangers to ourselves: Discovering the adaptive unconscious.* Cambridge, MA: Belknap Press.

Wilson, T. (2003). Knowing when to ask: Introspection and the adaptive unconscious. *Journal of Consciousness Studies, 10,* 131–140.

Winchester, S. (2001). *The map that changed the world: William Smith and the birth of modern geology.* New York: HarperCollins.

Windholz, G. (1990). Pavlov and the Pavlovians in the laboratory. *Journal of the History of the Behavioral Sciences, 26,* 64–74.

Windholz, G. (1997). Ivan P. Pavlov: An overview of his life and psychological work. *American Psychologist, 52,* 941–946.

Windholz, G., & Lamal, P. A. (1985). Köhler's insight revisited. *Teaching of Psychology, 12,* 165–167.

Winston, A. S. (1996). "As his name indicates": R. S. Woodworth's letters of reference and employment for Jewish psychologists in the 1930s. *Journal of the History of the Behavioral Sciences, 32,* 30–43.

Winkielman, P., Berridge, K., & Wilbarger, J. (2005). Unconscious affective reactions to masked happy versus angry faces influence consumption behaviors and judgments of value. *Personality and Social Psychology Bulletin, 31,* 121–135.

Witmer, L. (1996). Clinical psychology. *American Psychologist, 51,* 248–251. (Original work published in *The Psychological Clinic,* 1907, *1,* 1–9)

Wolpe, J., & Plaud, J. J. (1997). Pavlov's contributions to behavior therapy: The obvious and the not so obvious. *American Psychologist, 52,* 966–972.

Wong, W. (2009). Retracing the footsteps of Wilhelm Wundt: Explorations in the disciplinary frontiers of psychology and in *Volkerpsychologie. History of Psychology, 12,* 229–265.

Wood, G. (2002). *Edison's Eve: A magical history of the quest for mechanical life.* New York: Knopf.

Woodworth, R. S. (1918). *Dynamic psychology.* New York: Columbia University Press.

Woodworth, R. S. (1921). *Psychology.* New York: Holt.

Woodworth, R. S. (1938, 1954). *Experimental psychology.* New York: Holt.

Woodworth, R. S. (1943). The adolescence of American psychology. *Psychological Review, 50,* 10–32.

Woodworth, R. S. (1958). *Dynamics of behavior.* New York: Holt.

Woolley, H. T. (1910). Psychological literature: A review of the recent literature on the psychology of sex. *Psychological Bulletin, 7,* 335–342.

Woolley, H. T. (1914). The psychology of sex. *Psychological Bulletin, 11,* 353–379.

Wundt, W. (1858–1862). *Contributions to the theory of sensory perception.* Leipzig: Winter.

Wundt, W. (1863). *Lectures on the minds of men and animals.* Leipzig: Voss.

Wundt, W. (1873–1874). *Principles of physiological psychology.* Leipzig: Engelmann.

Wundt, W. (1888). *Zur Erinnerung an Gustav Theodor Fechner. Philosophische Studien, 4,* 471–478.

Wundt, W. (1896). *Outline of psychology.* Leipzig: Engelmann.

Wundt, W. (1900–1920). *Cultural psychology.* Leipzig: Engelmann.

Wynne, C. D. L. (2001). *Animal cognition: The mental lives of animals.* New York: Palgrave/St. Martin's.

Xu, J., & Roberts, R. (2010). The power of positive emotions. *Health Psychology, 29,* 9–19.

Yerkes, R. M. (1961). Autobiography. In C. Murchison (Ed.), *A history of psychology in autobiography* (Vol. *2*, pp. 381– 407). New York: Russell & Russell. (Original work published 1930)

Yerkes, R. M., & Morgulis, S. (1909). The method of Pavlov in animal psychology. *Psychological Bulletin*, *6*, 257–273.

Young, J. (2010). E. B. Titchener's brain on display. *Advances in the History of Psychology* (AHP.APPS01. YORKU.CA/?P=826)

Young-Bruehl, E. (1988). *Anna Freud: A biography*. New York: Summit Books.

Youniss, J. (2006). G. Stanley Hall and his times: Too much so, yet not enough. *History of Psychology*, *9*(3), 224–235.

Zagrina, N. (2009). Ivan Petrovich Pavlov and the authorities. *Neuroscience and Behavioral Physiology*, *39*, 383–385.

Zaretsky, E. (2004). *Secrets of the soul: The social and cultural history of psychoanalysis*. New York: Alfred A. Knopf.

Zeigarnik, B. (1938). On finished and unfinished tasks. In W. D. Ellis (Ed.), *A source book of Gestalt psychology* (pp. 300–314). London: Routledge & Kegan Paul.

Zenderland, L. (1998). *Measuring minds: Henry Herbert Goddard and the origins of American intelligence testing*. New York: Cambridge University Press.

Zimmer, C. (2004). *Soul made flesh: The discovery of the brain and how it changed the world*. New York: Free Press.

# Name Index

# Subject Index